Biochemistry

SCHAUM'S
outlines

Biochemistry

———————————————Third Edition

Philip W. Kuchel, Ph.D.

Coordinating Author

Simon B. Easterbrook-Smith, Ph.D.

Vanessa Gysbers, MSc (Med)

J. Mitchell Guss, Ph.D.

Dale P. Hancock, Ph.D.

Jill M. Johnston, BSc (Hons)

Alan R. Jones, Ph.D.

Jacqui M. Matthews, Ph.D.

Biochemistry in the School of Molecular and Microbial Biosciences
The University of Sydney
Sydney, Australia

Schaum's Outline Series

New York   Chicago   San Francisco   Lisbon   London
Madrid   Mexico City   Milan   New Delhi   San Juan
Seoul   Singapore   Sydney   Toronto

PHILIP W. KUCHEL, BMedSc(hons), MBBS, PhD, Dr(hc Cluj), FAA is McCaughey Professor of Biochemistry at the University of Sydney, Australia. He wrote and coordinated the writing of this book with contributions from other members of the academic staff in Biochemistry at the University of Sydney.

Schaum's Outline of BIOCHEMISTRY

Copyright © 2009, 1998, 1988 by the McGraw-Hill Companies, Inc. All rights reserved. Printed in the United States of America. Except as permitted under the Copyright Act of 1976, no part of this publication may be reproduced or distributed in any form or my any means, or stored in a data base or retrieval system, without the prior written permission of the publisher.

8 9 0 CUS/CUS 0 1 6

ISBN 978-0-07-147227-2
MHID 0-07-147227-4

McGraw-Hill books are available at special quantity discounts to use as premiums and sales promotions, or for use in corporate training programs. To contact a representative please e-mail us at bulksales@mcgraw-hill.com

Sponsoring Editor: Charles Wall
Production Supervisor: Tama Harris McPhatter
Editing Supervisor: Maureen B. Dennehy
Project Manager: Vastavikta Sharma, International Typesetting and Composition

Library of Congress Cataloging-in-Publication Data

Biochemistry / Philip W. Kuchel, coordinating author ; Simon B.
Easterbrook-Smith ... [et al.].—3rd ed.
        p.   cm.—(Schaum's outline series)
  ISBN-13: 978-0-07-147227-2
  ISBN-10: 0-07-147227-4
  1. Biochemistry—Outlines, syllabi, etc.   2. Biochemistry—Problems,
exercises, etc.   I. Kuchel, Philip W.
  QP518.3.B563 2010
  612'.015—dc22

                                                      2009022077

Preface

Dear Student,

Much has changed in the world as a whole and the world of science in particular, since the second edition of this book was written over 10 years ago. And we are still saddened by the death from cancer, early in his career, of Greg Ralston, my co-editor on the first two editions. Our Department of Biochemistry is now part of a larger school of Molecular and Microbial Biosciences, and the academic staff have almost completely turned over in the past 10 years. The nature of what is taught to our students has changed, caught up in the whirlwind of the molecular biology revolution. So, this Third Edition has been transformed, and it reflects all these changes. We have kept the foundations that were laid in the First and Second Editions, and yet even in the more traditional areas, such as metabolism, the perspective from which the topic is viewed has been changed. We hope that this new perspective appeals to you, and engages your curiosity!

It is worth reminding you about the tradition, or philosophy, that guides the way a book in the *Schaum's Outline Series* is designed and written: Each chapter begins with clear statements of pertinent definitions, principles, and central facts (in mathematics these are the main theorems) together with illustrative Examples. This is followed by a section of graded Solved Problems that illustrate and amplify the outlined theory and bring into focus those points without which you might feel that your knowledge is "built upon sand." The Solved Problems also provide the repetition of ideas, viewed from different angles, that is so vital to learning. Finally, the Supplementary Problems, together with their answers, serve to review the topics in the chapter. They have also been designed to stimulate further self-motivated inquiry by you.

This book contains more material than would reasonably be covered in a conventional second-year Bachelor of Science course in Biochemistry and Molecular Biology. It has been written as a *vade mecum* for you to take with you for foundational insights, from your third year of university and beyond, along whichever career path you construct, or follow.

When the idea to bring out a Third Edition of this book was raised, a new group of 10 authors met to discuss a format that was more in line with how we now teach the subject. Many of us got to work straightaway, while others waited to see what progress was being made before committing fingers to keyboard. Unanticipated professional forces deflected some, so others had to take up the mantles left by them. Nevertheless, I record our thanks to Joel Mackay, Merlin Crossley, and Gareth Denyer: Joel for drafting many of the figures in the first chapters, Merlin for advice on aspects of molecular biology, and Gareth for mapping out the presentation of the four chapters on metabolism. Dr Hanna Nicholas is thanked for critical comments on Chap. 9, Merilyn Kuchel for help with compiling the Index, and PhD students Tim Larkin and David Szekely thanked for their willing advice and assistance with drawing figures.

The authorship team is very grateful to the authors of the two previous editions, especially those who were formally contracted to do the writing, for relinquishing their contracts to allow us a free hand to rearrange and revise the text and figures.

We thank the tireless and attentive Vastavikta Sharma of ITC, India, and Charles Wall, our editor at McGraw-Hill, for their cheerful perseverance and cooperation in bringing into full view our attempt at a multifaceted pedagogic prism.

PHILIP W. KUCHEL
Coordinating Author

Preface to the Second Edition

In the time since the first edition of the book, biochemistry has undergone great developments in some areas, particularly in molecular biology, signal transduction, and protein structure. Developments in these areas have tended to overshadow other, often more traditional, areas of biochemistry such as enzyme kinetics. This second edition has been prepared to take these changes in direction into account: to emphasize those areas that are rapidly developing and to bring them up to date. The preparation of the second edition also gave us the opportunity to adjust the balance of the book, and to ensure that the depth of treatment in all chapters is comparable and appropriate for our audiences.

The major developments in biochemistry over the last 10 years have been in the field of molecular biology, and the second edition reflects these changes with significant expansion of these areas. We are very grateful to Dr. Emma Whitelaw for her substantial efforts in revising Chapter 17. In addition, increased understanding of the dynamics of DNA structures, developments in recombinant DNA technology, and the polymerase chain reaction have been incorporated into the new edition, thanks to the efforts of Drs. Anthony Weiss and Doug Chappell. The section on proteins also has been heavily revised, by Drs. Glenn King, Mitchell Guss, and Michael Morris, reflecting significant growth in this area, with greater emphasis on protein folding. A number of diagrams have been redrawn to reflect our developing understanding, and we are grateful to Mr. Mark Smith and to Drs. Eve Szabados and Michael Morris for their art work.

The sections on lipid metabolism, membrane function, and signal transduction have been enlarged and enhanced, reflecting modern developments in these areas, through the efforts of Drs. Samir Samman and Arthur Conigrave. In the chapter on nitrogen metabolism, the section on nucleotides has been enlarged, and the coverage given to the metabolism of specific amino acids has been correspondingly reduced. For this we are grateful to Dr. Richard Christopherson.

In order to avoid excessive expansion of the text, the material on enzymology and enzyme kinetics has been refocused and consolidated, reflecting changes that have taken place in the teaching of these areas in most institutions. We are grateful to Dr. Ivan Darvey for his critical comments and helpful suggestions in this endeavor.

The style of presentation in the current edition continues that of the first edition, with liberal use of *didactic questions* that attempt to develop concepts from prior knowledge, and to promote probing of the gaps in that knowledge. Thus, the book has been prepared through the efforts of many participants who have contributed in their areas of specialization; we have been joined in this endeavor by several new contributors whose sections are listed above.

PHILIP W. KUCHEL
GREGORY B. RALSTON
Coordinating Authors

Preface to the First Edition

This book is the result of a cooperative writing effort of approximately half of the academic staff of the largest university department of biochemistry in Australia. We teach over 1,000 students in the Faculties of Medicine, Dentistry, Science, Pharmacy, Veterinary Science, and Engineering. So, for whom is this book intended and what is its purpose?

This book, as the title suggests, is an *Outline* of Biochemistry—principally mammalian biochemistry and not the full panoply of the subject. In other words, it is not an encyclopedia but, we hope, a guide to understanding for undergraduates up to the end of their B.Sc. or its equivalent.

Biochemistry has become the language of much of biology and medicine; its principles and experimental methods underpin all the basic biological sciences in fields as diverse as those mentioned in the faculty list above. Indeed, the boundaries between biochemistry and much of medicine have become decidedly blurred. Therefore, in this book, either implicitly through the solved problems and examples, or explicitly, we have attempted to expound *principles* of biochemistry. In one sense, this book is our definition of biochemistry; in a few words, we consider it to be the description, using *chemical* concepts, of the processes that take place in and by living organisms.

Of course, the chemical processes in cells occur not only in free solution but are associated with macromolecular structures. So inevitably, biochemistry must deal with the structure of tissues, cells, organelles, and of the individual molecules themselves. Consequently, this book begins with an overview of the main procedures for studying cells and their organelle constituents, with what the constituents are and, in general terms, what their biochemical functions are. The subsequent six chapters are far more chemical in perspective, dealing with the major classes of biochemical compounds. Then there are three chapters that consider enzymes and general principles of metabolic regulation; these are followed by the metabolic pathways that are the real soul of biochemistry.

It is worth making a few comments on the *style* of presenting the material in this book. First, we use so-called *didactic questions* that are indicated by the word *Question*; these introduce a new topic, the answers for which are not available from the preceding text. We feel that this approach embodies and emphasizes the inquiry in any research, including biochemistry: the answer to one question often immediately provokes another question. Secondly, as in other Schaum's Outlines, the basic material in the form of *general* facts is emphasized by what is, essentially, optional material in the form of *examples*. Some of these examples are written as questions; others are simple expositions on a particular subject that is a specific example of the general point just presented. Thirdly, the solved problems relate, according to their section headings, to the material in the main text. In virtually all cases, students should be able to solve these problems, at least to a reasonable depth, by using the material in this outline. Finally, the supplementary problems are usually questions that have a minor twist on those already considered in either of the previous three categories; answers to these questions are provided at the end of the book.

While this book was written by academic staff, its production has also depended on the efforts of many other people, whom we thank sincerely. For typing and word processing, we thank Anna Dracopoulos, Bev Longhurst-Brown, Debbie Manning, Hilary McDermott, Elisabeth Sutherland, Gail Turner, and Mary Walsh and for editorial assistance, Merilyn Kuchel. For critical evaluation of the manuscript, we thank Dr. Ivan Darvey and many students, but especially Tiina Iismaa, Glenn King,

Kiaran Kirk, Michael Morris, Julia Raftos, and David Thorburn. Dr. Arnold Hunt helped in the early stages of preparing the text. We mourn the sad loss of Dr. Reg O'Brien, who died when this project was in its infancy. We hope, given his high standards in preparing the written and spoken word, that he would have approved of the final form of the book. Finally, we thank Elizabeth Zayatz and Marthe Grice of McGraw-Hill; Elizabeth for raising the idea of the book in the first place, and both of them for their enormous efforts to satisfy our publication requirements.

PHILIP W. KUCHEL
GREGORY B. RALSTON
Coordinating Authors

Contents

CHAPTER 1

Cell Ultrastructure

1.1 Introduction

Question: Since biochemistry is the *study of living systems at the level of chemical transformations,* it would be wise to have some idea of our domain of study, so we ask, "What is life?"

There is no universal definition, but most scholars agree that life exhibits the following features:

1. *Organization* exists in all living systems since they are composed of one or more *cells* that are the basic units of life.

2. *Metabolism* decomposes organic matter (digestion and *catabolism*) and releases energy by converting nonliving material into cell constituents (synthesis).

3. *Growth* results from a higher rate of synthesis than catabolism. A growing organism increases in size in many of its components.

4. *Adaptation* is the accommodation of a living organism to its environment. It is fundamental to the process of evolution, and the range of responses of an individual to the environment is determined by its inherited traits.

5. *Responses to stimuli* take many forms including basic neuronal reflexes through to sophisticated actions that use all the senses.

6. *Reproduction* is the division of one cell to form two new cells. Clearly this occurs in normal somatic growth, but special significance is attached to the formation of new individuals by sexual or asexual means.

EXAMPLE 1.1   What is the general nature of cells?

All animals, plants, and microorganisms are composed of cells. Cells range in volume from a few attoliters among bacteria to milliliters for the giant nerve cells of squid; typical cells in mammals have diameters of 10 to 100 μm and are thus often smaller than the smallest visible particle. They are generally flexible structures with a delimiting membrane that is in a dynamic, undulating state. Different animal and plant tissues contain different types of cells that are distinguished not only by their different structures but also by their different metabolic activities.

EXAMPLE 1.2   Who first saw cells and sparked a revolution in biology by identifying these units as the basis of life?

It was Antonie van Leeuwenhoek (1632–1723), draper of Delft in Holland, and science hobbyist who ground his own lenses and made simple microscopes that gave magnifications of ~200 ×. On October 9, 1676, he sent a 17½-page letter to the Royal Society of London, in which he described *animalcules* in various water samples. These small organisms included what are today known as protozoans and *bacteria*; thus Leeuwenhoek is credited with the first observation of bacteria. Later work of his included the identification of spermatozoa and red blood cells from many species.

There are thousands of different types of molecules in living systems; many of these are discussed in the following pages. As we continue to understand more and more of the intricacies of the regulation of cell function, metabolism, and the structures of macromolecules made by them, it seems natural to ask where the original molecules that made up the first living systems might have come from.

EXAMPLE 1.3   What type of experiments can we carry out that might shed light on the origin of life?

A landmark experiment that was designed to provide some answers to this question was conducted by Stanley Miller and Harold Urey, working at the University of Chicago (see Fig. 1-1). Electrical discharges, which simulated lightning, were delivered in a glass vessel that contained water and the gases methane (CH_4), ammonia (NH_3), and hydrogen (H_2), in the same relative proportions that were likely on prebiotic Earth. The discharging went on for a week, and then the contents of the vessel were analyzed chromatographically. The "soup" that was produced contained almost all the key building blocks of life as we know it today: Miller observed that as much as 10–15% of the carbon was in the form of organic compounds. Two percent of the carbon had formed some of the amino acids that are used to make proteins. How the individual molecules might have interacted to form a primitive cell is still a mystery, but at least the building blocks are known to arise under very plausible and readily reproduced physical and chemical conditions.

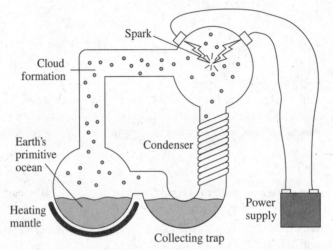

Fig. 1-1   The Miller-Urey experiment inspired a multitude of further experiments on the origin of life.

In higher organisms, cells with specialized functions are derived from *stem cells* in a process called *differentiation*. Stem cells have many of the features of a primitive unicellular *amoeba*, so in some senses differentiation is like evolution, but it is played out on a much shorter time scale. This takes place most dramatically in the development of a fetus, from the single cell formed by the fusion of one spermatozoon and one ovum to a vast array of different tissues, all in a matter of weeks.

Cells appear to be able to recognize cells of like kind, and thus to unite into coherent organs, principally because of specialized glycoproteins (Chap. 2) on the cell membranes and through local hormone-receptor interactions (Chap. 6).

1.2   Methods of Studying the Structure and Function of Cells

Light Microscopy

Many cells and, indeed, parts of cells (*organelles*) react strongly with colored dyes such that they can be easily distinguished in thinly cut sections of tissue by using light microscopy. Hundreds of different dyes with varying degrees of selectivity for tissue components are used for this type of work, which constitutes the basis of the scientific discipline *histology*.

EXAMPLE 1.4   In the clinical biochemical assessment of patients, it is common practice to inspect a blood sample under the light microscope, with a view to determining the number of inflammatory white cells present. A thin film of blood is smeared on a glass slide, which is then placed in methanol to fix the cells; this process rigidifies the cells and preserves their shape. The cells are then dyed by the addition of a few drops of each of two dye mixtures; the most commonly used ones are the *Romanowsky* dyes, named after their nineteenth-century discoverer. The commonly used hematological dyeing procedure is that developed by J. W. Field: A mixture of *azure I* and *methylene blue* is first applied to the cells, followed by *eosin*; all dyes are dissolved in a simple phosphate buffer. The treatment stains nuclei blue, cell cytoplasm pink, and some subcellular organelles either pink or blue. On the basis of different staining patterns, at least five different types of white cells can be identified. Furthermore, intracellular organisms such as the malarial parasite *Plasmodium* stain blue.

The *exact* chemical mechanisms of tissue staining are largely poorly understood. This aspect of histology is therefore still empirical. However, certain features of the chemical structure of dyes allow some interpretation of how they achieve their selectivity. They tend to be multiring, heterocyclic, aromatic compounds in which the high degree of bond conjugation gives the bright colors. In many cases they were originally isolated from plants, and they have a net positive or net negative charge.

EXAMPLE 1.5 *Methylene blue* stains cellular nuclei *blue*.

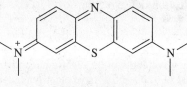

Methylene blue

Mechanism of staining: The positive charge on the N of methylene blue interacts with the anionic oxygen in the phosphate esters of DNA and RNA (Chap. 7).

Eosin stains protein-rich regions of cells red.

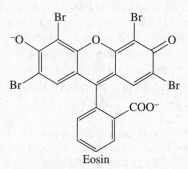

Eosin

Mechanism of staining: Eosin is a *dianion* at pH 7, so it binds electrostatically to protein groups, such as arginyls, histidyls, and lysyls, that have positive charges at this pH. Thus, this dye highlights protein-rich areas of cells.

Periodic acid Schiff (PAS) stain is used for the histological staining of carbohydrates; it is also used to stain *glycoproteins*—proteins that contain carbohydrates (Chap. 2) in *electrophoresis gels* (Chap. 4). The stain mixture contains *periodic acid* (HIO_4), a powerful oxidant, and the dye *basic fuchsin*.

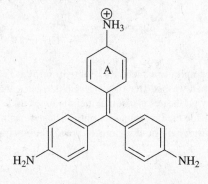

Basic fuchsin

Mechanism of staining: Periodic acid *opens* the sugar rings at *cis-diol* bonds (Chap. 2; i.e., the C_2—C_3 bond of glucose) to form two aldehyde groups and iodate (IO_3^-). Then the $=N^+H_2$ group of the dye reacts to form a *Schiff base* bond with the aldehyde, thus linking the dye to the carbohydrate. The basic reaction is

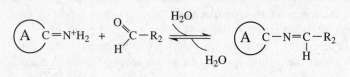

The conversion of ring A of basic fuchsin to an aromatic one, with a carbocation (positively charged carbon atom) at the central carbon, renders the compound pink.

Electron Microscopy

Image magnifications of thin tissue sections of up to 200,000 × can be achieved by using this technique. The sample is placed in a high vacuum and exposed to a narrow beam of electrons that are differentially scattered by different parts of the section; therefore, in staining the sample, we substitute differential electron density for the colored dyes used in light microscopy. A commonly used dye is *osmium tetroxide* (OsO_4) that binds to *amino groups* of proteins, leaving a black, electron-dense region.

EXAMPLE 1.6   The wavelength of electromagnetic radiation (light) limits the *resolution* attainable in microscopy. The resolution of a device is defined as the smallest gap, perceptible as such, between two objects when viewed with it; resolution is approximately one-half the wavelength of the electromagnetic radiation used. Electrons accelerated to high velocities by an electrical potential of ~100,000 V have electromagnetic wave properties, with a wavelength of 0.004 nm; thus a resolution of about 0.002 nm is theoretically attainable with electron microscopy. This, at least in principle, enables the distinction of certain features even on *protein molecules,* since the diameter of many globular proteins, e.g., hemoglobin, is greater than 3 nm; in practice, however, such resolution is not usually attained.

Histochemistry and Cytochemistry

Histochemistry deals with whole tissues, and *cytochemistry* with individual cells. The techniques of these disciplines give a means for locating specific compounds or enzymes in tissues and cells. A tissue slice is incubated with the substrate of an enzyme of interest, and the product of this reaction is caused to react with a second, pigmented compound that is also present in the incubation mixture. If the samples are adequately *fixed* before incubation, and the fixing process does not damage the enzyme, the procedure will highlight, in a thin section of tissue under the microscope, those cells that contain the enzyme or, at higher resolution, the subcellular organelles that contain it.

EXAMPLE 1.7   The enzyme *acid phosphatase* is located in the *lysosomes* (Sec. 1.3) of many cells, including those of the liver. The enzyme catalyzes the hydrolytic release of phosphate groups from various phosphate esters including the following:

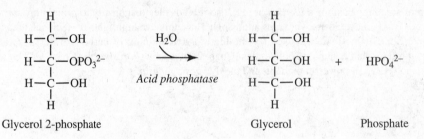

Glycerol 2-phosphate   Glycerol   Phosphate

In the *Gomori* procedure, tissue samples are incubated for ~30 min at 37°C in a suitable buffer that contains glycerol 2-phosphate. The sample is then washed free of the phosphate ester and placed in a buffer that contains lead nitrate. The glycerol 2-phosphate freely permeates lysosomal membranes, but the more highly charged phosphate does not, so that any of the latter released inside the lysosomes by phosphatase remains there. As the Pb^{2+} ions penetrate the lysosomes, they precipitate as *lead phosphate*. These regions of precipitation appear as dark spots in either an electron or light micrograph.

Autoradiography

Autoradiography is a technique for locating radioactive compounds within cells; it can be conducted with light or electron microscopy. Living cells are first exposed to a *radioactive precursor* of some intracellular component. The labeled precursor is a compound with one or more hydrogen (^1H) atoms replaced by the *radioisotope tritium* (^3H); e.g., [^3H] thymidine is a precursor of DNA, and [^3H] uridine is a precursor of RNA (Chap. 3). Various tritiated amino acids are also commercially available. The precursors enter the cells and are incorporated into the appropriate macromolecules. The cells are then fixed and the samples embedded in a resin or wax and then sectioned into thin slices.

The radioactivity is detected by applying (in a darkroom) a photographic silver halide emulsion to the surface of the section. After the emulsion dries, the preparation is stored in a light-free box to permit the radioactive decay to expose the overlying emulsion. The length of exposure used depends on the amount of radioactivity in the sample, but it is typically several days to a few weeks for light microscopy and up to several months for electron microscopy. The long exposure time in electron microscopy is necessary because of the *very* thin sections (<1 μm) and thus the minute amounts of radioactivity present in the tiny samples. The preparations are developed and fixed as in conventional photography. Hence, the silver grains overlie regions of the cell that contain radioactive molecules; the grains appear as tiny black dots in light micrographs and as twisted black threads in electron micrographs. Note that this whole procedure works only if the precursor molecule can traverse the cell membrane and the cells are in a phase of their life cycle that involves incorporation of the compound into macromolecules.

EXAMPLE 1.8 The sequence of events involved in the synthesis and transport of *secretory proteins* from glands can be followed using autoradiography. For example, rats were injected with [³H] leucine, and at intervals thereafter they were sacrificed and radioautographs of their *prostate glands* were prepared. In electron micrographs of the sample obtained 4 min after the injection, silver grains appeared overlying the *rough endoplasmic reticulum* (RER) of the cells, indicating that [³H] leucine had been incorporated from the blood into protein by the *ribosomes* attached to the RER. By 30 min the grains were overlying the Golgi apparatus and secretory vacuoles, reflecting intracellular transport of labeled secretory proteins from the RER to these organelles. At later times after the injection, radioactive proteins were released from the cells, as evidenced by the presence of silver grains over the glandular lumens.

Ultracentrifugation

The *biochemical* roles of subcellular organelles could not be studied properly until they had been separated by fractionation of the cells. George Palade and his colleagues, in the late 1940s, showed that *homogenates* of rat liver could be separated into several fractions by using *differential centrifugation*. This procedure relies on the different velocities of sedimentation of various organelles of different shape, size, and density through a solution. A typical experiment is outlined in Example 1.9.

EXAMPLE 1.9 A piece of liver is suspended in 0.25 *M* sucrose and then disrupted using a rotating, close-fitting Teflon plunger in a glass barrel (known as a *Potter-Elvehjem homogenizer*). Care is taken not to destroy the organelles by excessive homogenization. The sample is then spun in a centrifuge (see Fig. 1-2). The nuclei tend to be the first to sediment to the bottom of the sample tube at forces as low as 1000*g* for ~15 min in a tube 7 cm long.

High-speed centrifugation, such as 10,000*g* for 20 min, yields a pellet composed mostly of mitochondria, but mixed with lysosomes. Further centrifugation at 100,000*g* for 1 h yields a pellet of ribosomes and *microsomes* that contain endoplasmic reticulum. The soluble proteins and other solutes remain in the supernatant (overlying solution) from this step.

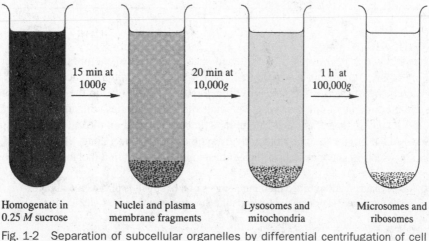

| Homogenate in 0.25 *M* sucrose | 15 min at 1000*g* → | Nuclei and plasma membrane fragments | 20 min at 10,000*g* → | Lysosomes and mitochondria | 1 h at 100,000*g* → | Microsomes and ribosomes |

Fig. 1-2 Separation of subcellular organelles by differential centrifugation of cell homogenates.

Density gradient centrifugation (also called *isopycnic* centrifugation) can also be used to separate the different organelles (Fig. 1-3). The homogenate is layered onto a discontinuous or continuous concentration gradient of sucrose solution, and centrifugation continues until the subcellular particles achieve density equilibrium with their surrounding solution.

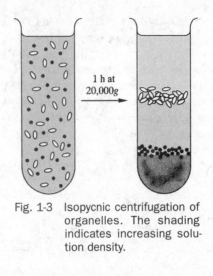

1 h at
20,000g

Fig. 1-3   Isopycnic centrifugation of organelles. The shading indicates increasing solution density.

Question: Can a procedure similar to isopycnic separation in a centrifugal field be used to separate different *macromolecules*?

Yes, in fact one way of preparing and purifying DNA fragments for molecular biology uses density gradients of CsCl. Various proteins also have different densities and thus can be separated on sucrose density gradients; however, the time required to attain equilibrium is much longer, and higher angular velocities are needed than is the case with organelles.

1.3   Subcellular Organelles

Question: What does a typical animal cell look like?

There is no such thing as a typical animal cell, since cells vary in overall size, shape, and contents of the various subcellular organelles. Figure 1-4 is, however, a composite diagram that indicates the relative sizes of the various subcellular organelles.

Endoplasmic Reticulum (ER)

The endoplasmic reticulum is composed of flattened sacs and tubes of membranous bilayers that extend throughout the cytoplasm, enclosing a large intracellular space. The *luminal* space (Fig. 1-5) is continuous with the outer membrane of the *nuclear envelope* (Fig. 1-10). It is involved in the synthesis and transport of proteins to the cytoplasmic membrane (via *vesicles*, small spherical particles with an outer bilayer membrane). The *rough* ER (RER) has flattened stacks of membrane that are studded on the outer (cytoplasmic) face with *ribosomes* (discussed later in this section) that actively synthesize proteins (Chap. 9). The *smooth* ER (SER) is more tubular in cross section and lacks ribosomes; it has a major role in lipid metabolism (Chap. 12).

EXAMPLE 1.10   What mass fraction of the lipid membranes of a liver cell is plasma membrane?

Only about 10%; the remainder is principally ER and mitochondrial membrane.

Golgi Apparatus

The Golgi apparatus is a system of stacked membrane-bound flattened sacs organized in order of decreasing breadth (see Fig. 1-6). Around this system are small *vesicles* (50-nm diameter and larger); these are the secretory vacuoles that contain protein that is released from the cell (see Example 1.8).

The pathway of secretory proteins and glycoproteins (proteins with attached carbohydrate) through *exocrine* (secretory) gland cells in which *secretory vacuoles* are present is well established. However, the exact pathway of exchange of the *membranes* between the various organelles is *less clear* and could be either one or a combination of both of the schemes shown in Fig. 1-7.

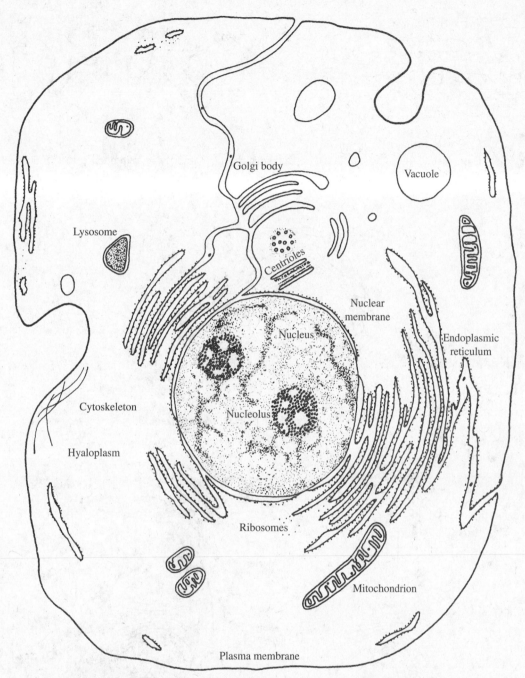

Fig. 1-4 Diagrammatic representation of a mammalian cell. The organelles are approximately the correct relative sizes.

In the *membrane flow* model of Fig. 1-7 membranes move through the cell from ER to Golgi to secretory vacuoles to plasma membrane. In the *membrane shuttle* proposal, the vesicles *shuttle* between ER and Golgi apparatus, while *secretory vacuoles* shuttle back and forth between the Golgi apparatus and the plasma membrane.

Question: What controls the *directed flow* of membranous organelles?

It is one of the great wonders of cell physiology that is yet to be fully understood. However, much progress has been made in the past decade. Some structural proteins self-associate adjacent to a lipid biolayer; as they build up an igloo-like structure they enclose a small spherical vesicle that moves to a new site in the cell.

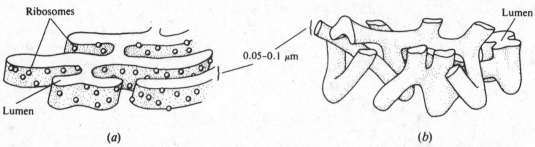

Fig. 1-5 Endoplasmic reticulum. (a) Rough endoplasmic reticulum and (b) smooth endoplasmic reticulum.

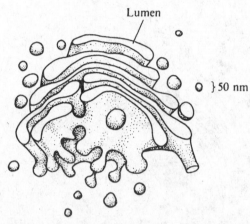

Fig. 1-6 Golgi apparatus and secretory vesicles.

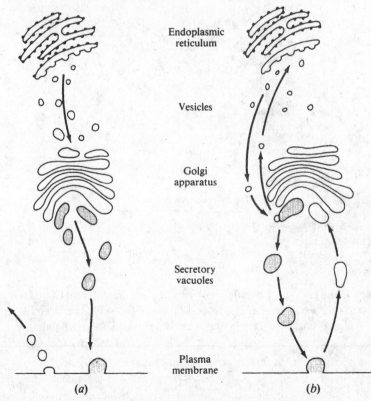

Fig. 1-7 Possible membrane-exchange pathways during secretion of protein from a cell. (a) Membrane flow and (b) membrane shuttles.

Lysosomes

Lysosomes are membrane-bound vesicles that contain *acid hydrolases*; these are enzymes that catalyze hydrolytic reactions and function optimally at a pH of ~5 that is found in these organelles. Lysosomes range in size from 0.2 to 0.5 μm. They are instrumental in intracellular digestion (*autophagy*) and the digestion of material from outside the cell (*heterophagy*). Heterophagy, which is involved with the body's removal of bacteria, begins with the *invagination* of the plasma membrane, a process called *endocytosis*; the whole digestion pathway is shown in Fig. 1-8.

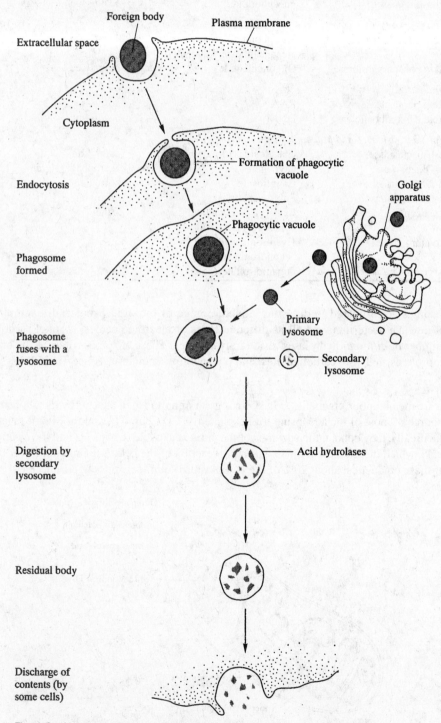

Fig. 1-8   Heterophagy in a mammalian cell, typically in a *macrophage*.

Table 1-1   Mammalian Lysosomal Enzymes and Their Substrates

Enzyme	Natural Substrate	Tissue Location
Proteases		
Cathepsin	Most proteins	Most tissues
Collagenase	Collagen	Bone
Peptidases	Peptides	Most tissues
Lipases		
A range of esterases	Esters of fatty acids	Most tissues
Phospholipases	Phospholipids	Most tissues
Phosphatases		
Acid phosphatase	Phosphomonoesters (e.g., 2-phosphoglycerol)	Most tissues
Acid phosphodiesterase	Oligonucleotides	Most tissues
Nucleases		
Acid ribonuclease	RNA	Most tissues
Acid deoxyribonuclease	DNA	Most tissues
Polysaccharidases and Mucopolysaccharidases		
β-Galactosidase	Galactosides of membranes	Liver, brain
α-Glucosidase	Glycogen	Macrophages, liver
β-Glucosidase	Gangliosides	Brain, liver
β-Glucuronidase	Polysaccharides	Macrophages
Lysozyme	Bacterial cell wall and mucopolysaccharides	Kidney
Hyaluronidase	Hyaluronic acid and chondroitin sulfate	Liver
Arylsulfatase	Organic sulfates	Liver, brain

Since lysosomes are involved in digesting a whole range of biological material, exemplified by the destruction of a whole bacterium with all its different types of macromolecules, it is not surprising to find that a large number of *different* hydrolases reside in lysosomes. These enzymes catalyze the breakdown of nucleic acids, proteins, cell wall carbohydrates, and phospholipid membranes (see Table 1-1).

Mitochondria

Mitochondria are membranous organelles (Fig. 1-9) of great importance in the energy metabolism of the cell; they are the source of most of the adenosine triphosphate (ATP) (Chap. 10) and the site of many metabolic reactions. Specifically, they contain the enzymes of the citric acid cycle (Chap. 11) and the electron transport chain (Chap. 11), which includes the main O_2-utilizing reaction of the cell. A mammalian liver cell contains about 1000 of these organelles; about 20% of the cytoplasmic volume is mitochondrial.

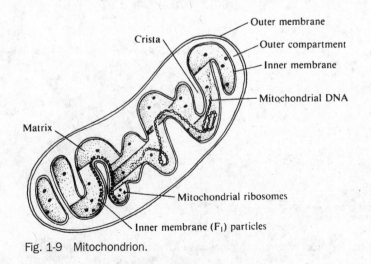

Fig. 1-9   Mitochondrion.

EXAMPLE 1.11 Mitochondria were first observed by *Altmann* in 1890. He named them *bioblasts* because he speculated that they and chloroplasts (the green cholorphyll-containing organelles of plants) might be intracellular *symbionts* that arose from bacteria and algae, respectively. This idea lay in disrepute until the recent discovery of mitochondrial nucleic acids.

In histology mitochondria can be stained *supravitally*; i.e., the metabolic activity of the functional (vital living) organelle or cell allows selective staining. The *reduced* form of the dye *Janus green B* is colorless, but it is *oxidized* by mitochondria to give a light green pigment that is easily seen in light microscopy.

Mitochondria are about the size of bacteria. They have a diameter of 0.2–0.5 μm and are 0.5–7 μm long. They are bounded by *two* lipid bilayers, the inner one being highly folded. These folds are called *cristae*. The inner space of the mitochondrion is called the *matrix*. Their own DNA is in the form of *at least* one copy of a circular double helix (Chap. 7) about 5 μm in overall diameter; it differs from nuclear DNA in its density and denaturation temperature by virtue of being richer in guanosine and cytosine (Chap. 7). The different density from nuclear DNA allows its separation by *isopycnic centrifugation* (Fig. 1-3). Mitochondria also have their own type of *ribosomes* that differ from those in the cytoplasm but are similar to those of bacteria.

Most of the enzymes in mitochondria are *imported* from the cytoplasm; i.e., the enzyme proteins are largely *coded* for by *nuclear DNA* (Chap. 8). The enzymes are disposed in various specific regions of the mitochondrion; this has important bearing on the *direction* of certain metabolic processes. See Table 1-2.

Peroxisomes

These are about the same size and shape as lysosomes (0.3–1.5 μm in diameter). However, they do *not* contain hydrolases but *oxidative* enzymes instead that generate *hydrogen peroxide*; they do so by catalyzing the combination of oxygen with a range of compounds. The various enzymes in *high* concentration (even to the extent of forming *crystals* of protein) are (1) urate oxidase; (2) D-amino acid oxidase; (3) L-amino acid oxidase; and (4) α-hydroxy acid oxidase (includes lactate oxidase). Also, most of the *catalase* in the cell is contained in peroxisomes; the enzyme catalyzes the conversion of hydrogen peroxide, produced in other reactions, to water and oxygen.

Table 1-2   Enzyme Distribution in Mitochondria

Location	Characteristics
Outer Membrane	
Monoamine oxidase	Neurotransmitter; catabolism
Rotenone-insensitive NADH-cytochrome *c* reductase	Chap. 10
Kynurenine hydroxylase	Tryptophan *catabolism* (Chap. 14)
Fatty acid CoA ligase	Chap. 13
Space Between Inner and Outer Membrane	
Adenylate kinase	$AMP + ATP \rightleftharpoons 2ADP$
Nucleoside diphosphokinase	$XDP + YTP \rightleftharpoons XTP + YDP$
	X and Y any of several ribonucleosides
Inner Membrane	
Respiratory chain enzymes	Chap. 10
ATP synthase	Chap. 10
Succinate dehydrogenase	Chap. 10
β-Hydroxybutyrate dehydrogenase	Chap. 13
Carnitine fatty acid acyl transferase	Chap. 12
Matrix	
Malate and isocitrate dehydrogenase	Chap. 10
Fumarase and aconitase	Chap. 10
Citrate synthase	Chap. 10
2-Oxoacid dehydrogenase	Chap. 10
β-Oxidative enzymes for fatty acids	Chap. 10
Carbamyl phosphate synthetase I	Chap. 14
Ornithine transcarbamoylase	Chap. 14

Cytoskeleton

In the cytoplasm, and especially subjacent to the plasma membrane, are networks of protein filaments that stabilize the lipid membrane and thus contribute to the maintenance of cell shape. In cells that grow and divide, such as liver cells, the cytoplasm appears to be organized from a region near the nucleus that contains the cell's pair of *centrioles* (see below). There are three main types of *cytoskeletal filaments*: (1) microtubules, 25 nm in diameter, composed of organized aggregates of the protein tubulin; (2) actin filaments, 7 nm in diameter; and (3) so-called intermediate filaments, 10 nm in diameter.

Centrioles

These exist as a pair of hollow cylinders that are composed of nine triplet tubules of protein. The members of a pair of centrioles are usually orientated at right angles to each other. Microtubules form the fine weblike protein structure that appears to be attached to *chromosomes* (see next page) during cell division (*mitosis*); the web is called the *mitotic spindle* and is attached to the ends of the centrioles. While they are thought to function in chromosome segregation during mitosis, it is worth noting that cells of higher plants, which clearly undergo this process, lack centrioles.

Ribosomes

These are the site of protein synthesis and exist (1) as *rosette*-shaped groups (polysomes) in the cytoplasm (in immature red blood cells there are usually five per group); (2) bound to the RER; or (3) in the mitochondrial matrix, although the latter are different in size and shape from those in the cytoplasm. Ribosomes are composed of RNA and protein and range in size from 15 to 20 nm. Their central role in protein synthesis is described in Chap. 7.

EXAMPLE 1.12   Ribosomes were first isolated by differential centrifugation and then examined by electron microscopy. This and related work by George Palade in the early 1950s eventually earned him the Nobel Prize in 1974. For a time ribosomes were known to electron microscopists as *Palade's granules*.

Nucleus

This is the most conspicuous organelle of the cell. It is delimited from the cytoplasm by a membranous envelope called the *nuclear membrane*, which actually consists of two membranes forming a flattened sac. The nuclear membrane is perforated by *nuclear pores* (60 nm in diameter) which allow transfer of material between the *nucleoplasm* and the cytoplasm. The nucleus (Fig. 1-10) contains the *chromosomes* that

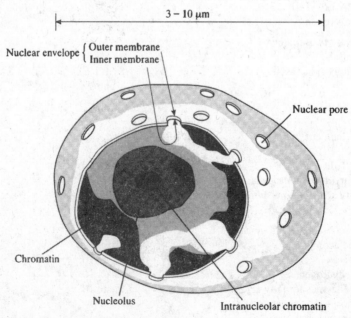

Fig. 1-10   Mammalian cell nucleus.

consist of *DNA* packaged into *chromatin* fibers by association of the DNA with an equal mass of *histone* proteins (Chap. 8).

Two obviously important features of the nucleus are the following:

Nucleolus

The nucleolus is composed of 5–10% RNA, and the remainder of the mass is protein. In light microscopy it appears to be spherical and *basophilic* (Prob. 1.1). Its function is the synthesis of ribosomal RNA (Chap. 9). There may be more than one per nucleus.

Chromosomes

Chromosomes are the bearers of the *hereditary instructions* in a cell; thus they are the overall regulators of cellular processes. Important features to note about chromosomes are the following:

1. *Chromosome number.* In animals, each *somatic cell* (body cells excluding sex cells) contains one set of chromosomes inherited from the *female parent* and a comparable (*homologous*) set from the *male parent*. The number of chromosomes in the *dual set* is called the *diploid number*; the suffix *ploid* means a set, and *di* refers to the *multiplicity* of the set. Sex cells (called *gametes*) contain one-half the number of chromosomes of somatic cells and are therefore referred to as *haploid* cells. A *genome* is the set of chromosomes that corresponds to the haploid set of a species.

EXAMPLE 1.13   Human somatic cells contain 46 chromosomes; cattle, 60; and fruit fly, 8. Thus, the diploid number bears no relationship to the species' position in the phylogenetic scheme of classification.

2. *Chromosome morphology.* Chromosomes become visible under the light microscope only at certain phases of the nuclear division cycle. Each chromosome in the genome can usually be distinguished from the others by such features as (1) relative length of the whole chromosome; (2) the position of the *centromere*, a structure which divides the chromosome into a crosslike structure with two pairs of arms of different length; (3) the presence of knobs of chromatin called *chromomeres*; and (4) the presence of small terminal extensions called *satellites*. (See Fig. 1-11.)

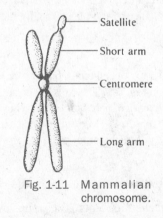

Fig. 1-11   Mammalian chromosome.

EXAMPLE 1.14   In the clinical investigation of infants or fetuses with possible inborn errors of metabolism or morphology, it is common practice to prepare a *karyotype*. Usually, white cells are cultured and then stimulated to divide. The predivision cells are squashed between glass slides, and the cellular nuclei disgorge their chromosomes that are then stained with a blue dye. The chromosomes are photographed and then ordered according to their length, with the longest pair being numbered 1. The sex chromosomes do not have a number.

The inherited disorder Down syndrome (also called mongolism) involves mental retardation and distinctive facial features. It results from the inclusion of an extra chromosome number 21 in each somatic cell of the body. Hence the condition is called *trisomy 21*.

3. *Autosomes and sex chromosomes.* In humans, sex is associated with a morphologically dissimilar pair of chromosomes called the *sex chromosomes*. The two members of the pair are labeled X and Y, with X being the larger. Genetic factors on the Y chromosome, though, determine *maleness*. All chromosomes exclusive of the sex chromosomes are called *autosomes*.

1.4   Cell Types

There are over 250 different histological types of cells in the human body. These are arranged in a variety of different ways, often with mixtures of cell types, to form tissues. Among this vast array of types are some highly specialized ones.

Red Blood Cell (Erythrocyte)

Erythrocytes are small compared with most other cells and are peculiar because of their *biconcave disk* shape (see Fig. 1-12). They have no nucleus because it is extruded just prior to the release of the cell into the bloodstream from the bone marrow where it develops. The cytoplasm has no organelles and is full of the protein hemoglobin that binds O_2 and CO_2. In the cytoplasm are other proteins: (1) the submembrane cytoskeleton, (2) enzymes of the glycolytic (Chap. 11) and pentose phosphate pathways (Chap. 11), and (3) a range of other hydrolytic and *special function* enzymes that will not be discussed here. In the membrane are specialized proteins associated with (1) anion transport and (2) carrying the carbohydrate cell surface antigens (blood group substances).

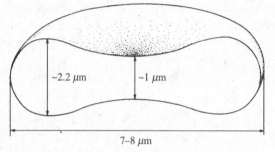

~2.2 μm   ~1 μm

7–8 μm

Fig. 1-12   Human erythrocyte.

Adipocyte

Adipocytes are the specialized cells of fat tissue (Fig. 1-13). The cells range in size from 60 to 120 μm in diameter and have the characteristic feature of a huge vacuole that is full of triglyceride. The nucleus and mitochondria are flattened on one inner surface of the plasma membrane, and there is only a small amount of endoplasmic reticulum.

Liver Cell (Hepatocyte)

The liver is one tissue in which there are an array of cell types, but the preponderant one is the hepatocyte. It has an overall structure much like that of the cell in Fig. 1-3. The cells are arranged in long branching columns of about 20 cells in a cross section around a *bile cannaliculus* (channel). Into the cannaliculus the cells secrete bile. The liver is the main organ that excretes urea (Chap. 14), stores glycogen (Chap. 11), synthesizes many of the amino acids used by other tissues (Chap. 14), and produces serum proteins, among many other metabolic roles.

Muscle Cell (Myocyte)

Muscle cells produce mechanical force by contraction. In vertebrates there are three basic types:

1. *Skeletal muscle* moves the bones attached to joints. These muscles are composed of bundles of long, multinucleated cells. The cytoplasm contains a high concentration of a special macromolecular contractile protein-complex *actomyosin*. There is also an elaborate membranous network called the *sarcoplasmic reticulum* that has a high Ca^{2+} content. The contractile protein complex has a banded appearance under microscopy.

2. *Smooth muscle* is the type in the walls of blood vessels and the intestine. The cells are long and *spindle-*shaped, and they lack the *banding* of skeletal muscle cells.

3. *Cardiac muscle* is the main tissue of the heart. The cells are similar in appearance to those of skeletal muscle but in fact have a different biochemical makeup.

Epithelia

Epithelial cells (Fig. 1-14) form the contiguous sheets that line the inner and outer surfaces of the body. There are many specialized types, but the main groups are as follows:

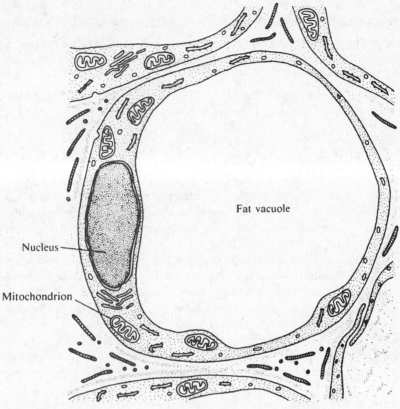

Fat vacuole

Nucleus

Mitochondrion

Fig. 1-13   Adipocyte.

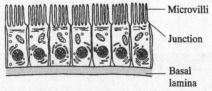

Microvilli

Junction

Basal lamina

(*a*) Absorptive cells

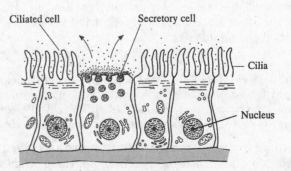

Ciliated cell   Secretory cell

Cilia

Nucleus

(*b*) Ciliated and secretory cells

Fig. 1-14   Epithelial cells.

1. *Absorptive cells*. These have numerous hairlike projections called *microvilli* on their *outer* surface; these increase the surface area for absorption of nutrients from the gut lumen and other areas.

2. *Ciliated* cells. These have small membranous projections (*cilia*) with interior contractile proteins; they beat in synchrony and serve to sweep away foreign particles on the surface of the *respiratory tract,* i.e., in the lungs and the nasal lining.

3. *Secretory* cells. Most epithelial surfaces have specialized secretory cells associated with them; e.g., sweat gland cells in the skin as well as mucus-secreting cells in the intestine and respiratory tract.

1.5　The Structural Hierarchy in Cells

The organic molecules that are *building blocks* of biological macromolecules are very small; e.g., the amino acid alanine is only 0.7 nm long whereas a typical globular protein, hemoglobin (Chap. 4), which consists of 574 amino acids, has a diameter of ~6 nm. In turn, protein molecules are small compared with the ribosomes that synthesize them (Chap. 9); these macromolecular aggregates are composed of over 70 different proteins and four nucleic acid strands. They have an M_r of around 2.8×10^6 and a diameter of ~20 nm. In contrast, mitochondria contain their own ribosomes and DNA and range in length up to 7 μm. Intracellular vesicles are often seen to be about the same size as mitochondria, and yet the Golgi apparatus, or the lipid vacuole of an adipocyte is much larger. The nucleus is larger again and also contains some ribosomes and other macromolecular aggregates including, most importantly, the chromosomes. Even though the building blocks of macromolecules are small in relation to the size of the cell (e.g., the ratio of the volume of one molecule of *alanine* to that of the red blood cell is $1:10^{11}$), a defect in the order of addition of one amino acid in a particular type of protein can profoundly affect not only the copies of this protein but also the cell structure. Furthermore, an altered enzymic activity or binding affinity can greatly influence the survival of not only the cell but also the whole being.

EXAMPLE 1.15　In the human inherited disease called *sickle cell anemia,* the hemoglobin molecules of the erythrocytes are *defective*; 2 of the 574 amino acids in the protein are substituted for another. Specifically, glutamate in position 6 of each of the two β chains of the hemoglobin *tetramer* (see Chap. 4) is replaced by a valine. This single change increases the likelihood of the molecules to *aggregate* when they are *deoxygenated*. The aggregated protein forms large *paracrystalline structures* (called *tactoids*) inside the cells and distorts them into a relatively inflexible *sickle* shape. These cells tend to clog small blood vessels and capillaries and lead to poor oxygen supply in many organs. Also, the red blood cells are more fragile and thus rupture, reducing the number of cells in the blood and causing anemia.

SOLVED PROBLEMS

METHODS OF STUDYING THE STRUCTURE AND FUNCTION OF CELLS

1.1. Basic dyes such as *methylene blue* (Example 1.5) or *toluidine blue* are positively charged at the pH of most staining solutions used in histology. Thus the dyes bind to acidic (negatively charged) substances in the cell. These acidic molecules are therefore referred to as *basophilic* substances in cells. Give some examples of basophilic substances.

SOLUTION

Examples of basophilic components are *DNA* and *RNA*; the latter includes messenger RNA (Chap. 9) and ribosomes. The youngest red blood cells in the blood circulation contain a basophilic *reticulum* (network) in their cytoplasm; this is composed of messenger and ribosomal RNA. The network is slowly dissolved over the first 24 h of the cell's life in the circulation. This readily identifiable red cell type is called the *reticulocyte*.

1.2. Acidic dyes such as *eosin* (Example 1.5) and *acid fuchsin* have a net negative charge at the pH of usual staining solutions. Therefore they bind to many cellular proteins that have a net positive charge. Give some regions of a liver cell that might be *acidophilic*.

SOLUTION

The cytoplasm, mitochondrial matrix, and inside the smooth endoplasmic reticulum; all regions have a high protein content.

1.3. Describe a possible means for the cytochemical detection and localization of the enzyme glucose-6-phosphatase: it exists in liver and catalyzes the following reaction:

$$\text{Glucose 6-phosphate} \xrightarrow{\;H_2O\;} \text{Glucose + Phosphate}$$

SOLUTION

Incubate a tissue slice at 37°C with glucose 6-phosphate in a suitable buffer solution. The tissue is washed free of the substrate, and the phosphate ions are then precipitated by the addition of lead nitrate to the tissue slice. The remainder of the preparation is as described in Example 1.7. In liver cells the reaction product is found *within* the endoplasmic reticulum, thus indicating the location of the enzyme.

1.4. How may cells be disrupted in order to obtain subcellular organelles by centrifugal fractionation?

SOLUTION

There are several ways of disrupting cells:

1. *Osmotic lysis.* The plasma membranes of cells are water-permeable but are impermeable to large molecules and some ions. Thus if cells are placed into water or dilute buffer, they swell due to the *osmotically driven* (Chap. 2) influx of water. Since the plasma membrane is not able to stretch very much (the red cell membrane can only stretch by up to 15% of its normal area before disruption), the cell bursts. The method is effective for isolated cells but is not so effective for tissues.
2. *Homogenizers.* One of these is described in Example 1.9.
3. *Sonication.* This involves the generation of shear forces in a cell sample in the vicinity of a titanium probe (0.5 mm in diameter and 10 cm long) that vibrates at ~20,000 Hz. The device contains a crystal of lead zirconate titanate that is *piezoelectric;* i.e., it expands and contracts when an oscillatory electric field is applied to it from an electronic oscillator. The ultrasonic pressure waves cause *microcavitation* in the sample, and this disrupts the cell membranes, usually in a few seconds.

SUBCELLULAR ORGANELLES

1.5. On the basis of the pathway of heterophagy (Fig. 1-8), make a proposal for the pathway of *autophagic* degradation of a mitochondrion.

SOLUTION

Figure 1-15 shows the scheme for autophagic degradation of a mitochondrion. Note that once the *phagosome* has been formed, the process of digestion, etc. is the same as for heterophagy.

1.6. There is an *inherited* disease in which a person's lysosomes lack the enzyme β-glucosidase (Table 1.1). What are the clinical and biochemical consequences of this deficiency?

SOLUTION

The disease is called *Gaucher disease,* and it is the most common of the *sphingolipidoses*; its incidence in the general population is ~1:2500. This class of disease results from defective hydrolysis of membrane components, *sphingolipids* (Chap. 3), that are normally turned over in the cell by hydrolytic breakdown in the lysosomes. The sphingolipids are lipid molecules with attached carbohydrate groups. A failure to be able to remove glucose from these molecules results in their accumulation in the lysosomes. In fact, over a few years, the cells which have rapid membrane turnover, such as the liver and spleen, become engorged with this lipid breakdown product. Clinically the patients have a large liver and spleen and may show signs of mental deterioration if much of the lipid accumulates in the brain as well.

CELL TYPES

1.7. How many red blood cells are there in an *average* 70-kg person?

SOLUTION

There are $\sim 2.6 \times 10^{13}$, or 26 trillion. The total blood volume is ~5.5 L, and ~40% of that is red blood cells; i.e., there are ~2.2 L of red cells. Since each cell has a volume of $\sim 86 \times 10^{-15}$ L (see Fig. 1-12), the result follows from dividing 2.2 L by this number.

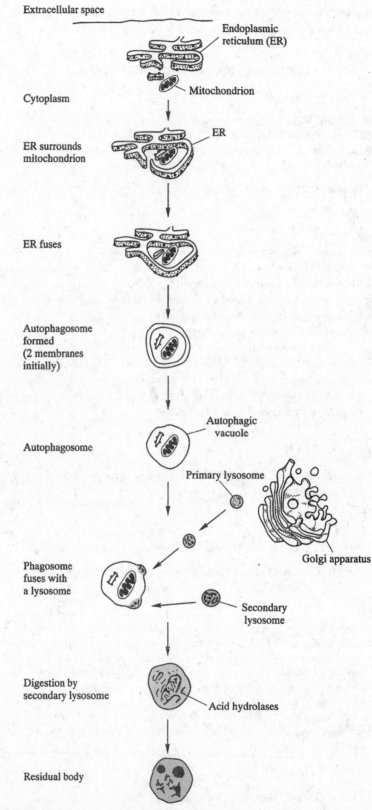

Fig. 1-15   The process of autophagy of a mitochondrion.

1.8. How many red blood cells are produced in an average 70-kg person every second?

SOLUTION

The number is 2.5 million! The average life span of a human red cell is 120 days; therefore the number produced per second is simply given by the answer from Prob. 1.7, divided by 120 days and expressed in seconds.

1.9. A *macrophage* (Fig. 1-16) is a cell type that is involved in engulfing foreign material such as bacteria and damaged host cells. In view of this specialized phagocytic function, draw what you think an electron microscopist would see in a cross section of the cell.

SOLUTION

The key features of a macrophage are its large system of *lysosomes* and *invaginations* of the *cytoplasmic membrane* (Fig. 1-16). Also, there is a rich, rough endoplasmic reticulum where the lysosomal hydrolytic enzymes are produced. Mitochondria are abundant since the highly active protein synthesis is very demanding of ATP. Certain of the white blood cells are macrophages.

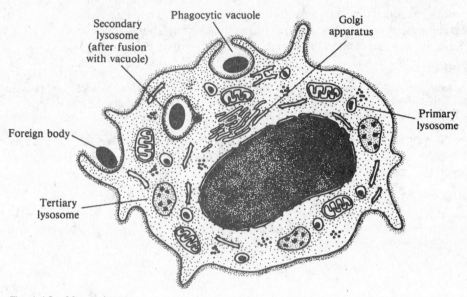

Fig. 1-16   Macrophage.

1.10. PAS staining (Example 1.5) of microscope sections of red blood cells gives a pink stain on only one side of the cell membrane. Which side is it, the extracellular or the intracellular side?

SOLUTION

Extracellular. All glycoprotein and glycolipids of the plasma membrane of red and *all* other cells are on the outside of the cell. No oligosaccharides are present on the inner face of the cell membrane.

1.11. Why do the vesicles of *mast* cells, which contain large quantities of histamine, stain red with eosin?

SOLUTION

Eosin is negatively charged, and histamine has the following structure

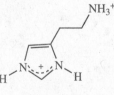

Histamine

The two types of molecules interact electrostatically inside the vesicles, and thus the red eosin stains the vesicles red.

THE STRUCTURAL HIERARCHY IN CELLS

1.12. The concentration of hemoglobin in human red cells is normally 330 g L^{-1}. The relative molecular weight M_r of hemoglobin is 64,500, and the volume of a red blood cell is ~86 fL. How many molecules of hemoglobin are there in one human red blood cell?

SOLUTION

There are ~3×10^8 molecules of hemoglobin in one erythrocyte. The number of moles of hemoglobin in one cell is

$$(330 \times 86 \times 10^{-15})/64{,}500 = 4.4 \times 10^{-16}$$

Since *Avogadro's number* is the number of molecules per mole of a compound, the previous number is multiplied by Avogadro's number to give the required estimate.

$$4.6 \times 10^{-16} \times 6.02 \times 10^{23} \approx 2.6 \times 10^8$$

1.13. The mean generation time, of a red cell, from the *stem cell* to a mature reticulocyte is ~90 h. The phase in the cell generation pathway in which most of the hemoglobin is synthesized is ~40 h. How many hemoglobin molecules are synthesized per human red blood cell per second?

SOLUTION

Since from Prob. 1.12 we saw that the cell contains ~2.6×10^8 hemoglobin molecules, we proceed by simply dividing this number by the time taken to generate them, 40 h. This gives the rate of production, namely, ~1800 molecules per second.

1.14. It has been estimated that it takes ~1 min to synthesize one hemoglobin subunit from its *constituent* amino acids. Using this fact, calculate the number of hemoglobin molecules produced on average at any one time in the differentiation of the red blood cell.

SOLUTION

From Prob. 1.13, ~1800 hemoglobin molecules are produced per second; this is equal to ~1.1×10^5 per minute. However, hemoglobin is a *tetrameric* protein (Chap. 4; four subunits), so $4 \times 1.1 \times 10^5$ chains are produced per minute, or 4.4×10^5.

SUPPLEMENTARY PROBLEMS

1.15. A commonly used test of the viability of cells in tissue culture is whether or not they exclude a *supravital dye* such as *toluidine blue*. If the cells exclude the dye, they are considered to be viable. What is the biochemical basis of this test?

1.16. The chemical compound *glutaraldehyde* has the structure

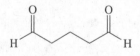

Glutaraldehyde

It is used as a fixative of tissues for light and electron microscopy. What chemical reaction is involved in this fixation process?

1.17. Outline the design of a histochemical procedure for the localization of the enzyme arylsulfatase in tissues; the enzyme catalyzes the following reaction type:

$$R\!-\!O\!-\!\overset{\overset{\textstyle O^-}{|}}{\underset{\underset{\textstyle O}{\|}}{S}}\!=\!O \; + \; H_2O \;\; \xrightarrow{\text{\textit{Aryl-sulfatase}}} \;\; R\!-\!OH \; + \; HO\!-\!\overset{\overset{\textstyle O^-}{|}}{\underset{\underset{\textstyle O}{\|}}{S}}\!=\!O$$

1.18. In an attempt to determine the location of *glycogen* in the liver, could there be any problems of interpretation of the electron microscopic radioautographic images if tritiated *glucose* were used as the radioactive precursor molecule of glycogen?

1.19. *Microsomes* are small spherical membranous vesicles with attached ribosomes. They sediment, during differential sedimentation, only in the late stages of a preparation when very high centrifugal velocities are used. They don't appear in electronmicrographs of a cell. From where do they arise?

1.20. There are two forms of the enzyme *carbamyl phosphate synthetase*, one in the mitochondrial matrix and the other in the cytoplasm. What might be the consequence and role of this *compartmentation* of enzymes?

1.21. Human *reticulocytes* (Prob. 1.1) continue to synthesize hemoglobin for approximately 24 h after release into the circulation. Design an electron microscopic experiment using autoradiography so that you can identify *which* of the cells are actively synthesizing the protein.

1.22. (a) From what *primary source* is the DNA in *your* mitochondria, your mother or your father? (b) Speculate on possible inheritance patterns if there were a defect in one or the other parent's mitochondria.

1.23. Given that mitochondria do *not* have the same *aggressive* autolytic capacity as lysosomes, what might be the significance of having such a complex membranous structure? After all, the endoplasmic reticulum and the plasma membrane could potentially support those enzymes found in mitochondrial membranes.

1.24. The disease *epidermolysis bulosa* involves severe skin ulceration and even loss of the ends of the ears, nose, and fingers. It is the result of a primary defect in the stability of lysosomal membranes.
(a) How does this lead to the signs, just mentioned, of the disease?
(b) What biochemical procedures might you suggest to treat the disorder?

1.25. In some sufferers of Down syndrome, the somatic cell nuclei do not contain three chromosomes number 21. There is a chromosomal defect relating to chromosome number 21; what might it be?

ANSWERS TO SUPPLEMENTARY PROBLEMS

1.15. The membranes of all living cells are selectively permeable to ions and other chemical species. This selectivity is in many cases linked to the supply of ATP (Chap. 10), and one feature of cell death is a low concentration of ATP. In this state, the cell no longer excludes foreign compounds, such as *toluidine* dye.

1.16. Glutaraldehyde forms a Schiff base between side-chain amino groups of neighboring protein molecules, thus cross-linking them (Chaps. 3 and 4).

1.17. The arylsulfatase substrate *p*-nitrophenyl sulfate is used together with lead nitrate in a manner analogous to the Gomori reaction (Example 1.7).

1.18. Yes, problems would arise in interpreting the autoradiograph because the [^{3}H]-glucose not only would be incorporated into glycogen but also would be metabolized via glycolysis (Chap. 12) to yield amino acids and fatty acids; these could appear in a whole array of cellular organelles.

1.19. Fragments of endoplasmic reticulum are transformed from lipid bilayer sheets, with attached ribosomes, into spherical vesicles. This is a result of the homogenization used in preparing the samples and also the tendency of lipid bilayers (Chap. 3) to spontaneously reseal.

1.20. It enables *separate* control over the rates of urea and pyrimidine synthesis (Chap. 14).

1.21. Incubate the reticulocytes with [^{3}H]-L-leucine, which will be incorporated into proteins. Prepare electron microscope autoradiographs, and count the number of silver grains per cell and the number of polysomes. The latter appear as rosettes of five ribosomes in each cell. A statistical comparison between the number of polysomes and the amount of protein synthesized during the incubation time (proportional to the number of silver grains) indicates whether there are nonactive polysomes. In fact, many of the polysomes are inactive; i.e., they are "switched off" (see Chap. 9 for a discussion of the control of protein synthesis).

1.22. (a) Mother. (b) If a defect exists in a mitochondrial gene, all progeny from that *female* will carry the defect. Several well-defined diseases resulting from such a defect have been described.

1.23. In fact, bacteria do not have mitochondria, but some types do have membranous intrusions into the cytoplasm called *mesosomes*. These are similar in function to the inner membrane of mitochondria (Chap. 10). The reason mitochondria are distinct from other membranous structures in higher cells is possibly due to their evolutionary origin as *intracellular symbionts* and to the fact that the spatial separations of functions lead to more advantageous (in terms of natural selection and *selective advantage*) control of the various metabolic processes that are now distributed between distinct compartments.

1.24. (a) The release of peptidases, in particular, leads to tissue-protein hydrolysis and hence breakdown. (b) Treatment is aimed at reducing inflammation with anti-inflammatory steroid drugs that also serve to stabilize the lysosomal membranes.

1.25. A fragment, usually the short arm, of chromosome 21 is translocated onto another chromosome; thus, there are three copies of a fragment of the short arm in any one cell. This is a relatively rare occurrence.

CHAPTER 2

The Milieux of Living Systems

2.1 Biomolecules

Question: What types of molecules are the foundations of life?

There are four major classes of *biomolecules* that are synthesized by living systems: *nucleic acids*, *proteins*, *lipids*, and polysaccharides (*carbohydrates*). They are all *polymers* of simple building blocks (see Chap. 3): sugar, phosphate, and a nitrogenous base for the nucleic acids; amino acids for proteins; glycerol and fatty acids for lipids; and simple *sugars* (monosaccharides) for polysaccharides. These can be combined in some specialized biomolecules such as carbohydrate and protein in *glycoproteins*; lipid and protein in *lipoproteins*; and carbohydrate and lipid in *glycolipids*.

All biomolecules are remarkably similar throughout the evolutionary or *phylogenetic tree*. Since living systems primarily exist within an aqueous environment, the unique structures and properties of biomolecules are determined by their reactions within this environment. The reactions between small molecules that take place in living systems depend on higher-order interactions between the larger biomolecules that modify the aqueous environment.

EXAMPLE 2.1   DNA (deoxyribonucleic acid) is the nucleic acid that carries genetic information. Hemoglobin is a protein that transports oxygen in red blood cells (Chap. 1). Triacylglycerides are the main lipid storage molecules. Cellulose is the polysaccharide structural molecule in plants.

2.2 Interactions between Biomolecules—Chemical Bonds

Question: What is the nature of the interactions between biomolecules?

Interactions between biomolecules depend on the forming and breaking of chemical bonds.

The *covalent bond* is the strongest chemical bond. It links individual atoms within a molecule and involves sharing of a pair of electrons between adjacent atoms. Its formation requires considerable energy, and its breakage releases this energy. The formation and breakage of covalent bonds are not *readily* reversible processes.

Noncovalent bonds are weaker and are often readily *reversible*. The four major ones differ in their *length*, *strength*, *specificity*, and *response to water*. Although noncovalent interactions are weaker than covalent bonds (Table 2-1), they are numerous in biological systems, and the accumulated strength of many of them can be enormous.

Electrostatic Interactions

These occur between two atoms bearing opposite electrical charges. The energy of the interaction depends on the distance between the charged atoms, the size of the charge (valency), and the dielectric constant of the intervening medium; this constant describes the extent to which the medium becomes polarized by partial separation of bound charges within it.

EXAMPLE 2.2

Table 2-1   Types of Bonds and Interactions that Occur between Biomolecules

Interaction	Example	Bond Energy (kJ mol^{-1})^a	Bond Length (Å = 0.1 nm)
Covalent bond	—C—C—	356	1.5 for a typical —C—C— bond 0.96 for O—H in water
Electrostatic interaction	—COO$^-$ ... H$_3$N$^+$—	12–20	3 for two atoms bearing a single opposite charge in water (Fig. 2-1)
Hydrogen bond	—N—H ... O=C—	10–20	1.8 for O...H in water
Van der Waals interaction	C—H ... H—C	1–5	2.6 for O...H in water
Hydrophobic interaction^b	Burial of —CH$_2$—	12–15	

^{a}The bond energy is the energy required to break the interaction.
^{b}This value represents the free energy required to transfer a —CH$_2$— group of a nonpolar side chain from a protein interior to water.

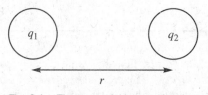

Fig. 2-1   Electrostatic interaction between two charged groups in
a molecule. If the charges q_1
and q_2 have opposite signs,
the groups will be *attracted*
to each other; if of the same
sign, they will be *repelled*.

Hydrogen Bonds

These are *polarization bonds*. They result from a distortion of the charge distribution around molecular groups; electrostatic interactions occur between a *hydrogen atom* that is covalently bound to an *electronegative* atom such as O, N, or S, and a second electronegative atom with a lone pair of nonbonding electrons (Fig. 2-2).

$$\delta- \quad \delta+ \quad \delta-$$
$$N—H----N$$

$$N—H----O$$

$$O—H----N$$

$$O—H----O$$

Fig. 2-2   Hydrogen bond donor/
acceptor systems.

van der Waals Interactions

These interactions are also due to polarization of the charge distributions around atoms in molecules. A dipole in the charge distribution induces a dipole in an adjacent atom, resulting in attraction that causes the atoms to move closer. The atoms approach each other, and the equilibrium distance between them is called the *van der Waals contact distance*. When the atoms are closer than this, there is strong repulsion between them (Fig. 2-3).

Hydrophobic Interactions

Placing a nonpolar molecule in water leads to an organization of water molecules around it that is *energetically unfavorable*; in other words, energy is expended in creating this organization. The organization of water molecules around the nonpolar molecule in a *shell* means that there is a decrease in the *entropy* of the solution. When two nonpolar molecules combine, some of the water molecules are displaced from the shells and there is a further increase in the *entropy* of the solution. This aggregation of nonpolar molecules in water is termed a *hydrophobic interaction* and sometimes *hydrophobic bonding* (Fig. 2-4).

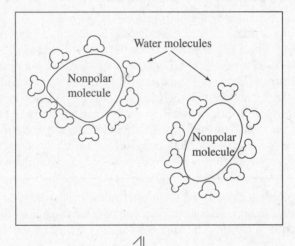

Fig. 2-3   van der Waals force between atoms.

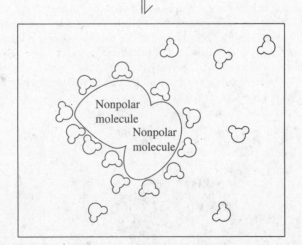

Fig. 2-4   Hydrophobic effect between molecules.

2.3   The Cellular Environment

Question: What is inside a living cell?

The inside of a cell is crowded with molecules, and these are in continuous vigorous motion that is driven by thermal energy.

In prokaryotic cells the *cytoplasm* is the only compartment; in most eukaryotic cells it is still the largest single compartment. The cytoplasm (also called the *cytosol*) is so crowded with small and large molecules that it is significantly more viscous than a typical aqueous solution encountered in laboratory experiments. As molecules in random motion collide, they diffuse throughout the cell; large molecules diffuse more slowly than small ones. It is the diffusion and collisions between molecules that enable biochemical reactions to occur.

EXAMPLE 2.3   The average mammalian cell is ~70% by weight water and 18–30% protein. In the erythrocyte (red blood cell), the average concentration of hemoglobin is 33%, or 330 g (L red blood cells)$^{-1}$.

2.4   The Aqueous Environment

Question: Why is water such an important molecule in living systems?

The strength and specificity of interactions between biological molecules depend on the medium in which they reside. The major biological solvent is water, although fat deposits readily dissolve hydrophobic molecules such as some pesticides and various drugs. Because of the large electronegativity of oxygen relative to hydrogen, the oxygen atom attracts electrons from the two hydrogen atoms, making them more negative and leaving the hydrogen atoms with a net positive charge. Thus, water molecules are highly polarized, and they associate with one another through hydrogen bonds. The angle between the two O—H bonds in water is not 180°; hence the molecule is bent, and hydrogen bonds form in which each water molecule interacts with several neighbors in a three-dimensional network. Without these interactions, water with a molecular weight of 18 would be a gas at normal atmospheric temperatures and pressures, like dinitrogen of molecular weight 28.

Water is an excellent solvent for polar and ionic molecules, hence they are termed *hydrophilic*; they dissolve in water because their charged regions interact with water as well as with one another. If molecular interactions with water are stronger than with their own kind, the substance will be soluble in water.

EXAMPLE 2.4   Proteins are polymers of polar and nonpolar amino acids; the amino acid units in the polymer are called *residues* because when the *peptide bond* between an amino acid and a peptide is formed, water is removed in a *condensation reaction,* leaving a residue of the amino acid. Amino acid residues that have polar side chains form hydrogen bonds with water so they are *hydrophilic* (Fig. 2-5). Nonpolar side chains of amino acid residues do not form hydrogen bonds with water, so they do not dissolve readily in it; they are said to be *hydrophobic*. Thus proteins tend to fold up so that their hydrophobic residues are clustered in an interior *core*, away from contact with the aqueous environment; and the hydrophilic residues tend to be arranged on the exterior interacting with water. Interactions also occur with other proteins and other biomolecules in general.

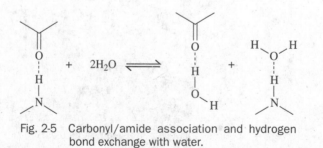

Fig. 2-5   Carbonyl/amide association and hydrogen bond exchange with water.

2.5   Acids and Bases

Most of the substances found in living systems, in the aqueous cytosol and in extracellular fluids, including ions such as Na$^+$, Cl$^-$, and biomolecules of all sizes, carry ionizable groups that are critical for their biological activity. The acid-base behavior of dissolved biomolecules is intimately linked with the dissociation of water.

A water molecule is a weak electrolyte that dissociates into a *proton* (H^+) and a *hydroxyl ion* (OH^-). In this process, the proton binds to an adjacent water molecule to which it is hydrogen bonded to form a *hydronium ion* (H_3O^+). This interaction is characterized by an equilibrium constant that for acetic acid is

$$K_a = \frac{a_{H_3O^+}\, a_{CH_3COO^-}}{a_{CH_3COOH}\, a_{H_2O}} \tag{2.1}$$

where *a* denotes the activity of the solute and solvent (see more on this below).

In pure water at 25°C, at any instant, there is 1.0×10^{-7} mol L^{-1} H_3O^+ and an equal concentration of OH^- ions. Note that the proton is hardly ever *bare* in aqueous solutions because of the very high affinity between it and water molecules. The dissociation of water is a dynamic exchange process for which we can write an equilibrium constant K_e, where *e* refers to equilibrium, and *a* in the equation refers to the *thermodynamic activity* of the various components:

$$K_e = \frac{a_{H_3O^+}\, a_{OH^-}}{a_{H_2O}^2} \tag{2.2}$$

In dilute solutions, the activity of water is constant and very close to 1.0, so the activities of solutes may be represented by their concentrations. Thus we define a practical constant K_w, called the *ionic product* of water:

$$K_w = [H_3O^+]\,[OH^-] \tag{2.3}$$

or, as is often used, $K_w = [H^+]\,[OH^-]$, where the hydration of the proton is ignored for simplicity and where the square brackets denote concentration in mol L^{-1}.

EXAMPLE 2.5   At 25°C in pure water, $K_w = 10^{-14}$ (mol L^{-1})$^{-2}$.
   The value of K_w is temperature-dependent; at 37°C, for example, $K_w = 2.4 \times 10^{-14}$.
   Since in pure water at 25°C $[H_3O^+] = [OH^-]$, then $[H_3O^+] = (10^{-14})^{-2} = 10^{-7}$ mol L^{-1}.
   Because the ionic product is constant in acid solution, since $[H_3O^+]$ is raised, then $[OH^-]$ is correspondingly lowered.

pH

The Danish chemist Søren P. L. Sørensen, in 1909, defined the term *pH* (*potentia hydrogenii*) as

$$pH = -\log[H^+] \tag{2.4}$$

Neutral solutions are defined as those in which $[H^+] = [OH^-]$, and for pure water at 25°C, $[H^+] = [OH^-] = 1 \times 10^{-7}$ mol L^{-1}. Therefore the value of the pH is $-\log[H^+] = -\log(1 \times 10^{-7}) = 7.0$.

Deionized water normally used in the laboratory is not absolutely pure. Traces of CO_2 dissolved in it produce carbonic acid which increases the H^+ concentration to $\sim 10^{-5}$ mol L^{-1}, meaning that the pH is ~5.

A solution with pH = 7.0 is said to be neutral.
A solution with pH < 7.0 is said to be acidic.
A solution with pH > 7.0 is said to be basic.
An increase of 10 fold in $[H^+]$ corresponds to a decrease of 1.0 in pH.

EXAMPLE 2.6   Calculate the pH of a 4×10^{-4} mol L^{-1} solution of HCl.

SOLUTION   At this low concentration, we may consider HCl to be completely dissociated to H^+ and Cl^-. Therefore
   $[H^+] = 4 \times 10^{-4}$ mol L^{-1}
   $pH = -\log 4 \times 10^{-4}$
   Therefore pH = 3.40.

Weak Acids and Bases

Acids: The Brønsted definition of an *acid* is a compound capable of donating a proton to another compound. Some acids are completely dissociated in water; these are termed *strong acids*. Thus,

$$HA + H_2O \rightarrow A^- + H_3O^+$$

Hydrochloric acid HCl is a strong acid.

Some acids are not completely dissociated in water; these are termed *weak acids*.

EXAMPLE 2.7   Acetic acid CH_3COOH is a weak acid because the dissociation of an H^+ from the carboxyl group, averaged over the whole population of carboxyl groups in the solution, is not complete when the acid is dissolved in water. The dissociation reaction is as follows:

$$CH_3COOH \ + \ H_2O \ \rightleftharpoons \ CH_3COO^- \ + \ H_3O^+$$

$$CH_3COOH \ (H^+ \ donor, \ acid) \ + \ H_2O \ (H^+ \ acceptor, \ base) \ \rightleftharpoons \ CH_3COO^- \ (conjugate \ base) \ + \ H_3O^+ \ (conjugate \ acid)$$

The donating and accepting of the proton is a dynamic two-way process. The H_3O^+ ion that is formed is capable of donating a proton back to the acetate ion to form acetic acid. Thus the H_3O^+ ion is considered to be an *acid*, and the acetate ion is considered to be a *base*. The acetate ion is called the *conjugate base* of acetic acid.

The two processes of association and dissociation reach equilibrium, and the resulting solution will have a higher concentration of H_3O^+ than is found in pure water; i.e., it will have a pH below 7.0.

A measure of the *strength* of an acid is its *acid dissociation constant* K_a, where the subscript a denotes *acid*:

$$K_a = \frac{a_{H_3O^+} \times a_{A^-}}{a_{HA} \times a_{H_2O}} \tag{2.5}$$

So for acetic acid, K_a is as in Eq. (2.1):

$$K_a = \frac{a_{H_3O^+} \ a_{CH_3COO^-}}{a_{CH_3COOH} \ a_{H_2O}}$$

where a denotes the *thermodynamic activity* of the chemical species; this is a factor that compensates for nonideality of the solution. In an *ideal solution*, there are no interactions (attractive or repulsive) between solute molecules. In reality, this is most unlikely to be the case, especially in moderately concentrated solutions of ions. The activity of a solute molecule is related to its concentration C by an activity coefficient γ by the equation

$$a = \gamma C \tag{2.6}$$

The activity of pure water, by convention, is taken to be 1.0. In dilute solutions the concentration of water is very close to that of pure water, and in dilute solutions the activity of a solute may be closely approximated by its concentration. Thus for most practical purposes the acid dissociation constant K_a is defined as

$$K_a = \frac{[H^+][A^-]}{[HA][H_2O]} \tag{2.7}$$

Rearranging this, Eq. (2.7) gives

$$[H^+] = \frac{K_a'[HA]}{[A^-]} \tag{2.8}$$

The *larger* the value of K_a' (note the prime denotes the fact that the *concentration of water* is included in the overall parameter value), the greater is the tendency of the acid to dissociate a proton, so the *stronger* is the acid.

In a manner similar to the definition of pH, we can define pK_a [dropping the prime in Eq. (2.8)] as

$$pK_a = -\log K_a \tag{2.9}$$

Thus, the *lower* the value of pK_a of a chemical compound, the higher the value of K_a, and the *stronger* acid it is.

For example, for acetic acid

$$K_a = \frac{[CH_3COO^-][H^+]}{[CH_3COOH]}$$

EXAMPLE 2.8   Which of the following acids is the *stronger*, (a) boric acid, $pK_a = 9.0$ or (b) acetic acid, $pK_a = 4.6$?

SOLUTION
For boric acid, $K_a = 10^{-9}$ mol L^{-1}.
For acetic acid, $K_a = 10^{-4.6} = 2.5 \times 10^{-5}$ mol L^{-1}.
Thus, acetic acid has the larger K_a and is therefore the stronger acid.

Bases: The *Brønsted* definition of a base is a compound that accepts a proton from an acid. When methylamine dissolves in water, it accepts a proton from water, thus leading to an increase in the OH$^-$ concentration and thus a higher pH.

$$CH_3NH_2 \text{(base)} + H_2O \text{ (H$^+$ donor, acid)} \rightleftharpoons CH_3NH_3^+ + \text{(conjugate acid)} + OH^- \text{ (conjugate base)}$$

As with acetic acid, as the concentration of OH$^-$ increases, the equilibrium moves to the left. An expression for a *basicity constant* is

$$K_b = \frac{[CH_3NH_3^+][OH^-]}{[CH_3NH_2]} \tag{2.10}$$

The use of this constant can be confusing, as we would need to keep track of two different types of constant, K_a and K_b. Since chemical equilibrium is a two-way process, it is perfectly correct, and more convenient, to consider the behavior of bases from the point of view of the conjugate acid. The latter is considered to donate a proton to water as follows:

$$CH_3NH_3^+ \text{(acid)} + H_2O \text{ (base)} \rightleftharpoons CH_3NH_2 \text{(conjugate base)} + H_3O^+ \text{(conjugate acid)}$$

$$K_a = \frac{[CH_3NH_3^+]}{[CH_3NH_2][H^+]} \tag{2.11}$$

EXAMPLE 2.9   Calculate [OH$^-$] in an aqueous solution when $[H^+] = 0.1$ mol L^{-1}. What is the pH?

SOLUTION
Since $[H^+][OH^-] = 10^{-14}$,
$pH = -\log 10^{-13} = 13$.

2.6 Buffers

A buffer is a system that absorbs some form of shock. In the case of a *pH buffer*, it is a solution containing an acid and its conjugate base that is capable of resisting changes in pH when small amounts of additional acid or base are added.

Consider the dissociation of acetic acid in water (Example 2.7):

$$CH_3COOH + H_2O \rightleftharpoons CH_3COO^- + H_3O^+$$

Adding extra acid leads to the recombination of H_3O^+ and CH_3COO^- to form acetic acid; so the net buildup of H_3O^+ is less than it might have been if there were no CH_3COO^-. Conversely, addition of NaOH causes dissociation of acetic acid to acetate, minimizing the decline in H_3O^+ concentration (See Fig. 2-6).

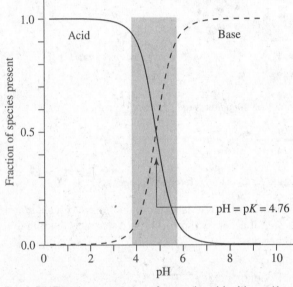

Fig. 2-6   Titration response of a weak acid with a pK_a of 4.76. The gray zone indicates the approximate range of effective pH buffering.

The prediction of the behavior of buffers can be quantified by rewriting the general equation for dissociation of a weak acid and taking logarithms of both sides of the equation:

$$K_a = \frac{[H^+][A^-]}{[HA]} \tag{2.12}$$

$$\log K_a = \log[H^+] + \log[A^-] - \log[HA]$$

Multiplying both sides by -1 gives

$$-\log K_a = -\log[H^+] - \log[A^-] + \log[HA]$$

From Eq. (2.4), $pH = -\log[H^+]$, and from Eq. (2.9), $pK_a = -\log K_a$, therefore

$$pH = pK_a + \log\frac{[A^-]}{[HA]} \tag{2.13}$$

This is the famous *Henderson-Hasselbalch* equation that relates the pH of a salt solution to the concentration and pK_a of the salt.

If [HA] = [A⁻], then pH = pK_a. This useful relationship enables the calculation of the composition of buffers that have a specified pH; as well as the pH range over which buffering occurs. The useful buffering range is ~p$K_a \pm 1$ pH units.

EXAMPLE 2.10

(a) Calculate the pH of a 0.2 M acetate buffer (a solution containing 0.1 mol L⁻¹ acetic acid and 0.1 mol L⁻¹ sodium acetate), given that the pK_a of acetic acid is 4.7.
(b) What would be the pH value after adding 0.05 mmol of NaOH to 1 L of 0.2 mol L⁻¹ acetate buffer?
(c) Compare the latter pH value with that obtained after adding 0.05 mmol NaOH to 1 L of water (a simple solution of 0.05 mol L⁻¹ NaOH).
(d) How much acid or base can be added to 1 L of the 0.2 M acetate buffer so that the pH does not change appreciably, i.e., what is its buffer range?

SOLUTION

(a) There is 0.1 mol acetic acid and 0.1 mol sodium acetate in 1 L of solution. Using the Henderson-Hasselbalch equation, Eq. (2.13), we obtain

$$pH = 4.7 + \log \frac{0.1}{0.1} = 4.7 + 0.0 = 4.7$$

(See the fifth row of Table 2-2.)

Table 2-2   Change in pH of 0.2 mol L⁻¹ Acetate Buffer after Addition of Acid or Base

Addition	[Base]:[Acid]	pH
HCl 0.095 mol	0.005:0.195	3.1
HCl 0.075 mol	0.025:0.175	3.9
HCl 0.05 mol	0.05:0.15	4.2
HCl 0.025 mol	0.075:0.125	4.5
	0.1:0.1	4.7
NaOH 0.025 mol	0.125:0.075	4.9
NaOH 0.05 mol	0.15:0.05	5.2
NaOH 0.075 mol	0.175:0.025	5.5
NaOH 0.095 mol	0.195:0.005	6.3

(b) On adding 0.05 mmol NaOH, the concentration of undissociated acetic acid falls to 0.05 mol L⁻¹, while the acetate concentration rises to 0.15 mol L⁻¹. Therefore,

$$pH = 4.7 + \log \frac{0.15}{0.05} = 4.7 + \log 3.0 = 4.7 + 0.48 = 5.18$$

(See the seventh row of Table 2-2.)
(c) The pH of 0.05 mol L⁻¹ NaOH is −log [H⁺] in the solution. If we assume the NaOH is fully dissociated in water, the value of [OH⁻] is 0.05 mol L⁻¹.
From the known value of the ionic product of water, 10^{-14} (mol L⁻¹)²,

$$[H^+] = 10^{-14}/0.05$$

Therefore pH = 12.7.
Observe the large increase in pH on adding NaOH to water, compared with the very small increase in pH on adding the same amount of NaOH to the buffer solution in (b).
(d) Suppose 0.025 mmol NaOH is added to the solution in (c), the concentration of undissociated acetic acid falls to 0.075 mol L⁻¹, while the acetate anion concentration rises to 0.125 mol L⁻¹. Perform this calculation for a series of additions, and it becomes clear that the pH does not vary greatly with the addition of acid or base until there is predominantly one form of solute present, at which point the pH changes rapidly. This is consistent with a buffer range for acetic acid of 3.7–5.7 pH units.

EXAMPLE 2.11   Nearly all biological fluids are pH-buffered; and the pH is maintained within a small range for which the interaction between biomolecules has been naturally selected. The pH of plasma is normally ~7.4. Phosphate ions ($pK_{a2} = 6.8$; the subscript $a2$ denotes the *second* acid dissociation reaction) and bicarbonate ($pK_a = 6.3$) are important biological buffers. Many biomolecules including proteins, lipids, and nucleic acids have ionizable groups with pK_a values in the physiological pH range. Because there are so many of these groups in any biological system, they make a significant contribution to the pH-buffering capacity. The first and second dissociation reactions for phosphoric acid are shown below, with the second dissociation being the most physiologically relevant.

$$H_3PO_4 + H_2O \rightleftharpoons H_2PO_4^- + H_3O^+$$

$$H_2PO_4^- + H_2O \rightleftharpoons HPO_4^{2-} + H_3O^+$$

2.7   Thermodynamics

Notwithstanding their obvious complexity, living organisms can still be viewed as physicochemical systems that interact with their surroundings. *Thermodynamics* is a theory that is concerned with the *energetics* and *macroscopic, bulk* properties of matter. It deals especially well with large amounts of matter and the properties of matter under changes in temperature and pressure. The link between thermodynamics and molecular processes is provided by the theory of *statistical mechanics*.

Basic Concepts

Several fundamental definitions are used in the thermodynamic descriptions of systems.

- *System*—that part of the universe with which the experimentalist is concerned, e.g., an organism or a glass vessel in which a chemical reaction is occurring.

- *Open system*—one in which both *matter* and *heat* exchange with the surroundings.

- *Closed system*—one in which *only heat* exchanges with the surroundings.

- *Isolated or adiabatic system*—(Greek *a*: without; *dia*: through; *bata*: flow) one in which neither matter nor heat exchanges with the surroundings.

- *State functions*—properties relating to changes in a system which are dependent only on its initial and final states. Many of the important system properties discussed in the next sub-sections such as *internal energy*, *enthalpy*, *entropy*, and *Gibbs free energy* are called state functions.

The SI unit of energy is the joule (J). The units commonly used in thermodynamic studies are shown in Table 2-3.

EXAMPLE 2.12   Are living organisms classified as thermodynamically *open*, *closed*, or *isolated* systems?
They are *open* systems because they exchange both heat and matter (nutrients, excreta) with their surroundings.

Table 2-3   Constants and Units of Thermodynamics

Joule (J)	$1\ J = 1\ kg\ m^2\ s^{-2}$
Calorie (cal)	1 cal of heat raises the temperature of 1 g water 1°C from 15 to 16°C; 1 cal = 4.184 J
Avogadro's number N	$N = 6.023 \times 10^{23}$ molecules mol^{-1}
Coulomb (C)	1 C = charge on 6.241×10^{18} electrons
Electron charge	1.60×10^{-19} C
Kelvin temperature scale (K)	0 K = absolute zero 273.15 K = 0°C
Gas constant (R)	$R = 8.3145\ J\ K^{-1}\ mol^{-1}$
Faraday (F)	1 F = N electron charges 1 F = 96,485 C mol^{-1} = 96,485 J V^{-1} mol^{-1}

First Law of Thermodynamics

"The total energy of a system *and its surroundings* is constant" is the *first law*. In other words, energy cannot be created or destroyed; it can only be changed from one form into another. If a system exchanges heat with its surroundings, or does work on its surroundings, then there is a change in its internal energy (ΔU) where the Greek letter delta Δ denotes change or *difference*. This is expressed mathematically as

$$\Delta U = \Delta U_{final} - \Delta U_{initial} = \Delta q + \Delta w \tag{2.14}$$

where Δq is the amount of heat exchanged with the surroundings and Δw is the work done by the system on the surroundings.

Question: What determines whether Δq and Δw are positive or negative?

If Δq is positive, then by convention this means that heat has been transferred *to the system*, giving an increase in internal energy; and the process is therefore termed *endothermic* (Latin *endo*, meaning *inside*). When Δq is negative, heat has been transferred to the surroundings, giving a decrease in internal energy, and the process is termed *exothermic*. When Δw is positive, work has been done on the system, giving an increase in internal energy. When Δw is negative, work has been done on the surroundings, giving a decrease in internal energy.

Enthalpy

Enthalpy H is the heat content of a system, in joules. Many chemical reactions are conveniently studied at constant pressure so the heat change ΔH during such a reaction is called the *enthalpy change* and is related to the change in internal energy, ΔU, and the work done by the system in making a volume change $P \, \Delta V$:

$$\Delta H = \Delta U + P \, \Delta V \tag{2.15}$$

Most biochemical reactions occur in solution; in these cases volume changes are negligible so Eq. (2.15) becomes

$$\Delta H = \Delta U \tag{2.16}$$

EXAMPLE 2.13 The changes in internal energy ΔU for the total oxidation of glucose ($C_6H_{12}O_6$) and stearic acid ($C_{18}H_{36}O_2$) at 310 K (37°C) are -2.9×10^3 kJ mol^{-1} and -11.36×10^3 kJ mol^{-1}, respectively.

(a) Calculate ΔH for these reactions.
(b) Which substance is more likely to be useful for energy storage in the body?

SOLUTION

(a) For glucose the reaction is

$$C_6H_{12}O_6 + 6O_2 \rightarrow 6CO_2 + 6H_2O$$

In this case there is no volume change in the reaction (both O_2 and CO_2 are gases at 310 K). Hence, $\Delta U = \Delta H = -2.9 \times 10^3$ kJ mol^{-1}.

For stearic acid the reaction is

$$C_{18}H_{36}O_2 + 26O_2 \rightarrow 18CO_2 + 18H_2O$$

In this case 8 mol of gas is consumed per mole of stearic acid ($26O_2$—$18CO_2$). Assuming that the *ideal gas law* (also called *Boyle's law*) applies, i.e.,

$$P \, \Delta V = \Delta n \, RT$$

then

$$\Delta H = \Delta U + \Delta n\, RT$$
$$\Delta H = -(11.36 \times 10^3 + 8 \times 8.314 \times 310/1000)\ \text{kJ mol}^{-1} = -11.38 \times 10^3\ \text{kJ mol}^{-1}$$

(b) Thus, more heat is given out by the oxidation of 1 mol of stearic acid, each molecule of which has 18 carbon atoms (11.38 MJ), than for 3 mol of glucose that also has a total of 18 carbon atoms (8.7 MJ). Clearly stearic acid is a far more energy-rich storage substance, for a given number of carbon atoms, than is glucose; the main reason for this is that glucose with its five —OH groups is already substantially more oxidized than stearic acid.

Overall, the first law of thermodynamics provides a description of the energy balance for a given reaction; the net change is the enthalpy of the system.

Second Law of Thermodynamics

"The total entropy of a system and its surroundings always increases for a spontaneous process"—this is the formal statement of the second law. The law provides a way of gaining an indication of the *disorder* or randomness of a system; this is the entropy S. It also provides a means of predicting whether a process will occur spontaneously. Thus the change in entropy ΔS associated with a change in a system in terms of the heat absorbed by the system at constant temperature T is given by

$$\Delta S \geq \Delta q/T \tag{2.17}$$

The equality in Eq. (2.17) applies in cases of reversible processes, while the *in*equality applies to irreversible processes.

As a system becomes more disordered, its entropy increases (see Fig. 2-7).

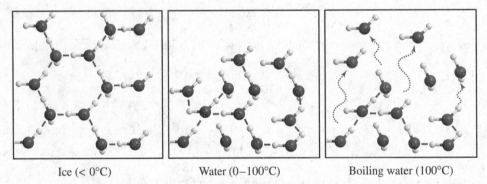

| Ice (< 0°C) | Water (0–100°C) | Boiling water (100°C) |

Fig. 2-7   Three different states of water and the various extents of bulk order.

Gibb's Free Energy

The second law of thermodynamics indicates that a process will occur spontaneously if $\Delta q < T\, \Delta S$. For processes occurring at constant temperature and pressure, $\Delta q = \Delta H$, so for a spontaneous process

$$\Delta H - T\, \Delta S < 0$$

The quantity $\Delta H - T\, \Delta S$ is called ΔG, and if a process occurs spontaneously, $\Delta G < 0$. Here G refers to *Gibb's free energy* and is therefore defined as

$$G = H - TS \tag{2.18}$$

and for a reaction at constant temperature and pressure,

$$\Delta G = \Delta H - T\, \Delta S \tag{2.19}$$

The value of ΔG gives the maximum *work* available from the process, apart from work associated with changes in pressure or volume referred to as *non-PV* work. PV work is generally not important in biological systems.

Spontaneous processes are termed *exergonic* and have a negative value of ΔG; processes which require energy input to drive them have a positive ΔG and are termed *endergonic*; processes which are at equilibrium have $\Delta G = 0$.

The fact that a reaction has a large negative ΔG does not mean that it will proceed spontaneously at a significant rate. Most biological reactions that are thermodynamically favorable (negative ΔG) proceed at an almost infinitely slow rate. It is only when the appropriate enzyme is present that a reaction will proceed at a reasonable (to enable life) rate. Thus, an enzyme accelerates the attainment of thermodynamic equilibrium. An enzyme does not alter the equilibrium constant and hence bias a system which is thermodynamically unfavorable (i.e., one with a positive ΔG).

EXAMPLE 2.14   Most of the energy that is transduced by higher animals is derived from the oxidation of glucose, in the following overall reaction:

$$C_6H_{12}O_6 + 6CO_2 \rightarrow 6CO_2 + 6H_2O$$

Given that $\Delta H = -2808$ kJ mol^{-1} and $\Delta S = 182.4$ J T^{-1} mol^{-1} for this reaction, how much energy is available from the oxidation of 1 mol of glucose at 310 K?

SOLUTION

$$\Delta G = \Delta H - T\,\Delta S = -2808 + (310 \times 182.4 \times 10^{-3}) \text{ kJ mol}^{-1} = -2865 \text{ kJ mol}^{-1}$$

Hence, absorption and oxidation of 1 mol (180.16 g) of glucose at 310 K provides an animal with 2865 kJ of non-PV work/energy, as noted in Example 2.13.

Standard States

The *standard state* of a substance is defined as that form of the substance at a specified temperature that is stable at 1 atm of pressure (101.325 kPa). For a *solute*, its standard state is defined as a solution of concentration 1 mol L^{-1}. For chemical reactions in solution, the *standard free energy change* (ΔG^0, where ^{0} denotes standard state) is that for converting 1 mol L^{-1} of reactants to 1 mol L^{-1} of products:

$$\Delta G^0 = \Delta H^0 - T\,\Delta S^0 \tag{2.20}$$

Biochemical Standard States

An activity (Sec. 2.5) of 1.0 is assigned to a solute in solution at a concentration of 1.0 mol L^{-1} at 25°C and 1 atm of pressure. Many biochemical reactions involve H$^+$ ions, or *protons*. The standard state of an H$^+$ solution is defined as a 1 mol L^{-1} solution, but it has a pH of 0 ($-\log 1.0 = 0.0$). This low pH is *in*compatible with most forms of life; therefore it is convenient to define a *biochemical* standard state for solutes in which all components except H$^+$ are at a concentration of 1 mol L^{-1}, but H$^+$ is present at a concentration of 10^{-7} mol L^{-1} (i.e., pH 7).

Free energy changes for systems described in terms of *biochemical standard states* are symbolized with a prime, such as $\Delta G^{0\prime}$, $\Delta H^{0\prime}$, $\Delta S^{0\prime}$.

2.8   Free Energy and Equilibrium

Free Energy

Every living organism requires a continuous input of energy. This energy is involved in the synthesis and maintenances of macromolecules, synthesis of small molecules, overall cell growth and differentiation, and movement. These outcomes are achieved through the action of a large number of enzymes, catalyzing reactions in complex networks of chemical transformations collectively known as *metabolism*.

A global overview of bioenergetics can be obtained by using thermodynamic ideas in the study of networks of reactions. The detailed chemistry of metabolic processes is discussed later (Chaps. 10 to 14). The key concepts are as follows.

Equilibrium and Free Energy

The free energy change for the reaction

$$a\text{A} + b\text{B} \rightleftharpoons c\text{C} + d\text{D}$$

is given by

$$\Delta G = \Delta G^0 + RT \ln \{[\text{C}]^c\,[\text{D}]^d/([\text{A}]^a\,[\text{B}]^b)\} \tag{2.21}$$

where ΔG^0, the *standard Gibb's free energy change*, is the free energy change at 25°C, 1 atm pressure, and unit *activities* of reactants and products. [A], [B], [C], and [D] are the concentrations of the reactants, while $a, b, c,$ and d are the so-called *stoichiometries* of the reactants in the reaction, and it is assumed that the concentrations of the reactants in their standard states ($[\text{A}]^0$, $[\text{B}]^0$, $[\text{C}]^0$, and $[\text{D}]^0$) are all 1 mol L^{-1}.

When the reaction attains equilibrium (i.e., a reversible process), $\Delta G = 0$.
Hence,

$$\Delta G^0 = RT \ln\{[\text{C}]^c\,[\text{D}]^d/([\text{A}]^a\,[\text{B}]^b)\} \tag{2.22}$$

where $[\text{A}]_e$, $[\text{B}]_e$, $[\text{C}]_e$, and $[\text{D}]_e$ are the equilibrium concentrations of the reactants.
Since K_e is the equilibrium constant of the reaction, then

$$K_e = \frac{[\text{C}]_e^c[\text{D}]_e^d}{[\text{A}]_e^a[\text{B}]_e^b} \tag{2.23}$$

$$\Delta G^0 = -RT\ln K_e \tag{2.24}$$

and

$$K_e = e^{-\Delta G^0/RT} \tag{2.25}$$

When the reactants are in excess, the reaction proceeds in the net-forward direction until equilibrium is reached; and when products are in excess, the reaction will proceed in the net-reverse direction until equilibrium is reached. Note that this discussion applies to the *net* production of products and depletion of substrates; but in reality, there are backward and forward exchanges of molecules in a process often termed *tandem exchange* that goes on all the time.

EXAMPLE 2.15   *Phosphoglucomutase* catalyzes the reversible reaction

$$\text{Glucose 1-phosphate} \rightleftharpoons \text{Glucose 6-phosphate}$$

The reaction has a standard free energy change at equilibrium of $\Delta G^0 = -7.3$ kJ mol^{-1}. If the enzyme is added to a 0.2 mmol L^{-1} solution of glucose 1-phosphate at 310 K, what will the equilibrium composition of the solution be?

SOLUTION   From Eq. (2.25)

$$K_e = e^{-\Delta G^0/RT} = e^{7.3 \times 10^3/8.314 \times 310} = 17.0$$

Thus, [glucose 6-phosphate]$_e$ = 17.0 [glucose 1-phosphate]$_e$.
As [glucose 1-phosphate] + [glucose 6-phosphate] = 0.2 mmol L^{-1},
then [glucose 6-phosphate]$_e$ = 0.189 mmol L^{-1} and [glucose 1-phosphate]$_e$ = 0.011 mmol L^{-1}.

Temperature Dependence of Equilibrium Constants
From Eqs. (2.20) and (2.24),

$$\ln K_e = -\Delta G^0/(RT)$$

and

$$G^0 = \Delta H^0 - T\Delta S^0$$

hence

$$\ln K_e = -\Delta H^0/(RT) + \Delta S^0/(RT) \tag{2.26}$$

This equation is called the *van't Hoff isochore* (Greek *iso*, same; *chora*, place, implying a constant volume). If ΔH^0 and ΔS^0 are independent of temperature (as they generally are), a plot of $\ln K_e$ versus $1/T$ gives a straight line. The intercept is $\Delta S^0/R$ and slope is $\Delta H^0/R$, so that ΔS^0 and ΔH^0 can be calculated for the various values of K_e measured at various temperatures. The corresponding plot is known as a *van't Hoff* plot (Fig. 2-8).

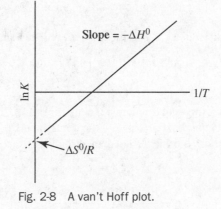

Fig. 2-8   A van't Hoff plot.

2.9   Oxidation and Reduction

Chemical reactions involving oxidation and reduction processes (*redox reactions*) are central to metabolism. The reactions involve the transfer of electrons between molecules; such reactions provide most of the energy in living systems.

Most life on earth is dependent upon a series of redox reactions in *photosynthesis* by which solar energy is used to produce ATP and O_2, and to synthesize carbohydrates from CO_2. The energy derived from the oxidation of carbohydrates is coupled to the synthesis of ATP via a series of redox reactions, the mitochondrial electron transport chain.

Basic Concepts

* *Oxidation reaction*—one in which a substance *loses* electron(s)

* *Reduction reaction*—one in which a substance *gains* electron(s)

* *Half-cell reaction*—the oxidation *or* reduction step in a *redox reaction*

EXAMPLE 2.16   What are the half-cell reactions in the following redox reaction?

$$Zn + Cu^{2+} \leftrightarrow Zn^{2+} + Cu$$

SOLUTION   The *oxidation* half-cell reaction is $Zn \rightarrow Zn^{2+} + 2e^-$.

The *reduction* half-cell reaction is $Cu^{2+} + 2e^- \rightarrow Cu$.

In the oxidation reaction, Zn is the electron donor, Zn^{2+} is the electron acceptor, and the two forms of zinc are a redox pair (in the same way that a weak acid has a conjugate base, making up an acid-base pair, HA and A^-).

The sum of the two half-reactions is the whole reaction.

Free Energy Changes in Redox Reactions

The free energy change in a redox reaction is given by

$$\Delta G = - nFE \tag{2.27}$$

where n electrons are transferred from each mole of the species being oxidized to that being reduced; E is the *electromotive force* (in volts) required to inhibit the electron transfer; and F is the *Faraday constant* which is equal to 96.5 kJ V^{-1} mol^{-1}. Recall that a measure of electric potential, the volt, is equal to one joule per coulomb of electric charge, so Faraday's constant is also the charge, in coulombs, of 1 mol of electrons.

When the components of a redox reaction are in their *standard states*

$$\Delta G^0 = - nFE_0 \tag{2.28}$$

EXAMPLE 2.17   Suppose that the ΔG^0 of the reaction below is -213 kJ mol^{-1}. What is the value of E_0 of this reaction?

$$Zn + Cu^{2+} \rightleftharpoons Zn^{2+} + Cu$$

SOLUTION   By rearranging Eq. (2.28), with $n = 2$, because *two* electrons are transferred, we obtain

$$E_0 = \Delta G^0/nF = 213/(2 \times 96.5) = 1.1 \text{ V}$$

Electrochemical Cells

Redox reactions can be studied by using electrochemical cells (Fig. 2-9). In contrast to the components of a conjugate acid-base pair, which cannot exist separately, the components of a conjugate redox pair can exist separately. Such a physical separation is achieved in an electrochemical cell.

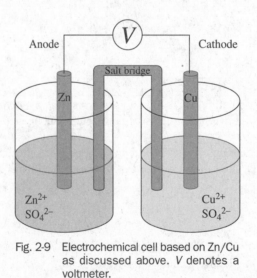

Fig. 2-9   Electrochemical cell based on Zn/Cu as discussed above. *V* denotes a voltmeter.

The Cu and Zn electrodes dip into solutions of their respective cations at 1 *M* concentration (for *standard* conditions), and the *salt bridge* (containing concentrated KCl) maintains electrical continuity between the two solutions. Electrons flow from the Zn *half-cell* to the Cu *half-cell* when Zn is oxidized to Zn^{2+}, with concomitant reduction of Cu^{2+} to Cu in the Cu half-cell. The value of E for this reaction is determined by measuring the potential difference (in volts) that must be applied to the cell to reduce the electron flow to zero.

Half-cell Electrode Potentials

Half-cell reactions cannot be studied in isolation; all that can be measured is the difference in potential (ΔE) when two half-cells are linked to form an electrochemical cell. *Relative* electrode potentials for half-cells are obtained by reference to a standard half-cell, the *hydrogen electrode* that is assigned an E_0 of 0.0 V.

The half-cell reaction for hydrogen is

$$H^+ + e^- \rightarrow H_2(Pt)$$

where Pt specifies a platinum electrode.

Hydrogen gas is bubbled over the platinum electrode at 1 atm of pressure, in an H^+ solution of 1 mol L^{-1}. The E_0 value for another half-cell reaction (with its components in their standard states as well) is measured by linking its electrochemical cell with the standard hydrogen cell.

By convention, the standard potential of a half-cell is expressed as a *reduction potential*; i.e., larger negative values indicate a greater tendency to lose electrons.

Table 2-4 lists some of the important biological reduction potentials. Oxygen has a strong tendency to accept electrons as deduced from the fact that its E_0' is positive, thus it is a strong oxidizing agent; its conjugate redox partner, water, is a weak electron donor, and thus it is a weak reducing agent. *Hydrogen has a strong tendency to donate electrons, and thus it is a strong reducing agent*.

In biological systems the properties of redox partners are modified by their surroundings, their proximity to water, or their protein carriers to which they are bound. This is shown in the cases of various *cytochromes*, all of which involve the Fe^{3+}/Fe^{2+} redox couple, but they have a range of reduction potentials.

Table 2-4   Standard Reduction Potentials of Reactions in the Electron Transport Chain (see Chap. 10)

Half-reaction		E_0' (V)
$\frac{1}{2} O_2 + 2H^+ + 2e^-$	$\rightarrow H_2O$	0.82
Cytochrome a_3 $(Fe^{3+}) + e^-$	$\rightarrow$ Cytochrome a_3 (Fe^{2+})	0.39
Cytochrome c $(Fe^{3+}) + e^-$	$\rightarrow$ Cytochrome c (Fe^{2+})	0.24
Cytochrome c_1 $(Fe^{3+}) + e^-$	$\rightarrow$ Cytochrome c_1 (Fe^{2+})	0.22
Cytochrome b $(Fe^{3+}) + e^-$	$\rightarrow$ Cytochrome b (Fe^{2+})	0.07
Ubiquinone (oxidised) $+ 2H^+ + 2e^-$	$\rightarrow$ Ubiquinone (reduced)	0.10
$FAD + 2H^+ + 2e^-$	$\rightarrow FADH_2$	−0.22
$NAD^+ + H^+ + 2e^-$	$\rightarrow NADH$	−0.32
$H^+ + e^-$	$\rightarrow \frac{1}{2} H_2$	−0.42

Relationship between E_0 and E

The free energy change for the general redox reaction occurring in solution

$$A_{ox} + B_{red} \rightleftharpoons A_{red} + B_{ox}$$

is

$$\Delta G = \Delta G^0 + RT \ln\left(\frac{[A_{red}][B_{ox}]}{[A_{ox}][B_{red}]}\right)$$

From Eq. (2.27), $\Delta G = -nFE$, and by recalling that the concentrations of solutes in their standard states are at 1 mol L^{-1}, then $[A_{red}]^0 = [B_{ox}]^0 = 1$ mol L^{-1}, hence

$$E = E_0 - (RT/nF) \ln\left(\frac{[A_{red}][B_{ox}]}{[A_{ox}][B_{red}]}\right) \tag{2.29}$$

This is called the *Nernst redox* equation; it provides a way of relating E and E_0 for any full redox reaction, or half-cell reaction.

EXAMPLE 2.18   What is E for the half-cell reaction shown below, at pH 7, 298 K, for 1 mol L^{-1} solutions of NAD^+ and NADH, given that E_0 is -0.11 V (Table 2-4)?

$$NAD^+ + H^+ + 2e^- \rightarrow NADH$$

SOLUTION   The Nernst redox equation in this case is

$$E = E_0 - (RT/2F)\ln\left(\frac{[NADH]}{[NAD^+][H^+]}\right)$$

Substituting in values for E_0, [NADH], and $[NAD^+]$, we obtain

$$E = -0.11 - (8.314 \times 298)/(2 \times 96.5 \times 10^3)\ln[1/(1 \times 10^{-7})] = 0.32 \text{ V}$$

Since the components of the reaction are in their *biochemical* standard states, this value of E is in fact E_0' for the half-cell reaction.

2.10   Osmotic Pressure

Question: What fundamental physicochemical phenomenon determines the distribution of water between the inside and outside of cells?

The plasma membranes of cells are *semipermeable*; in other words they are permeable to water and a *select group* of small molecules, but are impermeable to large molecules and many ions. If the total concentrations of solutes on either side of a semipermeable membrane are different, water diffuses from the region of low solute concentration to the region of high solute concentration until the solute concentrations are the same on both sides. This process is called *osmosis*, and the difference in water pressure across the cell membrane is called the *osmotic pressure*.

The interior of the cell has a high concentration of solutes. If cells are placed into water or dilute buffer, they swell. Since the plasma membrane does not stretch to any large extent, the cell bursts owing to the osmotically driven *influx* of water (Fig. 2-10). Conversely, if cells are placed in solutions of high solute concentration, they shrink owing to the osmotically driven *efflux* of water from the cells.

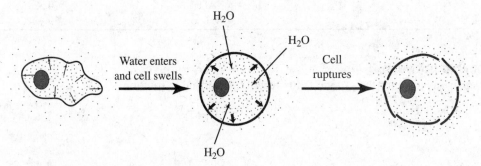

Fig. 2-10   Osmotically induced lysis of a cell.

Plant and prokaryotic cells are surrounded by a rigid *cell wall* that protects them against *osmotic stress*, but eukaryotic cells exist in vivo in tissues where the extracellular medium has very similar *osmolarity* to that inside the cells; thus there is normally no net osmotic pressure difference across the plasma membrane.

When performing experiments on eukaryotic cells, the cells are usually suspended in solutions of the same osmotic pressure as that inside the cells. Such solutions are said to be *isotonic* or *iso-osmotic* with respect to blood plasma. For practical purposes, an isotonic solution is 300 mOsmol L^{-1}.

Osmolarity depends on the total number of moles of solute *particles* (ions or molecules) in the solution. For most ions or molecules in physiological solutions, the activity γ is close to 1, so 1 mol of solute particles is equivalent to 1 Osmol. On the other hand, 1 mol of NaCl when added to water dissociates into 2 mol of particles, that is, 1 mol of Na^+ and 1 mol of Cl^- ions. In contrast, glucose does not dissociate in this way so 1 mol of glucose gives only 1 mol of particles in aqueous solution.

EXAMPLE 2.19 Is 0.9% (w/v) NaCl isotonic with plasma?

SOLUTION Yes. Every liter of solution contains 9 g NaCl; since the M_r of NaCl is 58.44, the concentration of this solution is 154 mmol L^{-1}. Since NaCl dissociates into two solute particles in water, the solution has an osmolarity of 308 mOsmol L^{-1}. This is very close to being isotonic with plasma.

In fact this estimate of osmolarity is *not* strictly correct; even at low concentrations around 300 mmol L^{-1}, a measurement in an osmometer shows the solution to be thermodynamically *nonideal* with a value less than that predicted. The value is actually 285 mOsmol L^{-1}, implying that the activity coefficient [Eq. (2.6)] is 0.93.

EXAMPLE 2.20 What is the molarity of a glucose solution that is isotonic with plasma (M_r glucose = 180.16) given that the osmolarity of plasma is 300 mOsmol L^{-1}?

SOLUTION Since glucose contains 1 mmol of solute particles per mmol of glucose, the solution needs to be 300 mmol L^{-1} to give an osmolarity of 300 mOsmol L^{-1} and to be isotonic with plasma. When measured with an osmometer (Example 2.19), the osmolarity is the same as predicted, implying that the thermodynamic activity [Eq. (2.6)] of glucose in dilute solutions like those found in living systems is 1.0. This turns out to be true for most other simple sugars.

2.11 Thermodynamics Applied to Living Systems

Thermodynamic analysis in the laboratory usually relates to reversible processes in closed systems that are at or close to equilibrium. The contrast with living systems is great! These are open systems that exchange matter and energy with their surroundings, and they are not at equilibrium.

Living systems overall are far from thermodynamic equilibrium. At equilibrium there is no energy available for useful work such as that required to synthesize structural or information-containing polymers and to pump ions to create transmembrane ionic disequilibria, i.e., $\Delta G \neq 0$. Only systems far from equilibrium have free energy available for useful work.

Living systems take in nutrients from their surroundings. These nutrients have high enthalpy and are often ordered such as the tissue of a higher organism, so they have *low entropy*. The organism converts these nutrients to products that have *low enthalpy* and *high entropy*, with the release of energy.

The biochemical processes that occur in living systems are relatively constant over time even though there is a continual flux of energy and matter through them. This is referred to as a steady state, or if there are still small variations, a *quasi-steady state*. Like the equilibrium state of a closed system, the quasi-steady state of an open system is usually a stable state. Overall, in living systems, some reactions operate near to equilibrium while others operate well away from equilibrium. The flow of energy and materials through a living system is controlled by enzymes, the activities of which are controlled by numerous regulatory mechanisms that are described in detail especially in Chaps. 5 and 10 to 14.

EXAMPLE 2.21 Starch is a storage carbohydrate in plants and is eaten as food by many organisms including humans. It is a polymer of glucose units (Chaps. 3 and 10), so the ordering involved in making the polymer means that entropy is less than in a solution of glucose molecules of the same number as are in the polymer. In the digestion process, starch is converted back to its individual glucose molecules by the action of the enzyme α-amylase (official name *α-1,4-glucan-4-glucanohydrolase*), increasing the entropy again.

Glucose is converted via a series of enzyme catalyzed reactions to carbon dioxide and water with the release of energy in reactions that overall are *exothermic*. The energy is used in driving movement, and also in reactions that build up molecular structures. The excess heat leaves the system by thermal conduction and convection.

2.12 Classification of Biochemical Reactions

Thousands of different reactions occur in living systems, and most of these are intrinsically slow. Life as we know it has only been made possible by catalysts known as enzymes. Enzymes are remarkable for the diversity of their selectivity, specificity, and catalytic power. Nearly all enzymes are proteins, but the importance of catalytically active RNA (*ribozymes*) is increasingly being recognized.

Protein enzymes have been classified into six major classes according to the nature of the reaction they catalyze. Enzyme Commission (EC) numbers have been assigned to all enzymes by the Nomenclature Committee of the International Union of Biochemistry and Molecular Biology. Generally, each enzyme has a unique number, but there are exceptions—the *restriction enzymes* which cut nucleic acids are one such exceptional group. The official name and number for this group of enzymes (and there are thousands of them) is Type II site-specific deoxyribonuclease, EC 3.1.21.4. Many other details of enzymes and their kinetics are given in Chap. 5.

SOLVED PROBLEMS

ACIDS, BASES, AND BUFFERS

2.1. The pK_a values for acetic acid and trichloracetic acid are 4.7 and 0.7, respectively. Which is the stronger acid?

SOLUTION

From Eq. (2.9),
$pK_a = -\log K_a$ or
$K_a = 10^{-pK_a}$
For acetic acid,
$\log K_a = -4.7$
$K_a = 1.8 \times 10^{-5}$
For trichloracetic acid,
$\log K_a = -0.7$
$K_a = 2.0 \times 10^{-1}$

The dissociation constant for trichloracetic acid is greater than the dissociation constant for acetic acid. Therefore, trichloracetic acid is the stronger acid.

2.2. (a) What is the pH of 100 mL of a solution made using 5 mL of 1 M Na_2HPO_4 and 5 mL of 1 M NaH_2PO_4?

SOLUTION

The pK_a for $H^+ + HPO_4^- \rightleftharpoons H_2PO_4^{2-}$ is 6.82.
For 1 M Na_2HPO_4, 5 mL contains 5 mmol.
For 1 M NaH_2PO_4, 5 mL contains 5 mmol.

Hence there are 5 mmol of the acid form and 5 mmol of the base form in 100 mL of the solution.
Using the Henderson-Hasselbalch equation,

$pH = pK_a + \log([A^-]/[HA])$
$pH = 6.82 + \log(5/5) = 6.82 + \log 1 = 6.82$

The pH of a buffer is the pK_a value when there are equal numbers of molecules of the acid and base forms of the buffer in solution.

(b) What is the maximum volume of 1 M HCl that this buffer can hold before the pH falls by more than 1 pH unit?

SOLUTION

When the pH drops by 1 unit
$5.82 = 6.82 + \log([A^-]/[HA])$
Therefore, $\log([A^-]/[HA]) = -1$, and
$[A^-] = 0.1 \times [HA]$
We know that the total amount of base and acid is 10 mmol in 100 mL of solution, thus
$[A^-] + [HA] = 0.1 \text{ M}$
Combining these two equations gives
$1.1[HA] = 0.1 \text{ M}$

[HA] = 0.1/1.1 = 0.0909 M
[A⁻] = 0.00909 M

So when the pH drops by 1, [A⁻] goes from 5 mmol/(100 mL) (or 0.05 *M*) to 0.0091 *M* which corresponds to a change of 4.09 mmol.

Hence we would need to add 4.09 mmol HCl to get a pH change of 1 in this buffer.

This corresponds to 4.09 mL of 1 *M* HCl added to the 100 mL of buffer.

THERMODYNAMICS

2.3. A sample of acetic acid (1 mol) was completely oxidized to CO_2 and H_2O in a constant-volume adiabatic calorimeter, at 298 K. The heat released in the oxidation was 874 kJ. Calculate ΔH for the oxidation of acetic acid.

SOLUTION

At constant volume, the heat absorbed by the system (Δq_V) is equal to ΔU. Hence, because heat is released (transferred *from* the system *to* the surroundings),

$\Delta U = \Delta q_V = -874$ kJ mol⁻¹

ΔU is related to ΔH by the equation $\Delta H = \Delta U + P\,\Delta V$.

However, given the reaction for oxidation of acetic acid,

$$CH_3COOH + 2O_2 \rightarrow 2CO_2 + 2H_2O$$

there is no volume change (as both O_2 and CO_2 are gases at 298 K) and hence ΔH for the oxidation is −874 kJ mol⁻¹.

2.4. The ΔH^0 value for oxidation of fumaric acid (HOOC—CH=CH—COOH) is −1336 kJ mol⁻¹. Calculate the enthalpy of formation (ΔH_f^0) of fumaric acid from its elements, given the following data:

$C + O_2 \rightarrow CO_2$ $\Delta H^0 = -393$ kJ mol⁻¹

$H_2 + 0.5O_2 \rightarrow H_2O$ $\Delta H^0 = -285.5$ kJ mol⁻¹

SOLUTION

Because enthalpy is a *state function*, we can calculate ΔH_f^0 by summation of the enthalpy changes for the following reactions:

$4C + 4O_2 \rightarrow 4CO_2$ $\Delta H^0 = -1572$ kJ
$2H_2 + O_2 \rightarrow 2H_2O$ $\Delta H^0 = -571$ kJ
$4CO_2 + 2H_2O \rightarrow C_4H_4O_4 + 3O_2$ $\Delta H^0 = 1336$ kJ
Net equation:
$4C + 2H_2 + 2O_2 \rightarrow C_4H_4O_4$ $\Delta H^0 = -807$ kJ mol⁻¹

This procedure, which is an example of *Hess' law of constant heat summation*, relies upon the fact that ΔH for any reaction depends only on the initial and final states, and illustrates a convenient method for calculating ΔH values which would be difficult to measure experimentally.

2.5. The respective concentrations of Na⁺ and K⁺ ions in tissues are ~10 mmol L⁻¹ and 90 mmol L⁻¹ inside cells, and 140 mmol L⁻¹ and 4 mmol L⁻¹ outside cells. Calculate the free energy requirements for maintenance of these ion gradients.

SOLUTION

We can represent the ion gradients by the equilibria:

Na⁺$_{in}$ ⇌ Na⁺$_{out}$
K⁺$_{in}$ ⇌ K⁺$_{out}$

In both cases, the ΔG values are given by the expression

$$\Delta G = \Delta G^0 + RT \ln\left(\frac{[\text{ion}]_{out_e}}{[\text{ion}]_{in_e}}\right)$$

where the subscript e indicates the equilibrium concentrations of the ions. However, at equilibrium it is expected that the concentrations of the ions inside and outside the cells would be equal. Hence, $\Delta G^0 = 0$, and therefore the free energy required to maintain the ion gradients is

$$\Delta G = RT \ln\left(\frac{[\text{ion}]_{\text{out}}}{[\text{ion}]_{\text{in}}}\right)$$

Substituting the Na^+ and K^+ concentrations into this equation, we have

$$\Delta G_{Na^+} = 6.8 \text{ kJ mol}^{-1}$$

$$\Delta G_{Cl^-} = 8.0 \text{ kJ mol}^{-1}$$

We have made a number of assumptions in this calculation, the most notable being that the solution of ions is *ideal*, in that there are no interactions (attractive or repulsive) between solute molecules. This is most *un*likely to be the case, especially in moderately concentrated solutions of ions. To correct for *nonideality* (interactions between solute molecules), we need to substitute the *activities* of solute molecules for their *concentrations* in all thermodynamic calculations. The activity a of a solute molecule is related to its concentration C by the *activity coefficient* γ as shown in Eq. (2.6):

$$a = \gamma C$$

For solutions of electrolytes, γ can be calculated by using the *Debye-Hückel theory*. The mean activity coefficient $\gamma_{+/-}$ of positively and negatively charged ions in a solution at 25°C is given by

$$\log \gamma_{+/-} = -0.5 z_+ z_- I^{0.5} \tag{2.30}$$

where z_+ and z_- are the charges carried by the ions and I is the *ionic strength* of the solution that is defined as

$$I = 0.5 \, \Sigma C_i z_i^2 \tag{2.31}$$

where the sum is carried out over all ion types in the solution.

2.6. Calculate the mean *activity coefficient* in a solution of 0.25 mol L^{-1} Na_3PO_4.

SOLUTION

This salt is completely dissociated in water. First, we calculate the ionic strength:
$I = 0.5(C_{Na^+} \times z_{Na^+} + C_{PO_4^{3-}} \times (z_{PO_4^{3-}})^2$
$I = 0.5(0.75 \times 1^2 + 0.25 \times 3^2) = 1.5 \text{ mol } L^{-1}$

Now, using Eq. (2.29), with $z_+ = 1$, and $z_- = 3$,
$\log \gamma_{+/-} = -1.837$
$\gamma_{+/-} = 0.0146$

Strictly, this value is valid only at 298 K (25°C) as the constant (0.5) in the equation for $\log \gamma_{+/-}$ is slightly different at other temperatures.

OXIDATION AND REDUCTION

2.7. Calculate $\Delta G^{0\prime}$ for the following reactions.

Pyruvate + NADH + H$^+$ $\rightleftharpoons$ lactate + NAD$^+$
given the half-cell reactions
Pyruvate + 2H$^+$ + 2e^- $\rightarrow$ lactate $E_0' = -0.19$ V
NAD$^+$ + H$^+$ + 2e^- $\rightarrow$ NADH $E_0' = -0.32$ V

SOLUTION

From the half-cell reactions, E_0' for the overall reaction is
$-0.19 - (-0.32) = 0.13$ V

Now, using Eq. (2.28) (below), with $n = 2$ in this case,

$$\Delta G^{0\prime} = -nFE_0^\prime$$

$$\Delta G^{0\prime} = -2 \times 96.5 \times 0.13 \text{ kJ mol}^{-1} = -25.1 \text{ kJ mol}^{-1}$$

Note that a *positive* $E_0^\prime$ value for a redox reaction implies that it is thermodynamically *favorable* with a *negative* value of $\Delta G^{0\prime}$.

2.8. The electrochemical potential μ of an ion of charge z in an electrostatic field ψ is (assuming ideal behavior) defined by the equation

$$\mu = zF\psi + \mu^0 + RT \ln X \tag{2.32}$$

where μ^0 is the *chemical potential* of the ion in its *standard state* and X is the *mole fraction* of the ion in the solution, given by the expression

$$X = (\text{mol of ion})/(\text{mol of ion} + \text{mol of solvent})$$

For dilute solutions, (mol of solvent) >> (mol of ion), hence

$$X = (\text{mol of ion})/(\text{mol of solvent})$$

In the *chemiosmotic theory* for oxidative phosphorylation (Chap. 10), electron flow in the electron transport chain is coupled to generation of a *proton concentration gradient* across the inner mitochondrial membrane.

Derive an expression for the difference in *electrochemical potential* for protons across the membrane.

SOLUTION

The difference in chemical potential is given by the expression

$$\Delta\mu = \mu_{in} - \mu_{out}$$

From Eq. (2.32),

$$\Delta\mu = z\,F(\psi_{in} - \psi_{out}) + RT \ln\left(\frac{[H^+]_{in}}{[H^+]_{out}}\right)$$

Hence

$$\Delta\mu = zF\,\Delta\psi - 2.3\,RT\,\Delta pH \tag{2.33}$$

where $\Delta\varphi$ is the *membrane potential* across the membrane and $\Delta pH = pH_{out} - pH_{in}$ is the pH difference across the membrane. This is the *Nernst potential equation*.

SUPPLEMENTARY PROBLEMS

2.1. (i) Given that the pK_a for phosphate buffer is 6.8, calculate the pH of the final solution when (a) 1 mL of 1 M HCl and (b) 1 mL of 1 M NaOH is added to 100 mL of 100 mM phosphate buffer at pH 7.0.

(ii) Given that the pK_a for Tris buffer is 8.1, calculate the pH of the final solution when (a) 1 mL of 1 M HCl and (b) 1 mL of 1 M NaOH is added to 100 mL of 100 mM Tris buffer at pH 7.0.

What observations can you make based on these results, and how do you account for these observations?

2.2. Blood contains dissolved oxygen and carbon dioxide. When carbon dioxide dissolves in aqueous solution, a mixture of carbonic acid, hydrogen carbonate (bicarbonate), and carbonate is formed. Given that the pK_{a1} of carbonic acid is 6.4 while its pK_{a2} is 10.3, which species would you expect to be present in blood at the physiological pH of 7.4? What would you expect the molar ratio of hydrogen carbonate and carbonic acid to be?

2.3. The *osmotic pressure* (π) of a solution is given by the equation

$$\pi = RTa \tag{2.34}$$

where a is the activity of the solute. Sketch the curve you would expect to see for the relationship between the osmotic pressure of a solution of NaCl and the concentration of NaCl.

2.4. (i) Calculate the ionic strengths of solutions of $NaCl$ at (a) 0.01 mol L^{-1}, (b) 0.05 mol L^{-1}, (c) 0.1 mol L^{-1}, (d) 1.0 mol L^{-1}.

(ii) Calculate the ionic strengths of solutions of Na_2SO_4 at (a) 0.01 mol L^{-1}, (b) 0.05 mol L^{-1}, (c) 0.1 mol L^{-1}, and (d) 1.0 mol L^{-1}.

(iii) Calculate the ionic strengths of solutions of $Na_3C_6H_5O_7$ (sodium citrate) at (a) 0.01 mol L^{-1}, (b) 0.05 mol L^{-1}, (c) 0.1 mol L^{-1}, and (d) 1.0 mol L^{-1}.

What observations can you make, based on these results, and how do you account for these observations?

2.5. Given the half-cell potentials:

$$0.5O_2 + 2H^+ + 2e^- \rightleftharpoons H_2O \qquad E_0' = 0.82 \text{ V}$$
$$NAD^+ + H^+ + 2e^- \rightleftharpoons NADH \qquad E_0' = -0.32 \text{ V}$$

calculate $\Delta G^{0\prime}$ across the electron transport chain.

2.6. Given that $\Delta G^{0\prime}$ for the synthesis of ATP from ADP and phosphate is 30.5 kJ mol^{-1}, and assuming that two protons are translocated by the mitochondrial ATP synthase per molecule of ATP synthesized, use the *Nernst potential equation* to calculate the *minimum* value of $\Delta\mu$ necessary for synthesis of ATP. (*Hint:* $\Delta\mu$ has units of kJ mol^{-1}; how can this be converted to units of mV to give $\Delta\mu$ as *proton-motive force* Δp?)

2.7. The enzyme pyruvate carboxylase from chicken liver is an oligomer of four identical subunits. The enzyme loses its catalytic activity when cooled below 277 K. Assuming that this loss of activity reflects dissociation of the tetrameric enzyme into its subunits, what can you deduce about the relative importance of *enthalpic* and *entropic* effects in the association of the subunits in the tetrameric enzyme?

2.8. For the ionization of acetic acid,
$$CH_3COOH \rightleftharpoons CH_3COO^- + H^+$$
ΔG^0 and ΔH^0 values at 298 K are 27.1 and -0.39 kJ mol^{-1}.
Calculate ΔS^0 for the reaction at 298 K.
Evaluate the equilibrium constant for the reaction at 323 K, noting any assumptions necessary for the calculation.
What does this value tell you about the ionization of acetic acid?

2.9. The formation of glucose 6-phosphate from glucose and ATP is catalyzed by *hexokinase*.
Given the ΔG^0 values for glucose 6-phosphate (-13.9 kJ mol^{-1}) and ATP (-30.5 kJ mol^{-1}), calculate values for the standard state free change and the equilibrium constant of the reaction at 298 K.
What do these values indicate about the net direction of the reaction?

2.10. On average, an adult human requires ~6000 kJ per day to maintain basal levels of activity. Given the ΔH values at 37°C of the compounds shown below as representative of the three major nutrient classes, how much of each of these nutrients would need to be consumed per day to maintain basal levels of activity, assuming that all food is ultimately burned to produce heat?
(a) Fat   stearic acid ($C_{18}H_{36}O_2$) $\Delta H = -1.1 \times 10^4$ kJ mol^{-1}
(b) Carbohydrate   glucose ($C_6H_{12}O_6$) $\Delta H = -3 \times 10^3$ kJ mol^{-1}
(c) Protein   glycine ($C_2H_5O_2N$) $\Delta H = -5 \times 10^2$ kJ mol^{-1}

ANSWERS TO SUPPLEMENTARY PROBLEMS

2.1. (i) (a) 6.80; (b) 7.21; (ii) (a) 2.62; (b) 7.32
At the starting point of pH 7.0, the phosphate buffer is close to its pK_a value of 6.8. Upon addition of acid or base, there is little change in pH.
At the starting point of pH 7.0, the Tris buffer is well below its pK_a value of 8.1. Upon addition of acid, it moves even further below its pK_a value, and there is a large fall in pH. Upon addition of base, it moves nearer to its pK_a value and there is little change in pH.

2.2. H_2CO_3 and HCO_3^- in a 1:10 molar ratio; there will be negligible CO_2 present.

2.3. Use Eqs. (2.6) and (2.30) for the activity and activity coefficient.

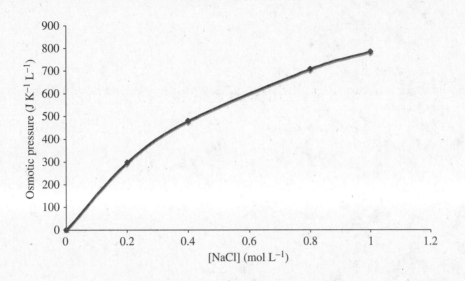

2.4. (i) (a) 0.01 mol L^{-1}; (b) 0.15 mol L^{-1}; (c) 0.1 mol L^{-1}; (d) 1.0 mol L^{-1}; (ii) (a) 0.03 mol L^{-1}; (b) 0.15 mol L^{-1}; (c) 0.3 mol L^{-1}; (d) 3.0 mol L^{-1}; (iii) (a) 0.06 mol L^{-1}; (b) 0.3 mol L^{-1}; (c) 0.6 mol L^{-1}; (d) 6.0 mol L^{-1}.
The ionic strength increases with concentration, and the increase is greater when there is a higher charge on one of the individual ionic species.

2.5. $\Delta G^{0\prime} = -220$ kJ mol^{-1}

2.6. Under biochemical standard-state conditions, the free energy of ATP synthesis is given by the expression

$$\Delta G^{0\prime} = -nF\Delta p$$

where n is the number of protons translocated per ATP molecule synthesized and p is the *proton-motive force*. Substituting values for $\Delta G^{0\prime}$ and n gives

$$\Delta p = -0.158 \text{ V}$$

where Δp is given by the expression

$$\Delta p = \Delta\psi - 2.3RT/F\ \Delta\text{pH}$$

which is Eq. (2.33) in which both sides have been divided by F.
Hence,

$$\Delta\mu = \Delta p \times F$$
$$\Delta\mu = -15.25 \text{ kJ mol}^{-1}$$

2.7. Using Eq. (2.19), it can be seen that below 277 K, dissociation becomes spontaneous. Thus, ΔG must be < 0, and enthalpic (ΔH) effects become less important than the entropic (ΔS) effects at the lower temperature.

2.8. Using Eq. (2.19),

$$\Delta S = -92.2 \text{ J K}^{-1} \text{ mol}^{-1}$$

Assuming that ΔH^0 and ΔS^0 are independent of temperature over the range 298 to 323 K,

$$K_e = 1.31 \times 10^{-5}$$

There is little ionization of acetic acid at 323 K; it is a weak acid.

2.9. $\Delta G^{0\prime} = 13.9 - 30.5 \text{ kJ mol}^{-1} = -16.6 \text{ kJ mol}^{-1}$

$$K_e = 812$$

The formation of glucose 6-phosphate is heavily favored; in other words, the reaction is strongly biased to the right.

2.10. (a) Fat   stearic acid ($C_{18}H_{36}O_2$)   155 g
       (b) Carbohydrate   glucose ($C_6H_{12}O_6$)   360 g
       (c) Protein   glycine ($C_2H_5O_2N$)   900 g

Building Blocks of Life

In this chapter we describe and discuss the classes of *bio*chemicals that yield the structural components, those that mediate the transfer of energy from food to the living cell and those that are involved in prescribing the genetic blueprint that orchestrates the whole organism, its replication and evolution.

3.1 Carbohydrates—General

Question: What is a carbohydrate?

The term *carbohydrate* means hydrated carbon atoms; literally the generic formula is $(CH_2O)_n$ with as many water molecules, attached as —H and —OH groups, as there are carbon atoms in the molecule. They are polyhydroxy aldehydes, or ketones, or compounds derived from these. They range in molecular size from < 100 to well over 10^6 Da. The smaller compounds, containing three to nine carbon atoms, are called monosaccharides. The larger compounds are formed by *condensation* of monosaccharides through *glycosidic* bonds. A disaccharide consists of two monosaccharides linked by a single glycosidic bond; a trisaccharide is three monosaccharides linked by two glycosidic bonds, etc. The words *oligo-* and *poly*saccharides describe carbohydrates with few (up to ~10) and many monosaccharide units, respectively. Note that many carbohydrates have a sweet taste, so they are often referred to as *sugars*.

Simple Aldoses and Ketoses

There are two series of simple monosaccharides: aldoses, which contain an aldehyde group, and ketoses, which contain a ketone group. Simple monosaccharides are also classified by the number of carbon atoms which they contain: e.g., trioses (3 C), tetroses (4 C), pentoses (5 C), and hexoses (6 C). The two naming systems are combined; e.g., glucose is an aldohexose as it is a six-carbon monosaccharide with an aldehyde group.

Simplest Aldose

The simplest carbohydrate is the aldotriose, glyceraldehyde (Fig. 3-1A).

Being an aldehyde, glyceraldehyde has reducing properties. The C-2 is a *chiral center* (also known as an *asymmetric center*), so there are two possible *stereo isomers*, known as *enantiomers*. The two enantiomers are shown in Fig. 3-1B and C. They can be drawn as in Fig. 3-1B, as *Fischer projection* formulas. This representation projects a three-dimensional molecule into the two dimensions of the page, with C-2 imagined to be in the plane of the paper, the aldehyde and the hydroxymethyl groups lying behind the plane of the page, and the —H and —OH in front of it. More standard chemical representation of the spatial arrangement of the groups around C-2 is given by solid and striped wedge-shaped bonds (Fig. 3-1C), with the solid bonds representing projection forward from the plane, and the striped bonds, away from the plane of the page.

Enantiomers are *mirror images* of each other: when placed in front of a mirror, one structure will give an image that has the spatial configuration of the four groups of the other. (Your hands, for example, are enantiomeric because they are *mirror images* of each other.) In the pairs of figures in Fig. 3-1B and C, those on the left are called D-*glyceraldehyde* and on the right L-*glyceraldehyde*. The prefixes D- and L- refer to the *overall shape* of the molecules; more specifically the letters refer to the *configuration*, or arrangement of

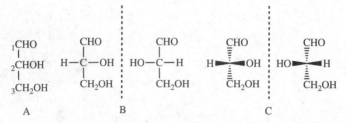

Fig. 3-1   Glyceraldehyde: various structural representations.

groups around the *chiral center*. The D- and L- notation is a standard one based on the representation of the H and OH groups of D- and L-glyceraldehyde.

Optical Activity

Generally, with compounds that have a single chiral carbon atom, there are only minor differences in physical and chemical properties of pure enantiomers. However, there is one physical property that is markedly different, and that is *optical activity*. This refers to the ability of a solution of an enantiomer to rotate the plane of polarization of plane-polarized light. One of a pair of enantiomers will rotate the plane of polarization in a clockwise direction when viewed toward the light source and is given the symbol (+). The other rotates the light counterclockwise and is given the symbol (−). The D enantiomer of glyceraldehyde is (+) and is described as *D-(+)-glyceraldehyde*; the other is *L-(−)-glyceraldehyde*. Mixtures of D- and L- enantiomers have a net rotation that depends on the relative proportions of each in the solution; equal proportions give zero rotation in which case the mixture is said to be *racemic*.

EXAMPLE 3.1   How is optical activity *measured* and what factors determine the *extent* of optical rotation?

Optical activity is measured in an instrument called a *polarimeter*. The magnitude of the optical activity is measured as an angle of rotation and is given the symbol α; it is expressed as either radians or degrees.

The factors that affect α are the *concentration* of the compound, the *length* of the light path in the solution, the *wavelength* of the polarized light, the *temperature*, and the *solvent*. Because of these variables a standard value for α is given for each compound and denoted by $[\alpha]_D^T$, where T refers to the temperature and D refers to the two *D lines of a sodium vapor lamp*, that is yellow, with wavelength of 589.0 and 589.6 nm.

$$[\alpha]_D^T = \alpha/[\text{length of sample cell (dm)} \times \text{concentration (g cm}^{-3})]$$

The name of the solvent is given in brackets after the value; e.g., $[\alpha]_D^{25} = +17.7°$ (in water).

More Complex Aldoses

These are related to D- and L-glyceraldehyde and can be viewed as having been structurally derived from them by the introduction of a hydroxylated chiral carbon atom between C-1 and C-2 (Fig. 3-2). Thus there are four aldotetroses.

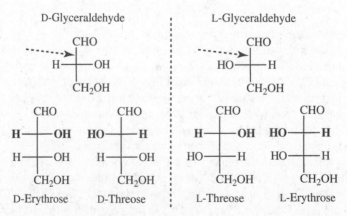

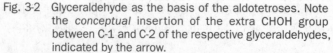

Fig. 3-2   Glyceraldehyde as the basis of the aldotetroses. Note the *conceptual* insertion of the extra CHOH group between C-1 and C-2 of the respective glyceraldehydes, indicated by the arrow.

Two simple aldopentoses can be derived structurally from each of the four aldotetroses described, making a total of eight aldopentoses (Fig. 3-3). There are 16 aldohexoses that have linear carbon chains, but the most abundant in higher organisms are glucose, galactose, and mannose, all of the D-form.

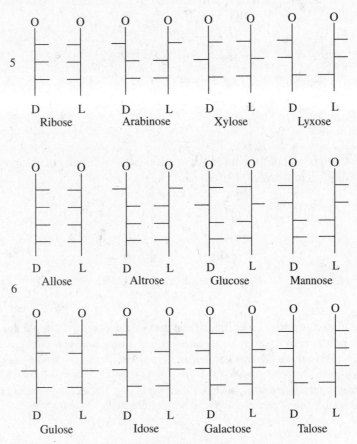

Fig. 3-3   All possible linear aldopentoses and aldohexoses.

EXAMPLE 3.2   Simplified structures of the eight aldopentoses and 16 aldohexoses are shown; — represents an OH group, C atoms lie at the ends of lines and at their intersections, and H atoms are omitted.

While glyceraldehyde has one chiral center, aldotetroses, -pentoses, and -hexoses have two, three, and four, respectively. Each chiral center gives rise to optical activity, and the net optical activity of an aldose will depend on contributions from each chiral center and will be (+) or (−).

EXAMPLE 3.3   D-erythrose was dissolved in water. Would you predict the solution to have a (+) or (−) optical rotation?
This is impossible to predict. The prefixes D- and L- refer to the *shape* of the molecule and imply nothing regarding the optical activity. In fact, a solution of D-erythrose is (−).

When more than four chiral carbon atoms are present, an aldose is given two configurational prefixes; one for the four lower-number chiral centers and one for the rest of the molecule. The configuration of the *highest*-number group is stated first.

EXAMPLE 3.4   The aldo-octose shown in Fig. 3-4 has an L-galactose-like configuration in the first five carbon atoms, and in the last three carbon atoms a configuration like the lower three of D-erythrose. Accordingly it is called D-*erythro*-L-*galacto*-octose. This is a rarely encountered monosaccharide and is only given here as an example of the use of the standard nomenclature for carbohydrates.

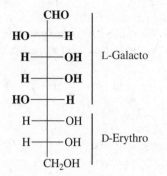

Fig. 3-4   D-Erythro-L-galacto-octose.

Ketoses

Structurally, the parent compound of the simple ketoses is the three-carbon compound *dihydroxyacetone*; it is a *structural isomer* of glyceraldehyde ($C_3H_6O_3$) (Fig. 3-5).

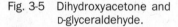

Fig. 3-5   Dihydroxyacetone and
D-glyceraldehyde.

Dihydroxyacetone does not possess a chiral carbon atom. However, the simple ketoses are related to it structurally by the introduction of hydroxylated chiral carbon atoms between the keto group and one of the hydroxymethyl groups. Thus, there are two ketotetroses, four ketopentoses, and eight ketohexoses.

EXAMPLE 3.5   The most common ketose, D-fructose, is shown in Fig. 3-6. Compare the configuration of the chiral carbon atom (C-5) most remote from the keto group with D-glyceraldehyde.

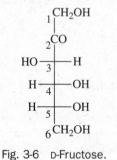

Fig. 3-6   D-Fructose.

Fructose was named long before its structure was known, because it is commonly found in fruit. The same is true for naming most aldoses. Names such as *glucose*, *mannose*, *ribose*, and *fructose* are called *trivial names*, i.e., they are *nonsystematic*.

EXAMPLE 3.6   How is it possible to tell if a monosaccharide is a ketose from its name?
    Apart from fructose, the name always ends in -ulose. Some ketoses are not related structurally to dihydroxyacetone. They are named by considering the configurations of all the chiral carbon atoms as a unit, ignoring the carbonyl group.

EXAMPLE 3.7   Consider the ketose shown in Fig. 3-7. It has three chiral carbon atoms in the D-arabino configuration (even though interrupted by a keto group). The keto group is at position 3. The ketose has six carbon atoms. It is therefore called D-*arabino*-3-hexulose.

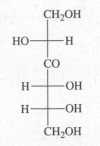

Fig. 3-7 D-Arabino-3-hexulose.

If the name of a ketose contains no number, it is assumed the ketose is related to dihydroxyacetone and the keto group is at position 2. There is no need to use numbers to indicate the position of the carbonyl group in aldoses because the aldehyde group must always be terminal to a chain of carbon atoms.

3.2 The Structure of D-Glucose

D-Glucose is the most common monosaccharide, occurring in the free state in the blood of animals and in a polymerized state as starch and cellulose. Tens of millions of tons of these polysaccharides are made on Earth by plants and photosynthetic microbes annually. Many of the structural features of all monosaccharides can be illustrated by using glucose as an example.

The *open* or *straight* chain configuration of D-glucose (Fig. 3-3) is only one of the possible conformations of glucose. In solution, glucose actually exists in an equilibrium reaction between the open form and two different ring forms (Fig. 3-8). These ring forms, denoted α and β, have different optical activities and form two different crystalline structures. The six-member rings contain five carbon atoms and one oxygen atom:

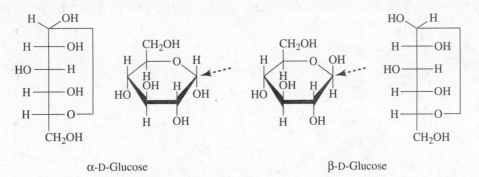

α-D-Glucose   β-D-Glucose

Fig. 3-8 The open chain and Haworth-projection representations of the two anomers of D-glucose. The arrows point to C-1.

EXAMPLE 3.8 The formation of a ring is the result of a reaction between the hydroxyl group on C-5 and the aldehyde group to give a *hemiacetal*. The aldehyde-carbon (C-1) becomes chiral as a result, giving rise to the α- and β- forms of D-glucose. These hemiacetals are known as *anomers*, and C_1 of the ring form is called the *anomeric carbon*. Whether an anomer is called α or β depends upon the configuration of the anomeric carbon relative to the configuration of the chiral atom that establishes whether the monosaccharide belongs to the L- or D- series; in the case of glucose, C-5. If the hydroxyl groups on these carbons are *cis* when the straight chain representation (Fischer projection) is used, the anomer is called α; if the hydroxyl groups are *trans*, the anomer is called β. Here the anomer with the anomeric hydroxyl below the plane of the ring is called α.

The Conformation of Glucose

The previous figures of glucose represent the arrangement of atoms, but not the structure of the molecule. The carbon atoms of glucose are all saturated, and the most stable form of a ring will be one in which the angles formed by the bonds at each carbon atom are the tetrahedral angle 109°, creating a *strain-free molecule*. Only two strain-free shapes or *conformations* of a six-member carbon ring are possible, a *chair* and a *boat*; they are interconvertible by various rotations of the C—C bonds, and they are referred to as *conformers* rather than isomers. Note that the presence of an oxygen atom in the ring structures means that there are two possible chair structures, CI and IC, which interconvert by rotation of the bonds, passing through a boat structure.

EXAMPLE 3.9   Of the carbon-linked atoms in the structure; six are in the general plane of the rings and are called *equatorial* (e); six are perpendicular to the general plane of the rings and are called *axial* (a) (Fig. 3-9).

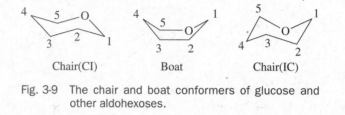

Chair(CI)   Boat   Chair(IC)

Fig. 3-9   The chair and boat conformers of glucose and other aldohexoses.

The chair conformations are more stable than the boat conformation because the boat conformation introduces steric overlap at some positions.

Monosaccharides have hydroxyl and hydroxymethyl groups replacing some of the H atoms substituted on the carbon atoms of the ring. These are much more bulky than H atoms and tend to be in equatorial positions around the edge of the ring rather than in axial positions on the faces of the ring, where they would be closer together and thus distort the ring.

3.3   Other Important Monosaccharides

Ribose and Deoxyribose

D-Ribose is the most common aldopentose, being the sugar present in RNA (Sec. 3.19). It exists in solution as a mixture of five- and six-member rings (Fig. 3-10).

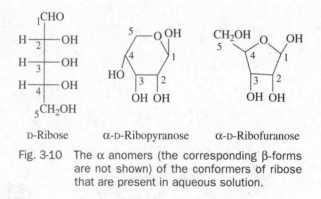

D-Ribose   α-D-Ribopyranose   α-D-Ribofuranose

Fig. 3-10   The α anomers (the corresponding β-forms are not shown) of the conformers of ribose that are present in aqueous solution.

EXAMPLE 3.10   There are reduced forms of sugars in which a hydroxyl group is replaced by a hydrogen atom. The most widely distributed deoxy sugar is 2-deoxy-D-ribose (Fig. 3-11); it is present in DNA (see Sec. 3.16).

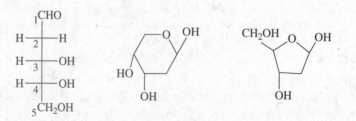

2-Deoxy-D-ribose   2-Deoxy-β-D-ribopyranose   2-Deoxy-β-D-ribofuranose

Fig. 3-11   The three main conformers of 2-deoxy ribose that exist in aqueous solution. Only the β anomers are shown.

Alditols, Uronic and Aldonic Acids

When the aldehyde group of an aldose has been reduced, it is referred to as an alditol. For example, the alditol produced from D-glucose is D-*glucitol* (the trivial name is *sorbitol*). The name of an alditol is obtained by adding "itol" to the root of the name of the aldose, except for glycerol (Sec. 3.6 on fatty acids), which is a reduction product of glyceraldehyde.

Oxidation of the aldehyde group of an aldose to a carboxylic acid group gives a derivative known as an aldonic acid. This occurs as a salt, *aldonate*, at physiological pH. If an aldonic acid contains five or more carbon atoms, a δ-*lactone* is formed spontaneously by the condensation of the carboxylic acid group and the hydroxyl group on C-5.

Uronic acids are sugars in which the hydroxymethyl group of an aldose has been oxidized to a carboxylic acid. These occur as salts, known as *uronates*, at physiological pH (Fig. 3-12).

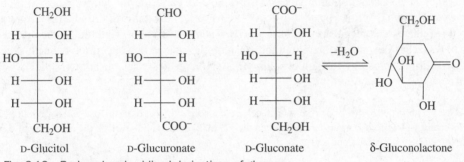

D-Glucitol   D-Glucuronate   D-Gluconate   δ-Gluconolactone

Fig. 3-12   Reduced and oxidized derivatives of glucose.

Amino Sugars, Phosphate and Sulfate Esters

Sugars in which a hydroxyl group has been replaced by an amino group are called amino sugars. The amino groups in these compounds are invariably acetylated. When hydroxyl groups are replaced by *phosphate* or *sulfate* groups they are known as phosphate and sulfate *esters*, respectively.

Amino sugars are widely distributed naturally and include molecules such as D-glucosamine (2-amino-2-deoxy-D-glucose), D-galactosamine (2-amino-2-deoxy-D-galactose), and sialic acid, a derivative of D-mannosamine (2-amino-2-deoxy-D-mannose).

In general, the phosphate esters exist as components of metabolic pathways within cells (e.g., fructose-1,6-*bis*phosphate and 6-phosphogluconate), whereas the sulfate esters exist in oligosaccharides and polysaccharides that are outside cells (e.g., D-galactose-4-sulfate and N-acetyl galactosamine-4-sulfate).

3.4   The Glycosidic Bond

The ability of many monosaccharides to form rings is important because the presence of oxygen in the ring increases the reactivity of the hydroxyl group which is attached to the anomeric carbon; e.g., only the anomeric hydroxyl group in monosaccharides reacts with alcohols and amines. The process is known as *glycosylation* (of the alcohol or amine), and the products are known as *O-glycosides* and *N-glycosides*, respectively (Fig. 3-13).

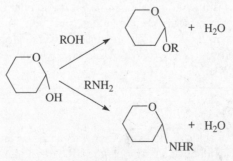
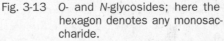

Fig. 3-13   *O-* and *N*-glycosides; here the hexagon denotes any monosaccharide.

EXAMPLE 3.11   In what respect does a glycoside ring differ from the ring structure of a monosaccharide?

The ring of a glycoside can no longer open to give a straight-chain structure. Consequently, glycosides have no reducing properties.

The glycosidic bond is present in a very wide range of biological compounds. In addition, there is a particularly important group of *O*-glycosides in which the glycosidic bond links two monosaccharides. Such compounds are called *disaccharides*. The anomeric hydroxyl group of the second monosaccharide can itself glycosylate a hydroxyl group in a third monosaccharide to give a *trisaccharide*, and so on.

Oligosaccharides and *polysaccharides* are polymers in which a few or a large number of monosaccharides are linked by glycosidic bonds, respectively.

The monosaccharide units in oligo- and polysaccharides are called *residues* because the formation of each glycosidic bond is a *condensation reaction* in which a water molecule is released. Effectively, all monosaccharides, except that at one end of an oligosaccharide, have lost a water molecule.

The name of a residue is formed by adding "osyl" to the root of the name of the sugar. Thus a trisaccharide made from three glucose molecules is *glucosyl-glucosyl-glucose*. To abbreviate the written descriptions for oligo- and polysaccharides, a shorthand method for naming residues has been introduced: Glc, glucosyl; Gal, galactosyl; Fru, fructosyl; GlcN, glucosaminyl; GlcNAc, *N*-acetyl glucosaminyl; GlcUA, glucuronyl; and NeuNAc, *N*-acetyl neuraminyl.

EXAMPLE 3.12   The structures of two different disaccharides, both composed of glucose, are shown in Fig. 3-14. The numbering indicates which carbon atoms are linked via the glycosidic bond and whether the bond is α or β with respect to the first residue (the glycosyl component).

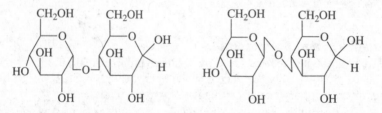

Maltose, α-D-Glucosyl-(1→4)-D-Glucose   Cellobiose, β-D-Glucosyl-(1→4)-D-Glucose

α-Glc-(1→4)-Glc   β-Glc-(1→4)-Glc

Fig. 3-14   Maltose and cellobiose differ only in the 1→4 linkage configuration.

The term *glycan* is used as an alternative to *polysaccharide*. This is a generic term, and names such as *glucan*, *xylan*, and *glucomannan* describe polymers composed, respectively, of glucose residues, xylose residues, and glucose and mannose residues.

3.5   Lipids—Overview

Question: What is a lipid?

Lipids are defined as water-insoluble compounds extracted from living organisms by weakly polar or nonpolar solvents. The definition is based on a *physical property* in contrast to the definitions of the other basic building blocks in this chapter (proteins, carbohydrates, and nucleic acids), which are based on chemical structure. Consequently the term *lipid* covers a structurally diverse group of compounds including *fatty acids*, *glycerolipids*, *sphingolipids*, *terpenes*, *steroids*, and *carotenoids*. There is no universally accepted scheme for their classification.

3.6   Fatty Acids

Over 100 naturally occurring fatty acids are known. They vary in chain length and *degree of unsaturation* (number of double bonds). Nearly all have an *even number* of carbon atoms. Most consist of linear chains of carbon atoms, but a few have branched chains. Fatty acids occur in very low quantities in the free state and are found mostly in an *esterified* state as components of other lipids.

Fatty acids are based on the following formula: $CH_3(CH_2)_nCOOH$.

The pK_a of the carboxylic acid group is ~5, and under physiological conditions it exists in an ionized state called an *acylate* ion; e.g., the ion of palmitic acid is *palmitate*, $CH_3(CH_2)_{14}COO^-$. Saturated fatty acids contain a double bond that is nearly always in the *cis* conformation. Polyunsaturated fatty acids have two or more double bonds that are rarely *conjugated* (i.e., adjacent to each other).

Table 3-1   Some Biologically Important Fatty Acids

	Saturated	Unsaturated
Common name	Palmitic acid	Palmitoleic acid
Proper name	Hexadecanoic acid	*cis*-9-Hexadecenoic acid
Formula	$CH_3(CH_2)_{14}COOH$	$CH_3(CH_2)_5CH{=}CH(CH_2)_7COOH$
Number notation	16:0	16:1$^{\Delta 9}$
		Polyunsaturated
Common name	Stearic acid	Linoleic acid
Proper name	Octadecanoic acid	*cis,cis*-9,12-Octadecadienoic acid
Formula	$CH_3(CH_2)_{16}COOH$	$CH_3(CH_2)_4CH{=}CH{-}CH_2{-}CH{=}CH(CH_2)_7COOH$
Number notation	18:0	18:2$^{\Delta 9,12}$

The *number notation* in the above examples indicates structural features. The first number gives the number of carbon atoms; the number to the right of the colon gives the number of double bonds. The position of the double bond is shown by the Greek letter Δ followed by the number of carbon atoms between the double bond and the end of the chain, noting that the carbon atom of the carboxylic acid group is designated number 1.

The melting points of different fatty acids differ markedly as shown in Table 3-2.

Table 3-2   Melting Points of Some Biologically Important Fatty Acids

Fatty Acid	Melting Temperature (°C)
Palmitic acid	63
Stearic acid	70
Oleic acid	13
Elaidic acid (*trans*-9-octadecanoic acid)	44
Linoleic acid	−5
α-Linolenic acid	−11

EXAMPLE 3.13   Differences in melting temperature exist between fatty acids containing the same number of carbon atoms because the preferred conformation of a chain of saturated carbon atoms is a long, straight structure. A *trans* double bond does not cause a bend in the chain, but a *cis* double bond causes a *bend* in the structure, making the chain less likely to pack into a solid crystal than a saturated molecule of the same length (Fig. 3-15). Straight molecules can pack together more densely and give crystals of higher melting temperature.

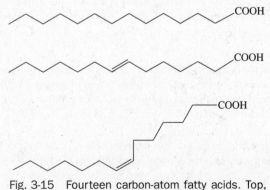

Fig. 3-15   Fourteen carbon-atom fatty acids. Top, a saturated chain; middle, a chain with one *trans* double bond; and bottom, a chain with one *cis* double bond.

The presence of *cis* rather than *trans* double bonds makes lipids that are built from such fatty acids have low melting temperatures, and they are fluid at physiological temperatures.

EXAMPLE 3.14 Branching can also affect melting temperature; e.g., 10-methyl stearic acid (Fig. 3-16) melts at only 10°C (Compare with Table 3-7).

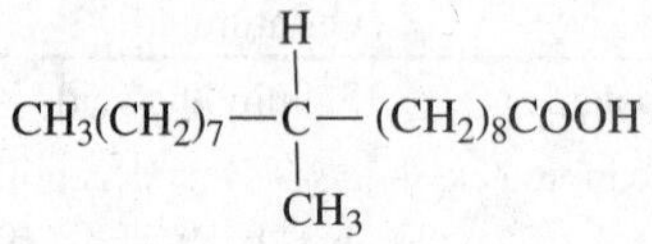

$$CH_3(CH_2)_7—\underset{\underset{CH_3}{|}}{\overset{\overset{H}{|}}{C}}—(CH_2)_8COOH$$

Fig. 3-16   10-Methyl stearic acid.

3.7   Glycerolipids

Glycerolipids are lipids that contain glycerol in which the three hydroxyl groups are substituted in some way. In terms of quantity, these are by far the most abundant lipids in mammals. Somewhat similar in structure, but occurring at concentrations of less than 1% of the glycerolipids, are lipids that contain diols, i.e., ethylene glycol (ethane diol) and 1,2- and 1,3-propanediol. Because of their rarity, lipids based on diols are not discussed further here.

Triacylglycerols (TAGs)

Triacylglycerols are *neutral* glycerolipids that are also known as *triglycerides*. In TAGs the three hydroxyl groups of glycerol are each esterified, invariably with three different fatty acids (Fig. 3-17). This makes the second carbon of the glycerol moiety chiral. However, by convention the *secondary hydroxyl group* or derivative is always drawn to the left.

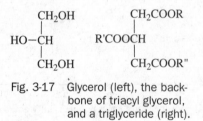

Fig. 3-17   Glycerol (left), the backbone of triacyl glycerol, and a triglyceride (right).

TAGs serve as food stores and are therefore the most abundant lipid in animals. They exist in most cell types but are especially prevalent in *adipose tissue* when they are known as *depot fat*. The hydrolysis of the ester bonds of TAGs and the release of glycerol and fatty acids from adipose tissue is referred to as fat *mobilization*. Depot fat is a water-free mixture of TAGs that differ from each other in the nature of the three fatty acyl groups which they contain.

EXAMPLE 3.15 Upon oxidation in the body, unsaturated fatty acids yield less energy than saturated ones of the same size. However, depot fat, which is an energy store, contains a high content of *unsaturated* fatty acids. This is thought to be so because the fat must be in a liquid state to present a large surface area to enzymes that hydrolyze it. Also, solid fat would render the adipose tissue rigid and unyielding during mechanical stress.

Usually the melting point of depot fat is only a few degrees below body temperature. The fatty acid composition of depot fat is thus a compromise between the need to keep the fat fluid and mobile and to store as much energy as possible.

Phosphoglycerides

These are *polar* glycerolipids derived from glycerol 3-phosphoric acid in which the phosphoric acid moiety is esterified with certain alcohols and the hydroxyl groups on C-1 and C-2 are esterified with fatty acids (Fig. 3-18).

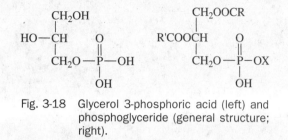

Fig. 3-18   Glycerol 3-phosphoric acid (left) and phosphoglyceride (general structure; right).

The similar term *phospholipid* describes any lipid containing phosphorus.

The phosphoglycerides are named and classified according to the nature of the alcohol that esterifies the glycerol phosphate (Table 3-3). Although they are referred to in the singular, phosphoglycerides exist as mixtures in which compounds with the same *X* group (Fig. 3-18) are esterified with a variety of different fatty acids. In most phosphoglycerides, the fatty acid on C-1 is *saturated* and that on C-2 is *unsaturated*.

Table 3-3   Three Major Classes of Phosphoglyceride

Name of X—OH	Structure of X	Name of Phosphoglyceride (symbol)
Choline	$-CH_2CH_2N(CH_3)_3$	Phosphatidylcholine
Serine	$-\underset{H_2}{C}-\underset{\underset{COO^-}{\mid}}{\overset{H}{C}}-NH_3^+$	Phosphatidylserine
Inositol	(inositol ring structure)	Phosphatidylinositol (PI)

Phosphoglycerides are often described as *polar* lipids because of the charges on the phosphate moiety. The term *polar* is used in a relative sense; i.e., relative to charge-neutral TAGs the phosphoglycerides are polar. However, in an absolute sense they are nonpolar overall and insoluble in water.

Glycoglycerolipids are similar to phosphoglycerides but contain a *carbohydrate* moiety in place of the esterified phosphate (Table 3-3).

3.8   Sphingolipids

These are built from long-chain hydroxylated bases, rather than glycerol (Fig. 3-19). *Sphingosine* is the most common form in animals. When the amino group of sphingosine is acylated with a fatty acid, the product is *ceramide*; and the primary hydroxyl group can be either esterified with choline phosphate to become *phosphosphingolipid* or substituted with a carbohydrate (i.e., glycosylated) to become a *glycosphingolipid* (Fig. 3-19).

Glycosphingolipids that contain the sugar *sialic acid* in the carbohydrate portion are called *gangliosides*.

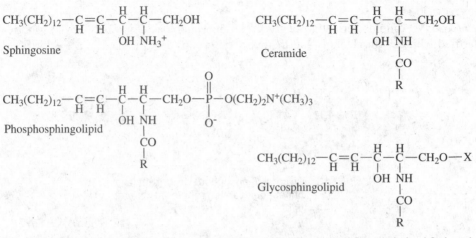

$$CH_3(CH_2)_{12}-\underset{H}{\overset{H}{C}}=\underset{H}{\overset{H}{C}}-\underset{\underset{OH}{|}}{\overset{H}{C}}-\underset{\underset{NH_3^+}{|}}{\overset{H}{C}}-CH_2OH$$

Sphingosine

$$CH_3(CH_2)_{12}-\underset{H}{\overset{H}{C}}=\underset{H}{\overset{H}{C}}-\underset{\underset{OH}{|}}{\overset{H}{C}}-\underset{\underset{NH}{|}}{\overset{H}{C}}-CH_2OH$$

Ceramide

$$CH_3(CH_2)_{12}-\underset{H}{\overset{H}{C}}=\underset{H}{\overset{H}{C}}-\underset{\underset{OH}{|}}{\overset{H}{C}}-\underset{\underset{NH}{|}}{\overset{H}{C}}-CH_2O-\overset{O}{\underset{O^-}{\overset{\|}{P}}}-O(CH_2)_2N^+(CH_3)_3$$

Phosphosphingolipid

$$CH_3(CH_2)_{12}-\underset{H}{\overset{H}{C}}=\underset{H}{\overset{H}{C}}-\underset{\underset{OH}{|}}{\overset{H}{C}}-\underset{\underset{NH}{|}}{\overset{H}{C}}-CH_2O-X$$

Glycosphingolipid

Fig. 3-19   Lipids that are based upon sphingosine, which is derived from palmitoyl-CoA and serine.

3.9   Lipids Derived from Isoprene (Terpenes)

Terpenes

The name *terpene* was applied originally to the steam-distillable oils obtained from turpentine (an extract of pine). Terpenes have a diverse range of structures but have the basic formula $C_{10}H_{15}$ (monoterpenes) or a larger number of carbon atoms that exist in multiples of five (Fig. 3-20). E.g., sesquiterpenes and diterpenes have 15 and 20 carbon atoms, respectively. Triterpenes (30 carbons) and tetraterpenes (40 carbons) give rise to steroids (see below) and carotenoid (Fig. 3-21); these are highly conjugated compounds that absorb visible light and hence are brightly colored. Most yellow and red pigments that occur naturally are carotenoids.

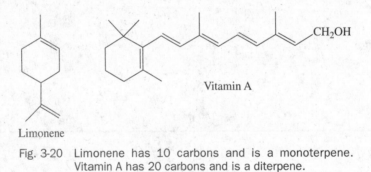

Vitamin A

Limonene

Fig. 3-20   Limonene has 10 carbons and is a monoterpene. Vitamin A has 20 carbons and is a diterpene.

Steroids

Steroids are derived from *isoprene* via *squalene*, and all share the same core structure; it is a fused ring that is essentially planar (Fig. 3-21). *Sterols* are steroids that contain one or more *hydroxyl* groups. E.g., cholesterol is an abundant component of cytoplasmic membranes of animal cells and is the precursor of the hormone testosterone.

3.10   Bile Acids and Bile Salts

The *bile acids* are produced in the liver by the modification of cholesterol, and are stored in the gall bladder as bile salts that have been conjugated in the hepatocytes with glycine or taurine (Fig. 3-22). They are *di-* and *trihydroxylated steroids* with *24 carbon atoms*, and the three main ones are *cholic acid*, *deoxycholic acid*, and *chenodeoxycholic acid* (see Chap. 12 for additional structures). All the hydroxyl groups lie on one face of the molecule while the methyl groups lie on the other. Thus one side of the molecule is more polar than the other, giving it detergent properties. This allows bile salts to emulsify dietary lipid in the intestine, making the lipid more accessible to attack by digestive enzymes. They are also needed for the absorption of

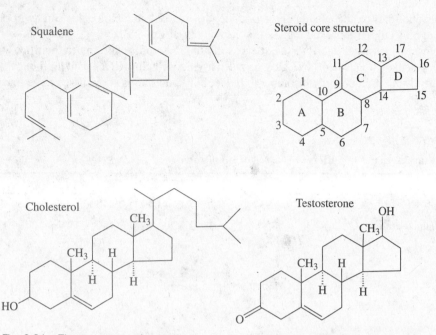

Fig. 3-21   The precursor of steroids is squalene that leads to the core structure of cholesterol, with its four carbon rings, and testosterone.

digested dietary lipids into the cells of the intestinal mucosa. Cholesterol with its four-ring hydrocarbon structure is hydrophobic, but the presence of its —OH group at the 3 position makes it hydrophilic at one end (Fig. 3-22).

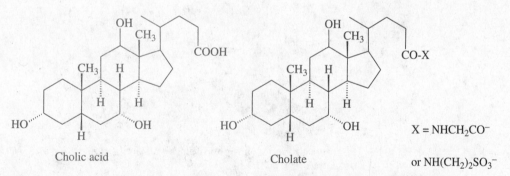

Fig. 3-22   Cholic acid and its anion, showing the site of conjugation with glycine or taurine.

3.11   Behavior of Lipids in Water

By definition lipids are insoluble in water, yet they exist in an aqueous environment. Therefore their behavior with water is critical for biology.

Many types of lipid are *amphiphilic* or *amphipathic*, meaning they have both polar and nonpolar parts.

EXAMPLE 3.16   The following lipids are amphiphilic: acylate ions, phosphoglycerides, phosphosphingolipids, and glycosphingolipids. They all possess at least one *formal charge* or have an abundance of hydroxyl groups in one part of the molecule. Although fatty acids, TAGs, and cholesterol have one or more polar groups, they are not amphiphilic and what polarity they have is extremely weak.

Plasma Lipoproteins

Blood plasma contains a number of different complexes that contain both protein and lipid. These lipoproteins are particles that consist of thousands of molecules that display the often small amounts of polar head groups of phospholipids on the outside of the particle; the hydrophobic molecules and hydrophobic regions of amphiphilic molecules are packed together in the centers (Fig. 3-23).

Lipoproteins are classified into four major types in human blood, according to their densities: chylomicrons, very low density lipoproteins (VLDL), low-density lipoproteins (LDL), and high-density lipoproteins (HDL). Isolated lipids are generally insoluble in blood, but lipoproteins allow lipids to be transported in the blood.

Table 3-4   Characteristics of Different Classes of Lipoproteins

	Chylomicrons	VLDL	LDL	HDL
Density (g mL^{-1})	< 0.95	0.95–1.006	1.006–1.063	1.063–1.21
Maximum diameter (nm)	500	70	25	15
% Composition*				
Protein	2	10	22	33
TAG	83	50	10	8
Phospholipid	7	18	22	29
Cholesterol and cholesterol esters	8	22	46	30

*Based on dry weight.

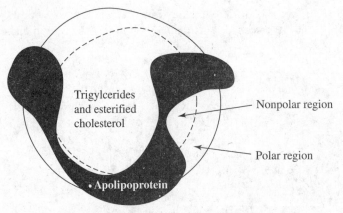

Fig. 3-23   Representation of a lipoprotein macromolecular assembly.

Intermediate-density lipoproteins (IDLs) have a density between those of VLDL and LDL. See Chap. 12 for greater discussion of these.

Monolayers and Micelles

When amphipathic molecules are dispersed in water, their hydrophobic parts (i.e., hydrocarbon chains) aggregate and become segregated from the solvent. This is a manifestation of the *hydrophobic effect* which comes about because of exclusion and hence ordering of water at the interface between these distinct types of molecule. Aggregates of amphipathic molecules can be located at a water-air boundary (*monolayers*) (Fig. 3-24); however, only a small quantity of an amphipathic lipid dispersed in water can form a monolayer (unless the water is spread as a very thin film). The bulk of the lipid must then be dispersed in water as *micelles* (Fig. 3-24). In both of these structures the polar parts, or heads (O), of the lipid make contact with the water, while the nonpolar parts, or tails (=), are as far from the water as possible. Micelles can be spherical as shown in Fig. 3-24, but can also form ellipsoidal, discoidal, and cylindrical structures.

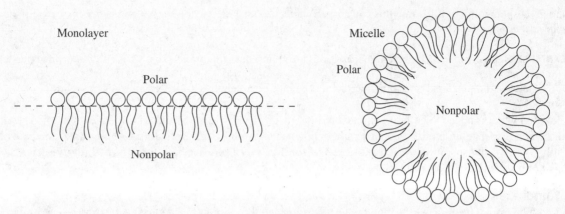

Fig. 3-24   Amphipathic molecules can form monolayers and micelles.

At very low concentrations of amphipathic lipids, micelles will not form; the transition from the unaggregated to the micellar state occurs over a narrow range of concentration known as the *critical micellar concentration* (CMC). This concenetration is dependent on both the solvent composition and the temperature.

Vesicles

In principle, amphipathic lipids can also form bilayers (Fig. 3-25), but some do so more readily than others; this ability depends on the diameter of the head group relative to the cross-sectional area of the hydrocarbon chain(s). More wedge-shaped molecules tend to favor the formation of micelles while cylindrical molecules tend to form bilayers. The latter consist of two sheets of lipid with opposed hydrocarbon chains. An isolated bilayer cannot exist in water because exposed hydrocarbon tails would exist at the edges and ends of the sheet. However, this is obviated by the sheet curving to form a self-sealed, hollow sphere. This type of bilayered micelle is referred to as a *vesicle* (Fig. 3-25).

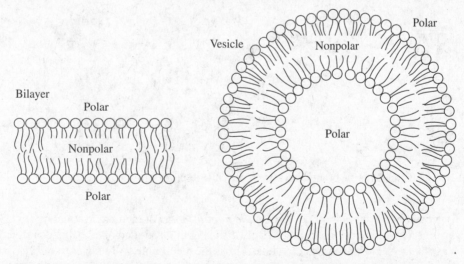

Fig. 3-25   Amphipathic molecules can self-assemble as bilayers and vesicles.

It is possible to make artificial vesicles or generate them from cytoplasmic membranes of cells (see Fig. 3-26) using a *sonification* procedure. Artificial vesicles and vesicles derived from natural membranes have proved to be very useful in studying *transport* phenomena across membranes. Vesicles also exist naturally, e.g., by the budding from the Golgi apparatus in eukaryotic cells.

EXAMPLE 3.17   Which particular lipids form vesicles and which ones form bilayers?

Whether or not a micelle forms, and what shape it takes up, is dependent on the length of the hydrocarbon chains relative to the size of the polar head group. Phosphoglycerides, phosphosphingolipids, glycoglycerolipids, and glycosphingolipids all fit into this category of molecules that are wedge shaped and hence pack readily in a spherical arrangement.

EXAMPLE 3.18   Question: If cholesterol can form mixed micelles with other lipids, what else can be incorporated into vesicles?

Mixtures of different lipids can form micelles, and a range of proteins can be incorporated into micelles.

When water is added to certain dry phospholipids with long hydrocarbon chains, the phospholipids swell, and when dispersed in more water, structures known as *liposomes* are formed. Liposomes are vesicles with multilayers of phospholipid. When subjected to sonification, liposomes are transformed into vesicles that have only a single bilayer of phospholipid.

Membranes

Lipid bilayers are the basis of the membranes that surround the cytoplasm (the plasma membrane) and subcellular structures such as the nucleus, mitochondria, and the endoplasmic reticulum. Membranes are made up of lipids (most commonly phosphogylcerides, phosphosphingolipid, and, in the plasma membranes of animals, cholesterol) and proteins. Although small amounts of carbohydrate are also present, this is usually present as a glycolipid or glycoprotein. The composition of membranes varies depending on the type of membrane.

EXAMPLE 3.19   Many different proteins are associated with membranes. These include proteins that can be readily removed from the membrane by using high salt or low denaturant concentrations. These are the *extrinsic* or *peripheral* membrane proteins. Other proteins, *intrinsic* or *integral* membrane proteins, can be removed only by treating the membranes with detergents or with organic solvents. Some proteins completely span the membrane, i.e., have parts that project on either side of the lipid bilayer, and may do so many times (see Chap. 4).

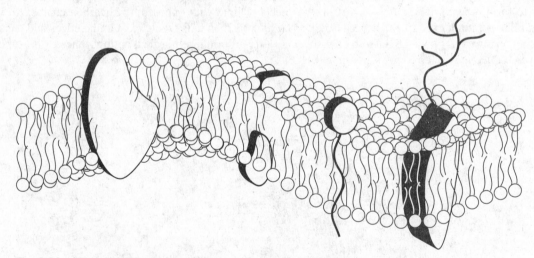

Fig. 3-26   Phospholipid membrane bilayer with associated proteins.

In 1972 Singer and Nicolson first proposed the *fluid mosaic model* of membrane structure (Fig. 3-26). The membrane exists as a two-dimensional fluid of freely diffusing lipids, dotted or embedded with proteins that may function as channels, or transporters of solutes across the membrane, as linkages to the cytoskeleton, or as receptors. Some membrane proteins perform two of more of these functions.

3.12   Nucleic Acids—General

Question: What are nucleic acids?

In 1868 Friederich Miescher isolated a substance from the nuclei of pus cells that he named *nuclein*. A similar substance was subsequently isolated from the heads of salmon sperm. Nuclein was later shown to be a mixture of a basic protein and a phosphorus-containing organic acid, now called *nucleic acid*. There are two forms of nucleic acids, DNA and RNA.

Deoxyribose Nucleic Acid (DNA)

This is the genetic material in most organisms. Its name is derived from the presence of the pentose sugar, deoxyribose, which is one of its major chemical constituents.

Ribonucleic Acid (RNA)

This plays major roles in the transmission and regulation of the genetic information encoded by DNA. It contains ribose instead of deoxyribose (Fig. 3-27).

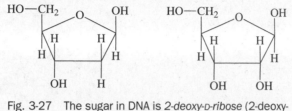

Fig. 3-27   The sugar in DNA is *2-deoxy-D-ribose* (2-deoxy-β-D-ribofuranose; left); in RNA it is *D-ribose* (β-D-ribofuranose; right). It is the β-*anomer* in each case that is present in the nucleic acid.

As well as ribose and deoxribose, DNA and RNA contain nitrogenous bases and phosphate groups. There are two general types of nitrogenous base (nucleobases) in both DNA and RNA, purines and *pyrimidines*.

3.13   Pyrimidines and Purines

These compounds are heterocyclic, nitrogen-containing bases that have the following structures (Fig 3-28).

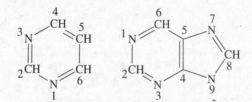

Fig. 3-28   The nucleobases of DNA and RNA and derivatives of pyrimidine (left) and purine (right).

Pyrimidines

The major pyrimidines found in DNA are *thymine* and *cytosine*; in RNA they are *uracil* and *cytosine*. These three pyrimidines vary in the types and positioning of chemical groups attached to the ring (Fig. 3-29).

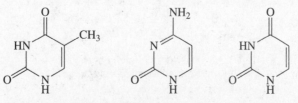
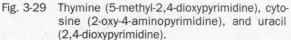

Fig. 3-29   Thymine (5-methyl-2,4-dioxypyrimidine), cytosine (2-oxy-4-aminopyrimidine), and uracil (2,4-dioxypyrimidine).

Modified Pyrimidines

Thymine can also be described as 5-methyluracil. Other methylated pyrimidines exist in some nucleic acids; e.g., methylation of cytosine (Fig. 3-30) in both DNA and RNA has important biological effects with respect to protection of the genetic material and its expression. Methylation is considered to be of central importance in controlling phenotypical traits whose inheritance appears to violate the usual "rules" of Mendelian genetics, and hence are termed *epigenetic* traits.

5-Bromouracil is an analoge thymine (Fig. 3-30) that differs only in the substituent on C-5 (Br rather than CH_3) that is found in some types of primitive organisms and viruses.

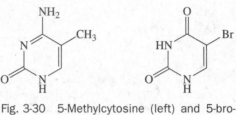

Fig. 3-30   5-Methylcytosine (left) and 5-bromouracil (right).

Purines

The major purine nucleobases that exist in DNA and RNA are derivatives of *adenine* and *guanine* (Fig. 3-31).

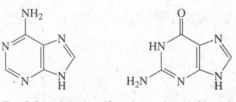

Fig. 3-31   Adenine (6-aminopurine; left) and guanine (6-oxy-2-aminopurine; right).

Tautomeric Forms of Pyrimidines and Purines

All pyrimidines and purines can exist in alternative isomeric forms called *tautomers*. Thus, uracil (Fig. 3-29), thymine (Fig. 3-29), and guanine (Fig. 3-31) and can exist in *keto* and *enol* forms (Fig. 3-32). The keto form dominates at neutral pH.

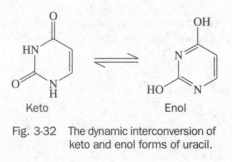

Keto   Enol

Fig. 3-32   The dynamic interconversion of keto and enol forms of uracil.

Enol forms of adenine and cytosine do not exist because they have no *keto* groups. However, they do isomerize to the tautomeric *imino* forms (Fig. 3-33). The *amino* form predominates under biological conditions.

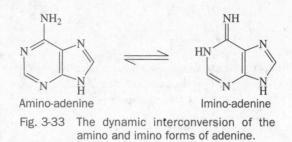

Amino-adenine   Imino-adenine

Fig. 3-33 The dynamic interconversion of the amino and imino forms of adenine.

3.14 Nucleosides

A base covalently linked to either D-ribose or 2-deoxy-D-ribose is known as a nucleoside (note the "s" replaces "t" in nucleotide, thus denoting sugar). Deoxyribonucleosides contain deoxyribose whereas ribonucleosides contain ribose.

Purine nucleosides have a β-*glycosidic linkage* from N-9 of the base to C-1 of the sugar (Fig. 3-34). In pyrimidine nucleosides the linkage is from N-1 of the base to C-1 of the sugar.

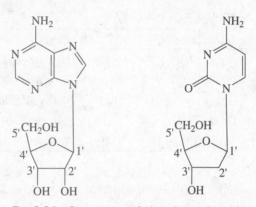

Fig. 3-34 Structures of the ribonucleoside that contains adenine, called *adenosine* (9-β-D-ribofuranosyl adenine; left), and the deoxyribonucleoside that contains cytosine, called *cytidine* (1,2′-deoxy-β-D-ribofuranosyl cytosine; right).

The N linkages in the nucleosides mean that they are referred to as *N-glycosides*. To distinguish the atoms in the furanose ring of the sugar from those in the ring(s) of the nucleobases, the former are designated $1', 2', \ldots, 5'$ as shown. This makes the formal chemical names of the nucleosides rather complex, but fortunately they are simplified as follows.

Table 3-5   Naming Conventions of Nucleosides

Base	Sugar	Name
Adenine	Ribose	Adenosine
Cytosine	Ribose	Cytidine
Guanine	Ribose	Guanosine
Uracil	Ribose	Uridine
Adenine	Deoxyribose	Deoxyadenosine
Cytosine	Deoxyribose	Deoxycytidine
Guanine	Deoxyribose	Deoxyguanosine
Thymine	Deoxyribose	Deoxythymidine

3.15   Nucleotides

Nucleotides

These are phosphoric acid esters of nucleosides in which there is a phosphate group at position C-5′. Nucleotides with phosphorylation at other positions do exist, but they are not components of natural nucleic acids.

Deoxyribonucleotide

These are nucleotides that contain deoxyribose.

Ribonucleotides

These are nucleotides that contain ribose.

Naming Conventions

The usual abbreviations for adenosine-5′-phosphate are AMP (adenosine monophosphate), or *adenylic acid*. If deoxyribose replaces ribose in AMP, the abbreviations are dAMP, or deoxyadenylic acid. The abbreviated names for the various ribonucleotides and deoxyribonucleotides are as follows.

Table 3-6   Naming Conventions for Nucleotides

Base		Ribonucleotide		Deoxyribonucleotide	
Adenine	A	Adenylic acid	AMP	Deoxyadenylic acid	dAMP
Cytosine	C	Cytidylic acid	CMP	Deoxycytidylic acid	dCMP
Guanine	G	Guanylic acid	GMP	Deoxyguanylic acid	dGMP
Uracil	U	Uridylic acid	UMP	Deoxyuridylic acid	dUMP
Thymine	T	Thymidylic acid	TMP	Deoxythymidylic acid	dTMP

All the common 5′-nucleotides also exist as 5′-diphosphates and 5′-triphosphates (Fig. 3-35). These molecules contain two and three phosphates, respectively. E.g., the corresponding adenosine-5′-nucleotides are referred to as ADP and ATP; the corresponding guanosine-5′-nucleotides are referred to as GDP and GTP; and so forth for the other nucleotides. The phosphorus atoms are designated α, β, and γ, with the α-phosphorus being attached to the C-5′ of the ribose. The phosphates of ADP are denoted α and β.

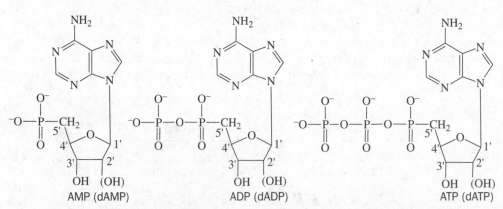

Fig. 3-35   Monophosphate, diphosphate, and triphosphate forms of adenosine. The deoxyribose form of each nucelotide is the same as the ribose form except that it lacks the 2′ hydroxyl group that is shown in brackets.

The ribonucleoside di- and triphosphates (NDPs, NTPs) and the deoxyribonucleoside di- and triphosphates (dNDPs, dNTPs) have important metabolic functions in the cell. They operate as *energy carriers* in many reactions and are also precursors in the synthesis of nucleic acids.

Polynucleotides

Nucleic acids, both DNA and RNA, are *polynucleotides* (Fig. 3-36). They are polymers that have nucleotides as their repeating subunits. The nucleotides are joined to one another through *phosphodiester bonds* between the C-3′ of one nucleotide and the C-5′ of the next. This linkage is repeated many times to build up a large structure (chain or strand) that contains hundreds to millions of nucleotides within the single macromolecule. Thus the sugar residues are each decorated by a nucleobase that is either a purine or a pyrimidine. It is these bases that make up a sequence that codes for a particular cellular outcome, be it a protein or a polynucleotide's structural element such as a ribosome (Chaps. 7 and 8).

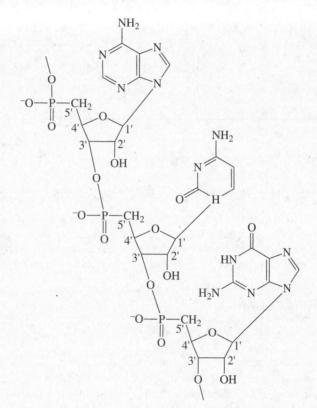

Fig. 3-36   Segment of a polyribonucleotide (RNA).

Because the phosphodiester linkages join different carbons, 3′ and 5′, in adjacent nucleotides the chain has a well-defined chemical direction or *polarity*. By convention the order of nucleotides is always written in the 5′→3′ direction.

The general term for structures containing a few nucleotides (~20–50 or less) is *oligonucleotide*.

3.16   Structure of DNA

DNA is a *polydeoxynucleotide* and is among the largest of all biological macromolecules. Some DNA molecules consist of more than 10^8 nucleotides. They contain adenine, thymine, guanine, and cytosine among the nucleobases present, and genetic information is encoded within the nucleotide sequence, which is precisely defined over the entire length of the molecule.

Base Composition of DNA

The total base composition of DNA varies from species to species (Table 3-7).

Table 3-7   **The Base Compositions for DNA from a Number of Species. (The ratio of purines (A + G) to pyrimidines (T + C) is close to unity in all cases. Perhaps more remarkable is that the ratios of both a to t and g to c are each close to unity. These reflect an important structural feature of most DNAs.)**

Species	Base Composition (Mol %)			
	G	A	C	T
Sarcina lutea (bacterium)	37.1	13.4	37.1	12.4
Alcaligenes faecalis (bacterium)	33.9	16.5	32.8	16.8
E. coli K12	24.9	26.0	25.2	23.9
Wheat	22.7	27.3	22.8*	27.1
Cattle	21.5	28.2	22.5*	27.8
Human	19.5	30.3	19.9	30.3
Saccharomyces cerevisiae (yeast)	18.3	31.7	17.4	32.6
Clostridium perfringens (bacterium)	14.0	36.9	12.8	36.3

*Cytosine + methylcytosine.

EXAMPLE 3.20   What is the base composition of DNA from a human kidney relative to that in liver and other tissues?

It is the same as for human liver, as shown in Table 7-1, because the base composition of DNA is a characteristic of a particular species and does not vary from one cell type to another. This reflects the fact that the nucleotide sequence and therefore the genetic information present in each type of cell within an organism start out being exactly the same. However, *somatic mutations* can occur that make a population of cells have a different coding sequence, and this is the basis of *tumor development*.

Double-Helical Structure of DNA

Question: What structural feature of DNA accounts for the ratio of A to T and G to C being close to unity?

DNA is a duplex molecule in which two polynucleotide chains (or strands) are linked to each other through specific *base pairing*. Adenine in one strand is paired to thymine in the other, and guanine is paired to cytosine. The two chains are said to be *complementary*. This was one of the essential features of Watson and Crick's proposal for the structure of DNA. Hydrogen bonds (H bonds) form between the opposing bases within a pair. In the structure proposed by Watson and Crick, A:T and G:C base pairs are roughly planar with H bonds (dotted lines) as shown in Fig. 3-37.

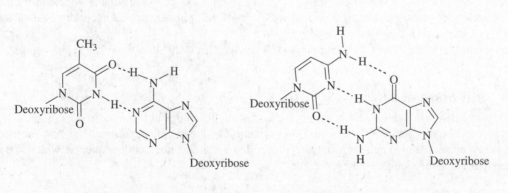

Fig. 3-37   Base pairing via hydrogen bonds (dashed lines) in DNA.

Note that two H bonds form in an A:T pair and three in a G:C pair (Fig. 3-37).

In the normal structure of DNA, the base pairs are aligned parallel with one another and with the plane of each base lying approximately perpendicular to the long axis of the two chains. This pair of chains is referred to as a *duplex*.

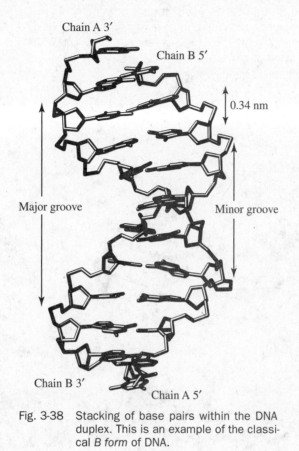

Chain A 3′

Chain B 5′

0.34 nm

Major groove

Minor groove

Chain B 3′

Chain A 5′

Fig. 3-38   Stacking of base pairs within the DNA duplex. This is an example of the classical *B form* of DNA.

The two strands of DNA run in opposite directions (Fig. 3-38). A model of DNA that incorporates base pairing between complementary strands and that is consistent with X-ray diffraction data was developed by James Watson and Frances Crick in 1953. In this model, the two strands twist around each other to give a *right-handed double-stranded helix*. To achieve a structure that was consistent with the structural data available at the time, it was necessary to orientate the complementary chains in opposite directions. Direct proof of this *opposite polarity* in chain direction was achieved ~10 years later.

EXAMPLE 3.21   How does twisting into a helix contribute to the stability of the overall structure of DNA, and its function?

One of the most significant effects of twisting DNA strands into a helix is to bring the stacked base pairs very close to one another (0.34 nm). Consequently, water is excluded from what becomes a hydrophobic core, and the negatively charged phosphates lie on the outer surface. The hydrophobic interactions within the core contribute, along with the H bonds between the base pairs, to the overall stability of the helix.

There is one complete twist of the helix every 10 base pairs, or 3.4 nm. This distance is referred to as the *pitch* of the helix. The surface of the helix shows alternating *major* and *minor grooves* that follow the twist of the double-stranded molecule along its entire length. The major groove accommodates interactions with proteins (transcription factors; see Chaps. 7 and 9) that recognize and bind to specific nucleotide sequences.

The structure of the double helix shown in Fig. 3-38 is called the *B form*. It appears to be the main form that occurs in vivo and in solutions of purified DNA. It also exists in fibers of DNA at high humidity. At lower humidities (<75%), a fiber of DNA will shorten; this is due to a change to the *A form* in which the base pairs are no longer perpendicular to the axis of the helix; but they are tilted by ~20°, and the pitch of the helix is reduced to 2.8 nm with 11 base pairs per turn. This A form may also occur in *hybrid pairings* between DNA and RNA strands.

A dramatically different form of the double helix has been observed in DNA molecules that contain an alternating d(GC)$_n$ structure along each strand. It is a *left-handed* rather than a right-handed helix and is known as the *Z form* of DNA. In the Z form, the repeating unit is a *dinucleotide* and the resulting structure gives a staggered zig zag shape, instead of a smoothly twisting helix, of the sugar-phosphate backbone. Segments of methylated DNA may adopt this Z geometry.

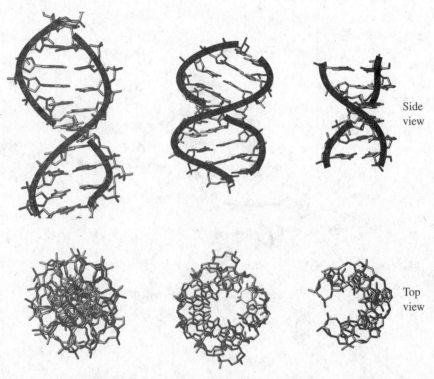

Side view

Top view

Fig. 3-39   B-DNA (left), A-DNA (center), and Z-DNA (right), side and top views.

Table 3-8   **Comparison of the Geometrical Features of Three Forms of DNA Helix**

Geometry Attribute	B-DNA	A-DNA	Z-DNA
Helix sense	Right-handed	Right-handed	Left-handed
Repeating unit	1 base pair	1 base pair	2 base pairs
Rotation per base pair	35.9°	33.6°	60°/2
Mean base pairs per turn	10.0	10.7	12
Inclination of base pair to axis	−1.2°	+19°	−9°
Rise per base pair along axis	3.32 Å	2.3 Å	3.8 Å
Pitch per turn of helix	33.2 Å	24.6 Å	45.6 Å
Diameter	20 Å	26 Å	18 Å

3.17   DNA Sequencing

Sanger or Dideoxy Method

Currently most methods for determining the sequence of DNA are carried out using the *chain termination method* developed by Frederick Sanger in the 1970s; this is also referred to as the *dideoxy* or *Sanger* sequencing method (Fig. 3-40). A sequencing primer (a short segment of DNA that is complementary to the strand being sequenced) is *annealed* to the target DNA strands near the start of the region to be sequenced. DNA polymerase and the four deoxynucleotides (dATP, dCTP, dGTP, and dTTP) are added, and the complementary strand of DNA is synthesized. The reaction is also supplemented with small amounts of dideoxy forms of the nucleotides. Whenever one of these dideoxynucleotides is added to the chain, it spontaneously terminates its elongation. This is a random event, so a pool of DNA molecules of different lengths accumulates in time.

In the classical Sanger method, a radiolabeled deoxynucleotide is incorporated into the strands, and four separate reactions are carried out, each supplemented with a different dideoxy nucleotide. The four reaction mixtures are then subjected to high-resolution polyacrylamide gel electrophoresis (PAGE) to separate the pools of different DNA molecules on the basis of their size; and these are visualized by detecting the radiolabelled polynucleotides (e.g., by exposure of a photographic film, or autoradiography). The sequence of the newly made strand, which is a perfect complement of the original DNA strand, is then simply read off sequentially from the film/autoradiograph.

In more modern methods, each of the dideoxy nucleotides carries a different fluorescent *tag* molecule, or *fluorophor*. Thus, all four chain-termination reactions can be carried out in a single sample tube. The different DNA strands are then separated by *capillary electrophoresis* and detected on the basis of their particular fluorescence.

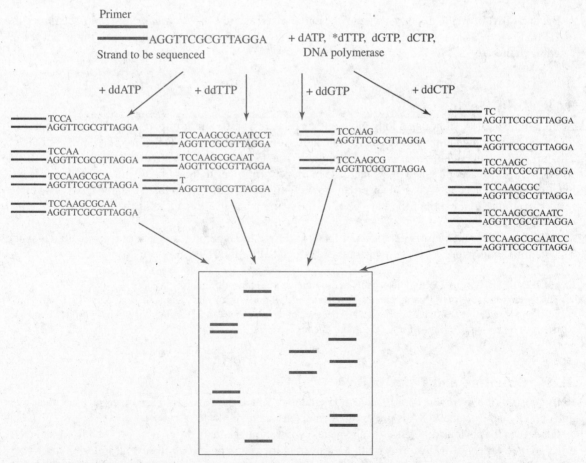

Fig. 3-40   Schematic representation of the Sanger or dideoxy method for sequencing a sample of multiple copies of a particular molecule of DNA.

EXAMPLE 3.22   How does a dideoxynucleotide terminate the chain extension reaction in the Sanger method of DNA sequencing?

The dideoxynucleotides lack the 3′ hydroxyl group on the deoxyribose moiety. This hydroxyl group forms part of the sugar phosphate backbone, so if it is missing, the chain cannot be further extended.

Pyrosequencing DNA Method

There are a number of other DNA sequencing methods becoming available; one of these, *pyrosequencing*, was developed initially by Mostafa Ronaghi in the late 1990s (Fig. 3-41). Like the chain termination method, it uses a sequencing primer and DNA polymerase to make a complementary copy of the DNA to be sequenced. However, rather than carry out a full sequencing reaction, followed by separation and detection of oligonucleotides, the incorporation of nucleotides into the growing strand is detected in real time.

Three additional enzymes are required for this process, i.e., *ATP sulfurylase*, *luciferase*, and *apyrase*, and the substrates *adenosine 5′ phosphosulfate* (APS) and *luciferin*.

The first of four dNTPs is added. If that dNTP is complementary to the one in the strand being sequenced, it is incorporated into the new strand by DNA polymerase, releasing pyrophosphate (PPi) in direct proportion to the amount of dNTP bound. ATP sulfurylase quantitatively converts PPi to ATP in the presence of APS. ATP drives the conversion of luciferin to oxyluciferin via luciferase that generates light in proportion to the amount of ATP present. This light is detected by a charge-coupled device (CCD) camera and is recorded as a peak in what is known as a *pyrogram*. The intensity of the light produced is proportional to the number of nucleotides incorporated into the emerging DNA. Apyrase degrades unincorporated dNTPs and excess ATP. When degradation is complete, another dNTP is added and the cycle begins again. This process continues in a cyclical manner as the sequence is read off the pyrogram.

Because dATP would directly activate the luciferase reaction, *deoxyadenosine α-thio triphosphate* (dATPαS) is used as a substitute for dATP. It is efficiently used by the DNA polymerase, but is not recognized by luciferase.

3.18   DNA Melting

Double-helical DNA, although a long molecule, is relatively stiff, and it imparts high viscosity to a solution. However, at high temperatures the double helix comes apart, and the DNA becomes single-stranded. This process is called *denaturation* or melting, and it is accompanied by a reduction in viscosity of the solution. It is also accompanied by an increase in the absorption of uv light at 260 nm. Thus, at this wavelength single-stranded DNA has an absorbance ~40% higher than that of double-stranded DNA. The effect results from the *unstacking* of the base pairs in the helix, and it is referred to as the *hyperchromic effect* of DNA denaturation.

DNA from different sources denatures or *melts* at different temperatures in a very reproducible manner. The melting temperature T_m is the temperature at which half of the DNA has been denatured.

EXAMPLE 3.23   Why do DNA molecules from different sources have different T_m values?

This occurs because the DNA molecules have different proportions of G:C and A:T base pairs. G:C base pairs confer a greater stability to double-stranded DNA because of the presence of three (rather than two) hydrogen bonds per base (Fig. 3-37). Thus, the higher the G:C content, the higher the T_m.

3.19   Structure and Types of RNA

RNA consists of *polyribonucleotide* molecular chains in which the bases are preponderantly adenine, guanine, uracil, and cytosine. RNA is present in the nucleus and cytoplasm of cells.

Other than the obvious differences in chemical composition, the main differences between RNA and DNA are a greater variety of RNA forms (with M_r values in the range of 25,000 to several million) and RNA's propensity to exist as a single polynucleotide chain that folds back on itself to form double-helical regions containing A:U and G:C base pairs (Fig. 3-42).

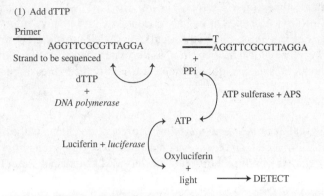

(1) Add dTTP

Primer

AGGTTCGCGTTAGGA   T AGGTTCGCGTTAGGA

Strand to be sequenced

dTTP + DNA polymerase

PPi

ATP sulferase + APS

ATP

Luciferin + *luciferase*

Oxyluciferin + light ⟶ DETECT

(2) Excess dNTPs degraded by apyrase

(3) Add dATPaS, dCTP, dGTP in sequence in an interative fashion

(4) Read pyrogram to determine sequence of the complementary strand

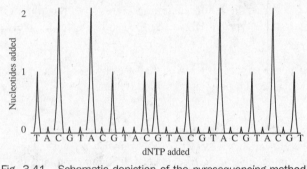
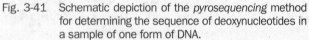

Fig. 3-41   Schematic depiction of the *pyrosequencing* method for determining the sequence of deoxynucleotides in a sample of one form of DNA.

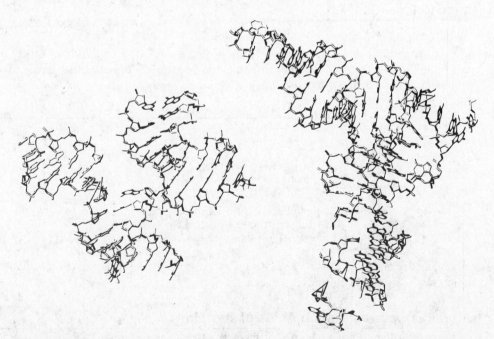

Fig. 3-42   Examples of RNA molecules that take on tertiary structures by hydrogen-bonded base pairing. Tertiary domain of mRNA is involved in the initiation of translation into protein (left) and yeast phenylalanine tRNA (right).

There are three major types of RNA: (1) *transfer RNA* (tRNA); (2) *ribosomal RNA* (rRNA); and (3) *messenger RNA* (mRNA). Recently it has also been shown that short segments of RNA (as small as 22 nucleotide residues long) are important in the regulation of cell function. These are known collectively as *small*, or *micro*, *RNAs*, and they form the basic tool in the experimented method known as RNA interference (RNAi); this is a method that is used to downregulate artificially the expression of target genes in cell lines and some organisms.

tRNA

This is RNA of M_r ~25,000. It serves as an *adaptor* in polypeptide chain synthesis (Chap. 8). It constitutes 10–20% of the total RNA in a cell, and there is at least one tRNA for each amino acid. tRNAs are unique in that they contain a relatively high proportion of nucleosides of unusual structure such as *pseudouridine*, *inosine*, and *2′-O-methylnucleoside*. There are also many types of modified bases such as those which are *methylated*, or *acetylated*.

rRNA

This is present in all *ribosomes*; these macromolecular complexes contain an approximately equal amount of protein and RNA. rRNA makes up ~80% of the total RNA in a cell and is of several types that are distinguished from one another by their sedimentation (S) rates in ultracentrifuge analysis (Sec. 4.14). E.g., bacterial ribosomes contain three types of RNA, 5S, 16S, and 23S, respectively.

mRNA

These are a very heterogeneous species of RNA as they are copies of DNA sequences. Each mRNA is translated in the cytoplasm to a particular polypeptide chain (Chap. 9).

Ribozymes

An additional *rare* form of RNA is the ribozyme (from *ribo*nucleic en*zyme*). As the name implies, these are RNA molecules that have enzymic activity (Chap. 5). Many ribozymes catalyze the hydrolytic cleavage of RNA of either other RNA molecules or their own RNA. They are also an integral part of ribosomes where they have *aminotransferase* activity. The discovery of ribozymes, along with the realization that RNA can act as a hereditary molecule, gave rise to the concept by Leslie Orgel of an "RNA world"; this idea posits that in the distant past, simple cells used RNA as structural, catalytic, and genetic elements (see Sec. 1.1).

3.20   Amino Acids—General

Question: What is an amino acid?

An amino acid is a molecule that contains an *amino* group and a *carboxyl* group. Although there are many different types of amino acid (for example, nonprotein amino acids used in metabolism), only a subset of these exist in proteins. These are the *α-amino acids*. The amino and carboxyl groups are *both* attached to the α-carbon atom (Fig. 3-43).

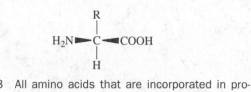

Fig. 3-43   All amino acids that are incorporated in proteins during synthesis on ribosomes are of the L- configuration shown here.

The α-carbon atom in amino acids is a *chiral center* except when the —R group, or *side chain*, is —H. Therefore amino acids display optical activity (Sec. 3.1).

3.21   Naturally Occurring Amino Acids of Proteins

There are *routinely* 20 different amino acids (but there is a twist; see Example 3.26) that are used in the synthesis of proteins, each of which can be represented by a single letter or a three-letter abbreviation. The three-letter symbols are easier to remember, but in writing down long sequences the single-letter symbols are usually used. Greek symbols are used to signify the position of carbon atoms in side chains in amino acids. The carbon atom to which the side chain, the amino group, and the carboxyl group are bound is labeled α, the next carbon is β, and so on (Fig. 3-44).

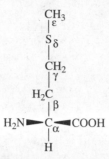

Fig. 3-44   Greek letter specification of carbon atoms in the side chain of an amino acid. Methionine is used here as an example.

The *side chains* of the amino acids do not form a natural series and can be classified according to several different properties (Figs. 3-45 to 3-49). In the following figures only the side chains are shown.

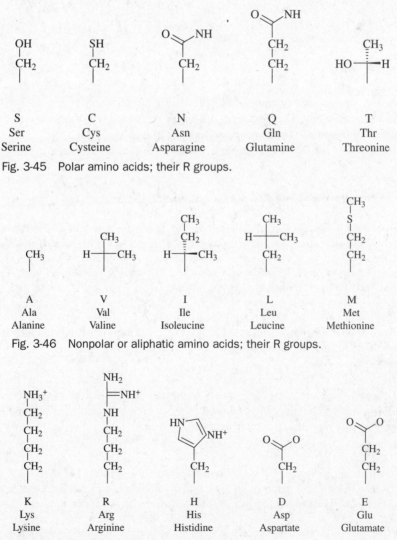

Fig. 3-45   Polar amino acids; their R groups.

Fig. 3-46   Nonpolar or aliphatic amino acids; their R groups.

Fig. 3-47   Charged amino acids; their R groups.

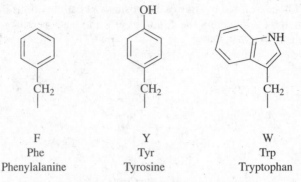

Fig. 3-48   Aromatic amino acids; their R groups.

The aromatic amino acids absorb light strongly in the ultraviolet region. This is useful in detecting them and in determining their concentration in solution.

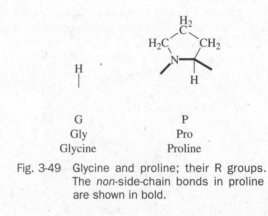

Fig. 3-49   Glycine and proline; their R groups. The *non*-side-chain bonds in proline are shown in bold.

Glycine and proline are often considered to be special because they are not typical α-amino acids.

EXAMPLE 3.24   Glycine is an amino acid that contains a simple H atom as its side chain. Thus it is *achiral* (i.e., not chiral) because it contains two H atoms bonded to the α-carbon. In normal solutions these H atoms are indistinguishable from one another, meaning that the mirror image of glycine can be superimposed on itself. However, when glycine is placed in an *asymmetric molecular environment* such as a solution of stretched gelatin-gel, each H atom gives a distinct ^{1}H NMR spectrum. The α-carbon is therefore said to be *prochiral*.

EXAMPLE 3.25   Is it strictly correct to call proline an amino acid?
   No. The side chain of proline bends around and is covalently linked to the backbone nitrogen atom replacing one of the hydrogen atoms. Thus it is actually an *imino* acid.

The classifications of the 20 amino acids in Figs. 3-45 to 3-49 are not mutually exclusive and are not the only way to classify these amino acids. E.g., *tyrosine* can be considered to be both *aromatic* and *polar*; the side chain of *arginine* has both polar and nonpolar properties; *glycine, alanine, serine,* and *cysteine* can be classed together as *small* amino acids, whereas *valine, leucine, isoleucine, methionine*, and the *aromatic* amino acids can be classed as having *bulky* side chains.

EXAMPLE 3.26   Are the 20 amino acids noted above really the only genetically encoded amino acids?
   No. In many proteins some of the amino acids are modified after their incorporation; e.g., in collagen a hydroxyl group is added to each of several proline residues to yield *hydroxyproline*, and this does not constitute direct genetic encoding.
   Recently two genetically encoded amino acids have been discovered. In 1986, *selenocysteine*, a selenium analog of cysteine, was discovered in a small number of proteins in most living species. One notable example in humans is

glutathione peroxidase that exists with high activity in erythrocytes. It contains the amino acid in its active site. The three-letter abbreviation for selenocysteine is Sec, and its one-letter symbol is U.

In 2002 *pyrrolysine* was discovered to be genetically encoded. Pyrrolysine exists only in the archaebacterium *Methanosarcina barkeri*. Its three-letter abbreviation is Pyl, and its one-letter symbol is O.

The amino acids are encoded by UGA and UAG stop codons, respectively. For selenocysteine incorporation, serine is first added to the nascent peptide (Sec. 9.8) via a special tRNA that recognizes not only the codon but also a peculiar tertiary loop structure in the upstream mRNA. Then the OH on the serine is modified to SeH via the high-energy intermediate *selenophosphate* that is generated using energy from ATP.

Less is known about *pyrrolysine* incorporation into proteins; but it is directly inserted by a special tRNA unlike selenocysteine that is fabricated in situ. Even less is known about how these two alternative processes evolved, but the systems are phylogenetically ancient.

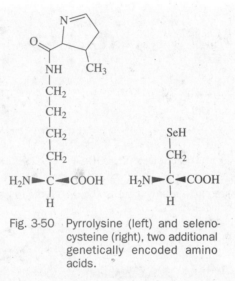

Fig. 3-50 Pyrrolysine (left) and seleno-cysteine (right), two additional genetically encoded amino acids.

3.22 Acid-Base Behavior of Amino Acids

Amino acids are *amphoteric* compounds; i.e., they contain both *acidic* and *basic* groups. Because of this, they are capable of bearing a net electric charge that varies according to the nature of the solution. These net charges can be important for the way in which proteins interact with other biomolecules and are often exploited when purifying proteins.

Acid-Base Behavior of Simple Amino Acids

When an amino acid is titrated by a strong base, the following type of titration curve is produced.

The curve in Fig. 3-51 shows two plateaux, one each at the pK_a value for the two titratable groups in alanine, pH ~3 and pH ~10. In the neighborhood of these points (~±0.5 pH units), alanine acts as a pH buffer.

The pH at which the molecule carries no net charge is called the *isoelectric point* (pI); for alanine the isoelectric point is pH 6.0. The molecule still carries charges, but they neutralize each other. The pH value of the isoelectric point is simply the average of the two pK_a values:

$$pI = (pK_{a1} + pK_{a2})/2$$

Acidic and Basic Amino Acids

Some amino acids bear a side chain that can be protonated or deprotonated (i.e., a *prototropic side chain*). Examples are aspartic acid and glutamic acid with their additional carboxyl group, histidine with an imidazole moiety, lysine with an ε-amino group, and arginine with its guanidino group. The structures of these side chains are given on the previous pages, and their pK_a values are listed in Table 3-9.

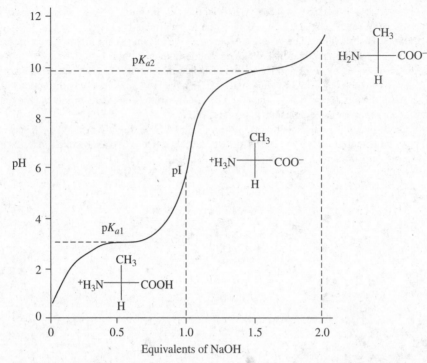

Fig. 3-51   Titration curve of the amino acid, alanine. Here pK_{a1} and pK_{a2} refer to the values for the amino and carboxyl groups, respectively; pI denotes the isoelectric point.

Table 3-9   The pK_a Values of Amino Acids

Amino Acid	pK_{a1} (α-COOH)	pK_{a2} (α-NH^{3+})	pK_{aR} (side chain)
Glycine	2.3	9.6	—
Serine	2.2	9.2	—
Alanine	2.3	9.7	—
Valine	2.3	9.6	—
Leucine	2.4	9.6	—
Aspartic acid	2.1	9.8	3.9
Glutamic acid	2.2	9.7	4.3
Histidine	1.8	9.2	6.0
Cysteine	1.7	10.8	8.3
Tyrosine	2.2	9.1	10.1
Lysine	2.2	9.0	10.5
Arginine	2.2	9.0	12.5

The protonated forms of the carboxyl groups and the tyrosine side chain are *uncharged*, while the deprotonated forms are negatively charged or *anionic*.

The protonated forms of the amino group, the *imidazolium* side chain of histidine, and the *guanidinium* group of arginine are positively charged (i.e., *cationic*) while the deprotonated forms are uncharged.

The titration curves of these amino acids have an extra inflection, e.g., aspartic acid as shown in Fig. 3-52.

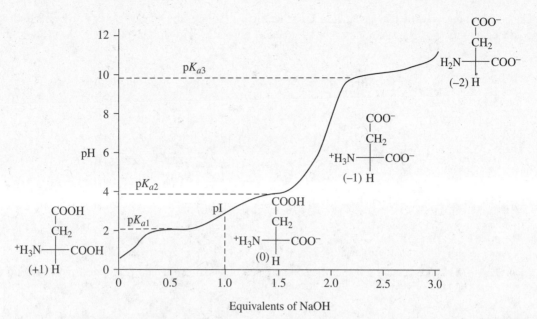

Fig. 3-52   Titration of 10 mM aspartic acid hydrochloride with NaOH. The structures indicate the various stages of protonation of the titratable moieties, and the number in brackets denotes the net change on the molecule.

Isoelectric Point

The isoelectric point of a *prototropic* (Greek, tropism means *change*) amino acid is the average of the pK_a values of the protonation transitions on *either side* of the isoelectric species. For aspartic acid the isoelectric species exists in the pH domain between pK_{a1} (2.1) and pK_{a2} (3.9). Thus, the pI of aspartic acid is 3.0.

EXAMPLE 3.27   What is the pI of arginine (Fig. 3-53)?

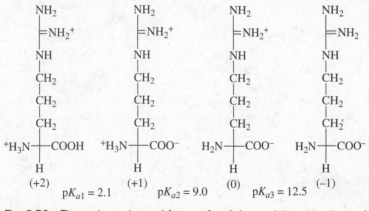

Fig. 3-53   The various charged forms of arginine and the pK_a values of each titratable group.

The isoelectric species exists in the pH domain between pK_{a2} and pK_{a3}; hence the pI of arginine is 10.25.

3.23   The Peptide Bond

In protein molecules, α-amino acids are linked in a linear sequence. The α-amino group of one amino acid is linked to the α-carboxyl group of the next through an amide bond, known as a *peptide* bond. The bond is special in that it is planar with the attached atoms not readily able to rotate around the bond; in other words it has *double-bond character*.

The peptide bond is formed in a condensation reaction that requires the input of energy, while its hydrolysis to yield free amino acids is a spontaneous process that is normally very slow in neutral solutions (Fig. 3-54).

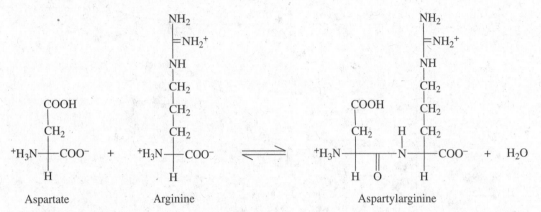

Aspartate   Arginine   Aspartylarginine

Fig. 3-54   The condensation reaction that takes place between two amino acids for a peptide bond and the release of a water molecule.

The acidic and basic characters of the carboxyl and amino groups that take part in forming the bond are lost after condensation.

Nomenclature

In naming short peptides, we begin with the amino acid that has the free α-NH_3^+ (the *N-terminus*) and replace the *-ine* endings (except the last one) with the ending *-yl*; the amino acids in the peptide are called *residues*, since they are the residue left after the removal of water during peptide-bond formation.

EXAMPLE 3.28   Distinguish between the dipeptides glycylalanine and alanylglycine (Fig. 3-55).

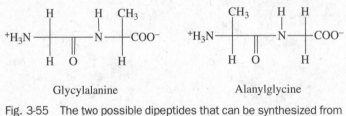

Glycylalanine   Alanylglycine

Fig. 3-55   The two possible dipeptides that can be synthesized from one molecule of glycine and one molecule of alanine.

Glycylalanine has a free α-amino group on the glycine residue, while the free carboxyl group is that of the alanine residue. Glycylalanine and alanylglycine are examples of *sequence isomers*; they are composed of the same amino acids, but they are combined in different sequences.

Compounds of two amino acids linked by a peptide bond are known as *dipeptides*, those with three amino acids are called *tripeptides*, and so on. *Oligopeptides* contain an unspecified but small number of amino acid residues, whereas polypeptides comprise larger numbers. Natural polypeptides *of 50 or more residues* are generally referred to as *proteins*.

All natural proteins are composed of α-peptide links (unless there have been postsynthetic modifications).

3.24   Amino Acid Analysis

The amino acid composition of a protein can be determined by methods that are referred to as *amino acid analysis*. The protein of interest is hydrolyzed in concentrated acid (usually $HClO_4$ or HCl) to generate the free amino acids which are separated from one another, usually by means of ion exchange chromatography.

Their *relative abundance* can be determined by first treating the amino acids with ninhydrin (see Fig. 3-56) to create a colored derivative, or fluorescamine to generate a fluorescent derivative. The concentration of each amino acid is proportional to the absorbance (or fluorescence) of the solution. The technique was originally used to help identify proteins, but it is now more commonly used as the most accurate way to determine the concentration of a protein sample.

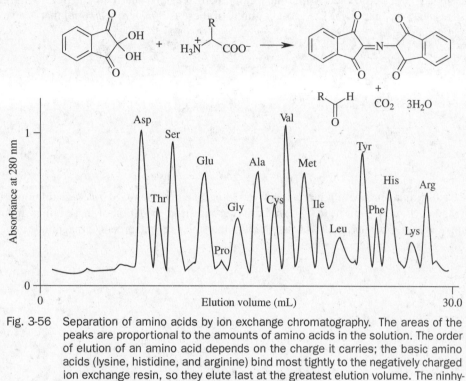

Fig. 3-56 Separation of amino acids by ion exchange chromatography. The areas of the peaks are proportional to the amounts of amino acids in the solution. The order of elution of an amino acid depends on the charge it carries; the basic amino acids (lysine, histidine, and arginine) bind most tightly to the negatively charged ion exchange resin, so they elute last at the greatest elution volume. The ninhydrin reaction is shown above the chromatogram.

Determination of the actual sequence of amino acids in a peptide or protein is considered in Sec. 4.4.

3.25 Reactions of Cysteine

The side chain of cysteine is very important because of its potential for oxidation, to form a disulfide bond with an adjacent cysteine, and thus form the amino acid *cystine*, as follows:

$$R—SH + R—SH + \frac{1}{2} O_2 \rightarrow R—S—S—R$$

Disulfide bonds often exist in proteins if the cysteine side chains are sufficiently close in the *tertiary structure* to form a bond or *bridge*. In addition, oxidation of free —SH groups on the surface of some proteins causes two different molecules to be linked covalently by such a disulfide bridge.

Disulfide bridges stabilize proteins, but they may also be undesirable, so cells contain reducing agents that prevent or reverse this reaction. The most common of these redox agents is the tripeptide γ-L-glutamyl-L-cysteinylglycine, or glutathione (Fig. 3-57). Its abbreviation is GSH; the SH emphasizes the reactive part of the peptide.

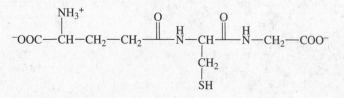

Fig. 3-57 Glutathione.

The redox potential of glutathione is sufficiently negative (i.e., a reducing agent that donates electrons to a recipient molecule) to reduce oxidized cysteines that are linked by a disulfide bond back to their sulfhydryl forms. In the process, glutathione becomes oxidized itself, forming two disulfide-linked glutathione molecules whose name is abbreviated as GSSG. Cells contain reducing systems, most notably NADPH/NADP$^+$, that are linked to metabolism that re-reduce oxidized glutathione.

Disulfide bonds can be cleaved in the laboratory with reagents that carry a free —SH group, like the cysteine residue of glutathione. The most common of these is *2-mercaptoethanol* that is also known as β-*mercaptoethanol* (Fig. 3-58).

$$HO—CH_2—CH_2—SH$$

Fig. 3-58　β-Mercaptoethanol.

Disulfide reducing agents with a more negative redox potential than GSH *include* dithiothreitol (DTT; Cleland's reagent) (Fig. 3-59). It bears two sulfhydryl groups, and oxidation of these brings about ring closure to form a stable disulfide bridge. As a result, dithiothreitol is several orders of magnitude more powerful as a reducing agent than β-mercaptoethanol.

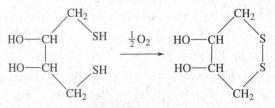

Fig. 3-59　Dithiothreitol or Cleland's reagent.

Yet another experimentally valuable reducing agent is tris(2-carboxyethyl)phosphine (TCEP) (Fig. 3-60). It employs a different type of chemistry from the sulfhydryl compounds, and it is used to retain proteins in a reduced state, in vitro. The redox potentials of phosphine are more negative at lower pH values than the sulfhydryl reducing agents.

$$(CH_2CH_2COOH)_3P: + RSSR + H_2O \rightarrow (CH_2CH_2COOH)_3P = O + 2RSH$$

Fig. 3-60　Reduction of disulfide bonds by TCEP.

It is experimentally desirable to prevent the oxidation of sulfydryl groups, as the presence of disulfide bonds can lead to insolubility of a protein and hence render it unsuitable for structural studies or amino acid sequencing. It is possible to *block* their active —SH groups with a range of chemical reagents.

EXAMPLE 3.29　Iodoacetate forms an S-carboxymethyl derivative of cysteine residues, thus blocking the —SH group and rendering it unavailable for disulfide bond formation. When it modifies the —SH group in the active site of an enzyme, it inhibits that enzyme.

$$RSH + ICH_2COO^- \rightarrow RSCH_2COO^- + HI$$

SOLVED PROBLEMS

CARBOHYDRATES

3.1. What is the difference between a sugar and a carbohydrate?

SOLUTION

Sugar is a term that is sometimes used incorrectly to refer to carbohydrates in general, because many carbohydrates have a sweet taste. But not all carbohydrates are sugars, e.g., starch. However, in common usage sugar usually refers specifically to sucrose, or perhaps to a few other simple carbohydrates such as fructose and glucose.

3.2. Which of the following compounds are carbohydrates?

$$
\begin{array}{ccc}
CH_3 & CHO & CH_2OH \\
| & | & | \\
CH_2OH & CH_2OH & CHOH \\
& & | \\
& & CHO \\
(1) & (2) & (3)
\end{array}
$$

SOLUTION

Only (3) is a carbohydrate. Although (1) contains a hydroxyl group, and (2) is an aldehyde with one hydroxyl group, carbohydrates are ketones or aldehydes with *multiple hydroxyl groups*, or are derivatives of them.

3.3. What is the chemical difference between a ketose and an aldose?

SOLUTION

Ketoses contain a ketone group whereas aldoses contain an aldehyde group.

GLUCOSE

3.4. β-D-Glucose is the most prevalent monosaccharide in the bloodstream. It can react with many different compounds. What is the chemical basis of this reactivity?

SOLUTION

Glucose is an aldehyde and hence is a reducing compound. The aldehyde group is reactive and can be reduced to form an alcohol, can be oxidized to form a carboxylic acid, or can react with many other compounds to form a glucosyl adduct with them.

3.5. What is the chemical/structural reason for β-D-glucopyranose being the dominant anomer over α-D-glucopyranose in an aqueous solution of glucose?

SOLUTION

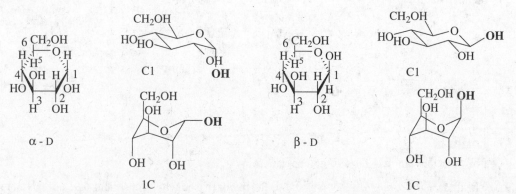

Draw the chair forms of both β-D-glucopyranose and α-D-glucopyranose from Fig. 3-9. It is easy to see that for each of the α and β forms the C1 conformation would be favored as most of the functional groups lie in the more stable equatorial plane, whereas in the 1C conformation most of the functional groups are in the less stable axial planes. The difference between the α and β forms in the C1 conformations (in bold) is that the hydroxyl group at position 1 is in the axial plane for the α form and in the equatorial plane for the β form. Thus, the β C1 conformation would be the most stable conformation overall, making β-D-glucopyranose the dominant anomer.

OTHER IMPORTANT MONOSACCHARIDES

3.6. What is the structural difference between L-ribitol-1-phosphate and D-ribitol-5-phosphate?

SOLUTION

Nothing. Ribitol can be numbered from either end because all the carbon atoms are in the same oxidation state, and the two differently named forms are the same structure turned upside down.

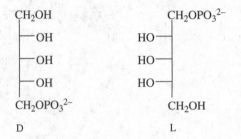

3.7. How does fructose, the most common dietary sugar other than glucose, differ from glucose?

SOLUTION

Like glucose, fructose is a six-carbon-atom carbohydrate, but it is a *ketose* rather than an *aldose*; i.e., it contains a ketone group at position C-2 rather than an aldehyde at position C-1.

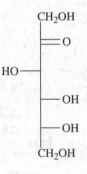

THE GLYCOSIDIC BOND

3.8. The disaccharide shown below is *lactose*. It is the main carbohydrate of mammalian milk. What is its detailed name?

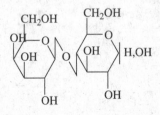

SOLUTION

β-D-Galactopyranosyl-(1→4)-D-glucopyranose.

3.9. The disaccharide *trehalose*, shown next, is the major reason why some plants and animals can withstand prolonged periods of dessication (severe dehydration). It is widely used in cosmetics and commercial foods, because of its high water retention properties. Is it a *reducing* or *nonreducing* disaccharide?

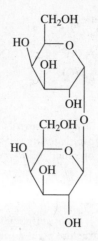

SOLUTION

The form of trehalose pictured is α-D-glucopyranosyl-(1→1)-β-D-glucopyranose. Other forms of trehalose are the α,β and β,β forms. The disaccharide bond is made through the *anomeric* carbon atoms of each constituent glucose molecule, thus trehalose is *nonreducing*.

LIPIDS

3.10. Draw the structure of the *essential* fatty acid all-*cis*, α-lineolic acid 18:3$^{\Delta 9,12,15}$.

SOLUTION

From the chemical composition α-lineolic acid contains 18 carbon atoms. Hence the backbone would be as follows, remembering that the carboxyl group is at position C-1:

The hydrocarbon chain also contains three double bonds, between carbon atoms 9 and 10, 12 and 13, and 15 and 16, and all the double bonds are specified as *cis*. So the structure is as follows:

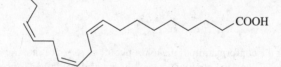

3.11. Is the melting temperature of this fatty acid likely to be higher or lower than the following all-*trans* form?

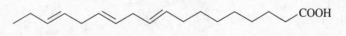

SOLUTION

The all-*cis* form has a lower melting temperature because the all-*trans* form packs together with its neighbors more tightly.

3.12. The pK_a values of phosphomonoesters are ~1 and ~6. In what form will glycerol 3-phosphoric acid exist at physiological pH?

SOLUTION

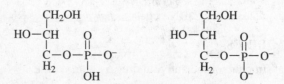

The dianion is the predominant species at pH 7.0, but small amounts of the monoanion will also be present because the pH is above but close to the second pK_a value.

3.13. What type of lipid is the following molecule?

$$CH_3(CH_2)_{14}CH \underset{\underset{OH}{|}}{} - \overset{\overset{H}{|}}{\underset{\underset{NH_3^+}{|}}{C}} - CH_2OH$$

SOLUTION

It is a long-chain *hydroxylated base*. Close inspection reveals the *serine* moiety on the right. Thus, it is a sphingolipid. More specifically, it is *dihydrosphingosine* (or sphinganine). It exists in animals as part of sphingolipids in membranes, although less commonly than sphingosine.

3.14. Can cholesterol form micelles and bilayers?

SOLUTION

Cholesterol does not form micelles because it is not sufficiently amphiphilic (even though it does have an —OH group) and its flat, rigid, fused-ring structure gives a solid rather than a liquid hydrocarbon phase at physiological temperatures. Such fluidity is required for micelle formation. However, cholesterol can form *mixed micelles* with amphiphilic lipids, and it enters monolayers as well where it constitutes ~25% of the mass of the lipid bilayer in the plasma membranes of mammalian cells.

3.15. What are the structural and chemical reasons why bile salts don't form typical micelles?

SOLUTION

Although bile salts possess a polar head group, the hydrocarbon tail usually contains polar hydroxyl groups. Therefore the rigid ring system gives a tightly packed, almost solid, nonpolar phase rather than a liquid one. However, like cholesterol, bile salts can form *mixed micelles* with phospholipids.

BEHAVIOR OF LIPIDS IN WATER

3.16. Do phospholipids with short hydrocarbon chains form lipid bilayers?

SOLUTION

No, the hydrocarbon chains must contain at least six carbon atoms for bilayers to form. Instead, they form micelles.

3.17. Which would be better for solubilizing the integral proteins from membranes, ionic or nonionic detergents?

SOLUTION

Ionic detergents alter the conformation of the hydrophobic portions of integral membrane proteins, whereas non-ionic detergents do not. Therefore, nonionic detergents are preferred; they form mixed micelles of detergent, lipid, and protein. Most integral membrane proteins need to be surrounded by lipids of some sort to remain active.

NUCLEIC ACIDS

3.18. Define a nucleic acid.

SOLUTION

Nucleic acids are polymers made up of nitrogenous bases, monosaccharides, and phosphate in a regular repeating structure. The monosaccharides are deoxyribose and ribose, and the bases are derivatives of purines and pyrimidines.

3.19. What is the major chemical difference between RNA and DNA?

SOLUTION

The sugar in RNA is *ribose* and the sugar in DNA is *2-deoxyribose*. Most of the bases (adenine, cytosine, and guanine) are the same; however, DNA contains *thymine* whereas RNA contains *uracil*.

PURINES AND PYRIMIDINES

3.20. Draw the chemical structure of the antiviral drug 5-fluorouracil.

SOLUTION

5-Fluorouracil is uracil with a fluorine atom attached to C-5 (see next). It inhibits the synthesis of RNA.

3.21. 5-Bromouracil is an analog of thymine, but 5-fluorouracil is not. Why?

SOLUTION

Thymine is 5-methyluracil so the halogen substituent needs to mimic a methyl group. A bromine atom is of a similar size to a methyl group, so this enables 5-bromouracil to mimic thymine, allowing its incorporation into RNA; but a fluorine atom is a similar size to a hydrogen atom. In addition, a fluorine atom forms hydrogen bonds with water and other hydrogen-bond donors, so it does not mimic the hydrophobic methyl group.

NUCLEOSIDES AND NUCLEOTIDES

3.22. Draw the structure of the ribonucleoside that contains thymine (called thymidine or 1-β-D-ribofuranosyl thymine).

SOLUTION

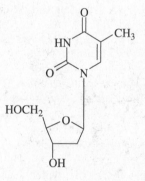

3.23. Draw the structure of the ribonucleotide that contains thymine (thymidine 5′-phosphate).

SOLUTION

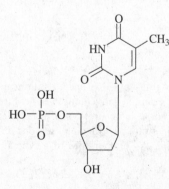

STRUCTURE OF DNA

3.24. You are given a sample of DNA that is the plasmid pXO1 from *Bacillus anthracis*, the causative bacterium of the disease *anthrax*. The pXO1 plasmid that carries the gene for producing *anthrax toxin* is circular, is double-stranded, and contains ~180,000 base pairs, with a G + C content of 32.5%. The pXO1 plasmid contains how many of the following?

(a) Deoxyribose residues
(b) Phosphate groups

(c) Purine nucleobases
(d) Adenine nucleobases
(e) Cytosine nucleobases
(f) Turns of the double helix
(g) Hydrogen bonds
(h) Would you expect this DNA to have a higher or lower melting temperature than a plasmid of the same size that has a G + C content of 67.5%?

SOLUTION

(a) Each base pair contains two nucleotides that contain a deoxyribose residue. So there are $180,000 \times 2 = 360,000$ deoxyribose residues.
(b) Each nucleotide contains a single phosphate group that is in the sugar-phosphate backbone. There are no free ends of the polymer as the plasmid is circular; so there are $180,000 \times 2 = 360,000$ phosphate groups.
(c) Each base pair consists of a purine and a pyrimidine moiety. So the plasmid contains 180,000 purine bases.
(d) The C + G content is 32.5%, so the A + T content is $100 - 32.5 = 67.5\%$. Hence there are $(67.5/100) \times 180,000 = 121,500$ base pairs that are A-T base pairs; so the plasmid contains 121,500 adenine bases.
(e) $(32.5/100) \times 180,000 = 58,500$ base pairs are G-C base pairs. Therefore the plasmid contains 58,500 cytosine moieties.
(f) If the tertiary structure of the DNA is the standard B form, then there will be 10 base pairs per turn, or $180,000/10 = 18,000$ turns.
(g) Hydrogen bonds are formed between the paired bases. Each G-C base pair forms *three* hydrogen bonds, and each A-T base pair forms two hydrogen bonds, so there are $3 \times 58,500 + 2 \times 121,500 = 418,500$ hydrogen bonds.
(h) A higher G + C content implies more hydrogen bonds and therefore increased stability. The pXO1 plasmid would therefore have a lower melting temperature than the other plasmid.

STRUCTURE AND TYPES OF RNA

3.25. What is the most abundant type of RNA in a typical bacterial or mammalian cell?

SOLUTION

Ribosomal RNA (rRNA) constitutes ~80% of all the RNA present in all cells. It is by far the most abundant RNA.

3.26. How would the melting curve for a sample of RNA compare with that of DNA?

SOLUTION

DNA is nearly always in the double-helical B form. Upon heating, and in a relatively narrow temperature range, it undergoes a transition from the native double-helical form to a denatured random coil. This change is accompanied by a ~40% increase in absorption of ultraviolet light at a wavelength of 260 nm, or A_{260}. However, RNA is largely single-stranded with small regions of intrastrand base pairing that vary in length and thermal stability. Increasing the temperature of a typical sample of RNA results in a very gradual increase in A_{260} that reflects the successive melting of short helical regions and not the concerted "unzipping" that occurs with DNA as it melts. So the extent of the increase in A_{260} would be significantly less for the sample of RNA.

AMINO ACIDS

3.27. Why is it not possible to distinguish between leucine and isoleucine by mass spectrometry?

SOLUTION

Although leucine and isoleucine have different chemical structures (see below), they have the same atomic composition so their mass is the same and the mass spectrometer "sees" them as the same.

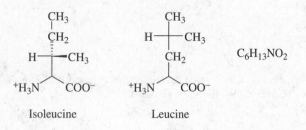

Isoleucine   Leucine

3.28. Which amino acids have a net positive charge in aqueous solutions at physiological pH?

SOLUTION

With side chain $pK_a > 10$, arginine and lysine will have a net positive charge. Histidine, with a side chain pK_a of 6, will be largely neutral, but will have a small proportion of positively charged side chains.

3.29. Which α-amino acids do *not* have a chiral carbon atom (also called a *chiral center*)?

SOLUTION

Only glycine with its —H side chain is *achiral*.

ACID-BASE BEHAVIOR OF AMINO ACIDS

3.30. What is the average net charge on the predominant form of lysine at pH values of (a) 2.0, (b) 5.0, and (c) 7.0?

SOLUTION

Draw the structure of lysine and show its different charged forms; then consider in which pH domains the pK_a values for deprotonation/protonation occur. These data are given in Table 3-9. The following scheme is the result.

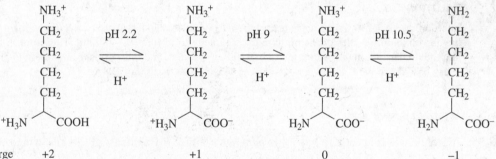

Net charge   +2   +1   0   −1

Thus, (a) at pH 2, the predominant form will have a net charge of +2; (b) at pH 5 the predominant form will have a net charge of +1; and (c) at pH 7.0 the predominant form will also have a net charge of +1.

3.31. What is the pI of the tripeptide alanyl-glutamyl-glycine?

SOLUTION

The pI is the pH at which the average charge is 0, and this exists at the average of the pK_a values for the reactions that occur on *either side* of the isoelectric species. From Table 3-9, the pK_a values for this tripeptide are 9.7 (alanine N terminus), 4.3 (glutamate side chain), and 2.3 (glycine C terminus). The isoelectric species is:

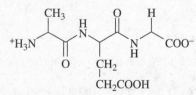

The glycine C terminus is deprotonated, but the glutamate side chain is not deprotonated, so the pI is the average of the pK_a values that describe those species, or (2.3 + 4.3)/2 = 3.3.

THE PEPTIDE BOND

3.32. Draw the structure of glycyl-seryl-cysteine.

SOLUTION

This is the name for a tripeptide with glycine having the free N terminus, followed by a serine residue, followed by a cysteine residue that has a free carboxy terminus.

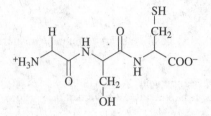

3.33. Why is the formation of a peptide bond called a *condensation reaction*?

SOLUTION

It involves the loss of a *water molecule*, an oxygen atom from the carboxyl group, and two hydrogen atoms from the amino group. Hence the two reacting amino acids are said to *condense*.

AMINO ACID ANALYSIS

3.34. Why is the extinction coefficient ($E_{1\%}$ at a wavelength of light of ~280 nm) for double-strand DNA (dsDNA) essentially constant regardless of the source of the DNA, whereas the same property for proteins varies considerably from protein to protein?

SOLUTION

In proteins only a few amino acids are aromatic (mainly Trp and Tyr), and they are the main contributors to the absorption properties of the protein at a wavelength of light at ~280 nm. Therefore, $E_{1\%}$ at that wavelength will depend on the proportion of Trp and Tyr present, and this varies from protein to protein, whereas every base is aromatic and every base pair contributes to the $E_{1\%}$ of DNA.

PROTEIN SEQUENCING

3.35. A protein was treated with *trypsin* to generate a series of fragments of the following sequences:

    Gly-Gly-Ile-Arg
    Ser-Phe-Leu-Gly
    Trp-Ala-Ala-Pro-Lys
    Ala-Glu-Glu-Gly-Leu-Arg

And the same protein was treated with *chymotrypsin* to generate the following fragments:

    Leu-Gly
    Ala-Glu-Glu-Gly-Leu-Arg-Trp
    Ala-Ala-Pro-Lys-Gly-Gly-Ile-Arg-Ser-Phe

Assemble the protein sequence.

SOLUTION

Trypsin cleaves a polypeptide backbone at the *C*-terminal side of Arg or Lys residues, whereas chymotrypsin cleaves after aromatic residues.

    Ser-Phe-Leu-Gly and **Leu-Gly** have neither an Arg nor a Lys, nor aromatic residue at their C terminus, suggesting that they are the C-terminal fragments of the original peptide. The remainder of the reassembly is achieved by making the appropriate overlaps as follows:

Leu-Gly

Ser-Phe-Leu-Gly

Ala-Ala-Pro-Lys-Gly-Gly-Ile-Arg-Ser-Phe

Gly-Gly-Ile-Arg

Trp-Ala-Ala-Pro-Lys

Ala-Glu-Glu-Gly-Leu-Arg-Trp

Ala-Glu-Glu-Gly-Leu-Arg

Noting that some of the information is redundant, the solution of this puzzle is

Ala-Glu-Glu-Gly-Leu-Arg-Trp-Ala-Ala-Pro-Lys-Gly-Gly-Ile-Arg-Ser-Phe-Leu-Gly

REACTIONS OF CYSTEINE

3.36. Using accurate mass spectrometry, how is it possible to determine if a small protein contains a pair of disulfide-bonded cysteine residues (i.e., cystine) or two reduced cysteine residues?

SOLUTION

The mass of a cystine-containing protein will be two mass units smaller than the equivalent cysteine-containing protein because two —SH groups are oxidized to —S—S—. To confirm this finding, it would be necessary to treat the protein with a reducing agent and compare the masses of the reduced and nonreduced samples.

3.37. A potent inhibitor of glycolysis in human erythrocytes is iodoacetate. How does this inhibition come about?

SOLUTION

Iodoacetate modifies a key —SH group in the active site of glyceraldehyde-3-phosphate dehydrogenase, a central enzyme of glycolysis. This —SH group is vital for the reaction mechanism of the enzyme. Thus the enzyme is rendered inactive and glycolysis stops.

SUPPLEMENTARY PROBLEMS

3.38. Which amino acids have chiral side chains?

3.39. A DNA solution with an absorbance of 1.0 at the wavelength of light of 260 nm has a concentration of 50 mg mL^{-1}. To achieve the equivalent absorbance at 280 nm, a protein solution must have a concentration of at least 0.5 and 2 mg mL^{-1}. Why is this so?

3.40. Two fragments of DNA of the same size but from different sources have the same G + C content. Which of the following properties—number of adenine bases, sequence, melting temperature—would you expect to change?

3.41. Draw the chemical structure of aspartylvalinylglycine. What is the pI of this peptide and what is its net charge at pH 7.4?

3.42. The differences in mass of a protein before and after treatment with TCEP or DTT is 6 Da. How many oxidized Cys residues or disulfide bonds does the protein contain?

3.43. A polypeptide is digested with trypsin, and the resulting segments are sequenced:

Val-Gly

Ala-Ala-Gly-Leu-Trp-Arg

Arg-Asp-Pro-Gly-Lue-Met-Val-Leu-Tyr-Ala-Ala-Asp-Glu-Lys

And the following fragments are produced by chymotrypsin fragmentation:

Met-Val-Leu

Ala-Ala-Gly-Leu

Trp-Arg-Arg-Asp-Pro-Gly-Leu

Tyr-Ala-Ala-Asp-Glu-Lys-Val-Gly

What is the sequence of the whole original polypeptide?

3.44. If a membrane contains 30% protein and 70% phospholipid by weight, with a molar protein-to-lipid ratio of $1 : 100$, and the average molecular size of the lipid being 1 kDa, what is the average molecular size of the proteins?

3.45. A compound with the chemical formula $C_5H_{10}O_5$ is likely to belong to what class of molecule?

3.46. Why are lipids poorly soluble in water whereas most low-molecular-weight carbohydrates are water-soluble?

ANSWERS TO SUPPLEMENTARY PROBLEMS

3.38. The β-carbon atoms of both isoleucine and threonine are chiral.

3.39. All the bases in DNA contribute to the absorbance at 260 nm, whereas only a few side chains of proteins contribute to absorbance at 280 nm; these are mostly Trp, Tyr, and disulfide-bonded Cys residues.

3.40. The melting temperature and number of adenine bases will be the same, but the sequence (i.e., the order of the different bases) is likely to be different.

3.41. pI ~3.0; net charge of –1 exists at pH 7.4.

3.42. Six Cys residues or three disulfide bonds.

3.43. Ala-Ala-Gly-Leu-Trp-Arg-Arg-Asp-Pro-Gly-Leu-Met-Val-Leu-Tyr-Ala-Ala-Asp-Glu-Lys-Val-Gly

3.44. ~43 kDa

3.45. Carbohydrate

3.46. Carbohydrates contain many polar hydroxyl and carbonyl groups, whereas lipids have low numbers of polar or charged functional groups.

CHAPTER 4

Proteins

Of the four major classes of biomacromolecules, proteins have the greatest diversity of structures and functions.

4.1 Introduction

Question: What are proteins?

   Proteins are polypeptides with >50 amino acid residues with a molecular weight greater than 5000. They may contain a variety of *cofactors* and other associated small molecules or may be modified by the addition of neutral and charged carbohydrates and ions. These *macromolecules* show great diversity in their physical properties, ranging from water-soluble enzymes to the insoluble keratin of hair, which is reflected in a wide range of biological functions.

What Biological Functions Do Proteins Perform?

Proteins fulfill the following biochemical roles:

1. *Enzyme catalysis*. Enzymes are protein catalysts, capable of enhancing the rates of reactions by factors of up to 10^{14}. For example, the enzyme *carbonic anhydrase* catalyzes the reaction $CO_2 + H_2O \rightleftharpoons H^+ + HCO_3^-$ by a factor of 10^7 over the uncatalyzed reaction.

2. *Transport and storage*. Many small molecules are transported both inside and outside cells bound to *carrier proteins*. Examples include the oxygen transport and storage proteins *hemoglobin* and *myoglobin*, respectively. The proteins in membranes often permit the passage of both small and large molecules through membranes.

3. *Mechanical structure and support*. *Collagen* provides the tensile strength in skin, teeth, and bone; *keratin* is the major component of hair and fur; and *fibroin* is one of two proteins that comprise spider silk.

4. *Motion*. Muscle contraction is accomplished by the interaction of filaments composed of two different proteins, *actin* and *myosin*. *Kinesin* moves protein cargoes around cells along microtubule "rails" formed by *tubulin*.

5. *Recognition*. *Antibodies* are proteins that form part of the immune response in mammals in the presence of foreign invaders. Other proteins form the *major histocompatibility complex* (MHC), which presents small peptides from viruses and other invaders for recognition by the immune system.

6. *Information and control*. Stimuli external to a cell, such as hormone signals or light, are detected by specific proteins, *receptors* and the *photosystem*, for example, that transfer signals to the cell interior. The visual protein *rhodopsin* is located in the membranes of retinal cells. Other proteins control the basic cellular functions of transcription and translation.

7. *Exotic functions*. Fish living in the very cold waters in the Antarctic Ocean require *antifreeze* proteins to prevent ice formation in their cells.

Question: What is a common feature among those functions listed above that may be explained in terms of protein structure?

In all the above examples, the phenomenon of *specific binding* is involved. For example, hemoglobin specifically binds molecular oxygen, antibodies bind to specific foreign molecules, and enzymes bind to specific substrate molecules, and in doing so bring about selective chemical bond rearrangement. The function of a protein, then, is understood in light of how the structure of the protein allows the specific binding of partner molecules.

4.2   Types of Protein Structure

Protein structures can be assigned to one of three broad structural classes: (1) *Fibrous* proteins generally form large, insoluble aggregates and are characterized by repeating primary structures and often contain a single type of secondary structure; (2) *Globular* proteins, as their name suggests, have a compact shape with hydrophilic residues on their outside surfaces, making these proteins water-soluble; (3) *Membrane* proteins interact with the hydrophobic *lipid bilayers* of the membranes surrounding cells and in subcellular organelles. Those parts of membrane proteins in contact with the hydrophobic lipids are also hydrophobic; the parts of the protein that extend into the aqueous phases on either side of the membrane resemble the domains of globular proteins.

4.3   Hierarchy of Protein Structure

It is possible to consider the structure of a protein on several levels, as originally proposed in 1951 by the Danish protein chemist Kai Linderstrøm-Lang:

1. *Primary structure*: the sequence of amino acids in the polypeptide chain. The sequence is generally listed, starting from the N terminus.

2. *Secondary structure*: the local conformation of the polypeptide chain that gives rise to regular repeating structures such as those first defined by Linus Pauling, the α helix and the β-pleated sheet. Assignment of the secondary structure reduces the complexity of a three-dimensional structure and often aids in finding relationships between the structures of different proteins. Topology diagrams are used to represent the secondary structural elements and their order of occurrence in a protein.

3. *Tertiary structure*: the way in which the polypeptide chains of a protein fold into a characteristic three-dimensional shape, stabilized by bonds between amino acids far apart in the sequence. These bonds may be strong covalent interactions such as disulfide bridges or weaker interactions involving hydrogen bonds or salt bridges.

4. *Quaternary structure*: the arrangement of the individual polypeptide chains in multi-*subunit* proteins.

4.4   Determining Sequences of Amino Acids in Proteins

The structure and properties of peptides and proteins depend critically upon the sequence of amino acids in the peptide chain. In 1953, Frederick Sanger determined the sequence of the 51 amino acid residues in insulin. The first step in determining the sequence was to ascertain the amino acid composition of insulin, i.e., the number of each type of amino acid residue in the protein. This was done by means of amino acid analysis (Sec. 3.24).

N-Terminal Analysis and Edman Degradation

The identity of the N-terminal residue, the first amino acid in the sequence of a peptide, can be found by its reaction with *phenylisothiocyanate*. At neutral pH this compound reacts with the α-amino group. After mild acid hydrolysis, the reaction product cyclizes, releasing the residue as a *phenylthiohydantoin* (PTH) derivative.

This process is called *Edman degradation* after its Australian discoverer (Fig. 4-1). The chemical nature and quantity of the derivative are readily determined as is its parent amino acid.

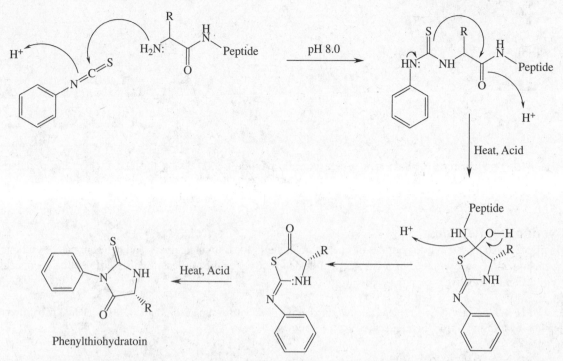

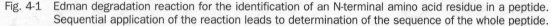

Phenylthiohydratoin

Fig. 4-1   Edman degradation reaction for the identification of an N-terminal amino acid residue in a peptide. Sequential application of the reaction leads to determination of the sequence of the whole peptide.

If the phenylisothiocyanate method is used, the cyclization and release of the N-terminal derivative occur under mild conditions that leave the rest of the chain intact. It is therefore possible to repeat the procedure on this shortened peptide to determine the second residue in the sequence, and so on. Like most chemical reactions, Edman degradation is not 100% efficient, meaning that at each step there is a chance of additional peptide hydrolysis or incomplete reaction; thus the method is not reliable for peptides with more than ~60 residues. However, this can be overcome by generating a series of peptides by specific protease pretreatment (see next section) and then separating the peptide fragments prior to using Edman analysis.

Specific Cleavage of Peptides

Many proteins contain hundreds of amino acid residues, so it may not be feasible to determine the sequence of the whole molecule in one operation, due to the accumulation of uncertainty in amino acid identity at each step. Therefore it is useful first to cleave the protein into smaller, more manageable segments. The protein may also contain *disulfide bonds* that link cysteine residues in different parts of the chain. These bonds must be broken to allow sequencing to continue.

Trypsin is one of the most frequently used enzymes for breaking polypeptides into smaller lengths. This digestive enzyme is normally secreted by the pancreas, and it hydrolyzes peptide bonds on the carboxyl side of *lysine* and *arginine* (i.e., positively charged) residues.

$$R_1\text{-Lys-Ala-}R_2 \rightarrow R_1\text{-Lys-COO}^- + {}^+\text{NH}_3\text{-Ala-}R_2$$

Chymotrypsin hydrolyzes peptide bonds on the carboxyl side of *phenylalanine*, *tyrosine*, and *tryptophan* (aromatic) residues.

$$R_1\text{-Phe-Ser-}R_2 \rightarrow R_1\text{-Phe-COO}^- + {}^+\text{NH}_3\text{-Ser-}R_2$$

Cyanogen bromide (CNBr) affords a nonenzymic, chemical means of specific cleavage of polypeptides on the carboxyl side of *methionine* residues (Fig. 4-2). Although popular in the past, CNBr is now less frequently used because it is a toxic gas.

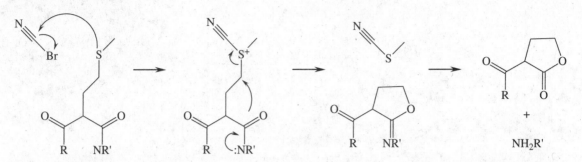

Fig. 4-2   Mechanism of CNBr cleavage of a specific peptide bond. During the last step in the reaction sequence, the intermediate undergoes Schiff base hydrolysis to release the cleaved peptide.

Overlapping Peptides

Having cleaved a protein into peptides of manageable length for Edman analysis, and determined the sequence of each peptide, next we need to order the peptides correctly. For this, at least two sets of peptide sequences, from different selective cleavage reactions, are required.

EXAMPLE 4.1   A peptide was cleaved into two smaller peptides with cyanogen bromide (CNBr) and into two different peptides by trypsin (Tryp). Their sequences were as follows:

    CNBr-1:   Gly-Thr-Lys-Ala-Glu
    CNBr-2:   Ser-Met
     Tryp-1:   Ser-Met-Gly-Thr-Lys
     Tryp-2:   Ala-Glu

What was the sequence of the parent peptide?

SOLUTION   By arranging the sequences in a way that leads to overlapping of the same residues, it is possible to infer the parent sequence as follows:

    Ser-Met
    Ser-Met-Gly-Thr-Lys
            Gly-Thr-Lys-Ala-Glu
                            Ala-Glu
    Ser-Met-Gly-Thr-Lys-Ala-Glu

As occurs in many real cases, some of this information is redundant; i.e., peptides Tryp-1 and CNBr-1 would be sufficient for unambiguous sequence determination. Also, in this case with only two peptides from each cleavage reaction, we can determine the sequence from the fact that the carboxyl sides of -Met- and -Lys- are the sites of cleavage with CNBr and trypsin, respectively.

Modern Methods of Peptide Sequencing

Dramatic advances in *mass spectrometry* (MS) have led to the new research field of *proteomics*. This analysis seeks to identify all the proteins that are present in an organism, an organelle, or a cell at a given time in its cycle of activity, or under specific conditions such as a disease state. The different states alter the range of proteins present and also their relative abundances. Rapid identification of thousands of proteins from very small samples is made possible by using proteases that cleave the proteins into small segments (Example 4.1). This treatment is followed by liquid chromatography, then mass spectrometry that enables the identification of the peptide fragments. This is followed by piecing together the whole sequence with the aid of a computer program.

MS measures the charge-to-mass ratio *m/z* of a molecule, by separating ions in a magnetic or electric field. Proteins and peptides are now able to be characterized by MS following the development of techniques to ionize large molecules and promote them into the gas phase without their destruction.

The approach taken to sequence a protein by MS depends on the characteristics of the protein that is to be identified, and this is best illustrated by considering the two following scenarios.

Scenario 1

The protein to be sequenced is from an organism for which the *genome has been sequenced*.
The amino acid sequences of the proteins in the genome are predicted from the DNA sequence. The fragmentation patterns that result from proteolysis by specific enzymes of these proteins are predicted using the genetic code. The target protein is digested with a specific protease, resulting in a group of peptide fragments that are then subjected to MS. The masses of the individual peptides in the group are compared by using a computer program with a database of predicted fragmentation patterns for various proteins (mass fingerprints). A positive match identifies the protein; this is shown for lysozyme in Fig. 4-3.

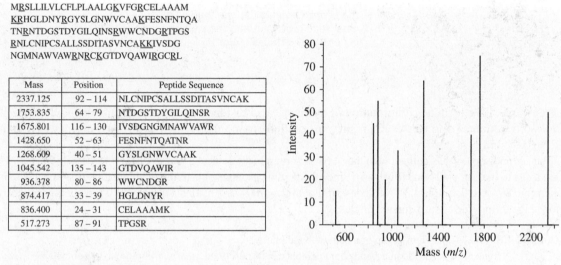

MRSLLILVLCFLPLAALGKVFGRCELAAAM
KRHGLDNYRGYSLGNWVCAAKFESNFNTQA
TNRNTDGSTDYGILQINSRWWCNDGRTPGS
RNLCNIPCSALLSSDITASVNCAKKIVSDG
NGMNAWVAWRNRCKGTDVQAWIRGCRL

Mass	Position	Peptide Sequence
2337.125	92 – 114	NLCNIPCSALLSSDITASVNCAK
1753.835	64 – 79	NTDGSTDYGILQINSR
1675.801	116 – 130	IVSDGNGMNAWVAWR
1428.650	52 – 63	FESNFNTQATNR
1268.609	40 – 51	GYSLGNWVCAAK
1045.542	135 – 143	GTDVQAWIR
936.378	80 – 86	WWCNDGR
874.417	33 – 39	HGLDNYR
836.400	24 – 31	CELAAAMK
517.273	87 – 91	TPGSR

Fig. 4-3 Theoretical and experimentally determined mass fingerprint of lysozyme.

Scenario 2

The protein to be sequenced is from an unidentified source, from an organism for which *no genome sequence is known*, or it cannot be positively identified (unlike the case above).
The target protein is digested with a specific protease, resulting in a group of peptide fragments that are then subjected to a combination of liquid chromatography and MS. The liquid chromatography separates the peptides, and the masses of the peptides are determined by MS. In addition, a high-energy heat pulse is applied to the peptide within the mass spectrometer; this causes the peptide to be broken into fragments. In different peptides the backbone will be fragmented between different residues, generating a series of fragments that differ by the mass of the various individual amino acid residues (see Fig. 4-4).

EXAMPLE 4.2 Generating B- and Y-series fragments within the mass spectrometer is shown in Fig. 4-5. The peptide sequence can be read from either the B-series or the Y-series fragments. The peptide series run in opposite directions, and there is potentially some redundancy of sequence information that facilitates sequence determination.

Protein sequences can be assembled from overlapping peptide sequences as shown in Fig. 4-5.
In the case of confirming the identity of a protein from an organism for which the genome has been sequenced, a short stretch of peptide sequence is often sufficient to positively identify the parent protein.

4.5 Descriptions of Protein Structure

We can completely describe the three-dimensional structure of a protein by listing the (x, y, z) coordinates of each atom. Indeed, this is how experimentally determined protein structures are stored in the *Protein Data Bank* (www.rcsb.org/pdb). However, the structure of a protein can be more succinctly described by listing the angles of rotation (*torsion angles*) of each of the bonds in the protein (see Fig. 4-6).

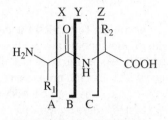

Fig. 4-4   The backbone of a peptide can be fragmented at three different positions
within each amino acid residue to generate the fragments A and X, B and Y, or
C and Z. Of the above covalent bonds,
the *peptide* bond is the one that is the
most readily broken, and the cleavage
generates the B and Y ions.

For example, the backbone conformation of an amino acid residue can be specified by listing the torsion angles ϕ (rotation around the N—C_α bond), ψ (rotation around the C_α—C′ bond), and ω (rotation about the N—C′ bond).

The zero position of ϕ is defined with the —N—H group *trans* to the C_α—C′ bond, and for ψ with the C_α—N bond *trans* to the —C═O bond (Fig. 4-6). Since the peptide group is planar, the peptide bond torsion angle ω is generally 180° (see Example 4.3). A full description of the three-dimensional structure of a protein also requires knowledge of the side chain χ torsion angles.

EXAMPLE 4.3   Why is the atom-group of a peptide bond planar?

The C—N bond has a partial double-bond character that can be described as an equilibration between two *resonance* forms as follows (see Fig. 4-7):

The C—N bond (~0.132 nm long) is intermediate in length between that of a C—N single bond (~0.149 nm long) and a C—N double bond (~0.129 nm long). The partial double-bond character restricts rotation of atoms around the C—N bond, such that the favored arrangement is for the O, C, N, and H atoms to lie in a plane, with the O and H atoms *trans* to each other; this corresponds to a torsion angle of $\omega = 180°$. The *cis* conformation that generally only occurs in proteins at X-Pro peptide bonds corresponds to $\omega = 0°$.

EXAMPLE 4.4   In the dipeptide *glycylalanine,* in which bonds of the backbone, is free rotation of the attached groups possible?

In this structure, the *peptide group* (also called an amide plane) is surrounded by dashed lines (Fig. 4-8). Because the peptide group itself is held rigidly planar, there is no rotation around the bond between the carbonyl carbon atom and the nitrogen atom (C′—N bond). However, free rotation is possible around the bond between the α carbon and the carbonyl carbon atom (the C_α—C′ bond) and about the bond between the nitrogen atom and the alanyl α-carbon atom (the N—C_α bond). Thus, for every peptide group in a protein, there are two *freely rotatable bonds* (i.e., two degrees of freedom), the relative angles of which define a particular backbone conformation.

4.6   Restrictions on Shapes that Protein Molecules Can Adopt

Not all combinations of ϕ and ψ angles are possible, as many lead to clashes between atoms in adjacent residues. For all residues except glycine, the existence of such steric restrictions involving side chain atoms drastically reduces the number of possible conformations. Since only two variable angles are involved, the possible combinations of ϕ and ψ angles that do not lead to clashes can be plotted on a *conformation map* (also known as a *Ramachandran plot*, after the Indian chemist who did much of the pioneering work in this field). Figure 4-9 shows such a plot for the allowed conformations of the dipeptide alanylalanine. The double-hatched areas represent conformations (combinations of ϕ and ψ) for which no *steric hindrance* exists. The single-hatched areas represent conformations for which some hindrance exists, but which may be possible if the distortion can be compensated for by strong interactions elsewhere in the protein.

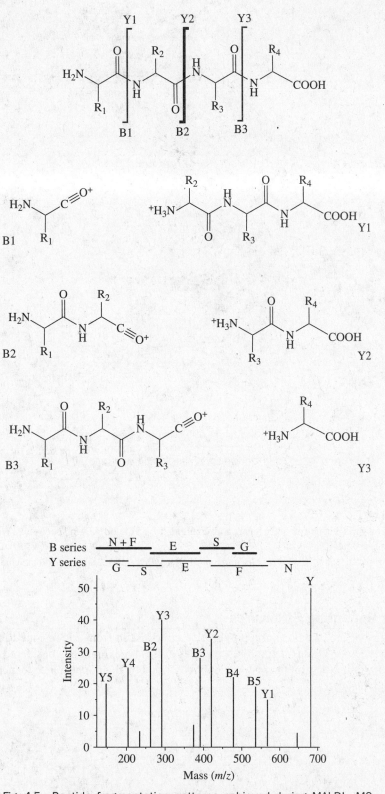

Fig. 4-5 Peptide fragmentation patterns achieved during MALDI MS (left); a possible mass spectrum (right); and above the spectrum is an attempt to align the peptide fragments to lead to a predicted complete amino acid sequence of the parent peptide or protein.

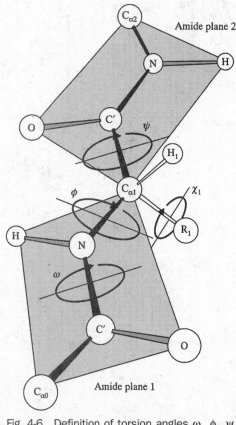

Fig. 4-6   Definition of torsion angles ω, ϕ, ψ,
and χ in a peptide. The conformation
shown is obtained when ω, ϕ, and ψ
are all set to 180°.

EXAMPLE 4.5   The right-handed α helix has ϕ and ψ angles of −57° and 47°, respectively. Would you expect the α helix to be a stable structure?

Yes. These values put the right-handed α helix into a particularly favorable area of the Ramachandran plot, indicated in Fig. 4-9 with the symbol α_R.

4.7   Regular Repeating Structures

If the torsion angles of the backbone of a polypeptide are constant from one residue to the next, a regular repeating structure results. While all possible structures of this type might be considered to be helices from a mathematical viewpoint, they are more commonly described by their appearance; hence they are called α *helices* and β-*pleated sheets*.

Fig. 4-7   The planarity of the peptide bond is due
to two structures that are in extremely
rapid exchange, called *resonance*.

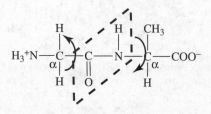
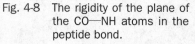

Fig. 4-8   The rigidity of the plane of
the CO—NH atoms in the
peptide bond.

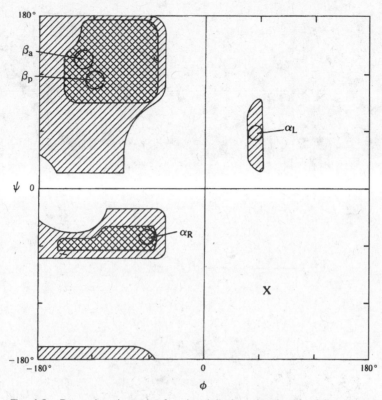

Fig. 4-9   Ramachandran plot for alanylalanine showing the fully allowed
regions (double-hashed) and partially allowed regions (single-
hatched) of ϕ and ψ angles (see Fig. 4-6). The coordinates for
the parallel and antiparallel β structures (β_p and β_a, respectively) and for the left-handed and right-handed α helices (α_L
and α_R, respectively) are indicated.

Given the usual van der Waals radii of the atoms, expected bond angles, and planarity of the amide group,
only two regular *repeating* structures exist without bond distortion and with a maximum of hydrogen bond
formation:

1. The α helix, which is found in almost all proteins, but is exemplified by the α-*keratins*.

2. The β-pleated sheets (parallel and antiparallel). These are also found in most proteins and are exemplified
    by the β form of stretched keratin and the silk protein fibroin.

These regular repeating structures are commonly found as elements of folding patterns in globular proteins,
as well as being the principal structure of fibrous proteins. In many globular proteins, a significant proportion
of the polypeptide chain displays no regular folding. These regions may have short sections of commonly found
structures such as *reverse turns* that link the strands of β-sheets. Regions without a regular repeating secondary
structure are often referred to as having a *random-coil* conformation; however, they may still be stable and hence
well defined in a structural analysis, even if they are not regular.

α Helix

In the α helix, the polypeptide *backbone* is folded in such a way that the —C=O group of each amino acid
residue is *hydrogen-bonded* to the —N—H group of the *fourth* residue along the chain; i.e., the —C=O
group of the first residue binds to the —N—H group of the fifth residue, and so on.

The backbone of the α helix winds around the long axis, as shown in Fig. 4-10. The hydrogen bonds are
all aligned approximately parallel to this axis, and side chains protrude outward. Each residue is spaced
0.15 nm from the next one along the axis, and *3.6 residues* are required to make a complete turn of the helix.

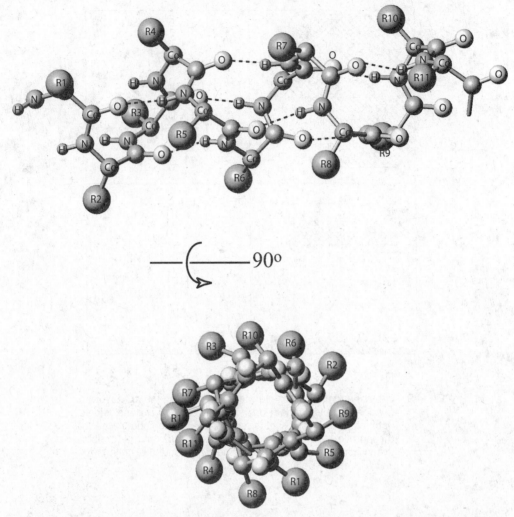

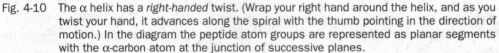

Fig. 4-10   The α helix has a *right-handed* twist. (Wrap your right hand around the helix, and as you twist your hand, it advances along the spiral with the thumb pointing in the direction of motion.) In the diagram the peptide atom groups are represented as planar segments with the α-carbon atom at the junction of successive planes.

Although both left- and right-hand screw senses are possible, the right-hand screw sense is energetically favored with peptides made from L-amino acids.

Because each —C═O and —N—H group is hydrogen-bonded (except for the four at each end), the α helix is very stable. However, for some amino acids, interactions involving the side chains may weaken the α helix, making this conformation less likely in polypeptide chains that contain a high proportion of such helix-destabilizing amino acids (Table 4-1).

Table 4-1   Tendency of Amino Acid Residues to Form α Helices

Helix formers	Glu, Ala, Leu, His, Met, Gln, Trp, Val, Phe, Lys, Ile
Helix breakers	Pro, Gly, Tyr, Asn
Indifferent residues	Asp, Thr, Ser, Arg, Cys

EXAMPLE 4.6   Do the —N—H groups on residues 1 to 4 of a peptide also hydrogen-bond to other groups in the α helix?

There are no available —C=O groups with which these amide groups can interact. Consequently, they remain *unbonded*. Similarly, at the other end of the chain, four —C=O groups remain unbonded. If the polypeptide chain is very long, the lack of bonding at the ends has a negligible effect on the overall stability. However, short α helical chains are less stable because the end effects are *relatively* more important.

β Sheet

The second major regular repeating structure, the β *structure*, differs from an α helix in that the polypeptide chains are almost completely extended, as in Fig. 4-11(a), and hydrogen bonding occurs *between* polypeptide segments, rather than *within* a single segment, as shown in Fig. 4-11(b).

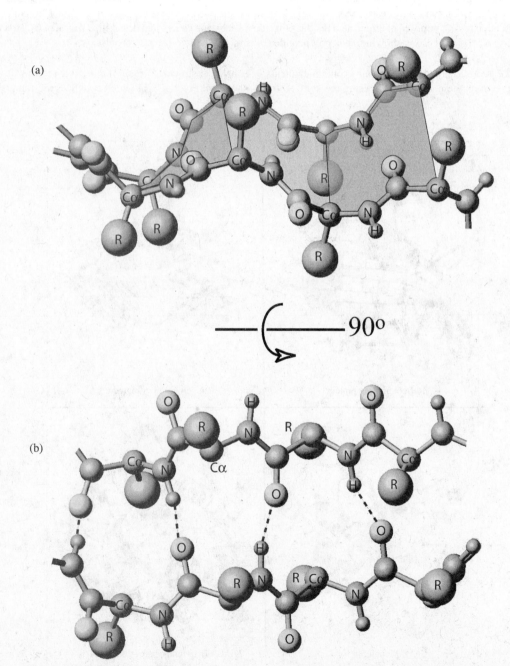

Fig. 4-11   β-Sheet structures: (a) sheet formed by the assembly of extended polypeptide chains side by side; (b) details showing hydrogen bonding between adjacent polypeptide chains in an antiparallel β sheet.

Adjacent segments can be aligned in the same direction (i.e., N terminus to C terminus), so they are called *parallel* β *sheets*; alternate chains may be aligned in opposite orientations, and these are called *antiparallel* β *sheets*, as shown in Fig. 4-11(b). These structures often form extensive sheets. Sometimes it is possible for several sheets to be stacked upon one another. Because the side chains tend to protrude above and below the sheet in alternating sequence [Fig. 4-11(a)], the β-sheet structures are favored by amino acids with relatively small side chains, such as alanine and glycine. Large, bulky side chains tend to have steric interference between the various parts of the protein chain.

EXAMPLE 4.7   Predict which regular repeating structure is more likely for the polypeptides (a) poly(Gly-Ala-Gly-Thr) and (b) poly(Glu-Ala-Leu-His).

Polypeptide (a) is composed largely of amino acid residues that have *small* side chains. Except for Ala, none of the residues favors helix formation, while Gly destabilizes α helices. Therefore, this polypeptide is more likely to form β structures.

Polypeptide (b) is composed of amino acid residues that have *bulky* side chains that destabilize β structures. However, all the amino acids are helix-stabilizing; thus polypeptide (b) is more likely to form an α helix.

EXAMPLE 4.8   Many globular proteins contain elements of α helix, β structures, plus *random-coil* regions. It is instructive to draw these structures by using the stylized forms shown in Fig. 4-12, in which α helices are represented

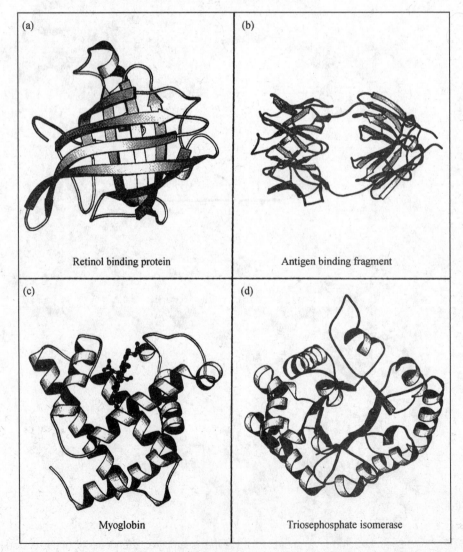

Fig. 4-12   Stylized drawings of protein structures in which α helices are represented as coiled ribbons and β strands are represented by arrows pointing in the N → C direction. (a) A β *protein*; (b) a β *protein*; (c) an α protein; and (d) an α-β protein.

by coiled ribbons and β structures are represented by flat arrows pointing in the N→C direction. Parallel β sheets have their arrows pointing in the same direction; antiparallel β sheets have their arrows alternating in direction. So-called β *proteins* (e.g., retinol binding protein, and antigen binding fragments of antibodies) contain predominantly β sheet secondary structure, while α *proteins* (e.g., myoglobin) are largely composed of α helices; so-called α-β *proteins* (e.g., triosephosphate isomerase) contain a mixture of α helices and β sheets (see Fig. 4-12).

Collagen Triple Helix

The protein *collagen,* from the dermis of the skin and tendons, is composed of ~30% proline and hydroxyproline and 30% glycine. This protein has an unusual structure in which *three* chains, each with a conformation very similar to the left-handed helix of polyproline, are twisted about each other to make a *right-handed* triple helix. The helix has a pitch of 0.96 nm with 3.3 residues per turn; thus the spiral is "steeper" than the α helix. The three strands are hydrogen-bonded to one another between the —NH of glycine residues and the —C=O groups of the other amino acids.

EXAMPLE 4.9   Why is proline rarely found within α-helical segments?

The α-amino group of proline is a *secondary* amino group. When proline participates in a peptide bond through its amino group, there is no longer an amide hydrogen to participate in the hydrogen bond stabilization of the α helix. In addition, because the side chain of proline is attached to the α-amino group, there is no free rotation about the $N—C_\alpha$ bond and proline therefore cannot take up the conformation that is required to form an α helix.

Although proline cannot participate in α-helical conformations, polypeptides composed only of proline can adopt a different type of helical conformation. This *polyproline helix* is *not* stabilized by hydrogen bonding, but rather by the steric mutual repulsion effects of the prolyl side chains. The polyproline helix is more extended than the α helix, with adjacent residues separated along the axis by 0.31 nm.

EXAMPLE 4.10   Why does collagen, with its polypeptide sequence that is largely (-Gly-Pro-X-)$_n$, where X is any other type of amino acid residue, form a triple helix, while polyproline does not?

In the collagen triple helix, every third residue is positioned toward the center of the helix and comes into close contact with another chain. Only glycine, with its side chain that consists of a single hydrogen atom, is sufficiently small to fit into this crowded space.

4.8   Posttranslational Modification

Many proteins are modified *after or during translation* from mRNA on a ribosome. These *posttranslational modifications* take many forms. The first residue in all peptides from bacteria is *N*-formylmethionine, or in eukaryotes it is *methionine*. The formyl group and the methionine are usually subsequently removed enzymically. In as many as 50% of eukaryotic proteins, the N-terminal residue is subsequently *acetylated*. Other amino acids in proteins are often modified by the addition of *phosphate* groups to the hydroxyl groups of serine, threonine, and tyrosine, or a nitrogen of the imidazole moiety of histidine. These phosphate groups are added enzymically by ATP-dependent *kinases* and are removed by hydrolysis that is catalyzed by *phosphatases*. Phosphorylated enzymes are often involved in *signaling pathways*. Proteins, usually those exported from cells, may be modified by the addition of covalently linked carbohydrate(s). The carbohydrate is enzymically added either to the amide side chain of asparagine residues or to the hydroxyl group of serine or threonine residues. Other posttranslational modifications include the hydroxylation of proline and lysine residues of collagen.

Some proteins also contain compounds in addition to their own amino acids. Such proteins are known as *conjugated proteins*, and the non-amino acid part is called a *prosthetic group*; the protein part is called the *apoprotein*. Glycoproteins and proteoglycans contain covalently bound carbohydrate, while *lipoproteins* (Chaps. 3 and 13) contain lipid as prosthetic groups.

4.9   Protein Folding

Proteins Fold into Compact, Well-Defined, Three-Dimensional Structures

To understand the mechanisms of operation of proteins, it is useful to understand the *conformation*, or the three-dimensional folding pattern, that is adopted by a polypeptide chain. Although many synthetic *poly-amino acids* have no well-defined conformation, and appear to exist in solution as nearly *random coils*, most biological polypeptides adopt a well-defined *folded structure*. Some proteins, such as the keratins of hair and feathers, are *fibrous*, and they are organized into sheetlike shapes with a regular repeating folding pattern. Others, such as most enzymes, are folded into compact, nearly spherical, *globular* shapes.

EXAMPLE 4.11   Why do proteins fold up into their own characteristic shape?

The folding of a protein into a compact structure is accompanied by a large *decrease in conformational entropy* (loss of disorder) of the protein; this is thermodynamically unfavorable. The native, folded conformation is maintained by a large number of *weak, noncovalent interactions* that act *cooperatively* to offset the unfavorable reduction in entropy. These *noncovalent interactions* include hydrogen bonds, and electrostatic, hydrophobic, and van der Waals interactions; they make the folded protein (often just marginally) more stable than the unfolded form.

The interactions that determine the final shape of a protein are mediated between amino acid residues in the protein. Since the sequence of amino acid residues determines the distribution of these interacting groups, the sequence *encodes* the overall fold of a native protein. The main interactions are as follows.

Electrostatic Interactions

Charged particles interact with one another with a force between them that is described by Coulomb's law:

$$F = (e^2/D)\, Z_A\, Z_B\, (1/r_{AB}^2) \tag{4.1}$$

where Z_A and Z_B are the number of electron charges on the two interacting groups, e is the charge on an electron, D is the dielectric constant of the medium, and r_{AB} is the distrance between the two charges. When the two charges are of opposite sign, the interaction force decreases as the groups approach each other, and under such circumstances the interaction is said to be *favorable*. Since the (virtual) work done (force × distance) to separate the charges by r_{AB} is the energy, this is written as

$$\Delta E = (e^2/D)\, Z_A'\, Z_B\, (1/r_{AB}) \tag{4.2}$$

Negatively charged groups in proteins (such as the carboxylates of Asp and Glu) frequently interact with positively charged side chains of Lys, Arg, or His residues. These electrostatic interactions result in the formation of a *salt bridge* in which there is also a degree of hydrogen bonding in addition to the electrostatic attraction. This is illustrated in Fig. 4-13.

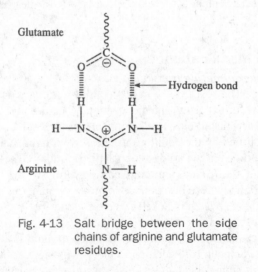

Fig. 4-13   Salt bridge between the side chains of arginine and glutamate residues.

Since water has a high dielectric constant of 80 (electric permittivity relative to a vacuum), the energy associated with an ion pair in a protein ranges from 0.5 to 1.5 kJ mol^{-1} for a surface interaction and up to 15 kJ mol^{-1} for an electrostatic interaction between residues that are buried in the interior of a protein, where the dielectric constant is low.

van der Waals Interactions

All atoms and molecules attract one another as a result of the induction of transient dipole-dipoles in them. A molecule need not have a net charge to participate in such dipolar interactions. In other words, electron density around an atom can be distorted and made highly asymmetric if adjacent atoms have markedly different *electronegativities*.

Atoms with the largest electronegativities have the largest *potential excess* of negative charge. The electronegativities of the atoms found in abundance in proteins are as follows: O, 3.44; N, 3.04; C, 2.55; and H, 2.20 (on a scale of 0.8 to 4).

Transient dipolar interactions are known as *van der Waals interactions*. Hence the bond is referred to as a *polarization bond*. (The hydrogen bond is also a polarization bond.) The bonds are weak and extend over a short range, their strength varying inversely as the sixth power of the interatomic distance. When atoms involved in a van der Waals interaction approach very closely, a *strong repulsive interaction* occurs. Thus, the van der Waals interaction energy is given by

$$\Delta E_{vdW} = a/d^{12} - b/d^6 \tag{4.3}$$

where *d* is the interatomic distance and *a* and *b* are positive constants. The first and second terms of the equation represent the repulsive and attractive parts of the van der Waals interaction, respectively. Equation (4.3) is often referred to as the *Lennard-Jones 6,12 potential*.

The optimal distance for a van der Waals interaction occurs when the interacting atoms are separated by 0.3 to 0.5 Å more than the sum of their van der Waals radii (defined as the minimum contact distance observed between the atoms in a crystal). The van der Waals interaction energy is small, being usually less than 1 kJ mol^{-1} or one-fifth of that of a typical hydrogen bond; however, there are usually many in a protein, so the sum of the interaction energies can be high.

Hydrogen Bonds

A hydrogen bond results from an electrostatic interaction between a hydrogen atom that is covalently bound to an *electronegative* atom (such as O, N, or S) and a second electronegative atom that has a *lone pair of nonbonded* electrons. It is a *polarization bond*, and the interaction takes place between the bonding partners because of charge *asymmetry*.

Although the hydrogen atom is covalently bonded to the *donor* group, it is partly shared between the *donor* and the *acceptor.* Hydrogen bonds are highly directional and are strongest when all three participating atoms lie in a straight line. Most hydrogen bonds in proteins occur between the backbone C=O and N—H groups, with an H—O distance of 1.9 to 2.0 Å. An average hydrogen bond of this type contributes ~5 kJ mol^{-1} to the stability of a protein in aqueous solution, although this value may vary from 2 to 7.5 kJ mol^{-1} (see Table 4-2).

Table 4-2 **Types of Noncovalent Interactions Involved in Stabilizing Protein Structure**

Interaction	Example	Bond Energy (kJ mol^{-1})*
van der Waals	C—H···H—C	0.4–2.0
Electrostatic	—COO$^-$···H$_3$N$^+$—	0.5–5
Hydrogen bond	—N—H···O=C—	2.0–7.5
Hydrophobic[†]	Burial of —CH$_2$—	~3

*The bond energy is the energy required to break the interaction.
[†]This value represents the free energy required to transfer a —CH$_2$— group of a nonpolar side chain from the interior of a protein to bulk water.

Hydrophobic Interactions

The placing of a nonpolar group in water leads to the ordering of the water molecules around it, i.e., a lowering of the entropy of the solution, and this is energetically unfavorable. Transfer of nonpolar groups from water to a nonpolar environment is therefore accompanied by an increase in entropy (of the water molecules) and is spontaneous (Chap. 2). The folding of a protein chain into a compact globular conformation removes nonpolar groups from contact with water; the increase in entropy arising from the liberation of water molecules compensates for the decrease in entropy of the folded polypeptide chain. Burial of a methylene (—CH$_2$—) group in the interior of a protein (referred to as a hydrophobic bond) is of comparable energy (~3 kJ mol^{-1}) to a hydrogen bond.

Hydrophobic interactions are such an important driving force in the folding of water-soluble globular proteins that a general rule is as follows: *Hydrophobic residues tend to be buried in the interior of proteins; this minimizes their exposure to water.*

EXAMPLE 4.12   If the overall folding energy of a particular protein is 40 kJ mol^{-1}, how many hydrogen bonds would have to be broken to disrupt its current folded structure?

Since each hydrogen bond contributes ~5 kJ mol^{-1} of stabilizing energy, the breaking of eight such bonds would be sufficient to disrupt the native structure.

Protein Denaturants

Because the stabilization energy of most proteins is so small, proteins show rapid, small fluctuations in structure, even at normal temperatures. In addition, it is easy to cause protein molecules to unfold, or *denature,* by using physical and chemical conditions as follows:

1. High temperature (> 60°C)

2. Extremes of pH

3. High concentrations of compounds such as urea or guanidinium hydrochloride (Fig. 4-14)

4. Solutions of detergents such as sodium dodecyl sulfate (SDS), $CH_3(CH_2)_{10}CH_2OSO_3^-Na^+$

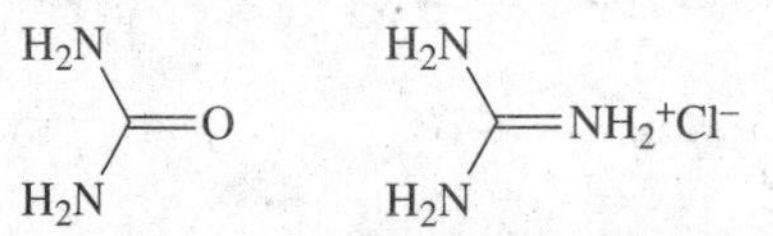

Fig. 4-14   Urea and guanidinium hydrochloride at high concentrations denature proteins.

Structure of a Protein Is Dictated by Its Amino Acid Sequence

Several proteins and enzymes, when completely unfolded by urea and with disulfide bridges reduced, are capable of refolding to give the active, native state on removal of the urea. This demonstrates that the *information* for the correct folding pattern exists in the sequence of amino acids.

EXAMPLE 4.13   *Ribonuclease,* the enzyme that hydrolyzes *ribonucleic acids,* contains *four disulfide bonds* that contribute to stabilizing its conformation. In the presence of 6 *M* guanidinium hydrochloride that weakens hydrogen bonds and hydrophobic interactions, and 1 m*M* mercaptoethanol that reduces disulfide bonds, all enzymic activity is lost. Also, according to circular dichroism analysis, there is no sign of residual secondary structure. On removing the guanidinium hydrochloride by dialysis, or gel filtration, the native conformation is regained, the correct pairing of cysteine SH groups occurs to make the normal disulfide bonds, and enzymic activity is restored.

Many larger proteins require interactions with *chaperones* (that are themselves protein molecules) to fold correctly. These chaperonins act by trapping incorrectly folded intermediates, causing them to unfold and thus allowing the protein to have another chance to fold correctly.

4.10   Hemoglobin

The ability of proteins to control biological reactions can be enhanced by the formation of complexes. The best-documented example of this is hemoglobin; it is a *tetramer* consisting of two α and two β chains. (Note that α and β here do not refer to the secondary structures, and are just the names of the polypeptides.) The chains are similar in *primary* structure to each other and to myoglobin. Each of the four chains folds into eight α-helical segments (the *globin fold*) designated A to H, starting from the N terminus.

Quaternary Structure

There are two types of contact between the hemoglobin chains. The contacts within both the $\alpha_1\beta_1$ and $\alpha_2\beta_2$ dimers involve the B, G, and H helices and the GH loop (Fig. 4-15). These are known as the *packing* contacts. The contacts between these two dimers (α_1 with β_2, and α_2 with β_1) involve the C and G helices and the FG loop (Fig. 4-15). These are called the *sliding* contacts because movement between dimers occurs here. About 20% of the surface area of the chains is buried when forming the tetramer. These contacts are mainly hydrophobic, with approximately one-third of the contacts involving polar side chains in hydrogen bonds and electrostatic interactions (salt bridges).

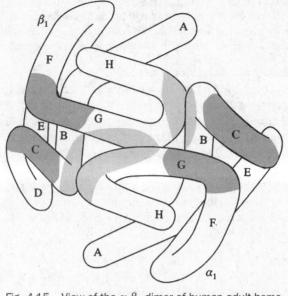

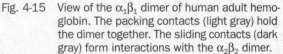

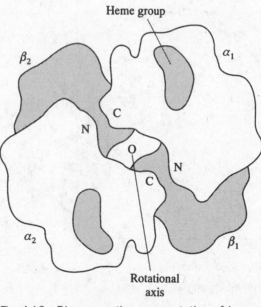

Fig. 4-15   View of the $\alpha_1\beta_1$ dimer of human adult hemo-
            globin. The packing contacts (light gray) hold
            the dimer together. The sliding contacts (dark
            gray) form interactions with the $\alpha_2\beta_2$ dimer.

The tetramer of hemoglobin is a *symmetric* molecule that is made up of two *asymmetric* but identical protomers, the $\alpha_1\beta_1$ and $\alpha_2\beta_2$ dimers. They are related by a twofold rotational axis of symmetry: if one dimer is
rotated by 180°, it is superimposable on the other, as seen in Fig. 4-16.

Fig. 4-16   Diagrammatic representation of human
            hemoglobin showing its cyclic symmetry.

If the α and β chains are considered to be identical, then hemoglobin has dihedral symmetry with two rotational axes whereby the four subunits are arranged at the apices of a tetrahedron.

EXAMPLE 4.14 Why do hemoglobin subunits associate to form a tetramer while myoglobin does not?
Although the amino acid sequences of myoglobin and hemoglobin are *homologous*, and they adopt the same globin
fold, there are important differences in patches where the polypeptide chains in hemoglobin make contact with one

another. In particular, some of the surface residues that are polar in myoglobin are hydrophobic in hemoglobin; e.g., residue B15 (the 15th residue in helix B) is a lysine in myoglobin and a leucine or valine in hemoglobin; and residue FG2 (the second residue in the loop between helices F and G) is a histidine in myoglobin and leucine in both chains of hemoglobin. In hemoglobin, both these residues are part of the *contact patch* between the α and β chains.

Oxygen Binding and Allosteric Behavior

When hemoglobin binds oxygen to form *oxyhemoglobin,* there is a change in its *quaternary* structure. The $\alpha_1\beta_1$ dimer rotates by 15° upon the $\alpha_2\beta_2$ dimer, sliding upon the $\alpha_1\beta_2$ and $\alpha_2\beta_1$ *contacts*, and the two β chains come closer together by 0.7 nm. This change in quaternary structure is preceded by changes in the tertiary structure that come about from the movement of the *proximal histidine* (the histidine nearest to the heme iron) when the heme iron binds *oxygen*. These shape changes break the constraining salt bridges between the terminal groups of the four chains. Deoxyhemoglobin is thus a structure with a low affinity for oxygen (it is the *tense* structure) while oxyhemoglobin has a structure with a high affinity for oxygen (the *relaxed* structure). Hence, as oxygen successively binds to the four heme groups of a hemoglobin molecule, the oxygen affinity of the remaining heme groups increases. This *cooperative* effect (Chap. 5) produces a sigmoidal oxygen dissociation curve, as shown in Fig. 4-17.

2,3-Bisphosphoglycerate

The compound *2,3-bisphosphoglycerate* (23BPG, previously known as 2,3-diphosphoglycerate or DPG; Fig. 4-18) is produced within the red blood cells of many animal species. It modifies the oxygen-binding affinity of hemoglobin.

    This *polyanionic* compound under physiological conditions carries five negative charges and binds in the central cavity (the β-β *cleft*) of *deoxy*hemoglobin, making salt bridges with cationic groups on the two β chains (Fig. 4-19). In oxyhemoglobin, the cavity is too small to accommodate 23BPG. The binding of oxygen and 23BPG are thus mutually exclusive, the consequence being that 23BPG reduces the oxygen affinity of hemoglobin. (Compare, in Fig. 4-17, the dissociation curve at pH 7.6, where 23BPG is present, with that labeled "No 23BPG").

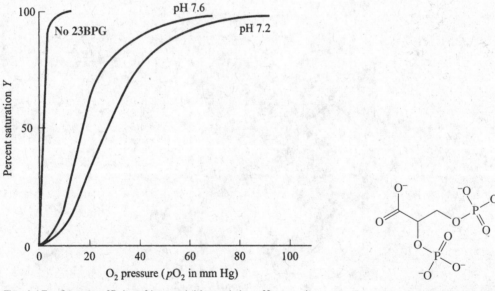

Fig. 4-17   Oxygen affinity of hemoglobin and the effect on it of pH and 23BPG.

Fig. 4-18   2,3-Bisphosphoglycerate (23BPG).

    As the concentration of 23BPG increases, the affinity of oxygen for hemoglobin decreases and more oxygen is released from the blood to the tissues at a given partial pressure (concentration). This effect compensates for the lowered arterial oxygen partial pressure as the blood passes through a tissue and oxygen is extracted from it.

pH and CO_2

Rapidly metabolizing cells require increased amounts of oxygen relative to the usage during their resting state, so there is a demand placed on oxyhemoglobin to release more oxygen to these tissues. Concomitantly

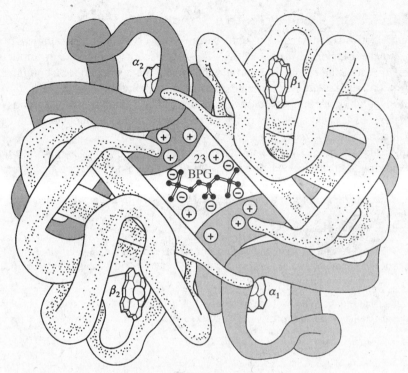

Fig. 4-19 · Deoxyhemoglobin with 23BPG binding in its β-β cleft.

there is a buildup of CO_2 from the oxidation of fuels, such as glucose and fatty acids. This causes an increase in proton concentration (decrease in pH) through the *carbonic anhydrase* reaction, as follows:

$$H_2O + CO_2 \rightleftharpoons HCO_3^- + H^+$$

Deoxyhemoglobin has a higher affinity for protons than does oxyhemoglobin, so that proton binding competes with the binding of oxygen (although at different sites) to displace oxygen, as follows:

$$Hb(O_2)_4 + 2H^+ \rightleftharpoons Hb(H^+)_2 + 4O_2$$

This is known as the *Bohr effect*, and it arises from the slightly higher pK_a of ionizing groups in deoxy-hemoglobin compared with oxyhemoglobin. One such group is histidine β146 in which the pK_a is raised as a consequence of its proximity to a neighboring aspartate in deoxyhemoglobin, and which therefore has a higher affinity for protons. In oxyhemoglobin, as a result of a changed geometry, histidine β146 is free and has a more normal pK_a. A decrease in pH from 7.6 to 7.2 can almost double the amount of oxygen released in the tissues (see Fig. 4-17). In the lungs, where oxygen partial pressure is very high, the two reactions shown above are biased to the left (net reversal), leading to the release of CO_2.

Although much of the CO_2 in the blood is transported as HCO_3^-, some also combines with the terminal amino groups of the β chains of hemoglobin and acts as an *allosteric effector* (Chap. 5). Specifically, CO_2 reacts with the unionized form of α-amino groups to form *carbamates* that in turn form salt bridges, thus stabilizing the tense (deoxyhemoglogin) structure. The reaction is as follows:

$$Hb—NH_2—CO_2 \rightleftharpoons Hb—NHCOO^- + H^+$$

In summary, the interactions between the subunits of hemoglobin allow the release of oxygen to be fine-tuned to physiological needs. The allosteric effectors 23BPG, H^+, and CO_2 all lower the affinity of hemoglobin for oxygen by increasing the strength of the subunit interactions in the tetramer.

4.11   Methods for Determining Protein Structure

Most of the structural information on proteins comes from X-ray crystallographic analysis of protein crystals or from the use of nuclear magnetic resonance (NMR) spectroscopy on proteins in solution. Each of these techniques has relative advantages and limitations which make them suitable for a complementary range of problems. The first protein structure determined at sufficient resolution to trace the path of a polypeptide chain was that of myoglobin, in 1960. Since then more than 50,000 structures of thousands of different proteins have been determined. The coordinates of the atoms of all protein and nucleic acid structures are stored in, and are available from, the *Protein Data Bank* (www.rcsb.org/pdb).

Other techniques such as circular dichroism (CD) spectrophotometry and fluorescence resonance energy transfer (FRET) spectrophotometry provide lower-resolution structural information.

EXAMPLE 4.15   What generalizations or folding rules can be inferred from the whole database of experimentally determined structures?

There are several key features, as follows:

1. Most electrically charged groups reside on the *surface of proteins* where they interact with water. Exceptions to this rule are the catalytically important residues in enzymes that are often partially stabilized by specific polar interactions within a hydrophobic pocket of the molecule.

2. Most nonpolar groups are in the interior of the molecule, thus avoiding thermodynamically unfavorable contact with water. Exceptions arise when *exposed hydrophobic* surfaces serve as binding sites for other proteins or ligands.

3. Maximal *hydrogen bonding* occurs within a molecule.

4. Repeating secondary structural elements, α helices and β-pleated sheets, make up a *large proportion* of most proteins.

5. Very large proteins fold into *semiautonomous domains* that resemble smaller proteins.

6. The tens of thousands of known protein structures can be grouped into fewer than 1000 *fold families*.

X-ray Crystallography

X-rays have a wavelength that approximates the distance between mutually bonded atoms in a molecule; e.g., a carbon—carbon single bond is 1.5 Å (0.15 nm) long, and the wavelength of X-rays from a copper target is 1.54 Å. When X-ray photons interact with a molecule, they are diffracted, and the resulting diffraction pattern contains information about the location of the atoms in the molecule. If the sample is dissolved in a solution, the individual molecules of the protein are randomly orientated by thermally driven motion, and only very low-resolution information on the shape of the molecules can be obtained. Fibrous proteins and nucleic acids can be induced to form orientated gels or fibers. X-ray scattering from these samples yields regular repeating spacings in diffraction patterns that led to the characterization of the α helix and β-pleated sheet in proteins, and the A and B forms of DNA and RNA. In these cases X-ray diffraction was capable only of refining a proposed geometric model, *not* of defining uniquely and objectively the structure.

The most valuable results from X-ray diffraction are obtained when the sample is a single crystal. Structures of molecules ranging in size from a few atoms to viruses with tens of thousands of atoms have been solved. In a single crystal all the molecules lie in a three-dimensional lattice with fixed relative positions and orientations. The intensities of each spot of light in a diffraction pattern can be measured and used to derive the full three-dimensional structure of the protein.

EXAMPLE 4.16   What are the advantages and limitations of X-ray crystallography for determining the structures of macromolecules?

As with all experimental methods, there are some advantages and some limitations. For X-ray crystallography they are as follows:

1. An advantage is that it is applicable to a wide range of samples that include proteins, enzymes, nucleic acids, and viruses and is not limited by the size of the molecules.

2. A disadvantage is that not all proteins can be crystallized. This is especially true of intrinsic membrane proteins that must be solubilized with detergents.

3. A disadvantage is that most protein crystals do *not* diffract to true atomic resolution. Due to an inherent lack of perfection in protein crystals, the *high angle component* of the diffraction pattern, which contains the fine detail on distances between atoms, is lost. For this reason, the protein sequence must generally be known before starting a structure calculation.

Nuclear Magnetic Resonance (NMR) Spectroscopy

Compared with X-ray crystallography, NMR spectroscopy has only recently become established as a technique for protein structure determination. The first complete three-dimensional protein structure solved using this technique was reported in 1986. The work followed the development of *two-dimensional* (2D) NMR spectroscopy that allowed the study of structures of much larger molecules than before, such as proteins.

The NMR phenomenon derives from the fact that the energy levels of nuclei with nonzero spin become unequally populated when the nuclei are placed in a magnetic field. The energy of nuclei can therefore be perturbed (i.e., moved between energy levels) by the application of radio-frequency pulses whose photons have energies that correspond to the energy gap between those of the energy levels of the nuclear magnets. The ability to perturb the nuclei in this way enables the observation of so-called scalar and dipolar nuclear interactions. The first type of interaction provides information on protein-bond torsion angles, while dipolar interactions provide information on internuclear distances. The structure of a protein is calculated using the *amino acid sequence* of the protein in combination with these measurements of dihedral angles and nuclear (usually proton-proton) distances.

Note that NMR studies of proteins are generally performed in solution, in which the molecules move around freely. NMR spectroscopy measures scalar quantities (torsion angles and distances), and this is fundamentally different from X-ray crystallography, which is essentially an imaging technique resulting in a molecular *image*. Since NMR spectra are most readily interpreted from solutions of molecules, the technique can provide details of the *dynamics* of a protein in solution.

EXAMPLE 4.17   What are the advantages and disadvantages of NMR spectroscopy relative to X-ray crystallography for determining the structure of macromolecules?

The technique is applicable to proteins and nucleic acids in their *solution state*. A few protein structures have been solved by using *solid-state NMR*, which involves spinning the sample at thousands of revolutions per second. This gives narrow spectral lines that are similar to those obtained from proteins in solution, but the instruments and data analysis are much more complex than for solution-state NMR spectroscopy.

1. There is an upper size limit of ~50 kDa, and yet this encompasses most proteins and/or their *domains*. This size limit is steadily increasing with the development of new radio-frequency pulse methods and higher magnetic fields. In special circumstances, structures of proteins of more than 500 kDa have been solved by NMR.

2. Large proteins need to be labeled with NMR-active ^{15}N or ^{13}C atoms. Incorporation of these nuclei by biotechnological means (gene expression) can be expensive.

3. In general, the final resolution of NMR spectroscopy is not as high as for X-ray crystallography, but one advantage is that additional information about the dynamics of the protein is obtained.

EXAMPLE 4.18   What is the relevance of a structure determined in the crystalline state to its native structure in solution?

Protein crystals have a solvent (water) content of 30 to 80% by volume. Thus, there are few direct intermolecular contacts between molecules that affect the structure. Structures of the same protein determined in different crystal forms, and therefore containing different packing contacts, have generally been found to be the same. This outcome is also true of structures determined using both NMR spectroscopy and X-ray crystallography. Some enzymes are fully active in the crystalline state, implying that crystallization has not altered their native conformation.

EXAMPLE 4.19   Given a 20 kDa protein, what preliminary steps could be taken to decide whether it was suitable for a structural study by X-ray crystallography or NMR spectroscopy?

1. Gel filtration, analytical ultracentrifugation (sedimentation equilibrium; see below), or light scattering experiments can be performed to determine if the protein is self-associated to form oligomers. Oligomerization often precludes structure determination with NMR spectroscopy, as even a dimer might be at the very upper molecular weight limit of this technique.

2. If the protein does not oligomerize, then NMR studies can begin as long as a sample volume of 250 μL and concentration of ~1 mM can be obtained. Good dispersion (separation) of the peaks in a one-dimensional spectrum indicates whether the protein is folded. The project can then proceed with the production of labeled protein and recording of 2D NMR spectra.

3. Oligomerization does not preclude attempts to crystallize a protein as long as the oligomers are all identical. Dynamic light scattering can be used to determine if the protein solution is *polydisperse*; if it is, it will probably not give rise to crystals. Protein crystals are most readily grown from monodisperse solutions. *Crystallization trials* can be commenced by using commercially available screening solutions with as many as 500 different conditions. These contain ranges of several different features of the solvent including the chemical nature of the buffer, a range of pH values, and various precipitating reagents.

Circular Dichroism (CD) Spectrophotometry

The aromatic amino acid residues in proteins (Phe, Try, and Trp) strongly absorb *ultraviolet* light in the region of the spectrum from 100 to 400 nm but not in the visible region of the spectrum from 400 to 800 nm. So, proteins are colorless, unless they contain a nonpeptide light-absorbing cofactor or *chromophore*. Proteins are asymmetric molecules composed of L-amino acids. Such molecules preferentially absorb either left- or right-handed plane or circularly polarized light. *Circular dichroism* (CD) spectrophotometry measures the difference in absorption of left- and right-handed circularly polarized light and is generally expressed as the difference in the *molar extinction coefficients* $\varepsilon_L - \varepsilon_R$ of the two forms of light. A plot of $\Delta\varepsilon = \varepsilon_L - \varepsilon_R$ versus the wavelength λ of the incident light is the CD spectrum of the sample. The interaction of the *chiral* amino acids with the different environments of secondary structure results in very different CD spectra for polypeptides in α-helical, β sheet, and random coil conformations. The net CD spectrum of a protein can be *deconvoluted* (mathematically unwrapped) to provide an estimate of the different proportions of secondary structure. A CD spectrum of a protein solution (e.g., Fig. 4-20) is often used as a rapid diagnostic tool to assess the folded state of the protein.

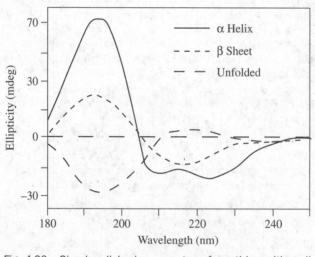

Fig. 4-20   Circular dichroism spectra of peptides with well-defined and known secondary structures. Note the ellipticity is expressed in millidegrees.

4.12   Comparing and Viewing Protein Structures

The Protein Data Bank

The *Protein Data Bank* (PDB) was established as a service to international science at the Brookhaven National Laboratory in the United States in 1971 to store and curate the atomic coordinates of macromolecular structures. Original versions of the whole data bank were distributed on magnetic tape to scientists, then on compact discs, and now they are freely available via the Internet (http://www.rcsb.org/). The PDB is part of the wwPDB whose mission is to ensure that the PDB archive remains an international resource with uniformly coded data. Other related sites are located in Japan (PDBj, http://www.pdbj.org/) and in Europe (MSD-EBI, http://www.ebi.ac.uk/msd/). In addition to coordinates, the PDB stores experimental diffraction data, and it provides many tools for analyzing and displaying structures. As of April 15, 2008, the PDB held 50,277 sets of atomic coordinates from proteins, nucleic acids, and carbohydrates determined by X-ray diffraction, NMR spectroscopy, and electron microscopy. About 5000 new structures are released each year, and the database is expected to treble to 150,000 by 2014.

Sequence Homology and Protein Evolution

The protein myoglobin serves as an oxygen binder in muscle. It was among the first to be studied with the aid of X-ray crystallography, and this revealed a *compact globular structure* consisting of eight segments of α helix that are linked via short nonhelical segments.

Hemoglobin, the oxygen-carrying protein of vertebrate blood, is similar in structure to myoglobin. However, hemoglobin is composed of four chains; i.e., it has a *quaternary structure*. The four chains are held together in a particular geometric arrangement by noncovalent interactions. There are two major types of hemoglobin polypeptide chains in normal adult hemoglobin: the α chain and the β chain (Sec. 4.10).

The polypeptide chain of myoglobin and the two chains of hemoglobin are remarkably similar in primary, secondary, and tertiary structures. They are said to be *homologous*. Myoglobin has 153 amino acid residues, the hemoglobin α chain has 141, while the β chain has 146; the sequence is identical for 24 out of 141 positions for the human proteins, and many of the differences show *conservative replacement*. This means that an amino acid residue in one chain has been replaced by a chemically similar residue at the corresponding position in another chain, e.g., the replacement of *glutamate* by *aspartate*, both of which contain a carboxyl group on their side chain.

Comparison of the amino acid sequences of hemoglobin and myoglobin from different species of animals shows that the chains from *phylogenetically* (evolutionarily) related species are similar. The number of differences increases with species that are phylogenetically more separated. On the assumption that proteins evolve at a constant rate, the number of differences between two homologous proteins is proportional to the time at which the species diverged during evolution.

EXAMPLE 4.20 Draw an evolutionary tree for the human, rabbit, silkworm, and the fungus *Neurospora* by using the data in the following table for differences in the respective cytochrome *c* sequences.

	Number of Sequence Differences			
	Human	Rabbit	Silkworm	*Neurospora*
Human	0	11	36	71
Rabbit		0	35	70
Silkworm			0	69
Neurospora				0

These data enable the construction of an *evolutionary tree*, with branch lengths that are approximately proportional to the number of differences between the species (see Fig. 4-21). The human and rabbit show greatest similarity and therefore are connected by short branches. The silkworm cytochrome *c* is closer to both mammalian forms than it is to *Neurospora*, so it should be connected to the mammalian junction. The length of the silkworm branch will be approximately three times the length of the rabbit and human branches. Finally, *Neurospora* shows approximately the same number of differences with all the animal species and therefore can be joined to their common branch.

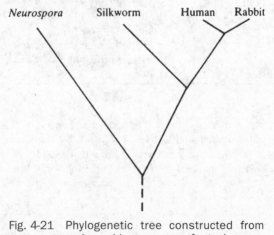

Fig. 4-21 Phylogenetic tree constructed from amino acid sequences of cytochrome *c*.

Protein Structure Prediction and Modeling of Shape

In principle, with sufficiently accurate force fields to describe bond lengths and the angles between subplanes that contain three or more atoms, it is often possible from the amino acid sequence alone to predict the full tertiary structure of a protein *ab initio* (from scratch). Approximations required to carry out these calculations with existing computer resources limit this approach to relatively small molecules. However, given the relatively large number of protein structures that have been determined already (see above), by either NMR spectroscopy or X-ray crystallography, unknown structures can be modeled, based on their *homology* with a known structure. This direct approach, known as *homology modeling*, first aligns the sequence of the protein of an unknown structure with those of homologous proteins or domains of a known structure from the PDB. The accuracy of the final model depends critically on this alignment process. A model is then created based on one or a composite of known structures incorporating changes in amino sequence, including insertions and deletions, to create the previously unknown structure. The model structure is then subjected to energy minimization to relieve any strain caused by changing the sequence. Homology modeling will almost certainly predict the correct fold if the sequence identity is 25% or greater. However, areas of the model where there are large insertions in the sequence are least likely to be correctly predicted.

More distantly related structures can be modeled by the use of the process of *threading*. This is a computational technique by which the sequence of the protein of an unknown structure is threaded through a nonredundant library of well-determined structures to determine which are compatible with the sequence. Basic statistical methods for predicting secondary structure, α helix and β sheet, have ~80% veracity.

4.13   Purification and Chemical Charcterization of Proteins

Purification

In general, in any separation and purification procedure, the target molecule (a protein in this case) must be able to be identified by some physical or chemical property. This might be the red color of myoglobin or a specific enzyme assay. Separation of molecules is carried out by exploiting physical or chemical differences between proteins in a mixture.

Physical Property	Experimental Technique
Solubility	Repetitive fractionation
Charge	Ion-exchange chromatography
	Electrophoresis
Isoelectric point	Isoelectric focusing
Polarity	Adsorption chromatography
	Reverse-phase chromatography
	Hydrophobic interaction chromatography
Size	Dialysis and ultrafiltration
	Gel electrophoresis
	Gel filtration chromatography
	Ultracentrifugation
Specific binding	Affinity chromatography

EXAMPLE 4.21   Since no separation method is perfect, to achieve high levels of purity, multiple separation steps are usually used. At each step some of the desired protein is lost, but its relative abundance is increased. In other words, the *specific activity*, which is the *total activity* relative to the *total protein*, increases in each step of the purification, while the *percentage recovery* decreases. An example of this is given in the following table that shows the purification of an enzyme from a tissue.

Fraction	Volume (mL)	Total Protein (mg)	Total Activity	Specific Activity	Percent Recovery
1. Crude extract	3800	22,800.00	2460	0.108	100
2. Salt precipitate	165	2800.00	1190	0.425	48
3. Ion-exchange chromatography	65	100.00	720	7.200	29
4. Gel filtration chromatography	40	14.5	555	38.300	23
5. Affinity chromatography	6	1.8	275	152.108	11

Molecular Weight Determination

Each protein has a unique *molecular weight*. Furthermore, the size or molecular weight of a particular protein, under specified conditions, distinguishes it from many other proteins. Note that the molecular weight (or more precisely, the *relative molecular weight*) MW is dimensionless and represents the mass of the molecule relative to one-twelfth of the mass of an atom of ^{12}C. Molecular *mass*, on the other hand, is usually expressed in units of daltons (Da) or kilodaltons (kDa), where 1 Da is one-twelfth of the mass of an atom of ^{12}C (1.66×10^{-24}g). The *molar mass* is the mass of 1 mol expressed in grams. All three quantities have the same *numerical* value, but have different units. For example, serum albumin could be described as having a molecular weight of 66,000, a molecular mass of 66 kDa, or a molar mass of 66 kg mol^{-1}.

The molecular weight is determined by the amino acid composition of the protein, any posttranslational modifications such as glycosylation, and the presence of bound nonpeptide groups such as metals and cofactors. While the exact weight of a polypeptide chain can be calculated from its amino acid composition, a *rule-of-thumb* calculation, based on the proportion of different amino acids found in most proteins, gives the molecular weight as the number of residues multiplied by 110.

EXAMPLE 4.22   Human cytochrome *c* contains 104 amino acid residues. What is its approximate molecular weight?
The molecular weight is approximately 11,900; it is the sum of the molecular weight of the polypeptide ($\sim$104 $\times$ 110) and that of the heme prosthetic group (412). Alternatively, the molecular size (or mass) is said to be 11.9 kDa.

Proteins that possess a *quaternary* structure are composed of several separate polypeptide chains held together by noncovalent interactions. When such proteins are examined under dissociating conditions (e.g., 8 *M* urea to weaken hydrogen bonds and hydrophobic interaction, plus 1 m*M* mercaptoethanol to disrupt disulfide bonds), the molecular weight of the component polypeptide chains can be measured. By comparison, with the *native* molecular weight it is often possible to determine how many polypeptide chains are involved in the native structure.

The molecular weight of a protein may be determined by the use of thermodynamic methods, such as *osmotic pressure* measurements and *sedimentation* analysis in an *ultracentrifuge*. Osmotic pressure is sensitive to the *number* of molecules (particles) in solution, and if the total mass of protein in solution is known, the molar weight can be estimated. The sedimentation of protein molecules in a centrifuge depends directly on the *mass* of each molecule.

Dialysis

Protein molecules have molecular weights that range from 5000 to several million. Synthetic membranes are available with fixed-size pores that allow the passage of molecules smaller than a defined size. This selective permeability is the basis of the process termed *dialysis*, which is usually carried out by placing the protein solution inside a bag or cell, which is then immersed in a relatively large volume of buffer. Smaller molecules diffuse across the membrane into the surrounding buffer, while the large proteins remain inside. Dialysis membranes can be obtained with molecular weight cutoff limits ranging from 1000 to more than 50,000. Dialysis membranes can be incorporated into centrifuge tubes, or high-pressure cells, to speed up the separation.

Selective Solubility

Proteins may be selectively precipitated from a mixture of different proteins by adding: (1) salts such as ammonium sulfate to increase the ionic strength of the medium (*salting out*); (2) organic solvents such as ethanol or acetone; or (3) potent denaturing agents such as trichloroacetic acid. Proteins are *least* soluble in any given solvent when the pH is equal to their *isoelectric point* pI. At the isoelectric point, the protein carries no net electric charge, and therefore electrostatic repulsion between protein molecules is minimal. Although a protein may carry both positively and negatively charged groups at its isoelectric point, the *sum* of these charges is zero. At pH values above the isoelectric point, the net charge will be *negative*, while at pH values *below* the pI, the net charge will be *positive*.

Electrophoresis

The movement of electrically charged protein molecules in an electric field, termed *electrophoresis*, is an important means of separating different protein molecules. Proteins are generally separated on polyacrylamide gels, hence the term *polyacrylamide gel electrophoresis* or PAGE. Microfluidic chips are now replacing traditional gels in high-throughput applications.

The terms *anode* and *cathode* are often used in electrophoresis and are often confused. Remember that an *anion* is a negatively charged ion; *anions* move toward the *anode*.

EXAMPLE 4.23   In which direction will the following proteins move in an electric field [toward the anode, toward the cathode, or toward neither (i.e., remain stationary)]? (1) Egg albumin (pI = 4.6) at pH 5.0; (2) β-lactoglobulin (pI = 5.2) at pH 5.0 and at pH 7.0.

1. For egg albumin, pH 5.0 is above its isoelectric point, and the protein will therefore carry a *small* excess negative charge. It will thus migrate toward the anode.

2. For β-lactoglobulin, pH 5.0 is below its isoelectric point; at this pH, the protein will be positively charged so it will move toward the cathode. At pH 7.0, on the other hand, the protein will be negatively charged and will move toward the anode.

Isoelectric Focusing

Isolectric focusing (IEF) electrophoresis separates a mixture of proteins based on their different isoelectric points (pI; the pH value at which a protein carries a *net* charge of zero). If a mixture of proteins is placed on a gel that contains a stable pH gradient in which the pH increases steadily from the anode to the cathode, each protein will migrate to a position in the gel corresponding to its own pI. Once it reaches this position, the charge on the protein will be zero and it will no longer be subject to a force due to the electric field. If the protein diffuses away from this position in either direction, it will be subjected to a force driving it back to the position of its pI. Each protein will therefore be *focused* into a narrow band on the gel corresponding to its pI.

Two-Dimensional Gel Electrophoresis

Proteomics is a new field of study in which an entire group of proteins or the *proteome* of an organism or organelle is studied at one time. This powerful technique enables us to compare, for example, the proteomes

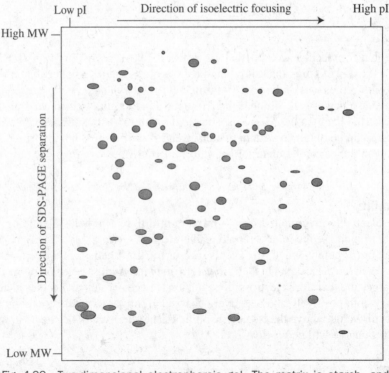

Fig. 4-22   Two-dimensional electrophorsis gel. The matrix is starch, and the dark spots indicate proteins that have been stained with the protein-selective dye Coomassie blue.

of normal and diseased tissue to identify which proteins are more or less abundant as a result of the disease, possibly identifying the cause. The heart of proteomics is the use of *two-dimensional* (2D) gel electrophoresis that combines SDS-PAGE or starch-gel electrophoresis with IEF. A single protein sample is loaded onto one edge of a large (up to 30 cm square) gel. The sample is subjected to IEF in one direction, and the separated proteins are then subjected to SDS-PAGE in the perpendicular direction. Each spot on this 2D gel is characterized by the pI of the protein and its molecular weight (Fig. 4-22). As many as 6000 proteins or the entire proteome of a bacterium such as *E. coli* can be separated in a single experiment. The resolution of the procedure can be increased or larger proteomes separated by using multiple gels with narrower pH ranges in the IEF direction. Individual spots can be excised, either manually or robotically, from 2D gels and identified using mass spectrometry (see Secs. 4.4 and 4.14 and Examples 4.3 to 4.5).

Ion-Exchange Chromatography

Ion-exchange chromatography relies on the electrostatic interaction between a charged protein and a stationary ion-exchange resin particle carrying a charge of the opposite sign. The strength of the interaction between the protein and the resin particle depends on the charge on the protein (and thus on the solution pH) and on the dielectric constant of the medium [Eq. (4.2)]. The interaction can be modified in practice by altering the pH or the salt concentration.

EXAMPLE 4.24   A solution containing egg albumin (pI = 4.6), β-lactoglobulin (pI = 5.2), and chymotrypsinogen (pI = 9.5) was loaded onto a column of diethylaminoethyl cellulose (DEAE-cellulose) at pH 5.4. The column was then *eluted* with a pH 5.4 buffer, with an increasing salt concentration. Predict the elution pattern.

The functional moiety of DEAE-cellulose is a quaternary ammonium group that carries a positive charge at pH 5.4. At this pH value, chymotrypsinogen also carries a positive charge and therefore does not bind. β-Lactoglobulin, carrying a small negative charge, binds only weakly and will be displaced as the salt concentration is raised. However, egg albumin, carrying a larger negative charge, binds tightly and will be displaced only at high salt concentrations, or on lowering the pH to a value at which the negative charge is reduced.

Gel Filtration

Separation of proteins on the basis of size can be achieved by means of *gel filtration*. This technique relies on diffusion of protein molecules into the pores of a *gel matrix* in a *column*. A commonly used gel matrix is *dextran*, a polymer of glucose, that is formed into very small beads for this purpose. The material is available commercially as *Sephadex* in a range of different pore sizes.

When a protein is larger than the largest pore of the matrix, no diffusion into the matrix takes place and the protein is eluted after only a small volume of solution has flowed through the column. Molecules smaller than the smallest pore can diffuse freely into all gel beads. The small molecules elute only after a larger volume of buffer has been passed through. Generally, gel filtration buffers do not dissociate oligomeric proteins into their subunits so that the proteins elute from the column according to their native size.

EXAMPLE 4.25   In what order would the following proteins emerge from a gel filtration column of Sephadex G200: myoglobin (M_r = 16,000), catalase (M_r = 500,000), cytochrome *c* (M_r = 12,000), chymotrypsinogen (M_r = 26,000), and hemoglobin (M_r = 66,000)?

Catalase is the largest protein in this set and would be excluded completely from the Sephadex beads (exclusion limit ~200,000). This means the beads appear to be solid to the catalase molecules, so it only dissolves in the fluid outside the beads (the *void volume*). Catalase would be eluted from the column when a volume of eluant equal to the void volume had passed through the column.

Cytochrome *c* is the smallest protein of the set and would be able to diffuse freely into all the spaces within the beads. The column would therefore appear to have a larger volume available to cytochrome *c*, so it would not emerge until the column had been flushed with a volume almost equal to its total volume.

Hemoglobin is a tetramer, with four protein chains. The buffer conditions used in gel chromatography do not normally dissociate oligomeric proteins into their subunits. Hemoglobin would therefore behave as a single-chain protein with the same total molecular weight.

The order of elution would therefore be catalase, hemoglobin, chymotrypsinogen, myoglobin, and then cytochrome *c*.

The *elution volume* from a Sephadex column is a monotonically decreasing function of molecular weight. Therefore, by comparing the elution behavior of an unknown protein with that in a series of standards of known molecular weight, an estimation of molecular weight can be interpolated.

EXAMPLE 4.26   What assumptions are inherent in both size-exclusion gel filtration and gel electrophoresis for deter-mining molecular weights of proteins?

1. In both cases the hydrodynamic behavior depends on the shape of the molecule. Therefore we assume that the shape (i.e., spherical, ellipsoidal, rod-shaped, etc.) of the unknown protein is the same as that of the standard proteins used to calibrate the column.

2. Gel filtration behavior depends on the effective size and not the mass of the protein. Therefore, if the protein differs from the standards in density (partial specific volume), an incorrect estimate of molecular weight will eventuate.

3. Proteins bind SDS, and to a first approximation the mass of SDS bound per gram of protein is the same for all pro-teins. Differences in mass of SDS bound per molecule of protein result in differences in the total charge (SDS is negatively charged), leading to differences in electrophoretic mobility, so aberrant SDS binding can lead to aberrant mobility and hence an incorrect estimate of molecular weight.

Affinity Chromatography

This is a form of chromatography in which the gel matrix (usually beads) has been chemically modified with a ligand that specifically interacts with the protein (often an enzyme) of interest. Thus, a crude mixture of proteins can be applied to the affinity column, and only those proteins that bind to the ligand are retained. Then after washing the column with an appropriate buffer, the selected protein(s) can be eluted by using a solution of the free ligand or by changing temperature or buffer conditions. Often an inhibitor of an enzyme can be used as the selective-affinity ligand.

4.14   Biophysical Characterization of Proteins

Mass Spectrometry

Mass spectrometry (MS) is a powerful technique for determining the mass-to-charge m/z ratio of ionized atoms or molecules (see also Sec. 4.4). The mass spectrum can easily be deconvoluted (unraveled) to yield the original mass of the entire molecule or subfragments of the molecule to yield structural information, in addition to its mass. The basic principle of a mass (m) spectrometer involves the evaporation and charging (z) of molecules and then separating them using electric and magnetic fields, according to their m/z ratios. Proteins are large molecules and tend to decompose if subjected to conditions that are used routinely for small organic molecules. The commonly used techniques are *matrix assisted laser desorption ionization* (MALDI), in which the sample is released from a matrix of a low-molecular-weight organic compound, and *electrospray ionization* (ESI), in which a solution containing the sample is sprayed from a fine capillary at high voltage, forming charged droplets from which the solvent evaporates, leaving a charged peptide.

Mass spectrometry is accurate to better than 0.01%, it requires only picomoles of sample, and it can be used to determine masses of molecules ranging in size from single amino acids to proteins larger than 100 kDa.

Analytical Ultracentrifugation (AUC)

Analytical ultracentrifugation is used to determine accurately the molecular weight and the hydrodynamic properties of proteins or other macromolecules, and it is particularly well suited to investigating self-associating systems. An analytical ultracentrifuge combines ultracentrifugation with a detection method for macromol-ecules, such as uv-visible is spectrophotometry, optical interference, or fluorescence spectrophotometry. A centrifugal force causes protein molecules, or other types of molecules, to sediment toward the bottom of a sample cell, increasing the concentration at the bottom of the cell. (The sample cells are constructed with windows on opposite faces so the motion of the molecules can be measured with the optical methods just mentioned.) An opposing force comes about from the concentration gradient that is formed by the sedimenta-tion, so random diffusion competes against the formation of the higher concentration.

In *sedimentation velocity* experiments, the centrifuge is run at high speeds (up to ~80,000 rpm), and the *rate* of sedimentation of the boundary between the solvent and the sedimenting protein is measured to yield the *sedimentation coefficient* of the molecule (or molecules). This value is related to the size and shape of the molecule and is measured in Svedberg units (denoted by S, and formally it is equal to 10^{-13} s). E.g., the 30S subunit of the ribosome has a sedimentation coefficient of 30 S. Thé Svedberg of Sweden invented the analytical ultacentrifuge, and he received the 1926 Nobel Prize in Chemistry for his work characterizing the hydrodynamic and mass properties of proteins.

EXAMPLE 4.27 A field is defined as a region of space in which a particle with a particular property experiences a force. Best known is the electric field in which an electrically charged particle experiences a force, and when it moves, it follows a path that is described by virtual lines, called *lines of force*.

A magnetic dipole placed in a magnetic field experiences a force on each pole that tends to turn the dipole about its center; i.e., the magnet experiences a *torque*.

In a gravitational field a mass experiences a force F_c. In a centrifuge the magnitude of the gravitational field is $r\omega^2$, and a mass m placed in this field experiences a sedimenting force of $F_c = mr\omega^2$.

A sedimenting molecule in a solution displaces solvent of mass m_0 in the direction opposite to its motion, so this contributes a buoyancy force $F_b = m_0 r\omega^2$. And the motion of the molecule through the solution with nonzero viscosity has a retarding force exerted on it that is proportional to its velocity, namely, $F_f = fv$, where f is the *frictional coefficient*. Taking these three forces together gives, under conditions of steady and uniform flow,

$$F_c - F_b - F_d = 0$$
$$mr\omega^2 - m_0 r\omega^2 - fv = 0 \tag{4.4}$$

For the mass of solvent displaced m_0, we substitute the product of the particle mass and its partial specific volume $\bar{v}$, which is the reciprocal of its density, times the solvent density ρ. Therefore,

$$mr\omega^2 (1 - \bar{v}\rho) - fv = 0 \tag{4.5}$$

To place the analysis onto a mole basis, we multiply by Avogadro's number and put the experimentally measured parameters on one side of the equation and the molecular ones on the other. We obtain

$$M(1 - \bar{v}\rho)/Nf = v/r\omega^2 = s \tag{4.6}$$

Thus we see that the sedimentation coefficient s is simply the velocity of sedimentation per unit of gravitational field. The larger the velocity, the larger the value of s.

In *sedimentation equilibrium* experiments, the centrifuge is run at slower speeds, and the opposing forces of sedimentation and diffusion are allowed to come to equilibrium. The resulting concentration distribution over the length of the cell is used to determine the molecular weight of the protein, the oligomeric state of the protein (e.g., monomers versus dimers or tetramers, etc.), and the association constant of self-association (e.g., dimerization, tetramerization, etc.).

EXAMPLE 4.28 Albert Einstein showed that the diffusion coefficient D of a particle is dependent on its size (mass) and shape and is a function of the temperature T and the universal gas constant R:

$$D = RT/Nf \tag{4.7}$$

where, as in Eqs. (4.4) to (4.6), N and f are Avogadro's number and the frictional coefficient of the particle, respectively. Equations (4.6) and (4.7) can be combined to give an expression for the molecular weight of the particles in an ultracentrifuge experiment:

$$M = RTs/D(1 - \bar{v}\rho) \tag{4.8}$$

This is the *Svedberg* equation.

Light Scattering

Two different light-scattering methodologies can be used to characterize proteins: *Classical light scattering* (also known as *static* or *Rayleigh* scattering, after Lord Rayleigh who had been simply J. W. Strutt before he became famous in the late 19th century) provides a direct measure of molecular mass. It is therefore very useful for determining whether the native state of a protein is a monomer or a higher oligomer, and for measuring the masses of aggregates or other nonnative species. The method can also be used for measuring the stoichiometry of complexes between different proteins (e.g., receptor-ligand complexes or antibody-antigen complexes). For globular proteins smaller than ~500 kDa, the intensity of the scattered light is uniform in all directions, so it is only necessary to measure scattering at a single angle (usually 90°). The relevant theory indicates that the intensity of light scattered at a given value is proportional to the product of the protein concentration (in mg mL^{-1}) and its molecular mass. For higher molecular masses or for proteins with an elongated shape, the scattering varies with angle. By measuring the scattering at additional angles (so-called multiangle laser light scattering, or MALLS), absolute measurements of masses into the megadalton range are possible, and the root-mean-square radius can also be determined.

This technique is often used online in conjunction with size-exclusion chromatography. Since the signal from the light-scattering detector is directly proportional to the molecular mass of the protein times the concentration (mg mL^{-1}), by combining this signal with that from a concentration detector (refractive index or absorbance) it is possible to measure the molecular mass of each protein coming off the column.

Dynamic Light Scattering (DLS)

This is also known as *photon correlation spectroscopy* (PCS) or *quasi-elastic light scattering* (QELS). It uses scattered light to measure the rate of diffusion of protein particles in a sample. The data on molecular motion are digitally processed to yield a size distribution of particles in the sample, where the size is given by the mean *Stokes radius* or *hydrodynamic radius* of the protein particles; this is the effective radius of a particle in its hydrated state. Clearly, the hydrodynamic radius depends on both mass and shape.

Dynamic light scattering is particularly useful for sensing the presence of very small amounts of aggregated protein (< 0.01% by weight) and for studying samples that contain a very large range of masses. The technique is one of the most popular ones for determining the size of particles. Shining a monochromatic light beam, such as a laser, onto a solution with spherical particles in Brownian motion causes a Doppler shift when the light hits a moving particle, changing the wavelength of the reflected light. This change is related to the velocity and hence the size of the particles in the sample.

Photon correlation spectroscopy has several important features, most notably the duration of the experiment is short, and it is readily automated so that reliable measurements can be made even by inexperienced operators. The method has modest development costs. Commercial particle sizing systems mostly operate at only one angle (90°) and use red light (wavelength, 675 nm). Usually in these systems the dependence of light-scattering intensity on concentration is neglected.

SOLVED PROBLEMS

TYPES OF PROTEIN STRUCTURE

4.1. What is the difference between a polypeptide and a protein?

SOLUTION

Proteins are all polypeptides that contain a large number (usually >50) of amino acids, but smaller polypeptides are not classified as proteins.

4.2. Are any of the following functions performed by proteins? (1) Efficient catalysis of chemical reactions; (2) storage and transport of oxygen; (3) tensile strength and elasticity in spiderwebs; (4) recognition of foreign antigens as part of the immune response; (5) transport of vesicles around cells; and (6) detection of light.

SOLUTION

Proteins carry out all these and many other functions. Any one type of protein usually carries out one function, but it is becoming increasingly obvious that many proteins perform at least two functions. Examples include enzymes that also serve as structural elements in the cytoskeleton of the cell, and integral membrane proteins that serve as points of attachment for the cytoskeleton. Such additional roles are referred to as moon lighting roles.

HIERARCHY OF PROTEIN STRUCTURE

4.3. An enzyme studied by means of gel filtration in aqueous buffer at pH 7.0 had an apparent M_r of 160,000. When studied by gel electrophoresis in SDS solution, a single band of apparent M_r of 40,000 was formed. Explain these findings.

SOLUTION

The detergent SDS causes the dissociation of quaternary protein structures and allows the determination of M_r of the component subunits. The data suggest that the enzyme comprises four identical subunits of $M_r = $ 40,000, yielding a tetramer of $M_r = 160,000$.

4.4. The artificial polypeptide poly-L-glutamate forms α helices at pH 2.0, but not at pH 7.0. Suggest an explanation for this.

SOLUTION

At pH 2, the side chains of poly-L-glutamate are largely uncharged and protonated. However, at pH 7 they are negatively charged. The negative charges lead to mutual repulsion of molecular groups and destabilization of the α helix.

4.5. The glycine residue at position 8 in the amino acid sequence of insulin has torsion angles of $\phi = 82°$ and $\psi = -105°$ that lie in the unfavorable region (marked X) of the Ramachandran plot in Fig. 4-9. How is this possible?

SOLUTION

Glycine has a very small side chain, i.e., a single hydrogen atom. The plot of Fig. 4-9 was determined for alanine that has a methyl group as the side chain. Thus, there are conformations allowed for glycine that are not possible for the methyl group of alanine.

SEQUENCING PROTEINS

4.6. (*a*) Which peptides would be released from the following peptide by treatment with trypsin?
Ala-Ser-Thr-Lys-Gly-Arg-Ser-Gly
(*b*) If each of the products were treated with fluoro-2,4-dinitrobenzene (FDNB) and subjected to acid hydrolysis, what DNP-amino acids could be isolated?

SOLUTION

(*a*) Trypsin hydrolyzes peptides at the carboxyl side of lysine and arginine residues. The resulting peptides would be Ala-Ser-Thr-Lys, Gly-Arg, and Ser-Gly.
(*b*) Treatment with FDNB and hydrolysis will liberate DNP derivatives of the N-terminal amino acids: DNP-Ala, DNP-Gly, and DNP-Ser. Note that the ε-amino group of lysine can also react with FDNB; however, the ε-DNP derivative of lysine can be distinguished from the α-DNP derivative by its chromatographic behavior.

4.7. The following data were obtained from partial cleavage and analysis of an octapeptide:

Composition:	Ala, Gly$_2$, Lys, Met, Ser, Thr, Tyr
CNBr:	(1) Ala, Gly, Lys, Thr
	(2) Gly, Met, Ser, Tyr
Trypsin:	(1) Ala, Gly
	(2) Gly, Lys, Met, Ser, Thr, Tyr
Chymotrypsin:	(1) Gly, Tyr
	(2) Ala, Gly, Lys, Met, Ser, Thr
N terminus:	Gly
C terminus:	Gly

Determine the sequence of the peptide.

SOLUTION

A set of overlapping peptides can be prepared from the above data by making use of the fact that one CNBr peptide must end in methionine, one tryptic peptide must end in either lysine or arginine, and one chymotryptic peptide must end in an aromatic amino acid. The sequence of the peptide is, therefore, Gly-Tyr-Ser-Met-Thr-Lys-Ala-Gly.

4.8. The enzyme *carboxypeptidase A* hydrolyzes amino acids from the C-terminal end of peptides, provided that the C-terminal residue is not proline, lysine, or arginine. Fig. 4-23 shows the sequential release of amino acids from a protein by means of treatment with carboxypeptidase A. Deduce the sequence at the C terminus.

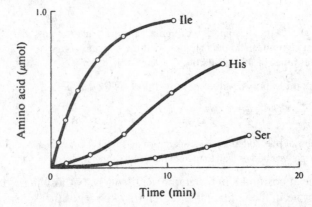

Fig. 4-23   Time course of the release of free amino acids from the digestion of a protein by carboxypeptidase.

SOLUTION

The sequence at the C terminus is -Ser-His-Ile.

4.9. Partial sequence determination of a peptide gave the following:
-Gly-Pro-Ser-Gly-Pro-Arg-Gly-Leu-Hyp-Gly-

What conclusions can be drawn about the possible conformation of the protein from which this peptide was derived?

SOLUTION

This sequence closely resembles that of collagen. In particular, the repeating Gly-Pro-X pattern and the occurrence of hydroxyproline are characteristic of collagen. It is possible, then, that the peptide was derived from a protein resembling collagen.

POSTTRANSLATIONAL MODIFICATION

4.10. Hydroxyproline is commonly found in collagen. It is not encoded by the genetic code, so how is it incorporated into collagen?

SOLUTION

Hydroxyproline is produced by the hydroxylation of the C-4 of proline by the vitamin C requiring enzyme *prolyl hydroxylase* after the protein has been synthesized. Thus it is referred to as *posttranslational modification*.

4.11. Which of the following amino acids could be a target for *phosphorylation*, and why? Phe, Tyr, Ala, Asp, Ser, Cys, Thr

SOLUTION

Phosphate groups are added enzymatically by *protein kinases* to the hydroxyl groups of Tyr, Ser, and Thr.

PROTEIN FOLDING

4.12. Insulin possesses two polypeptide chains denoted A and B that are linked by disulfide bonds. Upon denaturation by reduction of the SH groups of insulin, followed by reoxidation, only 7% of the hormone activity is recovered. This is the level of activity expected for random pairing of cysteine residues to form disulfide bonds. How can these data be reconciled with the hypothesis that *the amino acid sequence directs protein folding*?

SOLUTION

Insulin is synthesized as *preproinsulin* that is proteolytically processed in the β cells of the islets of Langerhans in the pancreas, to give *proinsulin*. After synthesis and folding, a section of the molecule (the C peptide) is excised, leaving the A and B peptides connected via disulfide bonds. Thus, native insulin, lacking the C peptide, lacks some of the information necessary to direct the folding process.

4.13. There are four disulfide bonds in ribonuclease. If these are reduced to their component sulfhydryl groups and allowed to reoxidize, how many different combinations of disulfide bonds are possible?

SOLUTION

In forming the first disulfide bond, a cysteine residue may pair with any one of the remaining seven. In forming the second bond, a cysteine residue may pair with one of the remaining five, and for the third bond, a cysteine residue may pair with one of three. Once three bonds have formed, there is only one way to form the last bond. Consequently, the number of possibilities is

$$7 \times 5 \times 3 = 105$$

Thus, the likelihood of achieving the correct pairing of cysteine residues, to make the requisite disulfide bonds, by chance alone is

$$1/105 = 0.0095, \text{ or } 0.95\%$$

4.14. Insulin and hemoglobin are both proteins that consist of more than one polypeptide chain. Contrast the interactions between the component polypeptide chains of the two proteins.

SOLUTION

The two chains of insulin are fragments of what was originally a single chain and are held together by covalent disulfide bonds. Hemoglobin has four polypeptide chains that are only held together by noncovalent interactions.

HEMOGLOBIN

4.15. Hemoglobin A (the major, normal form in adult humans) has an isoelectric point pI = 6.9. The variant hemoglobin M has a glutamate residue in place of the normal valine at position 67 of the α chain. What effect will this substitution have on the electrophoretic behavior of the protein at pH 7.5?

SOLUTION

Since pH 7.5 is above the isoelectric point of hemoglobin A, the protein carries a negative charge and will migrate to the anode. At pH 7.5 the glutamate side chain has a negative charge, while valine is uncharged. Hemoglobin M, therefore, carries an additional negative charge at pH 7.5 and will migrate *faster* toward the anode.

4.16. Human fetal hemoglobin (HbF) is a tetramer of two α chains and two γ chains. The γ chains are similar in folding shape to the β chains of HbA, but there are many sequence differences between them. One significant difference is that residue H21 is a positively charged histidine in the β chain, but it is a neutral serine in the γ chain. (*a*) Explain why HbF has a higher oxygen affinity than normal adult hemoglobin (HbA). (*b*) Why is this effect physiologically important?

SOLUTION

(*a*) The amino acid substitution at H21 affects the cleft between the β chains where 23BPG binds, there being two fewer positive charges in HbF. Thus, 23BPG is bound less strongly to HbF, and oxygen is more tightly bound and therefore is less readily released from HbF.

(*b*) This effect allows HbF to draw O_2 across the placenta from the maternal HbA for use by the fetus.

4.17. It is the tetramer of vertebrate hemoglobins that shows cooperation on binding with oxygen; the dimer shows no cooperative response. The *blood clam* has been shown to contain two types of hemoglobin: a tetramer consisting of two pairs of dissimilar chains and a homodimer of a third type of chain. Each of these chains has a tertiary structure that is similar to the globin fold. In the quaternary structure of the blood-clam hemoglobins, the E and F helices, which lie on the proximal and distal sides of the heme group, are involved in subunit interactions that form an extensive region of contact between the chains in the dimer. This is the *reverse situation* compared with the vertebrate hemoglobins, where the E and F helices are on the outside of the molecule. Notably, both the dimer and the tetramer blood-clam hemoglobins bind oxygen cooperatively. Explain how the mollusk dimer hemoglobin could demonstrate a cooperative effect.

SOLUTION

On combining with oxygen, the F helix, containing the proximal histidine residue, moves ~0.5 Å. With vertebrate hemoglobin, this movement, being on the surface of the molecule, has no direct effect since it acts only on the tetrameric structure (the $\alpha_1\beta_1$ dimers are quite rigid). In the clam hemoglobin, such movement *directly* affects the structure of the dimer and leads to an increase in the oxygen affinity, leading in turn to cooperation in oxygen binding.

4.18. There are many abnormal or mutant hemoglobins, some of which cause pathological clinical conditions. One is sickle-cell hemoglobin (HbS), in which the glutamate residue in the sixth position of the normal human hemoglobin (HbA) β chain has been replaced by valine. This position, referred to as $\beta6$, is on the outside of the hemoglobin molecule. Individuals who are homozygous for HbS suffer from poor circulation and anemia. This is so because the red blood cells become sickle-shaped in the venous circulation when the hemoglobin is deoxygenated, causing blockages in capillaries; and because of their abnormal shapes the cells are removed prematurely by the spleen, giving rise to anaemia. Why should such a small change, 2 amino acids in a total of 574, produce such a dramatic effect?

SOLUTION

Amino acid residues on the outside of soluble proteins are, almost without exception, polar. The replacement of the strongly polar glutamate in HbA by the nonpolar valine in HbS creates a hydrophobic patch on the exterior of the molecule. Such a *sticky patch* interacts with a complementary binding site on another molecule. HbS, but not oxyHbS, has such a site, and this causes HbS to polymerize into long fiberlike chains (called *tactoids*) that distort the red blood cell and produce the sickle shape. It is of interest that the *HbS* gene is common in tropical Africa, because the heterozygous individual who rarely has sickling episodes is protected against the most dangerous form of malaria. Should infection with malaria occur, the red cells tend to sickle because of the increased oxidative stress imposed on them by the parasite inside the cell; these cells are then removed from the circulation by the spleen. This situation is referred to in genetics as *balanced polymorphism*; it is the state of a population in which heterozygotes have selective advantage against a parasitic infection, but the infection has high morbidity and so does the homozygous genotype.

METHODS FOR DETERMINING PROTEIN STRUCTURE

4.19. How might you determine if a protein *in solution* contains α-helical structure?

SOLUTION

Far-uv *circular dichroism* is probably the most appropriate way to determine this structure. A helical protein exhibits double minima at wavelengths of 208 and 222 nm. However, this would only show that on average the protein contains some helical structure. To determine which residues contained helical structure, it would be necessary to use NMR spectroscopy to assign spectral peaks to residues and search for patterns of chemical shifts of peaks in the spectra, that are typical of α-helical structure. The first approach is rapid, the second takes longer but provides more information overall.

4.20. To determine the structure of a 300 kDa protein, would it be more appropriate to use X-ray crystallography or NMR methods?

SOLUTION

A 300 kDa protein is considered to be a *large protein*. It would be more suited to X-ray crystallography than NMR, which is better suited to small proteins. However, it would need to be crystallized first, and this can be a problem.

COMPARING AND VIEWING PROTEIN STRUCTURES

4.21. What are the ϕ (phi), ψ (psi), and ω (omega) angles?

SOLUTION

The ω angle describes the rotation of groups around the N—C' bond. As the peptide group is planar, this bond is ~180°. The ϕ angle describes the rotation of groups around the N—C$_\alpha$ bond, and the ψ angle describes the rotation of groups around the C$_\alpha$—C' bond. The ϕ and ψ angles define the structure of a protein backbone; α helices and β sheets each have characteristic values for ϕ and ψ angles.

4.22. Two proteins have a sequence identity of 40%. Are these proteins likely to have the same or different tertiary structures?

SOLUTION

Proteins that share sequence identities of >25% generally have the same fold. Thus, it is likely that these proteins will have very similar overall structures; however, some of the fine details of the structures will probably be different.

PURIFICATION AND CHEMICAL CHARCTERIZATION OF PROTEINS

4.23. The proteins ovalbumin (isoelectric point; pI = 4.6), urease (pI = 5.0), and myoglobin (pI = 7.0) were added to a column of the anion-exchange resin, DEAE-cellulose at pH 6.5. The column was eluted with a dilute pH 6.5 buffer and then with the same buffer as a gradient, containing an increasing concentration of NaCl. In what order will the proteins be eluted from the column?

SOLUTION

At pH 6.5, both ovalbumin and urease are negatively charged, and they will bind to the DEAE-cellulose. Myoglobin has a positive charge at pH 6.5 and will be eluted immediately. As the NaCl concentration increases, electrostatic interactions (salt bridges) are weakened. Hence urease will be eluted next and will be followed last by ovalbumin.

4.24. A sample of an enzyme of $M_r = 24,000$ and pI = 5.5 is contaminated with a protein of similar M_r but with a pI = 7.0, and a second protein of $M_r = 100,000$ and pI = 5.4. Suggest a purification strategy for the enzyme.

SOLUTION

Gel filtration will separate out the high-molecular-weight contaminant. The remaining mixture of low-molecular-weight proteins could be separated by anion-exchange chromatography as described in Prob. 4.23.

4.25. A series of standard proteins and an unknown enzyme were studied by gel filtration on a Sephadex G200 (the 200 refers to the maximum pore size size in kDa) column. The elution volume V_{el} for each protein is given below. (*a*) Plot the data in the form of log M_r versus elution volume. (*b*) From the line of best fit through the points for the standards, determine the M_r of the unknown enzyme. (*c*) Explain why ferritin and ovomucoid behave anomalously. The V_{el} versus M_r data were as follows:

Protein	M_r	V_{el} (mL)
Blue dextran*	10^6	85
Lysozyme	14,000	200
Chymotrypsin	25,000	190
Ovalbumin	45,000	170
Serum albumin	68,500	150
Aldolase	150,000	125
Urease	500,000	90
Ferritin[†]	700,000	92
Ovomucoid[†]	28,000	160
Unknown	—	139

*Blue dextran is not a protein but a high-M_r carbohydrate that has a covalently bound blue dye, and it elutes with the *void volume* of the column.
[†]Do not use for calibration curve.

SOLUTION

(*a*) Fig. 4-24 shows the line of best fit to the data and indicates coordinates for the unknown enzyme.

(*b*) From Fig. 4-24, Mr (M and subscript r both italics as in the text above the table) of the unknown enzyme = 126,000. (Please make that = an 'approximately equal' sign, namely one squiggle above a straight line)

(*c*) Ferritin contains a core of iron hydroxide, therefore its density is higher than that of the standards. Ovomucoid is a glycoprotein of different density, and probably different shape from the standards.

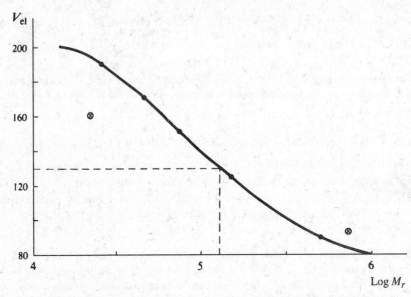

Fig. 4-24   Filtration of proteins from a column of Sephadex G200. The elution volume V_{el} is plotted for a series of different proteins of known M_r that had been applied in a mixture to the column.

4.26. Using the data from Prob. 4.25, estimate the molecular weight of an enzyme for which the elution volume was 155 mL.

SOLUTION

From Fig. 4-24, the value of log M_r corresponding to 155 mL elution volume is 4.8. Therefore M_r is 63,000, providing that the density and shape of the enzyme are similar to those of the calibration standards.

BIOPHYSICAL CHARACTERIZATION OF PROTEINS

4.27. A pure heme-containing protein is found to contain 0.426% by weight of iron. What is its minimum molecular weight (relative molecular weight M_r)?

SOLUTION

The mimimum M_r is that of a molecule that contains only a single iron atom. Thus, if 0.426 g of iron is contained in every 100 g of protein, then 1 mol (56 g) of iron is contained in

$$100 \times 56 \,/0.426 = 13{,}145 \text{ g of protein}$$

The mass of protein containing 1 g atom of iron is 13,145 g; therefore this represents the molar mass of the protein which is 13,145 (g mol^{-1}). This number is close to the M_r of the heme-containing protein, cytochrome c, so it is a plausible value. However, had the molecule of protein contained more than one atom of iron, the M_r would have been an *integer fraction* of 13,145.

4.28. Threonine constitutes 1.8% by weight of the amino acid content of insulin. Given that the M_r of threonine is 119, what is the minimum M_r of insulin?

SOLUTION

Since water is lost on the condensation of amino acids to form a peptide bond, the residue weight of threonine is $119 - 18 = 101$. If we assume there is a single threonine residue in each molecule, then 101 constitutes 1.8% of the M_r, and

$$M_r = 101/0.018 = 5600$$

Physical measurements in dissociating solvents confirm this value.

4.29. During an attempt to determine the molecular weight of the milk protein β-lactoglobulin, by means of gel filtration, the following data were obtained with different sample concentrations:

Protein Concentration	Apparent M_r
10 g L^{-1}	36,000
5 g L^{-1}	35,000
1 g L^{-1}	32,000
0.1 g L^{-1}	25,000

Electrophoresis in polyacrylamide gels that contained SDS led to an estimate of the apparent M_r of 18,000; this was consistent with the known amino acid sequence of this protein. Explain these data.

SOLUTION

These data show that the polypeptide chain of β-lactoglobulin has an M_r of 18,000, and that in high concentration, the protein exists as a dimer of $M_r = 36,000$. However, on dilution, the dimer, maintained by reversible, noncovalent interactions, undergoes a partial dissociation as follows: $A_2 \rightleftharpoons 2A$.

4.30. Calculate the M_r of a protein, given the following experimental data obtained at 25°C.

$$s = 4.2 \times 10^{-13} \text{ s}$$
$$D = 1.2 \times 10^{-10} \text{ m}^2 \text{ s}^{-1}$$
$$\bar{v} = 0.72 \text{ mL g}^{-1}$$
$$\rho = 0.998 \text{ g mL}^{-1}$$

SOLUTION

From Eq. (4.8)

$$M = RTs/D(1 - \bar{v}\rho)$$

where the gas constant $R = 8.314$ J K^{-1} mol^{-1} and 25°C corresponds to 293 K. Therefore, $M = 8.314 \times 293 \times 4.2 \times 10^{-13}/1.2 \times 10^{-10}(1 - 0.72 \times 0.998)$
$\qquad$ = 30 kg mol^{-1} or 30,000 g mol^{-1}
In other words the M_r is 30,000.

SUPPLEMENTARY PROBLEMS

4.31. List (*a*) the major proteins of muscle; (*b*) the major protein the dermis of skin, connective tissue like fascia and ligaments, and bone; and (*c*) the major protein of the epidermis of skin, hair, and feathers.

4.32. A pure heme protein was found to contain 0.326% iron. If the molecule contains only one iron atom, what is its molecular weight?

4.33. In what direction (toward the anode, toward the cathode, or toward neither) will the following proteins move in an electric field?
(*a*) Serum albumin (pI = 4.9) at pH 8.0
(*b*) Urease (pI = 5.0) at pH 3.0, and pH 9.0
(*c*) Ribonuclease (pI = 9.5) at pH 4.5, 9.5, and 11.0
(*d*) Pepsin (pI = 1.0) at pH 3.5, 7.0, and 9.5

4.34. In what order would the following globular proteins emerge on gel filtration of a mixture on Sephadex G200? Ribonuclease ($M_r = 12,000$), aldolase ($M_r = 159,000$), hemoglobin ($M_r = 64,000$), β-lactoglobulin ($M_r = 36,000$), serum albumin ($M_r = 65,000$)

4.35. Distinguish between the terms *primary, secondary,* and *tertiary* structures.

4.36. Of the residues of the following amino acids—methionine, histidine, arginine, phenylalanine, valine, glutamine, glutamic acid—which would you expect to find (*a*) on the surface of a protein and which would you expect to find (*b*) in the interior?

4.37. What functions would you expect to be served by residues such as (*a*) phenylalanine at the protein surface or (*b*) aspartic acid in the interior?

4.38. What is meant by a *domain* of protein structure? Give an example of a domain in a real protein.

4.39. What is meant by the statement that a particular conformation of an amino acid residue lies in an *unfavorable region* of the Ramachandran plot?

4.40. (*a*) Why does urea cause protein denaturation? (*b*) Why do our kidneys not denature in the presence of urinary urea?

4.41. (*a*) What are the important noncovalent interactions within proteins? (*b*) How do weak interactions result in a stable structure?

4.42. The *pitch p* of a helix is defined as $p = d\,n$, in which n is the number of repeating units per turn and d is the distance along the helix axis per repeating unit. Therefore, the pitch is a measure of the distance from one point on the helix to the corresponding point on the next turn of the helix.
(*a*) What is the pitch of an α helix and the axial distance per residue?
(*b*) How long would myoglobin be if it were one continuous α helix?
(*c*) How long would myoglobin be if it were one strand of a β sheet (axial distance/residue = 0.35 nm)?
(*d*) How long would myoglobin be if it were fully extended (axial distance/residue = 0.36 nm)?

4.43. Predict which of the following polyamino acids will form α helices and which will form no ordered structures in solution at room temperature.
(*a*) Polyleucine, pH = 7.0
(*b*) Polyisoleucine, pH = 7.0
(*c*) Polyarginine, pH = 7.0
(*d*) Polyarginine, pH = 13.0
(*e*) Polyglutamic acid, pH = 1.5
(*f*) Polythreonine, pH = 7.0

4.44. What forces hold protein subunits in a quaternary structure?

4.45. Poly-L-proline can form a single-stranded helix that is similar to a single strand of the collagen triple helix, but it cannot form a triple helix. Why not?

4.46. Poly(Gly-Pro-Pro) is capable of forming triple helices. Why?

4.47. Compare and contrast the structures of (*a*) insulin, (*b*) hemoglobin, and (*c*) collagen, all of which are proteins consisting of two or more chains but held together by different types of bonds.

4.48. What are the reasons for the marked stability of an α helix?

4.49. (*a*) In what important ways do the α helix and β sheet structure differ? (*b*) How are they similar?

ANSWERS TO SUPPLEMENTARY PROBLEMS

4.31. (*a*) Actin and myosin (also tropomyosin, troponin, myoglobin); (*b*) collagen; (*c*) keratin.

4.32. ~17,100 Da

4.33. (*a*) Anode
(*b*) Cathode; anode
(*c*) Cathode; neither; anode
(*d*) Anode in all cases

4.34. Order will be, biggest to smallest: aldolase, serum albumin/hemoglobin, β-lactoglobulin, ribonuclease.

4.35. Primary structure refers to the amino acid sequence; secondary is the local conformation of the polypeptide chain; tertiary is the overall three-dimensional fold of the polypeptide chain.

4.36. (*a*) Arginine, glutamine, glutamic acid, histidine
(*b*) Methionine, phenylalanine, valine

4.37. (*a*) Contribute to the hydrophobic core of the protein
(*b*) Catalytic site residue in an enzyme

4.38. Part of a protein sequence can function independently of the rest of the protein. For example, a protein may contain a DNA binding domain and an enzyme domain.

4.39. The φ and ψ angles (torsion angles of the polypeptide backbone) of the protein fall outside of the normal torsion angles seen in proteins, and atoms within the amino acid would be subjected to steric clashes.

4.40. (*a*) Urea can solubilize the hydrophobic portions of a protein, making the unfolded state with exposed hydrophobic regions more stable than in the absence of urea.

(*b*) The concentrations of urea in urine are not usually high enough to denature proteins.

4.41. (*a*) Electrostatic interactions/salt bridges; hydrogen bonds; hydrophobic and van der Waal's interactions.

(*b*) Proteins are only marginally stable, and many weak interactions (both favorable and unfavorable) combine to form an overall stable structure.

4.42. (*a*) 0.15 nm × 3.6 residues per turn = 0.54 nm/turn, as defined $d = 0.15$ nm

(*b*) Myoglobin has 153 residues; 153×0.15 nm = 22.95 nm

(*c*) 53.55 nm

(*d*) 55.08 nm

4.43. Helices: (a), (b), (d), (e)

No structure: (c), (f)

4.44. Noncovalent bonds: hydrogen bonds; hydrophobic interactions; charge-charge interactions; and van der Waals interactions

4.45. Proline is too bulky to accommodate the close approach at every third residue.

4.46. Glycine is small enough to accommodate the close approach at every third residue.

4.47. (*a*) Insulin is made up of two chains formed from a single-chain precursor and is held together by disulfide bonds.

(*b*) Hemoglobin is made up of two α and two β polypeptide chains held together by noncovalent interactions.

(*c*) Collagen has three chains and forms a triple helix. It is held together by hydrogen bonds and additional chemical (covalent) crosslinks.

4.48. Maximal backbone-backbone hydrogen-bond formation; all bond angles and bond lengths are normal; no clashes occur between atoms of the backbone; i.e., the helix maps to a favorable region of the Ramachandran plot.

4.49. (*a*) Differences: Hydrogen bonds in the α helix are formed between peptide groups of the same segment and are approximately parallel to the direction of the helix; in β sheets hydrogen bonds are formed between different segments of chains and are perpendicular to the direction of the chain. In the α helix, hydrogen bonds are approximately parallel to the axis of the helix while they are perpendicular to the chain in β sheets.

(*b*) Similarities: Both the α helix and β sheet are regular repeating structures that are stabilized by hydrogen bonds, and the bond angles map to favorable regions of the Ramachandran plot.

CHAPTER 5

Regulation of Reaction Rates: Enzymes

5.1   Definition of an Enzyme

Question: What are enzymes?

Enzymes are *proteins* and, much less commonly, *RNA* molecules that are catalysts of biochemical reactions. In cells they usually exist in very low concentrations where they increase the *rate* of a reaction without altering its equilibrium position; i.e., both forward *and* reverse reaction rates are enhanced by the same factor. This factor is usually around 10^3–10^{12}.

There are over 2500 different biochemical reactions with specific proteinaceous enzymes adapted for their rate enhancement. Since different species of organism produce different structural variants of enzymes, the number of different enzyme proteins in all of biology is many millions. Each enzyme is characterized by *specificity* for a narrow range of chemically similar *substrates* (reactants) and also other molecules that modulate their activities; these are called *effectors* and they can be *activators*, *inhibitors*, or both. In more complex enzymes, one compound may have either effect, depending on other physical or chemical conditions. Enzymes range in size from large multi-subunit complexes (called *multimeric* enzymes; $M_r \sim 10^6$) to small single-subunit forms.

EXAMPLE 5.1   Although the phenomena of fermentation and digestion of foodstuffs had long been known, the first clear recognition of an enzyme being involved was made by A. Payen and J. F. Persoz [*Ann. Chim. (Phys)*, **53**, 73, 1833] when they found that an alcohol precipitate of malt extract contained a thermolabile substance that converted starch to sugar.

EXAMPLE 5.2   The above-mentioned substance was called diastase (Greek, *separation*) because of its ability to separate soluble dextrin from insoluble envelopes of starch grains. The term *diastase* became generally applied to these enzyme mixtures until 1898 when V. Emile Duclaux suggested the use of –ase in the name of an enzyme; this classification procedure still holds today.

EXAMPLE 5.3   Many proteinaceous enzymes were purified from a large number of sources, but it was John B. Sumner who was the first to crystallize one. The enzyme was urease from jack beans. For his travail, which took over 6 years (1924–1930), he was awarded the 1946 Nobel Prize. The work demonstrated once and for all that proteinaceous enzymes are distinct chemical entities.

Question: Which part of an enzyme molecule is responsible for its substrate specificity?

The particular arrangement of its amino acid side chains in the *active site* of a protein determines the type of molecules that can bind *and* react there; there are usually about five such side chains in any particular enzyme. In addition, many protein-enzymes have nonprotein small molecules associated with or near the active site. These molecules are called *cofactors* if they are *non*covalently linked to the protein or *prosthetic groups* if covalently bound; alternatively, they might be *metal ions*.

In the case of RNA enzymes, the range of reactions and range of complexity of the active sites are much less.

EXAMPLE 5.4   Carbon dioxide gas dissolves readily in water and spontaneously hydrates to form carbonic acid, which rapidly dissociates to a proton and a bicarbonate ion:

$$CO_2 + H_2 \rightleftharpoons H^+ + HCO_3^-$$

The rate of the forward hydration reaction, for 20 mmol L^{-1} CO_2 at 25°C and pH 7.2, is ~0.6 mmol L^{-1} s^{-1}. In mammalian red blood cells the enzyme *carbonic anhydrase* is present at a concentration of 1–2 g (L cells)$^{-1}$; its M_r is 30,000, thus its *molar concentration* is ~50×10^{-6} M. The active site of carbonic anhydrase contains a zinc ion that is intimately connected to the catalytic process. The flux through the forward reaction in the presence of this concentration of enzyme, under the abovementioned conditions, is ~50 mol L^{-1} s^{-1}, a *rate enhancement* over the noncatalyzed process of 8×10^4.

EXAMPLE 5.5   Aspartate carbamoyl transferase, M_r 310,000, catalyzes the formation of carbamoyl aspartate from carbamoyl phosphate and aspartate in the first committed step of pyrimidine biosynthesis (Chap. 14). The enzyme from the bacterium *Escherichia coli* consists of six subunits, three *regulatory* and three *catalytic*. CTP is a *negative effector*; i.e., it inhibits the enzyme and does so through binding to the regulatory subunits. ATP is a *positive effector* that acts through the regulatory subunits, while succinate *inhibits* the reaction by direct competition with aspartate at the active site.

The surface area of even the smallest enzymes, such as ribonuclease M_r 12,000, that is occupied by the chemical groups to which the reactants bind, is less than 5% of the total area; this region is called the *active site*.

5.2   RNA Catalysis

Question: Which biochemical reactions do RNA enzymes catalyze?

RNA carries out its enzymic roles with many fewer chemical resources than its protein counterparts; it has a ribose-phosphate backbone (Chap. 3), with four rather similar heterocyclic nucleobases, plus attendant water molecules and metal ions. They carry out the water-elimination condensation reactions in splicing certain classes of introns (Chap. 7) and in the site-specific cleavage and ligation of small replicating RNA circles in some species of organism.

RNA provides much more than a messenger service for DNA in protein synthesis (Chap. 9). It has a role in almost every aspect of genetic function including: (1) self-processing by splicing together exposed ends of itself; (2) cleavage by hydrolysis of precursors; (3) site-specific editing and modification; (4) translation of the genetic code; and (5) regulation of genes.

Ribozymes could have played a key role in the early stages of evolution of life on earth, bridging the gap between a primitive metabolism and a crude translational apparatus where the RNA acted as both an informational molecule and a catalyst.

In the contemporary biosphere, though, overwhelmingly most enzymic action is carried out by proteins.

EXAMPLE 5.6   An example of an RNA-dependent catalytic reaction that is arguably one of the most important in any cell is the RNase P process in tRNA; it is present in all known forms of life. The reaction takes place on the large ribosomal subunit, hence the ribosome is an ancient ribozyme! The mechanism of the reaction involves stabilization of a transition-state complex (see Prob. 5.3) by the formation of hydrogen bonds, like that shown below.

EXAMPLE 5.7   An allosterically (see Sec. 5.12) controlled ribozyme is the GlmS *riboswitch* (Fig. 5-3) in which a metabolite, guanine, adenine, or thiamine pyrophosphate, regulates the expression of a gene. The metabolite controls the activity of the ribozyme that cleaves the mRNA in which it resides. Such riboswitches are typically located in the 5′ untranslated regions of mRNA. These ribozymes are members of a class that work by *transesterification* in which the adjacent 2′-hydroxyl group on the ribose backbone of an RNA residue is activated to attack the adjacent 3′-phospho-diester bond.

5.3   Enzyme Classification

Question: On what basis are enzymes given their particular names?

All enzymes are named systematically according to a classification scheme designed by the Enzyme Commission (EC) of the International Union of Pure and Applied Chemistry (IUPAC), based on the type of reaction they catalyze. Each enzyme type has a specific, four-integer, *EC number* and a complex, but unambiguous, name that obviates confusion between enzymes catalyzing similar but not identical reactions. In practice many enzymes are known by a *common name* that is derived from the name of its principal-specific reactant with the suffix *-ase*. Some common names do not even have -ase appended, but these tend to be enzymes that were studied in *the early days* before systematic classification of them had been undertaken (see Examples 5.1–5.3).

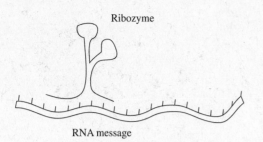

Ribozyme

RNA message

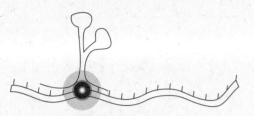

Ribozyme-mediated cut
introduced into RNA message

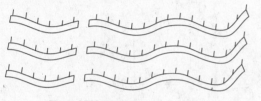

Cleaved RNA messages

Fig. 5-1 Ribozymes rely for their action on the great diversity of tertiary structures that RNA chains can adopt. A specific shape, so-called hammerhead RNA, has hydrolytic activity and cleaves mRNA at a specific sequence of bases.

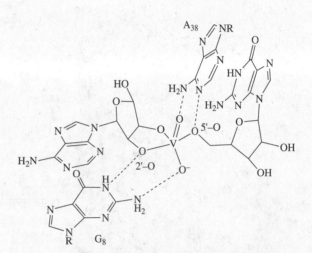

Fig. 5-2 The ribozyme active site is formed when the RNA folds into a hairpin structure. The cleaved (scissile) phosphate-ester bond is flanked by a guanine (G_8) and an adenine (A_{38}) moiety that stabilize a transition state by hydrogen bonding. The structure shown was prepared from the coordinates of the crystal structure of a vanadium salt, hence the V in the center of the structure. The dashed lines denote hydrogen bonds.

The first integer in the EC number designates to which of the six major classes an enzyme belongs; see Table 5-1 for details.

The second integer in an EC enzyme number indicates the *type of bond* acted upon by the enzyme (e.g., Table 5-2).

EXAMPLE 5.8 *Arginase* is a hydrolase that resides in the liver of urea-producing organisms (ureoteles). It catalyzes the reaction shown in Fig. 5-4.

The official EC name of this enzyme is *L-arginine amidinohydrolase*; the last word refers to the fact that the amidino group (the three-nitrogen group at the top of the structure above) is cleaved from arginine by the introduction of a water molecule across the C—N bond. In a reaction, a nonpeptide C—N bond is cleaved; thus, the second EC number for arginase is 5. Its whole EC number is 3.5.3.1.

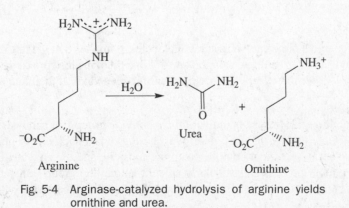

Fig. 5-4 Arginase-catalyzed hydrolysis of arginine yields ornithine and urea.

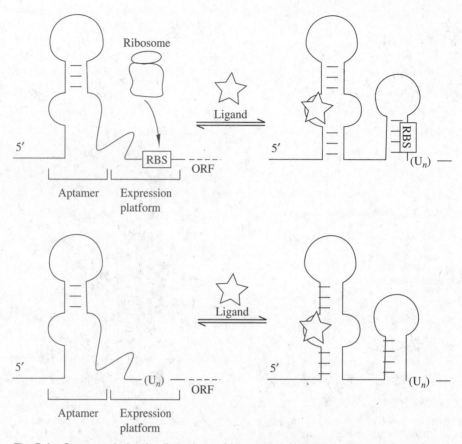

Fig. 5-4   Gene regulation by riboswitches. Upper panels: *translation control* occurs via riboswitch-mediated modulation of a stem that binds to a ribosomal binding site. When a metabolite binds to the *aptamer*, the ribosomal binding site is sequestered in a stem structure that prevents the ribosome from binding to the mRNA, thus stopping initiation of translation. The aptamer with its *stem-loop structure* assumes a different conformation when the metabolite (ligand) is bound. Lower panels: *transcription control* by riboswitches. Most commonly, gene expression is on when ligand concentrations are low, and high ligand concentrations turn gene expression off by forming a *strong stem* preceding a run of U nucleotides (U_n) that terminate transcription. Hence the open reading frame (ORF) that codes for protein is not produced.

5.4   Modes of Enhancement of Rates of Bond Cleavage

There are basically four groups of mechanism whereby enzymes increase the rates of chemical reactions.

Propinquity Effects

This is the facilitation of the proximity of reacting molecules. It implies that the rate of a reaction is enhanced by abstracting the molecules from dilute solution and holding them in close proximity in the active site of the enzyme. This process raises the *effective* concentration of the reactants at their site of interaction.

Covalent Catalysis

The side chains of amino acids present a number of *nucleophilic* groups for catalysis; these include $RCOO^-$, $R-NH_2$, aromatic—OH, histidyl, R—OH, and RS^-. These groups attack electrophilic (electron deficient) parts of substrates to form a covalent bond between the substrate and the enzyme, thus forming a *reaction intermediate*. This type of process is particularly evident among the group-transfer enzymes (EC class 2; see Table 5-1). In the formation of a covalently bonded intermediate, attack by the enzyme nucleophile

Table 5-1   Major Enzyme Classes

First EC Number	Enzyme Class	Type of Reaction Catalyzed
1	Oxidoreductase	Oxidation-reduction. A hydrogen or electron donor is one of the substrates. $AH_2 + B \rightarrow A + BH_2$ or $AH_2 + B^+ \rightarrow A + BH + H^+$
2	Transferase	Chemical group transfer of the general form $A\!-\!X + B \rightarrow A + B\!-\!X$
3	Hydrolase	Hydrolytic cleavage of C—C, C—N, C—O, and other bonds. $A\!-\!B + H_2O \rightarrow AH + BOH$
4	Lyase	Cleavage (*not* hydrolytic) of C—C, C—N, C—O, and other bonds leaving double bonds, or alternatively addition of groups to a double bond. $A = B + X\!-\!Y \rightarrow A\!-\!B$ with X and Y attached
5	Isomerase	Change of geometrical spatial arrangement of a molecule. $A \rightarrow B$
6	Ligase	Ligating (joining together) two molecules *with* the accompanying hydrolysis of a high energy bond N denotes nucleotide. $A + B + NTP \rightarrow A\!-\!B + NDP + Pi$ or $A + B + NTP \rightarrow A\!-\!B + NMP + PPi$

Table 5-2   Hydrolase Subclassification

First Two EC Integers	Type of Bond Acted Upon
3.1	Ester, —C(=O)—O—*R, or with S or P in place of C, or —C(=O)—S—R
3.2	Glycosyl, monosaccharide—C—O—*R, or with N or S in place of O
3.3	Ether, R—O—*R', or with S in place of O
3.4	Peptide, C—*N
3.5	Nonpeptide, C—*N
3.6	Acid anhydride, R—C(=O)—O—*C(=O)—R'
3.7	C—*C
3.8	Halide (X), C—*X, or with P in place of C
3.9	P—*N
3.10	S—*N
3.11	C—*P

*Denotes the bond acted upon by the enzyme.

(Enz-X in Example 5.10) on the substrate can result in acylation, phosphorylation, or glycosylation of the nucleophile.

Writing the chemical mechanism of a reaction involves describing the rearrangement of electrons as the substrate is converted to the product via a *transition state(s)*. A useful way of depicting the pathway of rearrangement of bonds is by use of curved arrows that show the directions of electron flow.

EXAMPLE 5.9   The electron flow diagram for the hydrolysis of a peptide bond is shown in Fig. 5-5.

The nucleophilic (electron-deficient) H_2O attacks the electrophilic carbonyl carbon, which is rendered electron-depleted by the electron-withdrawing action of the attached carbonyl oxygen. Note the so-called tetrahedral intermediates in the second and third structures; in these, the carbon has the usual tetrahedral arrangement of four bonds.

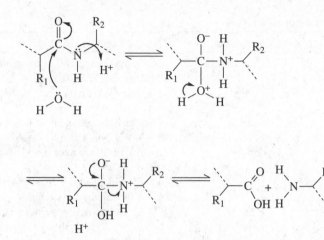

Fig. 5-5   Flow of electrons that occurs between atoms when a peptide bond is hydrolyzed.

EXAMPLE 5.10   A phosphoenzyme intermediate is formed in one type of covalent catalysis in enzymes:

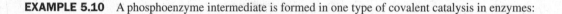

Fig. 5-6   Covalent catalysis via a phosphoenzyme intermediate.

Numerous examples of this basic mechanism of catalysis can be found among the enzymes of EC class 2. One example is *hexokinase*.

The covalent intermediates is attacked by a second nucleophile to bring about the release of the product. When the second nucleophile is water, the overall reaction is called *hydrolysis*. In many cases the nucleophile is not simply an amino acid side chain of the enzyme but a prosthetic group; an example is *pyridoxal phosphate* in the transaminases (Chap. 14).

General Acid-Base Catalysis

Acid-base catalysis is defined as the process in which there is *transfer of a proton* in the transition state of the reaction. It does not involve the formation of a covalent bond per se, but an overall enzyme-catalyzed reaction can involve this as well.

EXAMPLE 5.11   An example of general acid-base catalysis from organic chemistry illustrates the above-mentioned point, but note that *hemiacetals* also form in some enzymic reactions.
Overall reaction:

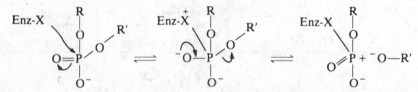

Acetaldehyde Methanol   **Hemiacetal**

Fig. 5-7   Overall reaction of acetaldehyde with Methanol to form a hemiacetal.

Reaction mechanism A: A *base* (OH^-) accelerates hemiacetal formation as follows:

$$CH_3-OH + OH^- \rightleftharpoons CH_3-O\colon^- + H_2O$$
Nucleophile

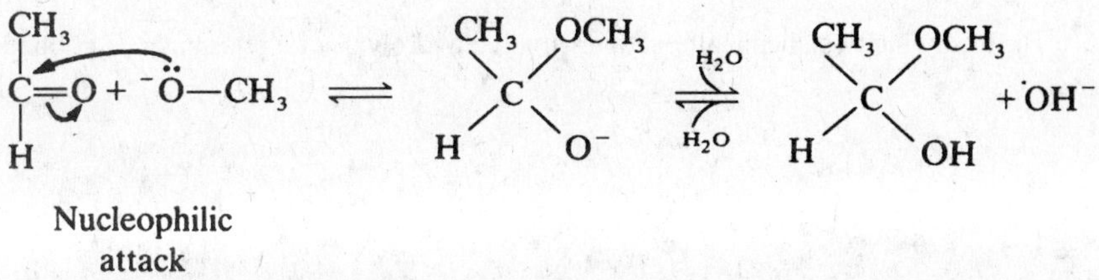

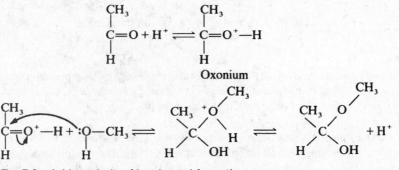

**Nucleophilic
attack**

Fig. 5-8   Base catalysis of hemiacetal formation. Nucleophilic attack by methanol
occurs onto the electrophile, acetaldehyde.

Note: The OH^- is recycled in the reaction; hence it can be considered to be a catalyst in the true sense of the word.

Reaction mechanism B: Acid catalysis also occurs in the reaction. It involves the formation of the oxonium salt, followed by reaction with the alcohol:

Oxonium

Fig. 5-9   Acid catalysis of hemiacetal formation.

In the preceding example, the rate of hemiacetal formation is enhanced in strong acid *or* strong base. In other cases, only one, either base or acid, might be the catalyst.

EXAMPLE 5.12   The hydrolysis of *nitramide* is susceptible to base, but not acid, catalysis. Elevation of pH leads to an increase in reaction rate with no net consumption of base, as can be inferred from the following reaction scheme:

$$NH_2NO_2 + OH^- \rightarrow H_2O + NHNO_2^-$$
$$NHNO_2^- \rightarrow NO_2 + OH^-$$

OH^- is not the only base that will catalyze the hydrolysis; other bases such as acetate also react; e.g.,

$$NH_2NO_2 + CH_3COO^- \rightarrow CH_3COOH + NHNO_2^-$$
$$NHNO_2^- \rightarrow NO_2 + OH^-$$
$$OH^- + CH_3COOH \rightarrow H_2O + CH_3COO^-$$

The above reaction illustrates a *Bronsted-Lowry acid*, which is defined as any chemical moiety that will *donate* a proton; while a *base* will *accept* a proton from another moiety.

Acid-base catalysis does not contribute to rate enhancement by a factor greater than ~100, but together with other mechanisms that operate in the active site of an enzyme it contributes considerably to increasing the rate of catalysis. The side chains of the residues of the amino acids, glutamic acid, histidine, aspartic acid, lysine, tyrosine, and cysteine, in their protonated forms can act as acid catalysts, and in their unprotonated forms as base catalysts (see Example 5.11). Clearly, the effectiveness of the side chain as a catalyst will depend on the pK_a (Chap. 3) in the environment of the active site and on the pH at which the enzyme is made to operate.

Strain, Molecular Distortion, and Shape Change

Strain in the system of bonds of reactants, and the release of the strain as the transition state converts to the products (like cutting a stretched helical spring), can provide rate enhancement of chemical reactions.

EXAMPLE 5.13   The following two chemical reactions involve hydrolysis of a phosphate ester bond.

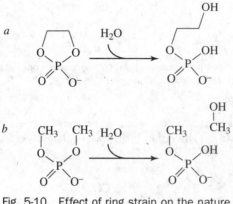

Fig. 5-10   Effect of ring strain on the nature of products of a reaction.

Under standard conditions, reaction (a) is 10^8 times faster than reaction (b). The explanation for this is that the cyclic compound has considerable *bond strain* (potential energy in this configuration is high) that is released on ring opening during hydrolysis. This type of strain is not present in the diester in (b).

In the case of enzymes, not only may the substrate be distorted (have strain), but also an extra degree of freedom is introduced via the enzyme with all its amino acid side chains. The binding of a substrate to an enzyme involves *interaction energy* that may facilitate catalysis. Also, for an increase in catalytic rate there must be an overall *destabilization* of the enzyme-substrate complex and an increase in the stability of the transition state. This idea is illustrated in Fig. 5-11.

In the *uncatalyzed reaction* (Fig. 5-11, left), the reactant has a relatively low probability of assuming the *strained* conformation necessary for interaction between the two reactive groups. For the reaction to take place, though, the molecule must cross this *activation energy barrier*. In the *catalyzed reaction* (Fig. 5-11, right), the *binding* of the reactant to the enzyme leads to the formation of a combined structure (enzyme-substrate complex) in which the tendency for the substrate to form into the *transition* state is greater; i.e., less energy is involved in bringing the reactive groups together. Therefore the reaction proceeds faster.

The destabilization of the enzyme-substrate complex can be imagined to be due to distortion of bond angles and lengths from their previously more stable configuration; this may be achieved by electrostatic attraction or repulsion by groups on the substrate and enzyme. Or, it could involve *desolvation* (removal of water) of a charged group in a hydrophobic active site. A further consideration is that of *entropy* change of the reaction; this is discussed in the next section.

Question: Does tight binding between an enzyme and its substrate imply rapid catalysis of the reaction?

If a substrate were to bind *without* significant transformation of binding energy into distortion strain, then binding would be stronger. But this would not necessarily mean that $\Delta G^{\ddagger}$ (see Fig. 5-11) is altered by the binding interaction. However, if some of the free energy of binding were used to distort the substrate more toward the shape of the transition state, or to distort the enzyme to be more complementary to the shape of the transition state, then binding of the enzyme to the substrate would be weakened, while binding to the transition state of the substrate would be correspondingly enhanced. Hence, it is important to dispel a common belief: tight binding of the *substrate* is *not* necessarily useful in enhancing the rate of an enzymic reaction.

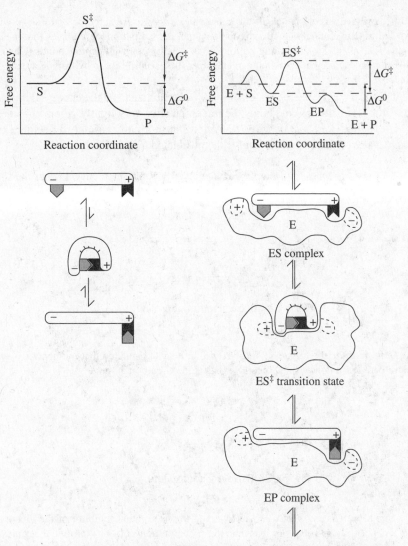

Fig. 5-11 Activation energy is lowered in catalyzed reactions. The graphs drawn above each of the reaction schemes indicate the energy of the substrate (depicted here as *potential* energy of the *bent* substrate) at each stage of the reaction. The arrows indicate, according to their length, the probability and in this case the rate of the reactions. $\Delta G^{\ddagger}$ is the activation energy of the transition state(s) molecule, and ΔG^0 is the *overall* free energy of the reaction (Chap. 2). NB changes in the enzyme and substrate lead to binding being tighter in the transition state than in either the ES or EP complexes.

EXAMPLE 5.14 Suppose a substrate half-saturates the active sites of a solution of enzyme when present at 10^{-7} mol L^{-1} (i.e., $K_d = 10^{-7}$ mol L^{-1}), but the concentration under *physiological conditions* is 10^{-3} mol L^{-1}. Under physiological conditions, the enzyme active sites are fully saturated (i.e., all sites are filled on average), so the enzyme rate enhancement is not what it could be if a large proportion of the binding energy were used for *destabilizing* the enzyme-substrate (E.S) complex.

If some of the binding energy were used to introduce strain or distortion within the enzyme or substrate molecules, such that tighter binding of the transition state were achieved, then the binding affinity of the enzyme for the substrate would be reduced.

Many enzymes have binding affinities for their substrates that are around the mean physiological concentrations, most probably as a result of *evolutionary pressure* for efficient catalysis.

EXAMPLE 5.15 X-ray analysis of crystals of the pancreatic *exopeptidase* carboxypeptidase A, with a bound *pseudo substrate* (a *false* substrate that is not degraded by the enzyme, i.e., an inhibitor) indicates that the *susceptible* peptide bond is twisted out of the *normal* planar configuration that is usually seen with peptide bonds (Chap. 4). This distortion leads to a loss of *resonance energy* in the bond, and enhances its susceptibility to hydrolytic attack.

Because in catalysis, the enzyme-substrate complex is destabilized and the energy so involved is released on forming the transition state, the enzyme binds the transition state very tightly. Some enzymes can be dramatically inhibited by *transition-state analogs*. The transition state normally has only a fleeting existence ($<10^{-13}$ s), but the analogs are stable structures that *resemble* the postulated transition-state.

EXAMPLE 5.16 *Proline racemase*, a bacterial enzyme, catalyzes the interconvention of the D- and L-isomers of proline:

D-Proline   L-Proline

Fig. 5-12   Racemisation of proline.

In proceeding from the D- to the L-isomer, and vice versa, it was postulated that momentarily a *planar* (rather than the usual tetrahedral) configuration of the molecule exists at the α-carbon atom.

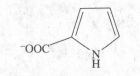

Fig. 5-13   Pyrrole 2-carboxylate.

A planar analog of proline is *pyrrole 2-carboxylate*, and this is a potent inhibitor of the racemase. It gives rise to 50% inhibition at a concentration 160 times less than the concentration of D- or L-proline that gives 50% saturation of binding. Therefore it is an excellent example of a *transition-state analog* of the enzyme.

Question: Do *both* the enzyme and substrate undergo a shape change when they interact?

Yes, the concept of *induced fit* of an active site to a substrate emphasizes the *adaptation* of the active site to match up with the functional groups of the substrate. A *poor* substrate or an inhibitor does not induce the catalytically favorable conformational response in the enzyme and its active site.

EXAMPLE 5.17 Hexokinase provides an example of the *induced fit* phenomenon; it catalyzes phosphoryl transfer from ATP to the C-6 hydroxyl of glucose, as follows:

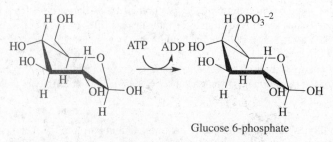

Glucose 6-phosphate

Fig. 5-14   Reaction catalyzed by hexokinase.

Hexokinase can also catalyze the transfer of the terminal phosphoryl of ATP to water; i.e., it acts as an *ATPase* but at a rate 5×10^6 times slower than for the above reaction. The basicity and nucleophilicity of water, versus the C-6 hydroxyl of glucose, are sufficiently similar to suggest that there would be no marked differences in rate. Therefore the explanation for the rate difference is that glucose induces a conformational change that *establishes* the correct active-site geometry in the enzyme, whereas a water molecule is too small to do so.

The induction of the correct geometry in the active site of an enzyme is *paid for* by a *good* substrate, with binding energy. An alternative explanation, to that of induced fit, is that some small molecules (e.g., H_2O in the hexokinase example) bind *nonproductively*; i.e., their small size allows them to assume many orientations with respect to the other substrate (ATP in the case of hexokinase) that do not lead to a reaction. Large substrates are restricted in motion and are held in a catalytically *correct* orientation millions of times more often during molecular vibrations than is, say, H_2O.

5.5 Rate Enhancement and Activation Energy

Question: Some biochemicals are stable when in pure form in a bottle on a shelf and yet in the presence of an enzyme they break down rapidly. Why?

There is an important distinction to be made between *thermodynamic stability* expressed in terms of the equilibrium constant of a reaction and the *kinetic stability* of a substance; the latter merely refers to how fast the reaction proceeds, the former to the final *position* of the reaction at equilibrium in terms of the relative amounts of substrate and product.

EXAMPLE 5.18 Most reduced organic molecules like glucose are *thermodynamically unstable* in the Earth's oxidizing atmosphere.

$$\text{Glucose} + 6\,O_2 \rightarrow 6\,CO_2 + 6\,H_2O \qquad -\Delta G^0 = 2872 \text{ kJ mol}^{-1}$$

Thus, from the value of the measured change in free energy of the reaction (Chap. 2) it is seen that the oxidation is *very exergonic* (heat-producing). In other words, the reaction is favored by the large $-\Delta G^0$ of the reaction. But we are all aware that glucose is stable *on the shelf*. Thus it is seen to be *kinetically stable* but *thermodynamically unstable*.

The distinction between kinetic and thermodynamic stability is explained by the concept of the *free energy of activation* that is necessary to convert a substrate to its transition-state form. For the substrate to convert to product(s) its internal free energy must exceed a certain value; i.e., it must *surmount an energy barrier*. The energy barrier is that of the free energy of the transition state $\Delta G^{\ddagger}$. The transition-state theory of reaction rates introduced by Henry Eyring relates the rate of the reaction to the magnitude of $\Delta G^{\ddagger}$.

Question: Is there a simple mathematical relationship between reaction rate and $\Delta G^{\ddagger}$?

Yes, in the 1880s Svante Arrhenius observed that the rate constant k for a simple chemical reaction varies with the temperature according to

$$k = Ae^{-E_a/RT} \tag{5.1}$$

where E_a is the *Arrhenius activation energy* of the reaction, A is called the *preexpontial factor*, R is the universal gas constant, and T is the temperature (K). However, it became apparent after many experiments that A is *not quite* temperature-independent, especially in catalyzed reactions. Therefore, Eyring proposed that *all* transition states break down with the same rate constant $\kappa T/h$, where κ and h are the Boltzmann and Planck constants, respectively. Therefore, he proposed that for any reaction

$$k = (\kappa T/h)\, e^{-\Delta G^{\ddagger}/RT} \tag{5.2}$$

where, again, $\Delta G^{\ddagger}$ is the activation energy of the *transition-state* complex.

In Chap. 2 it is shown that the Gibb's free energy of a system is made up of two components such that

$$\Delta G = \Delta H - T \, \Delta S \tag{5.3}$$

where ΔS is the *entropy* change and ΔH is the *enthalpy* change in the reaction system. Therefore Eq. (5.3) can be written as

$$k = (\kappa T/h) \; e^{\Delta S^{\ddagger}/R} \; e^{-\Delta H^{\ddagger}/RT} \tag{5.4}$$

Entropy is an equilibrium-thermodynamics entity that is *interpreted* mechanically as the *degree of disorder* in a system. From Eq. (5.4) it is seen that: (1) the preexponential factor A, of Eq. (5.1), can be interpreted as being related to the *organization* of a reactant in an enzyme as the transition-state complex is formed; and (2) the exponential factor relates to the enthalpy (heat) of the reaction.

Any molecular factors that tend to stabilize the transition state decrease $\Delta G^{\ddagger}$ and thus increase the rate of the reaction. Hence, this rate enhancement can result from either entropy or enthalpy effects, *or* from both.

5.6   Site-Directed Mutagenesis

Valuable insights into the mechanism of action of enzymes have been obtained by comparative studies of enzymes from different sources, e.g., different isoenzymes, or enzymes from different species. The amount of variation available by this means, however, is often limited. Further modification of enzymic activity has been discovered through the study of the effects on enzymic activity of specific chemical modifications. With the availability of methods for cloning and expressing DNA (Chaps. 7–9), methods have been developed for the specific modification of enzymes through *site-directed mutagenesis*, i.e., alteration of a gene to yield a protein with specific alterations in its amino acid sequence. Comparative studies of such mutant enzymes with one another, and with the wild type (or *naturally occurring* form), have provided valuable information on the roles of specific amino acid residues in the process of substrate binding, catalysis, enzyme stability, and regulation.

EXAMPLE 5.19   The specificity of trypsin toward peptide bonds adjacent to the carboxyl side of lysine and arginine residues has been altered by replacing a glycine residue in the active site by an alanine that carries an additional methyl group. This replacement favors the binding of lysine over the somewhat bulkier arginine.

EXAMPLE 5.20   In the catalytic mechanism of the *serine protease* (so called because of a catalytically important serine in the active site) *subtilisin*, the tetrahedral intermediate is thought to be stabilized by a hydrogen bond on the side chain of Asn155. Replacement of Asn155 with glycine leaves the binding unaffected, but inhibited in the catalytic step, confirming the proposed mechanism.

EXAMPLE 5.21   On the basis of chemical modification studies, Tyr198 of carboxypeptidase A was proposed to act as a proton donor (i.e., a general acid) in the mechanism of catalysis. However, if Tyr198 is replaced by phenyl alanine by means of site-directed mutagenesis, the modified enzyme retains substantial enzymic activity, indicating that the tyrosyl hydroxyl may not have a specific role in catalysis.

Question: Does the abolition of activity following mutagenesis unequivocally indicate a catalytic role for the mutated residue?

No, not necessarily! It is possible that replacement of one amino acid residue with another may abolish specific interactions that are critical for folding or even overall protein stability. It is essential in these types of studies to monitor protein conformation after mutagenesis. It is even more helpful if detailed structures, obtained either with X-ray crystallography or NMR spectroscopy (Chap. 4), are available for the wild-type and mutant forms of the enzyme.

5.7   Enzyme Kinetics—Introduction and Definitions

Enzyme kinetics is an area of science that seeks a general quantitative (mathematical) description of the rate of an enzyme-catalyzed reaction. The experimental aspects of enzyme kinetics are concerned with understanding those factors that affect the rate, with a view to determining the chemical mechanism of the reaction and, potentially, what controls it. The theoretical aspects of enzyme kinetics involve formulation of mathematical expressions for the rates of enzyme-catalyzed reactions and simulation of the progress of enzyme-catalyzed reactions either singly or in sequences of different reactions.

Question: What determines the rate of an enzyme-catalyzed reaction, and why is it important?

The important factors that influence the rate of an enzymic reaction are the concentration of the enzyme itself, the substrate concentration(s), and factors such as pH, temperature, presence of cofactors, and metal ions. In a practical sense, there may be occasions when we need to optimize the rate of a particular reaction. A study of the way the rate depends on experimental variables may allow us to discriminate between possible models that attempt to predict how the enzyme functions, and thus to suggest ways of affecting it with antimetabolites.

In addition to the experimental aspects of enzyme kinetics, the design of experiments, and the methods of determining the progress of an enzyme-catalyzed reaction, an important aspect is the *interpretation* of the data. This usually involves writing a mathematical expression for model reaction schemes that predict how the rate depends on reaction variables. These equations are then tested for consistency with experimental data that can allow the rejection of models that do not satisfactorily predict the measured behavior.

The basic principles and definitions that are used frequently in enzyme kinetic analysis are also the foundation of chemical kinetics in physical chemistry. Three key concepts in this area are as follows.

Principle of Mass Action

For a single, irreversible step in a chemical reaction, i.e., an *elementary* chemical process, the rate of the reaction is proportional to the concentrations of the reactants involved in the process. The constant of proportionality is called the *rate constant,* or the *unitary* rate constant, to highlight the fact that it applies to an elementary process. A subtlety that may be introduced into rate expressions is to use *chemical activities* (see Chap. 2) and not simply concentrations; but activity coefficients in biological systems are generally found to be near 1.0, so this is usually assumed to be the value for these dilute solutions.

EXAMPLE 5.22   Application of the principle of mass action to the reaction scheme

$$A + B \underset{k_{-1}}{\overset{k_1}{\rightleftharpoons}} P + Q \tag{5.5}$$

with forward and reverse rate constants k_1, and k_{-1} leads to the following expressions for the forward and reverse reaction rates or *fluxes* (Greek to *flow*):

$$\text{Forward rate} = k_1[A][B]$$
$$\text{Reverse rate} = k_{-1}[P][Q]$$

where the square brackets denote concentration in mol L^{-1}. At *chemical equilibrium*, the forward and reverse reaction rates are equal; so there is no *net* production of any of the reactants with time. Thus,

$$\frac{k_{-1}}{k_1} = \frac{[A]_e[B]_e}{[P]_e[Q]_e} = K_e \tag{5.6}$$

where K_e is termed the *equilibrium* constant, and the subscript e denotes the equilibrium value of the concentration.

Reaction rates are simply changes in concentration of a chemical species per unit of time. Therefore, they can be written mathematically as *derivatives*. Note, however, that the mathematical expression for the rate of change of, say, [A] must include forward and reverse fluxes from it:

$$\frac{d[A]}{dt} = -k_1[A][B] + k_{-1}[P][Q] \tag{5.7}$$

Molecularity

Molecularity refers to the *number of molecules* involved in an elementary reaction. Usually, only two molecules collide in one instant to give product(s) (molecularity = 2), or a single molecule undergoes *fission* (also called *scission*; molecularity = 1). Example 5.22 is of a reaction of which the forward and reverse processes have a molecularity of two.

Order of a Reaction

This is the *sum of the powers* to which the concentration (or chemical activity) terms are raised in a rate equation.

For example, Eq. (5.5) is a reaction scheme with a differential equation describing its rate [Eq. (5.7)] that has [A] and [B] each raised to the power 1; the sum is 2, so this reaction is said to be a second-order reaction.

EXAMPLE 5.23　In the first-order reaction

$$A \xrightarrow{\ k\ } P$$

the expression for the rate of change of [A] is

$$\frac{d[A]}{dt} = -k[A] \tag{5.8}$$

Since the left-hand side of the equation has the units of reaction rate (mol L^{-1} s^{-1}), these units must also apply to the right-hand side of the equation. The process of balancing dimensions in equations is called *dimensional analysis*; it is a most useful tool when checking kinetic (or any other physical) equations. Hence, the units of $k[A]$ must be mol L^{-1} s^{-1}, implying that k has units of s^{-1}. Simple dimensional analysis leads directly to the general expression for the units of a particular rate constant in a particular reaction scheme.

5.8　Dependence of Enzyme Reaction Rate on Substrate Concentration

Experimentally, the effect of substrate concentration on enzyme reaction rate is studied by recording the progress of an enzyme-catalyzed reaction, by using a fixed amount of enzyme and a series of different substrate concentrations. The *initial velocity* v_0 is measured as the slope of the tangent of the progress curve at time = 0. This *initial* velocity is used because enzyme degradation may occur during the reaction, or inhibition by reaction products may arise, thus yielding results that can be difficult to interpret.

When $[S]_0 \gg$ the enzyme concentration, v_0 is usually *directly proportional* to the enzyme concentration in the reaction mixture, and for most enzymes v_0 is a *rectangular hyperbolic function* of $[S]_0$ (see Fig. 5-15). If there are other (co-) substrates, then these are usually held constant during the series of experiments in which $[S]_0$ is varied.

The equation describing the rectangular hyperbola that usually represents enzyme reaction data (e.g., Fig. 5-15), is called the *Michaelis-Menten equation*:

$$v_0 = -\left(\frac{d[S]}{dt}\right)_{t=0} = \frac{V_{max}[S]_0}{K_m + [S]_0} \tag{5.9}$$

This equation has the property that when $[S]_0$ is very large, $v_0 = V_{max}$ (the *maximal velocity*); also when $v_0 = V_{max}/2$, the value of $[S]_0$ is K_m, the *Michaelis* constant.

5.9　Graphical Evaluation of K_m and V_{max}

Equation (5.9) can be rearranged into several new forms that yield straight lines when one *new* variable is plotted against the other. The advantages of this mathematical manipulation are that: (1) V_{max} and K_m can be determined readily by fitting a straight line to the transformed data; (2) departures of the data from a straight line are more easily detected than nonconformity to a hyperbola (these departures may indicate an

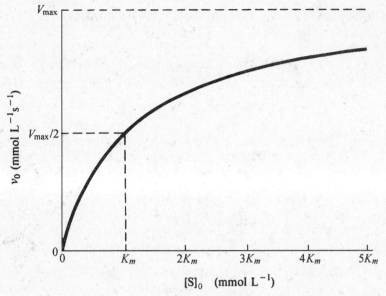

Fig. 5-15   The hyperbolic relationship between initial velocity v_0 and the initial substrate concentration $[S]_0$ of an enzyme-catalyzed reaction.

inappropriateness of the simple enzyme model to describe the data); and (3) the effects of inhibitors on the reaction can be analyzed more easily. It is also easier and more accurate to obtain an extrapolated intercept from a linear plot than to estimate by eye an asymptote to a rectangular hyperbola.

The most commonly used transformation of the Michaelis-Menten equation is that due to Hans Lineweaver and Dean Burk. Their equation was introduced in 1934: by taking reciprocals of both sides of Eq. (5.9) we obtain

$$\frac{1}{v_0} = \frac{K_m}{V_{max}} \frac{1}{[S]_0} + \frac{1}{V_{max}} \tag{5.10}$$

A plot of data pairs $(1/[S]_{0,i}, 1/v_{0,i})$, for $i = 1, \ldots, n$, where n is the number of data pairs, gives a straight line with ordinate and abscissa intercepts of $1/V_{max}$ and $-1/K_m$, respectively (Fig. 5-16).

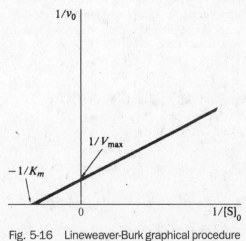

Fig. 5-16   Lineweaver-Burk graphical procedure for determining the values of the two steady-state kinetic parameters in the Michaelis-Menten equation.

5.10   Mechanistic Basis of the Michaelis-Menten Equation

Equilibrium Analysis

To explain their results on the hydrolysis rate of sucrose to glucose and fructose by the enzyme *invertase*, Lenor Michaelis and Maud Menten proposed, in 1913, the following scheme of reactions:

$$E + S \underset{k_{-1}}{\overset{k_1}{\rightleftharpoons}} ES \overset{k_2}{\longrightarrow} E + P \tag{5.11}$$

It was assumed that k_{-1} is large compared with k_2; thus the first part of the reaction can be described by the equilibrium constant for the dissociation of the enzyme-substrate complex, namely $K_S = [E][S]/[ES]$. The concentrations of S and E at any time are derived from the known initial conditions

$$[S]_0 = [S] + [ES] + [P] \tag{5.12}$$
$$[E]_0 = [E] + [ES] \tag{5.13}$$

Since experimentally $[S]_0 \gg [E]_0$, then $[S] \cong [S]_0$ early in the reaction, and by using the expression for K_S and Eq. (5.12), we obtain

$$K_S = \frac{([E]_0 - [ES])[S]_0}{[ES]} \tag{5.14}$$

This equation can be rearranged to give

$$[ES] = \frac{[E]_0[S]_0}{K_S + [S]_0} \tag{5.15}$$

The second step of the reaction is a simple first-order one, and thus

$$v_0 = k_2 [ES] \tag{5.16}$$

Hence the overall rate of appearance of the product is described by

$$v_0 = \frac{k_2[E]_0[S]_0}{K_S + [S]_0} \tag{5.17}$$

that is exactly of the form of Eq. (5.9), if we use the identities $V_{max} = k_2 [E]_0$ and $K_m = K_S$.

Steady-State Analysis

George E. Briggs and John B. S. Haldane, in 1925, examined the earlier Michaelis-Menten analysis and made an important development. Instead of assuming that the first stage of the reaction was at equilibrium, they merely assumed that, for all intents and purposes, the concentration of the enzyme-substrate complex scarcely changed with time; i.e., it is in a *steady state*. Written mathematically, this amounts to

$$\frac{d[ES]}{dt} = 0 \tag{5.18}$$

Next, the expression for the formation and dissociation of [ES] is

$$\frac{d[ES]}{dt} = k_1[E][S] - (k_{-1} + k_2)[ES] \tag{5.19}$$

and by using Eqs. (5.12) and (5.13) with $[S] \approx [S]_0$, then

$$0 = k_1[E]_0[S]_0 - (k_{-1} + k_2)[ES] \tag{5.20}$$

By rearranging this equation and using the fact that $v_0 = k_2 [ES]$, we obtain

$$v_0 = \frac{k_2[E]_0[S]_0}{k_{-1} + k_2/k_1 + [S]_0} \tag{5.21}$$

Again, Eq. (5.21) has the same form as Eq. (5.9), provided V_{max} is identified with $k_2 [E]_0$ and K_m is identified with $(k_{-1} + k_2)/k_1$.

Several features of Eq. (5.21) are worth noting:

1. Because k_2 describes the number of molecules of substrate converted to product per second per molecule of enzyme, it is called the *turnover number*. Generally, in more complex enzyme mechanisms the expression for V_{max} is complicated by k_2 being replaced by an expression that is a ratio of sums of products of unitary rate constants; this grouped expression is called k_{cat}.

2. If an enzyme is not pure, the concentration of its active form $[E]_0$ may not be able to be accurately determined. Nevertheless, V_{max} can still be obtained by steady-state kinetic analysis. Thus, to standardize experimental results, we refer to *one enzyme unit* (or *katal*) as the amount of enzyme solution required to transform 1 μmol of substrate into product(s) in 1 min, under standard conditions of pH, ionic strength, buffer type and temperature.

3. When $[S]_0$ is very large, compared with K_m, virtually all E is in the form of ES, so the enzyme is said to be *saturated* with the substrate; i.e., it is then operating at its maximum velocity.

5.11 Mechanisms of Enzyme Inhibition

Since the product of an enzymic reaction resides in the active site at the end of the reaction, it is not surprising that a high concentration of it might obstruct the active site in some way and thus inhibit the reaction. This phenomenon is called *product inhibition*. However, it is only one of many different ways in which products, substrates, and many compounds that are not directly related to the reaction could affect the operation of the enzyme. Such modulation of the activity of enzymes is central to the control of flux in metabolic pathways, which consist of sequences and cycles of enzyme-catalyzed reactions.

The mechanisms of enzyme inhibition fall into three main types, and they yield particular forms of modified Michaelis-Menten equations. These can be derived for single-substrate/single-product enzymic reactions using the steady-state analysis of Sec. 5.10, as follows.

Competitive Inhibition

The simplest reaction scheme in which the inhibitor I competes with the substrate S for binding to the enzyme E is as follows.

$$
\begin{array}{c}
\text{I} \\
+ \\
\text{E} + \text{S} \underset{k_{-1}}{\overset{k_1}{\rightleftharpoons}} \text{ES} \overset{k_2}{\rightarrow} \text{E} + \text{P} \\
k_{-I} \Big\Updownarrow k_I \\
\text{EI}
\end{array}
\qquad (5.22)
$$

where $K_I = k_{-I}/k_I$ is the dissociation constant of the enzyme-inhibitor complex.

Using the steady-state analysis of Briggs and Haldane (Sec. 5.10) coupled with the *conservation of mass equation* that is extended from Eq. (5.13) to include the EI complex,

$$[E]_0 = [E] + [ES] + [EI] \qquad (5.23)$$

yields the initial-velocity expression

$$v_0 = \frac{k_2[E]_0[S]_0}{\left(\dfrac{k_{-1} + k_2}{k_1}\right)\left(1 + \dfrac{[I]}{K_I}\right) + [S]_0} \qquad (5.24)$$

$$= \frac{V_{max}[S]_0}{K_m\left(1 + \dfrac{[I]}{K_I}\right) + [S]_0} \qquad (5.25)$$

The Lineweaver-Burk double reciprocal form of Eq. (5.25) is readily shown to be

$$\frac{1}{v_0} = \frac{K_m}{V_{max}}\left(1+\frac{[I]}{K_I}\right)\frac{1}{[S]_0} + \frac{1}{V_{max}} \tag{5.26}$$

This equation predicts that the slope of the Lineweaver-Burk plot will increase with increasing inhibitor concentration, but the intercept on the $1/v_0$ axis (namely $1/V_{max}$) does not change. A series of plots for several experiments with different concentrations of inhibitor will all have the same $1/v_0$ axis intercept as shown in Fig. 5-17a, indicating that competitive inhibition does not alter V_{max}.

Noncompetitive Inhibition and Mixed Inhibition

This type of inhibition involves the inhibitor binding to all forms of the enzyme, whether the enzyme is free or bound to its substrate(s). Hence the reaction scheme is based on that in Eq. (5.22) but with a second binding reaction in which I also binds to ES.

$$\begin{array}{ccc}
I & & I \\
+ & k_1 & + & k_2 \\
E + S & \rightleftharpoons & ES & \longrightarrow E + P \\
& k_{-1} & & \\
K_I \updownarrow & & K_I' \updownarrow & \\
EI & & ESI &
\end{array} \tag{5.27}$$

The corresponding conservation of mass equation for the enzyme and the rate equation derived using this information are:

$$[E]_0 = [E] + [ES] + [EI] + [ESI] \tag{5.28}$$

$$v_0 = \frac{V_{max}[S]_0}{K_m(1+[I]/K_I)+[S]_0(1+[I]/K_I')} \tag{5.29}$$

This equation corresponds to that of mixed inhibition if $K_I' \neq K_I$. However, if $K_I' = K_I$, then pure competitive inhibition is the result. Thus it can be seen that, *mechanistically speaking*, pure noncompetitive inhibition is a special case of mixed inhibition.

The double reciprocal form of Eq. (5.29) for pure noncompetitive inhibition is

$$\frac{1}{v_0} = \frac{K_m}{V_{max}}\left(1+\frac{[I]}{K_I}\right)\frac{1}{[S]_0} + \frac{1}{V_{max}}\left(1+\frac{[I]}{K_I}\right) \tag{5.30}$$

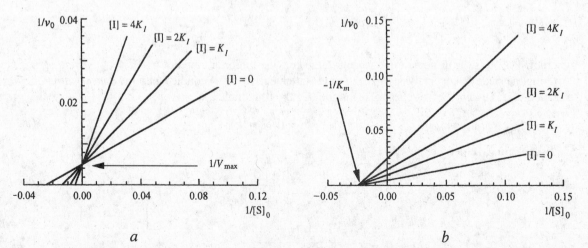

Fig. 5-17   Lineweaver-Burk plot: $1/v_0$ versus $1/[S]_0$ for (a) pure competitive inhibition and (b) pure noncompetitive inhibition.

This equation predicts that both the slope and the $1/v_0$ intercept of a Lineweaver-Burk plot increase with increasing inhibitor concentration, but the intercept on the $1/[S]_0$ axis (namely, $-1/K_m$) does not change. A series of plots from several experiments with different concentrations of inhibitors will all pass through the $1/[S]_0$ intercept as shown in Fig. 5-17b, indicating that pure noncompetitive inhibition does not alter the apparent K_m.

Anti- or Uncompetitive Inhibition

This strange-sounding form of inhibition comes about when the inhibitor binds only to the ES complex, and not the free enzyme. The simplest reaction scheme that describes this situation is

$$E + S \underset{k_{-1}}{\overset{k_1}{\rightleftharpoons}} \overset{\overset{\text{I}}{+}}{ES} \overset{k_2}{\rightarrow} E + P \tag{5.31}$$

$$K_I \updownarrow$$

$$ESI$$

And the corresponding rate equation is

$$v_0 = \frac{V_{max}[S]_0}{K_m + [S]_0(1 + [I]/K_I')} \tag{5.32}$$

In this case, the Lineweaver-Burk plots of $1/v_0$ versus $1/[S]_0$ for several experiments, with different concentrations of inhibitor, yield parallel lines of slope K_m/V_{max}.

5.12   Regulatory Enzymes

General

The enzyme kinetics discussed thus far are called *Michaelis-Menten* kinetics, since a plot of reaction rate versus substrate concentration is a pure rectangular hyperbola. Alternatively, a plot of reciprocal initial velocity versus reciprocal substrate concentration is linear. Many reactions involving *two or more substrates* also give such linear plots with respect to one substrate while the initial concentrations of the other substrate(s) are fixed. While many enzymes obey Michaelis-Menten kinetics, a significant number do not. The latter enzymes typically give velocity versus substrate curves that are *sigmoidal* rather than hyperbolic; they are called *control* or *regulatory* enzymes, and they are usually catalyze reactions that are at the *beginning* or at *branch points* of metabolic pathways.

EXAMPLE 5.24   The simplest form of regulation of a metabolic pathway is the *inhibition* of an enzyme that catalyzes the formation of a precursor compound, by the product of the pathway. In Fig. 5-18, the E_is denote enzymes and A and B denote metabolites; and the circled minus sign indicates *inhibition*. If there were no inhibitor of the enzyme E_1 that acts on A, then the concentration of B would depend entirely on its rate of synthesis, or utilization. If the rate of utilization of B decreased, or B were supplied by an outside source, its concentration would rise, perhaps even to toxic levels. However, if B is an *inhibitor* of the first enzyme, then as its concentration rises, the extent of inhibition will increase and its rate of synthesis will decrease. This effect is called *feedback inhibition* or *negative feedback control*; it is a concept that is also used in describing the behavior of electronic circuits.

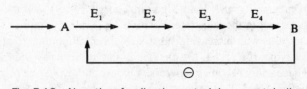

Fig. 5-18   Negative feedback control in a metabolic pathway.

EXAMPLE 5.25   Control of a *branched* pathway is more complex than in Fig. 5-18. Consider the metabolic scheme in Fig. 5-19. Here, B reacts with C, while D is produced further along the pathway. For most effective control of D, B should inhibit the first enzyme (E₁) and C should activate it. In this case, if B were supplied from an external source so that [B] ≫ [C], then B would inhibit its own synthesis from A and the concentrations of B and C would tend to become equal.

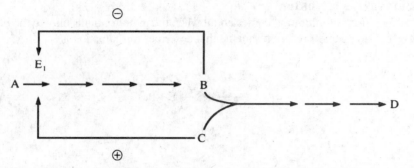

Fig. 5-19   Negative feedback control of a branched metabolic pathway.

Alternatively, if [C] ≫ [B], then C would activate the production of B, so this would tend to equalize [B] and [C]. This activation by C is usually the result of C competing for the same binding site as B on E₁, and thus reducing the inhibition by B. The first enzyme of pyrimidine synthesis, aspartate carbamoyltransferase, in *E. coli*, is subject to this type of control, in this case B is CTP, C is ATP, and D is a nucleic acid (see Chap. 14).

Other Forms of Control

Metabolic pathways are also controlled via enzyme *repression* and *derepression* (Chaps. 7 and 8) that occur in response to variations of metabolite levels. However, the time scale of this control is hours to days, in contrast to less than a few seconds for direct binding effects.

Finally, *molecular conversion*, namely, reversible covalent modification of enzymes, is another method of enzyme control. The best example of this is *enzyme phosphorylation* and *dephosphorylation* that occur in the control of glycogen synthesis and degradation (Chap. 11).

Kinetic Behavior of Regulatory Enzymes

Usually effector molecules bear few structural resemblances to those of the substrates of the enzymes that they control. The control is therefore not likely to be due to binding at the active site but at an alternative site, called an *allosteric site* (Greek: *allos* other, *stereos*, solid/site). The effect on the reaction at the active site is brought about by *conformational changes* in the protein.

If an effector of an enzyme is also a substrate, it is called a *homotropic* effector; while if it is a nonsubstrate, it is called *heterotropic*.

Regulatory enzymes are usually identified experimentally by the deviation of their kinetics from Michaelis-Menten kinetics: plots of velocity versus substrate concentration can be *sigmoidal* or a *modified hyperbola* [Fig. 5-20*a*]. If these curves are plotted in the double reciprocal (Lineweaver-Burk) form, then nonlinear graphs are obtained [Fig. 5-20(*b*)].

A useful quantitative measure for comparing the extent of regulation of an enzyme is the ratio R_S, defined as

$$R_s = \frac{\text{substrate concentration giving } 0.9V_{max}}{\text{substrate concentration giving } 0.1V_{max}} \tag{5.33}$$

For a Michaelis-Menten enzyme $R_S = 81$. For a sigmoidal curve $R_S < 81$, and the enzyme is said to exhibit *positive cooperativity* with respect to the substrate. Positive cooperativity implies that the substrate binding or catalytic rate, or both, increases with increasing substrate concentration more than would be expected for a simple Michaelis-Menten enzyme. If $R_S > 81$, the enzyme is said to display *negative cooperativity*; substrate binding or catalysis, while increasing, becomes progressively less than would be found with a simple enzyme, as substrate concentration is increased. The enzyme is said to show *negative cooperativity* with respect to the substrate.

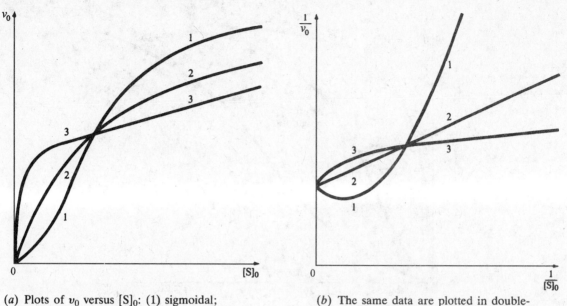

(*a*) Plots of v_0 versus $[S]_0$: (1) sigmoidal; (2) hyperbolic; (3) apparent hyperbolic.

(*b*) The same data are plotted in double-reciprocal form. Note that only (2) is linear and therefore indicative of hyperbolic kinetics, while (1) is concave and (3) convex.

Fig. 5-20   Possible kinetic behavior of regulatory enzymes. (*a*) Plot of v_0 versus $[S]_0$; (1) sigmoidal; (2) hyperbolic; and (3) apparent hyperbolic; (*b*) the same data plotted in double-reciprocal form.

EXAMPLE 5.26   Hetero- and homotropic effects also operate with *binding proteins*. Possibly the best example is O_2 binding to *hemoglobin*; the binding of one molecule of O_2 to hemoglobin *cooperates* in a *positive* way with the binding of the next molecule so that the apparent affinity of hemoglobin for O_2 increases as the *degree of saturation* by O_2 increases. When the fractional saturation is plotted against the partial pressure of O_2 (equivalent to O_2 concentration), the curve is not hyperbolic but *sigmoidal* (Fig. 5-20).

In human red blood cells the *heterotropic effector* 2,3-bisphosphoglycerate (23BPG) reduces the affinity of all four binding sites of the hemoglobin tetramers for O_2 (Fig. 4-17). On the other hand, myoglobin, the O_2-binding protein of muscle, is a single subunit and does *not* display sigmoidal O_2-binding behavior nor is it affected by 23BPG.

Mathematical Models of Cooperativity

Although hemoglobin is not an enzyme, but an O_2-*binding protein*, the study of it has contributed a great deal to our understanding of macromolecular cooperativity. Its cooperative O_2-binding behavior was first recognized by Christian Bohr in 1903, long before the effect was seen with any enzymes. Much effort was expended in developing theories to explain the effect. Therefore it is worth considering some of the earlier theories that still have relevance today.

Hill Equation

In 1909 Archibald V. Hill (Nobel Prize, 1922) proposed that the binding reaction between hemoglobin and O_2 could be described by a reaction of *molecularity $n + 1$*:

$$Hb + nO_2 \rightleftharpoons Hb(O_2)_n \tag{5.34}$$

where n is the number of O_2-binding sites on a hemoglobin molecule. The equation for the fractional saturation (the fraction of binding sites occupied by O_2 at any given partial pressure) Y is

$$Y = \frac{K_b(pO_2)^n}{1 + K_b(pO_2)^n} \tag{5.35}$$

where pO_2 is the partial pressure of O_2 (mmHg) and K_b is the *association* binding constant that is defined as

$$K_b = \frac{[Hb(O_2)_n]}{[Hb](pO_2)^n} \tag{5.36}$$

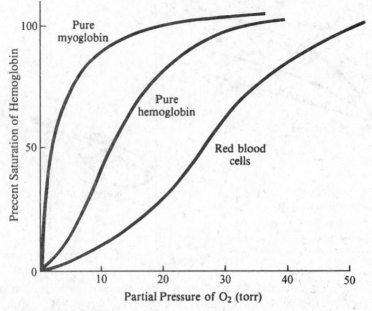

Fig. 5-21   Oxygen-binding curves for hemoglobin and myoglobin.

Note that Y is a dimensionless quantity that has the range 0–1, and n is called the *Hill coefficient*. For values of n around 2.5 a sigmoidal curve akin to those shown in Fig. 5-21 (lower curve) was obtained by Hill. The fact that n is *not an integer* raised some early problems in the mechanistic interpretations of the data analyzed with the Hill equation. This dilemma led to the development of other mechanistic models (see below).

EXAMPLE 5.27   If $n = 1$ in the Hill equation, what form does the equation take?

When $n = 1$, Eq. (5.36) yields a rectangular hyperbola. However, recall that the Michaelis-Menten expression is written with K_m being equivalent to (and having the units of) a *dissociation* constant, whereas binding equations such as the Hill equation are usually written with *association* constants (their numerical value being the reciprocal of the corresponding dissociation constant).

EXAMPLE 5.28   How is it possible to use experimental data to determine the values of K_b and n in the Hill equation?

By rearranging Eq. (5.36) and taking the logarithm of each side, we obtain

$$\log\left(\frac{[Hb(O_2)_n]}{[Hb]}\right) = \log K_b + n\log(pO_2) \tag{5.37}$$

Or a more general form of the expression, using the fractional saturation Y of a binding protein with substrate S, is

$$\log\left(\frac{Y}{1-Y}\right) = \log K_b + n\log[S]_0 \tag{5.38}$$

A plot of the left-hand side of Eq. (5.38) versus $\log [S]_0$ is called a *Hill plot*; it yields an estimate of n from the slope and K_b from the ordinate intercept.

EXAMPLE 5.29   For an *enzymic* reaction (in contrast to a *binding* process), the initial velocity v_0 is determined by the concentration of the enzyme-substrate complex; therefore, what form does Eq. (5.38) take when analyzing enzyme kinetic data?

A fractional saturation of unity corresponds to V_{max} so a Hill plot for an enzymic reaction consists of a plot of $\log[v_0/(V_{max} - v_0)]$ versus $\log [S]_0$. An initial estimate of V_{max} must be made before analyzing enzyme kinetic data in this way.

Adair Equation

Gilbert S. Adair in 1925 determined that the molecular weight of hemoglobin was about four times as great as previously thought. He postulated that a molecule of hemoglobin has four O_2-binding sites that are filled in a four-step process as follows:

$$
\begin{aligned}
\mathrm{Hb} + \mathrm{O_2} &\rightleftharpoons \mathrm{HbO_2} \\
\mathrm{HbO_2} + \mathrm{O_2} &\rightleftharpoons \mathrm{Hb(O_2)_2} \\
\mathrm{Hb(O_2)_2} + \mathrm{O_2} &\rightleftharpoons \mathrm{Hb(O_2)_3} \\
\mathrm{Hb(O_2)_3} + \mathrm{O_2} &\rightleftharpoons \mathrm{Hb(O_2)_4}
\end{aligned}
\tag{5.39}
$$

Consider *one* binding site on a totally empty (no sites filled) hemoglobin molecule; the binding reaction for this site can be characterized by the *association* equilibrium constant $K_1 = k_1/k_{-1}$, where k_1 and k_{-1} are the unitary rate constants for the forward and reverse reactions, respectively. This equilibrium constant is called an *intrinsic* constant since it refers to one site only. The *overall*, or *extrinsic*, binding constant relates to all four of the binding sites and thus has the value $4K_1$. The extrinsic binding constants for the other three sites are also expressed in terms of *intrinsic* binding constants and their *statistical factors* $(3/2)\,K_2$, $(2/3)\,K_3$, and $(1/4)\,K_4$. Thus the Adair binding function for four sites is expressed as follows:

$$
y = \frac{\text{number (or mol) of binding sites occupied}}{\text{total number (or mol) of binding sites}}
\tag{5.40}
$$

$$
= \frac{K_1[\mathrm{X}] + 3K_1K_2[\mathrm{X}]^2 + 3K_1K_2K_3[\mathrm{X}]^3 + K_1K_2K_3K_4[\mathrm{X}]^4}{1 + 4K_1[\mathrm{X}] + 6K_1K_2[\mathrm{X}]^2 + 4K_1K_2K_3[\mathrm{X}]^3 + K_1K_2K_3K_4[\mathrm{X}]^4}
\tag{5.41}
$$

where [X] denotes the partial pressure (concentration) of oxygen, in the particular case of hemoglobin binding to oxygen.

EXAMPLE 5.30   An alternative way of viewing the concept of *extrinsic binding constants* is as follows. The experimentally *measured* binding constant for each site of a polymeric protein, or enzyme, will depend on the number of available sites on each molecule; e.g., for the hemoglobin tetramer the first binding reaction Eq. (5.39) is

$$
\mathrm{Hb} + \mathrm{O_2} \rightleftharpoons \mathrm{HbO_2}
$$

There are four sites available for binding $\mathrm{O_2}$, but only one from which bound $\mathrm{O_2}$ can dissociate. Thus, by the law of mass action, the (overall) extrinsic equilibrium constant is equal to $4\,k_1/k_{-1} = 4K_1$. Similarly, the *extrinsic* constant denoted by K_2^e is given by $(3/2)\,K_2$, where K_2 is the intrinsic constant, and by the same reasoning $K_3^e = (2/3)\,K_3$ and $K_4^e = (1/4)\,K_4$.

EXAMPLE 5.31   If the hemoglobin tetramer had four *identical, noninteracting* binding sites, then what relative values would the intrinsic binding constants have?

They would all be equal, i.e., $K_1 = K_2 = K_3 = K_4$. There would be no cooperativity in this case (see Example 5.27). If each binding step facilitated the next, i.e., $K_1 < K_2 < K_3 < K_4$, then *positive cooperativity* would exist. Negative cooperativity at each stage in the binding requires that $K_1 > K_2 > K_3 > K_4$. Clearly more complex relationships between the values of the Ks *could* exist; e.g., $K_1 > K_2 < K_3 < K_4$.

EXAMPLE 5.32   Show that if $K_1 = K_2 = K_3 = K_4$, the four-site Adair equation becomes that of a rectangular hyperbola.

Note that the statistical factors in the numerator and denominator of the four-site Adair equation, and in fact in the general n-site equation, are the coefficients of the *binomial expansion*, i.e., the coefficients of the expansion of $(1 + x)^n$. In the present case with $n = 4$, Eq. (5.41) applies and

$$
Y = \frac{K_1[\mathrm{X}] + 3K_1^2[\mathrm{X}]^2 + 3K_1^3[\mathrm{X}]^3 + K_1^4[\mathrm{X}]^4}{1 + 4K_1[\mathrm{X}] + 6K_1^2[\mathrm{X}]^2 + 4K_1^3[\mathrm{X}]^3 + K_1^4[\mathrm{X}]^4}
$$

$$
= \frac{K_1[\mathrm{X}](1 + K_1[\mathrm{X}])^3}{(1 + K_1[\mathrm{X}])^4} = \frac{K_1[\mathrm{X}]}{(1 + K_1[\mathrm{X}])}
\tag{5.42}
$$

The final expression is that of an *hyperbola*; it is evident that it is equivalent to the Michaelis-Menten expression when it is recalled that K_1 is an *association* constant.

Model of Monod, Wyman, and Changeux (MWC Model) for Homotropic Effects

The cooperative binding of $\mathrm{O_2}$ by hemoglobin, and the allosteric effects in many enzymes, requires interactions between sites that are widely separated in space. The present model was proposed in 1965 to incorporate allosteric *and* conformational effects in an explanation of enzyme cooperativity. The seminal experimental observation was that most cooperative proteins have several identical subunits (*protomers*) in each molecule (*oligomer*); this situation is imperative for binding cooperativity. The MWC model is defined as follows:

1. Each protomer can exist in either of two *different conformations*, designated R and T; these originally referred to *relaxed* and *tense*, respectively.

2. All subunits of one oligomer *must* occupy the *same* conformation; hence for a tetrameric protein the conformational states R_4 and T_4 are the only ones permitted. Mixed states such as R_3T are forbidden. In other words, a *concerted* (Latin, *concert* all together) transition takes place in the conversion of R_4 to T_4 and vice versa.

3. The two states of the protein are in equilibrium *independent* of whether any ligand (substrate) is bound; the equilibrium constant is $L = [T_4]/[R_4]$.

4. A ligand molecule can bind to a subunit in either conformation, but the *association* constants are different for each conformation. For each R subunit,

$$K_R = [RX]/[R][X]$$

and for each T subunit,

$$K_T = [TX]/[T][X]$$

These postulates imply the following multiple-equilibrium scheme for the protein and ligand (X):

$$
\begin{array}{ccc}
R_4 & \rightleftharpoons & T_4 \\
4K_R[X]\ \updownarrow & & \updownarrow\ 4K_T[X] \\
R_4X & \overset{L}{\rightleftharpoons} & T_4X \\
\tfrac{3}{2}K_R[X]\ \updownarrow & & \updownarrow\ \tfrac{3}{2}K_T[X] \\
R_4X_2 & \overset{L}{\rightleftharpoons} & T_4X_2 \\
\tfrac{2}{3}K_R[X]\ \updownarrow & & \updownarrow\ \tfrac{2}{3}K_T[X] \\
R_4X_3 & \overset{L}{\rightleftharpoons} & T_4X_3 \\
\tfrac{1}{4}K_R[X]\ \updownarrow & & \updownarrow\ \tfrac{1}{4}K_T[X] \\
R_4X_4 & \overset{L}{\rightleftharpoons} & T_4X_4
\end{array}
\tag{5.43}
$$

By writing mathematical expressions for each of the free and bound states in terms of the free concentration of X, it can be shown that the saturation function of the four-site MWC model, with $c = K_T/K_R$ and $L = [T_4]/[R_4]$, is

$$Y = \frac{\alpha(1+\alpha)^{n-1} + Lc\alpha(1+c\alpha)^{n-1}}{(1+\alpha)^n + L(1+c\alpha)^n} \tag{5.44}$$

where this is the general form of the MWC expression for the particular case of four sites, i.e., $n = 4$.

EXAMPLE 5.33　The shape of the saturation curve defined by Eq. (5.44) depends on the values of L and c. If $L = 0$, then the T form of the protein does not exist and $Y = K_R[X]/(1 + K_R[X])$. This defines a hyperbolic binding function. Similarly, if $L = \infty$, $Y = K_T[X]/(1 + K_T[X])$. Thus deviations from hyperbolic binding occur only if both R and T forms exist; otherwise the situation described for the Adair equation in Example 5.31 applies since binding then is *independent* and *identical* at each site.

EXAMPLE 5.34 The fact that Eq. (5.44) defines a curve that is sigmoidal, or S-shaped, is not really obvious unless $c = 0$. In the case of $n = 4$,

$$Y = \frac{K_R[X](1 + K_R[X])^3}{(1 + K_R[X])^4 + L} \tag{5.45}$$

Hence when [X] is large and $K_R[X] \gg L$, L is negligible and $Y = K_R[X]/(1 + K_R[X])$; i.e., it is a hyperbolic binding equation. At *low* values of [X] the value of L dominates the denominator, and the *slope* of the binding curve as $[X] \to 0$ approaches $K_R/(L+1)$; this is in contrast to the hyperbola where the slope approaches K_R. Hence the binding or enzyme kinetic curve *must* be sigmoidal if L is much larger than 1, and in the limit of infinite L the initial slope is zero.

MWC Model for Heterotropic Effects

The MWC model of the previous section *only* accounts for *homotropic* effects that occur, for example, with O_2 binding to hemoglobin; but *heterotropic* effects are frequently observed with regulatory enzymes and with 23BPG binding to hemoglobin. To incorporate these effects into the MWC model, we introduce the binding of a second ligand to either the R or T state, or to both of them.

Consider a simplified model for which it is *assumed* that the substrate X (ligand) binds only to the R state. For the binding of another ligand A to bring about *activation* of the enzyme, it must promote a shift of the equilibrium between the R and T states toward the R state. An activator must therefore bind to the R state. By the same reasoning, an allosteric *inhibitor* I must bind to the T state and thus shift the equilibrium toward the inactive state of the enzyme. By an analysis of the multiple equilibria in the reaction scheme, similar to that used in the previous section, an expression for Y is obtained:

$$Y = \frac{\alpha(1 + \alpha)^{n-1}}{(1 + \alpha)^n + L(1 + \beta)^n/(1 + \gamma)^n} \tag{5.46}$$

where $\alpha = K_R[X]$, $\beta = K_I[I]$, $\gamma = K_A[A]$, and $L = [T_n]/[R_n]$. The term $L(1 + \beta)^n/(1 + \gamma)^n$ is known as the *allosteric coefficient*; if this term is zero, then Eq. (5.46) reverts to a hyperbolic binding function. Clearly, an increase in the activator term γ *decreases* the value of the allosteric coefficient, thus making the function more hyperbolic (see Example 5.34). An increase in the inhibitor concentration increases the inhibition term β, thus increasing L and making the curve more sigmoidal. Both of these effects are seen in Fig. 5-22.

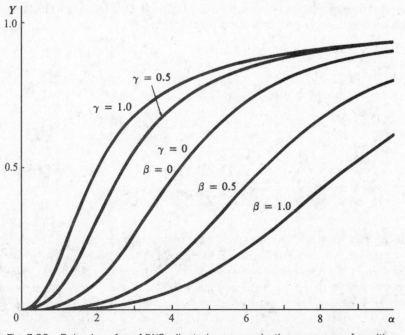

Fig. 5-22 Behavior of an MWC allosteric enzyme in the presence of positive and negative heterotropic effectors. The activator term γ in Eq. (5.46) causes the curve to become more hyperbolic whereas the inhibitor term β renders it more sigmoidal. The curves were constructed using Eq. (5.46) with $L = 1000$ and $n = 4$.

Model of Koshland, Nemethy, and Filmer (KNF Model)

The failure of the MWC model to describe negatively cooperative hetero- and homotropic effects in the binding function of an oligomeric protein led Daniel Koshland and colleagues in 1966 to develop a more general model of cooperativity in enzymes. Koshland's 1958 *induced fit hypothesis* for enzyme specificity had already extended Fischers' *lock and key* concept; he claimed that the binding of a substrate to an enzyme *creates* the correct three-dimensional arrangement of reactive groups for catalysis to occur. This abstract notion was advanced in the KNF model of oligomeric cooperative enzymes; in this case the change in conformation is assumed to *induce* (in contrast to the MWC model where the equilibrium between states of the subunits exists whether substrate is bound or not) *by the binding* of the substrate to a *protomer*. A change in the conformation of the protomer is transmitted to neighboring protomers to alter their binding and catalytic properties. This basic idea can explain both negative *and* positive cooperativity. Space limitations preclude the details of the model and the derivation of the binding and enzyme kinetic equations from being given here; nevertheless they do appear in the two previous editions of this book.

SOLVED PROBLEMS

DEFINITION OF ENZYMES

5.1. Justify the claim that the surface area of the active site of an enzyme is less than 5% of the total surface area of the protein. Consider the specific case of a 27 kDa globular enzyme with five amino acids in its active site.

SOLUTION

The ratio of the volume of the active site to that of the whole protein is $\sim 5/(27{,}000/110) = 0.02$; this comes about as follows: The mean amino acid residue weight is ~ 110. Assuming a spherical enzyme, the above volume ratio corresponds to a surface area ratio of $(0.02)^{2/3} \times 0.5$. The factor 0.5 accounts for the fact that one-half of the active-site residues face outward and contribute also to the total surface area; the answer is 0.04, or 4% of the surface area.

5.2. The nerve gas *di-isopropylfluorophosphate* (DFP) reacts with the serine -OH in some enzymes to form HF and the *O*-phosphoseryl ester as follows (Fig. 5-23):

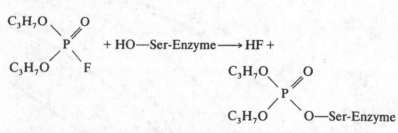

Fig. 5-23   Inhibition of an enzyme by the pesticide di-isopropylfluorophosphate.

In a chemical enzyme modification experiment conducted by Eugene F. Jansen and colleagues in 1949, chymotrypsin was incubated with ^{32}P-labeled DFP, and it was then hydrolyzed with a strong acid. Separation of the constituent amino acids revealed 1 mol of *labeled*, *O*-phophorylserine per 25,000 g of chymotrypsin. Since DFP is a potent inhibitor of the enzyme, what might we infer about the amino acid side chain composition of the active site?

SOLUTION

Since for chymotrypsin $M_r = 25{,}000$, only a single serine had reacted out of a total of 27. This indicated that a particular serine is an important component of the active site. The experiment is the archetypal form of many enzyme modification procedures that are now used routinely to identify active site constituents.

RNA CATALYSIS

5.3. On the basis of the RNase P reaction, postulate a mechanism for the splicing that occurs in the two-stage process that involves exon release and intron splicing from mRNA. The reaction is known to require two Mg^{2+} ions per active site.

SOLUTION

In the ligation reaction, one metal ion, usually Mg^{2+}, forms a bridge between the carbanion oxygen of the 5′-ribose residue and a phosphate oxygen atom. The second Mg^{2+} forms a tripartite bridge with the oxygen atoms of the phosphate and the 2′- and 3′-oxygens on the 3′-terminal ribose moiety (see Fig. 5-24).

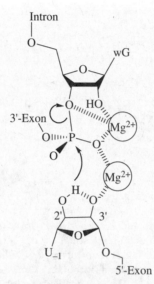

Fig. 5-24   Schematic representation of the active-site metal ion coordination within an RNA splicing complex.

ENZYME CLASSIFICATION

5.4. What is the order of abundance of enzymes in the six Enzyme Commision (EC) groups?

SOLUTION

The answer can only be given in general terms from a knowledge of all of metabolism, such as is given in this book; but since we emphasize mammalian biochemistry, is it not obvious that the relative abundance of enzyme types in mammals will be the same as in prokaryotes? However, a precise answer is obtained from the EC book on enzyme nomenclature.

Of the ~2500 different, named enzymes, the most abundant group is the oxidoreductases, group 1. Overall, the order is $1 > 2 > 4 > 3 > 6 > 5$.

5.5. Classify the following enzyme-catalyzed reactions into their major EC groups, and suggest possible names for each enzyme.

(*a*) D-Glyceraldehyde 3-phosphate + P_i + $NAD^+ \rightleftharpoons$ 1,3-*bis*phosphoglycerate + NADH

(*b*)

$$H_2N-\underset{\underset{NH_2}{|}}{\overset{\overset{O}{\|}}{C}} \; + \; H_2O \longrightarrow NH_4^+ \; + \; HCO_3^-$$

Urea

(*c*)

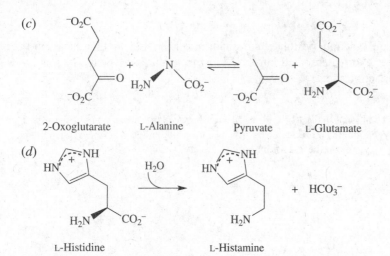

2-Oxoglutarate   L-Alanine   Pyruvate   L-Glutamate

(*d*)

L-Histidine   L-Histamine

(*e*) L-Alanine ⇌ D-Alanine

(*f*) L-Ribulose 5-phosphate ⇌ D-xylulose 5-phosphate

(*g*) The enzyme that catalyzes the rearrangement of S—S bonds in proteins

(*h*) $ATP + L\text{-tyrosine} + tRNA^{Tyr} \rightarrow AMP + PP_i + L\text{-Tyrosyl-}tRNA^{Tyr}$

(*i*) $ATP + \gamma\text{-}L\text{-Glutamyl-}L\text{-cysteine} + Glycine \rightarrow ADP + P_i + Glutathione$

SOLUTION

(*a*) Glyceraldehyde-3-phosphate dehydrogenase, EC 1.2.1.12. The systematic name is *D-glyceraldehyde-3-phosphate: NAD+ oxidoreductase (phosphorylating)*. It is an important glycolytic enzyme.

(*b*) Urease, EC 3.5.1.5. Its systematic name is *ureo amidohydrolase*. It was the first enzyme to be crystallized (by John B. Sumner in 1926), and interestingly, it contains *nickel*.

(*c*) Alanine transaminase, EC 2.6.1.12. The systematic name is *L-alanine:2-oxoglutarate aminotransferase*. Note that aminotransferases almost invariably contain *pyridoxal phosphate* as a cofactor.

(*d*) Histidine decarboxylase, EC 4.1.1.22. The systematic name is *L-histidine carboxylyase*; it, too, requires pyridoxal phosphate in animals, but the bacterial enzyme does not.

(*e*) *Alanine racemase*, EC 5.1.1.1; the systematic name is the same. It has the honor of being the first enzyme in Group 5! It also requires pyridoxal phosphate as a cofactor. A *racemic* mixture is a mixture of optical isomers of one chemical species.

(*f*) Ribulose phosphate epimerase, EC 5.1.3.4. Its official name is *L-ribulose-5-phosphate-4-epimerase*. This is a key enzyme in the pentose phosphate pathway. An *epimer* is a stereoisomer variant of a sugar differing in the configuration at only *one* carbon atom (see Chap. 11).

(*g*) Disulfide bond (S—S) rearrangease, EC 5.3.4.1. The official name is *protein disulfide-isomerase*. The common name is an example of naming the enzyme after the *phenomenon* with which it is associated; enzymes in this category are called *phenomenases*, and the EC of IUPAC generally disapproves of the use of such naming. Another common example is the use of the name *translocase* for an enzyme or protein carrier that catalyzes the movement of a moiety between biologically distinct compartments, e.g., *ATP translocase* in mitochondria (Chap. 10).

(*h*) Tyrosyl-tRNA synthetase, EC 6.1.1.1. The official name is *L-tyrosine:tRNA^{Tyr} ligase (AMP-forming)*. It is the first of the Group 6 enzymes but more importantly is essential to life because of its role in protein synthesis (Chap. 9).

(*i*) Glutathione synthetase, EC 6.3.2.3. The official name is *γ-L-glutamyl-L-cysteine:glycine ligase (ADP-forming)*. This is the final enzyme in glutathione production and is found in virtually all tissues in mammals and all organisms in general.

MODES OF ENHANCEMENT OF RATES OF BOND CLEAVAGE

5.6. Covalent enzyme catalysis involves the formation of a transient covalent bond between an enzyme and its substrate. Below are the general structures of commonly encountered *acyl-enzyme intermediates* and other covalent derivatives.

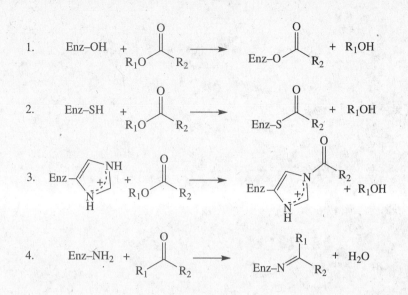

(*a*) Give examples of amino acid residues that have side chains with the reactive groups indicated above. (*b*) Give chemical names to the acyl-enzyme intermediates.

SOLUTION

(*a*) (1) Serine; (2) cysteine; (3) histidine; and (4) lysine.
(*b*) (1) Ester; (2) thioester; (3) acylimidazole; and (4) Schiff base.

5.7. The glycolytic pathway enzyme *fructose-1,6-bisphosphate aldolase* forms an acyl-enzyme intermediate with its ketone substrate *fructose 1,6-bisphosphate*. Given that the enzyme contains a lysine residue that is essential for its activity, what type of covalent intermediate is likely to be formed?

SOLUTION

The general structure is that of (4) in Prob. 5.6(*b*), namely a Schiff base, which is also called a *ketimine*.

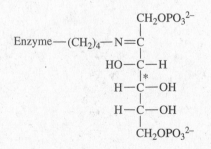

The formation of the ketimine labilizes the bond marked with the asterisk, leading to its cleavage.

5.8. *Propiniquity (proximity)* effects are important in the enhancement of reaction rates. In the case of the following compounds, anhydrides (products formed by the removal of water) form at different rates. Arrange the compounds in order of their rates of anhydride formation, and give your reasons for the ordering.

(*a*)

(b)

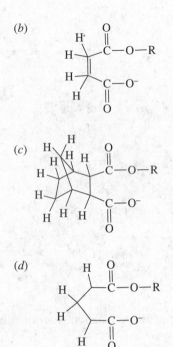

(c)

(d)

SOLUTION

The relative rates of anhydride formation are as follows: (*d*) 1; (*a*) 230; (*b*) 10,100; (*c*) 53,000. A greater rate enhancement occurs in the compounds in which the reacting carboxyl groups are held more rigidly; this prolongs the time during which a transition state can form and therefore increases the time during which the products can be formed.

5.9. Transition-state analogs are potent inhibitors of enzymes. In *cytidine deaminase* from the bacterium *E. coli*, the following chemical transformation takes place:

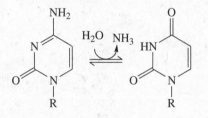

where R denotes a ribose residue.

(*a*) Draw a possible transition-state compound for the enzyme-catalyzed reaction.

(*b*) The two following compounds have different effects on the catalyzed reaction rate; one is a transition-state analog, while the other is a substrate. Give reasons for your proposal for which is the transition-state analog.

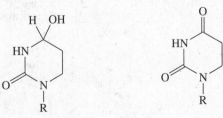

3, 4, 5, 6-Tetrahydrouridine   5, 6-Dihydrouridine

SOLUTION

(*a*) The likely transition-state compound is the *tetrahedral intermediate*, namely, an intermediate species in which the carbon has the usual four-bond arrangement for carbon atoms:

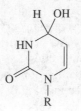

(*b*) It is clear that the compound on the left has a structure that is very similar to that of the intermediate in (*a*); it is indeed a potent inhibitor (transition-state analog) of cytidine deaminase.

5.10. The bacterial enzyme *chorismate mutase-prephenate dehydrogenase* is peculiar because it is a single protein unit with *two* catalytic activities. It catalyzes the sequential reactions of *mutation* of chorismate to prephenate, and then the reaction that leads to the formation of *phenylalanine* and *tyrosine*, through oxidation of prephenate. The first of these reactions is interesting because it is one of the mutases that are strictly *single substrate* enzymic reactions; it entails the migration of a side chain from one part of the ring to another, as shown in the scheme below.

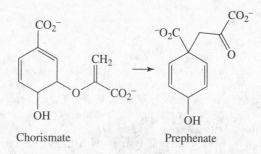

Chorismate   Prephenate

(*a*) Predict a likely *transition-state* structure for the reaction.

(*b*) Suggest a likely *transition-state analog* that might be a potent inhibitor of the enzyme.

SOLUTION

(*a*) By using molecular orbital calculations, Peter Andrews and Geoffrey Smith in 1973 suggested the following structure as that of the transition-state molecule:

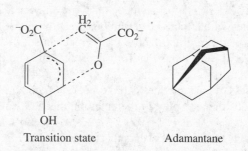

Transition state   Adamantane

(*b*) Andrews and Smith recognized the similarity between the structure of the transition state and *adamantane*.

   Adamantane has an *extra* methylene bridge linked to the six-membered ring that stabilizes a *cagelike* structure. The authors subsequently showed that some adamantane derivatives are potent inhibitors of chorismate mutase; thus these are examples of transition-state *analogs*.

   Note: Since the enzyme is not found in mammals, including humans, inhibitors of this enzyme *may* be an effective means of controlling bacterial infection. Certainly *species-selective toxicity* of the present kind is an important consideration in the development of new antimicrobial agents.

5.11. *Lysozyme* is an enzyme found in egg white and in tears. It hydrolyzes bacterial cell-wall polysaccharides, and it has one of the best understood of all enzyme mechanisms. The enzyme is a single polypeptide chain of 129 amino acids folded into a shape like a grain of puffed wheat, with a cleft along one side. Into the cleft fits the substrate, a polysaccharide made up of alternating units of *N*-acetylglucosamine (NAG) and *N*-acetylmuramic acid (NAM). Details of the binding of a competitive inhibitor (NAG)$_3$ to the active site have been obtained using X-ray crystallography. Using the X-ray structure, insights into the binding of substrates such as (NAG-NAM)$_3$ have been obtained (see Fig. 5-25 for a schematic model of the active site and the binding groups).

The enzyme catalyzes the cleavage of the bond between C-1 of residue 4 and the oxygen atom of the glycosidic linkage of residue 5 (see Fig. 5-25). Two amino acid side chains in the region of this bond can serve as proton donors or acceptors: Asp52 and Glu35, each of which is ~0.3 nm from the bond. Asp52 is in a polar environment and is ionized at the pH optimum of lysozyme (pH 5.0), whereas Glu35 is in a nonpolar region and is not ionized. The proposed catalytic mechanism is given in Fig. 5-26.

(*a*) To which EC group does lysozyme belong, and what are the first two integers in its EC number?

(*b*) Describe in words the various elementary chemical processes that take place in the cleavage of (NAM-NAG)$_3$, as shown in Fig. 5-26.

(*c*) What type of catalysis is operating here, covalent or noncovalent?

(*d*) What type of bonds are involved in the binding of the substrate (NAM-NAG)$_3$ to the enzyme?

(*e*) On binding to the enzyme, the sugar residue 4 is distorted from a *chair* conformation to that of a *half-chair* (Chap. 3). How might this aid catalysis?

SOLUTION

(*a*) Lysozyme is a *hydrolase*; therefore its first EC number (Table 5-1) is 3. Since is catalyzes the hydrolysis of a C—O bond its second number is 2 (Table 5-2).

(*b*) The carboxyl of Glu35 donates a proton, cleaving the C-1-O bond and releasing the disaccharide-5-6. The resulting *carbocation*, C-1 of ring-4, is stabilized by the negatively charged Asp52. The carbocation then reacts with the OH$^-$ from solvent water to release the tetrasaccharide 1-2-3-4. Glu35 is then reprotonated in readiness for the *next* round of reactions. The glutamic acid acts as a proton donor for the reaction, which is thus classified as *general acid catalysis*.

(*c*) Since proton donation is *central* to the catalytic process, this is an example of *general acid-base catalysis*; specifically, it is acid catalysis and it is *noncovalent*.

(*d*) In Fig. 5-26, the numerous dotted lines drawn between O's and NH's of amino acid residues and O's and NH's of the oligosaccharide indicate hydrogen bonding; however, van der Waals, noncovalent bonding also occurs.

(*e*) The binding of the substrate distorts the previous chair conformation of residue 4; this *reduces* the tendency for binding; i.e., ΔG for binding is elevated. This energy of distortion (strain) contributes to the total activation energy required for subsequent bond cleavage via formation of the carbonium ion.

5.12. *Carboxypeptidase A* (EC 3.4.17.1) is a pancreatic digestive enzyme that consists of a single polypeptide chain of 307 amino acids with a total M_r of 36,000. It catalyzes the cleavage of amino acid residues from C-termini of polypeptides. Importantly, for its mechanism of action, it contains one Zn^{2+} in its active site. The amino acid side chains that form its active site and the catalytic sequence are shown in Fig. 5-27.

(*a*) To what general class of enzyme does carboxypeptidase belong?

(*b*) What basic role does the Zn^{2+} play in the catalytic mechanism? What general type of catalysis occurs?

(*c*) Describe in words the sequence of events that is depicted in Fig. 5-27.

SOLUTION

(*a*) Carboxypeptidase is a hydrolase; i.e., it catalyzes the hydrolytic cleavage of a (peptide) bond. The second integer in its EC number sequence indicates that it cleaves a C—N bond (Table 5-2). It is an *exopeptidase*; i.e., it hydrolyzes amino acid residues from the carboxy terminus of a peptide. There also exist *amino*peptidases that catalyze the hydrolytic removal of the N-terminal amino acid residue of peptides. *Endo*peptidases are those hydrolases that hydrolyze peptide bonds, not at the C- or N-termini, but *within* the chain. Examples are *pepsin* from the stomach and the pancreatic peptidases, such as *chymotrypsin* and *trypsin*.

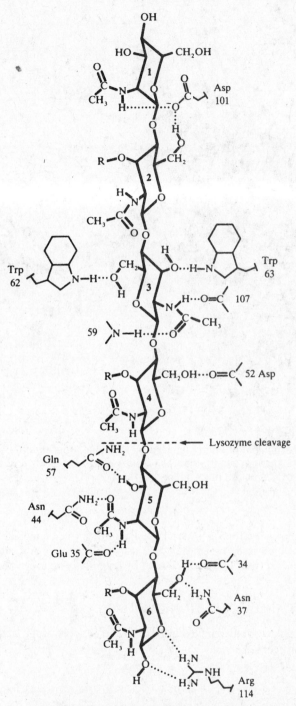

Fig. 5-25 Binding of the substrate (NAG-NAM)₃ to the active site of lysozyme. The substrate is drawn with boldface bonds, and the enzyme groups with lightface bonds. Hydrogen bonds are indicated by dotted lines.

(*b*) The Zn²⁺ acts as an *electrophile* that further polarizes the carbonyl oxygen [Fig. 5-26] before the formation of an ester linkage with the γ carboxyl of Glu270 in the enzyme. This linkage is covalent, so the reaction is an example of *covalent catalysis*.

(*c*) (1) The peptide substrate binds to the active site that contains Arg145, the Zn²⁺ ion, and the *hydrophobic pocket* that contains aromatic and aliphatic amino acid side chains. (2) Nucleophilic attack by Glu270 on the peptide bond is accompanied by the uptake of an H⁺ from Tyr248. (3) This results in cleavage

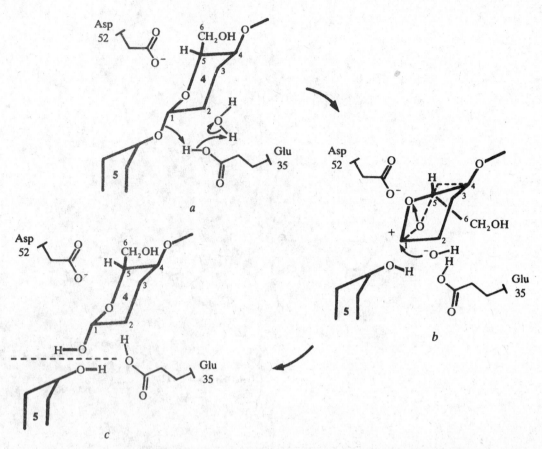

Fig. 5-26   Probable mechanism of bond cleavage by lysozyme. The structure drawn with thick solid lines is the substrate, and the lightface groups are on the enzyme. The small arrows indicate displacement of electron pairs during the reaction.

of the peptide bond and diffusion away of the C terminal, free amino acid. (4) The covalently bound polypeptide is then released to regenerate free enzyme by nucleophilic attack of an H_2O molecule on the anhydride bond of Glu270; this is followed by reprotonation of Tyr248.

RATE ENHANCEMENT AND ACTIVATION ENERGY

5.13. Calculate the rate enhancement achieved if the activation energy of the transition-state complex of an enzyme with its substrate is halved.

SOLUTION

From Eq. (5.2) the rate constant k is proportional to $e^{-\Delta G^{\ddagger}/RT}$. Thus,

$$k_{\text{NEW}} = k_{\text{OLD}}\, e^{-\Delta G^{\ddagger}/2RT}$$

It is clear that the rate enhancement is dependent upon both the original $\Delta G^{\ddagger}$ *and* the temperature. So unless these values are given, the rate enchancement cannot be calculated.

5.14. If $\Delta G^{\ddagger}$ and T in the previous example were -1 kJ mol^{-1} and 300 K, respectively, what would be the rate enhancement factor?

SOLUTION

$$k_{\text{NEW}} = k_{\text{OLD}} \exp[1000/(2 \times 8.314 \times 300)] = 1.22\, k_{\text{OLD}}$$

Thus, the rate enhancement would be 22%. Clearly, enzymes usually achieve far more dramatic rate increases than this. This suggests that $-\Delta G^{\ddagger}$ values are much larger in the first place (namely in free solution) and they are more dramatically reduced in enzymes than the twofold reduction discussed in this problem.

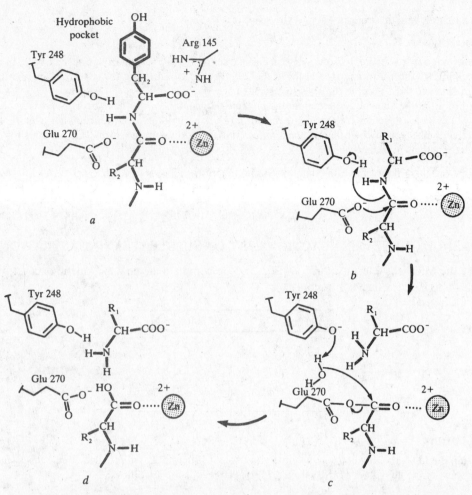

Fig. 5-27   Mechanism of the covalent catalysis of the hydrolysis of a C-terminal amino acid residue from a peptide by *carboxypeptidase A*. The reaction (a)→(d), and the bold-line structure is the peptide substrate. The C-terminal tyrosine side chain of the substrate shown in (a) is denoted by R1 in (b), (c), and (d).

ENZYME KINETICS—INTRODUCTION AND DEFINITIONS

5.15. Use the principle of mass action to write expressions for the rate equations for the following reactions:

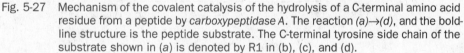

(a) $A \xrightarrow{k_1} P$

(b) $A \underset{k_{-1}}{\overset{k_1}{\rightleftharpoons}} P$

(c) $A + B \xrightarrow{k_1} P$

(d) $A + B \underset{k_{-1}}{\overset{k_1}{\rightleftharpoons}} P$

(e) $A + B \underset{k_{-1}}{\overset{k_1}{\rightleftharpoons}} P + Q + R$

SOLUTION

(a) $\dfrac{d[A]}{dt} = -k_1[A]$ $\qquad\qquad$ $\dfrac{d[P]}{dt} = -\dfrac{d[A]}{dt}$

(b) $\dfrac{d[A]}{dt} = -k_1[A] + k_{-1}[P]$ $\qquad$ $\dfrac{d[P]}{dt} = -\dfrac{d[A]}{dt}$

(c) $\dfrac{d[A]}{dt} = \dfrac{d[B]}{dt} = -k_1[A][B]$ $\qquad$ $\dfrac{d[P]}{dt} = -\dfrac{d[A]}{dt}$

(d) $\dfrac{d[A]}{dt} = \dfrac{d[B]}{dt} = -k_1[A][B] + k_{-1}[P]$ $\qquad$ $\dfrac{d[P]}{dt} = -\dfrac{d[A]}{dt}$

(e) $\dfrac{d[A]}{dt} = \dfrac{d[B]}{dt} = -k_1[A][B] + k_{-1}[P][Q][R]$ $\qquad$ $\dfrac{d[P]}{dt} = \dfrac{d[Q]}{dt} = \dfrac{d[R]}{dt} = -\dfrac{d[A]}{dt}$

5.16. What is the kinetic order of each of the reactions in Prob. 5.15?

SOLUTION

Reactions (*a*) and (*b*) are first-order, and in each direction for (*b*); (*c*) and (*d*) are second-order in the forward direction (left to right) and first-order in the reverse direction for (*d*); (*e*) is second-order in the forward direction and third-order in the reverse direction.

Note: For the uncatalyzed reaction, the *molecularity* and the *order* have been given as being the same. However, a trimolecular reaction, as depicted in (*e*), is an unlikely occurrence; what is more likely is the interaction between two of the reactants *followed* by reaction with the third. This amounts to two second-order reactions in sequence.

5.17. What are the units of the rate constants in the reaction schemes of Prob. 5.15?

SOLUTION

(*a*) k_1, s^{-1}; (*b*) k_1 and k_{-1}, s^{-1}; (*c*) k_1, $mol^{-1} L s^{-1}$; (*d*) k_1, $mol^{-1} L s^{-1}$, and k_{-1}, s^{-1}; (*e*) k_1, $mol^{-1} L s^{-1}$, and k_{-1}, $mol^{-2} L^2 s^{-1}$.

DEPENDENCE OF ENZYME REACTION RATE ON SUBSTRATE CONCENTRATION

5.18. Use the Michaelis-Menten equation [Eq. (5.9)] to complete the enzyme kinetic data set, when K_m is known to have a value of 1 mmol L^{-1}.

$[S]_0$ (mmol L^{-1})	v_0 (μmol L^{-1} min^{-1})
0.5	50
1.0	—
2.0	—
3.0	—
10.0	—

SOLUTION

Using Eq. (5.9), the first entry in the table gives $V_{max} = 150$ μmol L^{-1} min^{-1}. The other entries simply follow by substituting the values of $[S]_0$ into Eq. (5.9). The results are as follows:

$[S]_0$ (mmol L^{-1})	v_0 (μmol L^{-1} min^{-1})
0.5	50
1.0	75
2.0	100
3.0	112.5
10.0	136.4

5.19. Hexokinase catalyzes the phosphorylation of glucose and fructose by ATP. However, K_m for glucose is 0.13 mmol L^{-1}, whereas K_m for fructose is 1.3 mmol L^{-1}. Suppose that V_{max} is the same for both glucose and fructose and that the enzyme displays hyperbolic kinetics [Eq. (5.9)]. (*a*) Calculate the normalized initial velocity of the reaction (i.e., v_0 / V_{max}) for each substrate when $[S]_0 = 0.13$, 1.3, and 13.0 mmol L^{-1}. (*b*) For which substrate does hexokinase have the greater affinity?

SOLUTION

(*a*) For glucose the values of v_0/V_{max} are 0.5, 0.91, and 0.99, respectively; for fructose the values are 0.091, 0.56, and 0.91.

(*b*) Glucose; at lower concentrations the reaction rate is a greater fraction of V_{max} than it is with fructose.

GRAPHICAL EVALUATION OF K_m AND V_{max}

5.20. A constant amount of enzyme was added to a series of reaction mixtures containing different substrate concentrations. The initial reaction rates were measured from the initial slopes of progress curves of product formation. The data in Table 5-3 were obtained.

(*a*) What is V_{max} for this enzyme in the reaction mixture?

(*b*) What is K_m of the enzyme for the substrate?

Table 5-3 Steady-State Enzyme Kinetic Data	
$[S]_0$ (μmol L^{-1})	v_0 (μmol L^{-1} min^{-1})
0.1	0.27
2.0	5.0
10.0	20
20.0	40
40.0	64
60.0	80
100.0	100
200.0	120
1000.0	150
2000.0	155

SOLUTION

We can use the Lineweaver-Burk equation for the analysis. For this, the reciprocals of the entries in Table 5-3 must be calculated and then plotted as shown in Fig. 5-16. (Ignore the asterisks in Fig. 5-28, they refer to Prob. 5.22.) (*a*) From the reciprocal of the ordinate intercept, $V_{max} = 160$ μmol L^{-1} min^{-1}, and (*b*) from the reciprocal of the abscissal intercept, $K_m = 60$ μmol L^{-1}.

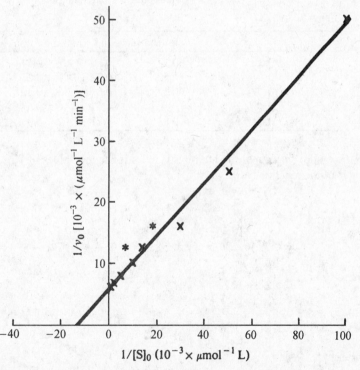

Fig. 5-28   Lineweaver-Burk plot of all but the first two data pairs in Table 5-3. (The asterisks refer to Prob. 5.22.)

5.21. One of the critical factors in the design of experiments to determine the values of steady-state enzyme kinetic parameters is the optimal choice of a range of substrate concentrations. On the basis of the data in Fig. 5-28, suggest a possible optimal range of substrate concentrations.

SOLUTION

The most useful concentrations for the purpose are those around K_m. In fact, a valuable *rule of thumb* is to use 1/5 to 5 times the expected value of K_m; by doing this v_0 will range from 0.17 to 0.83 times V_{max}. In other words, v_0 will be ~5 times greater at the highest concentration than at the lowest. However, if the initial concentrations are too low, then the velocity (initial slope) estimates become less precise because of the nonlinearity of the progress curves near zero time.

5.22. For the enzyme kinetic experiment described in Prob. 5.20, two additional data pairs were obtained: ($[S]_0 = 50$ μmol L^{-1}, $v_0 = 60$ μmol L^{-1} min^{-1}) and ($[S]_0 = 150$ μmol L^{-1}, $v_0 = 80$ μmol L^{-1} min^{-1}). Construct a Lineweaver-Burk plot from the whole data set. What are the estimated values of K_m and V_{max} now, as distinct from the results obtained in Prob. 5.20?

SOLUTION

The points marked by an asterisk in Fig. 5-28 are the new ones. When included in a visually weighted fit to the whole data set, they lead to the much lower estimates of K_m and V_{max} of 10 μmol L^{-1} and 25 μmol L^{-1} min^{-1}, respectively. Such changes in estimates brought about by using additional data, from a separate experiment, should alert the investigator to possible systematic artifacts in the outcome. The new analysis also shows the effects of outlying points on the parameter estimates. It alerts us to the idea that modern statistical methods of nonlinear regression analysis should be used to estimate parameter values in circumstances like the present. (We don't have the space to go into this here.)

MECHANISMS OF ENZYME INHIBITION

5.23. The effect of an inhibitor I on the rate of a single-substrate, enzyme-catalyzed reaction was investigated and gave the following results:

Substrate Concentration $[S]_0$ (mmol L^{-1})	Inhibitor Concentration (mmol L^{-1})		
	0	0.5	1.0
	Rate of reaction v_0 (mmol L^{-1} min^{-1})		
0.05	0.33	0.20	0.14
0.10	0.50	0.33	0.25
0.20	0.67	0.50	0.40
0.40	0.80	0.67	0.57
0.50	0.83	0.71	0.63

(*a*) What is the mode of action of the inhibitor? (*b*) Estimate the values of V_{max}, K_m, and the inhibition constant(s) of the reaction.

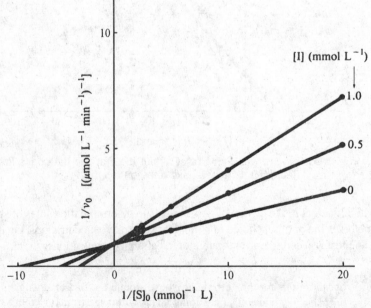

Fig. 5-29 Lineweaver-Burk plots showing the effects, on slope and abscissal intercept, of the presence of an inhibitor in the reaction mixture.

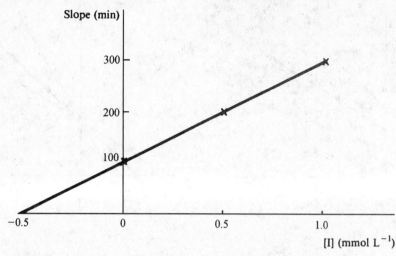

Fig. 5-30   Secondary plot of inhibition data given in Fig. 5-29.

SOLUTION

(a) The simplest way to deduce the mode of action of an inhibitor is to plot $1/v_0$ as a function of $1/[S]_0$ for each inhibitor concentration (Fig. 5-30).

   Equation (5.25) for pure competitive inhibition predicts that the slope of a Lineweaver-Burk plot will change with changes in inhibitor concentration, but the intercept on the $1/v_0$ axis (namely, $1/V_{max}$) will not. Thus, the above data are consistent with the inhibitor I acting as a *pure competitive* inhibitor.

(b) V_{max} is estimated from the intercept on the $1/v_0$ axis. We note from Eq. (5.25) that the slope of the plot is

$$Sl = \frac{K_m}{V_{max}}\left(1+\frac{[I]}{K_I}\right)$$

Thus, when Sl is plotted as a function of [I], we obtain the results shown in Fig. 5-30. The intercept of this *secondary plot* on the abscissa is $-K_I$; hence K_I is estimated to be 0.5 mmol L^{-1}. The intercept on the ordinate is K_m/V_{max}. Since we have already estimated V_{max}, then K_m can be calculated to be 0.1 mmol L^{-1}.

5.24. For each of the four types of inhibition of a Michaelis-Menten enzyme [competitive, Eq. (5.25); noncompetitive and mixed Eq. (5.29); and uncompetitive, Eq. (5.32)], derive the corresponding Lineweaver-Burk equations [Eqs. (5.26), and (5.30), respectively] and draw the *characteristic* plots that are the basis for the rapid visual identification of which type of inhibition applies when analyzing enzyme kinetic data.

SOLUTION

To derive the Lineweaver-Burk equations, we proceed by taking the reciprocals of each side of Eqs. (5.25), (5.29), and (5.32). The corresponding graphs of $1/v_0$ versus $1/[S]_0$ have various characteristic changes in slopes and intercepts as [I] is varied. Competitive inhibition gives lines that all intersect on the ordinate. Pure noncompetitive inhibition (in which $K_I' = K_I$) gives lines that all intersect on the abscissa. For anti- or uncompetitive inhibition, the *telltale* feature is that the set of lines are all parallel to each other. For mixed inhibition [$K_I' \neq K_I$ in Eq. (5.32)], both the slopes and the intercepts on the ordinate and abscissa differ for different values of [I]; see Fig. 5-31.

REGULATORY ENZYMES

5.25. The reaction scheme in Fig. 5-32 depicts isoleucine, E, synthesis from aspartate, A, by the bacterium *Rhodopseudomonas spheroides*. The control of flux through the pathway is via *sequential feedback control*. Describe, in words, the operation of this metabolic control system.

SOLUTION

Overproduction of E (isoleucine) inhibits enzyme E_6 (threonine deaminase), and the consequent rise in the concentration of D (threonine) reduces the rate of production of C (homoserine) *via* enzyme E_3 (homoserine dehydrogenase). The concentration of B (aspartate semialdehyde) rises, and this in turn inhibits E_1 (aspartokinase). Therefore it is obvious why the control system is called a *negative feedback network*, or that it displays *sequential feedback* control.

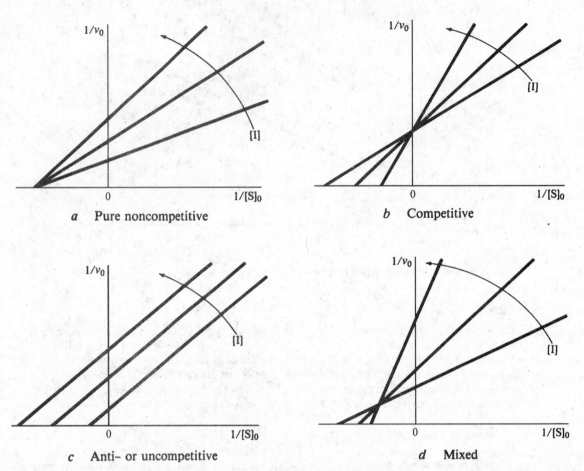

a   Pure noncompetitive   *b*   Competitive

c   Anti– or uncompetitive   *d*   Mixed

Fig. 5-31   Lineweaver-Burk plots for the four basic types of enzyme inhibition. The curved arrows indicate the direction of increasing [I].

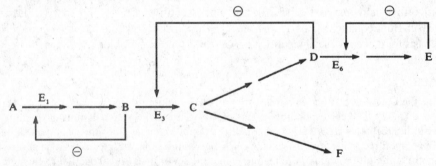

Fig. 5-32   Metabolic control network for isoleucine synthesis by *Rh. spheroides*.

5.26. For phosphofructokinase in the liver, ATP, ADP, and citrate are *effectors* of the reaction rate. Define what type of effectors they are, based on the information given in the reaction scheme shown in Fig. 5-33.

SOLUTION

1. ATP is a negative *homotropic* effector.
2. Citrate is a negative *heterotropic* effector.
3. ADP is a *positive homotropic* effector.

ATP exerts *negative feedforward* control (contrast with Example 5.24), while ADP exerts *positive feedback* control.

5.27. Describe the shapes of $1/v_0$ versus $1/[S]_0$ curves for enzymes exhibiting *positive cooperativity*, *no cooperativity*, and *negative cooperativity* of the kinetics of the reaction on substrate S.

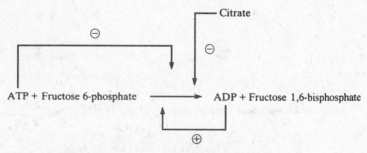

Fig. 5-33   Effector control of phosphofructokinase.

SOLUTION

In plots of $1/v_0$ versus $1/[S]_0$, the *slope* of the line is directly proportional to K_m. In a *positively cooperative* case, the affinity of the enzyme for the substrate *increases* and hence K_m *decreases* with increasing $[S]_0$ (or decreasing $1/[S]_0$ in the Lineweaver-Burk plot). Therefore, the slope of the plot of $1/v_0$ versus $1/[S]_0$ will decrease as $1/[S]_0$ decreases (Fig. 5-34*a*). In the case of *no cooperativity,* the affinity of the enzyme for the substrate, and hence K_m, is *constant* with changing $[S]_0$; therefore the slope of the plot of $1/v_0$ versus $1/[S]_0$ will be constant with $1/[S]_0$, giving Fig. 5-34*b*.

In the case of *negative cooperativity*, the affinity of the enzyme for the substrate *decreases* with increasing $[S]_0$, hence K_m *increases* with increasing $[S]_0$. Therefore the slope of the $1/v_0$ versus $1/[S]_0$ plot will *increase* with *decreasing* $1/[S]_0$, giving Fig. 5-34*c*.

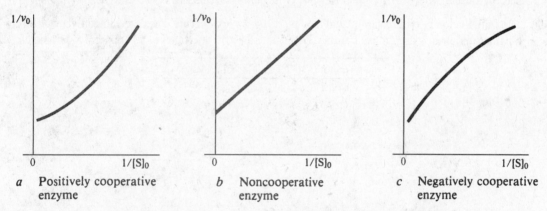

| *a* Positively cooperative enzyme | *b* Noncooperative enzyme | *c* Negatively cooperative enzyme |

Fig. 5-34   Characteristic Lineweaver-Burk plots for different types of control enzymes.

5.28. Prove that for a Michaelis-Menten enzyme, the control ratio R_S of Eq. (5.33) is equal to 81.

SOLUTION

The rate equation is

$$v_0 = \frac{V_{max}[S]_0}{K_m + [S]_0}$$

The equation is rearranged to give an expression for $[S]_0$, since we seek the ratio of the concentrations of S that give reaction velocities that are 0.9 and 0.1 of V_{max}. Thus,

$$[S]_0 = \frac{v_0 K_m}{V_{max} - v_0}$$

$$R_S = \frac{0.9V_{max}K_m(V_{max} - 0.1V_{max})}{0.1V_{max}K_m(V_{max} - 0.9V_{max})}$$

$$= \frac{0.9(0.9)}{0.1(0.1)} = 81$$

5.29. Derive the Hill equation [Eq. (5.35)].

SOLUTION

From the definition of K_b in Eq. (5.36), the concentration of the hemoglobin-O_2 complex is given by

$$[Hb(O_2)_n] = K_b[Hb](pO_2)^n$$

The fractional saturation of all the hemoglobin binding sites Y is given by

$$Y = \frac{\text{concentration of } Hb(O_2)_n}{\text{total concentration of } Hb}$$

$$Y = \frac{K_b[Hb](pO_2)^n}{[Hb] + K_b[Hb](pO_2)^n}$$

Cancellation of [Hb] from the numerator and denominator yields Eq. (5.35).

5.30. Prove that for $n > 1$ the Hill equation describes *positive cooperativity* in binding, or kinetics, for an enzyme.

SOLUTION

The Hill equation for an enzyme can be rearranged to give

$$[S]_0 = \left(\frac{v_0 K_m}{V_{max} - v_0} \right)^{1/n}$$

Therefore, from Prob. 5.28, $R_S = (81)^{1/n}$. Hence, if $n > 1$, then $R_S < 81$, and according to the definition given in Sec. 5.12, under "Kinetic Behavior of Regulatory Enzymes," the enzyme is said to be *positively cooperative*.

5.31. The initial velocity of a reaction catalyzed by a *regulatory enzyme* was determined over the following range of initial substrate concentrations. Determine the Hill coefficient and apparent K_m of the enzyme.

$[S]_0$ (mmol L^{-1})	v_0 (mmol L^{-1} min^{-1})
0.1	1.6×10^{-4}
0.3	1.4×10^{-3}
0.5	4.0×10^{-3}
1.0	1.6×10^{-2}
3.0	0.14
5.0	0.39
10.0	1.45
100.0	14.6
500.0	15.9
1000.0	16.0

SOLUTION

It is clear that V_{max} is ~16.0 mmol L^{-1} min^{-1} since the values of v_0 when $[S]_0$ was 500 and 1000 mmol L^{-1} are very similar. Thus the enzyme is almost saturated at these high substrate concentrations. Assuming that V_{max} has this value, we construct the following table expressing $[S]_0$ as a molar concentration. A plot of these data gives Fig. 5-35, which yields a slope of n and an ordinate intercept of $\log(1/K_m)$; with these data $n = 2$ and $K_m = 1$ mmol L^{-1}.

$\log[v_0/(V_{max} - v_0)]$	$\log[S]_0$
−5.00	−4.00
−4.06	−3.52
−3.60	−3.30
−3.00	−3.00
−2.05	−2.52
−1.60	−2.30
−1.00	−2.00
+1.02	−1.00
+2.20	−0.30
—	0.00

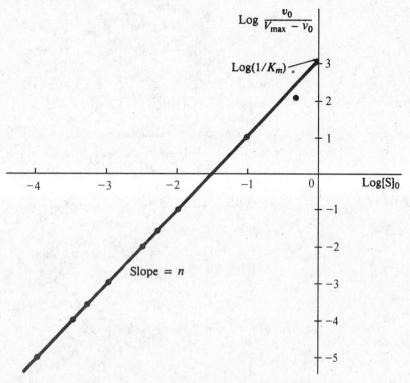

Fig. 5-35 Hill plot of an enzyme that displays positive cooperativity.

5.32. Derive an expression for the fractional saturation Y of the four-site homotropic effector system of the Monod-Wyman-Changeux type. Such a system provides a good description of oxygen binding to hemoglobin. This mechanism operates in addition to the heterotropic effector action of 23BPG on hemoglobin.

SOLUTION

Equation (5.43) describes the reaction scheme, where for oxygen binding to hemoglobin, X denotes O_2 and the R and T states are the relaxed and tense conformations of hemoglobin tetramers, respectively.

The concentration of the 10 states of the protein at equilibrium are related by the following expressions in which c is the ratio of the binding constants for the T and R states:

$$c = K_T/K_R$$

There are four binding sites for X on R_4 and T_4, and the Ks denote the intrinsic binding constant for each of these sites; therefore at equilibrium,

$$[R_4X] = 4\,K_R\,[R_4]\,[X] \qquad [T_4X] = 4\,K_T\,[T_4]\,[X] \tag{1}$$

The state R_4X has four possible arrangements of exactly one filled site, while R_4X_2 has six different possible arrangements of two filled sites. Therefore at equilibrium,

$$4\,[R_4X_2] = K_R\,6\,[R_4X][X] \qquad \text{or} \qquad [R_4X_2] = (3/2)\,K_R\,[R_4X][X]$$

and using Eq. (1), $[R_4X_2] = 6\,K_R^2\,[R_4][X]^2$ \hfill (2)

Similarly,

$$[T_4X_2] = 6\,K_T^2\,[T_4][X]^2 \tag{3}$$

The state R_4X_2 has six different possible arrangements of exactly two filled sites, while R_4X_3 has four possible arrangements of exactly three filled sites. Therefore at equilibrium,

$$6\,[R_4X_3] = K_R\,4\,[R_4X_2]\,[X] \qquad \text{or} \qquad [R_4X_3] = 2/3\,K_R\,[R_4X][X]$$

and using Eq. (2),

$$[R_4X_3] = 4 K_R^3 [R_4][X]^3 \tag{4}$$

Similarly,

$$[T_4X_3] = 4 K_T^3 [T_4][X]^3 \tag{5}$$

There is only one way of having R_4X_4, but R_4X_3 has four possible arrangements of exactly three filled sites, so

$$4 [R_4X_4] = K_R [R_4X_2] [X] \quad \text{or} \quad [R_4X_4] = 1/4 K_R [R_4X_3] [X]$$

and using Eq. (4),

$$[R_4X_4] = K_R^4 [R_4] [X]^4 \tag{6}$$

Similarly,

$$[T_4X_4] = K_T^4 [T_4][X]^4 \tag{7}$$

Finally, the relative concentrations of the R and T forms are determined by the value of the equilibrium constant L:

$$[T_4] = L [R_4] \tag{8}$$

The fractional saturation Y is defined as the sum of all occupied binding sites divided by the total of all the binding sites [see Eq. (5.40)], hence

$$Y = \frac{[R_4X] + 2[R_4X_2] + 3[R_4X_3] + 4[R_4X_4] + [T_4X] + 2[T_4X_2] + 3[T_4X_3] + 4[T_4X_4]}{4([R_4] + [R_4X] + [R_4X_2] + [R_4X_3] + [R_4X_4] + [T_4] + [T_4X] + [T_4X_2] + [T_4X_3] + [T_4X_4])}$$

$$= \frac{4K_R[R_4][X] + 12K_R^2[R_4][X]^2 + 12K_R^3[R_4][X]^3 + 4K_R^4[R_4][X]^4 + 4K_T[T_4][X] + 12K_T^2[T_4][X]^2 + 12K_T^3[T_4][X]^3 + 4K_T^4[T_4][X]^4}{4([R_4] + 4K_R[R_4][X] + 6K_R^2[R_4][X]^2 + 4K_R^3[R_4][X]^3 + K_R^4[R_4][X]^4 + [T_4] + 4K_T[T_4][X] + 6K_T^2[T_4][X]^2 + 4K_T^3[T_4][X]^3 + K_T^4[T_4][X]^4)}$$

$$= \frac{K_R[R_4][X](1 + 3K_R[X] + 3K_R^2[X]^2 + K_R^3[X]^3) + K_T[T_4][X](1 + 3K_T[X] + 3KT_R^2[X]^2 + K_T^3[X]^3)}{[R_4](1 + 4K_R[X] + 6K_R^2[X]^2 + 4K_R^3[X]^3 + K_R^4[X]^4) + L[R_4](1 + 4K_T[X] + 6K_T^2[X]^2 + 4K_T^3[X]^3 + K_T^4[X]^4)}$$

$$= \frac{K_R[X](1 + K_R[X])^3 + L_c K_R[X](1 + cK_R[X])^3}{(1 + K_R[X])^4 + L(1 + cK_R[X])^4}$$

$$= \frac{\alpha(1 + \alpha)^3 + L_c\alpha(1 + c\alpha)^3}{(1 + \alpha)^4 + L(1 + c\alpha)^4}$$

SUPPLEMENTARY PROBLEMS

5.33. Name the structures of the products of the following reactions and give the general EC classification of the enzyme involved:

(a) Glucose 6-phosphate + H_2O $\xrightarrow{\text{Glucose-6-phosphatase}}$

(b) Lactate + NAD^+ $\xrightleftharpoons{\text{Lactate dehydrogenase}}$ $NADH + H^+ +$

(c) Argininosuccinate $\xrightarrow{\text{Argininosuccinate lyase}}$ Fumarate +

(d) Fumarate + H_2O $\xrightarrow{\text{Fumarase}}$

5.34. Alcohol dehydrogenase catalyzes the oxidation of a variety of alcohols to their corresponding aldehydes. For a given amount of enzyme and a given substrate concentration (mol L^{-1}), the rates of the reaction with the following substrates are different. (*a*) Arrange the substrates in the order of decreasing reaction rate: methanol, ethanol, propanol, butanol, cyclohexanol, and phenol. (*b*) Give reasons for your speculations.

5.35. Glyceraldehyde-3-phosphate dehydrogenase has an essential cysteine residue in its active site. The enzyme forms a transient acyl compound with its substrate glyceraldehyde 3-phosphate. (*a*) What is the general chemical name of the compound? (*b*) Draw its likely structure.

5.36. What is the basic difference between the reaction catalyzed by: (*a*) a *mutase* enzyme and that catalyzed by an *isomerase*; (*b*) an *oxidase* and an *oxygenase*; and (*c*) the reverse reaction of a *reductase*? Give examples.

5.37. Given that the spontaneous hydration of CO_2 is reasonably fast, what might be a physiological rationalization for the need for the enzyme *carbonic anhydrase*?

5.38. What is a *suicide* substrate of an enzyme?

5.39. If the enzyme concentration in a reaction mixture at equilibrium is comparable to that of the reactants, is the ratio of the total product to the total substrate concentration(s) the same as if no enzyme were present?

5.40. Why are most enzymes so large relative to their substrates?

5.41. Give some examples of enzymes that are smaller than their substrates.

5.42. For the Michaelis-Menten equation, there are algebraic transformations in addition to the Lineweaver-Burk equation that yield straight-line plots from enzyme kinetic data. One such plot is due to G. S. Eadie and B. H. J. Hofstee; their equation takes the following form:

$$v_0 = -K_m \frac{v_0}{[S]_0} + V_{max}$$

Derive this equation.

5.43. (*a*) Draw the 5% coefficient of variation envelope around the data of Fig. 5-28. (*b*) Do this plot and its associated analysis yield unbiased estimates of the parameter values?

5.44. A fictitious enzyme from *Bettong* saliva was isolated and purified, and the following ATP-hydrolysis rates were obtained at an enzyme concentration of 10^{-8} mol L^{-1}:

[ATP] (μmol L^{-1})	5.0	1.7	1.0	0.7	0.56	0.56
v_0 (μmol L^{-1} min^{-1})	2.6	1.95	1.7	1.4	1.24	1.24

Estimate K_m, V_{max}, and k_{cat} of the enzyme.

5.45. In a Michaelis-Menten enzyme mechanism, what substrate concentrations (relative to K_m) are needed for the reaction rate to be: (*a*) 0.12 times V_{max}; (*b*) 0.25 times V_{max}; (*c*) 0.5 times V_{max}; and (*d*) 0.9 times V_{max}?

ANSWERS TO SUPPLEMENTARY PROBLEMS

5.33. (*a*) Glucose and phosphate, glucose-6-phosphatase, EC 3.1.3.9; (*b*) pyruvate, lactate dehydrogenase which is an oxidoreductase, hence its EC number begins with 1 and is 1.1.1.27; (*c*) arginine, argininosuccinate lyase, EC 4.3.2.1; (*d*) malate, fumarase which is a hydratase, EC 4.2.1.2.

5.34. (*a*) Ethanol > methanol > propanol > butanol > cyclohexanol > phenol. (*b*) Ethanol is the most favored substrate. Methanol is relatively too small for the active site, while the rest of the alcohols are too bulky or hydrophobic to be accommodated well in the active site.

5.35. (*a*) Thiohemiacetal.

(*b*)

5.36. (*a*) Mutases are members of the EC class 5, i.e., isomerases. The enzymes of class 5 catalyze geometrical structural changes *within* one molecule. When the isomerization consists of an intramolecular transfer of a *group*, the enzyme is called a mutase. Examples include phosphoglucomutase and chorismate mutase.

(*b* and *c*) These three types of enzymes are all members of EC class 1, namely, *oxidoreductases*. The enzymes of this class catalyze oxidation/reduction reactions, and the systematic name is *hydrogen donor:acceptor oxidoreductase*. The recommended name is *dehydrogenase* or, alternatively, *reductase*. *Oxidase* is a term that is used only in cases where O_2 is the electron acceptor. An example of a dehydrogenase is lactate dehydrogenase that catalyzes the formation of pyruvate and NADH from lactate and NAD^+. An example of an oxidase is choline oxidase (EC 1.1.3.4) that catalyzes the formation of betaine and H_2O_2 from choline and O_2.

5.37. In humans, the time spent by a red blood cell flowing through a capillary in the lung alveoli is ~0.3 s. In that time, HCO_3^- in the plasma reenters the red blood cell and is dehydrated to yield CO_2 that then diffuses across the plasma membrane of the red blood cell and adjacent capillary cells into an alveolus, from whence it is expelled into the atmosphere. In spite of its apparent speed, the spontaneous reaction is simply too slow for efficient expulsion of CO_2 in this process.

5.38. An analog of a substrate on which the enzyme operates but becomes covalently bound to a group in the active site, inhibiting it permanently.

5.39. No. The ratio of the *free* substrate and product will be the same, but the substrate and the product that are bound to the enzyme must be taken into account when the enzyme concentration is relatively high.

5.40. There is no single, simple answer to this question. Possible reasons are to: (1) provide the "correct" chemical environment for binding and catalysis, e.g., lower the pK_a of a binding or catalytic group; (2) absorb *energy of bombardment* from the diffusive (thermal) motion of water and "funnel" it into the active site to enhance the catalytic rate; (3) allow for *control* of catalysis via conformational changes that are induced by effectors that bind to other sites on the enzyme; (4) allow the fixing of enzymes in membranes or in large organized complexes; and (5) prevent their loss by filtration through membranes, e.g., from the plasma into the urine in the kidney.

5.41. DNA polymerase (Chap. 7), glycogen phosphorylase (Chap. 11).

5.42.
$$v_0 = \frac{V_{max}[S]_0}{K_m + [S]_0}$$

$$v_0(K_m + [S]_0) = V_{max}[S]_0$$

$$\frac{V_0(K_m + [S]_0)}{[S]_0} = \frac{V_{max}[S]_0}{[S]_0}$$

$$\frac{v_0 K_m}{[S]_0} + v_0 = V_{max}$$

$$v_0 = -K_m \frac{v_0}{[S]_0} + V_{max}$$

5.43. (*a*) Remember to use reciprocals. (*b*) No.

5.44. Use any of the graphical procedures. $K_m = 0.8$ μmol L^{-1}, $V_{max} = 3.0$ μmol L^{-1} min^{-1}, and from the expression $V_{max} = k_{cat}[E]_0$, $k_{cat} = 300$ s^{-1}.

5.45. (*a*) $(1/9)K_m$; (*b*) $(1/3)K_m$; (*c*) $1.0\ K_m$; (*d*) $9.0\ K_m$

CHAPTER 6

Signal Transduction

6.1   Introduction

Question: Do cells receive signals from their environment, apart from nutrients, that affect their metabolic behavior?

Yes, regardless of whether they are single-celled organisms like bacteria or protozoa or cells in the tissues of multicellular organisms, all cells sense changes in their extracellular environments and respond to these changes in a physiologically relevant way. Cells achieve this through the expression of specialized proteins called *receptors*.

Receptors for many different *ligands* are typically expressed on the cell's outer membrane. The event of binding extracellular molecules (*signaling ligands*) to their specific receptors is communicated to the cell interior; this is called *signal transduction*. Signal transduction is followed by sequential changes in the activities of proteins inside the cell. These *signaling pathways* allow cells to respond to the presence of the extracellular ligand in a relevant way; e.g., by activation or inactivation of enzymes already present in the cell, changing the pattern of genes expressed by the cell, etc.

Question: What kinds of extracellular molecules act as signaling ligands for receptors?

A wide range of extracellular molecules can act in this way. They include metal ions, low molecular weight compounds (e.g., amino acids and metabolites derived from them), peptides, and proteins. In particular physiological contexts, the signaling ligands for specific receptors are variously referred to as *hormones*, *neurotransmitters*, *growth factors*, *lymphokines,* or *cytokines*.

EXAMPLE 6.1   Insulin is a peptide hormone. It consists of two polypeptide chains, the A chain (2.4 kDa) and the B chain (3.4 kDa), that are linked by two disulfide bonds. Binding of insulin to its receptor (the insulin receptor) initiates a series of signaling pathways that (depending on the type of cell expressing the receptor) have consequences ranging from activation of some of the enzymes of *glycolysis* to up-regulation of the expression of proteins involved in energy metabolism.

6.2   General Mechanisms of Signal Transduction

In general terms, binding of a signaling ligand to a specific receptor can trigger signal transduction in two ways. As shown schematically in Fig. 6-1, ligand binding leads to a *structural change* in the receptor molecule. If this change is transmitted to the intracellular parts of the receptor, it alters the ways in which intracellular proteins that form part of a *signaling pathway* interact with the receptor. Alternatively, ligand binding can lead to *dimerization* of the receptor. The effect is to bring the cytoplasmic parts of the receptor molecules (together with any intracellular signaling molecules bound to them) into close physical proximity (Fig. 6-1). This initiates activation of an intracellular signaling pathway.

In Fig. 6-1(a), binding of a signaling molecule (black square) to a receptor (gray square) induces a structural change in it (gray circle) so that an intracellular signaling molecule (gray hexagon) can bind to it, initiating downstream signaling. In Fig. 6-1(b), the same effect is achieved through dimerization of the receptor.

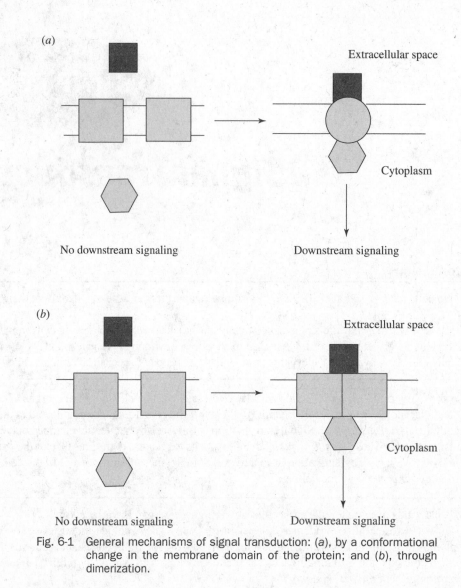

Fig. 6-1   General mechanisms of signal transduction: (*a*), by a conformational change in the membrane domain of the protein; and (*b*), through dimerization.

6.3   Classification of Receptors

Receptors can be classified in two general ways: in terms of signaling events, with respect to the anatomical relationship between the cells expressing the receptor and the cells that produce its ligand, and in terms of the structural properties of the receptor.

Anatomical Classification

Endocrine signaling

Endocrine signaling occurs when the cells that express the receptor are anatomically distant from those which produce its ligand.

Paracrine signaling

Paracrine signaling occurs when the cells that express the receptor are located in the same tissue as those which produce its ligand.

EXAMPLE 6.2   Transmission of a nerve impulse from one nerve cell to another is an example of *paracrine* signaling. Arrival of a nerve impulse at the end of an axon of a nerve leads to the release of ligand molecules (*neurotransmitters*) into the space (the synapse) between the axon of that nerve and an axon of a neighboring nerve. The neurotransmitter molecules diffuse across the synapse and bind to *specific receptors* that are expressed by the neighboring nerve. Signal transduction arising at the receptor initiates *propagation of a nerve impulse* in the neighboring nerve.

Autocrine signaling

Autocrine signaling occurs when the same cell produces *both the receptor and its ligand*.

EXAMPLE 6.3 Interleukin 12 (IL-12) is a cytokine that is produced by a class of T cells called *regulatory T cells* (TReg cells). Binding of IL-12 to its receptor on TReg cells induces them to become *tolerant to antigens* to which they would otherwise respond.

Contact signaling

Contact signaling occurs when a cell surface protein that is expressed by one cell binds to a cell surface protein that is expressed by another cell. In contact signaling (that requires the two cells to be in close physical contact) it is somewhat arbitrary to say that *one protein is the ligand* and the other is the *receptor*.

EXAMPLE 6.4 CD95L is a cell surface protein that is produced by cytotoxic T cells which have been activated by prior contact with a specific virus-derived peptide. In this case the peptide must be bound to a cell surface major histocompatibility complex (MHC) protein. If an activated cytotoxic T cell contacts a cell which is infected with the virus (through the presence of virus peptide:MHC complexes on the surface of the virus-infected cell), contact signaling between CD95L and a cell surface protein called CD95 on the virus-infected cell will occur. Signal transduction arising from this leads to induction of programmed cell death (apoptosis) in the virus-infected cell. The effect is prevention of replication of the virus in the infected cell.

Intracrine signaling

Intracrine signaling occurs when a receptor that is expressed on an *internal* cell membrane responds to a ligand produced inside the cell.

EXAMPLE 6.5 *Inositol trisphosphate* (IP₃) is often produced by cells in response to the binding of an extracellular ligand to a cell membrane receptor (see Sec. 6.3). Receptors for IP₃ are located on the membranes of the *endoplasmic reticulum*. Binding of IP₃ to these receptors leads to the release of Ca^{2+} from stores in the lumen of the endoplasmic reticulum. The IP₃ receptor is therefore an example of a *ligand-gated ion channel* (see below)

Structural Classification

Receptors are extraordinarily diverse with respect to both the chemical nature of their specific ligands and the mechanisms and physiological consequences of the signal transduction events that follow the binding of these ligands. Despite this, they can be classified into a number of major structural classes.

G Protein-Coupled Receptors

G protein-coupled receptors are the largest single class of receptors, with more than *1000* having been identified in the human genome. They have a common molecular architecture, containing seven *hydrophobic α-helices* that span the cell membrane. For this reason they are sometimes known as 7-transmembrane section (*7-TMS*) receptors. Their ligand-binding sites are located within the extracellular polypeptide chain loops (Fig. 6-2). Signal transduction from G protein-coupled receptors is mediated by *heterotrimeric G proteins* (see Sec. 6.8) that bind to the cytoplasmic loops in the polypeptide chain of the receptors.

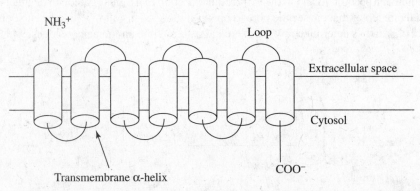

Fig. 6-2 Schematic depiction of a G protein-coupled receptor.

Cytokine receptors

Cytokine receptors are composed of two or more polypeptide chains. Some of these are shared between different receptors while others are unique to particular receptors. They all have: (1) an N-terminal extracellular domain that provides binding sites for their cytokine ligands; (2) a hydrophobic α-helix that spans the cell membrane; and (3) a C-terminal cytoplasmic domain that contains binding sites for *protein tyrosine kinases* that play roles in signal transduction from these receptors (see Fig. 6-3).

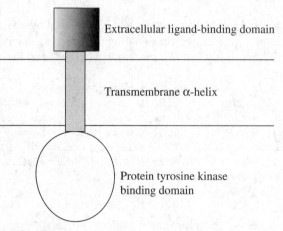

Extracellular ligand-binding domain

Transmembrane α-helix

Protein tyrosine kinase binding domain

Fig. 6-3   Schematic depiction of a cytokine receptor.

EXAMPLE 6.6   What are the physiological functions of *cytokine receptors*?

Cytokine receptors, such as those for interleukin 2 and erythropoietin, are typically involved in regulating the proliferation and differentiation of blood cells (hemopoietic cells).

Growth factor receptors

Growth factor receptors are structurally similar to cytokine receptors, being composed of: (1) an N-terminal extracellular domain that provides binding sites for their cytokine ligands; (2) a hydrophobic α-helix which spans the cell membrane; and (3) a C-terminal cytoplasmic domain. The cytoplasmic domains of growth factor receptors contain an *intrinsic* protein tyrosine kinase activity, in contrast to cytokine receptors, in which the associated protein tyrosine kinases are separate proteins.

EXAMPLE 6.7   What are the physiological functions of *growth factor receptors*?

As their name implies, growth factor receptors are particularly important in regulating cell division. Under most circumstances, normal mammalian cells are unable to divide unless they receive an external stimulus in the form of binding of a growth factor to its specific receptor.

Ligand-gated ion channels

Typically, ligand-gated ion channels are multi-subunit complexes with the polypeptide chains of each subunit forming a *transmembrane α-helical bundle*. Usually a *pore* is created at the interface between the subunits (Fig. 6-4). Binding of a specific ligand to the extracellular portion of a ligand-gated ion channel triggers a structural change in the receptor that causes the pore to open (or close). This allows (or prevents) entry of ions, the chemical nature of which is determined by the chemical nature of the amino acid residues, which line the pore.

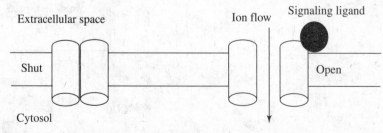

Extracellular space   Ion flow   Signaling ligand

Shut   Open

Cytosol

Fig. 6-4   Schematic structure and function of a ligand-gated ion channel.

EXAMPLE 6.8 The *nicotinic acetylcholine receptor* is a ligand-gated ion channel. This receptor is located in skeletal muscle cells at the synapses between them and motor neurons. The neurotransmitter *acetylcholine* that is released from the motor neuron binds to the receptor, leading to opening of its ion channels. This allows an influx of Na^+ ions into the muscle cell. In turn this leads to the release of Ca^{2+} ions from their intracellular store, the sarcoplasmic reticulum, into the cytosol; the resulting rise in cytosolic Ca^{2+} concentration induces *muscle contraction*.

Steroid receptors

Steroid receptors are an exception to the general rule that receptors are membrane proteins. Steroid receptors are normally present as soluble proteins in the cytoplasm. *Steroids* diffuse across the hydrophobic cell membrane and bind to their specific receptors. The receptors then *translocate* to the nucleus by simple diffusion, where they act as *transcription factors* by binding to specific regions of chromosomal DNA (*steroid response elements*), thus *controlling transcription* of particular genes.

Other receptors

Some receptors do not fall readily into the structural classes described above. Examples of these include: (1) *death receptors*, (2) guanylyl cyclase-coupled receptors, and (3) phosphoprotein phosphatase receptors.

 Death receptors are involved in signaling of programmed cell death (*apoptosis*). CD95 (Example 6.4) is a member of the death receptor family. Binding of specific ligands to death receptors leads to their trimerization. This triggers activation of an intracellular protease cascade. These proteases (the caspases) cleave many intracellular proteins, leading to cell death.

EXAMPLE 6.9 Natriuretic peptides (NP) regulate a variety of physiological functions, including control of blood pressure. The cytoplasmic domains of two of their receptors, NPR-A and NPR-B, are *guanylyl cyclases*. Binding of NP to these receptors activates the guanylyl cyclases, leading to increased intracellular levels of cGMP. Interestingly, one of the main peptide components of the venom of the duckbill platypus, an Australian marsupial, is a natriuretic peptide. Lowered blood pressure is a clinical sign in *platypus envenomation*.

EXAMPLE 6.10 *CD45* is an example of a *phosphoprotein phosphatase receptor*. CD45 is expressed on all leukocytes, including *T cells*. Contact signaling between CD45 on T cells and another protein called *CD22* (expressed by antigen-presenting cells) allows the phosphoprotein phosphatase that forms part of the cytoplasmic domain of CD45 to catalyze removal of phosphate groups from phosphorylated substrate proteins; this is important in antigen-driven activation of T cells.

6.4 Common Themes in Signaling Pathways

Despite the complexity of the details of individual signaling pathways (see Sec. 6.5), there are several *recurring biochemical themes* present in many of these pathways.

Activation of Protein Kinases

Most signaling pathways include steps in which *protein kinases are activated*. There are *three* major classes of protein kinases: (1) *Protein tyrosine kinases* catalyze the transfer of the γ-phosphate of ATP onto *tyrosine* residues in their substrate proteins; (2) *Protein serine/threonine kinases* similarly transfer the γ-phosphate of ATP onto *serine or threonine* residues; and (3) *Mixed-function protein kinases* catalyze the transfer of the γ-phosphate of ATP onto *tyrosine, serine,* or *threonine* residues.

EXAMPLE 6.11 What is the chemical nature of the reaction that is catalyzed by a *protein tyrosine kinase*?
 It is the transfer of the γ-phosphate of ATP onto the *phenolic –OH group* of a tyrosine residue on a substrate *protein*.

EXAMPLE 6.12 What is the chemical nature of the reaction that is catalyzed by a *protein serine/threonine kinase*?
 The enzyme catalyzes the transfer of the γ-phosphate of ATP onto the *side chain –OH group* of either a *serine* or a *threonine* residue on a substrate *protein*.

Protein Kinase Cascades

It is common for the substrates of protein kinases to include *other protein kinases*. This provides a mechanism for amplifying the initial signal of binding of a signaling ligand to its receptor, known as a *protein kinase cascade*. A protein kinase cascade occurs when activation of one protein kinase leads to phosphorylation (and consequent activation) of a second kinase, followed by phosphorylation and activation of a third kinase, etc.

Activation of Phospholipases

Many signaling pathways include steps in which phospholipases are activated.

EXAMPLE 6.13 What is the chemical nature of the reaction that is catalyzed by a *phospholipase*?

    Phospholipases catalyze the hydrolysis of bonds in phospholipids. As shown in Fig. 6-5, there are four major classes of phospholipases, which catalyze the hydrolysis of different bonds in phospholipids.

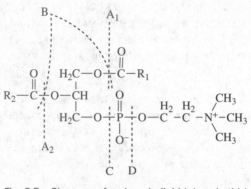

Fig. 6-5 Cleavage of a phospholipid (*phosphatidyl choline*) by different phospholipases. The dotted lines indicate bonds that are hydrolyzed by the respective phospholipases; the letters denote the type of phospholipase that catalyzes the hydrolysis; and R_1 and R_2 denote fatty acyl chains.

EXAMPLE 6.14 Which classes of phospholipases are important in signaling pathways?

    The C class of phospholipases (*PL-C*) is particularly important in signaling pathways. In this context, their primary substrate is *phosphatidyl inositol bisphosphate*. As shown in Fig. 6-6, cleavage of phosphatidyl inositol bisphosphate by a PL-C yields two products, IP_3 (see Example 6.5) and diacylglycerol (DAG). The D class of phospholipases (*PL-D*) is emerging as an important player in intracellular signaling; they were first revealed in humans in 1982 in red blood cells by one of us (Philip Kuchel) and his group, having previously been thought to exist only in plants.

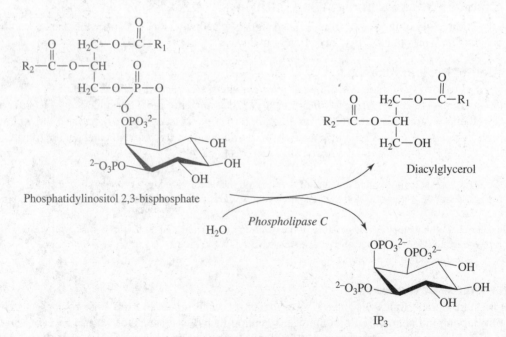

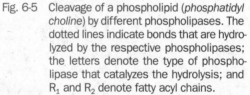

Phosphatidylinositol 2,3-bisphosphate

Diacylglycerol

H_2O

Phospholipase C

IP_3

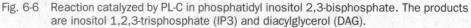

Fig. 6-6 Reaction catalyzed by PL-C in phosphatidyl inositol 2,3-bisphosphate. The products are inositol 1,2,3-trisphosphate (IP3) and diacylglycerol (DAG).

Regulated Protein Degradation

Many signaling pathways are controlled by regulating the degradation of key protein components in them. Intracellular proteins are degraded through the action of *proteasomes* that are large (~2 MDa) protein complexes present in the cytoplasm. Proteasomes contain a number of *proteases* that collectively degrade proteins to their constituent amino acids; these are then used to synthesize new protein molecules or are metabolized for energy.

EXAMPLE 6.15 What is the structural arrangement of a proteasome?

A proteasome has two components. First, the 20S catalytic core is a *hollow cylinder* in which proteolysis occurs. Second, the core is flanked by 19S *regulatory particles*; the protein subunits of these form a lid and baselike structure (Fig. 6-7).

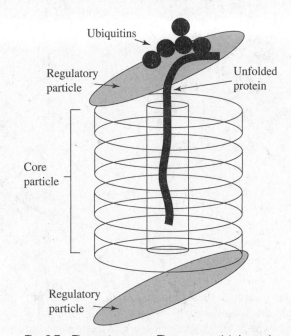

Fig. 6-7   The proteasome. The *core particle* is made up of two copies of each of 14 different proteins that are assembled in groups of seven forming a ring. The four rings are stacked on each other like four donuts. There are two identical *regulatory particles*, one at each end of the core particle. Each is made up of 14 different proteins, none being the same as those in the core particle; six of these are ATPases, and some of the subunits have binding sites that recognize the small (8.5 kDa) protein *ubiquitin*.

EXAMPLE 6.16 How does the proteasome recognize proteins that are to be degraded?

Proteins which are destined for degradation by proteasomes are targeted by covalent attachment of a protein called ubiquitin (Ub). Ub is a small protein (76 residues) that is linked to target proteins via *isopeptide* bonds, which form between lysine side chains (the ε-amino group) on the target protein and the carboxyl group of the C-terminal gly76 of Ub. After one Ub has been attached, polyUb chains are formed on the target protein through successive attachment of Ub molecules via Lys48-Gly76 isopeptide bonds.

Components of the 19S proteasomal particle recognize polyUb chains on target proteins (Fig. 6-7). Deubiqitinating enzymes then remove the Ub, which is recycled, and the target protein is delivered to the catalytic core (in an ATP-dependent fashion) where it is degraded.

It is of interest to know how polyUb is attached to target proteins: This is achieved through the consecutive action of four enzymes (Fig. 6-8). In the first stage, E_1 (Ub-activating enzyme) is linked to Ub via a thioester bond in an ATP-dependent reaction. The Ub is then transferred to E_2 (*Ub-conjugating enzyme*). The Ub is

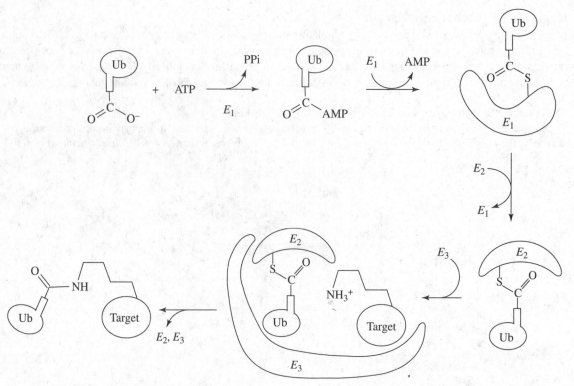

Fig. 6-8 The reactions of ubiquitinylation.

then linked to the target protein through the action of E_3 (*Ub ligase*). E_3 enzymes exist in two classes; one class is directly catalytic and the second class forms a scaffold, allowing E_2 to interact with the substrate protein. *HECT*-type and *SCF*-type E_3 enzymes are respective examples of these two classes.

EXAMPLE 6.17 A Ub ligase called *APC* is activated by signaling pathway-dependent phosphorylation as cells approach mitosis. This E_3 enzyme catalyzes the attachment of Ub to various proteins, including *lamins* that are components of the *nuclear membrane*. Degradation of lamins allows *dissolution* of the nuclear membrane, permitting release of chromatids in preparation for mitosis.

Adaptor Proteins
In many signaling pathways, different proteins (e.g., protein kinases and their substrates) must be brought into physical proximity to exert their effects. Often this arises through the action of one or more *adaptor proteins* that *link* the kinases and their substrates.

EXAMPLE 6.18 Proteins that bear *phosphotyrosine* residues can be linked to other proteins through the action of adaptor proteins that contain *SH2 domains*. These domains have a binding pocket that is specific for phosphotyrosine residues. Grb2 is a member of this group of adaptor proteins.

Short-Term and Long-Term Consequences of the Action of Signaling Pathways
In general, binding of a ligand to a specific receptor can have both short-term (time scale of minutes to hours) and long-term (time scale of hours to days) consequences. These different time scales usually reflect the effects on the cell of different downstream targets of the signaling pathway. In the case of short-term effects, the downstream targets are enzymes or other proteins that are already present in the cell. In contrast, long-term effects depend on the synthesis of new protein molecules; in this case the downstream targets of the signaling pathways are often *transcription factors*. A long chain of events must occur before the effects are manifest: namely, (1) activation of the transcription factor(s); (2) up-regulation of transcription of the gene(s) under their control; (3) assembly of ribosomes bearing cognate mRNA(s); and (4) production of sufficient amounts of the new protein(s) for the long-term effect to be sustained.

6.5 Complications in Signaling Pathways

There are several reasons why experimental attempts to understand signaling pathways have proved to be challenging. To explain these, let us first consider some terminology.

Nomenclature

Typically, when a new protein with a role in signal transduction is discovered, it is given a name, which makes sense to members of the laboratory concerned. These names are often abbreviated, and different laboratories, studying different facets of signaling pathways, may give the same protein different (abbreviated) names. The resulting 'tower of Babel effect' can hinder understanding, especially as different textbooks and research papers may use different names for the same protein or class of proteins.

EXAMPLE 6.19 SoS is a protein that is involved in signaling pathways that are initiated by growth factor receptors (see Sec. 6.7). It derives its name from a protein called *Sevenless*, which (when present in mutant form) leads to defects in the development of the fruit fly *Drosophila*. Proteins with sequence similarity to Sevenless were subsequently discovered in mammals. One of them was called *Son of Sevenless*, abbreviated as SoS. (Yes, molecular cell biologists do have a sense of humor!)

Convergent and Divergent Signaling Pathways

As shown in Fig. 6-9, a signaling pathway which is initiated by signal transduction from one type of receptor can be divergent, branching to reach two different downstream targets, e.g., two different transcription factors. Conversely, signaling pathways initiated by signal transduction from different types of receptors can be convergent, having the same downstream target. Convergence and divergence can pose significant experimental and conceptual difficulties when trying to understand the physiological consequences of ligand binding to a particular receptor.

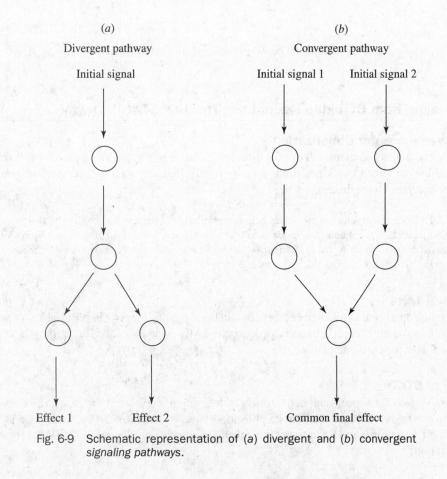

Fig. 6-9   Schematic representation of (*a*) divergent and (*b*) convergent *signaling pathways*.

Crosstalk between Signaling Pathways

It is very common for proteins that are involved in signaling to be members of *more than one* signaling pathway. This leads to *crosstalk* between the pathways. Because of this, the relative concentrations and activities of such proteins may affect the extent to which signaling occurs down the different pathways. This is shown schematically in Fig. 6-10, in which protein 3, which is activated as a consequence of signal transduction from receptor B, can activate protein 5; but it is also inhibited by protein 7, which is activated as a consequence of signal transduction from receptor C. Protein 1, activated by receptor B, is activated by protein 7 but inhibited by protein 6, both of which are activated by receptor C. Clearly, in this hypothetical example, the extent to which the downstream targets of the three pathways become activated will depend, in a very complicated way, on the activities of the proteins in all three pathways, because of *crosstalk* between the pathways.

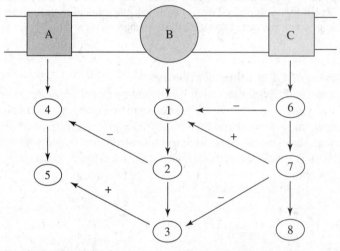

Fig. 6-10 Crosstalk between hypothetical signaling pathways.

6.6 Signaling from Cytokine Receptors: The JAK:STAT Pathway

Ligand-Driven Receptor Dimerization

In the absence of a specific cytokine, cytokine receptors are thought to exist as monomers in the plasma membrane. However, when cytokines bind to their specific binding sites on the external domains of the receptors, the receptors form dimers.

EXAMPLE 6.20 Does the structure of cytokines help to explain ligand-driven dimerization of their receptors?

Yes. Most cytokines have a common *four-helix bundle* structure. Experimental techniques including *scanning alanine mutagenesis* have been used to show that cytokines have several regions that are recognized by their receptors. Therefore, one cytokine molecule can act to cross-link two separate receptor molecules.

Activation of JAKs

The cytoplasmic domains of cytokine receptors contain binding sites for protein tyrosine kinases called JAKs (*Janus kinase*). In the absence of a bound cytokine, the JAKs have low catalytic activity but they become highly active following cytokine binding.

Activation of STATs

STAT proteins (*signal transducers and activators of transcription*) are a family of *transcription factors*. They contain specific *tyrosine* residues that can be phosphorylated by activated *JAKs*. Following this they form dimers that enter the nucleus and bind to specific *enhancer elements* on chromosomal DNA, eliciting specific gene transcription.

EXAMPLE 6.21 Why do phosphorylated STATs form dimers?

All STATs contain SH2 domains. These enable them to bind to *phosphotyrosine* residues on cytokine receptors. They can then be phosphorylated by the *activated JAKs*. Once this has occurred, they form dimers through interactions of mutual phosphotyrosine:SH2 domains.

Regulation of the Cytokine Receptor Signaling Pathway

The signaling pathway described above provides a mechanism by which the binding of a cytokine to its receptor leads to induction of the expression of specific genes. Physiologically, the proteins encoded by these genes play roles in the proliferation and differentiation of *hemopoietic* cells.

However, *constitutive expression* of these genes could have undesirable consequences. Therefore, there are a number of regulatory mechanisms that act to control signaling through the cytokine receptor pathway. One such mechanism involves a protein tyrosine *phosphatase* called *SHP2*; this catalyzes dephosphorylation of phosphotyrosine residues on the cytokine receptors, as well as on JAKs and STATs, and this inactivates the pathway.

EXAMPLE 6.22 How does SHP2 recognize its substrate proteins?

SHP2 contains *SH2 domains,* so it binds to *phosphotyrosine* residues; this leads to activation of the enzyme. Therefore, SHP2 could bind to phosphotyrosine residues on a cytokine receptor, become activated, and then catalyze the hydrolysis of phosphate groups from the phosphotyrosine residues of phosphorylated JAKs that are also bound to the cytokine receptor.

Among the genes whose transcription is enhanced by the JAK:STAT signaling pathway is a group that encodes for a family of proteins called the *SOCS proteins* (*s*uppressors *o*f *c*ytokine *s*ignaling). As their name implies, SOCS proteins inhibit signaling from cytokine receptors and therefore constitute a negative feedback loop for control of this pathway.

6.7 Signaling from Growth Factor Receptors

Families of Growth Factor Receptors

Amino acid sequence analyses reveal the existence of more than 50 different growth factor receptors. These can be grouped into at least *18 families*, notable examples of which include the (1) *platelet-derived* growth factor receptor family, (2) *fibroblast* growth factor receptor family, (3) *epidermal* growth factor receptor family, and (4) *insulin-like* growth factor receptor family.

The cytoplasmic domains of all of these receptors have an *intrinsic* protein tyrosine kinase activity, and all the receptors have hydrophobic transmembrane sequences. Their extracellular regions are more variable in structure. Depending on the receptor, they may contain a range of domains, including (1) immunoglobulin domains, (2) cysteine-rich motifs, (3) fibronectin type III repeats, and (4) EGF motifs. These can be present singly or in different combinations. Growth factor receptors are therefore examples of *mosaic proteins*.

Dimerization of Growth Factor Receptors

As is the case with cytokine receptors, growth factor receptors exist in the plasma membrane of a cell, predominantly as monomers in the absence of their specific ligands. Binding of a growth factor to the receptor is followed by the formation of *dimers* of the receptor.

Activation of the Protein Tyrosine Kinase

Activation of the protein tyrosine kinase occurs after dimerization of growth factor receptors. This arises from *transautophosphorylation*. Unphosphorylated protein tyrosine kinase domains have low enzymic activity, but when they are brought into proximity to each other by receptor *dimerization*, they can phosphorylate each other. The effect is to convert them to a *high-activity* state.

Recruitment of Adaptors and Effectors to Phosphorylated Growth Factor Receptors

Typically, the activated protein tyrosine kinases of growth factor receptors catalyze the autophosphorylation of a number of tyrosine residues on the cytoplasmic domains of the adjacent receptor molecule. These phosphorylated residues provide *docking sites* for both effector and adaptor proteins that mediate downstream signaling pathways.

EXAMPLE 6.23   PL-Cγ (see Sec. 6.4) binds to phosphotyrosine residues on the cytoplasmic domains of growth factor receptors via its SH2 domains. This has two consequences. First, it becomes activated by receptor tyrosine protein kinase-catalyzed phosphorylation. Second, PL-Cγ is normally found in the cytoplasm. Its recruitment to the cytoplasmic domains of growth factor receptors places it in proximity with the cytoplasmic leaflet of the cell membrane, where it is able to catalyze cleavage of the membrane phospholipid *phosphatidyl inositol bisphosphate* to yield two products, IP_3 and DAG (see Fig. 6-6).

EXAMPLE 6.24   What are the signaling consequences of IP_3 and DAG production?

IP_3 promotes release of Ca^{2+} into the cytoplasm from stores in the endoplasmic reticulum (see Example 6.5). One consequence is the binding of Ca^{2+} to the protein *calmodulin*. The calmodulin:Ca^{2+} complex binds to and activates members of a family of protein kinases, the *calmodulin-activated protein kinases*. This family of serine/threonine protein kinases has a large number of substrates, ranging from the light chain of the muscle protein myosin to transcription factors such as CREB (see Solved Problem 6.14).

Another consequence of the production of IP_3 and DAG is *activation* of protein kinase C. This serine/threonine protein kinase occurs in at least 10 different isoenzymic forms. Most of these forms require both bound Ca^{2+} and DAG for high enzymic activity. The nature of the substrates of protein kinase C depends both on the isoform and on the tissue(s) in which the isoform is expressed.

One of the best understood adaptor proteins that is involved in *downstream signaling* from growth factor receptors is *Grb2*. As shown in Fig. 6-11, binding of Grb2 (via its SH2 domain) to phosphorylated growth factor receptors is the first stage in linking these receptors to a signaling molecule called Ras.

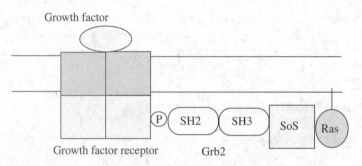

Fig. 6-11   Signaling between growth factor receptors and Ras.

The diagram (Fig. 6-11) shows a growth factor receptor that has dimerized after binding its cognate growth factor. Grb2 binds to phosphorylated tyrosine residues on the receptor through its SH2 domain. The SH3 domain of Grb2 binds to SoS, which in turn binds Ras.

Growth Factor Receptors and Protein Kinase Cascades

Activation of Ras initiates a complicated *protein kinase cascade* that culminates in the activation of a *mitogen-activated protein kinase* (MAP kinase). At its core are three protein kinases. The first, *Raf*, is activated by binding to Ras. Raf, which is functionally a *MAP kinase kinase kinase*, phosphorylates serine and threonine residues on the second kinase (known as *MEK* in mammals), leading to its activation. Functionally, MEK is a *MAP kinase kinase*. Finally, activated MEK phosphorylates specific serine and tyrosine residues on a MAP kinase (called *Erk* in mammals), which is then able to phosphorylate its downstream targets.

EXAMPLE 6.25   The downstream targets of the MAP kinase cascade include *transcription factors*, such as Fos and Myc. Among the genes whose expression is controlled by Fos and Myc are *G1 cyclins* (such as cyclin D; see Sec. 6.7) that are required for cell proliferation.

EXAMPLE 6.26   What are possible selective advantages of the MAP protein kinase cascade over less complicated schemes of reactions?

Phosphorylation of the tyrosine residues on growth factor receptors and activation of Ras are both short-lived events. Phosphoprotein phosphatases reverse the phosphorylation, and the GTP bound to Ras is rapidly hydrolyzed to GDP when a GAP (see Solved Problem 6.11) binds to Ras. Therefore, transducing these short-lived signals into longer-lived serine/threonine phosphorylations on MEK and MAP kinases allows the signal, which is initiated by binding of a growth factor to its receptor, to persist. The *selection* of a particular pathway is achieved at the level of the MAP kinases; these are inactive unless they are phosphorylated on specific serine and tyrosine residues, and the only known substrates for MAP kinase kinases are MAP kinases.

PI-3-Kinases and Cell Growth

The signaling pathways described above *stimulate cell division*. However, cell proliferation requires cell enlargement (cell growth) as well. Signaling pathways that involve *phosphatidylinositol-3-kinase* (PI-3-kinase) play a role in this. Activated PI-3-kinases catalyze phosphorylation of inositol phospholipids at the 3 position of the inositol ring to generate lipids called $PI(3,4)P_2$ or $PI(3,4,5)P_3$.

EXAMPLE 6.27   By what protein interaction is PI-3-kinase activated?

Typically, PI-3-kinases are composed of *regulatory* and *catalytic* subunits. Activation of them involves binding of the catalytic subunits to activated *Ras* and, depending on the particular enzyme, binding of the regulatory subunit to *phosphotyrosines* on activated *receptor tyrosine kinases* through its SH2 domains; or activation via G protein-coupled receptors.

EXAMPLE 6.28   How does activation of PI-3-kinases lead to cell growth?

This is still poorly understood. Proteins that bind to $PI(3,4)P_2$ or $PI(3,4,5)P_3$ have PH domains (pleckstrin homology domains). One example of such a protein is protein kinase B (*PKB*); this is activated by phosphorylation that is catalyzed by another PH domain kinase, *PDK1* (phosphatidylinositol-dependent kinase). Activated PKB phosphorylates a ribosomal protein, *protein S6*, which leads to increased rates of translation of selected mRNA molecules.

Signaling from Growth Factor Receptors and Cancer

In normal cells the process of cell proliferation is tightly controlled. It involves a series of coordinated events, occurring in what is known as the cell cycle (see Fig. 6-12).

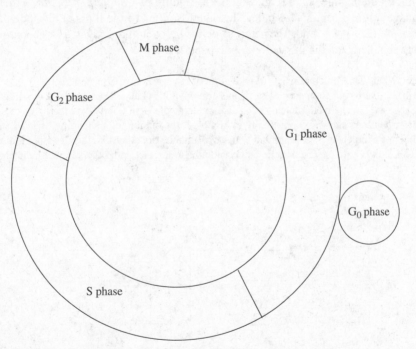

Fig. 6-12   The growth cycle of a cell, called *the cell cycle*.

Cell division (*mitosis*) occurs in the M stage of the cell cycle. This is followed by a gap (G1) in time, in which DNA damage that might have occurred in mitosis is detected and repaired. In the absence of external signals, typically the binding of growth factors to their receptors, mammalian cells are unable to proceed through a restriction point in the G_1 stage; they are said to be in the G_0 stage of the cell cycle. Passage through the restriction point commits cells to divide. This begins with synthesis of new DNA and proteins that occur in the S stage. Finally, the integrity of genomic DNA is checked in the G_2 stage, in preparation for mitosis.

This whole process is coordinated by complexes of *cyclins* and *cyclin-dependent protein kinases*. Specific cyclins are produced at different stages of the cell cycle and degraded through the action of the proteasome and regulated ubiquitinylation, when they are no longer required for cell function.

By definition, cancer cells proliferate in an *uncontrolled* manner. This lack of control usually arises from an accumulation of mutations in the genes of those proteins that have roles in cell proliferation. The *mutant proteins* either may have lost their normal functions or are locked into *permanently active* states.

EXAMPLE 6.29   Mutant forms of *Ras* are commonly found in human cancers. In some cases the mutations are in the *GTPase* active site of Ras, which makes it unable to hydrolyze GTP. The overall effect is that the mutant Ras is locked into a permanently active form; this leads to uncontrolled signaling down the MAP kinase and PI-3-kinase pathways, contributing to uncontrolled cell proliferation.

6.8   Signaling from G Protein-Coupled Receptors

Diversity of G Protein-Coupled Receptors

Although *G protein-coupled receptors* have a common molecular architecture (Sec. 6.3), they respond to a diverse range of signaling ligands, including proteins, small peptides, and derivatives of amino acids and fatty acids.

EXAMPLE 6.30   At least 9 distinct G protein-coupled receptors are activated by *epinephrine*, acetylcholine, and at least 15 activate another 5 by the neurotransmitter *serotonin*.

Activation of Heterotrimeric G Proteins

The binding sites for the signaling ligands of G protein-coupled receptors are contained within the *loops* of the extracellular polypeptide chain (e.g., Fig. 6-2). Binding of a *signaling ligand* to these sites triggers a structural change in the receptor molecule. This is transmitted to the intracellular polypeptide loops, to which *heterotrimeric G proteins* bind. The heterotrimeric G proteins are activated as a consequence of altered interactions between them and the intracellular polypeptide loops.

EXAMPLE 6.31   What is the structural basis of activation of heterotrimeric G proteins?

Heterotrimeric G proteins are composed of α, β, and γ polypeptide chains. Usually, the α and γ chains are anchored to the inner leaflet of the plasma membrane by lipid anchors that consist of a fatty acid that is linked to a cysteine side chain by a *thioester bond*. As shown schematically in Fig. 6-13, the binding of a signaling ligand leads to exchange of a molecule of GDP for a molecule of GTP, bound to the Gα subunit. Concurrently, the Gα subunit dissociates from the GβGγ subunit. This allows both the Gα and the GβGγ subunits to interact with other signaling molecules.

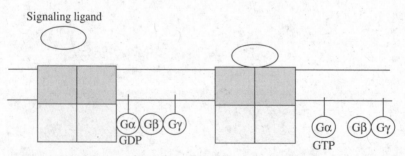

Fig. 6-13   Schematic representation of the activation of *heterotrimeric G proteins*.

There are multiple copies of the genes for the Gα, Gβ, and Gγ polypeptides in eukaryotic genomes. In the human genome there are at least 15 different Gα subunits, 5 Gβ subunits, and 10 Gγ subunits. Hence, there are potentially ~1000 different combinations of these subunits, with different possible physiological effects that depend on which G protein-coupled receptor(s) they become associated.

Regulation of Activation of Heterotrimeric G Proteins

The Gα subunits of heterotrimeric G proteins are *GTPases*; they are members of a large class of GTPases that also include Ras (Sec. 6.7) as well as the various GTP-dependent factors of protein synthesis. Once the Gα subunit hydrolyzes its bound GTP to GDP, it reassociates with the GβGγ complex to re-form an *inactive* G protein, thus reversing the activation process. The GTPase activity is typically enhanced when Gα subunits bind to their target protein(s). It is also enhanced by *regulator of G protein signaling* (RGS) proteins that are members of the GAP protein family (see Solved Problem 6.11). There are at least 25 RGS proteins in the human genome.

EXAMPLE 6.32   PL-Cβ is activated by binding of the Gα subunits of heterotrimeric G proteins (see Section 6.4). A member of the RGS family, RGS4, is thought to regulate activation of PL-Cβ in part by promoting the GTPase activity of these Gα subunits.

Activation of Adenylate Cyclase by Heterotrimeric G Proteins

Adenylate cyclase, which catalyzes the synthesis of cAMP from ATP, is an intrinsic membrane protein that has two *large cytosolic domains* that contain its *active site*. Adenylate cyclase is activated through the binding of Gα subunits that are released, for example, from G protein-coupled receptors like that for epinephrine. The binding site of these Gα subunits for adenylate cyclase is buried when they are in their inactive form bound to cognate GβGγ subunits. The effect of activation of adenylate cyclase is to increase the intracellular concentration of cAMP.

EXAMPLE 6.33   What are the consequences of increased cAMP concentration in the cytoplasm of a cell?

A major target of cAMP is *protein kinase A* (*PK-A*). PK-A is a heterotetramer that is composed of two catalytic (C) subunits and two regulatory (R) subunits. The C subunits are inactive when in the R_2C_2 heterotetramer. Binding two molecules of cAMP to each of the R_2 subunits of the heterotetramer leads to its dissociation; the released C_2 dimer is catalytically *active*.

PK-A catalyzes the phosphorylation of *serine* and *threonine residues* on its target proteins. It has many targets and therefore modulates many different cellular processes.

Sensory Perception and G Protein-Coupled Receptors

G protein-coupled receptors are important in *vision* as well as the perception of *smell* and *taste*. In general terms their role is to couple the primary stimuli, photons, odorants, or flavorants, respectively, to ligand-gated ion channels. Changes in ion flow through these channels lead to the induction of a nerve impulse that is transmitted from the sensory organ to the brain.

EXAMPLE 6.34   Rhodopsin is a G protein-coupled receptor that is present in the *rod cells* of the *eye*. It contains a chromophore, *retinal*, which isomerizes from 11-cis-retinal to all-trans-retinal upon absorption of a photon of light; this yields a form of rhodopsin called bathorhodopsin. This intermediate form is rapidly, within 1 ms, converted to metarhodopsin II.

Structural changes in metarhodopsin II compared to rhodopsin are sensed by a heterotrimeric G protein called *transducin*. The Gα subunit of transducin activates a cGMP phosphodiesterase that hydrolyzes cGMP to GMP. The resulting decrease in cGMP concentrations in the rod cell leads to closure of a cGMP-gated ion channel. This leads to hyperpolarization of the rod cell membrane and initiation of a nerve impulse.

SOLVED PROBLEMS

GENERAL MECHANISMS OF SIGNAL TRANSDUCTION

6.1.   Which types of receptors use the two general mechanisms of signal transduction mentioned in Sec. 6.1?

SOLUTION

Typically, signal transduction through *G protein-coupled receptors* and *ligand-gated ion channels* involves ligand-driven structural changes in the receptor, while signal transduction through *cytokine receptors* and *growth factor receptors* involves ligand-driven dimerization of the receptor molecules.

CLASSIFICATION OF RECEPTORS

6.2.   The interaction between insulin and its receptor is an example of which type of signaling?

SOLUTION

Signaling to the insulin receptor is an example of *endocrine signaling* because insulin is only produced by β cells within the pancreas, while the insulin receptor is expressed by many tissues that are distant from the pancreas (e.g., muscle and liver cells).

6.3. Is the structural similarity of G protein-coupled receptors matched by a corresponding functional similarity?

SOLUTION

No. G protein-coupled receptors are very diverse with respect to their physiological functions. They have been implicated in processes as diverse as *neurotransmission*, *regulation of metabolism*, *sensory perception,* and *cell proliferation*. The physiological functions of some G protein-coupled receptors are not yet known. These receptors are examples of *orphan receptors*. More experimental work is needed before we understand the functions of orphan receptors.

COMMON THEMES IN SIGNALING PATHWAYS

6.4. How is PL-C activated in signaling pathways?

SOLUTION

Two subclasses of PL-C are particularly important in signaling pathways. One subclass, PL-Cγ, contains SH2 domains, so the enzymes are activated through binding to proteins that have phosphotyrosine residues (see Secs. 6.4 and 6.7). Enzymes of the other subclass, PL-Cβ, are activated by heterotrimeric G proteins (see Sec. 6.8).

6.5. How is the specificity of ubiquitinylation achieved?

SOLUTION

In the human genome there are a small number of *isoforms* of E_1 enzymes, at least 50 E_2 enzymes, and at least 1000 E_3 enzymes. Particular combinations of E_2 and E_3 enzymes are specific for different substrate proteins.

6.6. Does signaling from the insulin receptor have short-term or long-term consequences?

SOLUTION

Both. Binding of insulin to its receptor can have both short-term and long-term consequences. In the short term, insulin stimulates the ability of cells to take up glucose. This reflects the translocation of preexisting molecules of the glucose transporter, GLUT4, from the cell interior to the cell surface as a consequence of signaling pathways that are initiated by binding of insulin to its receptor.

In the long term, insulin stimulates synthesis of new proteins, such as *apoAI*, which is a protein that is involved in the transport of cholesterol and other lipids in the blood plasma. In one set of experiments, using liver cells, apoAI was detected at increased concentrations 24 h after the cells had been exposed to insulin.

SIGNALING FROM CYTOKINE RECEPTORS: THE JAK:STAT PATHWAY

6.7. Why does cytokine binding lead to activation of the JAK enzymes?

SOLUTION

The JAK enzymes that are bound to the cytoplasmic domains of cytokine receptors are brought into close physical proximity following dimerization of the receptors. This allows JAKs bound to one receptor to catalyze phosphorylation of tyrosine residues of JAKs bound to the other in a process called *mutual auto-phosphorylation*. The effect is conversion of the JAKs into a *high-activity* form. They then phosphorylate tyrosine residues on the cytoplasmic domains of the receptors.

6.8. How do SOCS proteins inhibit intracellular signaling?

SOLUTION

They do this in at least two ways. First, because they contain SH2 domains, they can bind to the phosphotyrosine residues of proteins involved in the pathway. In doing this they act as *competitive inhibitors* of the pathway proteins that are activated by binding to these residues. Second, they contain a domain called a *SOCS box*. The SOCS box forms part of an E_3 *Ub ligase*. Therefore, binding of SOCS proteins to proteins in the pathway targets them for ubiquitinylation and subsequent *degradation*.

SIGNALING FROM GROWTH FACTOR RECEPTORS

6.9. What is the mechanism of dimerization of growth factor receptors?

SOLUTION

The three-dimensional structures of the extracellular domains of a few growth factor receptors (e.g., an epidermal growth factor and a fibroblast growth factor receptor), both free and complexed with their cognate growth factors, have been solved by *X-ray crystallography* (Sec. 4.11). These structures suggest that the receptors exist in two conformations: a *closed* conformation, in which the receptor is unable to form dimers, and an *open* conformation, in which it *can* form dimers. Binding of growth factor to these receptors promotes formation of the open conformation and hence dimerization of these receptors. In other cases (e.g., platelet-derived growth factor receptors), a different mechanism appears to apply: platelet-derived growth factor exists as a dimer and is therefore able to cross-link two receptor molecules to form a dimer.

6.10. Why does phosphorylation of growth factor kinase domains lead to their *activation*?

SOLUTION

Structural studies of some growth factor receptor protein *tyrosine kinases* have shown that the autophosphorylation occurs at tyrosine residues in an *activation loop* of the polypeptide chain. When this loop is not phosphorylated, it restricts access of ATP to the active site of the kinase. Upon phosphorylation it moves, so as to allow ATP ready access to the site, leading to the generation of a high-activity form of the enzyme.

6.11. How does SoS activate Ras?

SOLUTION

Ras is a member of the protein family called the *small GTP-binding proteins*. Members of this family are typically active when they have *bound GTP* and inactive when they have bound GDP. They have slow *GTPase* activity, which is enhanced when they are complexed to a *GTPase activating protein* (GAP) while exchange of bound GDP for GTP is favored when they are bound to a *guanine exchange factor* (GEF) protein. SoS is an example of a GEF. Therefore it promotes exchange of GDP that is bound to Ras for GTP, thus converting Ras into a *high-activity state*.

SIGNALING FROM G PROTEIN-COUPLED RECEPTORS

6.12. Why does binding of signaling molecules to a G protein-coupled *receptor* lead to exchange of GTP for GDP on the Gα protein?

SOLUTION

When the signaling molecule binds, there is a structural change in the nucleotide-binding site of the Gα protein, thus promoting release of GDP. GTP then binds and three sections of polypeptide of the Gα protein (called switch I, switch II, and switch III) interact with the γ-phosphate of GTP. A major consequence of these structural changes is a reduction in the affinity of Gα for GβGγ, leading to dissociation of the G protein heterotrimer.

6.13. How is the structure of the R subunits of PK-A related to their function?

SOLUTION

The R subunits of PK-A are composed of four domains: (1) the *N*-terminal *dimerization domain*, (2) the inhibitory region, and (3) two cAMP-binding domains. The R subunits interact with C subunits primarily through the inhibitory region. Cooperative binding of cAMP to the two cAMP-binding domains leads to structural changes in the inhibitory region, allowing dissociation of the R_2 dimer from the C_2 dimer of PK-A.

6.14. Does activation of PK-A have short-term or long-term consequences for cellular metabolism?

SOLUTION

This depends on the target of the activated PK-A; for example, PK-A phosphorylates enzymes that are involved in glycogen metabolism, thus promoting glycogen breakdown and inhibiting glycogen synthesis in the short term.

PK-A can also phosphorylate a transcription factor called *CREB* (*c*AMP-*r*esponse *e*lement *b*inding protein). The effect is to promote the binding of CREB to a coactivator, *CBP* (CREB *b*inding *p*rotein). Bioinformatics analysis has shown that expression of ~4000 genes in the human genome is potentially modulated by CREB/CBP, and these have functions ranging from regulating glucose metabolism through to regulation of cell division, and to *memory* storage in the brain.

SUPPLEMENTARY PROBLEMS

6.15. In functional terms, what do cAMP, Ca^{2+}, IP_3, and DAG have in common as components of signaling pathways?

6.16. What might happen if a·$G\alpha$ protein were unable to hydrolyze its bound GTP?

6.17. Cancer cells proliferate in an uncontrolled manner. How might this be linked to defects in signaling pathways?

6.18. What might happen if a $G\alpha$ protein were unable to bind GTP?

6.19. How might you measure the release of Ca^{2+} from the endoplasmic reticulum in response to IP_3 production?

6.20. If STAT dimers are to act as transcription factors, they must enter the nucleus. How is this achieved?

6.21. What do the letters SH in *SH2 domain* denote?

6.22. How might you measure the activation of protein kinase C that occurs in response to activation of a signaling pathway?

6.23. What is the biochemical basis of our ability to smell objects?

6.24. In a sample of cells, how might you measure the proportions of cells that are at different stages of the cell cycle?

ANSWERS TO SUPPLEMENTARY PROBLEMS

6.15. They are all produced as a consequence of the primary signaling event that is the binding of a signaling molecule to a receptor. For this reason, they are often called *second messengers*.

6.16. The $G\alpha$ protein would be locked into a permanently active state. This happens in cholera when the B subunit of the cholera toxin catalyzes the attachment of an ADP-ribose unit to an arginine residue of a $G\alpha$ protein that is present in intestinal epithelial cells. The permanently active $G\alpha$ protein continuously activates PK-A, thus leading to opening of an ion channel, through which Na^+, Cl^-, and water escape into the intestine.

6.17. Typically, cancer cells have accumulated a number of mutations in genes that code for proteins that are involved in signaling pathways, or in the cell cycle. These mutant proteins either are locked into a permanently active form or have lost the ability to carry out their normal regulatory functions. An example involves the platelet-derived growth factor receptor that in some human leukemias is locked into a permanently active state because of a chromosomal translocation. This mutation affects the N terminus of the receptor that is replaced by that of a *transcription factor* called Tel.

6.18. It would be trapped in an inactive form. This happens in whooping cough (*pertussis*). Pertussis toxin catalyzes the addition of an ADP-ribose unit to a $G\alpha$ protein (compare Supplementary Problem 6.16). In this case the effect is to *lower* the affinity of the $G\alpha$ protein for GTP. However, the link between this molecular event and the clinical signs of whooping cough is not clear.

6.19. This can be done by using fluorescent probes such as Fura-2 or Quin-1. These probes fluorescesce when they bind Ca^{2+}. Therefore, if the cytosol of a cell is loaded with one of these probes and IP_3 production is initiated by activation of an appropriate signaling pathway, you could then use fluorescence microscopy to observe the emergence of fluorescence in the cytoplasm that occurs as a result of the release of Ca^{2+} from the endoplasmic reticulum and mitochondria.

6.20. STAT dimers bind to an adaptor protein called *importin 5α*. This complex is then transferred to the nucleus via the *nuclear pore complex*. Upon arrival in the nucleus, the STAT dimers are released from importin 5α through the action of *Ran* that is a GTP-binding protein related to Ras.

6.21. SH stands for Src homology. Src is a tyrosine protein kinase that exits as a normal cellular protein (c-src) and as a protein that is encoded by the *Rous sarcoma virus* (v-src). The Rous sarcoma virus causes cancer in chickens, hence it is an example of an *oncovirus*. Oncogenesis occurs because the v-src protein, in contrast to the c-src form, is constitutively expressed in the cancer cells. The v-src gene is therefore an example of an *oncogene*.

6.22. Traditionally this was done by loading cells with γ-$[^{32}P]$-ATP. Activated protein kinase C catalyzes the transfer of the radioactive ^{32}P from the γ-phosphate of ATP onto target proteins. Their radioactivity can then be measured. More recently, nonradioactive assays have been devised. Many of these are based on fluorescence resonance energy transfer (FRET) that occurs between recombinant proteins that contain two naturally fluorescent proteins, such as *green fluorescent protein* (GFP) and a variant of it, EYGFP. Phosphorylation of these proteins leads to a change in the distance between the two naturally fluorescent proteins. This can be monitored by measuring differences in FRET intensities between them.

6.23. This is achieved through the action of *olfactory neurons*. These link the olfactory bulb of the brain and the nasal cavity. Each olfactory neuron expresses one of 500–700 different kinds of odorant receptor (OR). ORs are G protein-coupled receptors. Binding of an odorant to a specific OR triggers activation of the $G\alpha$ protein that is associated with the OR. The $G\alpha$ protein activates adenyl cyclase, and the cAMP consequently opens a cAMP-gated ion channel. The channel allows entry of Na^+ and Ca^{2+} into the neuron, thus triggering transmission of a nerve impulse to the brain. Our perception of particular smells is based on combinatorial activation of different ORs by different odorants in a sample that might have a complex mixture of odorants.

6.24. This can be done in various ways. One popular way is by *flow cytometry*. In a flow cytometer, particles such as cells in an aqueous suspension are passed through a beam of laser light, and their fluorescence is measured. Therefore, you could take a sample of cells, make holes in their plasma membranes with a low concentration of a suitable detergent, and incubate them with a dye such as propidium iodide, which fluoresces when it binds to DNA. Cells in the G_0 and G_1 phases of the cell cycle have the normal ($2n$) amounts of DNA while cells in the G_2 and M phases have twice the normal ($4n$) amount. Therefore G_2 and M phase cells will have twice the propidium iodide fluorescence of cells in the G_0 and G_1 phases. Cells in the S phase, during which DNA synthesis occurs, will have intermediate fluorescence levels.

CHAPTER 7

The Flow of Genetic Information

7.1 Molecular Basis of Genetics

Question: The rules of genetics that describe the transfer of characteristics from parents to offspring are well defined, but is there a molecular basis for these rules?

It is a matter of simple observation that offspring look like their parents. Animal breeders have known for centuries that certain traits are inherited and that by careful mating, *crosses* with unique characteristics can be bred. Classical genetics has formalized these observations into rules, and much can be predicted about the pattern of inheritance in animals and plants.

The discovery in the 1860s of a new phosphate-containing biopolymer in cell nuclei by Friedrich Miescher began an understanding of inheritance from a molecular perspective.

EXAMPLE 7.1   The abundant acidic polymer from the nuclei of cells that imparts a high viscosity to solutions became known as a *nucleic acid*. Frederick Griffith reported in 1928 on the transformation of a nonvirulent pneumococcus into a virulent form by incubating it with a killed virulent form; and Oswald Avery and his team in 1943 established the primary role of DNA as the carrier of this genetic virulence transformation. The chemical structure that was finally reported in 1953 by James Watson and Francis Crick relied on previous careful chemical analysis by Erwin Chargaff. He had shown that although the relative abundances of the nucleobases in DNA varied between animals, and in various microorganisms, the ratios of adenine:thymine (A:T) and guanine:cytosine (G:C) were always very similar.

EXAMPLE 7.2   Watson and Crick's proposed structure was derived from X-ray diffraction patterns from aligned fibers of DNA, meticulously prepared by Rosalind Franklin. It has two antiparallel strands arranged as a twisted ladder in which the rungs are base-paired nucleobases; the bases are all arranged so that A is only ever hydrogen-bonded in a specific way to T, and G to C (see Fig. 7-1). This is referred to as base pairing. With the DNA structure in hand, scientists began to form a view as to how genetic information is recorded in DNA and how this information might be transferred from parents to offspring. At the molecular level the information has to be translated into proteins within the cell. Evidence suggested another poly nucleic acid, RNA, was also involved. Although it is chemically very similar to DNA, the subtle differences in its structure are crucial to its function. The end product of gene expression are proteins are amazingly diverse in their structure, shapes, and functions.

There are two major cellular events in which genetic information is processed. The first is cell division, in which the DNA template is faithfully copied and transferred to the two daughter cells. The process is known as *replication*. The second process is *gene expression*, in which parts of the template are *transcribed* into RNA, an interim carrier molecule from which the coded message is *translated* into a sequence of amino acids, a protein. A cell nucleus can be viewed as a magnificent library of books. These books are only useful if they are read, and yet many of the books will be read only rarely while others are read a lot. This differential expression of parts of the DNA is under the control of *transcription factors*.

7.2 The Genome

Every cell of any organism that is able to reproduce itself contains the full genetic instruction set that is known collectively as its *genome*; double-stranded DNA makes up this coded set. In prokaryotic cells

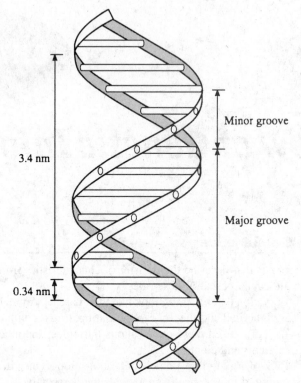

Fig. 7-1 Schematic representation of the so-called B
form of the DNA double helix.

(most notably bacteria), DNA is packaged into a single huge circular chromosome that is immersed in the cytoplasm. In eukaryotes, genomic DNA resides in a membrane-enclosed nucleus, *packaged* as a number of chromosomes. Most eukaryotic cells have two copies of the overall genetic information, one from the father and one from the mother. This situation is referred to as *diploidy*. The matching chromosomes form several pairs of *autosomes,* plus one pair of *sex chromosomes* that have a key role in determining the gender of the individual. (However, e.g., it has recently been shown that the determination of gender in the Australian platypus is via five different sex chromosomes.) The *two copies* of a gene that reside on each of a pair of the same autosomes are referred to as *alleles*.

Question: What is a gene, in molecular terms?

As is often the case with words that originated from an earlier period of understanding, the meaning of the word *gene* has evolved. It was originally used to describe a factor such as *eye color* that could vary from one organism in a species to another; but it now refers to *a length of DNA that is transcribed into a single RNA molecule*, that in turn might be translated into a protein. E.g., separate segments of DNA (genes) code for the α and β globin molecules of hemoglobin rather than there being a single gene for the hemoglobin tetramer (see Chap. 4). The terms *genome* and *genetics* and the adjective *genomic* were coined from the earlier term *gene*, and they now refer to DNA. The average length of a typical human gene, according to the human genome project, is 27,894 bases with on average 7 to 8 *exons* (see Chap. 9). There are ~30,000 genes in the human genome, although this estimate still varies depending on the source and method of analysis.

EXAMPLE 7.3   Multicellular organisms contain many different types of cells. In mammals these are recognized as different tissues such as skin, muscle, and liver. Since almost every cell type (for special exceptions see next Example) of a multicellular organism contains the same genomic DNA, what makes one cell type different from another?

The key concept is that of *differentiation*; this is the process by which the whole genome in each cell is selectively switched off or *silenced* in specific places on the chromosomal DNA, leaving only a subset of all possible genes available to be translated into proteins. It is the characteristics of the proteins in the set of all proteins in a cell, and their relative amounts, that are the fundamental determinants of the final nature of a cell, and hence what tissue name we might assign to it.

Cells of ordinary tissues are known as somatic cells (Greek *soma*, body). Different somatic cells in an organism express a very different set of these genes as proteins. The information about which genes are silenced is transferred from one somatic cell to the next when it divides in the normal process of tissue growth during embryogenesis, tissue repair, and normal turnover of cells.

EXAMPLE 7.4 Which cells do not contain a complete genome, namely, two copies of each gene, one from the male and one from the female parent?

The *germ cells* of the ovary and testis are not somatic cells, and they contain only a single copy of the genetic material; they are said to be *haploid*. These cells divide and become *ova* and *spermatozoa*, respectively.

Red blood cells have no nuclei (enucleated) and hence no DNA. And the outer layer of skin cells consists of little more than sacks of keratin in which the nuclei have degraded beyond recognition, but some DNA persists and it can be detected in forensic work.

EXAMPLE 7.5 Replication of chromosomes requires the copying of their full length of DNA whereas the copying of the messages in genes involves the making of copies of RNA. In other words, replication generates one complete copy of the genome, whereas in *gene expression* multiple copies of portions of the genome are made. Replication is a once-in-a-lifetime event for the cell, whereas gene expression occurs all the time as proteins are continually degraded and resynthesized in the cell.

Prokaryotes store their genetic information very efficiently. Their genome contains very little noncoding DNA. However, a large fraction of eukaryotic DNA is nonallelic. Despite the fact that it does not code for proteins, recent evidence suggests that this DNA is not *junk* but is transcribed and is involved in the control of cell function.

EXAMPLE 7.6 How much DNA is there in an average bacterial cell?

This depends on the type of cell, but in *E. coli* the total DNA content is 4.6 million pairs of nucleotides, or *base pairs* (bp). Suppose that each protein on average has a molecular weight of ~33,000. Then since the average mass of an amino acid residue is ~110, such a protein will contain ~300 amino acid residues. Since each amino acid is specified by an mRNA codon of three bases (Chap. 9), such a protein requires 900 bp to specify its amino acid sequence. Promoter regions and termination sequences are also part of a gene, and these add to the previous number to make it ~1100 bp. Thus the bacterium can code for $4.6 \times 10^6/1.1 \times 10^3$ or ~4000 proteins. The total number of proteins encoded by the *E. coli* genome has been determined experimentally to be ~4300; thus there is little *redundant* noncoding DNA in this organism's genome.

7.3 Base Composition of Genomes

The base composition of DNA in an organism is a fixed value, and it is expressed as the percent of G + C of the total genome. The variation of this value between different prokaryotes is large; this is surprising, given that many of the individual proteins produced by the species have similar amino acid sequences. Prokaryotic genomic DNA can have as little as 25% (G + C) in *Mycoplasma genitalium* to as high as ~72% in *Micrococcus lysodeikticus*.

There is redundancy in the triplet codes (codons) for many amino acids (Chap. 9), and which triplet is used by an organism is the subject of *selection pressure* during evolution of the species. Variation in *codon usage* arises from *directional mutations*, in which certain mutations are favored over others because of the differential availability of the four nucleotides during replication. In some prokaryotes, the reserves of each of the four nucleotides can differ markedly, and since their survival depends on the ability to divide rapidly, flexibility in the choice of nucleobases during replication is advantageous.

EXAMPLE 7.7 Does the base composition vary from gene to gene or chromosome to chromosome in a particular genome?

In prokaryotes, nucleobases are distributed throughout the genome with a slightly lower G + C content in *promoter* and *intergenic* regions; these often have (A + T)-rich segments that *melt* at higher temperatures more readily than the other. This feature can be exploited experimentally. The relatively constant base distribution within a given bacterial genome suggests that although there may be unequal nucleotide pool sizes inside the cell, the system will have evolved over many generations to be like this, and the rate of DNA replication is constant.

Eukaryotic genomic DNA does not display much variation between species. The %(G + C) composition of most plant and animal species falls within a narrow range, averaging 39% with a variation of only ±6%. The distribution of the G + C content throughout each genome, however, varies significantly, unlike prokaryotes. Whereas the mean variation in %(G + C) content throughout the *E. coli* genome is only 8.6%, in eukaryotes this variation is over 30%. Certain regions of eukaryotic genomic DNA are found to be (A + T)-rich, with a (G + C) content as low as 18%, while other regions have a G + C content as high as 70%.

EXAMPLE 7.8 Can general conclusions be drawn about the selective advantages of prokaryotes and eukaryotes from the patterns of their base compositions?

The survival of complex multicellular organisms does not rely greatly on their ability to proliferate rapidly, so their base composition and their nucleotide pool sizes have remained constant over millions of years. *E. coli* cells can divide every 20 min under optimal conditions, in contrast to eukaryotic cell cycles that take 18 to 24 h. Hence selection pressures such as the *rate of nucleobase supply* operate on prokaryotic genomes but not on eukaryotic genomes.

7.4 Genomic-Code Sequences

Any system of encryption involves a coded message and an algorithm (or cipher) that the recipient uses to translate the message into another series of characters. In espionage, the conversion of a plain text message to a seemingly nonsensical form requires a cipher and a key that only the intended recipient should know and use to revert the message to its original form. Scientists have discovered the rules that lead to deciphering the sequence of nucleobases in DNA into a sequence of amino acids in a protein. But note, the direction of information flow is only one way; protein sequences do not lead to the formation of DNA base sequences.

A simple place to begin a comparative analysis of the genomes of different organisms is to determine the frequencies of occurrence of *dinucleotides* in them. This is made possible by the availability of the complete sequences of the genomes from numerous organisms including humans and fast computers to count the millions of particular occurrences.

Dinucleotides are the shortest units of genetic information; there are only 16 possible different dinucleotides: there are four ways of choosing the first base and four ways of choosing the second one, namely $4 \times 4 = 16$. If the occurrence of each base pair were completely random, the frequency of each would be $1/16 = 6.25\%$. However, this is not the case in most organisms. In *E. coli* there is a 50% variation between the most frequently occurring dinucleotides GC (8.3%) and the least frequent one AT (4.5%).

The dinucleotide frequencies in the mouse, rat, and human genomes reveal a totally different order from that of *E. coli*; but in the three mammals the distributions are all similar. Some of the more common dinucleotides in the mammalian genomes are actually the least common in *E. coli*. The most striking finding is the low occurrence of the dinucleotide GC; the frequency is 75% less than the mean value (6.25%). The frequencies of the other 15 dinucleotides range from 23% more to 24% less than the mean frequency.

EXAMPLE 7.9 What is the explanation for the low frequency of CG dinucleotides in mammalian genomes?

In several mammalian genomes, between 2% and 7% of C residues in DNA are methylated, and more than 90% of these have a G following them. *Nearest-neighbor* analysis done with a computer also reveals that the dinucleotide of highest frequency in the mammalian genomes is TG. An explanation of this phenomenon is that thymine residues can be the product of the spontaneous deamination of methylcytosine (Fig. 7-2). Corruption of the code by this means may not be detected by DNA repair mechanisms (Chap. 8), so such a change in a somatic cell will persist into the next generation derived from it.

EXAMPLE 7.10 What is notable about the CG dinucleotide in eukaryotes?

It is not evenly distributed throughout the eukaryotic genome. There are some base clusters where this pair occurs at quite a high frequency; these are referred to as *CpG islands*. The *p* is inserted to distinguish these from standard CG dinucleotides. CpG islands are regions of DNA of at least 200 bp in length that have a much higher C + G content than expected (>50%) and much higher frequencies of the CG dinucleotide string. They are usually located *upstream of genes* in promoter regions. Methylation of the cytosine base in CpG islands is one means by which gene expression is regulated.

7.5 Genome Complexity

Question: Only ~2% of the DNA in the eukaryotic genome actually codes for proteins. What might the rest do?

A large amount of noncoding DNA is a feature of the genomes of higher eukaryotes. Scientists for some time have observed that the amount of genetic material does not correlate with the complexity of the

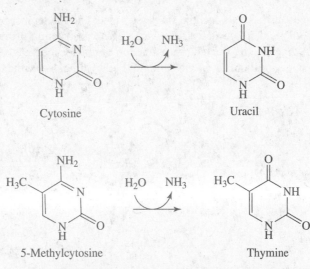

Cytosine

Uracil

5-Methylcytosine

Thymine

Fig. 7-2   The spontaneous *hydrolytic deamination* of cytosine to give uracil (top), and 5-methylcytosine to give thymine.

organism (see Solved Problem 7.7 and Table 7-1). This seemingly extra DNA was first discovered during experiments on features of melting and reannealing DNA. The human genome project has subsequently confirmed the presence of large amounts of noncoding DNA. Below in Table 7-1 are the general statistics gleaned from the sequencing of the human genome. An estimated 64–75% of the human genome is intergenic DNA, and of the remaining ~25% only 1.4% is exons.

A technique that is used to study the unraveling and reassociation of DNA was reported in 1968 by Roy Britten and Eric Davidson; it gained the name C_0t plot. The analysis provided the first hint of the abundance and diversity of noncoding sequences in various eukaryotic genomes.

DNA is isolated from tissue and sheared by sonification into consistent lengths (300 to 10,000 bp). It is then denatured by heating it to a temperature greater than the melting temperature T_M of the DNA (~80°C). This process can be monitored spectrophotometrically by light absorption at a wavelength of 260 nm (A_{260}). A few

Table 7-1   Numerical Data Relating to the Human Genome

Approximate size of the genome	2.9 Gbp
%(A + T)	54
%(G + C)	38
% undetermined bases in genome	9
Most GC- rich region 50 kb	Chr 2 (66%)
Most AT-rich region 50 kb	Chr X (25%)
Number of genes	26,383–39,114
Most gene-rich chromosome	Chr. 19 (23 genes/Mb)
Least gene-rich chromosomes	Chr. 13 (5 genes/Mb) and Chr. Y (5 genes/Mb)
Average gene length	27 kbp
Gene with the most exons	*Titin* (234 exons)
% of genome containing repeat sequences	35
% exon base pairs	1.1–1.4
% intron base pairs	24–36
% intergenic DNA (bp)	64–75

minutes later the DNA fragments have all become single-stranded; and the temperature is then reduced to an optimal renaturation temperature that is usually $T_M - 25°C$. The reassociation process is monitored by light absorption (A_{260}) as well. A graph is constructed of the fraction of reassociated DNA based on the A_{260}, versus the logarithm of the initial concentration, C_0, of DNA, multiplied by time, hence the term $C_0 t$.

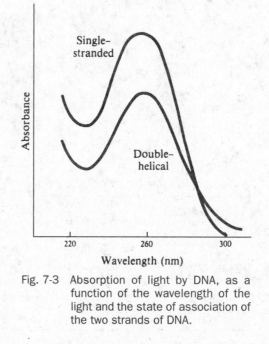

Fig. 7-3 Absorption of light by DNA, as a function of the wavelength of the light and the state of association of the two strands of DNA.

EXAMPLE 7.11 What form would a $C_0 t$ reassociation curve take if all the DNA sequences in a sample were represented only once in the genome?

If all the DNA sequences in a sample were represented only once in the genome, then a standard *reassociation curve* would result, since all the fragments would reanneal with their previous partners. If each strand had only one "complementary partner" then the reannealing rate would be the same for all fragments. *E. coli* DNA gives a very reproducible steep annealing curve that is characteristic of a genome with few repeated sequences (Fig. 7-4).

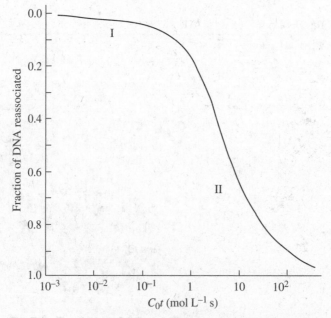

Fig. 7-4 The $C_0 t$ plot for *E. coli* DNA. The regions of the graph denoted I and II are referred to in Solved Problem 7.15.

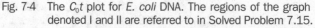

EXAMPLE 7.12   How does the C_0t plot change if some of the sequences appear more than once in the genome?

If the DNA sample contains some sequences that are represented more than once in the genome, then a much more interesting (and more difficult to analyze) plot is obtained. The time it takes to renature the strands depends on the number of copies of the sequence in solution. This is related to the complexity of the DNA. *Complexity* is defined as the number of bases in a *unique sequence*. Take the simplest possible sequence: Poly U has a complexity of 1, so in a poly U versus poly A reassociation experiment it does not matter where within the length of the two strands the two species encounter each other—they will match. The sequence AGTTC AGTTC AGTTC AGTTC has a complexity of 5. If the *E. coli* genome is composed of totally unique sequences, its complexity is the number of base pairs in the genome, or 4.6×10^6. The lower the complexity value, the quicker the reannealing time, hence the lower the C_0t range. Below is the C_0t analysis of DNA samples from various sources. Note the larger C_0t values in the more complex DNA.

Those sequences that have the most copies in solution will reanneal fastest, as there is a greater chance of encountering their matching complementary pair, while the more complex single-copy sequences take the longest to reanneal. Hence a sample of DNA that contains both single-copy sequences and sequences with multiple copies will give a C_0t plot that appears more like the one in Fig. 7-5.

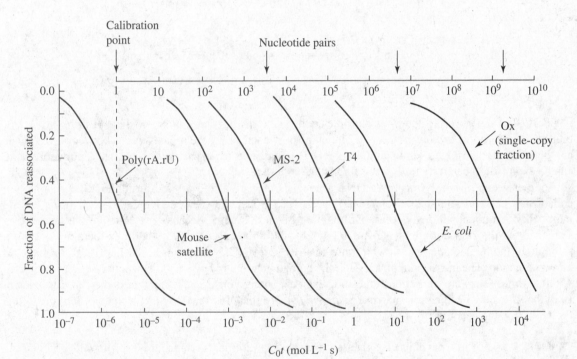

Fig. 7-5   The C_0t plots for genomes of different complexity. The figure is based on data from a real experiment.

The C_0t plot in Fig. 7-6 is from human DNA. What can be concluded from this analysis? The human genome (and other mammalian DNA) has a population of sequences that appear in high copy number (30–40%) and a population that is composed of highly complex single-copy sequences. These have been divided somewhat arbitrarily into four groups: (1) highly repetitive, (2) moderately repetitive, (3) small copy number, and (4) unique or single-copy sequences.

EXAMPLE 7.13   What types of sequences are found in the highly repetitive class of DNA sequences?

This group contains a number of classes of highly repetitive short repeat sequences: (1) short tandem repeats (STRs; 2–5 bp), (2) microsatellites (1–13 bp), and (3) minisatellites (14–500 bp).

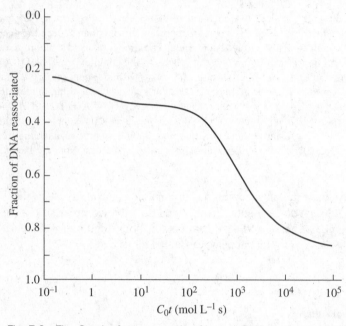

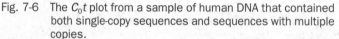

Fig. 7-6   The C_0t plot from a sample of human DNA that contained both single-copy sequences and sequences with multiple copies.

Short DNA repeats often appear as multiple copies in higher genomes, positioned in a *head-to-tail* orientation, and are known as *tandem repeats*. The number of copies of these repeats varies between individuals and between chromosomes within an individual's genome. This *hypervariability*, known as polymorphism, can be exploited in paternity testing and forensics.

Another group of highly repetitive DNA sequences that are also scattered throughout the genome are called SINES (*short interspersed elements*) and LINES (*long interspersed elements*). *Alu* repeats are the major SINE in mammalian genomes, and they are given this name because they contain the recognition sequence for the restriction enzyme *Alu*. They are ~300 bp long and ~1,000,000 of them are scattered throughout the human genome; they account for ~10% of it. They are transcribed into RNA but have no known function. The most common LINE in the human genome is L1, a 6000 bp sequence that is repeated ~50,000 times. They are transcribed and some even encode proteins. Their function in the cell is unknown. Both the *Alu* and L1 sequences are *transposable elements*, meaning that they are capable of moving to different sites in the genome.

EXAMPLE 7.14   What types of functions are served by the sequences that occur in moderately repetitive DNAs?

The sequences that have multiple copies in the genome often regulate other genes, increase the rate of gene expression, or by their multiplicity increase the amount of a specific gene product that is formed. Gene sequences such as those coding for ribosomal RNA and transfer RNA, that are present in the cell in large numbers, have many copies. Histone sequences also exist in large numbers in the genome.

EXAMPLE 7.15   What information is contained in the group of sequences for which there are only small numbers of copies in the genome?

Such sequences are genes that code for proteins whose expression is highly regulated; e.g., they include the globin genes. This family of genes contains a number of closely related sequences that differ from each other by only a few base pairs, so they will cross-hybridize if complementary strands are incubated together under annealing conditions (Example 7.12). These groups of genes are also known as *gene clusters*.

EXAMPLE 7.16   Which group noted under Fig. 7-5 contains most of the genes?

The final group, the *single-copy sequences*, makes up the vast majority of genes on the genome, with a gene being a functional unit that codes for a single polypeptide chain. This group is the most complex and takes the longest to reanneal, sometimes days, hence the use of the log scale on the time in a C_0t plot.

7.6 Other Noncoding DNA Species

Pseudogenes

The eukaryotic genome contains *pseudogenes* that occupy a significant proportion of the genome. There are two classes of pseudogenes. *Class I pseudogenes* have arisen by gene duplication and then have subsequently been inactivated by various mutations (insertions, substitutions, or deletions); they are often located near their functional-gene counterpart. *Class II pseudogenes* are processed sequences (lacking introns and often containing a vestigial poly A tail) and have originated during evolution from mRNA that was copied by *reverse transcriptase* back into DNA. The sequence was then inserted into the genome by a *retrotransposon* event. The footprints of this event are evident in the *direct repeats* that flank the pseudogene; the repeats have facilitated its insertion back into the genome. Such pseuogenes are usually located a long way from the functional parent gene.

Pseudogenes do not code for functional proteins, and they are not translated. The exact number of pseudogenes in the human genome is unknown, although some analyses have identified ~2900 regions that probably represent *processed* pseudogenes. The pattern that has emerged from analysis of the human genome is that those sequences which tend to give rise to pseudogenes have shorter than average transcripts and are sequences that are involved in nuclear regulation and translation. E.g., ribosomal proteins account for 67%; lamin receptors, 10%; and translation elongation factors, 5%. The common theme here is the increased level of transcription of these sequences.

Regulatory Regions

Other forms of noncoding DNA have an important role to play in gene transcription. The *promoter* regions of eukaryotic genomes are *substantially larger than their prokaryotic counterparts*. Transcriptional regulation in eukaryotes is a very complex process, often involving enhancers and upstream binding sites for regulatory elements. These regions can cover thousands of base pairs. Intergenic DNA occupies between 63 and 75% of the total base pairs in the human genome. The longest stretch of noncoding DNA, termed a *gene desert*, is on chromosome 13; it is 3,038,416 bp long.

7.7 Noncoding RNA

Question: Although it is known that very little of the human genome codes for proteins, a large amount of it is transcribed; some estimates are over 90%. What is the outcome of this extra transcription?

At first glance these findings only appear to add to the paradoxes of genome processing. RNA that does not code for proteins (*noncoding RNA*; ncRNA) consists of: (1) the introns from mRNA of protein-coding genes; (2) RNA that is transcribed from noncoding genes; and (3) sequences that are described as *antisense RNA*. The latter mRNA is derived from sequences that overlap genes that do code for proteins; however, they clearly have more sequences than are required to generate proteins.

Structural RNA

The RNA molecules that are transcribed from the genome, and which carry out well-characterized functions, are the structural or, more accurately, *infrastructural* RNAs such as *rRNA* and *tRNA*. These species are involved in translating mRNA into proteins. Vast numbers of copies of these genes are used to support protein synthesis. Numerous copies of these genes exist in the genome where they are termed *moderately repetitive sequences*, and they are transcribed at a high rate.

Over 90% of the total RNA content of a human cell, such as a hepatocyte, is rRNA and tRNA. The high steady-state concentration, given a moderately slow rate of rRNA and tRNA synthesis, is due to the inherently high stability of rRNA and tRNA.

EXAMPLE 7.17 Ribosomal RNA in eukaryotes is actually four separate RNA species: 28S RNA, 18S RNA, 5.8S RNA, and 5S RNA. (The S notation is related to how fast a molecule sediments in an analytical ultracentrifuge cell.) The larger the number, the faster the sedimentation rate. A globular protein of 100 kDa has an S value of ~6S, but note that the relationship between size and S value is a sublinear one; see Chap. 4. The 28S, 18S, and 5.8S rRNAs are transcribed as long precursor pre-rRNAs of size 45S.

Bacterial rRNAs (23S, 16S, and 5S) are also transcribed as one long molecule. In both eukaryotes and prokaryotes, the pre-rRNA is then cleaved in a sequence of reactions to produce the individual RNA species.

EXAMPLE 7.18 Like rRNA, tRNA is also transcribed as a long precursor molecule that is cleaved in specific sites in the sequence, to release several different tRNA molecules. *RNase P* is the specific enzyme that catalyzes the reactions that occur at the 5′ ends of the relevant sequences.

Other Noncoding RNA

Small nuclear RNA (*snRNA*) molecules form part of the *spliceosome* that is involved in cleaving introns out of mRNA precursors. There are five of these special snRNAs, called U1, U2, U4, U5, and U6. They range in size from 50 to 200 nucleotides and form complexes with proteins to form small nuclear ribonucleoprotein particles (snRNPs).

Small nucleolar RNAs (snoRNAs) contain between 60 and 300 nucleotides. They bind to specific target sequences by hydrogen-bond base pairing; and then specialized proteins bind to the complex. The complex catalyzes modifications of the target RNA molecule, thus snoRNAs are particularly important in processing rRNA in mammals.

MicroRNA (miRNA) and short interfering RNA (siRNA) are small RNA sequences that are from 21 to 25 nucleotides long. These recently discovered RNA molecules were the subject of the 2006 Nobel Prize in Physiology or Medicine awarded to Andrew Fire and Craig Mello. Their award was for "gene silencing by double-stranded RNA."

The two species are quite similar; the variations come from their source. MicroRNA comes from short endogenous hairpin loop structures, while siRNA molecules are produced from long double-stranded RNA molecules or giant hairpin molecules. The mature miRNA molecules are ~22 nucleotide duplexes and usually repress translation of target mRNA sequences. The siRNAs are part of the antiviral defense system of the cell.

Experimentally we can introduce synthetic double-stranded RNA into cells. This processed interfering RNA (RNAi) catalyzes the destruction of endogenous mRNAs of the same sequence, so it is possible to observe the effect of down-regulating the expression of a particular protein in a cell.

7.8 Nonnuclear Genetic Molecules

Question: In the eukaryotic cell, is there genetic material other than in the nucleus?

Yes. Some organelles have their own genomes, in particular the *mitochondrion* and the *chloroplast*. Mitochondria evolved from bacteria over a billion years ago; the bacteria had become incorporated into larger nucleated cells in a symbiotic relationship with their host. This phenomenon of *endosymbiosis* accounts for the genetic characteristics of the present-day mitochondrion, in particular the circular chromosome. In plants, the additional autonomous organelle is the chloroplast; its genome is similar to that of the mitochondrion, reflecting a bacterial origin.

Mitochondrial Genome

There can be multiple copies of a circular chromosome in any one mitochrondrion, and the chromosome size varies from species to species. Humans have 16,569 bp in their mitochondrial genome, and most other mammals have a similar number, whereas yeast cells have a ~80 kbp genome and some plants have 200–2000 kb mitochondrial chromosomes. Yet, all mitochondrial genomes code for essentially the same number of genes: 13 essential components of the electron transport pathway. Many of the proteins are embedded into a membrane as they are translated. The mitochondrial genome also encodes all the ribosomal RNA (16S and 12S) and tRNAs (22 in total) required to translate the specialized intramitochondrial proteins. The mitochondrial genome is *inherited maternally* as almost all mitochondria in a fertilized egg come from the mother. The paternally derived mitochondria are located in the proximal end of the tail of the spermatozoon. Hence, *maternal genetics* can be traced by using the mitochondrial genome.

Most of the proteins in mitochondria are encoded in the nuclear genome. These include all the enzymes required to synthesize the DNA in the mitochondrial chromosome, the enzymes of the citric acid cycle, and many of the soluble enzymes in oxidative phosphorylation.

The proteins are synthesized in the cytoplasm and transferred to the mitochondria once they have been completely translated. The sequences tagged for the mitochondria have a presequence at the N terminus of the protein. This 15–35 amino acid *signaling peptide*, containing a large number of positive side chains, is recognized by *specific receptors* that bring the proteins to the membrane surface of the mitochondrion. The partially folded proteins are then imported into the mitochondrion, passing through two membranes. The signaling peptide sequence is cleaved from the protein once it is localized, and folding is completed in the presence of *molecular chaperones*.

Chloroplast Genome

The chloroplast genome is similar to that of mitochondria, reflecting its similar bacterial origin. However, the circular chromosome is larger than its mitochondrial counterpart, encoding 30 membrane proteins that are involved in photosynthesis. It also encodes the four components of the bacterial ribosomal system (23S, 16S, 5S, and 4.5S), 20 ribosomal proteins, and 30 tRNAs. Notable among the proteins is one of the subunits of ribulose bisphosphate carboxylase (*Rubisco*). This enzyme catalyzes the carboxylation of ribulose 1,5-bisphosphate from CO_2 and is responsible for carbon fixation in plants. It is the most abundant protein on earth.

A vestigial chloroplast is present in the malarial parasite *Plasmodium*. It codes for some of the enzymes involved in fat synthesis. Because mammals do not have chloroplasts, this plasmodial organelle is a potential target for selective antimalarial therapy.

7.9   Genome Packaging

The genomes of all organisms, even the very simple *archaebacteria*, contain a massive amount of coded genetic information, so all chromosomal DNA molecules are extremely large. *E. coli* has one single circular chromosome containing a single DNA molecule that is 1.3 mm long; the cell that it fits into is a cylinder of diameter ~1 μm and length 3 μm. Thus the ratio of the length of the chromosomal DNA to that of the cell is 1000:1. Consequently DNA is *packaged*; it is looped and supercoiled, and it is associated with proteins that form a dense *scaffold* for the overall structure.

EXAMPLE 7.19   The DNA in the total human genome is contained in 46 chromosomes and is ~2 m long; this is packaged into a nucleus ~4 μm in diameter in each nucleated cell in the body. There are ~25×10^{13} cells in a typical adult human and excluding the ~25×10^{12} red blood cells that have no nucleus there are $(25 \times 10^{13} - 25 \times 10^{12}) \times 2/1000 =$ ~4.5×10^{11} km (2.8×10^{11} mi) of DNA. The distance from the earth to the sun is 150 million km (93 million mi), so the DNA from one human being would stretch this distance 4.5×10^{11} km/$150 \times 10^6 = 3000$ times. This is also ~10 times around the orbit of Pluto at the outer reaches of our solar system!

Eukaryotic chromosomes are formed from *linear DNA*. The DNA is wrapped around specialized proteins known as histone scaffolds; then it is folded into loops and is wrapped into *minibands*, and finally it is stacked as chromosomes. DNA in chromosomes is usually maintained in a slightly negative supercoil (Chap. 8).

Prokaryotic genomes consist of *circular DNA*; this is also the case for viruses (phages), mitochondrial genomes, chloroplast genomes, and plasmids. Circularizing the DNA protects the ends from exonuclease attack. This DNA does become supercoiled and must be maintained with an optimal balance between twisting stress and relaxation. Most naturally occurring circular DNA molecules are negatively supercoiled, in other words, *underwound*. This facilitates unwinding of the DNA prior to its replication and transcription.

7.10   Chromosome Characteristics

The number of chromosomes in each nucleus varies among species, but it is always the same within normal cells of a given species. The chromosome number is a multiple of the number of *sets* or the *ploidy*, and the *haploid number n*. Algae and fungi are haploid; most animals and plants are *di*ploid. Not only is the total amount of genetic material very variable between species, but also the number of pairs of chromosomes in the genome of different species seems bizarre (Table 7-2). Chromosomes also vary in size within a species. Within the human genome there is a fourfold difference in the size across the set of chromosomes.

EXAMPLE 7.20   Many varieties of cultivated grains are *multiploid*; e.g., wheat is *octaploid*. Many cancer cells are *polyploid*, and often the population of cells shows *aneuploidy*, namely, variations in the number of chromosomes throughout the tumor.

Table 7-2   Selected Organisms, Their Genome Size, Number of Genes, and Percent of Their Genome That Exists as a Single Copy

Organism	Size of Genome (kbp)	Estimated # Genes	% Single Copy
Viruses			
Simian virus 40 (SV40)	5.1		100
Bacteriophage φX174	5.4		100
Bacteriophage λ	48.5		100
Bacteria			
M. genitalium	580	470	>90
E. coli	4,639	4,405	92
Yeast			
S. cerevisae	12,100	6,200	90
Round worm			
C. elegans	97,000	19,000	
Fruit fly			
D. melanogaster	180,000	13,600	60
Mammals			
M. musculus	2,500,000	30,000	70
H. sapiens	3,240,000	30,000	64
Mustard plant			
A. thaliana	125,000	25,500	80

Molecular Features

All chromosomes have the following features:

Centromere: This is the region of the chromosome where the mitotic-spindle fibers attach. Attachment occurs via the *kinetochore* that consists of repeated segments of DNA located on either side of the centromere. The relative position of the centromere is constant, so the relative lengths of the two *arms* are constant for each chromosome. This is an important feature for chromosome identification.

Telomeres: These occur at the ends of the chromosome and consist of distinct repeated sequences that must be copied before the chromosome can replicate. Special enzymes, *telomerases*, catalyze the processing of the telomeres. Reduced activity and extent of this processing are implicated in cell aging.

Chromatids: During the period before cell division, each chromosome is *duplicated* by *replication*. At *metaphase* the chromosomes of the same type pair up, so at this stage each chromosome consists of two *sister chromatids*, attached at their centromeres.

Two arms: The short arm of the chromosome is denoted by *p* (French *petit*, small), and the long arm is denoted by *q* (French *queue*, tail, implying long).

Karyotyping

Chromosomes from any one individual species, when stained with special dyes, give a consistent and unique pattern, like a *bar code*. This is a very reproducible pattern, and the bands in human chromosomes have therefore been numbered.

When *Giesma* stain is applied after mild *trypsin* treatment, light (*G-light*) and dark (*G-dark*) bands can be seen under the light microscope. When viewed at a low magnification, the resolution is poor and only a few bands are evident. These are numbered p1, p2, p3, etc., counting out from the centromere. If stained chromosomes are viewed at higher magnification, many sub-bands can be seen; the labeling then is subdivided by addition of a second digit to the initial number, e.g., p11, p12, p13.

EXAMPLE 7.21   Suppose a DNA marker or *locus* (Latin, *place*) is identified as being at position 17p22. This means the locus is on chromosome 17 on the short, p, arm, in region 2, and the second band in that region.

Cytogeneticists refer to the material in the cell nucleus as *chromatin*. At the molecular level this is DNA and protein. When it is stained with DNA-reactive dyes and viewed under a light microscope, there appear

Arm Region Band

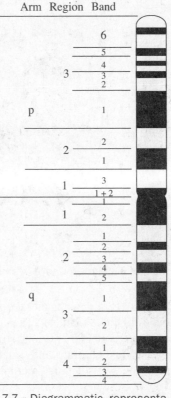

Fig. 7-7 Diagrammatic representation of the Giemsa-stained banding seen here in human chromosome 17. The arm, region, and band numbering systems are indicated.

to be two different regions: one with intense staining and one with much less. Densely stained regions are known as *heterochromatin* and the less-stained regions as *euchromatin*. Heterochromatin accounts for ~17–20% of the total DNA; it contains DNA, which is more condensed, and it is not actively transcribed, while the actively transcribed genes are located in the *euchromatin*. Satellite DNA and DNA of a repetitive nature are contained in heterochromatin.

7.11 Molecular Aspects of DNA Packing

In a chromosome, the DNA is wound around a series of very basic (positively charged) proteins called *histones*. These constitute approximately one-half of the total mass of nuclear chromatin, and hence chromosomes. In the 19th century these proteins were thought to be the genetic material, and DNA was assigned a mere structural role; this was so because DNA appeared not to have the large sequence variety of histones and that was deemed to be needed by a coded blueprint of a cell.

Histones are small proteins (11,000–23,000 Da) and contain a high proportion of lysine and arginine residues, giving them a high pI (~12) and hence a large positive charge at pH 7.

There are five separate histone isoforms: histones H1, H2A, H2B, H3, and H4. Histones H2A, H2B, H3, and H4 assemble as dimers to form an *octamer* ($2 \times 2A + 2 \times 2B + 3 + 4 = 8$). The DNA wraps 1.75 turns around this octamer. Histone H1 acts as a *linker* between the octameric units. When viewed under the electron microscope, the packaging yields a structure that is reminiscent of a *string of beads* in which octamers and associated DNA are the beads and the linker is the H1 bound to DNA. A bead and its linker are referred to as a *nucleosome*.

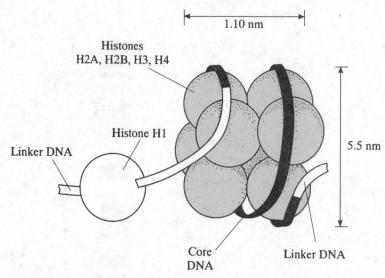

Fig. 7-8   Arrangement of histones and DNA in a *nucleosome*.

A string of nucleosomes is wrapped in a cylindrical manner to form a solenoid-shaped fiber; there are six nucleosomes per turn and the solenoid is 30 nm in diameter. Then the solenoid is folded into loops of 40 to 90 kb, which are tethered to nuclear *scaffold* proteins. This loop structure is then compacted further to form *minibands* that stack together to form the final chromosome structure. Thus the stages in folding DNA to make a chromosome are DNA → nucleosome → solenoid → miniband → chromosome.

EXAMPLE 7.22   Which forces hold a nucleosome together?

The major attractive force in the association between histones and DNA is *electrostatic* between the protonated (positively charged) amino groups of *arginine* and *lysine* residues and the unprotonated (negatively charged) *phosphoryl oxygen* atoms of DNA. Hydrogen bonds are also implicated; these form between amino hydrogen atoms of arginine and lysine residues and the bases of DNA. This hydrogen bonding does not depend on the particular base sequence. Thus histones are an example of non-base-sequence-specific interactions with DNA.

In carrying out experiments on chromatin structure, histones can be dissociated from the DNA by using high salt concentrations. The high ionic strength shields the ions from each other and leads to dissociation of the nuclear components.

SOLVED PROBLEMS

MOLECULAR BASIS OF GENETICS

7.1.   There are two fundamental and distinct processes that involve DNA and enable the flow of genetic information. What are these and when do they occur in the cell cycle?

SOLUTION

The first process is *DNA replication:* This can extend to duplicating the whole genome. It occurs immediately prior to cell division and is necessary for the transfer of genetic information from one generation to the next. The fidelity of the copying process must be as high as possible. There is little room for errors in this process, as these will be copied perhaps trillions of times in the offspring.

The second process is *DNA transcription*; it is the copying of special sections of the DNA as RNA, and the latter is then *translated* into protein. Collectively this is called *gene expression*; it occurs throughout the life of the cell and is essential for any new protein formation. Enzymes that are recycled and replaced, structural proteins, and hormones must all be synthesized by this process. Gene expression is obviously most active in rapidly growing tissue.

Transcription and translation of DNA are very different processes. Replication requires a single copy to be made of the whole genome once in the life of the cell. This must be highly accurate for healthy daughter cells. Gene expression involves the copying, sometimes carried out many thousands of times, of small sections of the genome that are then often translated to proteins. The copying process is not as accurate as for DNA replication, and because many copies are made, random errors occur but they are not usually repeated.

7.2. The flow of genetic information is analogous to the flow of information in a computer (*in silico*). Continuing this analogy, what are the computer equivalences of: (1) replication; (2) transcription; and (3) translation of DNA?

SOLUTION

The computer equivalent of the genome is the *hard drive* with its store of files; this constitutes a stable store of all information on the computer. The counterpart of RNA is the files that are transferred and linked into programs in the random access memory (RAM). The results of computations in the RAM, including output files and printed matter, are equivalent to the proteins. (1) Replication is tantamount to copying the contents of the hard drive onto another hard drive; this is done infrequently at the time of *backup* of all files. (2) Copying certain sections of the information of the hard drive into RAM is the equivalent of *transcription*. (3) The process of using the information on the RAM to create the file that generates graphical or printed output is equivalent to *translation*.

7.3. What properties must a polymer possess for it to be capable of carrying genetic information?

SOLUTION

It must be stable, with a *structural backbone* that is resistant to chemical attack from cellular components. It must have scope for *variation* with a range of different side chains that are covalently linked to the backbone. The side chains must be stable and distinguishable by other molecules through selective binding. There must be a chemical process for copying the polymer that faithfully preserves the order of the side chains in the copied version of the polymer.

7.4. Protein was originally thought to be the molecule responsible for carrying the genetic information in a cell. What particular properties of nucleic acids and protein would have led early researchers to this conclusion?

SOLUTION

Proteins are composed of a linear sequence of 20 different amino acids (in fact up to 22, but rarely so; Chap. 3) with different side chains, unlike nucleic acids that have only four. Hence proteins are capable of greater diversity than DNA and RNA. Thus it was originally thought that proteins would carry more genetic information. Nucleic acids seemed to be *monotonous* molecules that were likely to play a *structural role* in the nucleus rather than carry genetic information.

7.5. Nucleic acids are unique among the biopolymers in that they contain *phosphate*. How has this property been exploited experimentally in studies of protein synthesis?

SOLUTION

The use of ^{32}P (radioactive) to label DNA and RNA for *Southern* and *northern blotting* was a major technical advance. One of the earliest exploitations of the unique phosphorus content of nucleic acids was the Waring-blender experiment (first performed by Alfred Hershey and Martha Chase). This groundbreaking experiment proved that DNA (and not protein) was responsible for genetic information flow from one generation to the next. In this experiment the ability of T2 bacteriophage (a virus that infects bacteria) to inject DNA but not protein into the host bacterium during infection was conclusively shown with ^{32}P labeled (which labeled the nucleic acid) and ^{35}S labeled (which labeled proteins only) phage. When ^{32}P labeled phage, containing radiolabeled DNA, were allowed to attach briefly to the host bacteria (then removed with a Waring blender), a ^{32}P-labeled bacterial pellet was the result obtained after centrifugation of the sample. When ^{35}S-labeled phage were used, the bacterial pellet obtained after centrifugation was unlabeled. From this experiment it was finally established that the nucleic acid and not the protein coat was transferred to the host during viral infection. This DNA could then hijack the host's transcription and translation machinery to direct the synthesis of many copies of the virus, eventually leading to host cell.

THE GENOME

7.6. What is the molecular weight of the DNA in an *E. coli* chromosome? What is the mass of the DNA in a typical bacterial cell?

SOLUTION

Calculation: The molecular weight of a dAMP residue in DNA is 313 and that for dCMP is 275; so a round number for a deoxynucleotide residue is 300. Since the *E. coli* genome consists of 4.6×10^6 bp, the molecular weight of the DNA in the chromosome is $4.6 \times 10^6 \times 2$ (both strands) $\times 300 = 2760 \times 10^6$. This means 1 mol of *E. coli* DNA weighs 2.7×10^6 kg! The total weight of one molecule of DNA in the cell is $4.6 \times 10^6 \times 2$ (bp) $\times 300/6.022 \times 10^{23}$ (Avogadro's number) $= 4.6 \times 10^{-15}$ g. Expressed another way, DNA from ~220 *E. coli* cells weighs ~1 pg.

7.7. How many base pairs of DNA are there in a typical eukaryotic cell?

SOLUTION

The fraction of the total DNA used for coding proteins in eukaryotes is much less than in prokaryotes. Many eukaryotic species have nuclear DNA with an order-of-magnitude more base pairs than are required to encode all the different proteins. Note also that the size of the genome has little correlation with the complexity of the organism. This observation is referred to as the *C*-value paradox. The *C* value is the total number of DNA base pairs in the genome (per haploid set of chromosomes). When we compare this with the complexity of the organism, there is a massive discrepancy. Some species seem to have far too much DNA for their limited complexity. Humans have 23 pairs of chromosomes (22 pairs of autosomes and one pair of sex chromosomes), cows have 39, carp have 52, and alligators have 16. The sizes of chromosomes also differ markedly among species. And the largest number of chromosomes is found in a flowering plant. It is clear that the position of a species in the evolutionary tree or in the food chain has little bearing on the size of its genome.

BASE COMPOSITION OF GENOMES

7.8. In *E. coli* the G + C content is ~51%. How many adenine, thymine, cytosine, and guanine bases does one copy of the genome contain?

SOLUTION

Calculation: From Prob. 7.6 there are $4.6 \times 0.51 \times 10^6 = $ ~2.35×10^6 G:C base pairs; therefore there are 2.35×10^6 guanine bases, 2.35×10^6 cytosine bases, and 2.25×10^6 adenine and thymine bases. If there are 4.6×10^6 base pairs, there are 9.2×10^6 bases $[(2.35 + 2.35 + 2.25 + 2.25) \times 10^6$ bases]. There are 9.2×10^6 deoxyriboses and phosphates as well.

7.9. Does the base composition of the RNA (the *transcriptome*) reflect that of the DNA *genome*, in prokaryotes and eukaryotes?

SOLUTION

In prokaryotes a large fraction of the genome contains coding sequences, hence large sections are copied into RNA. Thus the transcriptome of a bacterium will reflect the base composition of its respective genome. However, only one strand of DNA is copied at any one time, and some sequences are copied far more often than others. The *promoter regions*, although quite short in bacteria, are *rich in A and T* and these regions are not copied into RNA. These factors could alter the measured base composition so the relative proportions of the bases of RNA do deviate from the relative proportions of the bases in the genome.

Much of the eukaryotic genome is noncoding, although a large proportion of it is still transcribed. The promoter regions, which are characteristically more A-T rich and much larger than their prokaryotic equivalents, are not transcribed, so this can alter the base composition of the transcriptome relative to the genome.

Some of the noncoding RNA has a short lifetime in the cell, and this can become an important factor when considering the base composition of the transcriptome under steady-state conditions.

7.10. How does degeneracy of the genetic code (different codons that code for the same amino acid) enable bacteria to have different genomic base compositions yet to code for similar proteins?

SOLUTION

With degeneracy of the genetic code it is possible to have different base sequences in a gene and yet code for the same sequence of amino acids. In coding for leucine, e.g., the RNA codons for leucine are CUU and CUA which correspond to 33.3% (G + C), while its other two RNA codons are CUC and CUG and these are 66.7% (G + C). If the first codon only were used to code for leucine in a gene, and all other amino acids were coded with a similar bias in G + C, then the gene would have a G:C/A:T ratio of 1:2. This extreme situation never actually arises in nature because not all amino acids have four different codons.

GENOMIC-CODE SEQUENCES

7.11. How does the spontaneous deamination of cytosine affect the distribution of dinucleotide pairs in *eukaryote genomes*?

SOLUTION

Deamination of cytosine yields uracil, which is thought to be why DNA has evolved to contain methyl uracil (thymine), to enable the correction of this chemically inevitable *corruption* of the coded message. However, there are regions of the genome that contain significantly higher proportions of methyl cytosine, often preceding a G in the sequence. These regions are associated with *gene silencing* in promoter regions, rather than protein-encoding portions of the DNA. Deamination of methyl cytosine yields thymine that has the effect of increasing the proportion of TG dinucleotides and reducing the abundance of CG dinucleotides; this outcome is seen in dinucleotide analysis of eukaryotic genomes. The most commonly occurring dinucleotide pair is TG, and the least common is CG; the incidence of CG is significantly lower than for any of the other dinucleotide pairs.

7.12. Why does the spontaneous deamination of cytosine *not* affect the distribution of dinucleotide pairs in *prokaryote genomes*?

SOLUTION

Bacteria usually do not methylate cytosine residues and do not use methyl CpG as a means of regulating gene expression. Bacteria typically *methylate* adenine residues, which protect genomic DNA from restriction by restriction endonucleases (Chap. 8), and *tag* the parent strand during mismatch repair (Chap. 8).

7.13. Is cytosine the only base that is spontaneously deaminated? What are the consequences of other deaminations to the genetic code?

SOLUTION

While adenine and guanine also contain amino groups that can be spontaneously hydrolyzed from the nucleobase, the resultant bases are *hypoxanthine* and *xanthine*, respectively. Neither of these bases is typically found in the genetic code. Thus a system of molecular machinery has evolved whereby they are identified and removed (Chap. 8).

7.14. What is the scientific value of analyzing the frequency of occurrence of the various nucleotide pairs? What information is yielded by this that a knowledge of the base composition does not provide?

SOLUTION

Base composition analysis only yields the relative proportions of the four bases in the genome. Two totally different genomes, coding for vastly different proteins, could have very similar base compositions and vice versa. This is seen with two different *Micrococcus* species that are from the same genus but can have very different base compositions, and yet code for similar proteins. This is particularly evident when there are only four bases in the code. It is the order of these bases that is important for coding a message. The simplest *string of information* is the dinucleotide. Hence the frequency of the different strings will reveal more about the actual similarities of stored information than mere base compositions.

GENOME COMPLEXITY

7.15. A C_0t plot of *E. coli* genomic DNA is like that shown in Fig. 7-4. What are the physical units on the abscissa and ordinate; and why are these two variables plotted and not some other potential candidates? What is the state of the DNA in phases I and II of the graph?

SOLUTION

The unit on the y axis is the fraction of the DNA that is unrenatured. This is calculated from the uv absorbance. Double-stranded DNA has 1.4 times less light absorption at a wavelength of 260 nm than that of the equivalent concentration of single-stranded DNA (Fig. 7-4). Phase I on the graph is 100% single-stranded and would have a higher A_{260}. The DNA would be all renatured (double-stranded) by phase II, and its A_{260} would be 1.4 times lower. The fraction of unrenatured DNA is determined from the A_{260} of the sample at time t, divided by the A_{260} of the same sample when it is completely denatured (when its temperature has been raised to well above its melting temperature, T_M).

The units of the x axis are C_0t, expressed in mol L^{-1} s. Here C_0 refers to the initial concentration of DNA and t to the time after the DNA is allowed to reanneal. The extent of renaturation is dependent on both the concentration of the DNA and the time.

7.16. How is the value of DNA complexity measured from a C_0t plot?

SOLUTION

Those DNA molecules that have the most copies of a given sequence will reanneal fastest in solution because there is a higher probability of encounter between complementary sequences. Hence more complex single-copy sequences take the longest to reanneal. The probability of a long sequence encountering its *complementary* sequence in a mixture of sequences in a given time is small because of its lower concentration when compared with other multiple-copy sequences. This situation can be modeled by assuming *second-order kinetics* (Chap. 5) for reannealing, because the rate of association is proportional to the concentration of each strand. The parameter of greatest interest is $C_0t_{1/2}$ that is estimated by regression of an exponential function onto the experimental data. This is the time taken for 50% of renaturation to occur.

7.17. The estimate of genome complexity, indicated by the value of $C_0t_{1/2}$ is derived from a C_0t graph as described in Prob. 7.16. For the nonrepetitive fraction of calf thymus DNA, $C_0t_{1/2}$ is ~10,000 times greater than the value for T4 bacteriophage DNA. What do you conclude from these values?

SOLUTION

The same concentration of calf thymus DNA takes 10,000 times longer to reanneal complementary strands than do the DNA fragments from T4 phage. The interpretation of this result is that the strands of DNA from calf thymus have many noncomplementary sequences, so the concentration of each is much lower than for the same total amount of DNA from T4 phage. Therefore the time for collision and binding between complementary strands is much longer for the thymus DNA; i.e., a concentration of calf thymus DNA that is 10,000 times greater than that of T4 phage would be required to observe the same $C_0t_{1/2}$ value.

7.18. How might you deduce from a C_0t plot that the *gene density* in higher eukaryotes, e.g., from calf thymus DNA as in Prob. 7.17, is much lower than in *E. coli*?

SOLUTION

E. coli DNA has a $C_0t_{1/2}$ value of ~10 mol L^{-1} s while the nonrepetitive fraction of calf thymus (Prob. 7.17), which makes up 60 to 70% of the genome, has a $C_0t_{1/2}$ value of ~10^4 mol L^{-1} s. Thus calf thymus DNA takes 1000 times longer to reanneal than does *E. coli* DNA. As noted in Prob. 7.17, 1000 times more calf thymus DNA is required in the starting solution for the measurement to achieve the same value of $C_0t_{1/2}$. The *E. coli* genome is 4.6 million bp while the human genome is ~3 billion bp. Even after accounting for the repetitive fractions from the human genome, there is a ~1000-fold larger fraction of unique sequences in the human genome than in the *E. coli* genome.

7.19. DNA sequence analysis reveals that *E. coli* cells synthesize ~4000 different proteins while mammals have ~30,000 protein-encoding genes, but they make many more different proteins from these genes due to alternative splicing of mRNA (Chap. 9). Thus mammals have only ~7 times as many structural genes as does *E. coli*, but their genomes are ~500–1000 times larger. What is the basis for this disparity in genome size? Are the gene sequences simply longer, or are there other unique noncoding sequences among the genes?

SOLUTION

The answer is that both aspects are relevant to the explanation. The vast majority of mammalian genes contain *introns* that make up as much as 90% of a gene. Introns are unique sequences of noncoding RNA. The coding sequences are usually longer on average; the average polypeptide in mammals is ~50 kDa whereas in bacteria it is 40 kDa. The mammalian genome also contains repetitive DNA sequences that are not present in bacteria, and they have much longer promoters and other regulatory sequences than in bacteria.

7. 20. Draw a C_0t plot derived from human genomic DNA.

SOLUTION

Human genomic DNA gives a C_0t curve (e.g., Fig. 7-6) that has 30–40% fast annealing, called *low C_0t sequence elements*, and 60–70% of slow annealing, called *high C_0t*, unique sequences. The human genome is divided into four classes of sequence repetition: (1) highly repetitive, with hundreds to millions of copies; (2) moderately repetitive with tens to hundreds of copies; (3) slightly repetitive, with 1–10 copies; and (4) single-copy sequences.

7.21. In the DNA that makes up a genome, what are the fast-annealing low C_0t sequence elements?

SOLUTION

They are the repetitive DNA sequences. Sequence analysis reveals them to contain the short repeated sequences in what is called *satellite DNA*, and longer sequences from genes that have a large number of copies. The term *satellite* derives from their behavior in samples that are subjected to CsCl density-gradient centrifugation. Because much of the DNA in simple sequences is rich in A and T, it has a lower density than the more (G + C)-rich DNA; therefore it forms a *band* (satellite) above the main ones in the density gradient. Repeated sequences account for 10–20% of higher eukaryotic DNA. The highly repetitive DNA reanneals in seconds. Repetitive DNA sequences are clustered around the *centromeres* and *telomeres* in the genome.

7.22. Which of the four classes of *sequence repetition* contains most of the genes (Prob. 7.20)?

SOLUTION

The final group; these are the single-copy sequences that make up the vast majority of genes in the genome. This group has the greatest size and sequence variation. The sequences account for the longest reannealing time in C_0t analysis; this time can be days, which is the reason that the log scale is used on the abscissa.

7.23. Can repetitive DNA alone account for the additional DNA in a mammalian genome, compared with, say, *E. coli*?

SOLUTION

No, although 30–40% of the DNA is not single-copy sequences, the other 60–70% *is* single-copy. If single-copy DNA contains most of the coding DNA, why is only 2% of the DNA estimated to be coding DNA? (This paradox was also explored in Prob. 7.17.) Study of eukaryotic genes found that they are interrupted by large sections of noncoding regions called *introns*. These stretches of DNA, which make up over 90% of some genes, are excised after transcription when the mRNA is *processed*.

NONCODING RNA

7.24. Which RNA is referred to by the term *noncoding RNA*?

SOLUTION

Noncoding RNA is RNA that is *generated by transcription* from DNA but that is not translated into protein. It includes the major structural RNAs: rRNA and tRNA as well as *small nuclear RNA* (snRNA), *small nucleolar RNA* (snoRNA), *microRNA* (miRNA), and *short interfering RNA* (siRNA).

7.25. If one of the principal functions of RNA is to act as an interim molecule in the transfer of information between DNA and proteins, why is so much of the RNA noncoding?

SOLUTION

To translate these mRNA sequences into proteins requires large amounts of rRNA and tRNA. This accounts for the large copy-number of these sequences in the genome. The other smaller RNA species have roles in the regulation of gene expression, probably in controlling the stability and localization of specific mRNA species.

7.26. Why has the mechanistic requirement for mRNA evolved in protein synthesis? In other words, why are proteins not directly translated from DNA?

SOLUTION

RNA acts as an interim molecule that can *amplify* gene expression much better than directly translating the protein from the DNA. An interim template offers *multiple levels of regulation* that proceeding directly from DNA to the protein does not. By regulating the stability of the mRNA, the up-regulation of more copies of the protein is ensured. It also allows for greater flexibility when down-regulating gene expression; in other words, without mRNA it would be difficult to down-regulate gene expression. Translation would become incredibly complicated as it would have to both ensure correct translation and regulate the rate of initiation of translation. Repressors, activators, and enhancers would need to work on the ribosome. This would add another level of complexity to an already complex process of translation. Without mRNA, eukaryotic translation could not occur in the cytoplasm, nor could *alternative splicing* produce a wide variety of proteins from one gene.

7.27. Speculate on the possible regulatory roles played by noncoding RNA in protein synthesis.

SOLUTION

Noncoding RNAs can recruit proteins to certain RNA sequences. These proteins can then modify the RNA (as occurs with snoRNA), regulate the stability of specific sequences by orchestrating their destruction or protecting them from destruction, altering the rate of translation by binding to 5′-UTR or 3′-UTRs, and localize specific sequences within the cytoplasm.

7.28. Organelles such as mitochondria and chloroplasts are thought to have arisen by *endosymbiosis*. What clues as to their origin do we see from their genomes?

SOLUTION

Their genomes, like prokaryotic genomes, are *circular* and usually very efficient, containing no repetitive sequences or introns. The ribosomes used in translation are closer to those in the bacterial protein synthesis system than in the eukaryotic one; e.g., 12S and 16S rRNAs are used. Other clues include the number of membranes surrounding the organelle; some organelles have more than one membrane, such as the *apico-plast* in *Plasmodium* sp, suggesting more than one endosybiotic event had occurred.

7.29. Why may it be necessary to have some proteins encoded by organelle-specific genomes?

SOLUTION

Proteins whose folding must occur in the membrane, such as integral membrane proteins, need to be translated within the organelle so they can dock with the membrane in the folding process. They often have to be embedded with a surface on the inner face of the organelle membrane. These proteins cannot be synthesized in the cytoplasm and then exported to the organelle, as the folding environment of the cytoplasm would probably produce an incorrect fold.

7.30. The *universal genetic code* has been viewed from the time of its discovery ~50 years ago as a *frozen accident*. Some organelle genomes show a deviation from this universal code. Do these genomes provide evidence for this view of the code?

SOLUTION

The mitochondrion in particular shows some deviation from the universal genetic code. If we view the genetic code as a frozen accident, then prior to its adoption by all cells there must have been some *sloppi-ness* in the translation process, whereby a particular sequence could be translated to *a number of different* protein sequences. As life-forms became more complex, this ambiguity could be no longer tolerated and the code would have been adopted by life from then on. Deviations from this code could be the result of changes introduced after the *frozen accident event* or vestiges of the previous more promiscuous times. There is evidence of recoding in some yeast species and amino acids, such as *selenocysteine* (Chap. 3), which were added to the code, but whether the organelle codes represent earlier versions or later evolution in isolation is still open to debate. The deviations in the mitochondrial code enable the mitochondrion to translate its proteins with only 22 tRNAs. This makes the genome considerably smaller and hence more efficient for the organism, as each tRNA must be coded in the genome.

GENOME PACKAGING

7.31. You plan to isolate the *histone protein* fraction from *calf thymus*. Which properties of these proteins might you employ to separate them from the rest of the proteins in the cells? How many different polypeptide chains would you expect to isolate?

SOLUTION

Histones are located in the nucleus and are associated with DNA, so an initial subcellular fractionation procedure such as differential centrifugation (Chap. 1) could be used to isolate the nuclei. The histones could then be separated from the DNA by using a solution with high ionic strength to shield the electrostatic interactions between the polycationic histones and the polyanionic DNA. The high pI of histones, coupled with their low molecular weight relative to DNA, makes a combination of ion exchange and Sephadex size-exclusion chromatography an ideal approach.

There would be five different separate polypeptide chains: histones H1, H2A, H2B, H3, and H4.

7.32. Based on the number of base pairs in the *E. coli* chromosome, and the fact that each turn of a DNA helix has 10 base pairs and a pitch of 3.4 nm, calculate the length of DNA in one *E. coli* cell.

SOLUTION

There are 4.6×10^6 base pairs with 10 bases per turn that advance the helix by 3.4×10^{-9} m each turn; this leads to the product $4.6 \times 10^6 \times 10^{-1} \times 3.4 \times 10^{-9}$ which is equal to 1.56 mm.

7.33. What effect might the acetylation of lysine residues on a histone (Fig. 7-9) have on DNA packaging?

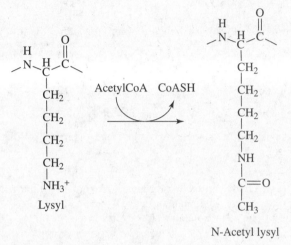

Fig. 7-9   Acetylation of a lysine residue in a histone.

SOLUTION

The acetylation of the lysine side chain neutralizes the positive charge of the lysine and hence will loosen the association between the histone and DNA. This should facilitate greater access of enzymes to the DNA sequence.

7.34. What are the roles of histones in the assembly of chromosomes?

SOLUTION

Packaging: The tight packaging of the DNA around the histones is achieved because the histones shield the negatively charged phosphate groups from each other. Otherwise the DNA would repel itself and could not fold up tightly.

Transcriptional control: The tight packing of DNA makes it less accessible for transcription that requires open access to the base sequence. Transcription factors (proteins) bind and interact with specific base sequences and achieve this more readily in histone-free DNA or in DNA that is more loosely packed. Thus the extent of DNA packaging in a cell regulates gene expression. In other words, one of the first steps in activating the transcription of a gene is to loosen the packaging by modifying the histones in specific ways, such as by methylation.

7.35. Below is a hypothetical chromosome that is part of the karyotype of a cell. Give the arm-region-band specification for each of the regions of the chromosome that are indicated by the arrows labeled A–D.

SOLUTION

A, p35; B, p13; C, q25; and D, q31. The upper arm is labeled p and the lower one q. The numbering of the regions and the bands within them, by convention, increases *out* from the *centromere*.

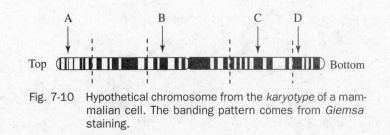

Fig. 7-10   Hypothetical chromosome from the *karyotype* of a mammalian cell. The banding pattern comes from *Giemsa* staining.

SUPPLEMENTARY PROBLEMS

7. 36. Which process is responsible for the transfer of information from one generation to the next?
A. Replication
B. Transcription
C. Translation
D. Transformation
E. Integration

7.37. It is said that retroviruses do not obey the *standard central dogma* for the flow of genetic information. Is this statement true?

7.38. What does the term *gene* mean in molecular biology?

7.39. Do all genes code for proteins?

7.40. What is meant by *diploid* and *haploid*? Which organisms are diploid?

7.41. How is the base composition of genomes measured and expressed? What is meant by different base compositions?

7.42. Which statement is incorrect?
A. Bacterial genomes have a fairly constant base composition throughout the genome.
B. Eukaryotes show greater diversity within the genome.
C. The %(G + C) content is very similar among all bacteria.
D. Mammalian base compositions vary by less than 12% between various species.

7.43. Why is CG the lowest-frequency dinucleotide, and TG the dinucleotide with the highest frequency, in the mammalian genome?

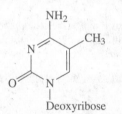

Fig. 7-11 5-Methylcytosine.

7.44. In relation to the methylcytosine, which statement is correct/incorrect?
A. 5-Methyl substituted cytosine is actually thymine.
B. The addition of the methyl group disrupts the normal hydrogen bonding.
C. The addition of the methyl group causes a bulge in the double helix.
D. The deamination of methyl cytosine gives thymine.
E. Methylcytosine base pairs with adenine rather than guanine.

7.45. What do C_0t plots reveal about genome complexity?

7.46. Give an example of a sequence with a complexity of 4.

7.47. Why do sequences with a lower complexity have a lower C_0t?

7.48. Why do mammalian genomes have a very different shaped C_0t plot (e.g., Fig. 7-6) from the equivalent bacterial graph (e.g., Fig. 7-4)?

7.49. How do we account for the large fraction of a mammalian genome that is *transcribed* but not *translated*?

7.50. Which noncoding RNA is responsible for recruiting RNA-modifying proteins that are necessary for rRNA processing?

7.51. What roles do interfering RNA sequences play in vivo?

7.52. Give two examples of nonnuclear genomic DNA. How do these genomes arise in the cell?

7.53. What is the function of the genomes mentioned in Prob. 7.52?

7.54. Why does the genome become packaged?

7.55. How does prokaryotic genome packaging differ from eukaryotic genome organization?

7.56. Why do DNA isolation methods usually include incubation of the sample in a high-ionic-strength buffer early in the procedure?

7.57. You have isolated and separated a number of proteins from a cell lysate by 2D gel electrophoresis. You then estimate the molecular weight and pI of these proteins. The properties of a number of your proteins, labeled A–E, are presented in the table below. Which one(s) could be histones?

Protein Label	Molecular Weight	pI
A	69,000	4.8
B	12,000	12
C	20,000	10
D	70,000	6.5
E	10,500	7.4

7.58. Micrococcal nuclease is a nonspecific *exo-endonuclease* (cuts both in the middle and at the ends of RNA and DNA polymers; single- and double-stranded) that will cleave any *naked* or unpackaged DNA. Once the DNA is packaged, or masked, it is no longer exposed to the nuclease. After briefly treating isolated chromatin with micrococcal nuclease, DNA is isolated and separated by gel electrophoresis. The gel reveals bands every ~200 nucleotide pairs. Can you explain this observation and how the gel pattern might change if you digested the chromatin for longer?

ANSWERS TO SUPPLEMENTARY PROBLEMS

7.36. A

7.37. The statement is true. Retroviruses store their genetic information as RNA that is converted to DNA via *reverse transcriptase* upon infection. As the standard flow of genetic information is from DNA to RNA, they do not follow the standard central dogma.

7.38. It is a distinct sequence of DNA that is transcribed by an RNA polymerase. It has a defined region for the *start* of transcription, and a defined *stop* region.

7.39. No, a significant part of the genome contains genes that code for RNA species such as rRNA and tRNA.

7.40. A diploid organism is one where the somatic cells contain two copies of the genome. Most plants and animals are diploid. Haploid organisms contain only one copy of their genome. Most fungi, algae, and bacteria are haploid.

7.41. The base composition is the percent of each base (A, G, C, and T) in the total genome. As G = C and A = T, the base composition is expressed as %(G + C). Different organisms, even within the same species or genus, will have different %(G + C) content.

7.42. C

7.43. Because cytosines in C.G islands are often methylated in the mammalian genome. If they then spontaneously deaminate, the C.G becomes T.G. Over evolutionary time there has been a drift in this direction.

7.44. D

7.45. The most surprising feature revealed by C_0t analysis is the amount of repetitive DNA that exists in complex organisms such as mammals. While a large amount of the mammalian genome is complex (single-sequence), a significant proportion shows very low complexity.

7.46. AGTCAGTCAGTCAGTC is a sequence with a complexity of 4. The unique repeat sequence is AGTC. It will not matter how many times this tetramer is repeated, the sequence will still have a complexity of 4.

7.47. Because there are more copies of the particular sequence, the complementary partner will find its match more rapidly.

7.48. Mammals have different classes of genomic DNA when classified by *complexity*. Broadly speaking, there are four classes; *highly repetitive, moderately repetitive, slightly repetitive* and *unique (simple copy) sequences* (Prob. 7.20). Each class has its own typical C_0t plot. The net plot is a summation of the four classes. Bacterial genomes contain only unique sequences so they have a single annealing curve.

7.49. RNA species whose final product is RNA, e.g., the structural RNAs, tRNA and rRNA, make up a large proportion of the *transcriptome* and have many copies in the genome. Other regulatory RNA species, e.g., *snoRNA, snRNA,* and *miRNA*, must all be transcribed from the genome. Many mammalian genes contain *introns* that can make up to 90% of the gene. These introns are excised before the processed mRNA transcript is exported to the cytoplasm. Many of the *small regulatory RNAs* are produced from the introns.

7.50. This is small nucleolar RNA or snoRNA. These RNA species recognize their target sequence by *base-pairing* and then recruit specialized proteins that perform nucleotide modifications to these RNAs; usually 2′ *O*-ribose *methylation*, base *deaminations* such as adenine-to-inosine conversions, and the addition of *pseudouridines*. These modifications are *crucial* to ribosome biogenesis.

7.51. Interferring RNA species bind to the 3′ UTR (3′ *untranslated region*) of endogenous mRNA species and either inhibit their translation or initiate the destruction of the molecule.

7.52. The *mitochondrial* genome and the *chloroplast* genome are the best known examples, although the *apicoplast* in certain protozoans such as the malarial parasite also has its own genome. These organelles are thought to have arisen by endosymbiosis whereby the larger nucleated cell engulfed a smaller bacterial cell and together they set up a symbiotic relationship.

7.53. These genomes code for proteins that, during translation and folding, become embedded into the organelle membrane. Most of the proteins that are required by the organelle are of nuclear origin, and they are imported *after translation*.

7.54. The nucleus is *as big as it needs to be* to enclose the genome! The compaction of the genome reduces the time taken for transcription factors to locate specific DNA sequences and for various substrates to interact with the enzymes that act upon them.

7.55. The prokaryotic genome is very economical in terms of size (there is little noncoding DNA), but even so it is packaged into the cell. Scaffold proteins enable the DNA to be compacted into the small volume of a bacterial cell. The *E. coli* DNA is over 1 mm in length (Prob. 7.32), yet it is packaged into a cell with a diameter in micrometers.

7.56. The high ionic strength (high salt concentration) shields the charges on the histones and DNA and enables the proteins to dissociate from the DNA. Electrostatic interactions are rendered much weaker in a high-ionic-strength environment.

7.57. Protein B could be a histone. The low molecular weight and high pI make it an ideal candidate. Protein C could also be a histone, although the larger size would fit the profile of histone H1 (the clamp) rather than a component of the octamer (H2A, H2B, H3, or H4).

7.58. This is the classical discovery of Dean Hewish and Leigh Burgoyne in 1973 at Flinders University in South Australia. The brief digestion allowed the cleavage of the string of the nucleosome units, leaving the beads protected by the histone core octamer. Because of the brief time of digestion, only some of the interspersed sites are digested, so a series of fragments containing the DNA from 1, 2, 3, etc. nucleosome units are seen. If the chromatin were exhaustively digested, only a fragment at ~200 nucleotide pairs would be seen.

CHAPTER 8

DNA Replication and Repair

8.1   Introduction

The flow of genetic information from an individual cell to its next generation requires the duplication of its genetic blueprint, the *genome*. Central to this information transfer is the *replication of DNA*.

Question: What process ensures the transfer of genetic information from one generation to the next?

DNA replication is the process whereby a single copy is made of both strands of the whole genome in the cell. It is highly regulated and is carried out once in the life of a cell, just before it divides. The fidelity of the copying process is paramount, as this is the template for the next generation of cell. The process is closely coordinated with cell division.

8.2   Chemistry of DNA Replication

An understanding of the chemical reactions involved in the replication of DNA helps us to see the close links between metabolism that supplies ATP and the process of assembly of these complicated polymers.

New DNA strands are synthesized in the 5′→3′ direction. This means that new deoxyribonucleotide tri-phosphates (dNTPs) are added onto the 3′-OH of the growing chain in a template-directed manner by *DNA polymerase*. The polymerization involves the formation of a *phosphodiester bond* between the α-phosphate of the incoming nucleotide and the 3′-OH of the nascent chain. Only the deoxyribonucleotide monophosphate (dNMP) is incorporated into the growing chain; the pyrophosphate (PPi) is cleaved off during polymerization. The cleavage of the phosphodiester bond provides the energy for the polymerization reaction. The resulting pyrophosphate ion is rapidly hydrolyzed to two phosphate ions by the ubiquitous and abundant enzyme *pyrophosphatase*, and this reaction drives the polymerization in the direction of polymer formation (Fig. 8-1).

8.3   Semiconservative Nature of DNA Replication

There are three possible mechanisms that describe the fates of the DNA strands that are copied and where they will ultimately end up in the two daughter cells after mitosis. *Conservative replication* posits that one daughter cell will contain both parent strands and the other daughter cell will contain the two newly synthesized strands of DNA. *Semiconservative replication* posits that the DNA of both daughter cells contains one strand from the parent and one newly synthesized strand. The *dispersive model* posits that sections of parental and newly synthesized DNA are scattered throughout both strands of the daughter genomes. Experimental evidence shows that DNA replication is *semiconservative*.

EXAMPLE 8.1   A series of experiments by Matthew Meselson and Franklin Stahl proved that DNA replication was semiconservative. Cells were grown on the heavy isotope of nitrogen ^{15}N (denoted H for heavy); then the medium was changed to one containing the light isotope of nitrogen ^{14}N (denoted L for light) as the sole nitrogen source. DNA was isolated at various time points after the medium was changed, and applied to a CsCl density gradient. This technique separates molecules by density differences (Chap. 1); DNA containing two light strands (L:L) will form a band at a different density from a hybrid H:L duplex, or the H:H form of DNA. If replication were *conservative*, the DNA in one cell

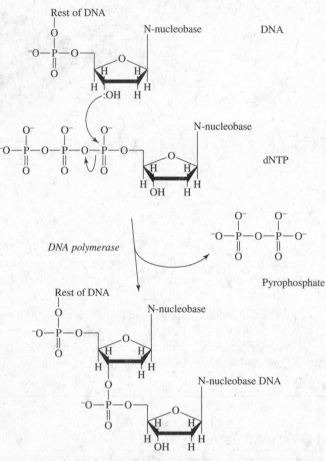

Fig. 8-1   Chemistry of DNA replication catalyzed by *DNA polymerase*. dNTP denotes deoxynucleotriphosphate, and N-nucleobase denotes a purine or a pyrimidine.

A T	A T	A T	A T	A T
G C	G C	G C	G C	G C
C G	C G	C G	C G	C G
T A	T A	T A	T A	T A
T A	T A	T A	T A	T A
A T	A T	A T	A T	A T
A T	A T	A T	A T	A T
G C	G C	G C	G C	G C
C G	C G		C G	C G
C G	C G		C G	C G
G C	G C		G C	G C
T A	T A		T A	T A
A T	A T		A T	A T
C G	C G		C G	C G
G C	G C		G C	G C
A T	A T		A T	A T

(a)   (b)   (c)

Fig. 8-2   Unwound DNA as a template for replication. The bold letters denote newly synthesized DNA.

division after the medium change would be composed of H:H and L:L in equal proportions. In the second generation there should be a ratio of 3 L:L to 1 H:H. If replication were *semiconservative*, the first generation after medium change would show DNA composed solely of the hybrid H:L. In the next generation we would expect H:L and L:L in a ratio of 1:1. In the following generation the H:L and L:L would have a ratio of 1:3. In the next generation it would be 1:7. *This is what was found experimentally*. If replication were *dispersive*, hybrid H:L DNA would result; but if the individual strands were analyzed under denaturing conditions (in CsCl with NaOH to keep the strands apart), they would also have an intermediate density. The individual DNA strands would always be either H or L in the other models.

8.4 DNA Replication in Bacteria

Bacterial DNA replication, especially that in *E. coli*, has been extensively studied. The *E. coli* chromosome is a single circular DNA molecule, composed of ~4.6×10^6 base pairs.

Replication of the bacterial chromosome is divided into three stages: *initiation, elongation,* and *termination*. Under optimal growth conditions *E. coli* can double their cell number every 20 min. They can take up to 10 h to double their number in less nutritious circumstances. However, irrespective of the nutritional status, DNA replication occurs at a constant rate of ~1000 nucleotides s^{-1}.

Replication in *E. coli* is a bidirectional process and is described by the *theta* model of replication. In this model the new strands peel from the parent strand, appearing like a Greek letter theta (θ). There is strong evidence to support a model with two *replication forks* that work in concert in opposite directions starting from a well-defined *initiation* site. By the time the forks meet up, a complete second copy of the genome has been made (Fig. 8-3).

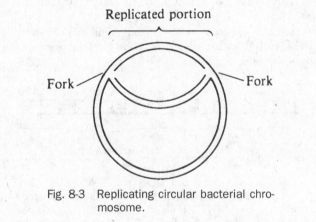

Fig. 8-3 Replicating circular bacterial chromosome.

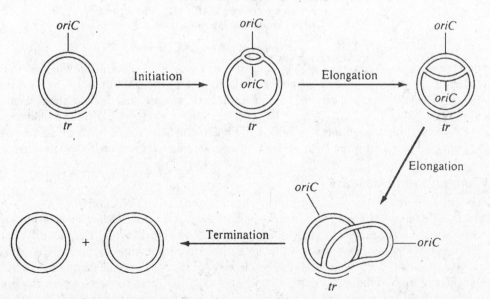

Fig. 8-4 Stages in the replication of a bacterial chromosome. The origin of replication is *oriC* and *tr* is the termination region.

8.5   Initiation of DNA Replication in Bacteria

A number of proteins are involved in initiation of replication of the genome in bacteria (Table 8-1).

Table 8-1   Proteins Needed for Initiation of Replication

Protein	Function
DnaA	Recognizes *oriC* sequences
DnaB	Unwinds DNA
DnaC	Needed for DnaB binding
HU	Stimulates initiation
SSB	Binds single-stranded DNA
RNA polymerase	Facilitates DnaA activity
DNA gyrase	Relieves torsional strain caused by DNA unwinding
Dam methylase	Methylates GATC sequences at *oriC*
Primase	Synthesizes RNA primers

The initiation of DNA replication occurs at a defined site on the bacterial chromosome called *oriC*.

EXAMPLE 8.2   What are the defining features of *oriC*, the site of initiation of DNA replication in *E. coli*?

As shown in Fig. 8-5, *oriC* consists of a stretch of 245 bp of DNA within which are three highly conserved 13-mer sequences and four highly conserved 9-mer sequences.

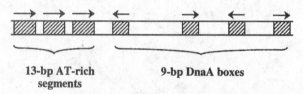

13-bp AT-rich   **9-bp DnaA boxes**
segments

Fig. 8-5   Arrangement of nucleobase sequences in *oriC*. The 13-bp AT-rich segment has the sequence GATCTNTTTNTTT, where N denotes any nucleobase. The group of 9 bp segments has the consensus sequence TTATCCACA. The arrows indicate the orientation of the base segments in each case.

Initiation of replication commences with binding of complexes of the protein DnaA to each of the 9-mer sequences in *oriC*. This is followed by *unzipping* (denaturation) of the DNA in the 13-mer sequences, in a process that is ATP-dependent and that requires the protein HU. DnaB then binds to the unwound region, facilitated by DnaC. DnaB is a *DNA helicase* that catalyzes the unwinding of DNA in a bidirectional way, creating two potential replication forks. Single-strand binding (SSB) protein-binds to the single-stranded DNA, preventing renaturation while *DNA gyrase* relieves the torsional stress caused by the unwinding.

8.6   Elongation of Bacterial DNA

At least six different proteins are involved in the elongation of bacterial DNA (Table 8-2).

Elongation of bacterial DNA involves two different but related processes: leading strand synthesis and lagging strand synthesis. It is pertinent to ask why these two processes are different. They are different because DNA polymerases synthesize DNA in a way that involves adding nucleotides to the 3′-OH of deoxyribose. *Leading strand* synthesis is relatively straightforward, because the 3′→5′ strand of parental DNA serves as a template. *Lagging strand* synthesis is more complicated; the 5′→3′ strand of DNA serves as a template for synthesis of short DNA fragments called *Okazaki fragments* after their discoverer Reiji Okazaki (Fig. 8-6).

Table 8-2   Proteins Involved in the Elongation of Bacterial DNA

Protein	Function
SSB	Binding to single-stranded DNA
DnaB	DNA unwinding
DnaG	RNA primer synthesis
DNA polymerase III	New strand elongation
DNA polymerase I	Primer excision, filling in gaps
DNA gyrase	Supercoiling

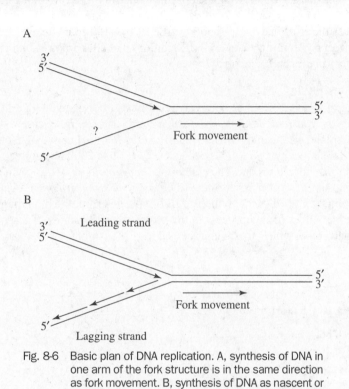

Fig. 8-6   Basic plan of DNA replication. A, synthesis of DNA in one arm of the fork structure is in the same direction as fork movement. B, synthesis of DNA as nascent or *Okazaki* fragments in one arm of the replication fork.

EXAMPLE 8.3   One enzyme, *DNA polymerase III*, is responsible for DNA synthesis in both the leading and lagging strands. Knowing its three-dimensional structure helps explain how this is possible (Fig. 8-7).

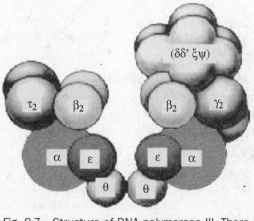

Fig. 8-7   Structure of DNA polymerase III. There are several different protein subunits.

DNA polymerase III is an asymmetric dimer. It contains two copies of the core *polymerase*, subunits α, ε, and θ. The α subunit has polymerase activity while ε is a $3'\rightarrow5'$ proofreading *exonuclease*. A τ_2 subunit is associated with one arm and a $(\delta\delta'\xi\psi)_2$ subunit with the other. These serve as the *clamp-loading complex*. The β_2 subunits form ringlike structures that serve as sliding DNA clamps.

Leading Strand Synthesis

This begins with the synthesis of an RNA primer at *oriC* by *DnaG*. DNA polymerase III then adds bases to this, moving along the DNA as it unwinds. In part, this is achieved because the *DNA helicase*, *DnaB*, binds to DNA polymerase III. If the incorrect nucleotide is added to the growing chain, the altered geometry of the base pairing causes the polymerase to *stall* and reduce its affinity for the 3'-OH end of the deoxyribose moiety. The end then moves to the $3'\rightarrow5'$ *exonuclease* site, allowing the enzyme to cleave off the offending nucleotide. A new dNTP is then added by the polymerase. This *proofreading* ability, which corrects the error at the time of the addition of a nucleotide, reduces the error rate of DNA polymerase III by ~100-fold. On average, DNA polymerase III alone inserts the incorrect nucleotide once every ~10^5 additions, but after proofreading via the exonuclease, this error rate is reduced to 1 in every ~10^7 incorrect bases.

Lagging Strand Synthesis

Synthesis of the lagging strand of DNA is relatively complicated compared with that of the leading strand. The synthesis depends on *transient interactions* between *DnaG* and *DnaB* helicase, as the latter moves along the lagging strand template. As this movement occurs, a *short RNA primer* (~10 nucleotides long called an *Okazaki fragment*) is laid down by *DnaG*. This occurs every 1000 to 2000 nucleotides on the single strand of the lagging strand template that loops out. The *clamp-loading subunit* of DNA polymerase III then positions a new β_2 sliding clamp on the primer, and synthesis of a new *Okazaki fragment* commences. When this is complete, the core component of DNA polymerase III dissociates from the β_2 sliding clamp and associates with a new one. The net effect of this process is the production of a series of discontinuous segments of complexes of DNA and RNA, which are then processed into one continuous DNA strand.

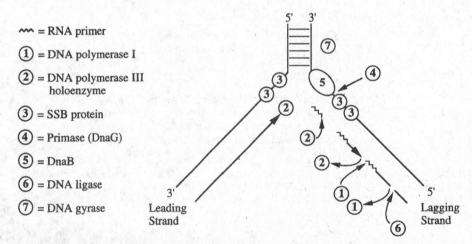

Fig. 8-8 Events involved in the growth of a DNA molecule at its replication fork.

8.7 Termination of Bacterial DNA Replication

The two replication forks (Fig. 8-4) eventually meet at the terminus region of the circular chromosome. Termination of DNA replication is restricted to this region.

EXAMPLE 8.4 How is termination of DNA replication restricted to a particular region of the bacterial chromosome?

The terminus region of *E. coli* covers ~25% of the genome. It contains six DNA terminator sequences (*TerA–F*), each of 23 bp. They are arranged as two opposing groups of three, as shown in Fig. 8-9. The terminators bind a terminator protein *Tus* (terminator utilization substance) forming a Tus-Ter complex. This complex blocks the approaching fork in *one direction only*. *TerB*, *TerC*, and *TerF* arrest the *clockwise* moving fork (and not the counterclockwise approaching fork), and *TerA*, *TerD*, and *TerE* stop the *counterclockwise*-moving fork. Because of the arrangement of the six *Ter* sites, a trap is formed; forks may enter the region but they cannot leave it.

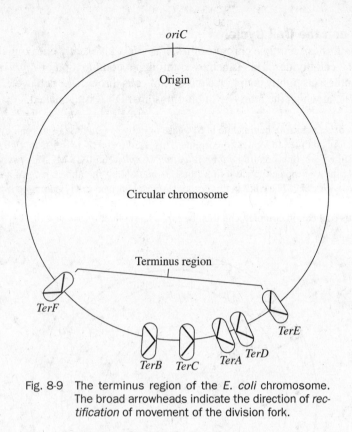

Fig. 8-9   The terminus region of the *E. coli* chromosome. The broad arrowheads indicate the direction of *rectification* of movement of the division fork.

8.8   DNA Replication in Eukaryotes

DNA replication in eukaryotes is fundamentally similar to that in prokaryotes. It is catalyzed by DNA polymerases which synthesize new DNA strands in a 5′→3′ direction. Synthesis of leading strand eukaryotic DNA is continuous while synthesis of lagging strand DNA entails the production of Okazaki fragments. However, there are a number of differences between prokaryotic and eukaryotic DNA replication.

EXAMPLE 8.5   As is the case in prokaryotes, eukaryotes express a number of different DNA polymerases. DNA polymerase α has no exonuclease activity and therefore cannot proofread. It is tightly associated with a *primase*. This primase component of the complex is thought to produce ~10 base RNA primers which are extended by the polymerase by ~15 deoxyribonucleotides. These oligonucleotides serve as primers for lagging strand DNA synthesis. DNA polymerase δ is functionally analogous to prokaryotic DNA polymerase III; it has a 3′→5′ proofreading exonuclease activity and, when associated with proliferating cell nuclear antigen (PCNA), shows *high processivity*. This is so because PCNA acts as a sliding clamp in the same way as the β subunits of DNA polymerase III. The structures of PCNA and the β clamp are very similar, even though they have no significant amino acid sequence identity.

EXAMPLE 8.6   Which of the differences in the *organization* of prokaryotic and eukaryotic genomes have implications for *eukaryotic* DNA replication?
   There are three major differences: (1) Eukaryotic genomes are much larger than prokaryotic ones; e.g., the *E. coli* chromosome contains 4.6×10^6 base pairs while the 23 human chromosomes contain $\sim 3 \times 10^9$ base pairs; (2) Prokaryotic chromosomes are usually *circular* while eukaryotic chromosomes are *linear*; (3) Eukaryotic chromosomal DNA is packaged into *nucleosomes* through specific interactions with *histones* and other proteins while prokaryotic DNA is not.

EXAMPLE 8.7   One way in which difference 1 in Example 8.6 is addressed is that, in contrast to the single initiation site for DNA replication in prokaryotes, there are *multiple initiation sites*, between 3×10^4 and 3×10^5 base pairs apart, on eukaryotic chromosomes. Therefore, even though replication fork movement is slower in eukaryotes than in prokaryotes (about 50 nucleotides s^{-1}), the presence of multiple sites of initiation allows chromosome replication to occur on a time scale of ~10 h whereas it would take ~500 h if there were only a single initiation site.

DNA Replication and the Cell Cycle

Because eukaryotic cells have multiple chromosomes, it is vital that exactly one copy of the DNA in *each* be synthesized before the cell divides. This is achieved through a combination of *replication licensing*, which ensures that DNA synthesis is tightly coupled to passage of cells through the cell cycle, and a series of *checkpoints* in the cell cycle, at which the *integrity* of chromosomal DNA is evaluated.

EXAMPLE 8.8   *Replication licensing* begins late in M phase or early in G_1 phase of the cell cycle, with the binding of the hexameric ORC protein complex to replication origins. This is followed by recruitment of the *MCM2–7* complex by replication licensing factor *Cdt1*, thus creating *a prereplication complex* (preRC). MCM2–7 is a *DNA helicase*. Passage of the cell from the G_1 phase of the cell cycle into S phase is marked by the appearance of a *cyclin:cyclin-dependent protein kinase complex*, cycA:cdk2. The cdk2 in this complex phosphorylates cdt1, leading to its release from the preRC. Also MCM2–7 is phosphorylated, leading to activation of its *helicase* function and allowing recruitment of PCNA and *DNA polymerase* δ. This replication complex can then begin DNA replication.

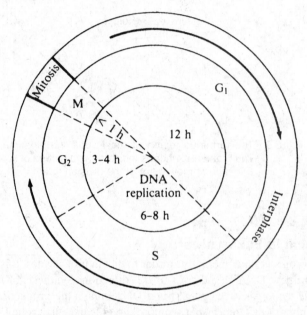

Fig. 8-10   The eukaryotic cell cycle. The duration of the four phases as shown is typical of higher eukaryotic cells grown in tissue culture.

EXAMPLE 8.9   There are a number of checkpoints in the cell cycle. G_2 has a checkpoint that prevents progression into M phase unless replication of all chromosomal DNA is complete. The M phase checkpoint ensures that the chromosomes have been correctly attached to the *mitotic spindle*. Checkpoints in the G_1 and S phases lead to arrest of the cell cycle if damaged DNA is detected by the relevant protein complex.

Examination of replicating eukaryotic DNA by electron microscopy shows the presence of many tandemly arranged bubbles separated by only 30–300 kb and clustered in groups of 20–80 in various regions of the DNA. Both forks of each bubble represent sites of replication that move in opposite directions, until they fuse with an approaching fork from an adjacent bubble. Thus eukaryotic DNA contains many tandemly arranged *replicons*, each with an origin of replication. While the rate of fork movement in eukaryotes is less than 10% of the rate in bacteria, the genome can be replicated in the available time during cell division because of the multiple origins of replication.

Telomeres and Telomerase

The fact that eukaryotic chromosomes are linear poses a problem for their replication. Because DNA polymerase can only synthesize new DNA in the 5′→3′ direction, and because it requires an RNA primer, it is unable to synthesize the 5′ end of the lagging strand. Therefore, if there were no mechanism for completing the lagging strand, both ends of a chromosome would be shortened by the length of an RNA primer after every round of replication.

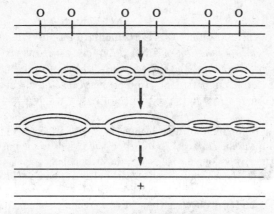

Fig. 8-11   Tandemly arranged *replicons* in eukaryotic DNA generate a chain of *replication bubbles.* O denotes an origin of replication.

EXAMPLE 8.10   The ends of linear eukaryotic chromosomes are called *telomeres*. The ends of telomeres are capped by specific telomere-binding proteins. This prevents end-to-end fusion of chromosomes. DNA sequencing experiments have shown that telomeric DNA is composed of ~1000 *tandem repeats* of the sequence TTAGGG in humans and TTGGGG in protozoa, with a 12–16 base pair *overhang* on the 3′ strand. This overhang serves as the primer for synthesis of the last Okazaki fragment of the lagging strand. Telomeres are maintained by a ribonucleoprotein called *telomerase*; its RNA component acts as a template for addition of bases to the 3′ end of telomeric DNA, a process that is catalyzed by the protein component that is therefore *homologous* to the enzyme, *reverse transcriptase*.

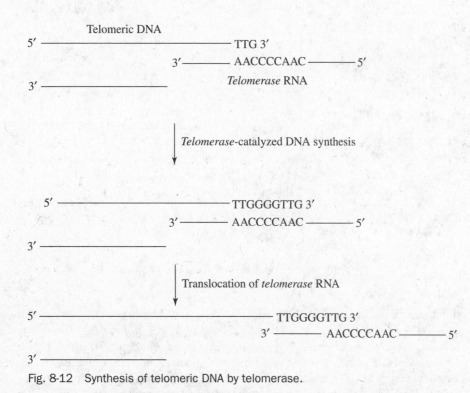

Fig. 8-12   Synthesis of telomeric DNA by telomerase.

EXAMPLE 8.11   Telomerase is *not* expressed in somatic cells in mammals. This explains why they exhibit senescence. When grown in culture, they only divide a limited number of times before they die. After each cell division the telomeres become shorter to the extent they are unable to be capped. The resulting chromosomal instability leads to cell death.

8.9　Repair of Damaged DNA

Maintenance of the integrity of chromosomal DNA is essential for the survival of all forms of life. In part this is achieved through the *proofreading function* of DNA polymerases. However, errors in DNA polymerization occasionally escape this proofreading, and the sequence of bases in the DNA is altered by agents that are present in a cell or in its external environment. Both prokaryotes and eukaryotes have evolved elaborate DNA repair mechanisms to correct errors in the sequence of bases in DNA.

EXAMPLE 8.12　Errors arising from failure of proofreading in *E. coli* are corrected by a process called *mismatch repair*. Several proteins are involved in this process. A dimer of *MutS* binds to the mismatched base pair, recruiting a dimer of *MutL*. This complex then moves along the DNA, creating a loop that contains the mismatched base pair. When it encounters a *hemimethylated* GATC sequence (marking the parent DNA strand; see Prob. 8.3), the endonuclease *MutH* cleaves the phosphodiester bond on the 5′ side of the unmethylated (daughter) strand. *UvD helicase* then unwinds the parent strand and daughter strands, and an exonuclease removes the daughter strand. Then *DNA polymerase III* replaces the excised strand.

EXAMPLE 8.13　One of the most common ways in which bases in DNA become damaged is through hydrolytic *deamination*. In this way cytosine, adenine, and guanine are converted to uracil, hypoxanthine, and xanthine, respectively (Fig. 8-13).

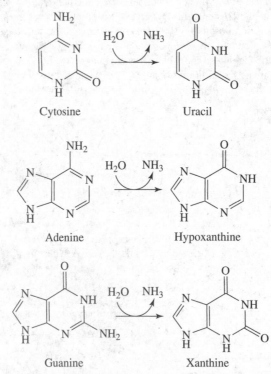

Fig. 8-13　Hydrolytic deamination of nucleobases.

Deamination damage is corrected by *base excision repair*. All cells contain several different *DNA glycosylases*, each being for a specific type of damaged base as shown in Fig. 8-13. These enzymes cleave the glycosidic bond of the damaged base, giving an *apurinic* or *apyrimidinic* (AP) site. This site is recognized by an *AP endonuclease* that cleaves the phosphodiester bond on one side of the AP site. Several bases around this point of cleavage are then removed by an *exonuclease*. The nucleotides are then replaced by *DNA polymerase I* and *sealed in* (via phosphate ester bonds formed on the ends) by *DNA ligase*.

EXAMPLE 8.14　DNA damage, in which bases acquire bulky substituents, or when they are displaced from their normal hydrogen-bonded positions, is remedied by *nucleotide excision repair*. A common example of such damage is formation of *pyrimidine dimers*. These form through photochemical reactions that are initiated by utlraviolet light. Carbon atoms 5 and 6 of two consecutive pyrimidines form covalent bonds with each other, forming a *cyclobutane* ring. This occurs most often with adjoining thymine nucleotides. The cyclobutane bonds are ~1.6 Å long which is much shorter than the normal distance between bases (~3.4 Å) in a DNA double helix. This causes a *bulge* in the double helix.

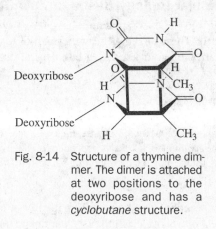

Fig. 8-14   Structure of a thymine dimmer. The dimer is attached at two positions to the deoxyribose and has a *cyclobutane* structure.

In *E. coli*, nucleotide excision repair (Example 8.14) is carried out by the *UvrABC endonuclease*. The enzyme cleaves the damaged DNA strand at the seventh and third or fourth phosphodiester bonds at the 5′ and 3′ sides adjacent to the damaged base. The resulting oligonucleotide is removed by *helicase II*, and repair is carried out by *DNA polymerase I* and *DNA ligase*.

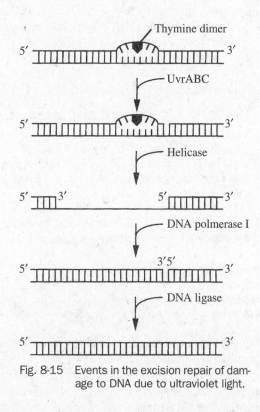

Fig. 8-15   Events in the excision repair of damage to DNA due to ultraviolet light.

EXAMPLE 8.15   Ionizing radiation and the free radical by-products of oxidative metabolism can both cause breaks in each strand of a DNA molecule. These *double-strand breaks* (DSBs) are especially serious because exonucleases may then degrade DNA at a DSB, leading to irrevocable loss of genetic information. Eukaryotic cells have two mechanisms for repairing DSB, *nonhomologous end joining* and *recombination repair*.

In nonhomologous end joining of DNA, the Ku70Ku80 protein heterodimer binds to DNA at the site of a DSB, aligning the halves of the DSB. The strand ends are accessible to nucleases, DNA polymerases, and DNA ligases that collectively repair the DSB.

8.10 Techniques of Molecular Biology Based on DNA Replication

Many of the enzymes that are involved in DNA replication have now been identified and purified, and they are available as commercial products. These enzymes lie at the heart of *recombinant DNA technology*, which not only is a cornerstone of modern biomedical research but also forms the basis of a multi-billion-dollar pharmaceutical industry.

Polymerase Chain Reaction (PCR)

EXAMPLE 8.16   Often only trace amounts of a specific DNA sample of interest are available. Larger amounts can be produced using the *polymerase chain reaction* (PCR) that is dependent on the availability of *thermostable* DNA polymerases, e.g., *Taq polymerase*, that is produced by the thermophilic bacterium *Thermus aquaticus*. It is purified in large quantities and is available commercially.

The steps involved in a PCR experiment are shown schematically in Fig. 8-16. The method uses (1) the *thermostable* DNA polymerase, *Taq polymerase*; (2) the DNA template that is to be amplified; (3) *two* primers, each usually of ~20 nucleotides that can anneal to distinct parts on the complementary strands of the target DNA and serve as sites for commencing the action of DNA polymerase; and (4) a solution that includes the four deoxynucleotides dATP, dCTP, dGTP, and dTTP, Mg^{2+}, some other salts, and pH buffer.

In step 1 the DNA containing the target region to be amplified (thin lines) is heated (~94°C) to separate the strands; synthetic oligonucleotide primers complementary to the 5′ *and* 3′ regions of the target are added (bold and bold-dashed lines, respectively), and the sample is cooled (~55°C), allowing the primers to anneal to the target. These primers are in excess to allow sufficient material to generate the required amount of amplified product.

In step 3, conducted at ~72°C, the thermostable DNA polymerase catalyzes the 5′→3′ DNA synthesis. Subsequent steps entail repeating steps 1–3 through multiple (typically ~25) cycles leading to an exponential accumulation of the target region (~10^6-fold from 25 cycles).

EXAMPLE 8.17   Among the most important enzymes of recombinant DNA technology are the *restriction enzymes*. These are endonucleases that cleave DNA only at specific sequences of bases (called *restriction sites*). Typically, restriction sites are *palindromic*; in other words, the sequences are the same in the 5′→3′ and 3′→5′ strands. Restriction enzymes are produced by bacteria as an antiviral defense, and they cleave the DNA of viruses (*bacteriophages*) that infect them. However, they do not cleave host bacterial DNA. Fig. 8-17 shows the restriction sites of three common restriction enzymes, *BamHI, EcoRI*, and *PvuII*. Because *BamHI* and *EcoRI* cleave their restriction site asymmetrically, they produce overhangs in the cleaved DNA, called *sticky ends*. Conversely, *PvuII* cleaves symmetrically, producing *blunt ends*.

Often the primers used in PCR are designed to contain restriction sites for appropriate restriction enzymes, as well as regions that are complementary to the target DNA sequence.

Plasmid Vectors

EXAMPLE 8.18   DNA samples produced by PCR are usually incorporated into other DNA molecules called *vectors*. Vectors are commonly circular DNA molecules, up to 200 kb pairs in size, known as *plasmids*.

As shown schematically in Fig. 8-18, plasmid vectors typically contain several key regions. They normally contain a gene for a protein that confers resistance against an antibiotic; in this case the *AmpR* gene product confers resistance against the antibiotic, ampicillin. Plasmids typically contain a *multiple cloning site* (MCS) that has cleavage sites for many different *restriction enzymes*. Recombinant DNA is incorporated into the plasmid at these sites, exploiting the *sticky ends* produced by many restriction enzymes. For example, if a PCR product were designed to have an *EcoRI* site at one end and a *BamHI* site at the other, then cleavage of a plasmid with both of these enzymes, followed by the introduction of the PCR product, would lead to annealing of the complementary sticky ends of the plasmid and the PCR product. *DNA ligase* would then be used to link the two DNA molecules.

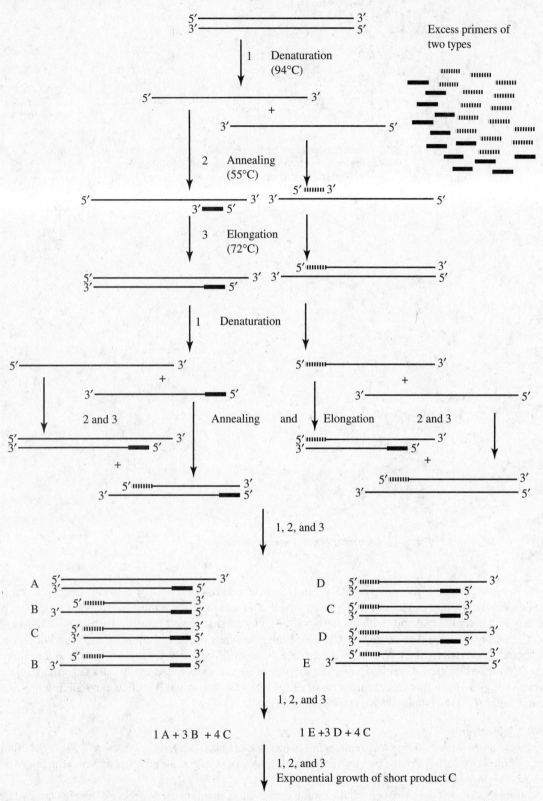

Fig. 8-16 Stages in a polymerase chain reaction.

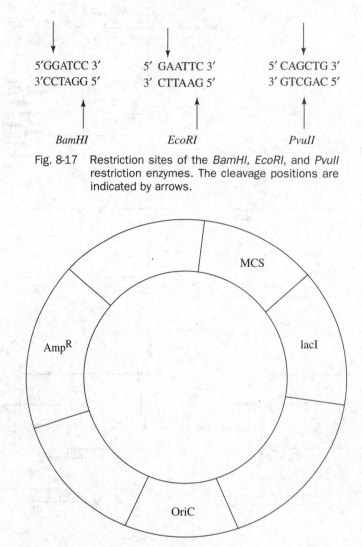

BamHI	EcoRI	PvuII
5′GGATCC 3′	5′ GAATTC 3′	5′ CAGCTG 3′
3′CCTAGG 5′	3′ CTTAAG 5′	3′ GTCGAC 5′

Fig. 8-17 Restriction sites of the *BamHI*, *EcoRI*, and *PvuII* restriction enzymes. The cleavage positions are indicated by arrows.

Fig. 8-18 A hypothetical plasmid vector.

Plasmids that contain recombinant DNA can be introduced into bacteria by *transfection*. Bacterial cells that contain the plasmid can be selected by using a growth medium that contains the relevant antibiotic; only bacteria that carry the plasmid (with its antibiotic resistance marker) will grow under these conditions. The transfected bacteria can then be grown to produce large amounts of the recombinant DNA and/or recombinant protein encoded by the DNA. In the latter case, production of mRNA that corresponds to the recombinant DNA insert is often controlled using the *lac repressor* that is encoded by the *lacI* gene in the plasmid shown in Fig. 8-19. In this case, repression of mRNA production would be relieved by adding the lactose analog, isopropyl β-D-1-thiogalactopyranoside (*IPTG*).

DNA Sequencing

The most common method for *DNA sequencing* makes use of bacterial DNA polymerase I. Frederick Sanger, was awarded two Nobel Prizes, one for discovering a way of sequencing proteins and one for discovering how to sequence DNA!

This method, called the *dideoxy* or chain termination method, involves using a piece of single-stranded DNA as the template and an oligonucleotide that is complementary to its 3′ end as a *primer*. In its initial form, dideoxy sequencing entailed setting up four separate reaction vessels. All contained the template, primer (which was labeled with radioactive ^{32}P), the *Klenow fragment* of DNA polymerase (in which the 5′→3′ exonuclease activity is missing), dATP, dTTP, dCTP, and dGTP. Each vessel also contained a small amount (~1% relative to the deoxytriphosphates) of one of the dideoxy (dd) nucleotide triphosphates, ddATP, ddTTP, ddCTP, and ddGTP.

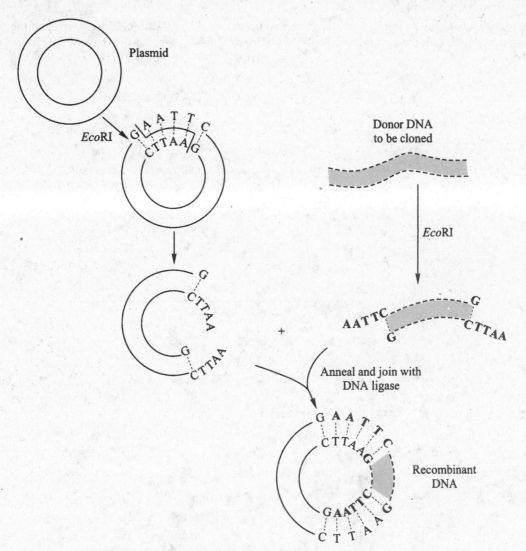

Fig. 8-19   Steps in the formation of a joint or recombinant DNA molecule.

As shown in Fig. 8-20 for ddATP, because dideoxy nucleotides have a hydrogen atom and not an OH at the 3′ position of the pentose ring, when they are incorporated into a DNA chain that is being synthesized, addition of further bases is not possible. This will occur in only a minority of the DNA chains being synthesized in the solution, because of the trace concentrations of the dideoxy nucleotides. The outcome is a series of fragments of DNA that can be resolved by gel electrophoresis and visualized by autoradiography, exploiting the fact that the primers are radioactive.

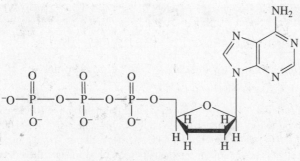

Fig. 8-20   Structure of dideoxyATP.

As shown schematically in Fig. 8-21, the pattern of fragments allows the sequence to be read off the gel by scanning across the four lanes and recording the next dark band in sequence toward the lower end of the gel.

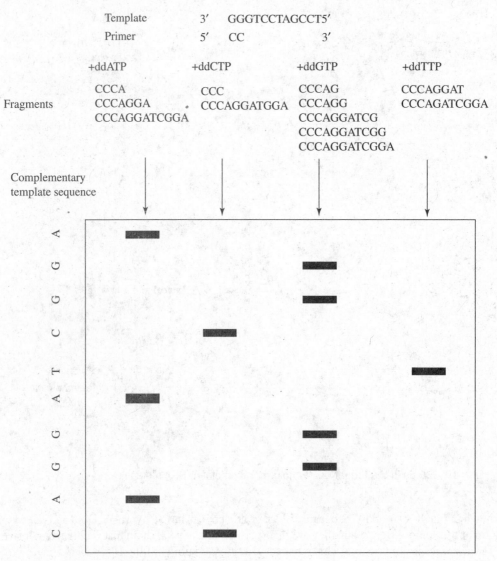

Fig. 8-21   Diagrammatic *dideoxy sequencing* gel.

SOLVED PROBLEMS

DNA REPLICATION IN BACTERIA

8.1. How much time will it take to copy the entire *E. coli* chromosome?

SOLUTION

Since the replication fork moves at ~1000 bases s^{-1} and there are 4.6×10^6 base pairs in the chromosome, it will take the two replication forks (that copy both strands simultaneously) $4,600,000/(1000 \times 2 \times 60) = $ ~38 min to copy the whole *E. coli* genome. It will then take another ~20 min to separate the cellular components. To double the cell number in less than 60 min means the cell must initiate the next round of replication before the previous one has finished. This results in multiforked chromosomes.

INITIATION OF BACTERIAL DNA REPLICATION

8.2. What is meant by torsional stress in DNA and how can it be relieved?

SOLUTION

The torsional stress that arises in DNA replication is a consequence of the fact that unwinding of DNA at *oriC* introduces *supercoiling* (coiling of the coiled DNA helix).

Double-stranded DNA that is coiled in the direction of the double helix is described as *positively supercoiled*, while DNA coiled in the opposite direction to the turns of the helix is termed *negatively supercoiled*.

The torsional stress introduced by this supercoiling is relieved by *DNA gyrase*, which is a *type II topoisomerase*. DNA gyrase relieves the torsional stress of supercoiling by cutting *both* DNA strands in an ATP-dependent reaction, thus relieving positive supercoiling and keeping the DNA slightly negatively supercoiled. DNA gyrase is so crucial to the survival of the bacterial cell that it has become a target for some antibiotics, e.g., nalidixic acid.

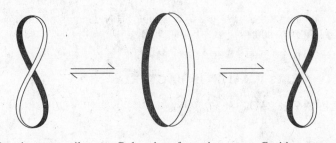

Negative supercoil   Relaxed conformation   Positive supercoil

Fig. 8-22   Diagrammatic representation of supercoiling in double-stranded DNA.

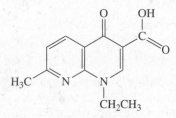

Fig. 8-23   Nalidixic acid.

8.3. How is initiation of bacterial DNA replication controlled?

SOLUTION

This is still not well understood, but the enzyme *Dam methylase* is involved. This enzyme *methylates* cytosine residues in the sequence GATC within *oriC*. After DNA replication is complete, the parent DNA strands are methylated but the daughter strands are not. This *hemimethylated DNA* binds to the bacterial cell membrane. It must be released from the membrane and fully methylated by Dam methylase before DnaA can bind to *oriC*, thus initiating another round of DNA replication.

ELONGATION OF BACTERIAL DNA

8.4. What characteristics of DNA polymerase III make it an ideal enzyme for replicating the whole genome?

SOLUTION

The key features of DNA polymerase III are its catalytic potency, its fidelity, and its *processivity*. It is able to catalyze the addition of $\sim10^3$ bases per second, compared to only about 10 per second for DNA polymerase I, with an error frequency of about $1:10^4-10^5$. One of the unique features of DNA polymerase III is its ability to continuously synthesize very long (thousands of bases) stretches of DNA, unlike DNA polymerase I. This is a consequence of its processivity; the β2 sliding clamps ensure that it remains bound to the template strand DNA. In contrast, DNA polymerase I, without a sliding clamp, is much more likely to dissociate from the template strand after synthesis of short (tens of bases) stretches of DNA.

8.5. How are the primers removed during lagging strand DNA synthesis?

SOLUTION

The primers are removed by the $5' \rightarrow 3'$ exonuclease activity in DNA polymerase I. It then uses its polymerase activity to fill in the gap created by the primer removal, working from the 3'-OH end. The nucleotide additions are proofread with the 3' exonuclease activity. DNA polymerase I is incapable of sealing the nick as there is no energy source to form the phosphoester bond between the 3'-OH and the 5' phosphate. Another enzyme, DNA ligase, performs this task, using NAD^+ as an energy source (cleaving the NAD at the diphosphate linkage, releasing nicotinamide mononucleotide and AMP). The final product is one continuous strand of DNA.

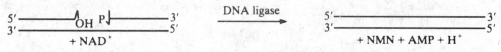

Fig. 8-24   Reaction catalyzed by DNA ligase in *E. coli*. NMN denotes nicotinamide mononucleotide. Eukaryotic ligases use ATP instead of NAD^+ as the high-energy coreactant.

TERMINATION OF DNA REPLICATION IN BACTERIA

8.6. Why might it be advantageous to *E. coli* to have *six* replication terminators in its chromosome?

SOLUTION

Usually the replication forks meet and fuse in the vicinity of *TerC*. *TerC* appears to be the most frequently used terminator, probably because the clockwise fork would get to this site before the counterclockwise fork reached *TerA*. Presumably the terminators flanking the innermost ones are backups when *TerA* or *TerC* fail.

DNA REPLICATION IN EUKARYOTES

8.7. The primers for lagging strand eukaryotic DNA synthesis are a *hybrid* of RNA and DNA. How are they removed?

SOLUTION

Two enzymes are required for this. *RNase H1* removes most of the RNA, leaving a single ribonucleotide next to the DNA component. *Flap endonuclease*-1 (FEN1) then removes this ribonucleotide and also any mismatched bases in the DNA component. In this way the inability of DNA polymerase α to proofread is overcome. The excised section of DNA is replaced by DNA polymerase δ as it synthesizes the next Okazaki fragment.

8.8. What prevents rereplication of DNA during S phase in a eukaryotic cell?

SOLUTION

A number of regulatory processes prevent this. Some of them are focused on the phosphorylated Cdt1 which is produced during the transition from a prereplication complex (preRC) to a replication complex (RC). *Phosphorylated* Cdt1 binds to an inhibitory protein called *geminin* and is also targeted for regulated protein degradation (see Sec. 6.4) through the action of two E3 *ubiquitin ligases*, SCF^{skp2} and Cul4 DDB1^{Cdt2}. The net effect is to ensure that there is no active Cdt1 in S phase, thus preventing rereplication of DNA.

8.9. What molecular events take place if damaged DNA is detected at the G_1 or S phase cell-cycle checkpoint?

SOLUTION

DNA damage leads to activation of two protein kinases, ATM and Chk2. These phosphorylate an E3 ubiquitin ligase called Mdm2, leading to its inactivation. The major target of Mdm2 is a transcription factor called *p53*. Normally, p53 is targeted for regulated protein degradation by Mdm2; its cellular concentration is therefore very low. However, its concentration will rise in response to the inactivation of Mdm2 following DNA damage. Factor p53 controls the expression of a number of genes. Among these is one coding for a protein called p21, which binds to cyclin-dependent protein kinases and to PCNA, leading to their inhibition in both cases. The effect is to prevent further progression through the cell cycle and DNA replication until the damaged DNA has been repaired. Also p53 controls the expression of a number of genes that code for proteins involved in programmed cell death (apoptosis). Up-regulation of these genes by p53 will therefore lead to the death of the cell in the event that the DNA damage cannot be repaired.

8.10. *Werner's progeria* is a premature-aging disease; people with this disease usually die in their mid-40s. How is this inherited disease related to DNA replication?

SOLUTION

One of the signs of Werner's progeria is *rapid aging* of the skin. Skin fibroblasts of Werner's progeria patients have unusually short *telomeres*, a phenotype that can be rescued in vitro by expression of the catalytic subunit of telomerase. Molecular genetics studies have shown that Werner's progeria arises from defects in WRN, a *helicase* that can physically associate with telomere-binding proteins.

8.11. Why don't cancer cells exhibit senescence in the same way that normal body cells do?

SOLUTION

Their persistence occurs because telomerase is constitutively active in cancer cells. This means that telomerase is an attractive target for the development of new cancer chemotherapeutic drugs.

DNA DAMAGE AND REPAIR

8.12. What is the basis of mismatch repair in eukaryotes?

SOLUTION

This is incompletely understood. Eukaryotic cells express proteins that are homologous to *MutS* and *MutL* but do not express a homolog of *MutH*. Therefore, they must use a mechanism other than the methylation state of DNA to distinguish between parent and daughter DNA strands.

8.13. Why might thymine rather than uracil have been naturally selected to be part of DNA?

SOLUTION

It is used to maximize the maintenance of the integrity of the information encoded by DNA. Cytosine can spontaneously deaminate to form uracil; this damage is repaired by base excision repair. If uracil rather than thymine were used in DNA, then correctly positioned uracil would be indistinguishable from that arising from cytosine deamination. Use of thymine (methylated uracil) in DNA avoids this problem.

8.14. How do eukaryotes carry out nucleotide excision repair?

SOLUTION

The mechanism is essentially the same as in *E. coli* although 16 different proteins are involved and a larger oligonucleotide (~30 bases) is removed. Understanding this process has come from studies of genetic diseases. In one of them, *xeroderma pigmentosum*, skin cells are unable to repair the DNA damage caused by uv light. Because of this, patients with xeroderma pigmentosum are ~2000-fold more likely to develop skin cancers than normal individuals.

8.15. How does recombination repair lead to the repair of double-strand breaks (DSBs)?

SOLUTION

As shown in Fig. 8-25, there are several stages in this process. In stage 1, *exonucleases* convert a DSB in one chromosome (thick lines) into a gap, with more extensive degradation of 5′ ends than 3′ ends. In stage 2, a 3′ end on the chromosome with the DSB base-pairs with the corresponding region of the sister chromosome (thin lines). In stage 3, DNA replication occurs, using the sister chromosome as a template. This creates two *crossover* points, called Holliday junctions (named after Robin Holliday). In stage 4, the Holliday junctions are cleaved. Depending on the site of cleavage, DNA in the two chromosomes may be recombined in different ways. Recombination also occurs during meiosis, where it has two functions: (1) providing a brief physical link between chromatids, allowing chromosome segregation, and (2) providing a mechanism for the generation of genetic diversity.

MOLECULAR BIOLOGY TECHNIQUES DERIVED FROM REPLICATION

8.16. It is often desirable to analyze mRNA from a tissue sample. However, RNA is much less stable than DNA. How can the sequence information in mRNA be converted into sequence information in DNA?

SOLUTION

This can be done by using *reverse transcriptase*, an enzyme derived from retroviruses, such as the AIDS virus. Reverse transcriptase synthesizes DNA using RNA as a template, producing complementary DNA (*c*DNA). In the case of eukaryotic mRNA, an oligo-dT primer is used, exploiting the 3′ poly A tail on eukaryotic mRNA.

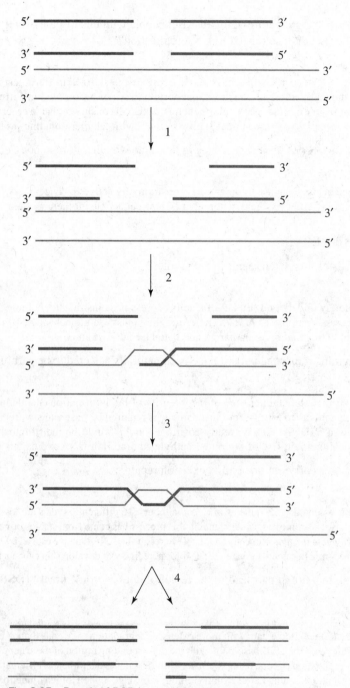

Fig. 8-25 Repair of DSB by recombination repair.

8.17. How can PCR be used to estimate the relative amounts of different mRNA species in a sample?

SOLUTION

This can be done using *real-time PCR* (RT-PCR). This entails first making cDNA copies of the mRNA species using reverse transcriptase. PCR is then carried out, using primers specific for the cDNA of interest. The more mRNA there was in the sample (and therefore more cDNA after the reverse transcription stage), the higher the levels of double-stranded PCR DNA product will be after each cycle of the PCR reaction. The amount of this product can be measured using dyes (for example, SYBR Green), which fluoresce when they bind to double-stranded DNA.

8.18. The restriction enzymes *PvuII* and *HaeIII* both have blunt end restriction sites. Would this have any disadvantages when trying to insert a piece of recombinant DNA flanked by *PvuII* and *HaeIII* sites into the multiple closing site (MCS) of a plasmid?

SOLUTION

Yes, there would be two disadvantages. First, the efficiency of ligation would be very low because there would be no annealing between the recombinant DNA and the plasmid DNA. Second, in the absence of annealing, the recombinant DNA could be incorporated into the plasmid in either orientation, but only one of these would be useful. To avoid these problems, it is usual to ensure that the piece of recombinant DNA to be incorporated into a plasmid is flanked by *sticky end restriction sites* at one or preferably both ends.

8.19. The human genome contains ~3×10^9 base pairs. Was it sequenced using the methods described in Fig. 8-21?

SOLUTION

The fundamental strategy was the same, but the process was automated. Each of the dideoxy nucleotides was tagged with a different fluorescent dye. The four separately reacted mixtures were combined and electrophoresced in a single lane using a robotically controlled sequencer, which can analyze 96 samples simultaneously. As each fragment reached the bottom of the electrophoresis lane, its dideoxy nucleotide was identified from its characteristic fluorescence. Automatic sequencers can sequence ~5×10^5 bases per day compared to ~3×10^4 per year using the manual methods described in Fig. 8-21.

SUPPLEMENTARY PROBLEMS

8.20. Approximately how many Okazaki fragments are synthesized in the replication of the *E. coli* chromosome?

8.21. Is DNA helicase a topoisomerase?

8.22. The *oriC* region of the *E. coli* chromosome is rich in A:T base pairs. Why might this be?

8.23. What structural features of the ends of DNA chains at a nick are necessary for *sealing* by DNA ligase?

8.24. The S phase of the cell cycle is very short (~20 min) in some embryonic cells. How might such rapid complete replication of chromosomal DNA occur?

8.25. What effect would an inhibitor of RNA polymerase be expected to have on bacterial DNA replication?

8.26. What will happen in a DNA sequencing experiment when (a) too little ddNTP is added and (b) too much ddNTP is added?

8.27. What would happen in a PCR experiment in which one of the primers were inadvertently omitted?

8.28. What might happen to cells in which p53 had been mutated so that its transcription factor activity was lost?

8.29. Why is the Klenow fragment of DNA polymerase, rather than the whole enzyme, used in DNA sequencing?

ANSWERS TO SUPPLEMENTARY PROBLEMS

8.20. Okazaki fragments are ~1500 bases long, and the *E. coli* chromosome contains 4.6×10^6 base pairs. Therefore, ~3000 Okazaki fragments are produced.

8.21. No.

8.22. AT-rich DNA is less stable than GC-rich DNA, and it therefore takes less energy for its strands to be separated.

8.23. A 3′ hydroxyl group on one chain and a 5′ phosphate group on the other.

8.24. The distance between one replication complex and the next is much shorter in these cells than in terminally differentiated cells. Therefore, there are more replication complexes per chromosome in these cells, and hence each replication fork has to move a relatively small distance until the next replication complex is reached.

8.25. It would block initiation of replication at *oriC*.

8.26. (*a*) Bands representing truncated fragments would be faint because DNA synthesis would be terminated infrequently. (*b*) Longer fragments would be less abundant because DNA synthesis would be terminated more frequently.

8.27. Single DNA strands of variable length would be produced, and the number of such strands would increase linearly rather than exponentially with the number of PCR cycles.

8.28. It is likely that they would progress through the cell cycle regardless of the extent to which their DNA had been damaged, and they would be unable to enter apoptosis. Such p53 mutants are very common in human cancers.

8.29. Use of the Klenow fragment (without $5' \rightarrow 3'$ exonuclease activity) ensures that all fragments have the same $5'$ terminus, which is necessary if a sequence is to be assigned according to fragment length.

CHAPTER 9

Transcription and Translation

9.1 Introduction

Question: How is the DNA of the genome translated into functional proteins?

The original definition of the term *gene* was based on the capacity of sections of DNA to be translated into protein. The process by which this is accomplished is called gene expression. In this process a sequence of deoxynucleotides in DNA (which defines the gene) is first *transcribed* into a sequence of ribonucleotides in RNA. Messenger RNA (mRNA) is then *translated* into a sequence of amino acids by ribosomes and related molecular machinery to give a *polypeptide* of defined length. The amino acid sequence determines the manner in which a polypeptide folds upon itself to yield a biologically active protein.

In bacterial cells there is no membrane surrounding the DNA *nucleoid*, and both *DNA transcription* and *RNA translation* proceed within the one-cell compartment. A ribosome can begin translation of mRNA before transcription is complete. In contrast, in eukaryotes the nucleus is bounded by a double membrane. Transcription occurs within the nucleus, and the completed mRNA must pass into the cytoplasm to be translated. Frequently, the immediate polypeptide product of translation is subsequently modified, sometimes in a process that enables it to be transported around or out of the cell.

The sequence of nucleotides in a *single-stranded* mRNA is assembled according to complementary base pairing with one of the two strands of duplex DNA that contains the gene. One DNA strand thus provides the template for transcription; it is called the *template* or *antisense* strand (Fig. 9-1). The other DNA strand has the same sequence as the mRNA (except with T in place of U) and is called the *coding*, or *sense*, strand. Generally, it is the coding strand of DNA that is quoted when a DNA sequence is written.

Question: How is a nucleotide sequence of mRNA translated into an amino acid sequence of a polypeptide?

The basis is the genetic code, which describes how various combinations of nucleotides (of which there are only four types in DNA or RNA) can be interpreted as individual amino acids (of which there are 20 types, plus two special atypical ones, as described in Chap. 3). The *cipher* of the genetic code was cracked in the 1960s.

9.2 The Genetic Code

There are 20 amino acids that need to be coded for, and only four nucleotides, so there must be a combination of at least three nucleotides to define each amino acid. A code based on two nucleotides would provide only $4^2 = 16$ combinations, which is insufficient to code uniquely for 20 different amino acids. Proof that the *codon* for each amino acid consists of three nucleotides was provided by genetic studies of the effects on the polypeptide product of nucleotide addition or deletion from a gene.

5′ . . . A T G A A G T C A A G A C T G A C T . . . 3′   Sense strand of DNA = *coding*
3′ . . . T A C T T C A G T T C T G A C T G A . . . 5′   Antisense strand of DNA = *template*

Transcription of antisense strand

5′ . . . A U G A A G U C A A G A C U G A C U . . . 3′   mRNA

Translation of mRNA

Met - Lys - Ser - Arg - Leu - Thr -   Peptide

Fig. 9-1   Transcription of a sequence of deoxynucleotides in DNA into a sequence of nucleotides in mRNA, and translation of mRNA into a sequence of amino acids in a protein.

EXAMPLE 9.1   A trinucleotide-based code provides $4^3 = 64$ codons. Are the extra codons used?

Yes, it turns out that they are all used. In the vast majority of cases a single amino acid can be coded for by more than one codon. For this reason the code is said to be *degenerate*. Degeneracy of the code is very obvious from an examination of the codon assignments shown in Table 9-1. E.g., there are six different codons for leucine.

Table 9-1   Codon-Amino Acid Assignments of the Genetic Code*

First Position	Second Position				Third Position
	U	C	A	G	
U	Phe	Ser	Tyr	Cys	U
	Phe	Ser	Try	Cys	C
	Leu	Ser	CT*	CT*	A
	Leu	Ser	CT*	Trp	G
C	Leu	Pro	His	Arg	U
	Leu	Pro	His	Arg	C
	Leu	Pro	Gln	Arg	A
	Leu	Pro	Gln	Arg	G
A	Ile	Thr	Asn	Ser	U
	Ile	Thr	Asn	Ser	C
	Ile	Thr	Lys	Arg	A
	Met (CI)†	Thr	Lys	Arg	G
G	Val	Ala	Asp	Gly	U
	Val	Ala	Asp	Gly	C
	Val	Ala	Glu	Gly	A
	Val (CI)†	Ala	Glu	Gly	G

*Note that the nucleotide components of each triplet are written in terms of the ribonucleotides A, U, C, G, which are present in mRNA. The first position refers to the initial nucleotide of the triplet, positioned at its 5′ end. The third nucleotide is at the 3′ end.
†CT = chain termination.
‡CI = chain initiation.

Alternative representation of the same genetic code as shown a wheel:

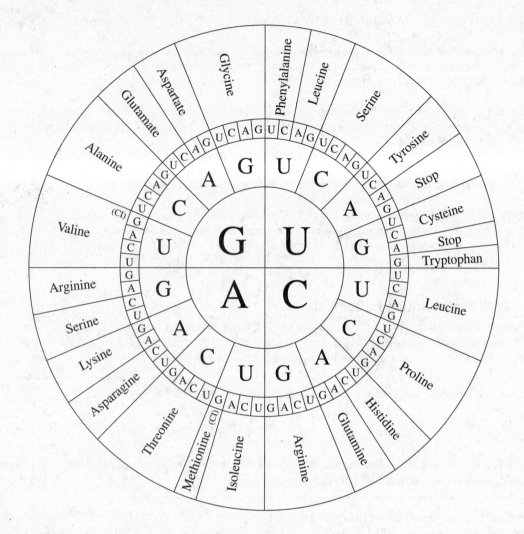

EXAMPLE 9.2 What is the codon for methionine?

From Table 9-1 the codon for methionine is seen to be AUG. Methionine is one of two amino acids for which there is only one codon.

EXAMPLE 9.3 What is the significance of the term CI in Table 9-1?

This stands for *chain initiation* and indicates that the codon for methionine, AUG, defines where translation will begin on mRNA. This means that methionine is the first amino acid to be incorporated into the polypeptide chain. Less frequently GUG, which normally codes for valine, can serve in place of AUG as the chain initiation codon that incorporates methionine. The initiating amino acid is always incorporated at the *N terminus*. Subsequent amino acids are sequentially added to the carboxyl (*C*) end of the growing chain, so the direction of assembly of a chain is $N \rightarrow C$.

EXAMPLE 9.4 Is there also a codon that defines the site on mRNA where polypeptide chain formation will terminate?

There are actually three codons that function in this way. They are UAA, UGA, and UAG and are referred to as the *chain termination* triplets, or *stop codons* (see Table 9-1).

EXAMPLE 9.5 Write down a sequence of ribonucleotides that would define a short polypeptide with the following amino acid sequence:

Met-Leu-Arg-Asn-Ala-Val-Glu-Ser-Ile-Cys-Phe-Thr

A possible sequence is as follows:

5′ AUG.UUA.CGU.AAU.GCU.GUC.GAA.UCU.AUU.UGC.UUU.ACA.UAA 3′

Note the presence of chain initiation and termination codons, respectively, at the beginning and end of the sequence. In translating this sequence into a sequence of amino acids, it has been assumed that the codons do not overlap. This has been established experimentally: the triplet genetic code is said to be *nonoverlapping* for all but a few organisms.

EXAMPLE 9.6 In the ribonucleotide sequence shown in Example 9.5 there is also an AUG triplet which could be formed by joining portions of two adjacent triplets, starting from A at the 11th position. Is it possible for this to function as an alternative initiation codon?

For this to be so, the overall *frame of reading* would be different and an alternative set of triplets would be read after this position (CUG UCG etc.). As shown just after Example 9.8, there are sequences in mRNA *upstream* (to the left) of a potential translation start site (e.g., AUG) which define the frame of reading.

EXAMPLE 9.7 Is the dictionary of amino acid codons shown in Table 9-1 the same for all organisms?

The genetic code dictionary was originally established from studies on the bacterium *Escherichia coli*. It is now known to be the same for all organisms; i.e., it is *universal*. The only exceptions, for a small number of codons, occur in mitochondria from a number of species.

9.3   DNA Transcription in Bacteria

The present detailed knowledge of the mechanism of *DNA transcription* to produce RNA rests largely upon studies with bacteria, particularly *E. coli*. It is convenient to discuss transcription in bacteria first. The enzyme *RNA polymerase* is responsible for transcription of all genes in bacteria.

Question: What is the nature of the chemical reaction catalyzed by RNA polymerase?

$$\text{The overall reaction is} \quad n\text{NTP} \xrightarrow{\text{Mg}^{2+}} (\text{NMP})_n + n\text{PPi}$$

where NTP and n denote nucleotide triphosphate and number of these molecules, respectively. NMP denotes nucleotide monophosphate and PPi denotes pyrophosphate.

RNA polymerase uses the four ribonucleoside triphosphates (ATP, GTP, UTP, and CTP) to assemble an RNA chain, the sequence of which is determined by complementary base pairing to the *template* strand of DNA. RNA chain growth is in the 5′ → 3′ direction, with each nucleotide added sequentially to the 3′ end of the growing RNA chain. The phosphodiester bond is formed by the same mechanism as for DNA polymerase. An important distinction between RNA polymerase and DNA polymerase, however, is the ability of the former to start a new chain de novo. Unlike DNA polymerase, it does not have an obligatory requirement for a *primer*. The first nucleotide to be incorporated into the chain of RNA contains either adenine or guanine and retains its 5′ triphosphate.

EXAMPLE 9.8 A single DNA molecule contains, within a continuous nucleotide sequence, a multitude of genes. How does RNA polymerase recognize where to start transcribing a particular gene and which strand to copy?

To transcribe a particular stretch of sequence, RNA polymerase binds to the DNA at a specific site, called a *promoter*, just *upstream* (i.e., on the 5′ side) of the *transcriptional start site* that is defined by the *sense* strand.

Many bacterial promoters have been sequenced, and it has been found that while the sequence of the region is not the same in all cases, there are two segments located ~10 and 35 base pairs upstream of the start site that vary only slightly from one another, such that a *consensus sequence* can be defined for each. The closer the promoter sequence is to the consensus sequence, the more likely it is to be recognized by RNA polymerase, and the more often transcription is likely to be initiated. This is known as the *strength* of a promoter. Figure 9-2 shows sequences from a number of promoter regions, with the *–10 region* underlined. The –10 region is also called the TATAAT box or the *Pribnow box* (after David Pribnow who discovered it with Heinz Schaller).

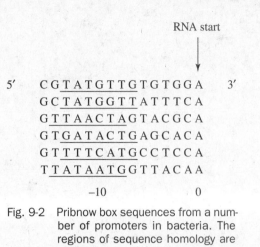

Fig. 9-2   Pribnow box sequences from a number of promoters in bacteria. The regions of sequence homology are underlined.

Another conserved region is centered around 35 base pairs upstream of the start site (i.e., at the –35 position). The consensus sequence is TTGACA. In more detailed form, the sequence is

$$T_{82} \; T_{84} \; G_{65} \; A_{65} \; C_{54} \; A_{45}$$

where the subscript indicates the percentage occurrence of the base that is most commonly found at each position. Although the actual sequence between the –10 and –35 regions is not important, the distance separating them is crucial for positioning RNA polymerase on the promoter.

EXAMPLE 9.9   How does RNA polymerase recognize the promoter?

Bacterial RNA polymerase is a multisubunit enzyme of M_r 480,000. The four major subunits—β, β′, α, and σ (M_r = 150,000; 160,000; 36,500; and 86,000, respectively)—are present in the ratio $1:1:2:1$, and the total complex is more correctly called the *RNA polymerase holoenzyme*. The σ subunit is involved directly in *promoter recognition*. The complex without the σ subunit is called the RNA polymerase *core enzyme*. To start transcription, α-helices in the σ subunit simultaneously contact base pairs in the –10 and –35 regions of the promoter. This directs the holoenzyme to the promoter site to form a *binary complex* in which there is a limited unwinding of the DNA duplex to generate an *open promoter complex*. This is the first step in the overall *transcription cycle* and is called *template binding*. The sequence of events in the transcription cycle is illustrated in Fig. 9-3.

Following template binding, the β subunit initiates an RNA chain by catalyzing formation of a phosphodiester bond between the first nucleotide (ATP or GTP) and the next nucleotide defined by the template. Thus

$$ppp^A_G + pppN \rightarrow ppp^A_GpN + PPi$$

Figure 9-3 shows diagrammatically that following initiation, the σ subunit is released and an additional protein (NusA) binds to the core enzyme. The β subunit then elongates the RNA chain by sequentially adding nucleotide units to the 3′-OH of the previously incorporated nucleotide (as described for the DNA polymerases in Chap. 8). Transcription is terminated when the core enzyme reaches a *termination sequence*. Two types of termination sequence have been identified in *E. coli*. One type requires an additional protein, called *rho*, to effect termination; the other does not (intrinsic terminators). Rho binds a specific sequence on the growing RNA chain and derives energy from ATP to unwind and release RNA from the DNA in the elongation complex. Intrinsic termination sequences are relatively long (up to ~50 nucleotides) and function through the formation of *hairpins* in the single-stranded RNA transcript. Hairpins result from *inverted repeat* sequences that allow the RNA chain to bend back on itself and become stabilized through complementary base pairing. Following release of the RNA transcript from the DNA, the core enzyme is also released. It is then available, after interaction with the σ subunit, for a further cycle of transcription. The RNA released upon termination is called a *primary transcript* because, in some cases, it is modified before being used in subsequent processes.

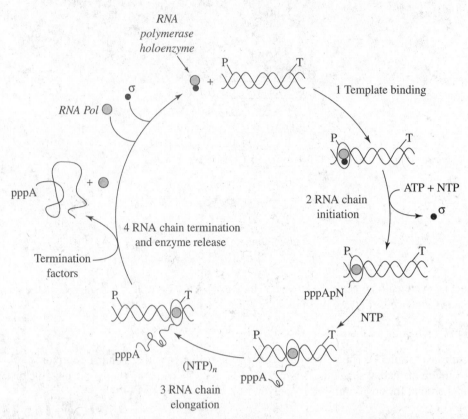

Fig. 9-3 The transcription cycle in bacteria. P and T refer to promoter and termination sites, respectively, for a single RNA transcript, and pppA denotes triphosphate ATP.

9.4   DNA Transcription in Eukaryotes

The process of transcription in eukaryotes is similar to that in bacteria, but there are important differences, as described next.

EXAMPLE 9.10   Is there a single type of RNA polymerase involved in eukaryotic transcription?

No. Eukaryotic RNA polymerases have been isolated from many tissues, and in all cases *three* distinct enzymes have been found in the nucleus. All are complex in structure and contain a number of polypeptide subunits. *RNA polymerase I* is known to be involved specifically in the transcription of rRNA genes. *RNA polymerase II* gives rise to transcripts that are subsequently processed to yield mRNA. *RNA polymerase III* is responsible for the transcription of the tRNA genes and a small ribosomal RNA gene that yields a species called 5S RNA. There is also a distinct RNA polymerase found in mitochondria, which is similar to *bacterial* RNA polymerase.

Each of the three types of eukaryotic *RNA polymerase* requires distinct *promoter* elements. Reflecting the more complex regulation of gene expression in multicellular organisms, eukaryotic promoters are generally more complex and varied than those of prokaryotes, and require additional proteins to assemble before RNA polymerase can bind. As with bacterial promoters, consensus sequences near the start point of transcription have been identified. Promoters for RNA polymerase I are usually *upstream* of the transcription start site and contain two conserved regions separated by ~70 nucleotides. The majority of RNA polymerase III promoters lie within the transcribed region at around + 55 base pairs. Genes transcribed by RNA polymerase II are those that are translated to proteins, and many are tightly regulated and unique to a particular cell type. Therefore promoters for RNA polymerase II are the most complex and diverse, and they determine where, when, and how frequently a gene is transcribed. Each particular promoter may contain some, but usually not all, of several different *core (basal) promoter* sequence elements. Most RNA polymerase II promoters contain six or more of these elements, with the position and combinations of these sites varying between different promoters. Certain sequences are found in nearly all promoters; these generally control genes that have *constitutive expression*. Other promoter sequences are associated with genes that are expressed only at certain times (*temporal regulation*) or in certain tissues (*spatial regulation*). The most highly conserved region is 25 nucleotides upstream of the start site. This consensus sequence is referred to as the TATA or *Hogness box* (after its discoverer David Hogness). Further upstream are generally a number of less highly conserved sequences. Other consensus sequences surround or are downstream of the transcription start site.

Enhancers are sequences that are positioned up to 60 kb from the start site. They greatly influence the frequency at which the gene is transcribed. The position of enhancers, relative to a promoter, can vary substantially; they can lie on either side of the gene and can operate in either orientation.

9.5 Transcription Factors

For any RNA polymerase to recognize a eukaryotic promoter and initiate transcription, ancillary proteins called *general transcription factors* must bind. Assembly of these proteins at the promoter is absolutely essential for eukaryotic transcription and is highly regulated. Some promoter sequences are fairly common, and they bind to transcription factors that are present in all cell types. Other transcription factors are specific only to certain cell types, but they all influence the ability of RNA polymerase to transcribe a gene (Table 9-2).

Table 9-2   Common Transcription Factors and the Promoter Sequences to Which They Bind

Factor	Sequence	Distribution
TFIID	TATAA	General
CTF/NF-1	CCAATC	General
SP1	GGGCGG	General
Oct1	ATTTGCAT	General
Oct2	ATTTGCAT	General
NFκB	GGGACTTTC	Lymphoid
Erf1	AGATAG	Erythroid

For a gene that is transcribed by RNA polymerase II, the formation of a *preinitiation complex* begins with binding of TFIID (Transcription Factor for RNA polymerase II D) to the TATA box and other core promoter elements (Fig. 9-4). β-sheets in the TATA-binding protein (TBP), a subunit of TFIID, distort the DNA and allow binding of another transcription factor, TFIIB, to the core promoter. The preinitiation complex is completed by assembly of other transcription factors which eventually recruit RNA polymerase II. Assembly of this preinitiation complex is followed by ATP-dependent *melting of DNA*, mediated by the *helicase* activity of TFIIH. To initiate the elongation state of transcription, a heptapeptide repeat in the C-terminal domain *tail* of RNA polymerase II is *phosphorylated* (by TFIIH and other kinases). Following phosphorylation of its tail, RNA polymerase II leaves the promoter, and most of the transcription factors, behind and begins elongation of the mRNA.

An important subgroup of transcription factors regulates expression of genes that determine the identity of body regions. These transcription factors are encoded by *homeobox* genes that were first discovered in the fruit fly *Drosophila* and later in other organisms from plants to humans. They regulate many embryonic developmental patterns, including anterior-posterior *polarity*, *limb* development, and *organogenesis*. The name *homeobox* was derived from the fact that mutations in these transcription factors lead to *homeotic transformations*, where one body part is displaced or duplicated. The best-known homeobox genes are the *Hox* family. They are present in large clusters, suggesting they

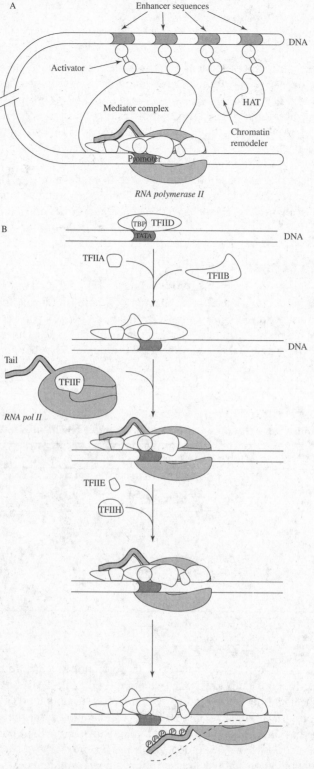

Fig. 9-4 Promoters interact with distant enhancers via looping,
facilitated by the mediator complex. (A) DNA looping
around so its enhancer sequences, via activator transcription factors, interact with the complex that forms around
RNA polymerase II. (B) RNA polymerase II, like other
eukaryotic RNA polymerases, is recruited by transcription factors which assemble step-wise at the promoter.
Its C terminal tail is phosphorylated to recruit elongation factors which permit it to leave the promoter and
commence transcription. The various transcription factors (TFIIA, TFIIB, etc.) are indicated by their abbreviated
names, unlike HAT which is histone acetyl transferase.

have been held together during natural selection. Interestingly, expression of these transcription factors is determined by their position in the cluster; e.g., 5′ and 3′ homeobox genes are expressed in posterior and anterior segments of an embryo, respectively. In addition, genes at one end tend to be expressed first, or more strongly than genes at the other end of the cluster. Such an expression pattern is described as *collinear*.

EXAMPLE 9.11   Predict the general structure of transcription factors.

   Transcription factors must recognize and bind to specific DNA sequences as well as activate transcription. These different functions generally occur via a physically independent domain of the protein. There are many types of DNA-binding domains; perhaps the best understood are the *zinc fingers* in which a group of conserved amino acids bind a *zinc ion*. Activation domains are less well understood. It is thought that they are involved in protein/protein interactions to recruit other transcription factors and/or RNA polymerase.

EXAMPLE 9.12   How is the production of a tissue-specific protein restricted to a particular tissue when the gene is present in the nucleus of all cells?

   Most of the control of tissue-specific gene expression occurs at the level of transcription; this is achieved with *tissue-specific transcription factors*. E.g., all the genes that are to be expressed in erythroid cells (such as globins, spectrin, and the erythropoietin receptor) have the site -AGATA- in their promoters. This promoter is only active when bound by a transcription factor, called GATA-1, which is present only in erythroid cells.

EXAMPLE 9.13   Most of the information about sequence requirements of promoters has been provided by *mutations*. Mutations in promoters affect the frequency of expression of the gene that they control, without altering the gene product. Are there any human promoter mutants?

   There are a number of diseases that are caused by mutations of a single base pair (*point mutations*) in the promoters of important genes. E.g., β thalassemia is a genetic disease in which anemia results from a reduced production of β globin; it is due to a mutation (at several possible sites) in the promoter of the gene. The mutation is usually associated with reduced binding affinity of the promoter for a positive *transcription factor*.

EXAMPLE 9.14   The general transcription factors alone cannot initiate efficient transcription by RNA polymerase *in vivo*. Is transcription affected by the interaction of *histone* with DNA in *nucleosomes*?

   In vivo, DNA is associated with histone proteins and packaged into nucleosomes to form chromatin (Section 6.10). This interaction is dynamic: the position and structure of nucleosomes can be regulated to control access to DNA by the transcription machinery. Histones interact with the DNA through positive charges on their basic amino acids, thus chemical modifications that alter this charge may directly affect nucleosome structure. For example, acetylation of arginine residues by histone acetylases removes positive charges, while phosphorylation and poly(A)denosine diphosphate ribosylation add negative charges. These modifications can affect the function of chromatin. For instance, acetylated nucleosomes are associated with regions of active transcription, while deacetylated nucleosomes are associated with transcriptionally repressed regions. The precise mechanism by which such modifications influence the interaction between DNA and nucleosomes is currently unknown. It is thought that modifications of various combinations of residues in histone tails form a 'histone code'. This code results in patterns of modification that are recognized by effector proteins (eg, chromatin remodelling proteins). These protein complexes mediate access to DNA, activating or repressing transcription by regulating chromatin condensation and altering the position of nucleosomes.

EXAMPLE 9.15   How can enhancer sequences influence transcription at promoters that are so far away?

   Enhancers and promoters come into proximity by *looping* of the intervening DNA (Fig. 9-4). The mediator complex also contributes to this process, acting as a *molecular bridge*. Transcription factors that bind to enhancers have additional sites that bind to other transcription factors, and the mediator, that are coassembled at the promoter of the gene. *Silencers* are DNA sequences that function similarly, but they inhibit transcription by binding to *repressive transcription factors*. As they can function across large distances, enhancers and silencers are separated from promoters by DNA sequences called *insulators* that prevent inappropriate activation of other genes in the same region.

9.6   Processing the RNA Transcript

In bacteria, and prokaryotes in general, the primary transcript provides functional mRNA that is ready for immediate *translation*. In eukaryotes, the vast majority of primary transcripts are chemically modified and have sequences removed from within them before becoming mature *functional* mRNAs that are transported out of the nucleus for translation. Eukaryotic genes that are expressed as protein contain nontranslated *intervening* sequences called *introns*. These are *excised* or *spliced out* of the *primary transcript* to leave the segments that are to be expressed, called *exons*, in the mRNA. A representation of the β-globin gene with its introns and exons is shown in Fig. 9-5.

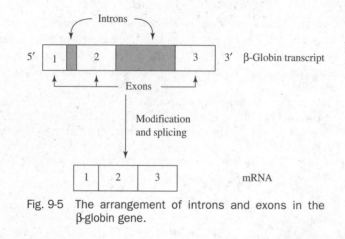

Fig. 9-5   The arrangement of introns and exons in the β-globin gene.

A *primary transcript* corresponding to the full length of the gene is made first; this is then chemically *modified,* and *introns* (two in the case of β-globin) are removed by *splicing*. The mixture of primary transcripts present in the nucleus is known as *heterogeneous nuclear RNA* (hnRNA).

The splicing out of introns is a very precise reaction; it avoids changes in the reading frame so that a functional message is the result. Splicing is mediated by a large complex called the *spliceosome,* consisting of proteins and five different snRNA (small nuclear RNA) molecules. There are consensus sequences at the 5′ exon-intron junctions and at the *branch site* in introns that are complementary to one of the snRNAs in the *spliceosome.* The snRNA forms base pairs with these two adjacent consensus sequences, forming a secondary structure that accurately juxtaposes the ends of *neighboring* exons. This process forces the intervening introns into a loop (called the *lariat*) that is excised, and the adjacent exons are ligated together by other snRNAs in the spliceosome.

In the case of an rRNA from *Tetrahymena thermophila,* a single intron is autocatalytically spliced out in the presence of only GTP and certain cations in a process known as *self-splicing*. The RNA acts as an enzyme and is called a *ribozyme* (see Sec. 5.2).

EXAMPLE 9.16   Why might introns have evolved to be present in most eukaryotic genes?

The precise function of introns is unknown. Nevertheless, it appears that exons, or coding sequences, code for structural domains, or units, in the final protein product. Therefore *interrupted genes*, as they are called, may reflect an evolutionary process in which combinations of various exons gave rise to different proteins through the joining together of different protein *domains*.

EXAMPLE 9.17   What modifications other than intron removal and exon splicing occur in the primary mRNA transcript?

Processing mRNA of occurs during transcription, and many of the enzymes involved are recruited by the *C*-terminal tail of *RNA polymerase II. Capping* occurs at the 5′ end of the transcript shortly after its initiation. In the first step of capping, GTP is used to add a guanine-containing nucleotide that is linked to the chain through its triphosphate bridge; this reaction is catalyzed by *guanyl transferase*. In subsequent reactions, both the added guanine and the first two nucleotides in the primary transcript are *methylated*. The 5′ cap is thus relatively complex in structure. It has an important role in the subsequent initiation of translation (Sec. 9.10). *Poly(A)denylation* results in the nontemplate directed addition of a *poly(A) tail* of 40–200 residues at the 3′ end of the transcript. The enzyme responsible for this addition is *poly(A) polymerase*. The poly(A) tail is believed to stabilize mRNA and play a role in initiation of translation.

Much less is known about termination of transcription in eukaryotes than in bacteria. Once transcribed, specific termination sequences of mRNA are bound by protein complexes (such as CPSF: cleavage and poly(A)denylation specificity factor, and CstF: cleavage stimulation factor) that process cleavage of the message and subsequent poly(A)denylation. RNA polymerase continues transcription for up to several hundred nucleotides before dissociating from the DNA.

EXAMPLE 9.18   The steps involved in the production of a functional mRNA from a typical eukaryotic gene are shown in Fig. 9-6. In this example, a gene is shown with six *introns* (labeled A – F) and seven *exons* labeled 1–7. Not illustrated is the fact that there is probably a defined order in which individual introns are spliced out.

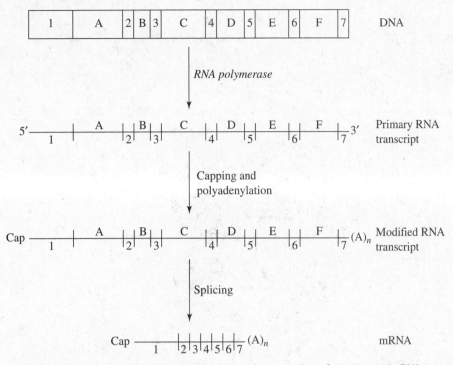

Fig. 9-6 Steps involved in the transcription and processing of a eukaryotic RNA transcript into mRNA.

EXAMPLE 9.19 Does transcription of DNA always give rise to mRNA?

Much of the DNA that is transcribed gives rise to mRNA that is translated into protein. However, the most abundant species of RNA are of other types that are not subsequently translated into protein. They are *ribosomal RNA* (rRNA) and *transfer RNA* (tRNA) that participate in mRNA translation; they are formed in a high rate of transcription of a relatively small number of genes (called *rRNA and tRNA genes*) by RNA polymerases I and III.

9.7 Inhibitors of Transcription

The three eukaryotic *RNA polymerases* are distinguishable from one another by their differential sensitivity to the drug α-*amanitin* (the toxic principle of the mushroom *Amanita phalloides*) which does not affect bacterial RNA polymerases. RNA polymerase II is very sensitive to α-amanitin, while RNA polymerase I is completely resistant. RNA polymerase III is moderately sensitive to this inhibitor. Mitochondria have yet another type of RNA polymerase, which is unaffected by α-amanitin but is sensitive to drugs that inhibit bacterial RNA polymerase. A number of antibiotics also act through their inhibition of transcription; e.g., *actinomycin D* exerts its effect by binding to DNA templates, and it also blocks *DNA replication*.

EXAMPLE 9.20 Would actinomycin D be expected to inhibit transcription in both bacteria and eukaryotes?

Yes, because when binding to the template it recognizes a structural feature of the DNA double helix and therefore cannot discriminate between the two sources of DNA.

EXAMPLE 9.21 Are there inhibitors that discriminate between transcription in bacteria and eukaryotes?

Yes. Examples are *rifampicin* and *streptolydigin* which bind only to bacterial RNA polymerase and inhibit its action; α-*amanitin* binds only to eukaryotic RNA polymerase II and to a lesser extent to RNA polymerase III to inhibit their action. The structures of these three inhibitors are shown in Fig. 9-7.

EXAMPLE 9.22 Bacterial RNA polymerase is a multi-subunit enzyme. Are there particular subunits to which *rifampicin* and *streptolydigin* bind?

Yes, both bind only to the β subunit. But rifampicin blocks only *initiation* of RNA synthesis while streptolydigin preferentially blocks *elongation*. This shows that the β subunit is involved in both initiation and elongation of RNA chains.

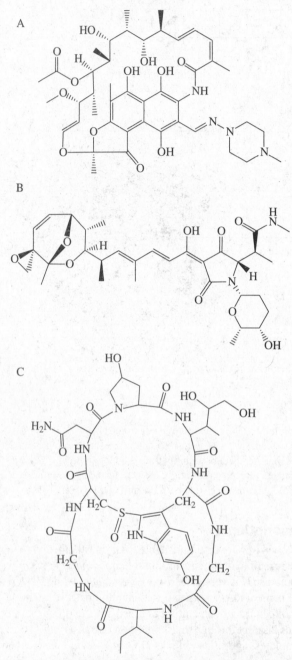

Fig. 9-7   Inhibitors of DNA transcription: (A) rifampicin,
(B) streptolydigin, and (C) α-amanitin.

9.8   The mRNA Translation Machinery

The sequence of nucleotides in mRNA is converted through the translation machinery into a sequence of amino acids that constitutes a *polypeptide*. The translation machinery includes tRNA and ribosomes (that contain rRNA and a set of unique proteins). The tRNA acts as an *adaptor* between the nucleotide sequence that defines the order of codons and the amino acid sequence that is assembled into a polypeptide.

EXAMPLE 9.23   How does a tRNA molecule serve as an *adaptor* between a codon and an amino acid?

There is at least one tRNA corresponding to each amino acid. One part of each tRNA molecule is involved in the binding of an amino acid, and another part contains a sequence of three unpaired nucleotides (the *anticodon*) that is complementary to one (or more) of the codons for this amino acid. The anticodon in each tRNA forms complementary base pairs with codons in the mRNA, thus determining the sequence of amino acids that are added during the process of translation.

The nucleotide sequences of many tRNAs from a wide variety of organisms are known. They all contain ~80 ribonucleotides, and many of them have unusual structures. While the sequences of different tRNAs vary, they all form a common secondary structure in which the RNA chain folds back on itself and engages in a maximum amount of base pairing. Figure 9-8 illustrates tRNA folded into this typical *cloverleaf* structure that contains several base-paired stems and loops. While sequences differ between individual tRNA molecules, there are regions that are *invariant*. Most of these regions are in the *loops*, within which the unusual bases are concentrated, and at the 3′ end of the molecule within the *acceptor stem*. The nucleotide sequence at this end is always CCA, and it is to the 3′-OH that the appropriate amino acid is attached through its carboxyl group. The cloverleaf is stabilized in an elongated L-shaped structure by additional hydrogen bonds, with the acceptor sequence at one end and the anticodon loop at the other.

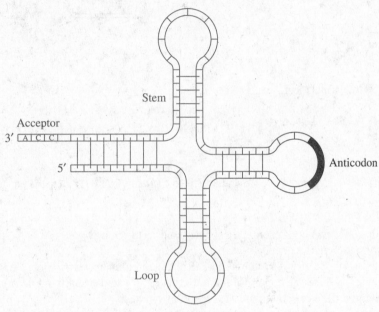

Fig. 9-8   Folded cloverleaf structure of tRNA.

EXAMPLE 9.24   While there is at least one tRNA for each amino acid, there is *not* a separate one for each codon. How can a single tRNA molecule accommodate more than one type of codon?

This can be accounted for by what is known as the *wobble hypothesis*. It appears that when a codon in mRNA interacts with the anticodon, unconventional pairing can form between the alternative bases in the third position of the codon (3′ end of triplet) and the first position of the anticodon. The unusual nucleoside *inosine* frequently resides in the first position of the anticodon, and it can pair with A, U, or C. The possibility of more than one type of pairing in this position accounts for the fact that when there is more than one codon for a single amino acid, called *synonyms* (Table 9-1), the differences are usually in the third position only.

The attachment of an amino acid to an appropriate tRNA is accomplished via the enzyme *aminoacyl-tRNA synthetase* and the hydrolysis of ATP. There is a separate synthetase enzyme that is *specific* for each amino acid, and it will recognize all tRNAs for that amino acid. The activation reaction proceeds in two steps and requires Mg^{2+} (Fig. 9-9). The first step, *amino acid activation*, results in the formation of an *aminoacyl-AMP-enzyme* intermediate. In the second step, the aminoacyl group is transferred to the 3′-OH of its appropriate (*cognate*) tRNA, through an *ester* bond. Recognition between the synthetase and tRNA is achieved through very precise contact between the two molecules, with single contact points distinguishing one tRNA from another. The first reaction is driven to completion by the enzymic hydrolysis of PPi. Thus, the overall activation and attachment

Reaction 1

Reaction 2

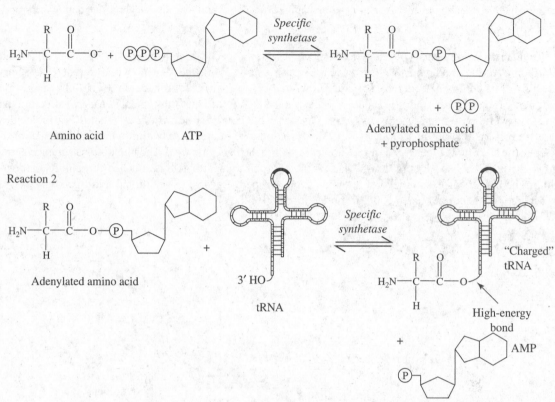

Fig. 9-9 Reactions in the attachment of an amino acid to its cognate tRNA. R refers to the amino acid side group.

of an amino acid consumes two high-energy phosphate bonds. This energy is stored in the ester bond and later contributes to the formation of the peptide bond.

mRNA and aminoacylated tRNAs ("charged" tRNAs) interact on *ribosomes*. The initial interaction occurs in such a way as to allow the codon for the initiating amino acid (usually methionine) to interact with its appropriately charged tRNA to commence polypeptide synthesis.

Ribosomes are large macromolecular complexes of protein and RNA that are assembled in the *nucleolus*. Almost two-thirds of the mass of the ribosome is composed of ribosomal RNAs (rRNAs), which are first chemically modified by small nucleolar RNAs (snoRNAs) before assembly. Ribosomes consist of small and large subunits; some details are listed in Table 9-3. Subunits are distinguishable from one another by their different rates of sedimentation in an ultracentrifuge cell (Sec. 4.14). In bacteria the small and large subunits have sedimentation coefficients of 30S and 50S, respectively. During translation, they interact to form a 70S ribosome only after tRNA and mRNA are assembled on the 30S subunit. In eukaryotes, the makeup of the subunits is similar, although both subunits are slightly larger. The small (40S) and large (60S) subunits yield an 80S ribosome. The individual subunits in both types of ribosome have similar functions that are determined by the types of rRNA and proteins present within them; e.g., the small subunit has a special role in initiating polypeptide synthesis.

Table 9-3   Components of Bacterial and Eukaryotic Ribosomes

Bacteria	Eukaryotes
70S ribosome:	*80S ribosome:*
30S subunit	40S subunit
= 16S RNA + 21 proteins	= 18S RNA + ~30 proteins
50S subunit	60S subunit
= 23S RNA + 5S RNA + 34 proteins	= 28S RNA + 5.8S RNA + 5S RNA + ~50 proteins

A considerable amount of information is available on the precise architecture of the small and large sub-units of bacterial ribosomes, the surface location of the many proteins, and the manner of interaction of the subunits. Some of this is illustrated in Fig. 9-10.

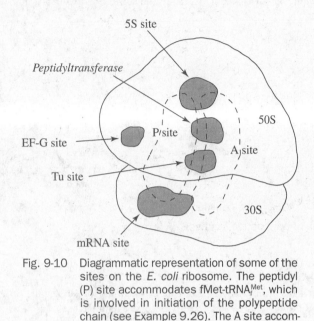

Fig. 9-10   Diagrammatic representation of some of the sites on the *E. coli* ribosome. The peptidyl (P) site accommodates fMet-tRNA$_f^{Met}$, which is involved in initiation of the polypeptide chain (see Example 9.26). The A site accommodates the incoming aminoacyl-tRNA. The protein Tu releases the aminoacyl-tRNA to the A site. EF-G refers to elongation factor G, a translocase. Refer to subsequent text for explanation of terms.

9.9   RNA Translation in Bacteria

Because we have a clearer idea of the way in which ribosomes interact with mRNA and assemble poly-peptides in bacteria than in eukaryotes, here the bacterial system is considered first. The overall process in eukaryotes is very similar, and the *special* features of eukaryotes are covered later. Translation of an RNA message into a polypeptide occurs in three stages: *initiation*, *elongation*, and *termination*. Translation in prokaryotes begins soon after transcription begins, and long before the 3′ end of mRNA is completed, thus confirming that mRNA is read from 5′→3′. Initiation in bacteria involves the interaction of the 30S ribosomal subunit at the appropriate location on mRNA.

EXAMPLE 9.25   What features of the structure of mRNA enable its interaction with the 30S subunit?

Toward the 5′ end of mRNA there is a region of ~20 nucleotides prior to the initiation codon AUG. This *leader* region contains a purine-rich sequence that is responsible for the interaction of the mRNA with the 30S subunit. It is known as the *Shine-Dalgarno* sequence (after John Shine and Lynn Dalgarno, the Australians who made the discovery); it can bind to a complementary sequence at the 3′ end of the 16S rRNA to orient the 30S subunit appropriately for initiation. The Shine-Dalgarno sequence distinguishes the initiating AUG, which also determines the reading frame, from an AUG that encodes an internal methionine. Other sequences in the *leader region* are possibly involved in the overall process of initiation of translation, which also involves the binding of the appropriately charged methionyl-tRNA opposite the AUG codon.

EXAMPLE 9.26   Is there any special feature of methionyl-tRNA, in addition to the presence of an anticodon for AUG that is required for its participation in initiation of translation?

Yes. There are two different tRNAs for methionine, one involved in initiation and the other that adds methionine to the growing chain. The two species are called tRNA$_f^{Met}$ and tRNA$_m^{Met}$. The former is capable of being *formylated* by a *transformylase* to yield *N*-fomylMet-tRNA$_f^{Met}$ (or fMet-tRNA$_f^{Met}$, for short) and is the species that is involved exclusively in the initiation of polypeptide synthesis. Presumably, unique features of the structure of the tRNA in this case are required for the initiation process. In addition to mRNA, fMet-tRNA$_f^{Met}$ and the ribosome subunits, three protein *initiation factors* (IF1, IF2, and IF3) and GTP are involved in initiation of polypeptide synthesis. Initiation factors in the 30S initiation complex bind GTP and enable mRNA and then fMet-tRNA$_f^{Met}$ to join the complex. The fMet-tRNA$_f^{Met}$ occupies the *peptidyl* (P) site of the ribosome (Fig. 9-10). Another site, the *acceptor* (A) site, is empty at this stage; it is aligned with the next codon (shown as xxx in Fig. 9-11) in the mRNA and will accommodate each subsequent incoming aminoacyl-tRNA.

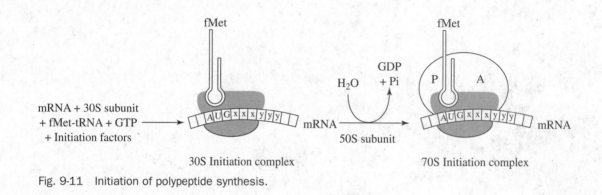

Fig. 9-11   Initiation of polypeptide synthesis.

EXAMPLE 9.27   What is the mechanism for filling the A site of the ribosome with the appropriate aminoacyl-tRNA?

Transport of the appropriately activated tRNA to the A site requires association with a protein-GTP complex. The protein, called Tu (so named because it is a *transfer* factor and is *unstable* when heated), is known as an *elongation factor*. Upon releasing the aminoacyl-tRNA to the A site, the GTP in Tu-GTP is hydrolyzed to Tu-GDP + Pi. Tu-GTP is then regenerated from Tu-GDP through reactions that involve another protein, Ts (a heat-*stable transfer* factor) and GTP. Thus one high-energy phosphate bond is consumed in delivering each aminoacyl-tRNA into the A site. The delay while GTP hydrolysis occurs is important for fidelity of translation. An incorrect tRNA, more weakly bound to the codon, has time to diffuse away before the irreversible formation of the peptide bond. The GTP in the 30S initiation complex is also hydrolyzed upon binding the 50S subunit to form the 70S complex. Initiation factors prevent formation of this 70S elongation complex until tRNA and mRNA are in place. Everything is now ready for peptide bond formation, i.e., elongation.

EXAMPLE 9.28   The initiator codon specifies that the polypeptide chain is initiated by *methionine*. Does this mean that all "mature" protein sequences begin with methionine?

No. The first few amino acids are often removed during or after translation. The formyl group at the N terminus is also removed.

The elongation phase of polypeptide synthesis is depicted in Fig. 9-12. The 50S subunit is a *peptidyl transferase* that catalyzes the formation of a peptide bond between amino acids. The 23S rRNA is responsible for this catalytic activity. As its name implies, it transfers the fMet (and in later reactions a peptide) from the tRNA that occupies the P site to the amino acid on the tRNA in the A site. To do this, the amino group of

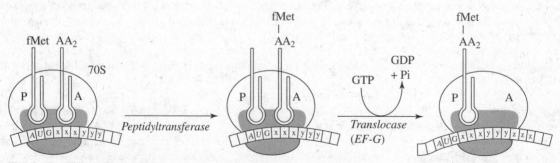

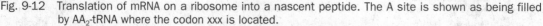

Fig. 9-12   Translation of mRNA on a ribosome into a nascent peptide. The A site is shown as being filled by AA$_2$-tRNA where the codon xxx is located.

the aminoacyl-tRNA in the A site attacks the ester bond between fMet and its tRNA to form the first peptide bond. The fMet (or later the peptide) is thereby transferred to the A site (AA$_2$-tRNA in Fig. 9-12). In the next step, another protein, *translocase* or *elongation factor G* (EF-G), in association with GTP hydrolysis, shifts or *translocates* the ribosome by one codon to position the dipeptidyl-tRNA in the P site, leaving the A site available for the binding of another aminoacyl-tRNA. This process of aminoacyl-tRNA binding, peptide bond formation, and translocation continues until a *stop codon*, which defines the completion of the poly-peptide chain, is aligned with the empty A site. There are no tRNAs that recognize stop codons; rather, stop codons are recognized by *protein release* factor proteins.

EXAMPLE 9.29 How is the completed polypeptide chain released from its ester linkage to the tRNA in the P site if there is no tRNA in the A site?

In bacteria there are three *release factor* proteins: RF1, RF2, and RF3. In response to the stop codons they bind (in various combinations) to the A site and activate *peptidyl transferase* that hydrolyzes the ester bond using water rather than an amino group as the acceptor of the peptide. This releases the chain from the tRNA in the P site and generates the free carboxy-terminus of the polypeptide. Also 16S rRNA plays a role recognizing stop codons. Once the peptide leaves the ribosome, the ribosome subunits dissociate and are recycled.

EXAMPLE 9.30 During translation the ribosome moves along the mRNA and leaves the leader region (containing the *Shine-Dalgarno* ribosome binding site) empty. Is it possible for initiation of a new polypeptide chain to occur before completion of the previous one?

Yes. It is common for any single mRNA to be translated simultaneously by many ribosomes. They give rise to structures called *polyribosomes*, or *polysomes*. Each ribosome independently synthesizes a complete polypeptide chain.

9.10 RNA Translation in Eukaryotes

The molecular mechanism of translation in eukaryotes is very similar to that in bacteria. The activation of amino acids and their attachment to tRNA molecules, and the steps of initiation, elongation, and termination of polypeptide chains, are essentially the same in overall terms. The small and large ribosomal subunits of bacteria and eukaryotes, although different is size and composition, are equivalent with respect to their roles in initiation and elongation of polypeptide chains. Differences lie mainly in the details of some steps, particularly initiation, and in the greater number of accessory proteins involved in each step.

EXAMPLE 9.31 As discussed in Sec 9.1, the processes of transcription and translation are separated in space and time in eukaryotes. What are the other *significant* differences between the mechanism of translation of mRNA in bacteria and eukaryotes?

The main differences relate to the initiation step. For translation to be initiated, the ribosome must be recruited to mRNA and correctly positioned over the start codon; and a charged tRNA must be placed in the P site of the ribosome. Due to the dissimilar structures of their mRNA molecules, prokaryotes and eukaryotes process their in different ways. The order of events during initiation is also different. In prokaryotes, the small subunit of the ribosome and mRNA can interact before recruiting initiator tRNA. In eukaryotes, initiator tRNA is brought to the small (40S) subunit *before* the ribosome interacts with the mRNA; this is mediated by interaction between *eukaryotic initiation factors* (eIFs), includ-ing eIF2 on the tRNA (forming a *ternary complex*), and other eIFs on the ribosome. The complex composed of the small subunit and its associated initiator tRNA and eIFs is called the *43S pre-initiation complex*. Like prokaryotes, eukaryotes also have two forms of tRNA for methionine, one of which is used in initiation (tRNA$_i^{Met}$). However, neither activated form is *formylaled*. There is *no transformylase* in eukaryotes, although eukaryotic [Met-tRNA$_i^{Met}$] is able to be formylated by the bacterial transformylase.

Another difference, of more significance, is the involvement of the methylated 5′ cap of eukaryotic mRNA in initia-tion of translation. In contrast to this step in prokaryotes, complementarity between rRNA in the small ribosomal subunit and sequences at the 5′ end of mRNA does not appear to be important in eukaryotes. Instead, interaction of ribosomes and mRNA requires the 5′ cap, and is mediated by eIF4, a multisubunit factor. Messages from which the 5′ cap has been removed are not translated efficiently.

The 43S complex recruite mRNA by interaction between specific eIFs. Some eIFs (e.g. eIF3) associate with the 43S complex and others (e.g eIF4) associate with the 5′ cap of mRNA. eIF4 has helicase activity that unwinds secondary and tertiary structures in the mature mRNA. It also associates with proteins that are bound to the poly(A) tail. The interaction of mRNA with the 43S complex appears to be facilitated by *looping* that results from interactions between eIF complexes at the 5′ and 3′ ends. The looping of the mRNA also permits efficient reinitiation of translation by ribosomes that have previously completed a round of translation.

Once associated with mRNA, the pre-initiation complex scans downstream to locate a start codon (AUG). This process is driven by ATP, and requires the helicase activity of an eIF. The start codon is recognised by base paring between the anti-codon on tRNA and the AUG on the mRNA. Codon-anticodon interaction is facilitated by yet more eIFs. Usually, the first AUG codon that is encountered is used, especially if it is surrounded by the so called *Kozak* consensus sequence (named after its discoverer Marilyn Kozak). Occasionally a later AUG is used if the first AUG not in the context of a consensus Kozak sequence, or is very close to the 5′ cap. This is in contrast to prokaryotes, where the AUG that will act as a start codon is located at the future P site by the position of the ribosome after base-pairing between the 16S rRNA of the ribosome and the Shine Dalgarno sequence.

Following recognition of the start codon in eukaryotes, initiator tRNA bound to the start codon is delivered to the P site after hydrolysis of the GTP on eIF2. eIF2 dissociates, and is recycled for another round of translation: GDP is replaced with fresh GTP by a *guanine exchange factor* called eIF2B. Finally, other eIFs dissociate, permitting the large (60S) subunit to join forming the 80S complex to begin the elongation phase (which, like termination, is very similar to that in prokaryotes).

9.11   Inhibitors of Translation

Because of the large number of steps associated with the translation of mRNA into protein, there are numerous opportunities available for blocking it with inhibitors. The action of many antibiotics is based upon blocking translation in bacteria.

EXAMPLE 9.32   Which inhibitors block translation in both bacteria and eukaryotes?

Representative examples are *fusidic acid* and *puromycin* (Fig. 9-14A). Fusidic acid inhibits the binding of charged tRNA to the *A site* of the ribosome. Puromycin acts by virtue of its similarity in structure to an aminoacyl-tRNA. It competes with aminoacyl-tRNAs as an acceptor in the peptidyl transfer reaction. The growing chain is transferred to the−NH$_2$ group of puromycin and is prematurely terminated.

EXAMPLE 9.33   Do different inhibitors act on analogous targets in protein synthesis in bacteria and eukaryotes?

Yes. *Chloramphenicol* (Fig. 9-15A) inhibits the *peptidyl transferase* of the 50S ribosomal subunit in bacteria, while *cyclohexamide* (Fig. 9-15B) inhibits the analogous enzyme activity of the 60S subunit of *eukaryotic* ribosomes. It is interesting to note that chloramphenicol also inhibits translation in eukaryotic mitochondria, indicating the similarity of mechanisms of gene expression in mitochondria and bacteria.

EXAMPLE 9.34   Many inhibitors are specific for either bacterial or eukaryotic cells. An interesting one is *diphtheria toxin* that is effective only in eukaryotes. *Corynebacterium diphtheriae* produces diphtheria toxin, a single polypeptide ($M_r = 63,000$) with two intrachain disulfide bonds. Through a complex process, the molecule is cleaved on the membrane surface to yield fragments A and B. The latter facilitates entry of the A fragment ($M_r = 21,000$) into the cytoplasm of the cell where it exerts its toxic effects. The A fragment specifically catalyzes the chemical modification (ADP-ribosylation) of the eukaryotic translocase (elongation factor 2: EF2) to inactivate it and therefore inhibit the growth of a polypeptide chain.

9.12   Posttranslational Modification of Proteins

Most polypeptides that are synthesized on ribosomes are chemically modified. The formyl group on the N-terminal methionine in bacteria is removed by a *deformylase*. In both bacteria and eukaryotes the N-terminal methionine, sometimes along with a few additional amino acids, is removed by *aminopeptidases*. Other chemical modifications that are known to occur are the *attachment of sugars (glycosylation)* to asparagine, serine, and threonine residues. *Phosphorylation* of serine, tyrosine, and threonine residues is often important in activating or deactivating proteins, for example, in signal transduction pathways (Chap. 6).

EXAMPLE 9.35   The amino acids *hydroxyproline* and *hydroxylysine* are absent from Table 9-1 which describes the genetic code. How do these amino acids arise in some proteins?

Hydroxyproline and hydroxylysine are prominent in *collagen* (Sec. 4.7). They are formed by the modification of proline and lysine residues by specific enzymes *after* synthesis of the collagen chains. The enzyme that hydroxylates proline, *prolyl hydroxylase*, requires *ascorbate* (vitamin C) as a coreactant.

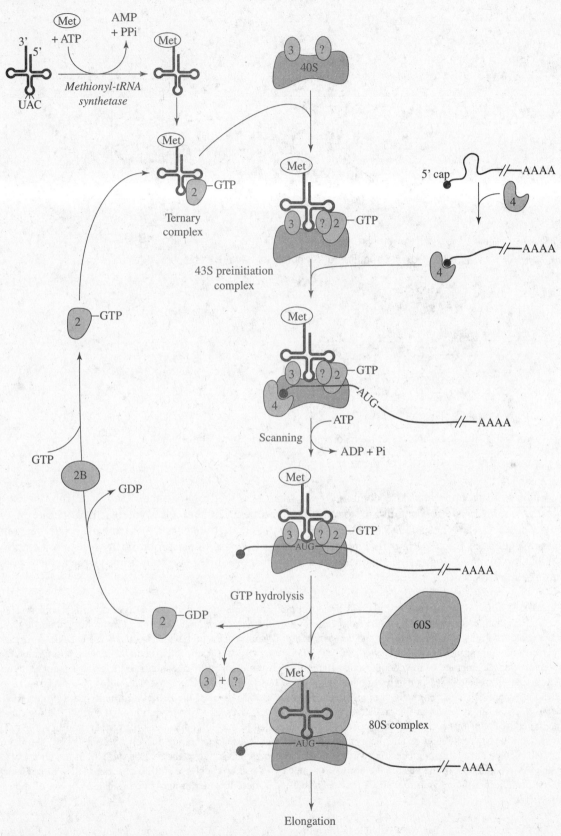

Fig. 9-13 Translation of mRNA into a polypeptide in eukaryotes.

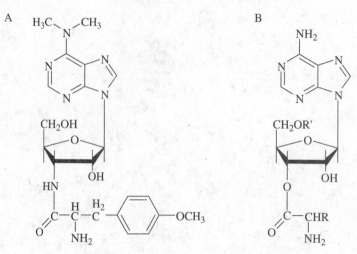

Fig. 9-14   Structures of (A) puromycin and (B) aminoacyl-tRNA.

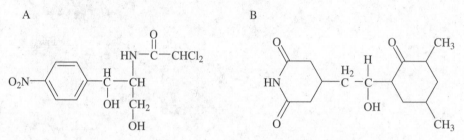

Fig. 9-15   Structures of (A) chloramphenicol and (B) cyclohexamide.

Eukaryotic proteins may also contain *signal sequences* that regulate their transport from the cytoplasm, where translation begins, to specific compartments of the cell. Proteins that operate in the nucleus, such as histones and *DNA-* and *RNA-polymerases*, are transported by virtue of short N-terminal signal sequences. Such *nuclear localization signals*, which are often rich in positively charged amino acids, bind to *importin* proteins that mediate active transport of large proteins through the nuclear pores into the nucleus.

EXAMPLE 9.36   How can proteins be transported through a hydrophobic membrane and out of a eukaryotic cell?

Proteins that are destined for *secretion* from cells are usually synthesized in a precursor form. This contains a signal sequence that is relatively hydrophobic and consists of 15–30 amino acids at the N terminus. As soon as it is formed at the ribosome, this sequence binds a *signal recognition particle,* a complex of proteins and RNA, which in turn binds a receptor in the membrane of the endoplasmic reticulum. (The attachment of ribosomes to the endoplasmic reticulum through peptide chains is responsible for what is known as the *rough endoplasmic reticulum*, Fig. 1-5). As translation of the polypeptide chain continues, it elongates and passes to the lumen of the ER. Here it undergoes further modification, including removal of the signal sequence by a *signal peptidase*, glycosylation, and correct folding that is facilitated by *chaperone* proteins. The protein is then transported to the Golgi apparatus for further modification and is subsequently packaged into a vesicle that is transported through the cell membrane. Proteins destined to be retained on the cell surface have large stretches of hydrophobic amino acids that lodge in the hydrophobic lipid membrane, first in the vesicle and then in the plasma membrane. In the case of bacterial cells, a similar process can lead to transport of the protein into the *periplasmic space* (between the inner and outer membranes at the surface) or out of the cell altogether.

EXAMPLE 9.37   Insulin is a good example of the transport (or secretion) of a protein out of a eukaryotic cell following extensive posttranslational modification. Insulin is formed in the pancreas by β cells of the islets of Langerhans. The immediate product of mRNA translation is a single polypeptide called *preproinsulin*. The modifications associated with the conversion of *prepro*insulin to insulin are shown in Fig. 9-16.

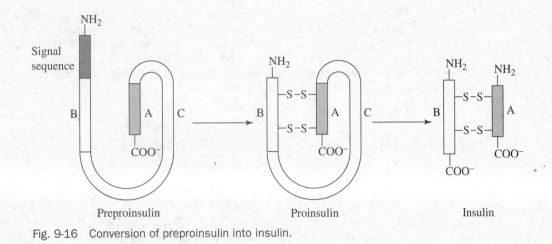

Fig. 9-16   Conversion of preproinsulin into insulin.

Porcine preproinsulin is a single polypeptide chain of 107 amino acid residues. After the signal peptide is synthesized on the ribosome, it recognizes a receptor on the endoplasmic reticulum and attaches to it. The polypeptide chain passes through the membrane and into the lumen. Here the signal peptide of 16 residues is cleaved off to yield a shortened chain of 84 residues which folds on itself to form intramolecular disulfide bridges that join cysteine residues. This folded molecule is called *proinsulin*. Proinsulin is packaged into membrane vesicles and transported to the *Golgi apparatus* (Fig. 1-6) where conversion to insulin begins. This involves cleavage of the single chain to remove the connecting (C) peptide. Cleavage is completed as it is transported *via secretory granules* from the Golgi to the *plasma membrane* with which the granules fuse to release mature insulin, now consisting of two disulfide-crosslinked polypeptide chains, into the circulation.

9.13   Control of Gene Expression

Question: With few exceptions, every cell in an organism contains the same DNA genome. What, then, accounts for the differences between cells?

Differences between cells are due to differences in *gene expression*, i.e., changes in the abundance and diversity of mRNA sequences in the cell. A gene is said to be *expressed* if its mRNA is found in the cell, which usually means its protein product is also present. Expression of certain genes may be subject to *spatial* control and expressed only in specific cell types and/or *temporal* control, such that they are expressed only at specific times during development or in response to a particular hormonal signal.

The end products of gene expression are proteins, and it is essential that their concentrations be strictly controlled. There are many potential sites of control in both bacteria and eukaryotes. In Chap. 8 the occurrence of *gene amplification* in eukaryotes is considered. This is one way of responding to the need for more of a protein product; if there are more copies of the gene, then transcription can occur more often. Usually control is achieved at the level of either transcription or translation, with the former generally being more important for both bacteria and eukaryotes. One of the most widely used strategies is to control where, and how often, transcription is initiated. Different genes are controlled by different promoters; the efficiency and specificity with which a promoter is recognized depend on *upstream promoter sequences* that are recognized by more specialized transcription factors (in eukaryotes) or by σ-subunits of RNA polymerase (in prokaryotes, Fig. 9-3).

Transcriptional control in bacteria is particularly effective because of the very short half life (a few minutes) of mRNA in such cells; it is longer in eukaryotes. The prototype for transcriptional control is the *lactose operon* in *E. coli*.

EXAMPLE 9.38   The *lactose* operon (or *lac* operon) is a region of 5.3 kb of the *E. coli* chromosome that contains the genes that encode the three enzymes that catabolize lactose. The cell stringently controls expression of the *lac* genes; it expresses them only if it needs to metabolize lactose. Furthermore, when glucose is also present, there is no need for high levels of expression of the *lac* operon. Therefore, as detailed in Fig. 9-17, the *lac* operon is under both negative and positive feedback control. The genes for the three enzymes involved, β-*galactosidase, galactoside permease,* and *thiogalactoside transacetylase,* are situated next to one another in a segment of DNA. They are transcribed as a single unit of RNA, transcription being controlled by sequences (control elements) toward the 5′ end of the 5.3 kb segment of DNA. The control elements consist of a *promoter* (to which RNA polymerase binds) and an adjacent *operator* (to which a *repressor protein* binds to inhibit transcription by RNA polymerase). The repressor is produced by a separate gene that is located on the 5′ side of the operon. This is illustrated in Fig. 9-17.

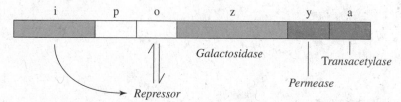

Fig. 9-17   The *lactose* operon of *E. coli*. Here *i, p, o, z, y,* and *a* denote the *repressor gene, promoter, operator, β-galactosidase gene, permease gene,* and *transacetylase* genes, respectively. Because the three genes, *z, y,* and *a,* are transcribed as a single unit (*polycistronic mRNA*), they are said to be expressed *coordinately*. When transcription is blocked by the binding of the repressor to the operator, none of the genes are expressed.

EXAMPLE 9.39   How does the cell overcome repression to express the genes of the *lac* operon?

When lactose is present, a small amount of it enters the cell and is converted to *allolactose*. This metabolite binds to the repressor to alter its conformation and cause its release from the operator. RNA polymerase is now free to access the promoter and *transcribe* the three genes. The allolactose is said to be acting as an *inducer*. The relief of repression by an inducer is an example of *negative control* of expression. There is also an aspect of *positive control* in the *lac* operon. When glucose is absent and the cell is relying on lactose for energy, expression of the *lac* operon must increase greatly. This response is mediated by another protein, CAP (*catabolite activator protein*). CAP has a direct positive effect on transcription by binding to a distinct control element (the CAP binding site) and recruiting RNA polymerase to the promoter. However, CAP can only bind to its control element when first bound by cAMP, a metabolic indicator of low glucose. Once glucose concentrations rise again, the concentration of cAMP falls such that CAP no longer binds much of it and so is unable to exert its positive effect. This reflects the preference of the cell to use glucose rather than lactose as a carbon source.

In addition to the *lac* operon, there are several other examples of transcriptional control in bacteria that illustrate some additional features. The *tryptophan operon* (Fig. 9-18) is a cluster of several genes that are involved in tryptophan synthesis. The *trp* operon is a single transcriptional unit that is under *negative control*. In contrast to the *lac* repressor, however, the *trp* repressor (or *apo-repressor*) does not bind to the operator unless tryptophan is bound to it. Thus, tryptophan acts as a *corepressor* and switches off transcription when the cell has achieved a sufficiently high concentration of tryptophan. In addition to this repressor-mediated on/off mechanism, the expression of the *trp* operon is controlled by a type of fine-tuning called *attenuation*. This peculiar mechanism involves premature termination of transcription in the presence of moderately low concentrations of tryptophan, but the generation of proper full-length transcripts when the tryptophan concentration is *critically low*. It relies on a DNA-base sequence called the *attenuator,* which lies between the promoter and the initiation codon of the first gene *trp E,* and is the first part to be transcribed. Its mRNA has four regions that have self-complementary sequences that can form two different *hairpin stem loop structures* that are involved in attenuation. Region 3 forms a stem loop structure that causes transcription to terminate when it binds with region 4, but can be prevented from participating in the termination structure by forming a stem loop with region 2.

The attenuator also contains two *trp* codons. If sufficient tRNA^{Trp} is present (even if there may be no free tryptophan), the ribosome that is translating the growing mRNA can continue translation of the *leader peptide* past these *trp* codons. This blocks region 2 and permits formation of the terminator stem loop that causes the ribosome, RNA polymerase, and mRNA to dissociate before the other genes in the operon are transcribed or translated. However, if tryptophan is so scarce that even tRNA^{Trp} is reduced, the ribosome stalls at the *trp* codons, leaving region 2 free to bind region 3 preventing formation of the terminator stem loop and permitting transcription to continue. Other ribosomes are then able to translate the genes that are required for tryptophan synthesis.

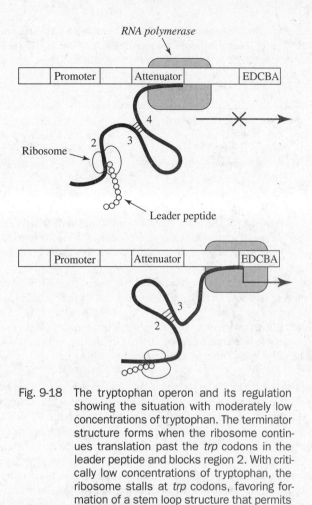

Fig. 9-18   The tryptophan operon and its regulation showing the situation with moderately low concentrations of tryptophan. The terminator structure forms when the ribosome continues translation past the *trp* codons in the leader peptide and blocks region 2. With critically low concentrations of tryptophan, the ribosome stalls at *trp* codons, favoring formation of a stem loop structure that permits transcription to continue.

The operon system is an economical method of coordinately regulating multiple genes. In the larger genomes of eukaryotes, genes that encode proteins for steps within a given pathway may be widely distributed among chromosomes, rather than being organized as operons. This contributes to the fact that regulation of gene expression in eukaryotes is considerably more complex than in prokaryotes. More significantly, eukaryotes are generally multicellular with a variety of different cell types, each requiring expression of particular genes at specific times and in specific locations.

EXAMPLE 9.40   Does transcriptional control also occur in eukaryotes?

Yes. Eukaryotes commonly control transcription via regulation of *transcription factors*. A transcription factor might be expressed only in a specific tissue and/or at a specific time. Transcription factors may also require activation by an environmental signal (Chap. 8); e.g., genes that are expressed in response to *interferons* are activated by STATs (signal transducers and activators of transcription). STATs remain inactive in the cytoplasm until they are phosphorylated by a *kinase* that is associated with the cell surface *interferon receptor*. This allows *dimerization* of STATs and their entry into the nucleus where they activate transcription of interferon-responsive genes by interacting with their *gene control elements*. Controlling the entry of transcription factors into the nucleus is a common method of transcriptional control.

Many of the *steroid hormones* (Sec. 12.8) act by stimulating transcription. Through a series of complicated steps, involving interaction with a cytoplasmic receptor, the hormone enters the nucleus where it binds, either by itself or in association with the receptor or other proteins, to a specific site on the DNA. Exactly how it then induces transcription is still not clear, but one hormone can invoke both positive and negative control mechanisms. A well-studied example of this is the *estrogen*-mediated induction of ovalbumin mRNA synthesis in the *chicken oviduct*.

EXAMPLE 9.41   What other mechanisms exist for controlling gene expression in eukaryotes?

The separation of transcription and translation means there are many more opportunities for control in eukaryotes. For example, expression can be controlled at a *posttranscriptional* level. The cell can alter the rate at which RNA transcripts are processed while still within the nucleus. It is known that RNA is not transported across the nuclear membrane until all introns are spliced out. A more subtle form of control involves *alternative modes of splicing* of a particular transcript. Certain splice sites may be blocked so that different exons are excluded from the mature mRNA. There are now many known examples (about 60% of human genes) where this occurs to yield a great diversity of mRNA molecules from a single gene.

EXAMPLE 9.42　Cells can also alter the rate at which mRNA molecules are degraded. The sequences involved in regulating mRNA stability are usually in the 3′ untranslated region. Some elements in this region, such as AU-rich elements (AREs), bind proteins that recruit *RNA hydrolyzing nucleases*, whereas other elements recruit proteins that protect the mRNA from degradation.

　Genes involved in iron uptake and storage are coordinately controlled at several levels in response to the concentration of iron in the cell. When iron is low, the cell increases expression of transferrin that promotes iron uptake. Its mRNA has a stem loop structure in the 3′ untranslated region that binds the enzyme *aconitase*, which protects the mRNA from degradation. Ferritin lowers the concentration of free iron by sequestering it, so it is not required when iron concentrations are low. In this situation, aconitase binds to the 5′ untranslated region of ferritin mRNA and prevents translation. When iron concentrations rise again, aconitase can no longer bind to either mRNA, transferrin mRNA is degraded and ferritin mRNA is translated, so iron in the cell is restored to a normal concentration.

EXAMPLE 9.43　In 2006, a Nobel Prize was awarded for the discovery of RNA interference (RNAi). This is an exquisitely specific and sensitive process in which double-stranded RNA (dsRNA) guides distinct nucleases to degrade only mRNA that shares its sequence. As dsRNA is not a normal component of the *transcriptome*, it is believed that RNAi is part of a *genome surveillance system* that is used to repress transposons and viruses that have dsRNA as part of their replication cycle. Similar short sequences of RNA, called *microRNAs*, repress translation when they are bound to almost-complementary sequences in the 3′ untranslated region of mRNA.

EXAMPLE 9.44　Perhaps one of the best-known examples of a special form of control of protein concentration in eukaryotes is that of *translational control* of *globin* synthesis; this ensures that almost equal amounts of heme and globin are synthesized for the production of hemoglobin. Globin is synthesized in *reticulocytes* (Chap. 1, Prob. 1.1) which have no nucleus, only a pool of already transcribed mRNA, and therefore cannot use transcriptional or other modes of control. Control of globin synthesis from the pool of globin-enriched mRNA is related to the level of *hemin* (Fe III-protoporphyrin; Fig. 14-30) in the cell. When the globin concentration is low, heme accumulates and is oxidized to hemin. Excess hemin inactivates a *translational inhibitor* of protein synthesis. The inhibitor is a *protein kinase* that *phosphorylates* and *inactivates* eIF2, one of the initiation factors involved in translation. Inactivation of the kinase prevents the phosphorylation of eIF2 and therefore permits initiation of globin translation (Example 9.31). In contrast, an excess of globin prevents the accumulation of heme and its oxidation to hemin. As a result, the kinase is active, and the subsequent phosphorylation of eIF2 prevents translation of the globin chain. This homeostatic mechanism can only operate in cells such as reticulocytes that are dedicated predominantly to the production of only one type of protein. Inhibition of translation by phosphorylation of eIF2 can also be triggered in response to stressors such as hypoxia, infection, and starvation.

　The most important form of regulation of protein production occurs at the level of transcription. The human genome is 1000 times larger than that of *E. coli,* but the number of genes is only about 50 times greater. All the proteins are, on average, no larger. So what does this extra DNA do? The answer is that it is possible that much of the eukaryotic genome is involved in gene regulation, i.e., the "decision" *to transcribe DNA or not*. Enhancer elements clearly play a role in this process. Some elements, called locus control regions (LCRs), many of which also function as enhancers, maintain large regions of chromatin in an open structure that is accessible to the transcription machinery. Open chromatin is called *euchromic* as opposed to *heterochromic*. Heterochromatin is generally made up of repetitive, or otherwise transcriptionally inactive, DNA. The LCRs are tissue-specific; they only operate in the cell type in which the gene is selected to be active. It appears that most genes in eukaryotic cells are maintained in an inactive state except those in which transcription is activated by specific *positive regulatory mechanisms*. Transforming particular regions of chromatin into an open configuration in particular cell types may be the major means by which gene expression is regulated in eukaryotes.

9.14　Techniques to Measure Gene Expression

Question:　The differential expression of genes regulates the development of a single cell to a multicellular organism, determines the response of cells to external signals, and distinguishes a brain cell from a bone marrow cell, and a healthy cell from a diseased cell. How can differences in gene expression be measured?

Gene expression refers to the production of mRNA that may be reflected in the presence of the corresponding protein. A variety of quantitative and qualitative methods are used to detect the abundance and diversity of mRNA or proteins within a cell. Generally, these rely on the use of a *labeled probe* molecule to detect the presence of a specific RNA sequence or protein among the *total transcriptome* or *proteome* isolated from the cell. In the case of RNA, the probe is often a complementary nucleic acid sequence which hybridizes only to the sequence of interest by base-pairing. To detect a particular protein, antibodies are employed which bind specific regions, known as *epitopes*, on a protein. The *label*, which permits visualization of the probe, often emits a radioactive signal, is fluorescent, or is an enzyme that catalyzes the formation of a colored product (a *chromophore*). The intensity of the signal from a label is proportional to the amount of specific RNA or protein to which the probe binds, and it can be quantified relative to a standard sample of known concentration. Gel electrophoresis is used to determine the size of the detected molecule. To study the function of regulatory sequences, the gene under its control can be replaced by, or fused to, a *reporter gene*. These are genes whose protein products are readily detected. The enzyme β-galactosidase is often used for this purpose as it catalyzes the formation of a blue product from a colorless substrate (X-gal). Fluorescent proteins (*fluorochromes*, e.g., aequorin), originally isolated from jellyfish and corals, are now commonly used as reporters and are available in a range of colors for simultaneous detection of multiple signals.

Measuring Changes in Transcription: Detecting RNA

A number of techniques are used to detect a particular RNA species that may be present at low concentrations in a mixture of other RNA sequences.

With a *northern blot*, named for its similarity to the Southern blot, total RNA (or total mRNA) is isolated from samples and run on an electrophoresis gel to separate sequences by their size. The RNA from the gel is then immobilized by transfer to a nylon membrane and incubated with a DNA probe labeled with ^{32}P. The probe molecule *hybridizes* only to the complementary sequence, which can then be visualized on the gel by exposing an X-ray film to it.

A more sensitive detection technique is the RNase protection assay (RPA). The *transcriptome* (mRNA) is isolated from cell samples and hybridized in solution to a *labeled antisense RNA probe*. A *single-strand-specific RNase* is added, and only double-stranded regions (where the probe has hybridized to target RNA) are protected from degradation. The sample is then subjected to electrophoresis, and the labeled probe, protecting target RNA, is detected on X-ray film. As RNA hybridizes to RNA with high affinity, this technique is very *sensitive* (able to detect low abundances of transcripts) and capable of high *resolution* (able to distinguish between similar sequences).

Both *northern blots* and RPAs detect the presence and size of a particular RNA sequence, and relative changes in expression levels can be inferred from the intensity of the autoradiography signal. A more accurately *quantitative* method of detecting changes in transcription is the reverse transcriptase polymerase chain reaction (RT-PCR). Reverse transcriptase is used to make a *cDNA* copy of the isolated transcriptome. PCR (Fig. 8-16) is then performed with primers that amplify only the sequences of interest, using the cDNA as a template. Quantification is achieved by including a fluorescent dye that binds only to double-stranded PCR products. In this way, the intensity of fluorescence is proportional to the amount of the product, which in turn is proportional to the amount of original RNA extracted from the sample. As each cycle of PCR results in a doubling of the product, the number of cycles taken to reach a *threshold* level of fluorescence is lower for more abundant transcripts. As a result of the amplification process, RT-PCR is *extraordinarily sensitive* and can theoretically detect a particular RNA from a single cell.

EXAMPLE 9.45 The preceding techniques require that the RNA sequence of interest be known so that a complementary probe or primer can be designed and synthesized. Is there an experimental technique that can detect changes in expression from multiple unknown genes?

Yes. A microarray is a glass slide onto which DNA representing up to 30,000 genes is bound in distinct spots, with each spot consisting of a different gene. To detect differences in gene expression between two cell samples, RNA is extracted from each and reverse-transcribed to yield cDNA. Each cDNA sample is labeled with a different fluorescent dye, mixed, and then hybridized to the DNA on the *microarray slide*. Each cDNA competes for binding to the DNA at each spot; thus the relative amounts of original RNA expressed from a gene can be inferred from the relative intensity of each dye at the corresponding gene spot.

EXAMPLE 9.46　You are interested in which genes change expression in response to a particular drug. cDNA prepared from cells treated with the drug is labeled with a red fluorescent dye, and cDNA from an untreated control is labeled with a green dye. The samples are mixed in equal concentrations and hybridized to genes spotted on a DNA-microarray slide. What can be concluded about a gene that results in a red spot on the array?

The red-labeled cDNA must be more abundant as it competes more successfully for binding to the DNA at that spot. It follows that the gene represented at that spot was more highly expressed in the treated sample. Similarly, a green spot would indicate a gene whose expression was reduced (down-regulated) by the drug. A gene whose expression is unchanged is represented by a yellow spot. A gene that is not expressed in either sample will result in a black or brown spot on the array, while a white spot indicates that the signal is overexposed because excess sample was loaded onto the DNA array.

Measuring Changes in Translation: Detecting Protein

Specific proteins can be detected and quantified from a mixture of proteins in a variety of ways by using gel electrophoresis and antibodies, direct functional assays, and construction of fusion proteins with tags that are easy to detect.

When a protein of interest is an enzyme, one of the most straightforward methods of detection is an enzyme assay. As long as the substrate is used in excess, the amount of enzyme present will be proportional to the rate of either the disappearance of the substrate or the appearance of its product. Synthetic substrates that form readily detectable colored compounds have been developed for this purpose. Antibodies used to detect proteins can also be visualized by conjugation with an enzyme that catalyzes formation of a colored product.

By modifying the techniques of *Southern* and *northern blots*, the *western blot* is a reasonably inexpensive and simple method to determine relative amounts and size of a particular protein in a mixture. Rather than a nucleic acid probe, the blot is incubated with a *primary antibody* that binds only to the protein of interest. Generally, the label is attached to a *secondary antibody* that binds the invariant fragment of the primary antibody. In this way, a band (or bands) representing the protein of interest is visualized.

Another technique, the *enzyme-linked immunosorbent assay* (ELISA), combines the specificity of antibodies with the sensitivity of an enzyme assay. The ELISA can be performed in a variety of combinations that involve either a specific antibody or the total cellular protein immobilized on a solid support, such as the wells of a plastic microplate. In one version of the method, the *sandwich ELISA*, the primary antibody is bound to the wells. When a mixture of proteins is added, the protein of interest binds to the antibody, and other proteins are washed away. A second labeled antibody, specific to a different epitope on the protein, is added, and the amount of signal is proportional to the amount of the particular protein in the sample. The method can be modified to detect specific antibodies in a mixture by using their antigen as the *immobilized bait*. ELISAs also have the advantage of being able to be performed in 96-well plates so many samples can be analyzed in one experiment.

Radio immunoassays (RIAs) are highly sensitive tests that rely on detection of protein by a radioactively labeled antibody. The amount of antigen bound to a microplate can be quantified by a γ-ray counter. Due to the expense and special precautions required with the use of radioactivity, this technique has largely been replaced by ELISAs.

EXAMPLE 9.47　Why are both primary and secondary antibodies used in western blots and ELISAs? Why is the primary antibody not simply labeled directly?

The primary antibody that recognizes the protein of interest is often *monoclonal* (identical antibodies to one specific epitope on a protein). The addition of a label may interfere with the specificity of binding. In contrast, secondary antibodies are generally *polyclonal* and recognize all other antibodies made by a single animal species. Thus, if the primary antibody was produced in rabbits, the secondary antibodies to be used should be antirabbit. This means that the secondary antibodies can be used to detect many different primary antibodies, avoiding the time-consuming and expensive process of labeling multiple primary antibodies. The use of secondary antibodies also provides *signal amplification*.

EXAMPLE 9.48　Are there any techniques that can detect where a gene is expressed within a cell or tissue?

Yes. A thin slice of tissue can be fixed to a microscope slide and incubated with a specific labelled probe molecule that hybridizes only to the transcript or protein of interest. The probe can be complementary DNA or antisense RNA; when RNA is the target, this is called *in situ hybridization* (ISH). Proteins in a tissue slice can be expressed as recombinant tagged fusion proteins or detected by antibodies; the latter is called *in situ immunocytochemistry*. The label can be radioactive, such as ^{32}P or commonly the more precise ^3H, fluorescent (FISH), or an enzyme that produces a colored product. The signal is then recorded by light microscopy to permit localization of the transcript or protein.

9.15 Techniques to Study Gene Function

Question: How do we study what function(s) a particular gene has in a cell?

One of the most informative ways to investigate the function of a gene is to determine its effect in vivo, by artificially introducing DNA into the cells of an organism. Such DNA is called a *transgene* (transferred gene), and such organisms are known as transgenic. Transgenes can be used to investigate gene function either by introducing a new gene, new regulatory regions, or a mutated version of an endogenous gene, or by inactivating an endogenous gene. A new or enhanced gene activity conferred by a transgene is known as a *gain-of-function mutation*, whereas a *loss-of-function mutation* results in reduced or abolished gene function.

Common transgenic animals, in order of complexity, include baker's yeast (*Saccharomyces cerevisiae*), the nematode worm (*Caenorhabditis elegans*), the fruit fly (*Drosophila melanogaster*), and the mouse (*Mus musculus*). Evolutionary conservation means that their genes share a degree of homology with human genes, so that discoveries about function made with these organisms frequently apply to humans. While similar genetic manipulations can be performed in vitro using cell culture, transgenic organisms provide more physiologically relevant data, resulting from the interaction of gene products with all components of an intact organism. Transgenic organisms therefore provide models to explore gene function, gene control, and human diseases.

In the early 1980s, methods were developed to introduce new or modified genetic material into eukaryotic cells and subsequently to generate mice with introduced foreign DNA. Following *microinjection* into the pronucleus of a fertilized egg, the foreign DNA incorporates in random locations into the genome; and following implantation into a surrogate mother, the egg develops into a mature organism. Transgenic mice aid understanding of the function of genes and the products they encode, although the usefulness of this method is limited as the location in the genome where the *transgene* integrates is unable to be controlled or predicted. As the actual site of integration influences the expression rate of genes, random insertion of a transgene can lead to an unpredictable *variety of phenotypes*. In addition, if a transgene randomly inserts into an endogenous gene, or its control region, the normal function of the endogenous gene can be disrupted; this is called *insertional mutagenesis*.

To overcome problems associated with random integration, the technique has been modified so a transgene can be targeted to a specific locus in the genome. The developers of this targeted mutation technique (Mario Cappechi, Martin Evans, and Oliver Smithies) were awarded a Nobel Prize in 2007. Crucially, the transgene is flanked by regions that are homologous to the endogenous locus to facilitate site-specific recombination. The transgene is also designed with *positive and negative selectable markers* so that cells that have undergone homologous recombination of the transgene can be detected (Fig. 9-19). The transgene is transferred into embryonic stem cells which, after selection for homologous recombination, are reintroduced into a blastula to generate a transgenic organism. Embryonic stem cells are pluripotent, which means they can develop into any cell type of an organism.

Targeted mutation technology is commonly used to determine the effect of eliminating a particular gene. This is known as a gene *knockout*: a specific endogenous gene is replaced with an inactivated copy (Fig. 9-19). A knockout transgene construct typically contains an antibiotic resistance gene (for example, neomycin resistance; neoR) interrupting a copy of an exon of the endogenous gene. This marker has a dual role of inactivating the target gene (loss of function) and permitting selection of cells containing the vector (positive selection). As there is a high incidence of random (nonhomologous) integration, the transgene typically also includes an additional marker for negative selection. The negative marker is located outside the region of homology, and therefore does not integrate when the transgene construct has undergone homologous integration. A typical negative marker is the thymidine kinase gene. Cells in which the transgene has undergone random integration express thymidine kinase positive and die when exposed to the prodrug *gancyclovir*, which is converted to a cytotoxic derivative by thymidine kinase.

The technique of targeted mutation can be modified to replace an endogenous gene with a copy that contains a mutation; this is called *gene knock-in*. This procedure permits investigators to examine the effects of changes in the amino acid sequence of the gene product. The endogenous gene is not inactivated but contains the introduced mutation. The principles of vector design and generation of the transgenic organism are similar to knockout targeted mutations. One important difference is that the antibiotic resistance gene is not located in an exon; rather it is located as a *cassette* with its own promoter in an intron so as not to disrupt expression of the transgene.

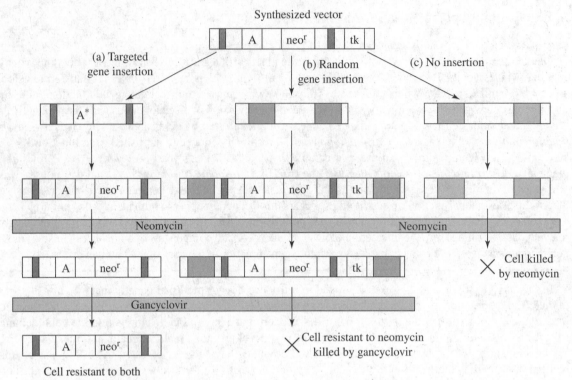

Fig. 9-19   Design and selection of a knockout transgene developed to replace an endogenous gene and eliminate its function. A denotes the transgene; neo^r, the neomycin resistance gene; tk, *thymidine kinase*. The transgene typically has two selectable markers, an inactivated copy of the endogenous gene, and regions of homology to the endogenous gene. (a) When integration has occurred at regions of homology, the endogenous gene is replaced by the inactive copy in the *transgene*. These cells survive neomycin treatment (positive selection) as they express the neomycin resistance gene that has replaced an exon of the endogenous gene. They also survive treatment with gancyclovir (negative selection) because the *thymidine kinase* gene, which is outside the region of homology, does not integrate during homologous recombination. (b) Cells in which the transgene has integrated randomly do not survive, as the thymidine kinase gene has integrated, and its product converts the nontoxic pro-drug gancyclovir to a cytotoxic derivative. (c) Cells in which the transgene has not integrated at all are not resistant to neomycin. Cells that survive both rounds of selection are used to generate the transgenic organism.

As an alternative to interrupting an endogenous gene using knockout technology, it is possible to down-regulate (i.e., *knockdown*) the expression of a gene with great specificity using RNA interference. Short double-stranded fragments of RNA that correspond to the gene of interest are added to cells where they act to guide specific nucleases to degrade homologous mRNA. Organisms can also be generated that carry transgenes that synthesize these short interfering RNAs for long-term knockdown of expression of specific genes. This technology has become so important that its discoverers (Andrew Fire and Craig Mello) were awarded a Nobel Prize in 2006.

EXAMPLE 9.49   How can essential genes be studied when eliminating their function may be lethal to a transgenic organism?

Conditional mutants can be produced in which the timing (temporal control) and/or location (spatial control) of gene expression is regulated. For example, it is possible to eliminate the function of a gene of interest only in a certain cell or tissue type by using the *Cre/lox* system. This system employs a site-specific recombination enzyme called *Cre recombinase*. This enzyme causes deletion of DNA that lies between specific sites called *loxP* sites. When loxP sites are engineered to flank a gene, Cre recombinase catalyzes the recombination between loxP sites, thus deleting the intervening gene sequence.

The Cre/lox system requires the generation of two separate lines of transgenic mice that are crossed to produce a conditional knockout in the offspring as follows (Fig. 9-20). One parental strain of transgenic mice is generated expressing

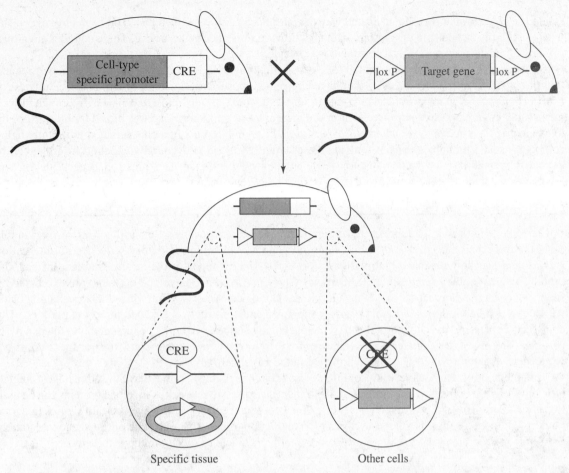

Fig. 9-20   The Cre/lox system for generating tissue-specific *deletion* of transgenes.

Cre-recombinase under the control of a *tissue- or cell-specific promoter*. A second line is generated in which the gene to be deleted in the offspring is replaced by a transgene that contains a copy of the gene surrounded by loxP sites; the gene is said to be *floxed*. These loxP sites are typically incorporated into the introns that are immediately flanking an exon, so they do not interfere with expression of the gene in this line. In the offspring that are produced by crossing these two strains, the gene surrounded by loxP sites is excised only in cells that express Cre-recombinase. Expression of the target gene is unaffected in cells that do not express Cre-recombinase.

EXAMPLE 9.50   Expression of a particular gene may be lethal to a transgenic organism in its embryonic form. How can such a gene be studied later in development?

To control the timing of gene expression, an *inducible system* can be used as a type of molecular switch. In this case, the transgene is designed so that it is only expressed when its promoter is bound by a *transcriptional activator* (the effector). Expression is inducible because binding of the effector is reversible; its conformation is altered in the presence of a specific inducer. A common inducible approach uses modified elements of the prokaryote tetracycline-inducible (tet) operon (Example 9.38). In this *tet-on system*, the effector is expressed in an inactive form, and cannot activate transcription of the transgene until the drug tetracycline (the inducer) is administered. By varying the concentration of tetracycline, the level of expression can also be controlled.

Question: Both in vivo and in vitro studies of gene function initially require introduction of new DNA into cells. Such methods predate the development of transgenic organisms. What methods are available for transferring DNA into cells today?

When the aim is to produce large amounts of transgene DNA or protein, the transgene vector (usually a plasmid) is *transformed* into bacteria for *amplification*. The bacterial membranes are first permeabilized (said to be made *competent*) and incubated with the plasmid. The cells are then plated on a *selective* agar plate, where only cells that contain the plasmid with an antibiotic resistance gene survive. These colonies are grown in culture, and the transgenic DNA or protein is extracted.

DNA can also be transferred into eukaryotic cells, usually with the aim of studying the function or regulation of a gene, or to produce proteins that have appropriate posttranslational modifications. The process of *transfection* uses calcium phosphate, or commercially available cationic lipids, to carry DNA through the cell membrane. DNA can also enter the cell after the membrane is temporarily permeablized by brief exposure to an electric field in a process called *electroporation*. Foreign DNA is often only retained transiently in the cell, as it usually remains *episomal* (outside the chromosome) and is eventually expelled from the cell or degraded. A small fraction of the transfected cells maintain stable transgene expression, because the foreign DNA has become integrated into the chromosome. Transgenes often carry antibiotic resistance genes to permit selection of cells that retain the transgene.

For more long-term gene expression, foreign DNA can be introduced to cells using *viral vectors*. In this case, the transgene construct is based on the viral genome, retaining regulatory sequence(s), integration signals, and packaging signals, but modified so no genes for viral coat proteins are included. Instead, the proteins that assemble to make the viral particles (such as *capsid* and envelope proteins) are expressed by separate packaging constructs. The transgene and packaging constructs are introduced into packaging cells, which express the viral coat proteins, but only the transgene construct is packaged into viral particles. The constructs expressing viral coat proteins have no packaging signals, so cannot be included into the new viral particles. This means that when a target cell is *transduced* by the viral particles, only the transgene construct is transferred, and the virus is unable to replicate in the target cell.

Viral methods of gene delivery are commonly used for gene therapy, as they have the advantage of higher efficiency of gene delivery and long-term stable transgene expression. Specific envelope proteins can be used to determine *tropism* of the viral particles, i.e., affinity for target cell type. However, certain viruses integrate randomly into the genome, so they can disrupt the regulation of genes near the site of transgene integration. Host immune responses to viral vectors can pose another obstacle to successful gene therapy.

SOLVED PROBLEMS

THE GENETIC CODE

9.1. Assuming that the first three nucleotides define the first codon, what is the peptide sequence coded for by (a) UAAUAGUGAUAA and (b) UUAUUGCUUCUCCUACUG?

SOLUTION

(a) None. These three codons are not translatable, they are signals for chain termination.
(b) (Leu)$_6$. This illustrates the degeneracy of the genetic code for leucine (Table 9-1); there are six codons for leucine, the most for any of the amino acids.

9.2. From within the sequence below, identify two possible sites from which initiation of translation could commence; and write out the sequence of the first three amino acids. AAUUAUGUUUCCAUGUCCACCU

SOLUTION

AUG is the most common initiation codon. The first one encountered in the sequence would give the following sequence for nine nucleotides from this position: AUGUUUCCA. This codes for Met-Phe-Pro. Further along there is the sequence AUGUCCACC that codes for Met-Ser-Thr.

9.3. Within the antisense strand of the DNA in a gene, the codon sequence ATA is changed by mutation to ATG. Following replication of the DNA, what change in the polypeptide product would this cause?

SOLUTION

The antisense strand of DNA gives the same sequence as the mRNA, except for T being present in place of U, in the DNA. Thus the codon will change from AUA to AUG. This causes isoleucine to be replaced by methionine.

9.4. An mRNA contains the following translated sequence, with the reading frame defined by the grouping of triplets.

AUG.CUC.ACU.UCA.GGG.AGA.AGC

(a) What is the amino acid sequence of the resulting polypeptide?
(b) If the first C (nucleotide encoding cytosine) encountered is deleted from the sequence, what new amino acid sequence will result?

SOLUTION

(a) The original sequence will give Met-Leu-Thr-Ser-Gly-Arg-Ser.
(b) Point deletions lead to frame shift mutations. The new sequence will be

AUG.UCA.CUU.CAG.GGA.GAA.GC

which codes for Met-Ser-Leu-Gln-Gly-Glu.

9.5. The DNA of the virus φX174 appears to contain insufficient nucleotide residues to code for the nine different proteins that are its gene products. How does this arise?

SOLUTION

In this case, the same sequence of nucleotides codes for more than one protein, by the use of more than one *reading frame*. Thus, the sequence of codons for one protein is out of phase with the sequence of the overlapping gene.

```
Gene E product            Met - Val  - Arg -
                           |      |      |       |
                         G U U U A U G G U A C G C
                           |    |    |    |       |
Gene D product           - Val -  Tyr -  Gly - Thr -
```

9.6. The fidelity of DNA replication is enhanced by a proofreading function, whereby errors in the complementary sequence are excised and repaired. Why is a similar mechanism not found in protein synthesis?

SOLUTION

Errors in protein synthesis are not so serious. A single defective protein molecule will, in general, not cause deleterious effects. While such a protein may not function properly or may be unstable, and may represent a waste of energy to the cell, however, such errors do not become perpetuated in future generations.

9.7. The template strand of a double helical segment of DNA contains the sequence

5′ GCTACGGTAGCGCAA 3′

(a) What sequence of mRNA can be transcribed from this strand?
(b) What amino acid sequence would be coded for, assuming that the entire transcript could be translated?

SOLUTION

(a) The transcribed RNA would be complementary to the above strand and would have U replacing T:

3′ CGAUGCCAUCCGUU 5′

Written in the 5′ → 3′ direction, this becomes

5′ UUGCGCUACCGUAGC 3′

(b) Translation occurs in the 5′ → 3′ direction, resulting in the following sequence:

-Leu-Arg-Tyr-Arg-Ser-

DNA TRANSCRIPTION IN BACTERIA

9.8. Would it be possible for a single strand of DNA to function both as *sense-* and *antisense* strands with regard to transcription?

SOLUTION

Yes. For this to occur, transcription by RNA polymerase would proceed through the segment of duplex DNA in *opposite directions* and use different promoters. Each strand of the duplex DNA would function as both *sense* and *antisense* strands, but for two different RNA transcripts.

9.9. Which of the following could not represent the 5′ end of an RNA transcript?
(a) pppApGpCpU···
(b) pppUpCpGpA···
(c) pppCpApGpA···

SOLUTION

Only (a) is possible, because RNA polymerase, when initiating transcription, always incorporates a pppA or a pppG in the first position.

9.10. Is the Pribnow box the same as a bacterial promoter?

SOLUTION

No. The Pribnow box is only *part* of the sequence that defines the promoter. It corresponds to the −10 region of ~7 nucleotides. There is another region centered on the −35 position that is also an essential part of the promoter.

9.11. Which subunits of bacterial RNA polymerase are needed for initiation of transcription from a promoter?

SOLUTION

First, the σ subunit is required for promoter binding and the formation of an *open promoter complex*. Subsequent to this the β-subunit, which can bind the inhibitor *rifampicin*, is essential for the formation of the first phosphodiester bond.

9.12. Is the transcription termination sequence incorporated into the RNA transcript?

SOLUTION

Yes. After the RNA polymerase transcribes the *inverted repeat* sequence, it is the ability of this region to form a *hairpin* in the single-strand transcript that is responsible, at least in part, for terminating the chain.

9.13. Can a single RNA transcript in bacteria carry information from more than one gene?

SOLUTION

Yes. Very frequently groups of adjacent genes are transcribed from a single promoter to give an RNA molecule that carries information for all of them. If this information is to be expressed as protein, as is normally the case, the single RNA molecule is called *polycistronic mRNA*. A cistron is a genetic unit equivalent to a gene. Each gene has its own start codon and ribosome binding sites from which translation of separate proteins can be initiated. Collections of rRNA and tRNA genes are usually transcribed as single units. In these cases the primary transcript is modified and subsequently cut by nucleases to yield individual rRNA and tRNA molecules. This is one example of processing of primary transcripts that is much more common in eukaryotes.

9.14. How many transcription termination sequences would be present in a polycistronic mRNA?

SOLUTION

Polycistronic mRNA, which forms as a primary transcript in bacteria, is a continuous length of RNA that is transcribed from a single promoter. Therefore it will contain only one normal termination sequence, ignoring a possible attenuator sequence prior to the first initiation codon.

9.15. Does processing of RNA transcripts occur in bacteria?

SOLUTION

Processing refers to modification of the primary transcripts that are formed by RNA polymerase. In bacteria it is restricted to the transcripts that contain rRNA and tRNA. In these cases, larger transcripts are chemically modified and then cut down to the smaller mature forms of rRNA and tRNA by nucleases.

DNA TRANSCRIPTION IN EUKARYOTES

9.16. How many types of *RNA polymerase* might you expect to find in a eukaryotic cell?

SOLUTION

Four. In the nucleus there are RNA polymerases I, II and III. In mitochondria there is another RNA polymerase that is similar to *bacterial* RNA polymerase.

9.17. With respect to the general mechanism of RNA chain growth, are there any differences between the various types of RNA polymerase in eukaryotic cells?

SOLUTION

No. All RNA polymerases use duplex DNA as a template and copy one of the strands, synthesizing RNA in the $5' \rightarrow 3'$ direction using *ribonucleoside triphosphates* as substrates.

9.18. Does transcription in eukaryotes yield polycistronic mRNA?

SOLUTION

No. This is in marked contrast to the situation in bacterial mRNA that may contain multiple Shine-Dalgarno sequences that permit binding by ribosomes to initiate translation from multiple start sites. In eukaryotes, the mRNA that codes for protein is *monocistronic* and hence codes for a single protein. One explanation for why this comes about is that each eukaryotic mRNA molecule has only a single 5' cap that recruits ribosomes, and thus translation cannot be initiated from multiple start sites on the same mRNA molecule, although alternative start sites may be used.

9.19. Would the major transcriptional activity of a eukaryotic cell be affected by α-amanitin?

SOLUTION

No. The most abundant RNA component of a cell is always rRNA. The rRNA genes are transcribed by RNA polymerase I that is resistant to α-amanitin.

9.20. Is it possible that α-amanitin exerts its inhibitory effect on certain eukaryotic RNA polymerases by affecting the availability of its substrates?

SOLUTION

No. All RNA polymerases use the same substrates, and α-amanitin inhibits some RNA polymerases and not others.

9.21. Does monocistronic mRNA of eukaryotes represent a primary RNA transcript?

SOLUTION

No. In the vast majority of cases, the mRNA in eukaryotes is formed by the processing (modification and splicing) of primary transcripts.

INHIBITORS OF TRANSCRIPTION

9.22. Would actinomycin D be expected to inhibit transcription of rRNA and tRNA genes, and those that code for protein products?

SOLUTION

Yes. Actinomycin D inhibits transcription by binding to the DNA template. In doing so, it recognizes a common structural feature of all duplex DNAs, binding by intercalation between stacked base pairs.

9.23. The bacterial RNA polymerase inhibitors *rifampicin* and *streptolydigin* each bind to the same subunit of the enzyme, but their overall effect on the activity of the enzyme is different. Why is this so?

SOLUTION

Each of these inhibitors binds exclusively to the β-subunit of RNA polymerase. This subunit is involved in both initiation and elongation of RNA chain growth. Rifampicin binds to the subunit in such a way to affect only the initiation step; it has no effect on elongation. Streptolydigin, on the other hand, binds in a manner that blocks *both* activities.

THE mRNA TRANSLATION MACHINERY

9.24. How many different rRNA and tRNA species that are present in a cell are actively involved in mRNA translation?

SOLUTION

At most there are 3 to 4 types of rRNA, depending on whether the cells are bacterial or eukaryotic. On the other hand there will be *at least* 20 types of tRNA, there being at least one for each amino acid, in any type of cell.

9.25. Why would it be necessary for all tRNAs to have similar overall dimensions?

SOLUTION

All tRNAs must have similar overall dimensions because, during translation, all activated tRNAs interact singly and very precisely with the same sites on the ribosome. The anticodon is positioned at one end of the tRNA to enable interaction of tRNA with the bound mRNA, and the amino acid at the other end is precisely located on the surface of the ribosome with respect to the location of the bound *peptidyl transferase*.

9.26. Would it be possible for a single tRNA molecule to accommodate all the codons for leucine?

SOLUTION

Leucine has six codons, the largest number for any amino acid. A single tRNA can accommodate more than one codon because the *wobble hypothesis* allows for up to three different nucleotides, at only the third position in the codon, to interact with a single nucleotide in the anticodon. The fact that there are six codons means that they must differ at other than the third position, so they could not be accommodated by a single anticodon in a particular tRNA molecule.

9.27. *Aminoacyl-tRNA synthetase* operates in two steps to bring about the attachment of an amino acid to its cognate tRNA. Does it possess specificity to either the amino acid or the tRNA at each of these steps?

SOLUTION

In the first step (amino acid activation) the enzyme recognizes its appropriate amino acid. In the second step the amino acid must be attached to the correct tRNA, and it is therefore essential that the latter be recognized by the enzyme. Sometimes, at a low frequency, a similar but incorrect amino acid is incorporated during the first step; when this occurs, the amino acid is released when the enzyme recognizes its appropriate tRNA.

RNA TRANSLATION IN BACTERIA

9.28. What is the *leader region* or *leader sequence* of bacterial mRNA?

SOLUTION

The *leader* is the region between the 5′ end of the RNA and the *initiation codon*. It contains untranslated sequences that are involved in ribosome binding. The latter step is essential for translation of the message into a polypeptide. It is also known as the *5′ untranslated region* (UTR).

9.29. Why does $tRNA_m^{Met}$ not function in initiation of polypeptide synthesis from an appropriate AUG codon?

SOLUTION

During initiation of translation, the methionyl-tRNA species, $tRNA_f^{Met}$ is used exclusively. Presumably, the unique nucleotide sequence of this tRNA molecule is required for the initial interaction with the small ribosomal subunit, the leader region of mRNA, initiation factors, and GTP, to give the first *initiation complex*. It is unlikely that formylation, which can only occur with methionyl- $tRNA_f^{Met}$, is essential for initiation, as this is not the case in eukaryotes. Therefore, it appears that $tRNA_m^{Met}$ is excluded from initiation because essential structural requirements in the tRNA are not present.

9.30. How many ATP *equivalents* are consumed with the incorporation of an amino acid into a polypeptide?

SOLUTION

One ATP is used for activation of the tRNA, and then one GTP is hydrolyzed on binding of the aminoacyl-tRNA binding to the A site on the ribosome, and another GTP is hydrolyzed on translocation. Thus the equivalent of three ATPs are used for each amino acid incorporated, ignoring initiation. Note that in amino acid activation, the products are AMP and PPi, the latter being hydrolyzed to Pi to drive the reaction to completion. Thus the equivalent of four high-energy phosphate bonds are used for each amino acid incorporated into the growing polypeptide.

9.31. In translocation, the peptidyl-tRNA is shifted from the A site to the P site on the ribosome. What happens to the peptidyl-tRNA anticodon-codon interaction?

SOLUTION

This must remain undisturbed; and it is simpler to imagine that the whole ribosome moves by one codon position with respect to the peptidyl-tRNA-mRNA complex.

9.32. What major structural requirement for initiation of translation of eukaryotic mRNA does not exist in bacterial mRNA?

SOLUTION

During the processing of primary transcripts that are destined for mRNA formation in eukaryotes, a methylated guanine *cap* is attached to the 5′ end. This is essential for efficient initiation of translation of the mature eukaryotic mRNA, and it *does not occur in prokaryotes*. In prokaryotes, rRNA in the small ribosomal subunit binds first to the Shine-Dalgarno sequence of the mRNA, before binding tRNA. In eukaryotes, the ribosome binds first to the 5′ *cap* and then scans along the mRNA, using the tRNA to detect the AUG codon.

9.33. Is there any obvious reason why polysomes could not form in eukaryotes?

SOLUTION

In prokaryotes polysomes form as the result of the loading of sequential ribosomes at the 5′ end of mRNA, such that many ribosomes can progress along a single strand of mRNA at any one time. Polysomes can also form in eukaryotes; once the first ribosome has moved a significant distance from the ribosome binding site at the 5′ cap, there is no reason why a subsequent one should not be loaded through the normal sequence of events. In fact the classical finding of *five ribosomes* per globin message in reticulocytes seen in electron micrographs is testament to this fact. These polysomes look like rosettes of five dots in the images.

9.34. *Coupled transcription translation* in prokaryotes refers to the commencement of translation of an RNA molecule before its transcription from the DNA template is complete. Could such a situation arise in eukaryotes?

SOLUTION

Clearly, the answer is no. Transcription in eukaryotes must be completed within the nucleus. The mRNA that is finally produced is transported to the cytoplasm where it is translated into a polypeptide.

POSTTRANSLATIONAL MODIFICATION OF PROTEINS

9.35. When proteins are hydrolyzed with acid at high temperatures, they are broken down to their constituent amino acids. Usually the amino acid *cystine* is found among them, but cystine is not included among the amino acids listed in the dictionary of codons. Why?

SOLUTION

Cystine is composed of two molecules of cysteine that are linked through oxidation of —SH groups to give a disulfide, S—S bond. Such oxidation, which is important in stabilizing the folded structure of proteins, is a *posttranslational modification* of a protein. Thus, cystine is never incorporated, as such, into a polypeptide during translation, and there is no codon that corresponds to it.

9.36. The signal sequence on a protein that is destined for export from a cell is never located at the *C* terminus of the polypeptide chain. Why is this so?

SOLUTION

This is so because the signal sequence is required for passage of the polypeptide chain as it is being translated through the membrane of the endoplasmic reticulum. The *C* terminus is always synthesized last, and a signal sequence at this location would not allow the threading of the growing peptide through the membrane.

INHIBITORS OF TRANSLATION

9.37. Why does puromycin inhibit mRNA translation in both bacteria and eukaryotes?

SOLUTION

Puromycin is similar in structure to the 3′ end of aminoacyl-tRNAs, most notably that of phenylalanyl-tRNA, with which it competes during translation. The 3′ end of aminoacyl-tRNA molecules is the same in all organisms.

9.38. Chloramphenicol is used as an antibiotic to treat bacterial infection of animals, but it has some severe side effects. What might contribute to these?

SOLUTION

Chloramphenicol blocks translation of mRNA in bacteria by inhibiting the *peptidyl transferase* of the large ribosomal subunit. It does not interfere with the peptidyl transferase in the large subunit of eukaryotic ribosomes. However, the mitochondrion of animal cells contains ribosomes that are similar to bacterial ribosomes, and chloramphenicol blocks protein synthesis in this organelle. This may cause side effects in humans, such as deafness due to cell death in the acoustic nerves from a lack of ATP supply in them.

CONTROL OF GENE EXPRESSION

9.39. Why is control of expression of the *lac* operon in *E. coli* said to be an example of *negative* control?

SOLUTION

This is so because control of expression is brought about by modulating the effectiveness of a *negatively acting* agent, the *repressor*. In other words, expression of the *lac* operon is achieved through negating the effect of the repressor. In *positive* control systems, expression is achieved through the immediate effect of an agent that positively induces or increases expression. The *catabolic activator protein* is one example of a positive control protein.

9.40. Describe the effect of a mutation in the *lac operator* in the *lac* operon.

SOLUTION

Most mutations in the sequence of the operator reduce the affinity for the repressor. By reducing the ability of the repressor to bind, such a mutation will permit expression of the lac genes in the absence of the inducer. This outcome is called *constitutive expression* of the genes.

9.41. What would be needed for the coordinated control of expression, at the transcriptional level, of a number of genes that are not located next to one another on a chromosome?

SOLUTION

Each gene would need to have common regulatory elements, promoters, and/or operators, associated with it. In this way a single control factor, such as a repressor or *positively acting substance*, could influence all genes simultaneously.

9.42. Transcriptional control of globin synthesis in reticulocytes is not possible because transcription does not occur in these cells. Does this mean that the overall control of globin synthesis is completely lacking any aspect of transcriptional control?

SOLUTION

No. Prior to the formation of a reticulocyte from its precursor cell during the process of erythropoiesis there must have been a stage of preferential transcription of the globin genes to yield the globin-enriched mRNA of the reticulocyte.

TECHNIQUES TO MEASURE GENE EXPRESSION

9.43. Why are techniques that detect changes in DNA not used to measure changes in gene expression?

SOLUTION

Changes in gene expression are, by definition, reflected in changes in the concentrations of mRNA and usually protein. DNA is not altered by changes in gene expression. DNA is the same, with some exceptions, in every cell in an organism.

9.44. Consider a northern blot. Which strand of a *double-stranded DNA probe* would bind to the sample on the membrane?

SOLUTION

In northern blots, mRNA is separated by size on an electrophoresis gel, then immobilized on a nylon membrane. Therefore, it is the template (*antisense*) strand of the probe that will hybridize to the mRNA.

9.45. A particular RNA sequence prepared from liver cells takes 30 cycles of RT-PCR to reach a prescribed fluorescence threshold. The same sequence prepared from brain cells takes 34 cycles to reach the same threshold. How many fold difference is there in transcription of this gene between the two cell types?

SOLUTION

The sample from brain cells took four more cycles to reach the same amount of product as the liver cell sample. As each cycle involves a doubling of the PCR DNA product, there would have been $2^4 = 16$-fold less of the particular RNA in the brain cell sample than in the liver.

9.46. What major factor must be taken into account when designing primers for RT-PCR compared with conventional PCR?

SOLUTION

The template for RT-PCR is the cDNA copy of the *transcriptome*, i.e., RNA; therefore, primers must be complementary to regions that are present in mature mRNA. In practice, primers are designed to target *exons*. Conventional PCR has genomic DNA as its template, so primers can be made to target introns, exons, or regions that flank the gene of interest.

TECHNIQUES TO STUDY GENE FUNCTION

9.47. When producing a gene *knockout* in embryonic stem cells, which cells survive after treatment with neomycin?

SOLUTION

The cells that survive are those in which the *transgene* has been inserted. This includes both insertion by *homologous recombination* and *random integration*, as the neomycin resistance gene is within the region of homology. Cells in which the transgene has undergone random integration are subsequently killed by negative selection with gancyclovir, which is converted to a toxic form by thymidine kinase that is expressed in these cells.

9.48. In the Cre/lox system, why is the gene of interest not simply expressed from a tissue-specific promoter?

SOLUTION

This system is designed to eliminate, not express, the gene of interest in a tissue-specific manner. The gene of interest is intended to be expressed in all other tissues. Thus, *Cre recombinase*, and not the gene of interest, is expressed in certain tissues and catalyzes the deletion of DNA between loxP sites, only in those tissues.

9.49. How is a transgenic animal produced to carry an endogenous gene surrounded by *lox* sites?

SOLUTION

The transgene that has a copy of the endogenous gene surrounded by lox sites must insert into the genome to replace the targeted endogenous gene. Therefore, the transgene must be introduced into embryonic stem cells to permit selection of only those cells in which the transgene has undergone homologous recombination. In effect this is a knock-in mutation. In contrast, the transgenic line that carries the *Cre-recombinase gene* can be produced by microinjection of the transgene into the pronucleus of a fertilized egg. Random insertion of the transgene is sufficient because the promoter is tissue-specific.

9.50. Why are target cells that have been transduced with a viral vector unable to produce new infectious viral particles?

SOLUTION

The transducing viral particles are produced in *packaging cells* where the viral genes that encode packaging proteins do not have signals that permit their inclusion in new virus particles. Thus, the transducing virus particles do not contain or deliver any viral genes encoding packaging proteins to the target cells.

9.51. Other than for investigations of gene function, what are some other applications of transgenic technology?

SOLUTION

Transgenic technology has been developed to produce transgenic *livestock* and *plants* that have nutritional and medical value. These include the ability to produce medically useful recombinant proteins and antibodies on an industrial scale, as well as disease-resistant or vaccine-containing crops.

9.52. In the original version of the tetracycline-inducible system of *conditional transgenesis*, tetracycline prevents transgene expression. Suggest how this *tet-off* system is regulated, compared with the *tet-on* system in Example 9.50.

SOLUTION

In the *tet-off* system, the effector is expressed in an active form. It binds the *transgene promoter* and activates transcription in the absence of *tetracycline*. Therefore, tetracycline is continuously administered to the transgenic organism until transgene expression is required.

SUPPLEMENTARY PROBLEMS

9.53. Decode the following RNA sequence into the corresponding amino acid sequence:

CAU AUU ACU CAU GAA CGU GAA

9.54. The following occurs at the start of the coding sequence of a eukaryotic mRNA. For which amino acid sequence does it code?

GUG UUU UUU GUG UUU

9.55. The following segment of duplex DNA contains the region defining the start codon for a protein.

5′-GATGTCTCCT- 3′

3′-CTACAGAGGA- 5′

Identify the template strand.

9.56. Which is the most abundant RNA species in a cell?

9.57. DNA polymerase requires a primer on which to attach a new nucleotide unit for chain growth. Is a primer obligatory for RNA polymerase action?

9.58. For which process is a promoter needed, for the initiation of RNA synthesis or of polypeptide synthesis?

9.59. The Pribnow box occurs ~35 nucleotides upstream of the initiation codon, true or false?

9.60. The σ subunit of RNA polymerase is required only for initiation of transcription, true or false?

9.61. Is the *termination sequence* for transcription near the 5′ or 3′ end of the mRNA transcript?

9.62. Can monocistronic mRNA represent a primary transcription product of bacterial cells?

9.63. In which are enhancer sequences found, bacteria or eukaryotes?

9.64. Would *phosphorylation* of *histones* decrease or increase the net positive charge on such molecules?

9.65. Genes of eukaryotes are generally made up of introns and exons. Are both these sequences transcribed and translated?

9.66. Does splicing occur in DNA, RNA, or polypeptides?

9.67. Does capping of an RNA molecule occur before or after splicing?

9.68. Can an exon contain an initiation codon?

9.69. Does *rifampicin* inhibit the transcription of histone genes?

9.70. In what species of RNA do codons and anticodons occur?

9.71. Why is the tRNA molecule so large, when the codon is only three nucleotide residues long?

9.72. tRNA is a single-stranded molecule, but much of its structure is double helical. How is this possible?

9.73. Does the acceptor stem of a tRNA molecule contain the 3′ or 5′ end?

9.74. Are there more species of aminoacyl-tRNA synthetase than tRNA in a cell?

9.75. Which of the subunits of a ribosome recognizes the nontranslated leader sequence of mRNA?

9.76. Subsequent to the formation of the 70S initiation complex in bacteria, at what steps of translation is energy consumed in the form of high-energy phosphate bonds?

9.77. Are termination codons associated with termination of transcription or termination of translation?

9.78. Is the methylated cap on eukaryotic mRNA attached to the RNA while it is in the nucleus or in the cytoplasm?

9.79. What is the first translational product of the insulin gene?

9.80. Does a *signal peptidase* cleave the nontranslated leader sequence of mRNA?

9.81. Does a bacterial repressor molecule bind to the promoter or operator site adjacent to a gene in DNA?

9.82. For the *lac* operon, describe the effect of a mutation in the lac I repressor.

9.83. What is the difference between a repressor and a corepressor in relation to transcription?

9.84. What techniques can be used to monitor changes in the mRNA levels of a particular gene?

9.85. What technique can be used to detect differences in the mRNA levels in cells of multiple genes in different tissues?

9.86. What type of macromolecule is detected in a western blot?

9.87. What techniques can be used to monitor changes in the concentration of a particular protein?

ANSWERS TO SUPPLEMENTARY PROBLEMS

9.53. His-Ile-Thr-His-Glu-Arg-Glu. (By using the single-letter notation for amino acids (Table 9-1), this sequence reads HI THERE!)

9.54. Met-Phe-Phe-Val-Phe.

9.55. The lower strand.

9.56. Ribosomal RNA (rRNA).

9.57. No. The RNA polymerases can start chains de novo.

9.58. RNA synthesis.

9.59. False.

9.60. True.

9.61. Near the 3′ end.

9.62. Yes. (For example, the lac repressor gene of *E. coli* would give rise to monocistronic mRNA.)

9.63. Eukaryotes.

9.64. Phosphorylation would decrease the net positive charge.

9.65. No. Introns and exons are both transcribed, but only exons are translated.

9.66. RNA.

9.67. Before splicing

9.68. Yes. The first exon (closest to the 5′ end) of the mRNA must contain the initiation codon.

9.69. No. Histones occur in eukaryotes, and rifampicin blocks transcription only in bacteria.

9.70. Codons occur in mRNA and anticodons occur in tRNA.

9.71. The tRNA molecule must recognize not only the codon, but also specific regions of the ribosome, elongation factors, and the appropriate *aminoacyl-tRNA synthetase*, each of which involves cooperative interactions through noncovalent bonds.

9.72. The single tRNA chain folds back on itself to allow the formation of several segments of double helix through intrastrand base pairing.

9.73. It contains both.

9.74. There are more species of tRNA.

9.75. The small ribosomal subunit.

9.76. At two steps; the binding of charged tRNA and translocation after the formation of each peptide.

9.77. Termination of translation.

9.78. Capping of the RNA occurs before splicing and therefore must occur in the nucleus.

9.79. Preproinsulin.

7.80. No. The signal peptidase cleaves the translated signal peptide that directs the nascent protein to the endoplasmic reticulum.

9.81. It binds to the operator site.

9.82. Mutations in the lac I gene that produce a repressor that cannot bind to the operator will lead to constitutive expression of the protein, as expression cannot be repressed in the absence of an inducer. Mutations that prevent the repressor binding to the inducer will prevent the repressor from being released from the operator. This results in a noninducible phenotype.

9.83. A repressor molecule can bind to an operator and block transcription. A corepressor is a compound that binds to a protein to give a functional repressor that can then bind to an operator.

9.84. Northern blot, real-time PCR, or RNase protection assays. These techniques require that the sequence sought be *known*, because the probe must be made to be complementary to the mRNA.

9.85. Microarrays. The cDNA copies of mRNA from two or more tissue samples can be labeled with different dyes. The cDNA of both samples is then simultaneously hybridized to thousands of genes that are bound to separate spots on a glass slide. The intensity of each dye at each spot is indicative of the ratio of each particular mRNA sequence in each sample.

9.86. Western blots use labeled antibodies to recognize and detect a particular protein in a mixture of proteins that are separated by electrophoresis according to molecular size.

9.87. ELISA, RIA, or western blots. If the protein of interest is an enzyme, an *assay* that detects the appearance of the product or disappearance of the substrate can be used.

CHAPTER 10

Molecular Basis of Energy Balance

10.1   Introduction to Metabolism

Question: Living systems require energy to build their own forms and structures, and in many bacteria and animals this construction and movement is obvious, but cell movement and cytokinesis take place even in plants. How is this energy supply achieved?

It is done via metabolism (Greek *metabole*, change) in which small molecules are directed by enzymes through pathways of reactions, and during changes in the structure of these molecules, energy is released and stored in other specialized molecules. This storage of energy is equivalent to having an *energy currency* that can be spent to drive even more reactions, especially those involving synthesis, and to generate movement, both of which require energy.

A key aspect of the regulation of metabolism occurs at the surface membrane of a cell where the selective uptake of small molecules takes place via specific transporter proteins. This is exemplified by the many different *isoforms* of glucose transporters that are differentially expressed in various tissues and that have various responses to hormones, especially insulin.

EXAMPLE 10.1   Elaborate on the description of the processes that consume energy in living systems.

Although there are many biochemical reactions that require an input of energy in order to proceed, a key aspect of growth entails the synthesis of macromolecules. In the formation of polypeptides from amino acids, or of DNA from nucleotides, a significant amount of energy is expended. The formation of polysaccharides (long chains of repeating sugar units, Chap. 3) and of triglycerides (molecules of fatty acids attached to a glycerol backbone, Chap. 11) also requires energy.

Energy is also required to drive the movement of ions across membranes against an electrochemical gradient, a process that occurs continuously, maintaining the potential difference across the membranes that is crucial for nerve conduction and muscle contraction.

10.2   Anabolism and Catabolism

The processes that involve the synthesis of complex molecules from simpler ones, and which therefore consume energy, are referred to as *anabolism* (Greek *ana*, again; as in *building up again*). These reactions are not restricted to the synthesis of biopolymers, but include the formation of relatively simple organic molecules such as amino acids and monosaccharides that are derived from inorganic precursors such as carbon dioxide, ammonia, and water. The opposite reactions, those that break down large molecules into smaller units, are part of what is called *catabolism* (Greek *cata*, down; as in breaking down).

The chemicals involved in metabolism are called *metabolites*.

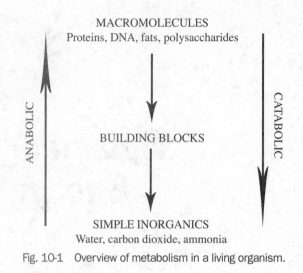

MACROMOLECULES
Proteins, DNA, fats, polysaccharides

BUILDING BLOCKS

SIMPLE INORGANICS
Water, carbon dioxide, ammonia

Fig. 10-1 Overview of metabolism in a living organism.

10.3 ATP as the Energy Currency of Living Systems

The energy released during catabolism is captured in a form that drives anabolic reactions. Energy that is *earned* by catabolism is *spent* on a wide variety of energy-consuming reactions. This currency role is fulfilled by adenosine triphosphate (ATP); its chemical structure is shown in Fig. 10-2.

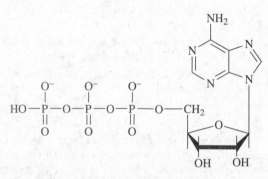

Fig. 10-2 Adenosine triphosphate (ATP).

Chapter 3 introduces ATP as a nucleoside triphosphate building block involved in RNA synthesis. The hydrolysis of the terminal phosphate anhydride bond when ATP is converted into adenosine diphosphate (ADP) releases energy. Further hydrolysis of ADP is possible, giving rise to adenosine monophosphate (AMP), with the release of a slightly smaller amount of energy.

EXAMPLE 10.2 How much ATP is there in a typical mammalian cell?
   The concentration of ATP in many types of healthy cells is ~5 mM, while the concentration of ADP is much less at ~0.2 mM. AMP concentrations are typically ~1 μM. The ratios of the concentrations of these adenine nucleotides are important in the control of metabolic processes. Except under extreme circumstances such as very fatigued muscle, the total concentration of the adenine nucleotide pool remains constant at ~5 mM. The constancy of the total amount of recycled metabolites such as ATP is referred to as *moiety conservation*; cells do this on time scales of hours to days.

EXAMPLE 10.3 How does the rate of ATP turnover compare to the total amount in a cell?
   A rapidly contracting muscle cell might use ATP at a rate of 3 mmol g^{-1} s^{-1}. From Example 10.2, each gram of muscle that has a volume of ~1 mL contains ~5 mmol of ATP. In just 1 s, the muscle cell will have used over one-half its available ATP. This outcome illustrates how important moiety conservation is with respect to ATP.

As the concentration of ATP diminishes, cellular reactions that depend on it decline. Many reactions slow down to a critical rate even before ATP is fully depleted, and a concentration of ATP less than ~2 mM is generally fatal to a cell. The critical need for a cell to maintain its concentration of ATP coupled with its relatively low intracellular stores means that the turnover of ATP is very rapid.

EXAMPLE 10.4 The enormous mismatch between the small size of the ATP *stores* in a cell and the rate of its *turnover* can be illustrated on the level of the whole body as well.

A typical human contains ~0.1 mol or ~50 g of ATP (M_r 505). This typical human turns over ~70 kg of ATP in a day, by hydrolyzing ATP and rephosphorylating the product, ADP. A sense of this amount is gauged from the knowledge that the average human consumes ~8000 kJ of energy in food each day. The energy stored in the terminal anhydride bond of ATP under standard conditions is 30.6 kJ mol^{-1}. If it is supposed that the dietary energy is channeled through ATP, then the number of moles of ATP turned over is 8000/30.6 = 260 mol; but the energy transfer is not 100% efficient. This lower efficiency is considered in Sec. 10.8, but if we suppose for the moment that the transfer is 50% efficient, then this amounts to 130 mol or 130 × 505 g = 66 kg.

Therefore, each molecule of ATP is turned over more than 1000 times a day. The additional condition that the ATP concentration in most living cells not drop below a critical threshold of ~2 mM means that the phosphorylation of ADP and hydrolysis of ATP are very closely controlled; for any anabolic, energy-consuming reaction to occur, a catabolic process simultaneously occurs, supplying the energy.

Any energy currency, if it is short-lived in a cell, would not have been naturally selected if it were chemically unstable. An important feature of ATP is that it does not spontaneously hydrolyze in aqueous solutions, and that its conversion to ADP only occurs in association with enzymes that specifically bind it and use it in their reactions.

Many metabolites, especially those involved in glycolysis (Sec. 10.6) and the Krebs cycle (Sec. 10.7), have high-energy phosphate-ester bonds. Compared with these metabolites, ATP is an intermediate with respect to the amount of energy stored in its phosphate anhydride bonds. This makes sense, because a denomination of currency would not be practical if it needed to be "changed" (the energy content split up into smaller packets) each time it was used.

10.4 Extracting Energy from Fuel Molecules: Oxidation

Energy transduction involves the oxidation of molecules such as monosaccharides, especially glucose, and fatty acids; these are the major fuels used by the human body. Oxygen is consumed with the consequent production of carbon dioxide and water, and the release of energy.

Gasoline consists of molecules that are chains of carbon atoms with attached hydrogen atoms (hence the name *hydrocarbon*); the chains of carbon atoms in fatty acids are also hydrocarbons (Sec. 10.5). Consider the energy available from a small volume of gasoline when it burns in the oxygen in the cylinders of an automobile engine.

The overall balanced equations for cellular fuel oxidation are identical to those for the simple combustion of commercial fuels. However, in the cell, oxidation takes place in a series of ordered enzyme-regulated steps in which energy is transferred in units whose values are similar to that of the terminal phosphate bond of ATP.

An *oxidized molecule* is one that contains a relatively large number of oxygen atoms. Conversely, a reduced molecule contains a relatively small number of oxygen atoms, and usually more hydrogen atoms. The process of *reduction* entails the removal of oxygen atoms or the addition of hydrogen atoms. Oxidation and reduction can also be described in terms of *electron transfer* since forming a bond between an oxygen atom and another, such as carbon, involves the transfer of electrons to form the bond with oxygen. Adding electrons to a molecule is termed *reduction*, while removal of electrons is termed *oxidation*; in other words, *oxidation is deelectronation*.

EXAMPLE 10.5 What are the initial and final points of fatty acid and carbohydrate catabolism?

Examination of a representative monosaccharide and a fatty acid (Fig. 10-3), which are fuels of catabolism, shows that they contain many hydrogen atoms, and their carbon atoms are, therefore, relatively reduced. During oxidation, hydrogen atoms and their associated electrons leave the carbon atoms and are replaced by oxygen atoms. As a result, the carbon atoms become incorporated into carbon dioxide. Thus the conversions of carbon atoms from —CH$_2$— and —C(OH)H— units to CO$_2$ are oxidative processes.

During oxidation, hydrogen ions (protons) and electrons are removed from fuel molecules and transferred to one of a small number of special carrier molecules. The most abundant such molecule is nicotinamide adenine dinucleotide (NAD$^+$). It forms an essential link between the oxidative part of catabolism and the generation of ATP.

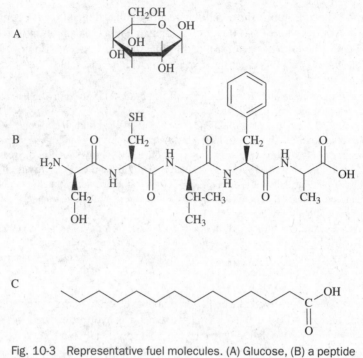

Fig. 10-3   Representative fuel molecules. (A) Glucose, (B) a peptide
(a pentapeptide), and (C) a fatty acid (myristic acid).

Since the word *nucleotide* refers to a *carbohydrate molecule containing a single monosaccharide* residue, the name of NAD$^+$ indicates two monosaccharide residues (riboses) on the compound. In contrast to nucleotides in a polynucleotide chain such as RNA, the two nucleotides are joined. While one of the nucleotides contains an adenine moiety (as in ATP, Fig. 10-2,) the other nucleotide has a nicotinamide moiety. It is this part of NAD$^+$ that receives a hydrogen atom from a fuel molecule, reducing it to NADH.

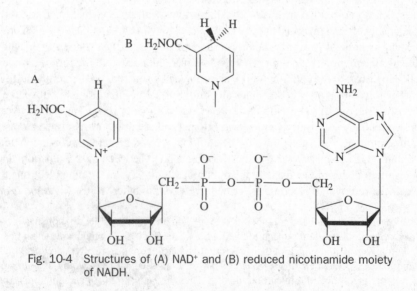

Fig. 10-4   Structures of (A) NAD$^+$ and (B) reduced nicotinamide moiety
of NADH.

EXAMPLE 10.6   What is the metabolic origin of nicotinamide?

Nicotinamide is derived from nicotinic acid that is synthesized by human cells from the *essential* amino acid tryptophan. Our diet is also a rich source of nicotinamide, so the body has adapted to synthesizing much less than the daily requirements. Many commercial breakfast cereals and spreads are supplemented with nicotinamide that is usually termed niacin or vitamin B3 on their Nutrition Fact labels.

EXAMPLE 10.7   Which chemical transformation takes place on NAD^+ when it accepts a hydrogen atom?

The nicotinamide moiety of NAD^+ contains a positive charge and an unsaturated six-atom pyridine ring containing three double bonds; it is therefore *aromatic*. Incorporation of a hydride ion (H^-, equivalent to H^+ and two electrons) neutralizes the positive charge, and the hydrogen atom attaches to C4, making the pyridine ring lose its aromatic character and become *aliphatic*. Removing two hydrogen atoms from a fuel molecule is equivalent to abstracting two protons and two electrons, but one of the protons escapes to the aqueous medium. For this reason, the NAD^+ reduction reaction is often written as $NAD^+ \rightarrow NADH + H^+$.

Fuel molecules are dismantled and their carbon atoms become oxidized progressively, finally producing CO_2. Obviously, this process does not occur in one step but within a series of coordinated reactions that are called *metabolic pathways*. This and the next three chapters are concerned with how the major metabolic pathways are configured, interrelated, and controlled.

10.5   β-Oxidation Pathway for Fatty Acids

Catabolism of fatty acids includes the reduction of NAD^+ and the sequential splitting of the fatty-acyl chain into 2-carbon acetyl units. A fatty acid enters the oxidative pathway only after it has become linked to the large molecule, coenzyme A (CoA). The abstraction of a *hydride ion* ($H^- = H^+ + 2e^-$) by NAD^+ does not immediately lead to the disassembly of the fatty acid, as it takes three more reactions before scission of a 2-carbon unit occurs from the carbon backbone to produce acetyl-CoA. NAD^+ is not the only oxidizing agent involved in the hydrogen extraction from the fatty acid; the compound flavine adenine dinucleotide (FAD) also accepts hydrogen atoms.

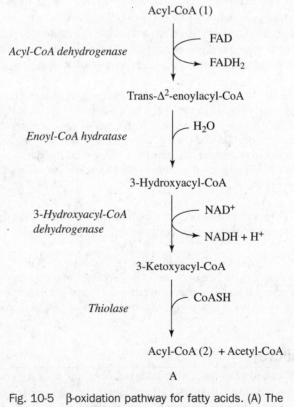

Fig. 10-5   β-oxidation pathway for fatty acids. (A) The overall scheme with enzyme names and (B) the details of the four reactions.

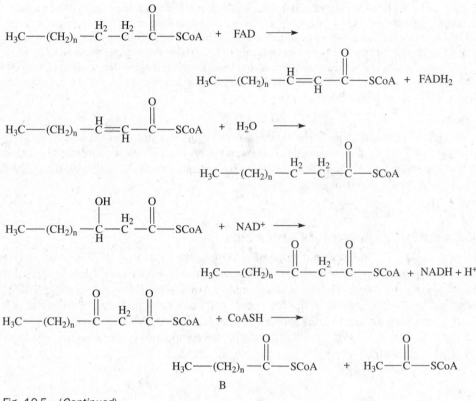

Fig. 10-5   (*Continued*)

For a fatty acid to be subdivided into acetyl-CoA units, several rounds of the sequence of reactions are required. This requires the ready availability of CoA, NAD^+, and FAD.

Like NAD^+ and ATP, coenzyme A is synthesized around an adenine nucleotide. Instead of having high-energy phosphate groups on the 5′ end of the molecule, coenzyme A has a *pantothenic acid* moiety that contains a free sulfydryl group that can form a thioester bond with an acyl group, such as the —COOH portion of a fatty acid.

EXAMPLE 10.8   The priming step of β-oxidation occurs in the cell's cytoplasm, while β-oxidation takes place in the mitochondrial matrix. What physical phenomena have been "addressed" for this to take place in the cell?

The *addition of CoA* to the fatty acid prevents it from diffusing across the inner mitochondrial membrane (Chap. 1) into the matrix. Transfer of the fatty acyl portion takes place onto a smaller molecule, *carnitine*, that has a specialized transporter in the inner mitochondrial membrane to enable the acyl carnitine molecules to enter the matrix. Once inside the matrix, the fatty acyl moiety is reattached to mitochondrial CoA, and the carnitine diffuses back into the cytoplasm to participate in another transfer reaction.

Carrier proteins located in membranes are very important sites of metabolic regulation. If the carriers are in short supply, the rapid operation of the entire pathway can be compromised.

EXAMPLE 10.9   What medical conditions might result from a deficiency of carnitine?

A deficiency of carnitine means that the rate of transport of fatty acids into the mitochondrial matrix is likely to be inadequate. Therefore energy supply from the oxidation of fats is impeded, and muscle weakness is an early symptom. Carnitine supplements may be beneficial to athletes for whom high rates of fatty acid oxidation are imperative. This is discussed in Chap. 12.

10.6   Glycolytic Pathway

In the sequence of reactions called *glycolysis*, glucose is oxidized and split into two 3-carbon molecules that ultimately both lead to pyruvate (Fig. 10-8). In cells in which oxygen is not consumed, the NAD^+ that is required for the reaction catalyzed by glyceraldehyde-3-phosphate dehydrogenase is regenerated via lactate dehydrogenase; this enzyme converts pyruvate to lactate while concomitantly oxidizing NADH.

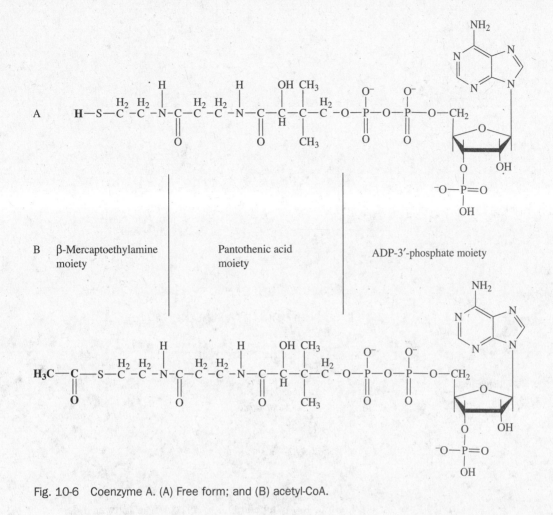

Fig. 10-6   Coenzyme A. (A) Free form; and (B) acetyl-CoA.

While NAD^+ is involved in abstracting hydride ions from the phosphorylated carbohydrate glyceraldehyde 3-phosphate, glucose is extensively altered before this key oxidation step. In oxygen-consuming cells, a major fate of pyruvate is further reaction with NAD^+ in processes catalyzed by the multienzyme complex *pyruvate dehydrogenase* (Fig. 10-8C). In this instance, the carboxyl group of pyruvate is released as CO_2, while the remaining two carbon atoms emerge as the acetyl moiety of acetyl-CoA.

The conversion of glucose to pyruvate occurs in the cytoplasm of the cell, and pyruvate is selectively transported into the mitochondrial matrix where it encounters the pyruvate dehydrogenase complex.

EXAMPLE 10.10   From Figs. 10-7 and 10-8, deduce the general principles of fuel oxidation that are common to both pathways.

Fuel molecules must be transported into cells in order to be processed, and this occurs via reactions that involve oxidation. Although fatty acids with their hydrophobic hydrocarbon chain readily diffuse across the plasma membrane of the cell, the more hydrophilic glucose requires a special transport protein. The integral membrane proteins that mediate the exchange of glucose from the bloodstream into the cytoplasm belong to the GLUT (GLU = glucose, T = transporter) family.

The release of fatty acids from triglycerides before their unaided transport into the cell and the glucose transport via GLUTs into cells represent quite different points of regulation in their metabolism. These aspects are discussed further in Chaps. 11 to 13.

EXAMPLE 10.11   GLUTs transport *glucose* and *related hexoses* across cell membranes. They are *integral membrane proteins* that contain 12 membrane-spanning helices with both the amino and carboxyl termini on the cytoplasmic side of the plasma membrane. Their kinetics is described by a model that has *alternative conformations* that face one way or the other across a cell membrane. Binding of glucose to one site provokes a conformational change that is associated with transport, and the conformational change leads to the release of glucose to the other side of the membrane.

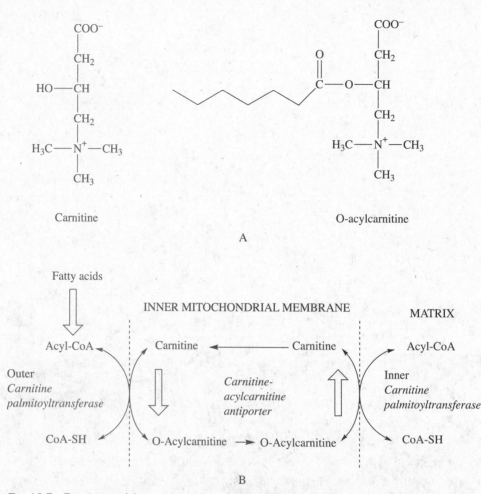

Carnitine   O-acylcarnitine

A

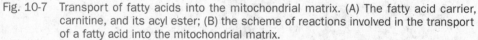

Fatty acids

INNER MITOCHONDRIAL MEMBRANE   MATRIX

Acyl-CoA   Carnitine ⟵ Carnitine   Acyl-CoA

Outer   Carnitine-   Inner
Carnitine   *acylcarnitine*   *Carnitine*
palmitoyltransferase   *antiporter*   *palmitoyltransferase*

CoA-SH   O-Acylcarnitine ⟶ O-Acylcarnitine   CoA-SH

B

Fig. 10-7   Transport of fatty acids into the mitochondrial matrix. (A) The fatty acid carrier,
carnitine, and its acyl ester; (B) the scheme of reactions involved in the transport
of a fatty acid into the mitochondrial matrix.

EXAMPLE 10.12   Not all fuel molecules require transport into the cell for their degradation; some, such as glycogen, are produced and stored within the cell so they are there already (Sec. 11.4).

Some classes of fuel molecules are attached to larger *carrier* molecules during oxidation, and these carriers are needed for transport across intracellular membranes. The attachment that commonly involves linkage to a charged group also serves to trap the molecule within the cytoplasm. The addition of a charged phosphate group, such as with the phosphorylated metabolites involved with glycolysis, traps the monosaccharide inside the cytoplasm. Although the phosphorylation involves the input of energy from ATP, the investment is returned during later oxidation; this first expenditure of ATP before any energy is extracted from the glucose is referred to as a *priming step* or *sparking reaction*.

Similarly, fatty acids are trapped and *primed* by addition of CoA, a step that also involves the investment of energy at an early stage of the operation of the pathway prior to the release of energy.

For both fatty acid and glucose oxidation, the initial oxidative removal of hydride ions from the carbon backbone gives rise to acetyl groups, which are carried on CoA. As metabolism of acetyl-CoA proceeds, further oxidation by NAD^+ and FAD occurs together with the release of CO_2.

10.7   Krebs Cycle

The Krebs cycle, also known as the *tricarboxylic acid* or *citric acid cycle*, operates within the mitochondria; it fully oxidizes the two carbon atoms in acetyl-CoA to CO_2. During the oxidation process, acetate groups are *carried* on a 4-carbon molecule, *oxaloacetate*. The fact that oxaloacetate is regenerated at the end of the process makes this pathway a *cycle*. Availability of the carrier is important in regulating the carbon flux around the cyclic pathway.

The combined operation of β-oxidation of fatty acids, glycolysis, and the Krebs cycle strips protons and hydride ions from the corresponding fuel molecules, thus fully oxidizing the carbon atoms to CO_2. Crucially, in the process, NAD^+ and FAD receive these protons and electrons and are reduced to NADH and $FADH_2$, respectively. Thus it is their *cargo* of protons and electrons that are used to generate ATP.

10.8   Generation of ATP

The chemical reaction between two hydrogen atoms and one oxygen atom generates a water molecule, with the release of a considerable amount of energy. Combinations of liquid hydrogen and liquid oxygen are used to power rockets; and hydrogen-filled airships (the Zeppelins) were notoriously prone to explosion. The hydrogen-burning reaction can be viewed as the *ultimate oxidation-reduction reaction*, with the classical reduced molecule H_2 reacting with the classical oxidized molecule O_2 to produce water which is redox-neutral.

Unlike a rocket, a cell performs this same reaction in a stepwise, controlled manner and harnesses the energy in the form of an electrochemical gradient across the inner mitochondrial membrane, which in turn is used to generate ATP.

Question: How is the reaction between hydrogen and oxygen *controlled* by a cell?

The reaction uses a series of specialized electron- and proton-transporting proteins that are formed into large complexes. These are embedded in the inner mitochondrial membrane and constitute the

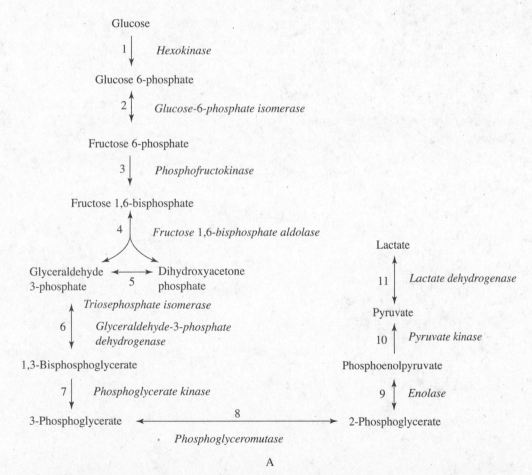

A

Fig. 10-8   Glycolysis. It produces pyruvate that leads to lactate or acetyl-CoA. (A) The 12 primary reactants and 11 enzymes; (B) details of the chemical transformations showing the recycling of NAD^+ that occurs under anaerobic conditions; and (C) how pyruvate forms acetyl-CoA under aerobic conditions.

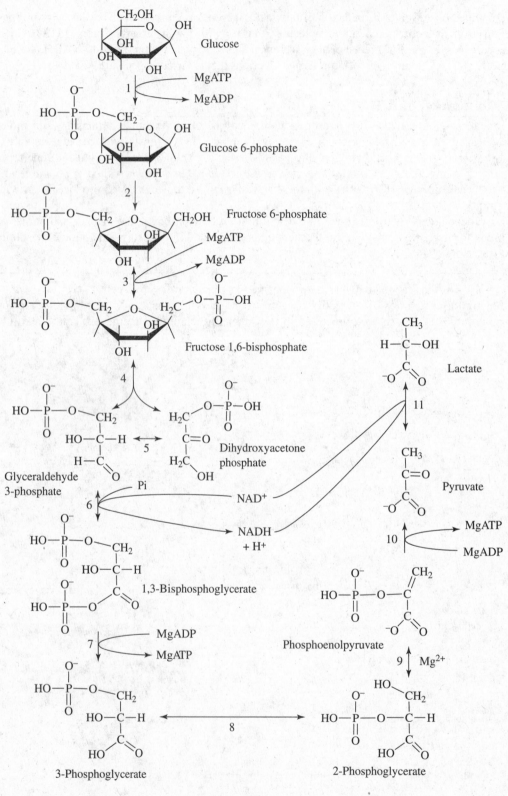

B

Fig. 10-8   (*Continued*)

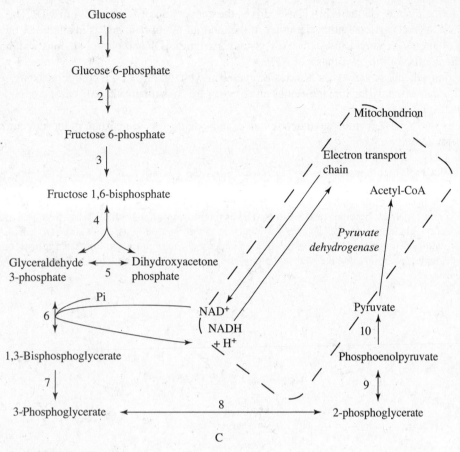

Fig. 10-8 (*Continued*)

electron transport chain (ETC). As electrons move along this chain of electron-conducting proteins, from NADH to oxygen, protons are pumped out of the mitochondrial matrix into the *intermembranous space*, and they then diffuse via *porin* proteins in the outer membrane, to the cytoplasm. Because the phospholipid bilayer of the inner mitochondrial membrane is impermeable to protons, the ejection of protons from the matrix by proteins establishes an *electrochemical gradient*. This gradient is composed of both a *proton chemical potential difference* and a *membrane potential* and is called the *proton motive force*. The donation of protons and electrons by NADH to the first complex in the ETC (Complex I) leads to the recycling of NAD^+ that is then available for oxidation of more fuel molecules (e.g., see Fig. 10-10A and B).

In the inner mitochondrial membrane there reside many copies of a molecular complex that is a marvel of nanoengineering: the F_0F_1ATPase. This consists of an intramembranous channel, the F_0 section, that conducts protons across the membrane, and another section of the complex located on the internal side of the inner mitochondrial membrane, F_1ATPase; it phosphorylates ADP with P_i to generate ATP. The three-dimensional structure and the molecular mechanism of this incredible ATP generator are discussed further in Sec. 10.11. The *mechanism of synthesis* of ATP by the F_0F_1ATPase that is coupled to the flow of electrons from NADH and $FADH_2$ along the ETC is called *oxidative phosphorylation*.

In summary, fuel molecules are oxidized by the removal of protons and electrons. This leads to the carbon atoms in the molecules being converted to carbon dioxide. The protons and electrons are combined with NAD^+ and carried on NADH to the electron transport chain located in the inner mitochondrial membrane. Movement of the electrons along this chain to oxygen results in the regeneration of NAD^+, the production of a proton gradient across the inner mitochondrial membrane, and the conversion of oxygen to water. The return of protons to the matrix, via the F_0F_1ATPase, drives the conversion of ADP and Pi to ATP. The ATP leaves the matrix via special carriers within the inner mitochondrial membrane and is available in the cytoplasm as a source of energy. When it is used, the ATP is converted into ADP and phosphate ions which must travel back into the matrix for the resynthesis of ATP.

The reaction scheme is viewed as a series of cycles in which many of the components are regenerated. During ATP synthesis, only the fuel molecules and oxygen are consumed, and only carbon dioxide and water are produced.

Although Fig. 10-12 lacks molecular detail, it does indicate the most important points of control of oxidative phosphorylation.

EXAMPLE 10.13   Which compounds are *recycled* during the operation of the overall scheme of oxidative phosphorylation?

Protons are pumped out of the matrix during the operation of the electron transport chain, and they reenter the matrix driving ATP synthesis. NAD^+ becomes reduced to NADH as it removes protons and electrons from fuel molecules, but it becomes NAD^+ again after it donates its cargo of reductant to the electron transport chain. ADP can also be viewed as a carrier; it is recycled during ATP synthesis when it condenses with a phosphate ion. Then it loses this phosphate during ATP-dependent reactions, and the ADP and phosphate ions return to the mitochondrial matrix for another round of ATP synthesis.

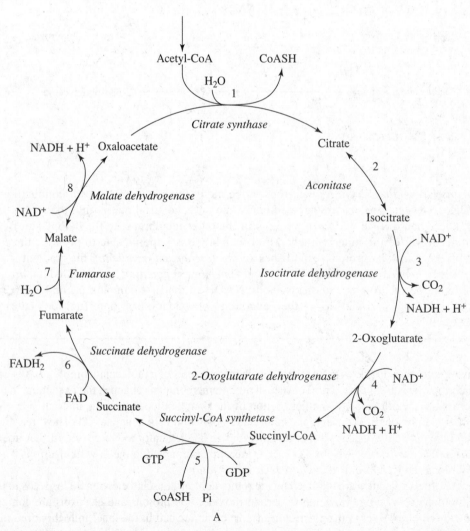

Fig. 10-9   The Krebs cycle. (A) Names of the enzymes and reactants and (B) details of the chemical transformations.

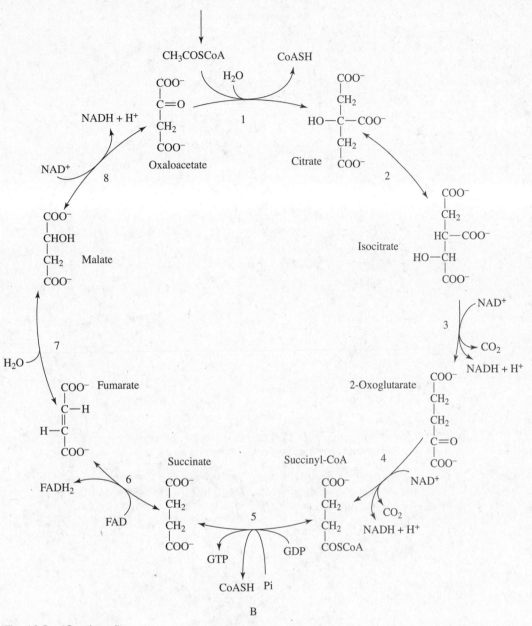

Fig. 10-9 *(Continued)*

10.9 Interconnection between Energy Expenditure and Oxidation of Fuel Molecules

The coordination of the oxidation of fuel molecules and the synthesis of ATP can be understood by drawing on the following concepts:

1. ATP is formed when protons enter the mitochondrial matrix via F_0F_1ATPase, but protons will *only* reenter the matrix if ADP is simultaneously converted to ATP. Thus ADP and phosphate must be available in the matrix. The movement of protons and the synthesis of ATP by the F_0F_1ATPase are so tightly linked that they do not occur independently.

2. The proton pumping (also called *vectorial transport* or *translocation*) and electron-transferring reactions in the electron transport chain are part of the same overall reaction. Just as the proton gradient is generated as electrons move along the electron transport chain from NADH to oxygen, the electrons only move along the electron transport chain if protons are simultaneously pumped out. In NADH and $FADH_2$ the

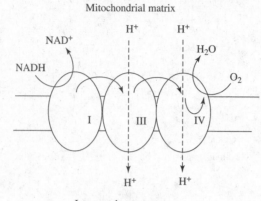

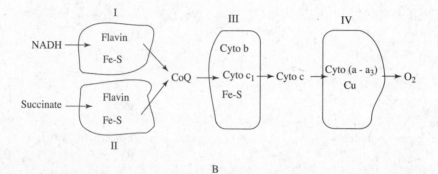

Fig. 10-10   Electron transport chain (ETC) in the inner mitochondrial membrane. The arrows indicate the flow of electrons along and between the complexes, denoted I–IV, to oxygen. Fe-S denotes iron-sulfur clusters; CoQ, coenzyme Q; and Cyto, cytochrome. (A) The three main complexes that vectorially pump H⁺ ions; (B) the linkage between the main protein complexes and the electron carriers in the ETC.

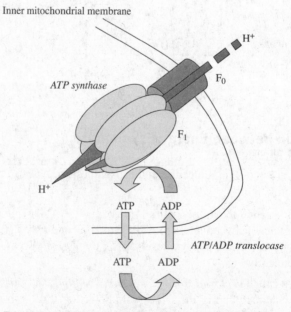

Fig. 10-11   Schematic representation of the F_0F_1ATPase, or ATP synthase complex.

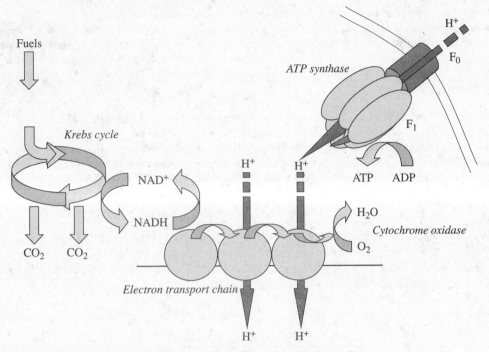

Fig. 10-12   Summary of fuel oxidation and ATP generation in a cell.

electrons have high energy, but by the time they are incorporated into water, they have low energy. The energy required for proton *translocation* is derived from the loss of energy by these electrons.

3. The higher the proton motive force, the larger the proton gradient, so the slower the rate of proton efflux from the matrix. Consequently, a high proton gradient slows the flux of electrons along the electron transport chain.

4. The electron carriers in the electron transport chain are limited in number. The concentration of ADP in the cell is low relative to ATP (Sec. 10.3), so once ADP is phosphorylated, no more ATP can be synthesized. Similarly, when NAD^+ is reduced to NADH, it is no longer available for further oxidation of fuel molecules. The individual components of the electron transport chain must also continually pass on their electrons to the next carrier; otherwise, they remain fully reduced and are unable to accept electrons from the preceding electron carrier. Even compounds that participate in the metabolic pathways that generate NADH are in limited supply (recall moiety conservation in Sec. 10.3), and they too can become limiting unless they are regenerated.

Using the simple rules of the system, it is easy to deduce that a *lack of work* equates with a *decrease in ATP consumption* that causes a slowing or even stopping of the oxidation of fuels by a cell. The driving force for the oxidation of fuels comes from the demand for ATP. It is not the *supply* of fuel but the *demand* for energy that determines if fuels are oxidized.

This *coupling* between energy demand and the oxidation of fuels is due to the interdependence of electron flow along the electron transport chain and the simultaneous proton flow across the inner mitochondrial membrane, which occurs back through the F_0F_1ATPase.

10.10   Inhibitors of ATP Synthesis

Poisons

A deeper understanding of the regulation of energy metabolism can be gained experimentally by examining the outcome when parts of the system are inhibited or activated by added chemical species.

It has been concluded that some inhibitors of energy conversion act on particular electron-transporting complexes. These compounds block electron transport.

EXAMPLE 10.14   Give an example of a poison that acts via the electron transport chain.

Rotenone interferes with the electron/proton transfer reaction at complex I, thus rendering all the subsequent complexes fully oxidized because they have nothing from which to accept electrons. This prevents proton pumping and therefore stops oxygen consumption. The lack of proton pumping leads to a collapse of the proton gradient and an inability of the system to synthesize ATP. As a consequence, ATP concentrations fall, and the cell dies. This is why rotenone is such an effective poison.

EXAMPLE 10.15   Which class of compounds might provide an antidote to cyanide poisoning?

Cyanide has a similar size to O_2 and binds to the site specific for O_2 on complex IV. A compound that binds to, and sequesters, cyanide would be ideal, but these are difficult to deliver *therapeutically*. But providing a bypass for the inhibited complex IV is also a possibility. The compound *methylene blue* accepts electrons in place of complex IV, thereby allowing electron transport to operate and allowing the proton gradient to be reestablished. Under these conditions, oxygen would not be consumed, and the number of protons pumped out per NADH is decreased. The lower yield of protons means that the rate of both electron transport and fuel oxidation must increase to maintain the proton motive force.

The electron transport system can be inhibited at many stages. If oxygen and/or fuel substrates are in short supply, then it is easy to see how the rate of electron transport will decrease and how there will no longer be the vital proton gradient to drive ATP synthesis. Clearly, a lack of oxygen has devastating consequences for ATP levels and hence cell survival.

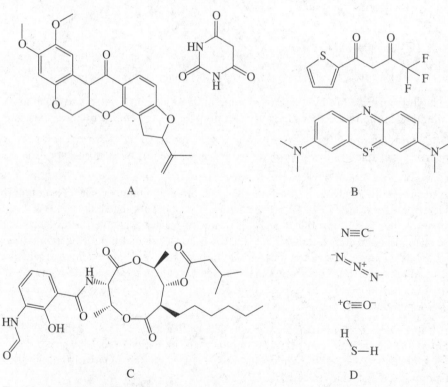

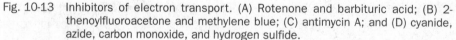

Fig. 10-13   Inhibitors of electron transport. (A) Rotenone and barbituric acid; (B) 2-thenoylfluoroacetone and methylene blue; (C) antimycin A; and (D) cyanide, azide, carbon monoxide, and hydrogen sulfide.

EXAMPLE 10.16   Fluoroacetate, commonly known as the poison *1080*, is used to eradicate feral animals.

It exerts its effect by being an inhibitor of the Krebs cycle. Fluoroacetate substitutes for acetate and is converted to fluoroacetyl CoA. This is condensed with oxaloacetate to produce fluorocitrate; in other words citrate synthase uses fluoroacetate as a substrate and forms *fluorocitrate* that inhibits *aconitase* (reaction 2 in Fig. 10-9A and B). If the Krebs cycle is not functioning correctly, the rate of NADH production will be insufficient to maintain the mitochondrial proton gradient, and the ATP concentration will decline. A further complication is that processes such as the Krebs cycle have an important role in regenerating *moiety carrier* molecules. If the cycle is inhibited, then vital carriers such as *oxaloacetate* and *coenzyme A* become depleted.

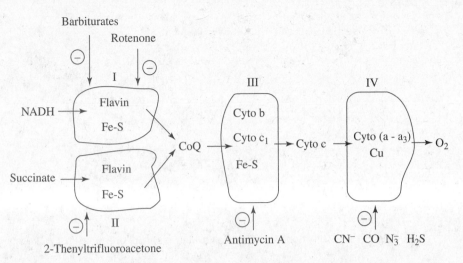

Fig. 10-14   Sites of action of the inhibitors of the electron transport chain.

ATP:ADP Translocase

The movement of ATP out of the mitochondrial matrix and the movement of ADP back in to it from the cytoplasm are catalyzed by the same membrane protein, ATP:ADP translocase. Inhibition of this transporter by the compound *atractyloside* (from the Mediterranean thistle) prevents ADP from being available to the F_1F_0ATPase. This causes ATP synthesis to stop, the proton gradient to stay high, and the proton pumps to be inhibited by the enormous backpressure of protons. Fuel oxidation will cease as will the ability for ATP to enter the cytoplasm. Thus the cytoplasmic ATP concentration will quickly fall.

Imagine if the protons did not have to pass through the F_0 channel to return to the matrix. Suppose there is a leak or hole in the inner mitochondrial membrane or another compound is able to carry the protons across the membrane. Such a situation is analogous to a *short circuit* in an electrical system. Under these conditions the proton gradient would rapidly dissipate, and the driving force for ATP synthesis would be lost. There would no longer be a backpressure to *control* H^+ pumping, and there would no longer be any restriction on the rate of electron movement along the electron transport chain. This would lead to a massive increase in oxygen consumption and rapid regeneration of NAD^+ from NADH. Fuel oxidation would occur at a high rate, even though there was little synthesis of ATP. The lack of ATP synthesis would rapidly deplete ATP concentrations and lead to cell death. In this situation fuel oxidation will have been *uncoupled* from its dependence on ATP demand, and the "rule" that it is impossible to burn fuels without doing work will have been broken.

Uncoupling by Chemicals and Natural Means

There is no formal *chemical* reason why the burning of hydrogen in oxygen in a test tube, or in a mitochondrion, should lead to the phosphorylation of ADP to make ATP. The process that achieves this linkage of energy transfer between two disparate reactions is oxidative phosphorylation; it takes place via an intermediate energy store that is the proton motive force. If this intermediate energy store is discharged nonproductively, the energy is simply given out as heat, i.e., the increased speed of the random motion of the molecules in the system.

EXAMPLE 10.17   2,4-Dinitrophenol (DNP) is a hydrophobic molecule that can move freely across membranes. Consider the mechanism of how this leads to uncoupling of oxidation of fuels from the phosphorylation of ADP.

The proton on the phenolic —OH group readily dissociates from it, so DNP is a *weak acid*. If DNP were to enter the mitochondrial matrix, which is a relatively basic environment, then the dissociation of this proton would reduce the transmembrane proton gradient. However, DNP can dissipate the proton gradient in an even more dramatic way. The negative charge remaining after proton dissociation can be delocalized around the DNP molecule, thus reducing its local electric field; so this enables the negatively charged DNP to escape from the matrix via the lipid bilayer to the outside of the mitochondrion where the environment is relatively acidic. There it accepts a proton and brings it into the matrix. This process bypasses the need for protons to enter via F_0 and thus brings about *uncoupling* of oxidative phosphorylation. Under these circumstances most of the energy liberated in the oxidation of fuels is not captured as ATP but is lost as *heat*.

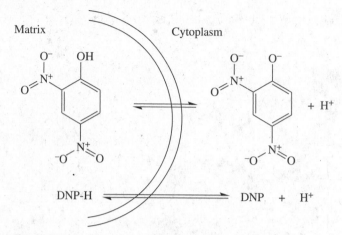

Matrix   Cytoplasm

+ H⁺

DNP-H ⇌ DNP + H⁺

Fig. 10-15   Dinitrophenol uncouples oxidative phosphorylation.

Despite the medical dangers of chemically mediated uncoupling of oxidative phosphorylation (see Example 10.17), there are examples of *deliberate* and *controlled* uncoupling that occur naturally. The mitochondria of *brown adipose tissue* (BAT) contain an intramembrane proton-conducting channel called *thermogenin* or *uncoupling protein-1* (UCP-1). This channel, when open, allows protons to flow back into the matrix, bypassing the F_0F_1ATPase. As with DNP (Fig. 10-15), such a short circuit means less ATP is produced and there is an increase in the amount of energy that is liberated simply as *heat*. In contrast to DNP, the channel is totally controllable and is restricted to BAT which makes this tissue a key *thermogenic organ*. While this feature is not necessarily required in adult humans, it plays a vital role in thermal homeostasis in neonates and smaller animals, such as rodents. In rodents, BAT is mainly located in a discrete depot between the shoulder blades, the *interscapular BAT*, where it is furnished with a very high supply of blood and extensive neuronal connections to thermoregulatory centers in the brain. In effect, BAT acts as a heat radiator for the bloodstream; and it is also important in the *metabolic arousal* of *hibernating* animals.

EXAMPLE 10.18   How is the extent of uncoupling of oxidative phosphorylation regulated in brown adipose tissue (BAT)?

BAT plasma membranes contain specialized β_3-*receptors* that are G protein-coupled receptors. Agonists of these receptors stimulate the elevation of intracellular cAMP concentration. Through mechanisms explained in Chap. 6, cAMP raises the concentration of fatty acids in the cytoplasm, and these bind to and open the *UCP-1* (*thermogenin*) H⁺ conduction channel. The natural agonist of the β_3-receptor is *norepinephrine* which is copiously released from nerve endings in BAT during exposure to the *cold*. The noradrenergic stimulus also causes thermogenesis in BAT in response to overeating, and it provides a way of oxidizing, rather than storing, excess fuel.

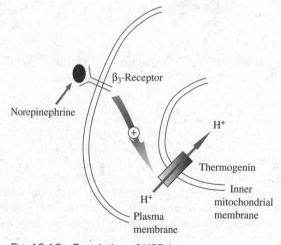

Fig. 10-16   Regulation of UCP-1.

Uncoupling proteins other than UCP-1 (Example 10.18) have been named UCP-2 and UCP-3. They are present in the mitochondria of the major tissues that have high metabolic rates, such as muscle, liver, and adipose tissue. Their precise role is unknown, but some lines of evidence point to reducing the production of reactive oxygen radicals (an unfortunate leakage of the electron transport chain which is discussed below) with others showing a role in ATP-level-dependent hormone secretion. A simple but intriguing suggestion is that the UCPs play a role in maintaining an "idling" rate of electron transport in cells even when ATP demand is very low—in much the same way as an automobile engine is not switched off but is left idling, when the vehicle stops at traffic lights, and yet it is poised ready for action.

10.11 Details of the Molecular Machinery of ATP Synthesis

Electron Transport Chain (ETC)
The ETC consists of four large protein complexes embedded in the inner mitochondrial membrane. The complexes are free to move laterally in the membrane, but the order of their interactions is strictly choreographed by two intercomplex carriers: the small, hydrophobic, intramembrane molecule *ubiquinone* and the water soluble protein *cytochrome c*. Complex II only has a face on the matrix side of the inner membrane while the other three complexes span the membrane and have portions that protrude into both the cytosolic and matrix spaces.

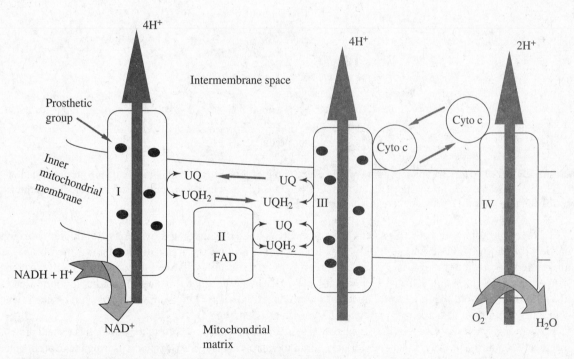

Fig. 10-17   ETC in the mitochondrial inner membrane.

Each complex consists of many proteins. Some of the proteins create the correct shape of the complex, fulfilling a purely structural role, while other proteins are involved in the transfer of hydrogen atoms (protons and electrons). These transfer reactions are mediated by *prosthetic groups*.

EXAMPLE 10.19 Human complex I contains 35 proteins. Key hydrogen and electron-transporting proteins within the complex contain the heme rings, copper atoms, and iron atoms.

The proteins are arranged so that as the hydrogen/electron transfers occur within the complex, protons are expelled on the outer, cytosolic side, and protons are brought in on the inner, matrix side. It is important at this stage to understand how the transfer of protons and electrons from one carrier to the next could result in the ejection or uptake of protons. Crucial to this is the recognition that carriers transfer hydrogen atoms (a proton and an electron) whereas others transfer only electrons.

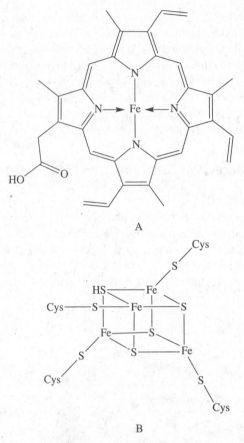

Fig. 10-18 Heme, copper, and iron serve as electron carriers.

EXAMPLE 10.20 Does the mitochondrial matrix ever run out of protons for pumping in oxidative phosphorylation?

No. Water is in a state of dynamic equilibrium; it is continually dissociating and reassociating to and from protons, hydroxide ions, and H_3O^+ ions, so there is a plentiful supply of all these.

Transfer of protons and electrons between complexes I and III is mediated by the hydrophobic hydrogen carrier ubiquinone. This compound, which is free to move around the inner mitochondrial membrane, is also called Coenzyme Q and Coenzyme Q_{10}. It carries hydrogens and is also involved in shuttling hydrogens from complex II to complex III. (It received its particular name because it is a quinonoid compound that is ubiquitous throughout the inner mitochondrial membrane. It has 10 linked isoprenoid units, and since it was originally thought to be a coenzyme, it became known as coenzyme Q_{10}.)

Cytochrome c transfers electrons from complex III to complex IV via a *heme* prosthetic group. It is a small protein that resides on the outer face of the inner mitochondrial membrane. It is readily displaced during the experimental preparation of mitochondria, and this leads to lower than expected rates of oxygen consumption in such samples.

Complex II does not accept electrons from NADH but hydrogen atoms carried on $FADH_2$. FAD is an integral part of the complex. And in both β-oxidation and the Krebs cycle, the relevant oxidation step for $FADH_2$ (step 1 in Fig. 10-5 and the reaction in step 6 in Figs. 10-9A and B) is actually catalyzed by complex II. In both cases, the FAD removes hydrogen atoms from a saturated hydrocarbon chain ($-CH_2-CH_2-$), thus creating a $-CH=CH-$ double bond. In contrast, NAD^+ tends to remove hydrogen atoms and electrons from an alcohol $-CH_2-CHOH-$ to create a carbonyl group $-CH_2(C=O)-$.

FAD, like NAD^+, is a dinucleotide with an adenine nucleotide joined "back to back" with one that contains a hydrogen-carrying group that is flavin. In its reduced state, the flavin heterocyclic ring carries two hydrogen atoms and is located on the matrix side of the inner mitochondrial membrane. The flavin moiety is derived from riboflavin (vitamin B_2) that is commonly added to foods as a nutritional supplement. The energy of the electrons in $FADH_2$ is not as great as in those in NADH. Consequently electrons in $FADH_2$ do not lead to translocation of as many protons from the ETC.

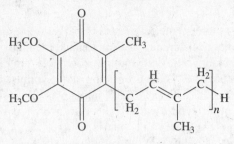

Fig. 10-19   Ubiquinone.

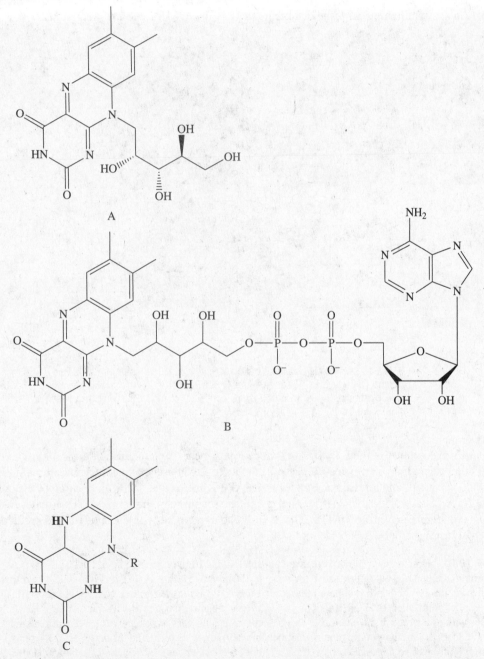

Fig. 10-20   (A) Riboflavin; (B) FAD; and (C) the reduced form, FADH$_2$, where R denotes the rest of the molecule shown in (B).

F_0F_1ATPase

One of the remarkable features of this enzyme complex is that it resembles a sophisticated motor or dynamo in that it transduces a potential energy difference into motion and then into chemical energy.

The complex consists of two major sections: the intramembranous proton channel F_0 and the intramatrix F_1ATPase. The most notable feature of F_0 is the protruding and asymmetric γ-subunit that resides inside a hydrophobic pocket in F_0, rather like a ball-and-socket joint. This allows the γ-subunit to rotate, and this rotation is driven by the turning of the cylindrical subunits of F_0 which, in turn, move as protons are passed between them from the intermembrane space to the matrix.

The rotating γ-subunit interacts with the α- and β-subunits of the F_1ATPase, causing adenine nucleotide binding sites on the enzyme to change conformation and thereby altering their affinity for the substrate. This leads to the formation of ATP from ADP and Pi. A key, but often overlooked, requirement for this assembly to work is the fact that the F_1ATPase portion should remain stationary and not be moved by the spinning γ-subunit. Thus, a stabilizing *stator*, the δ-subunit, anchors the F_1ATPase to the membrane.

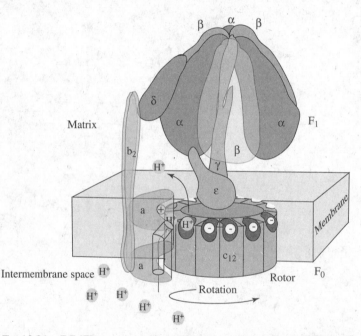

Fig. 10-21 F_0F_1ATPase, also called ATPsynthase. The γsubunit, attached to the C_{12} rotor, rotates inside the F_1 complex that is held stationary by the b_2 dimer. (Note, in E.coli there are 9-12 c subunits, while in yeast there are 10.)

The exact stoichiometry of the F_0F_1ATPase is not entirely clear. Each full turn of the γ-subunit must create three ATP molecules since, during a cycle, each of the three F_1ATPase adenine nucleotide binding sites will have bound, converted, and released one molecule of ATP. It seems that a shift in position of the cylindrical F_0 subunits is necessary to rotate the γ-subunit through one revolution. Therefore, most estimates predict that 10 protons are required to make 3 ATPs. This is in broad agreement with thermodynamic predictions and experimental measurements.

EXAMPLE 10.21   How many ADP molecules are phosphorylated from one molecule of NADH?

If 10 protons are pumped out of the matrix for every NADH oxidized (Fig. 10-17), and if it takes 10 protons to make 3 ATPs, then, in theory, it could be supposed that just over 3 ATPs are made for each NADH. However, this would be incorrect. First, the movement of an ATP (with its average of four negative charges at pH ~7) out of the matrix in exchange for an ADP (with its average of three negative charges) constitutes the loss of a negative charge from the matrix, which effectively reduces the strength of the proton-electrochemical gradient. Second, the synthesis of ATP from ADP and Pi (which, itself, contains two negative charges at pH ~7) has an effect on the electrochemical gradient. Third, the active transport of phosphate from the cytoplasm to the matrix is partially driven by the proton gradient, and part of the latter is dissipated during Pi uptake. A combination of these factors means that the real return is ~2.5 ATP molecules formed per NADH molecule oxidized.

EXAMPLE 10.22 How many ADP molecules are phosphorylated from the conversion of one molecule of $FADH_2$ to one molecule of FAD?

The major difference between the yield of ATP from NADH and $FADH_2$ is due to the fact complex II does not participate in proton pumping. Only complexes III and IV pump protons when $FADH_2$ is the source of reductant. This lowers the yield to ~1.5 ATPs per $FADH_2$.

10.12 Whole Body Energy Balance

Food Energy and Its Storage

At the molecular level, the rate of fuel oxidation is tightly linked to ATP demand. At the whole body level, fuel intake in the form of food is *not* linked to the immediate demand for ATP. In other words, we burn food at the same time as we ingest it. Thus there must be *fuel reserves*, and most of the food that we eat will initially be stored rather than immediately oxidized. The reserves are primarily *triglycerides*, which are the store of fatty acids, and glycogen, which is the store of glucose (see Chaps. 11 and 12 for the molecular details). Historically it is thought that we evolved with the need to store metabolic fuel for times of famine so that we are inclined to overeat in times of plenty, and store this fuel as triglycerides.

In conclusion, any net positive difference between the amount of energy consumed and the energy expenditure is stored.

Although there is discordance between daily whole body energy intake and expenditure, our fuel reserves and therefore our weight remain remarkably constant over a year or more. Without deliberate and drastic intervention, it is unusual for an individual to change body weight by much more than 1–2% in a year. Indeed, humans are very efficient at "defending" their fuel reserves, and they seem to have a *set point*, an intrinsic homeostatic value for fuel stores that operates in the long term. This is remarkable given the huge variations that occur in both energy expenditure and intake from one day to the next.

EXAMPLE 10.23 Our body weight is normally constant to within ~1 kg per year. Since adipose tissue contains ~30 MJ kg^{-1} of energy, the accumulation, or loss, of 1 kg represents an imbalance of ~30 MJ in a year, or ~70 kJ per day. This is a very small amount of energy and would be almost impossible to detect, during either normal intake or expenditure measurements, because it is the equivalent of a teaspoon of sugar (5 g) or some measure of physical activity such as a half-mile walk. An alternative, and equally important, way of viewing this is to note that only a tiny mismatch in the energy balance equation can have quite large ramifications on whole body mass, in the long term.

Measurement of Whole Body Energy Expenditure

At the level of the whole body, the two most practical methods of measuring energy expenditure are *indirect calorimetry* and the use of *doubly labeled water*.

Indirect calorimetry relies on the principle (introduced in Sec. 10.9) that energy expenditure drives fuel oxidation that in turn leads to the reduction of oxygen. Therefore, measuring the rate of oxygen consumption provides a rapid and convenient way of predicting energy expenditure. The only disadvantage of this technique is that it involves measuring gas intake so subjects must wear a restrictive hood or be placed in a sealed room, neither of which encourages long-term participation in these calorimetric measurements.

EXAMPLE 10.24 How can measuring both the rate of CO_2 production and the rate of oxygen production determine which fuels the body is oxidizing?

The quantitative analysis of oxidation of fuels shows that when most *carbohydrates* are oxidized, the ratio of carbon dioxide produced to oxygen consumed is 1. On the other hand, this ratio, which is called the *respiratory quotient* (RQ) or the *respiratory exchange ratio*, is ~0.7 when *fatty acids* are oxidized. The measurements of O_2 consumption and CO_2 emission only indicate which fuels are being oxidized *on average* by the whole body and do not necessarily reflect which fuel is being used selectively by particular cell types or tissues. As noted in Chap. 11, the synthesis of triglycerides raises the RQ above 1.

The technique that uses *doubly labeled water* measures the amount of CO_2 produced by the whole body, and this is a good indicator of the rate of fuel oxidation. The subject consumes a dose of water that contains isotopes of both hydrogen and oxygen. Specifically, the nonradioactive isotopes used are deuterium (^2H or D) and ^{18}O (as opposed to the usual ^{16}O). After consumption, the $D_2^{18}O$ diffuses within the unlabeled water throughout the body where it reacts with CO_2 to produce carbonic acid (H_2CO_3). Under the catalytic influence of carbonic anhydrase, carbonic acid is in rapid exchange with water and CO_2. Because the three oxygens in carbonic acid are chemically identical, during this equilibration the labeled ^{18}O enters CO_2. Over time, the ^{18}O is exhaled in CO_2 from the lungs, and the relative amounts of C $^{18}O_2$ in exhaled-gas samples are measured using mass spectrometry. The more CO_2 that is present, the faster the initial ^{18}O label in the C $^{18}O_2$ will be lost. Also ^{18}O can be excreted as water in sweat and urine. Cunningly, the rate of the latter processes can be estimated from the disappearance of the ^2H (again using mass spectrometry on the sweat and urine samples), so the difference between the rates of decay in ^{18}O and ^2H allows an estimation of the rate of net CO_2 production. This method has the disadvantage that it is expensive and requires specialized mass spectrometry equipment, but the significant advantage is that it can be performed over several weeks with the subjects in their natural environment.

Another method to estimate someone's basal metabolic rate (BMR) is to interpolate from equations called the Harris-Benedict equations, which have been derived on the basis of numerous experiments made on many human subjects, using the methods described above.

EXAMPLE 10.25   Using the *Harris-Benedict equations*, it is possible to gain a good estimate of an indivdual's BMR given the person's age, weight, and height. There is no biochemical rationale behind these equations, but they are useful for everyday approximation. Note that the equations return values as kilocalories. It is necessary to multiply by 4.184 to convert the results to kilojoules.

BMR estimator

Women:

$$BMR = 66 + (9.6 \times weight, kg) + (1.8 \times height, cm) - (4.7 \times age, years)$$

Men:

$$BMR = 66 + (13.7 \times weight, kg) + (5 \times height, cm) - (6.8 \times age, years)$$

A factor that is omitted in the Harris-Benedict equations is lean body mass. So formulas are quite accurate in all but the very muscular (where they underestimate BMR) and the very fat (where they overestimate BMR).

Multiply the BMR in kcal day^{-1} by 4.184 to get the value in kJ day^{-1}.

Fig. 10-22   Harris-Benedict equations.

Basal Metabolic Rate (BMR)

BMR refers to the energy that is expended by the body at rest, but not while asleep. It indicates the amount of energy that is required to keep the body alive and is strongly proportional to lean body mass, which is the amount of metabolically active tissue. This emphasizes the fact that even resting muscle is metabolically active. A great deal of energy is expended in maintaining ion gradients in resting muscle whereas adipose tissue is relatively inactive, being mainly lipid droplets and possessing little cytoplasm.

Surprisingly, overweight people do not on average have lower BMRs because the fat mass of an obese person is accompanied by extra lean body mass. In contrast, the body seems to be able to manipulate BMR in response to over- or underfeeding. The tendency of body mass (weight) to return to its *set point mass* means that individuals respond to a period of mass loss by *lowering* their BMR. Conversely, mass gain will generally lead to an adaptive *rise* in BMR.

This response seems to be contradictive because if energy expenditure and rates of fuel oxidation of the body are so well coupled, how can there be any latitude for an individual's BMR to be manipulated by, say, a personal trainer?

In fact, a great many factors have been hypothesized, and in many cases have been shown, to change the BMR. In the longer term, increasing lean body mass is an effective way of increasing the BMR, and there are many biochemical mechanisms that can operate in the short term; these are given in (Example 10.18) the following examples.

EXAMPLE 10.26   We have already discussed the presence and function of UCP-1 in BAT and the recently recognized importance of UCP-2 and UCP-3 in other tissues. Clearly the most obvious way of *dissipating* or *conserving* energy is to decrease or increase, respectively, the efficiency of oxidative phosphorylation by altering the activity of the UCPs. This is involved in the regulation of body temperature.

EXAMPLE 10.27   Whenever an energy-requiring process is reversed, it is likely that the ATP concentration will decline. Protein synthesis from amino acids consumes ATP; but if that protein is then hydrolyzed into amino acids, ATP is not regenerated and the net effect is ATP consumption. This is called a *futile cycle*; other examples include the *synthesis* and *hydrolysis* of triglycerides, glycogen, and nucleic acids. There are also examples within metabolic pathways; e.g., the trapping of glucose in cells by its conversion to glucose 6-phosphate consumes ATP, but glucose 6-phosphate can readily be hydrolyzed back to glucose by glucose 6-phosphatase which does not involve the production of ATP.

   The most physiologically important futile cycle results from cell membranes that are leaky. For example, in muscle cells ATP is consumed in pumping calcium ions into the sarcoplasmic reticulum. Leakage of calcium ions from this compartment forces the process to proceed faster than would be necessary if the membrane were totally impermeable to these ions.

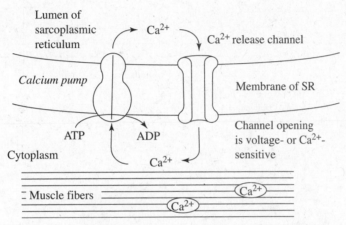

Fig. 10-23   Calcium movement across the sarcoplasmic reticulum in skeletal muscle. Note the potential futile cycle.

EXAMPLE 10.28   When muscle cells contract, Ca^{2+} ions are released from the sarcoplasmic reticulum into the cytoplasm. It is this sudden rise in cytoplasmic Ca^{2+} concentration that stimulates the molecular interactions that cause myofibrillar contraction. Much energy is required to pump Ca^{2+} ions into the sarcoplasmic reticulum against a concentration gradient, so if more Ca^{2+} ions are released than are required to stimulate contraction, then this overrelease represents a *waste of energy*. Such a situation might result from the ion gradient being maintained at too high a level in the first place. There is good experimental evidence that such a mechanism is involved in an increase in muscle efficiency as seen when animals, made to be less active than usual, are held below their energy expenditure *set point* and gain weight more rapidly than usual.

Shuttles

The discussion of glycolysis (Sec. 10.6) highlights the fact that it produces NADH in the cytoplasm. For the generation of ATP from NADH, and also for the regeneration of cytosolic NAD⁺, the hydrogen atoms and electrons must be transferred from the cytoplasm to the ETC within the mitochondria. As cytoplasmic NADH cannot cross the inner mitochondrial membrane, a redox shuttle system is required. There are two such shuttle systems. The first is *malate-aspartate shuttle* which relies on the cytoplasmic malate dehydrogenase converting cytoplasmic oxaloacetate to malate, thereby oxidizing cytoplasmic NADH to NAD⁺. The malate, so produced, is transported into the mitochondrial matrix, via a *dicarboxylate carrier protein*, which cannot translocate oxaloacetate, and is oxidized by a mitochondrial malate dehydrogenase to oxaloacetate with the concomitant production of mitochondrial NADH.

   The second shuttle system involves the cytoplasmic enzyme *glycerol-3-phosphate dehydrogenase* which reduces cytoplasmic dihydroxyacetone phosphate to glycerol 3-phosphate, thereby oxidizing NADH to NAD⁺. The glycerol 3-phosphate is oxidized to dihydroxyacetone phosphate by another glycerol 3-phosphate dehydrogenase which is embedded within the outer surface of the inner mitochondrial membrane. This enzyme uses FAD as a cofactor so that the protons and electrons originating in cytoplasmic NADH are transported to the inner mitochondrial membrane within $FADH_2$.

The malate-aspartate shuttle delivers the cytoplasmic electrons into the matrix at complex I, producing ~2.5 ATPs overall whereas the glycerol 3-phosphate shuttle transfers its electrons at a much lower energy into the matrix at complex II. Thus the electrons from NADH, originating from the malate-aspartate shuttle, will lead to the production of ~2.5 ATPs while the electrons from $FADH_2$, originating from the glycerol 3-phosphate shuttle, will produce 1.5 ATPs. Clearly, if a cell uses the latter shuttle, there will be a decrease in its energy efficiency. Not only has this mechanism of differential efficiency of the two shuttles been shown to contribute to adaptive changes in metabolic rate, but it can also explain many of the differences in metabolic rates between different species.

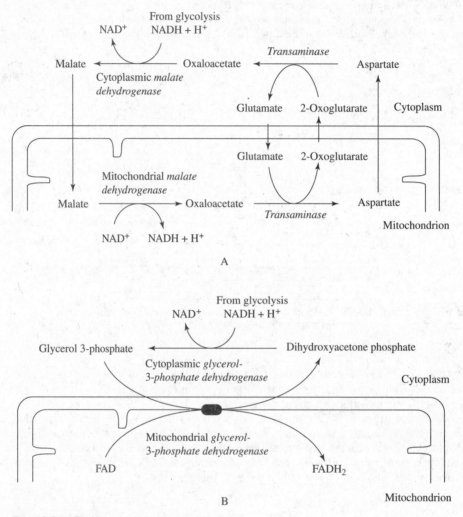

Fig. 10-24   The two main redox shuttles.

EXAMPLE 10.29   Variations in BMR are under tight control. One of the endocrine factors that participates in the regulation of BMR is thyroid hormone (T3). T3 increases BMR, and this is brought about through changes in gene expression since T3 acts via *nuclear receptors*. While the precise identity of the genes and signaling pathways involved are yet to be elucidated, recent studies have shown that T3 acts via several of the processes described above.

Leptin

The motion of the body-mass *set point* had led scientists to postulate that there must be a homeostatic signal from the fuel stores of the body to the brain. This has been referred to as a *lipostat* which can communicate the level of fuel stores to the brain to alter the *appetite* and *metabolic rate control centers* in the brain. In 1995, the hormone *leptin* was discovered. It is secreted by white adipose tissue at a rate that is proportional to the size of the fat reserves. The hypothalamus in the brain influences energy intake and expenditure, and it possesses receptors for leptin. Binding of leptin reduces food intake and increases whole body BMR.

ANABOLISM AND CATABOLISM

10.1. The most common of the reactions in *catabolism* is hydrolysis. Show how this process occurs in the degradation of the three classes of biopolymers: (a) the polymer of glucose, i.e., starch; (b) the polymer of amino acids, i.e., proteins; and (c) the storage form of fatty acids, i.e., triglycerides.

SOLUTION

(a) Starch comes in two structural forms, amylose and amylopectin. Amylose is primarily a linear polymer of glucose monomers that are connected by an anhydride linkage between the C-1 of one glucose and the C-4 of the next glucose molecule in the chain. The glucose units are in the α-anomeric conformation. Just the hydrolysis of amylose is shown in Fig. 10-25A.

(b) A representative peptide and the hydrolysis of one of its peptide bonds are shown in Fig. 10-25B.

(c) A representative triglyceride is shown in Fig. 10-25C. Note the three ester linkages that must be hydrolyzed to release the three fatty acids and glycerol.

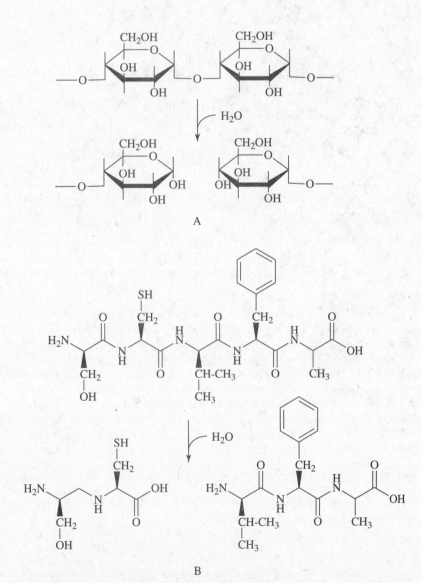

Fig. 10-25   Hydrolysis of three major *macronutrients*. (A) Starch, (B) peptides and proteins, and (C) triglyceride.

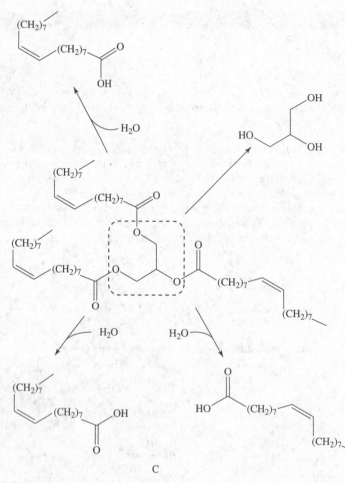

Fig. 10-25 (*Continued*)

10.2. Assign names to the enzymes that catalyze the hydrolytic reactions described in Prob. 10.1.

SOLUTION

(a) The general name would be *glucohydrolase*, but in practice the more specific term is *amylase*. There are many types of amylase, with different substrate specificities, found throughout living systems. The one that is produced in the human pancreas and that is secreted into the duodenum is called α-amylase, so named because it was deemed useful to indicate that it catlyzes the hydrolysis of α-anhydride bonds. Furthermore it hydrolyzes bonds within the amylose chain as well as at the end, so it is called a mixed *endo-* and *exoamylase*. On the other hand, glucohydrolase that is located on the surface of the human small-intestine mucosa is an exoamylase.

(b) The enzyme is called an *endopeptidase*, or if the enzyme operates on long peptide chains, it is called an endoprotease.

(c) The enzyme is called a *lipase*.

ATP AS THE ENERGY CURRENCY OF LIVING SYSTEMS

10.3. Why might such a relatively complicated molecule as ATP have been naturally selected in living systems as the *energy currency* in most cells?

SOLUTION

While the free energy of the anhydride bond in a simple anion-like pyrophosphate is similar to that of the terminal anydride bond of ATP, the value of having the large adenosine moiety present on this currency molecule is that it places many more constraints on the binding sites of those enzymes that use it as a substrate. In other words, the specificity, selectivity, and hence control of the reactions that use it are enhanced.

EXTRACTING ENERGY FROM FUEL MOLECULES: OXIDATION

10.4. (a) What is the pathway from glucose molecules to acetyl-CoA? (b) Which cellular compartments are involved? (c) Are reducing equivalents generated in different cellular compartments?

SOLUTION

(a) Figure 10-26 shows that glucose enters the cell via a GLUT transporter and is phosphorylated via hexokinase. This phosphorylation locks the glucose inside the cell. Glycolysis proceeds in the cytoplasm to yield pyruvate.

(b) Glycolysis takes place in the cytoplasm, and the conversion of pyruvate to acetyl-CoA and the subsequent oxidation of these two carbon units to CO_2 and H_2O take place in the mitochondrial matrix.

(c) Yes, NADH is generated in the glycolytic (cytoplasmic) reaction that is catalyzed by glyceraldehyde-3-phosphate dehydrogenase.

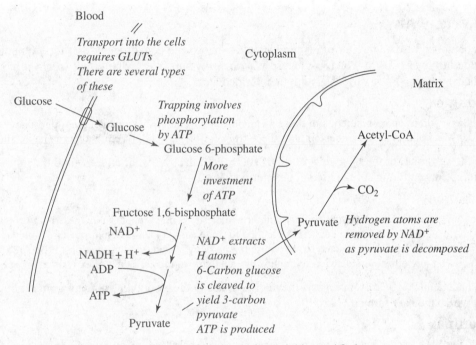

Fig. 10-26 Metabolism of glucose via glycolysis to yield acetyl-CoA.

β-OXIDATION PATHWAY FOR FATTY ACIDS

10.5. How much energy, in the form of ATP, is obtained from β-oxidation of 1 mol of palmitoyl-CoA?

SOLUTION

One mole of palmitoyl-CoA yields 8 mol of acetyl-CoA by β-oxidation. The overall equation is
Palmitoyl-CoA + 7FAD + 7NAD⁺ + 7CoA + 7H₂O → 8Acetyl-CoA + 7FADH₂ + 7NADH + 7H⁺.
FADH₂ and NADH + H⁺ are oxidized in the ETC of the mitochondria:

$$7FADH_2 + 7NADH + 7H^+ + 7O_2 \rightarrow 7FAD + 7NAD^+ + 14H_2O$$

During electron transport, coupled with ATP synthesis, each mole of $FADH_2$ that is oxidized yields 1.5 mol of ATP; therefore, 7 mol of $FADH_2$ yields 10.5 mol of ATP. Each mole of NADH that is oxidized yields 2.5 mol of ATP; therefore, 7 mol of NADH plus 7 mol of H⁺ yields 17.5 mol of ATP. Hence the total yield is 28 mol of ATP.

10.6. What is the complete sequence of events in the complete oxidation of linoleic acid?

SOLUTION

β-Oxidation proceeds normally to shorten the 18-carbon-chain linoleic acid to dodecadienoic acid, $C_{12:2}\Delta 3,6$; three molecules of acetyl-CoA are produced as follows:

$$CH_3-(CH_2)_4-CH=CH-CH_2-CH=CH-(CH_2)_7-COO^- \rightarrow$$

$$CH_3-(CH_2)_4-CH=CH-CH_2-CH=CH-CH_2-COO^- + 3\,CH_3-COSCoA$$

Before the next round of β-oxidation can proceed, the double bond of *cis* Δ^3 is converted to *trans* Δ^2 by the enzyme Δ^3-cis- Δ^2-trans-*enoyl-CoA isomerase* as follows:

$$CH_3-(CH_2)_4-CH=CH-CH_2-CH=CH-CH_2-COO- \rightarrow$$
$$\text{cis}$$
$$CH_3-(CH_2)_4-CH=CH-(CH_2)_2-CH=CH-COO^-$$
$$\text{trans}$$

After one further cycle of β-oxidation, a 4-*cis*-enoyl CoA intermediate is formed. It is acted upon by *enoyl-CoA dehydrogenase* to give 2-*trans*, 4-*cis*-dienoyl CoA. Further metabolism of this intermediate proceeds through one cycle of β-oxidation and requires a second *auxiliary* enzyme, 2,4-*dienoyl-CoA reductase*, that has high activity in mitochondria. Thus, nine molecules of acetyl-CoA are produced from the oxidation of one molecule of linoleic acid.

GLYCOLYTIC PATHWAY

10.7. A compound is an inhibitor of glyceraldehyde-3-phosphate dehydrogenase. If this compound were added to liver cells in which D-glucose was the only substrate, what effect would it have on the concentrations of the various glycolytic intermediates?

SOLUTION

There would be an accumulation of those metabolites in the pathway from glucose 6-phosphate to glyceraldehyde 3-phosphate and a depletion of those from 1,3-bisphosphoglycerate to pyruvate and lactate.

10.8. If the substrate for the liver cells in Prob. 10.7 were L-lactate, what effect would the inhibitor have on the concentrations of the glycolytic intermediates?

SOLUTION

There would be no effect on the glycolytic intermediates except, perhaps, an increase in the concentration of pyruvate. The cells would convert the lactate to pyruvate via lactate dehydrogenase, and the pyruvate would then be converted to acetyl-CoA via pyruvate dehydrogenase, and then on to the Krebs cycle. If glucose or any other suitable carbohydrate is not available to the cell, then glycolysis cannot proceed.

10.9. What chemical constraint prevents the intermediates of the glycolytic pathway from leaving the cell in which they are formed?

SOLUTION

All glycolytic intermediates derived from glucose are phosphorylated. At physiological pH values, phosphate groups are ionized so that each intermediate is negatively charged. Charged molecules are not readily able to cross cell membranes unless they have a specific transport protein, so the intermediates are confined to the cytoplasm of the cell.

10.10. What is the net change in oxidation state when glucose is converted to lactate?

SOLUTION

There is no overall change in the oxidation state when glucose is converted to lactate, because glyceraldehyde-3-phosphate dehydrogenase catalyzes the *oxidation* of glyceraldehyde 3-phosphate to 1,3-bisphosphoglycerate, but lactate dehydrogenase catalyzes the *reduction* of pyruvate to lactate. In combination these two reactions reduce NAD^+ to NADH, then oxidize NADH back to NAD^+.

10.11. If all the glycolytic enzymes, ATP, ADP, NAD^+, and glucose were incubated together under ideal conditions, would pyruvate be produced?

SOLUTION

No, because an important omission is inorganic phosphate, or Pi. Even if phosphate were added to the incubation mixture, pyruvate would be produced only in an amount equivalent to that of the NAD^+ present. Glycolysis requires NAD^+ for step 6 (Fig. 10-8A), the reaction catalyzed by glyceraldehyde-3-phosphate dehydrogenase.

10.12. What is the metabolic fate of lactate in mammalian cells?

SOLUTION

Lactate can undergo only one reaction: it is oxidized to pyruvate via lactate dehydrogenase.

10.13. In red blood cells, *2,3-bisphosphoglycerate* binds to hemoglobin and reduces its oxygen affinity (Chap. 4). This negative heterotropic effector of hemoglobin is synthesized in one step from a glycolytic intermediate and is converted to yet another also in one step, What are the two glycolytic intermediates and which enzymes are involved in the reactions?

SOLUTION

2,3-bisphosphoglycerate is synthesized from *1,3-bisphosphoglycerate* in a reaction that is catalyzed by *2,3-bisphosphoglycerate synthase*. The enzyme *2,3-bisphosphoglycerate phosphatase* catalyzes the hydrolysis of the 2-phosphate to make 3-phosphoglycerate. This detour from glycolysis (Fig. 10-27) is called the *Rapoport-Luebering shunt* after its discoverers.

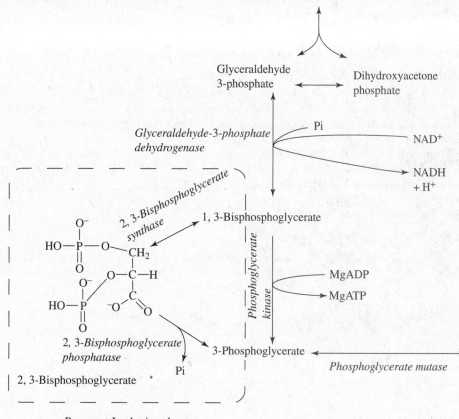

Rapoport-Luebering shunt

Fig. 10-27   Rapoport-Luebering shunt of glycolysis. It is present in red blood cells of most mammals.

KREBS CYCLE

10.14. What are the overall chemical changes that occur during one complete turn of the Krebs cycle?

SOLUTION

The overall reactions are: (1) the complete oxidation of one molecule of acetyl-CoA; (2) the production of two molecules of CO_2; (3) the reduction of three molecules of NAD^+ and one of FAD; and (4) the phosphorylation of GDP.

10.15. The overall reaction of the Krebs cycle is:

$$CH_3COSCoA + 2H_2O + 3NAD^+ + FAD + GDP + Pi \rightarrow 2CO_2 + 3NADH + 3H^+ + FADH_2 + GTP$$

Is only one ATP equivalent (GTP) produced for each molecule of acetyl-CoA consumed?

SOLUTION

Only one ATP equivalent is *directly* produced (reaction 5 in Fig. 10-9B), but the oxidation of NADH and $FADH_2$ (reactions 3, 4, and 8, and reaction 6 respectively, in Fig. 10-9B) yields a further ~ $(3 \times 2.5 + 1 \times 1.5) \cong 9$ molecules of ATP via the ETC and oxidative phosphorylation.

10.16. In the Krebs cycle (Fig. 10-9) how many steps involve: (a) oxidation-reduction; (b) hydration-dehydration; (c) substrate-level phosphorylation; and (d) decarboxylation? List the enzymes responsible for these reactions.

SOLUTION

(a) Four steps involve oxidation-reduction. The enzymes involved are isocitrate dehydrogenase, 2-oxoglutarate dehydrogenase, succinate dehydrogenase, and malate dehydrogenase.

(b) Two steps involve hydration-dehydration reactions. The enzymes that catalyze these reactions are aconitase and fumarase.

(c) One step involves substrate-level phosphorylation, and the enzyme is succinyl-CoA synthetase.

(d) Two steps involve decarboxylation. The enzymes are isocitrate dehydrogenase and 2-oxoglutarate dehydrogenase.

10.17. Two molecules of CO_2 are produced each time a molecule of acetyl-CoA is oxidized. Do the carbon atoms of *this* acetyl-CoA molecule directly become the CO_2 in the first turn of the cycle?

SOLUTION

No, Fig.10-28 shows the fate of the carbon atoms of one molecule of acetyl-CoA in *two* turns of the cycle. The two carbon atoms can be followed as a *single unit* until step 5, the formation of the symmetric molecule succinate, when they become *randomized*. This means that the two methylene carbon atoms of succinate have equal probability of arising from the methyl group of acetyl-CoA. Steps 3 and 4 of the *second* turn each yield CO_2, which constitutes at each step 50% of the original carboxyl carbon of acetyl-CoA. During the *third* turn of the cycle, these two steps collectively liberate 50% of the remaining labeled methyl carbons as CO_2, and so forth for subsequent turns of the cycle.

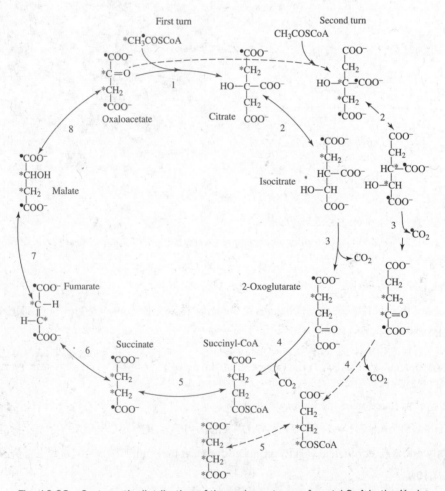

Fig. 10-28   Systematic distribution of the carbon atoms of acetyl-CoA in the Krebs cycle among the various metabolites. The dot and asterisk identify those carbon atoms from the initial acetyl-CoA.

10.18. Citrate is bilaterally symmetric about C-3, yet in step 2 (Fig. 10-9 and 10-28) of the Krebs cycle, aconitase catalyzes the removal of the elements of water from only *half* of the molecule and not from the *structurally identical* other half. How can this be explained?

SOLUTION

Hans Krebs, the discoverer of the cycle, also pondered this question and at one stage came to the conclusion that citrate could not be an intermediate in the cycle. However, in 1948, Alexander ("Sandy") Ogston provided the explanation, called the *three-point attachment* proposal, that was to initiate the concept of *prochirality*. If citrate is represented as a three-dimensional structure, as in Fig. 10-29, then on the assumption that a three-point attachment to a surface in aconitase is necessary for catalysis, it is seen that citrate can only be accommodated in *one orientation*. The removal of the elements of water can then only occur from one particular half of the symmetric molecule. Thus a combination of the binding site and the *prochiral* citrate is, overall, asymmetric or has *handedness*.

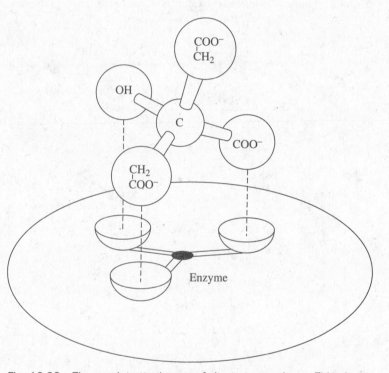

Fig. 10-29   Three-point attachment of citrate to aconitase. This shows how only one *particular* —CH$_2$—COO$^-$ group binds to the enzyme.

10.19. Assuming that aspartate is the only major carbon source supplied to a preparation of mammalian cells in culture, outline all reactions whereby the Krebs cycle would operate in the mitochondria.

SOLUTION

Aspartate would be *transaminated* (Chap. 14) to yield oxaloacetate. Oxaloacetate would then be converted to acetyl-CoA by the following sequence of reactions:

Oxaloacetate $\xrightarrow{1}$ Malate $\xrightarrow{2}$ Oxaloacetate $\xrightarrow{3}$ Phosphoenolpyruvate $\xrightarrow{4}$ Acetyl-CoA

The enzymes are, respectively, (1) mitochondrial malate dehydrogenase; (2) cytoplasmic malate dehydrogenase; (3) phosphoenolpyruvate carboxykinase; and (4) pyruvate kinase and pyruvate dehydrogenase. The acetyl-CoA could then condense with oxaloacetate (produced from a second molecule of aspartate) to yield citrate. Aspartate would therefore continue to supply acetyl-CoA, which would continue to fuel the Krebs cycle.

INTERCONNECTION BETWEEN ENERGY EXPENDITURE
AND OXIDATION OF FUEL MOLECULES

10.20. Using the principles espoused in Secs. 10.8 and 10.9, deduce a link between work done by a cell and its production of ATP.

SOLUTION

Cells maintain their internal environment in a relatively stable state, continuously pumping ions in and out, turning over proteins, etc. If a cell is not doing work, it is not using ATP and making ADP, so all adenine nucleotides in the cell will be predominantly in the form of ATP. If ADP were not available, the H^+ ions would not pass through the F_0F_1ATPase. In this case the proton gradient would remain high and not be dissipated. Protons would not be pumped out against the large electrochemical gradient, so electrons would *not* proceed along the ETC and on to oxygen. In effect, there would be a *traffic jam*, and all carriers would exist in the fully reduced state. Under these circumstances, NADH would not pass its electrons to the ETC so no NAD^+ would be formed. Since NAD^+ would not be regenerated, it would not be available to remove protons and electrons from fuel molecules and their oxidation would cease. This is summarized in Fig. 10-30.

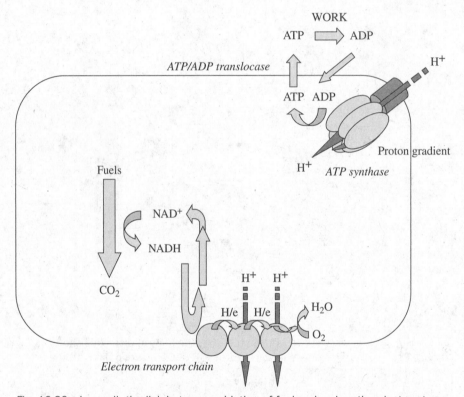

Fig. 10-30   In a cell, the link between oxidation of fuel molecules, the electron transport chain, the supply of ATP, and work done by the cell, e.g., a contractile muscle cell.

INHIBITORS OF ATP SYNTHESIS

10.21. Predict the effect on a cell of cyanide, an inhibitor of complex IV and hence of ATP production.

SOLUTION

A block at the last complex in the electron transport chain (ETC) prevents the reduction of oxygen and causes all the electron transport complexes to become fully saturated (reduced) with electrons. As with rotenone (Example 10.14), a lack of electron/proton movement along the chain means that NADH is not reoxidized and fuel oxidation ceases. Similarly, the lack of electron transport activity means that the proton gradient soon dissipates and there is no driving force for ATP synthesis. ATP levels falls rapidly and the cell dies.

10.22. What is the physiological effect of ingesting dinitrophenol (DNP)?

SOLUTION

If consumed, DNP will cause a rapid elevation in fuel oxidation and oxygen consumption. The metabolic effects of DNP were first discovered when it was noted that munitions workers rapidly lost weight after contact with the compound as it was used in the manufacture of explosives. During the first half of the 20th century, DNP was sold as a weight loss agent, ignoring the fact that it also causes depletion of ATP which renders it highly dangerous. Another side effect of DNP consumption is a marked elevation in body temperature as a consequence of an increased loss of NADH energy as heat.

10.23. Could UCP-1 be exploited for antiobesity therapy?

SOLUTION

Many pharmaceutical companies are interested in designing agonists of the β-3 receptor (Fig. 10-16). However, excessive cross reactivity between β-3 agonists and other beta receptors is a problem. Perhaps a more fundamental problem is that adult humans do not contain very much BAT, probably as a consequence of a low surface area/mass ratio and a lifetime of living in centrally heated environments and wearing warm clothes. Set against this, it is easy to show that even a small rise in daily energy expenditure can have significant repercussions for body weight reduction in the long term; and new methods of histological tissue screening have revealed that even adult humans may have more BAT than was previously thought.

DETAILS OF THE MOLECULAR MACHINERY OF ATP SYNTHESIS

10.24. Propose a simple mechanism that leads to the directional (vectorial) expulsion of H⁺ ions as electrons flow through an electron transfer protein complex.

SOLUTION

Imagine that a hydrogen-atom carrier X (carrying a proton and an electron) passes its electron onto an electron carrier Y. The latter will only accept an electron, so in the transfer process the H⁺ will diffuse into the surroundings. Now imagine that the reduced electron carrier has the potential to pass its electron to another hydrogen atom carrier Z. The latter requires a proton as well as the electron, thus the transaction will require that a proton be taken up from the surroundings. During the net movement of hydrogen atoms from X to Z, protons are both ejected and regained. Clearly if the proton ejection reaction occurs on the cytosolic face and the H⁺ uptake reaction occurs on the matrix face, the net effect will be the movement of protons from the matrix.

Note that the H⁺s that are pumped out come from the matrix and are not necessarily those directly from NADH. The one hydride ion on NADH causes the translocation of 10 H⁺s as it goes along the chain.

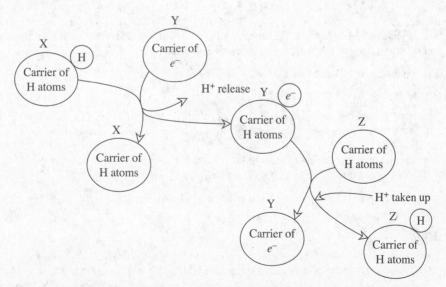

Fig. 10-31   Schematic representation of proton pumping in a protein complex situated between two compartments.

10.25. Using Fig. 10-21, postulate how changing the affinity of the adenine nucleotide binding sites in the F_1ATPase causes the formation of ATP.

SOLUTION

Each of the three binding sites on the F_1ATPase can exist in one of three conformations; loose, tight, and open. The loose form has a high affinity for ADP and Pi. As the site changes to the tight form, the ADP and Pi react to produce ATP. At any one time, each of the three sites on the F_1ATPase will exist as loose, tight, or open. It is the interaction with the γ-subunit (Fig. 10-21) that causes the transition, making it like a camshaft that moves the valves in an internal combustion engine to open and close at the correct times. This model was first proposed by Paul Boyer and called the *binding change model*. It is discussed in his Chemistry Nobel Prize citation of 1997.

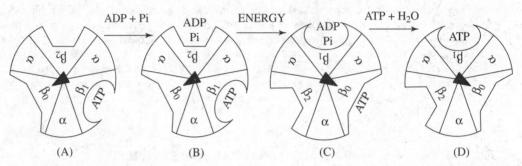

Fig. 10-32   Boyer's binding change model of F_1ATPase. The black triangle represents the γ subunit.

10.26. Can the F_1ATPase run in reverse?

SOLUTION

Yes. The F_1ATPase, in isolation from the F_0 channel, can catalyze the hydrolysis of ATP. In fact, there is an example, in nature, of a proton pump that is fueled by ATP that works like the F_1F_0ATPase in reverse. But the intact F_1F_0ATPases in mitochondria do not act as ATPases.

WHOLE BODY ENERGY BALANCE

10.27. Speculate on the major components of whole body energy expenditure.

SOLUTION

The three main components are *basal metabolic rate* (BMR), which constitutes 60% of daily whole body expenditure; *physical activity*, which generally contributes ~30% of the total; and *diet-induced thermogenesis*, making up the remaining 10%. These proportions vary among individuals, but the figures do illustrate the general dominance of BMR in the daily metabolic rate.

10.28. What is the meaning of the term *diet-induced thermogenesis*?

SOLUTION

This refers to the energy that is expended in: (1) the digestion of food; (2) the transport of molecules derived from food into and around the body; (3) the increased metabolic rate as these molecules are assimilated into the body; (4) energy demands associated with synthesis and storage of fuel molecules; and (5) the effect that feeding can have on the stimulation of brown adipose tissue; in other words a psychological effect. The last is often referred to as the *thermic effect of food*.

10.29. What are likely possible problems with using the Harris-Benedict equations (Example 10.25) to calculate someone's BMR?

SOLUTION

The major inaccuracy in the Harris-Benedict equation is that it relies on *total weight* and not lean body weight (or mass) that is the primary determinant of BMR. It is not accurate in the *very muscular*, where it underestimates BMR, and the *very obese*, where it overestimates the BMR. Other equations have been formulated that allow rapid prediction of BMR from whole body parameters.

10.30. What might be the effect of a mutation in the leptin gene that prevents production of active leptin?

SOLUTION

Patients with a rare leptin gene mutation have an insatiable appetite. While this inevitably leads to obesity, the condition can be managed with *injections of leptin.*

10.31. Draw a bar graph to show possible food-energy intake by an adult human over a period of 24 h. Draw a second graph to show possible energy consumption.

SOLUTION

The intake of food is usually in three to five meals and snacks a day. It is episodic. But the body's use of energy is highest during the day and not coordinated with meals. It is low during sleep.

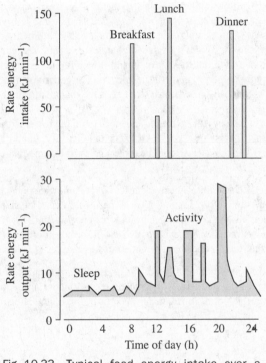

Fig. 10-33 Typical food energy intake over a 24 h period by an adult human (upper graph), and corresponding energy expenditure by the body.

SUPPLEMENTARY PROBLEMS

10.32. Glucose transporters (the GLUTs) play a major role in making this ubiquitous substrate accessible to the metabolic machinery in the cell cytoplasm. However, not all cells have the same level of control over glucose entry such as the insulin dependence of glucose uptake by skeletal muscle. How do the classes of GLUTs differ from one another and hence attain their various attributes?

10.33. If 1 molecule of glucose produces 2 molecules of ATP by substrate-level phosphorylation in glycolysis and the resulting 2 molecules of pyruvate can each yield 12.5 molecules of ATP when oxygen is available, how many glucose molecules will be necessary to produce 135 molecules of ATP by yeast grown under (a) aerobic and (b) anaerobic conditions?

10.34. In Prob. 10.33, how many molecules of CO_2 would be evolved in producing 135 molecules of ATP during growth under (a) aerobic and (b) anaerobic conditions?

10.35. Human red blood cells contain no mitochondria so they derive their energy from glucose purely on the basis of anaerobic glycolysis. Thus, from Prob. 10.33, it might be expected that each glucose molecule would generate two molecules of ATP. However if 1,3-bisphosphoglycerate were detoured via the Rapoport-Luebering shunt, what would be the stoichiometry between glucose and ATP?

10.36. Could leptin be used to treat obesity?

ANSWERS TO SUPPLEMENTARY PROBLEMS

10.32. Each isoform of glucose transporter has a specific action in glucose metabolism that is determined by its pattern of expression in tissues, its substrate specificity, transport kinetics, and how its expression is regulated under different physiological conditions. Thirteen members of the GLUT family have been identified. The family has been divided into three subclasses.

  1. Class I consists of the well-characterized glucose transporters GLUT-1 to GLUT-4.
    (a) GLUT-1 is widely distributed in fetal tissues. In the adult, it is expressed at the highest levels in erythrocytes and also in the endothelial cells of *barrier tissues* such as in the blood-brain barrier. It is also responsible for the low level of basal glucose uptake in all cells. Its levels in cell membranes in those cells with nuclei, so not in erythrocytes, are increased by reduced glucose levels and decreased by increased glucose levels.
    (b) GLUT-2 is expressed by renal tubular cells and the epithelial cells of the small intestine that transport glucose, hepatocytes, and the β cells of the islets on Langerhans in the pancreas.
    (c) GLUT-3 is expressed mostly in neurons, where it is the main isoform of GLUT, and in the placenta. It has a high affinity for glucose.
    (d) GLUT-4 is found in adipocytes, skeletal, and cardiac myocytes. It is the *insulin-regulated* isoform.
  2. Class II consists of the fructose transporter GLUT-5 and GLUT-7, 9, and 11.
  3. Class III consists of GLUT-6 , 8, 10, 12 and the proton *symport* that mediates polyol transmembrane exchange, i.e., the *H^+/myoinositol transporter* (HMIT).

Most members of classes II and III have been identified in genomewide database searches. The function of these newly discovered transporter isoforms is not yet well defined. Several of them (GLUT-6 and 8) contain motifs that lead to their retention inside the cell, and therefore this prevents their involvement in glucose transport at the plasma membrane. Whether mechanisms exist to invoke cell surface insertion of these transporters is unknown, but it has been established that insulin does *not* promote translocation of GLUT-6 and GLUT-8 to the cell surface.

10.33. (a) Growth under aerobic conditions can produce $2 + 25 = 27$ molecules of ATP per molecule of glucose. To produce 135 molecules of ATP, $135/27 = 5$ molecules of glucose are required.
    (b) Growth under anaerobic conditions can produce only 2 molecules of ATP per molecule of glucose. To produce 135 molecules of ATP, $135/2 = 67.5$ molecules of glucose are required.

10.34. (a) Aerobic: 1 Glucose $\rightarrow$ 6 CO_2
                 $\therefore$ 5 Glucose $\rightarrow$ 30 CO_2

    (b) Anaerobic: 1 glucose $\rightarrow$ 2 pyruvate but this must be converted to lactate to recycle NAD^+. So pyruvate does not pass into pyruvate dehydrogenase which would otherwise release 2 molecules of CO_2. So the answer is 0. Five molecules of glucose would also give 0 molecules of CO_2.

10.35. If all the carbon atoms in glycolysis flowed through the Rapoport-Luebering shunt, then the ATP-generating step catalyzed by phosphoglycerate kinase would be bypassed. Two ATP molecules are consumed in the first part of glycolysis, and one is recovered at each of two steps in the lower part of glycolysis when the intermediates have only three carbon atoms, so there is a net of 2 ATP molecules produced. But if one of the ATP-generating steps is bypassed entirely, then net ATP production would be 0. In fact, experiments show that a maximum of only ~20% of the carbon flux in glycolysis can be via the Rapoport-Luebering shunt. However, variations in this flux leads to a variation in the number of molecules of ATP that are produced from each molecule of glucose. This phenomenon is called *variable stoichiometry* and it is very important in balancing the varying demands for ATP and reducing equivalents in red blood cells in circulating blood.

10.36. The discovery of leptin caused great excitement for this very reason. However, injections of leptin are relatively ineffective at reducing food intake or in raising energy expenditure in obese patients, except in those rare cases noted in Solved Problem 10.30. This is so partly because obese patients already have high circulating concentrations of leptin. It is also so because obese patients appear to be *leptin-resistant*, which implies that a given concentration of leptin is less effective in obese patients than in lean individuals. In addition, it is possible that an appetite suppressant such as leptin may not be fully effective in subjects whose metabolism has settled on a *high-mass set point*. But the meaning of the latter statement in molecular terms is yet to be elucidated.

Fate of Dietary Carbohydrate

11.1   Sources of Dietary Carbohydrate

Question: What forms do carbohydrate molecules take in the diet and in the body?

As noted in Chap. 3, the term *carbohydrate* means hydrated carbon atoms. All living things make and store carbohydrates, so when one organism eats another organism, it acquires carbohydrates. Carbohydrates are present in three basic forms: *monosaccharides*; *disaccharides* that are dimers of monosaccharides; and *oligo-* and *polysaccharides* that are polymers of monosaccharides.

Starch, a polymer of glucose, is the most common source of dietary carbohydrate for humans because it is the main storage form of carbohydrate in plants; but significant amounts of the disaccharides, sucrose (which consists of a heterodimer of glucose and fructose), lactose (of glucose and galactose), and maltose (of two glucose molecules), are also consumed. Surprisingly only small amounts of carbohydrate arise from direct intake of the monosaccharides, but some glucose (mainly in confectionary) and fructose (in fruit and honey) are the two most commonly ingested forms.

Lactose is present in milk, so most dairy products contain this disaccharide.

EXAMPLE 11.1   Typical proportions of the various types of carbohydrates in a Western diet are as follows.

The total daily intake of carbohydrate is ~300 g: of this, ~250 g is starch, 30 g is sucrose, and 20 g is lactose. Cooked foods containing large amounts of starch include potatoes (average values) (12.4 g/100 g), rice (27.9 g/100 g), and pasta (24.6 g/100 g). A slice of bread weighing 30 g has 12.8 g of starch. Of the starches in a Western diet, bread contributes about one-half and potatoes about one-third.

EXAMPLE 11.2   The consumption of maltose has risen in recent years. Why might this be so?

Maltose, a disaccharide of glucose is derived commercially from the hydrolysis of starch obtained from corn. It is as maltose that glucose is introduced into many popular modern sports drinks.

11.2   Nomenclature of Carbohydrates

General Notation

Before going any further, we need to recall some of the commonly used chemical terminology of carbohydrates and how monosaccharides are bonded to each other to make oligo- and polysaccharides; more details are given in Chap. 3.

Because many mono- and disaccharides have a sweet taste, carbohydrates of low M_r are called *sugars*. However, it is advisable to use the words *carbohydrates* or *saccharides* or the correct name of the compound because *sugar* can mean many different compounds depending on the context in which it is used. The main sugar in your blood is glucose, the sugar in milk is lactose, the sugar in your coffee is usually sucrose, and the main sugar in fruit is fructose.

We restrict discussion here to simple monosaccharides, i.e., polyhydroxy compounds that contain a carbonyl functional group (Chap. 3). There are two series, the *aldoses* that contain an *aldehyde* group and

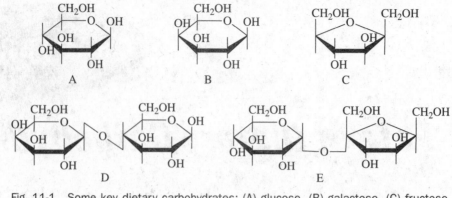

Fig. 11-1   Some key dietary carbohydrates: (A) glucose, (B) galactose, (C) fructose, (D) lactose, and (E) sucrose. An explanation of these *Haworth* projections is given in Sec. 11.2.

ketoses that contain a *ketone* group. Simple monosaccharides are also classified according to the number of carbon atoms that they contain: trioses, tetroses, pentoses, hexoses, etc. contain, three, four, five, and six carbon atoms, respectively. The two systems of names can be combined; e.g., glucose, the most common carbohydrate, is an *aldohexose*, and it has six carbon atoms and contains an aldehyde group.

EXAMPLE 11.3   The classification of each of the monosaccharides is given beneath its structure in Fig. 11-2.

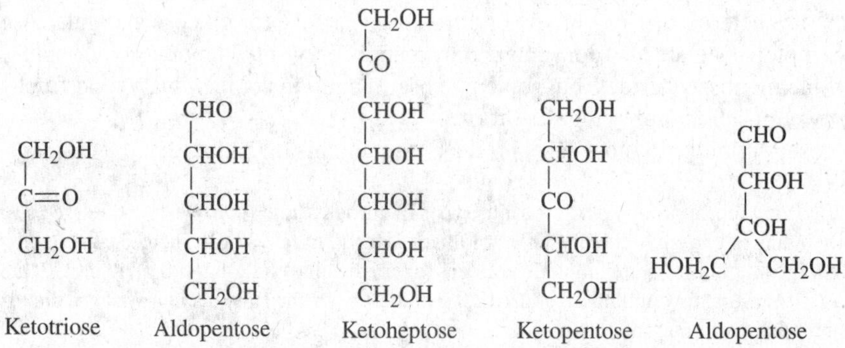

| Ketotriose | Aldopentose | Ketoheptose | Ketopentose | Aldopentose |

Fig. 11-2   Five different monosaccharides and their systematic biochemical classification.

Aldoses

The simplest carbohydrate is the aldotriose, glyceraldehyde (Fig. 3-1). The 4-carbon aldoses are related to D- and L-glyceraldehyde and can be viewed as having been structurally derived from them by the introduction of a hydroxylated chiral carbon atom between C-1 and C-2. Thus there are four aldotetroses. Two simple aldopentoses can be derived structurally from each of the four aldotetroses described, making a total of eight aldopentoses.

Ketoses

As noted in Chap. 3 structurally, the parent compound of the ketoses is dihydroxyacetone (Fig. 3-5); it is a *structural isomer* of glyceraldehyde (Fig. 3-1). There are two ketotetroses, four ketopentoses, and eight ketohexoses. The most common ketose is *fructose* (Fig. 3-6).

Glucose Structure

D-Glucose is the most abundant of the monosaccharides in human metabolism, and the *open-* or *straight-chain* structure only occurs when glucose is in solution; even then it represents only ~1% of the glucose molecules. The other forms are known as α- and β-anomers (Chap. 3). The two forms are represented in *Haworth projections*, as shown in Chap. 3, and we use these in the diagrams in this chapter.

Let us now return from this nomenclature detour to the main theme of the chapter.

11.3 Digestion and Absorption of Carbohydrates

In humans and other mammals, carbohydrate absorption from food occurs in the small intestine, primarily the jejunum. The substrate-specific transport proteins in the membranes of the epithelial cells transport only monosaccharides. Disaccharides and polysaccharides must be hydrolyzed into monosaccharides by specific enzymes in order to be absorbed.

EXAMPLE 11.4 The milk disaccharide lactose is hydrolyzed in the small intestine prior to the absorption of the constituent monosaccharides. Describe this process.

Lactose is hydrolyzed by the membrane-bound enzyme *lactase*. The enzyme is also known as a β-*galactosidase* because its action involves the cleavage of the β-anomer of galactose from its 1→4 bond with an α-anomer of glucose. Note this arrow nomenclature for the bond or linkage between the two monosaccharides.

EXAMPLE 11.5 What is the consequence of an acquired or *inherited* deficiency of lactase?

If the enzyme lactase is deficient, then lactose is not hydrolyzed in the small intestine and it passes unchanged into the large intestine. There it is fermented by bacteria that release volatile organic acids that irritate the mucosa of the bowel; and large volumes of gas such as hydrogen and methane are produced in the process. This, in turns, leads to the clinical signs of flatulence and loose stools, plus abdominal discomfort and a feeling of being "bloated." This negative response to the ingestion of lactose is called *lactose intolerance*, and if it occurs in babies prior to weaning, the condition is manifested as *explosive diarrhea*. Interestingly, the extent of lactose intolerance is seen to be strongly linked to ethnicity, with some populations having very low incidence (3% in Scandinavians) while other groups show very high prevalence (>90% in Thais).

In the small intestine, sucrose is cleaved to glucose and fructose by *sucrase*. In contrast to lactase, this enzyme is rarely deficient.

Starch digestion also occurs primarily in the small intestine, but some cleavage begins in the mouth and gastric contents since saliva contains the enzyme *ptyalin*, which is a form of α-amylase. It attacks the 1→4 glycosidic bond of an adjacent α-anomer of glucose. Ptyalin hydrolyzes the starch chains down into *di-* and *trisaccharides* (maltose and maltodextrins) that are further hydrolyzed by *maltase* to glucose in the small intestine.

Note that there are two forms of starch: amylase and amylopectin. In amylase, the glucose residues are joined end to end by 1→4 glycosidic bonds between α-anomers of glucose. This produces a linear, unbranched polysaccharide. Hydrogen bonds between amylose molecules twist the chains into large helical rodlike structures that stack to form sheets. These sheets impede digestion by amylase.

In contrast, amylopectin contains 1→6 glycosidic branch points at regular intervals. These result in an open, treelike structure. Amylopectin is more readily hydrolyzed by amylase, and this results in a mixture of small, branched maltodextrin molecules that are often referred to as *limit dextrins*. Limit dextrins are further hydrolyzed by maltase.

EXAMPLE 11.6 What are the respective dietary sources of the starches amylose and amylopectin?

Amylose is mainly found in legumes and pulses (such as peas, lentils, chick peas, and kidney beans). Older strains of grain contain more amylose than modern, agriculturally developed ones. Through successive generations, grain crops have been bred to contain a higher proportion of *amylopectin* because this form of starch makes flour that yields a more pleasing outcome when cooked (e.g., it makes lighter bread). Most of the pasta and bread used in the Western diet contains a high proportion of amylopectin. Increasing interest in the potential health benefits of amylose starch has led grain producers to explore the use of grains that contain a higher proportion of amylose.

As the di- and trisaccharides are hydrolyzed to glucose by *maltase* and *dextrinases*, respectively, in the small intestine, the glucose molecules enter the epithelial cells through specialized sodium-dependent GLUT transporters (Prob. 10.32). From there, the glucose crosses the enterocytes and enters the bloodstream via different GLUT transport proteins, thus elevating the blood glucose concentration.

11.4 Blood Glucose Homeostasis

The concentration of glucose in the blood of normal individuals is usually ~5 mM, a state that is referred to as *euglycemia* (Greek *eu-* = good or well, *glycemia* = glucose in the blood). If the concentration falls below 2–3 mM, this state is referred to as *hypoglycemia*; and because the brain has an obligatory requirement for glucose, hypoglycemia can lead rapidly to *unconsciousness*. Glucose is a relatively reactive molecule,

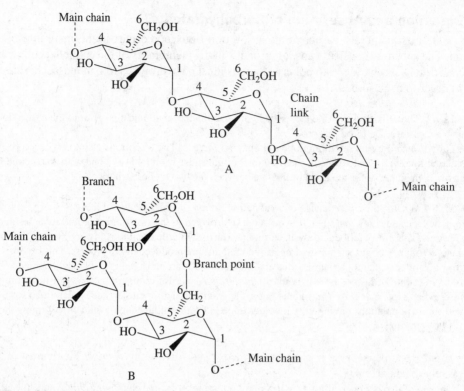

Fig. 11-3   Structures of (A) amylose and (B) amylopectin as chair projections of glucose residues.

because the open-chain form is a free aldehyde (see Sec. 11.2). Although a blood glucose concentration above 7 m*M* that is referred to as *hyperglycemia* is not dangerous in the short term, there are severe health consequences associated with hyperglycemia that lasts over periods of more than a few weeks.

EXAMPLE 11.7   What is the nature of the chemical reactivity of glucose?

The aldehyde group of the open-chain form of glucose, which is in chemical exchange with the α- and β- closed-ring forms, reacts with free amino groups on proteins, resulting in the covalent attachment of glucose residues to the protein. The product is called a Schiff base (Chap. 1). The extent of the reaction, that is spontaneous and not enzyme-catalyzed, depends on the concentration of glucose and the time of exposure to elevated concentrations of glucose.

After a carbohydrate-rich meal, glucose is distributed into tissues and then subsequently converted to the fuel stores of glycogen (glycogenesis) and triglyceride (lipogenesis), or catabolized by oxidation to carbon dioxide (via glycolysis and the Krebs cycle).

The liver is the first organ to receive blood that contains glucose absorbed from the intestine. The portal vein drains from the small intestine into the hepatic sinuses that are surrounded in a neat *columnar* fashion by hepatocytes. The arrival of glucose in the blood is detected by the β-cells in the pancreas, and they respond by secreting the peptide hormone *insulin*. Insulin facilitates glucose uptake by many cell types, from skeletal muscle to white blood cells (Fig. 11-4), but it has no effect on glucose uptake by the brain or red blood cells that rely on GLUT-1.

Glycemic Index (GI)

Because the maintenance of euglycemia is important for health, both the *disposal time* and the *amplitude* of the postmeal (*postprandial*) blood glucose concentration are useful measures when investigating patients with possible glucose-handling problems. Carbohydrates that are rapidly digested and absorbed lead to higher, and more prolonged, postprandial blood glucose concentrations. It is noted that the two starches amylose and amylopectin are digested at different rates, and as expected, they cause quite different effects on the time course of blood glucose concentration.

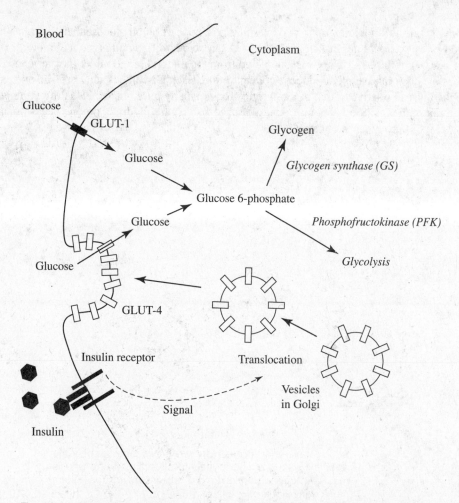

Fig. 11-4   Overview of glucose uptake and disposal in skeletal myocytes and adipocytes. Glucose enters the cell via GLUT-1 and via the insulin-stimulated insertion of GLUT-4 carriers into the plasma membrane. Glucose 6-phosphate is a point of *flux divergence* into glycolysis and glycogen synthesis.

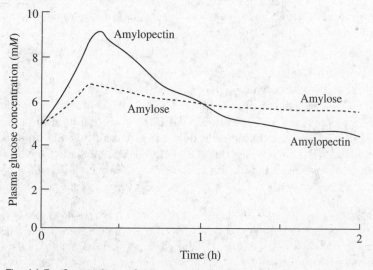

Fig. 11-5   Comparison of the postprandial glucose responses of amylose and amylopectin.

The different concentration maximum and overall time course of blood glucose that occur in a normal person in response to a standard dose of a particular food can be quantified and given a number; it is called the *glycemic index* (GI) of the food. The GI is calculated from the integral (area) under the curve, up to 120 min, that describes the postprandial blood glucose concentration. Each GI value is standardized and expressed as the ratio of the integral relative to that of a reference food, usually pure glucose. Healthy volunteers are fed a known amount of the test food containing 50 g of absorbable carbohydrate, on one occasion, and then an identical amount of pure glucose on another occasion.

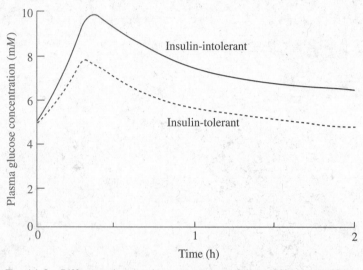

Fig. 11-6   Different plasma glucose response in two different patients after a meal; one who is insulin tolerant and one who is insulin intolerant, for example, as occurs in non-insulin dependent diabetes mellitus (NIDDM).

EXAMPLE 11.8   Which foods are expected to have a high GI?

Foods containing amylopectin or free glucose have high GI values. Examples are highly processed starch-rich foods that use modern grains. Some potato and rice products have GI values greater than 100; they give a postprandial glucose concentration that is much higher earlier after ingestion than pure glucose! This is due to the very rapid digestion of amylopectin starches and the fact that the high osmolality of a pure-glucose test solution delays stomach emptying and thus slows intestinal absorption.

Glucose Absorption into Cells

Although the metabolic fate of blood glucose varies from tissue to tissue, it commences with the transport of glucose from the blood across the plasma membrane of a cell. The family of integral membrane proteins, the GLUTs, mediates this uptake (see Prob. 10.32). GLUT-1 is present in all tissues where it provides a continuous, baseline flux of glucose; however, it does not give a sufficiently high rate of glucose transport to handle the sudden arrival of a postprandial glucose load. Some tissues have additional specialized GLUTs that are more responsive to the insulin signal (Chap. 13) which heralds a higher blood-glucose concentration.

EXAMPLE 11.9   Muscle and adipose tissue contain a member of the GLUT family of glucose transporters (GLUT-4) that normally resides in a *holding zone* in vesicles that are associated with the endoplasmic reticulum. On the binding of insulin to an insulin receptor on the cell surface, an intracellular signal is transmitted to the vesicles, which causes the transporters to be translocated to, and fuse with, the plasma membrane. This delivery of GLUT-4 transporters to the plasma membrane allows a potentially great increase in the flux of glucose into the cell. Interestingly, exercise is even more effective in stimulating GLUT-4 translocation than is insulin.

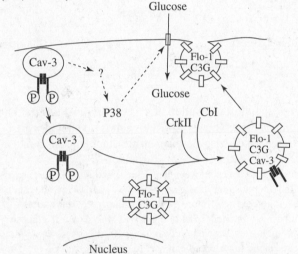

Phase 1 (early, 0–2 min)   Blood

Caveolae   Cytoplasm

Insulin receptor-β

Nucleus

Phase 2 (late, 2–5 min)

Glucose

Glucose

Nucleus

Fig. 11-7 Insulin stimulation of GLUT-4 translocation. This is rather
complex, so to capture the current understanding of
the system the diagram also needs to be complex: In
the first stage of activation of glucose uptake (phase 1),
the signaling protein, insulin receptor substrate 1
(IRS1), is phosphorylated by the insulin receptor. IRS1
then phosphorylates and activates phosphoinositol-3-
kinase (PI3K) that phosphorylates phosphoinositol
4,5-bisphosphate and 4-phosphate to form phosphoinositol 3,4,5-trisphosphate (PIP_3) and phosphoinositol
3,4-bisphosphate (PIP_2), respectively, in the cell membrane (e.g., Fig. 6-6). These phosphoinositides are
allosteric activators of phosphoinositide-dependent
kinase-1 (PDK-1) that in turn phosphorylates and
activates protein kinase B (also called Akt) as well as
atypical-protein-kinase C (PKC-ζ). These two enzymes
promote the translocation of perinuclear membrane
domains that contain the protein flotillin and GLUT-4
to the plasma membrane. Phase 2 sees caveolin-3
(Cav-3)-containing domains move from the sarcolemma
(endoplasmic reticulum) to the cytoplasm where they
interact with flotillin/GLUT-4 containing domains.
Insulin receptors now move from the plasma membrane attached to vesicles that contain Cav-3, which
in the presence of the regulatory proteins CrkII and
CbI, and with the GDP/GTP exchange activator protein
C3G, finalizes the movement of GLUT-4 to the plasma
membrane. Cavolin-3 also acts via p38 MAP kinase to
make GLUT-4 function in glucose transport.

Locking Glucose inside Cells

Once inside the cell, glucose is phosphorylated to produce glucose 6-phosphate; this has a net negative charge, rendering it unable to bind to the GLUT transporters. Thus the plasma membrane becomes impermeable to the modified glucose that is now locked within the cytoplasm (Prob. 10.9). Phosphorylation of a glucose molecule consumes a molecule of ATP. This constitutes an investment of energy in the metabolism of the molecule, so the step is often referred to as a *priming* or *sparking* reaction for the subsequent metabolic steps (Example 10.12).

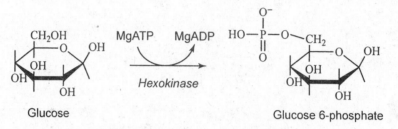

Glucose   Glucose 6-phosphate

Fig. 11-8　Phosphorylation of glucose by hexokinase.

Hexokinase catalyzes the phosphorylation of glucose in most tissues; but hepatocytes use an additional form of this enzyme, *glucokinase*. The ways in which the two enzymes are regulated are quite different, and this strongly influences the tissue-specific manner in which glucose is metabolized.

EXAMPLE 11.10　The key differences between hexokinase and glucokinase are as follows.

Hexokinase, in all cells, can phosphorylate other 6-carbon monosaccharides such as fructose and galactose, whereas glucokinase is specific for glucose and is only found in the liver. Hexokinase is inhibited by its product, glucose 6-phosphate, but glucokinase is not. Hence hexokinase will slow down if glucose 6-phosphate accumulates, whereas glucokinase will continue unabated; consequently glucose 6-phosphate concentrations do not become very high in peripheral tissues such as skeletal muscle, but can rise significantly in the liver. There it can be incorporated into large amounts of glycogen.

Another difference is that glucokinase has a high K_m for glucose (~10 mM), but that for hexokinase is ~100 times less (~0.1 mM). Enzymes operate near their maximal rate (V_{max}) when their substrate concentration is >10 times K_m; hence hexokinase is nearly always operating near its maximum rate. Conversely, the flux of glucose through glucokinase varies almost linearly within the normal blood glucose concentration range.

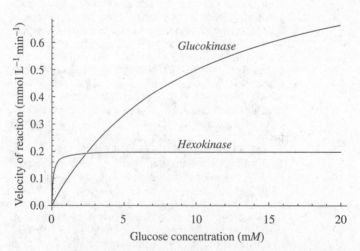

Fig. 11-9　Enzyme kinetics of glucokinase and hexokinase. This is a schematic only and shows glucokinase having a maximal velocity that is 10 times greater than that of hexokinase, while the K_m of hexokinase for glucose (0.1 mM) is 1/100th of that for glucokinase (10 mM).

Fate of Glucose 6-Phosphate

Glucose 6-phosphate has one of two major fates: either *glycogenesis* or *glycolysis*. The particular fate is determined by regulation of the fluxes via the enzymes in the two pathways. Even though both of these pathways contain multiple enzyme-catalyzed steps, each pathway has specific controls on the constituent enzymes.

EXAMPLE 11.11   What is the major flux-controlling step of glycogen synthesis?

Synthesis of glycogen from glucose 6-phosphate involves its conversion into glucose 1-phosphate and the transfer of this glucose residue onto the nucleotide UDP. Thus the glucose residue is *activated* for transfer onto a growing glycogen polymer. The protein *glycogenin* is at the core of glycogen molecules. It has the unusual property of catalyzing its own glycosylation, attaching C-1 of a UDP-glucose molecule to the –OH of a tyrosine residue. Therefore glycogenin serves as a primer for the synthesis of glycogen. After ~6 rounds of attachment of glucose residues via α-$(1{\to}4)$ linkages from UDP-glucose, glycogen synthase takes over the reactions. While glycogen synthase catalyzes the formation of the new glycosidic bonds, it is the slowest of the enzymes in the glycogenesis pathway. This step is effectively irreversible, and glycogen synthase is subjected to many regulatory effectors. Branching of the growing linear chains of glucose takes place at periodic intervals via the *branching enzyme*, as shown in Fig. 11-10.

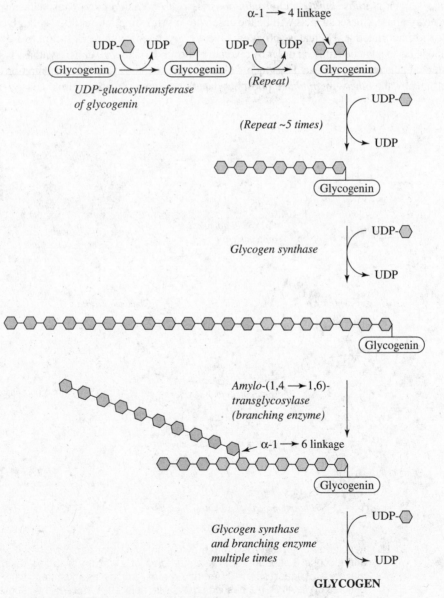

Fig. 11-10   Overview of glycogen synthesis.

EXAMPLE 11.12　What is the mechanism of insertion of branch points into a growing glycogen polymer?

An enzyme called *branching enzyme* catalyzes the hydrolysis of small sections, ~10–12 glucose residues in length, from the end of a growing glycogen chain. It then transfers this section to a region of the chain nearer the origin of the polymer and catalyzes the formation of an α-1→6 bond to another glucose residue. Branch points in glycogen occur once every ~10 residues.

Control of Glycogen Synthase and Phosphofructokinase

Because the fate of glucose 6-phosphate depends largely on the relative activities of *glycogen synthase* and *phosphofructokinase*, to understand the direction of carbon flow from glucose, it is necessary to understand how these enzymes are regulated.

Glycogen synthase is inactivated (*switched off*) when specific serine residues are *phosphorylated*. This reaction is catalyzed by *glycogen synthase kinase* that uses ATP as a cosubstrate. Glycogen synthase is reactivated (*switched on*) by *protein phosphatase 1* which catalyzes the hydrolysis of the phosphate groups from the enzyme. Protein phosphatase 1 in turn is *stimulated by insulin*. The binding of *insulin* to insulin receptors in the plasma membrane of the cell triggers a *signaling cascade* that stimulates protein phosphatase 1.

The total amount of glycogen synthase in the cell does not change in a few minutes or hours, but the proportion of the inactive and active forms does, and this is under the control of insulin. Insulin determines the relative activities of *glycogen synthase kinase* and *protein phosphatase 1*. When protein phosphatase 1 is more active than glycogen synthase kinase, such as will be the case with insulin stimulation of the cell, glycogen synthase becomes dephosphorylated and hence is activated. Overall, glycogen synthase is stimulated by insulin.

In addition to being switched fully *on* or *off* by reversible phosphorylation, glycogen synthase is subject to more subtle allosteric regulation. It is activated by glucose 6-phosphate, so if the cytosolic concentration of this metabolite rises sufficiently, the *otherwise inhibited* phosphorylated glycogen synthase is stimulated into activity.

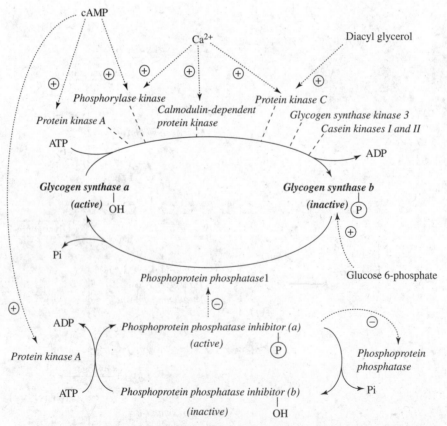

Fig. 11-11　Regulation of glycogen synthase by phosphorylation, dephosphorylation, and glucose 6-phosphate. Phosphorylation of glycogen synthase takes place via at least *seven* different *protein kinases* as indicated. cAMP denotes *cyclic AMP*. The dashed arrows with adjacent + and − signs denote activation or inhibition, respectively.

EXAMPLE 11.13 Phosphofructokinase is regulated allosterically.

In contrast to glycogen synthase, phosphofructokinase is *not* regulated by phosphorylation and dephosphorylation; instead it is *regulated allosterically* (Chap. 5). Phosphofructokinase contains several different allosteric sites that bind a variety of different metabolites. Most importantly it is very sensitive to changes in metabolite concentrations that reflect the *energy charge* of the cell. Energy charge is a convenient way of describing the availability of ATP in the cell and is defined as ([ATP] + 0.5[ADP])/([ATP] + [ADP] + [AMP]).

Binding of ADP or AMP allosterically *activates* phosphofructokinase, but high concentrations of ATP are *inhibitory*. At first sight this seems to be a contradictory response elicited by ATP since it is a substrate for the enzyme. However, careful analysis of the relationship between the activity of phosphofructokinase and ATP concentration shows that there is always sufficient ATP in the normal cell for the reaction to proceed, but that ATP inhibition becomes significant only when its concentration is very high. *Fructose 2,6-bisphosphate* is an *inhibitor*, as is *citrate*. The regulation of the concentration of fructose 2,6-bisphosphate is via a phosphorylation-dephosphorylation process as shown in Fig. 11-12.

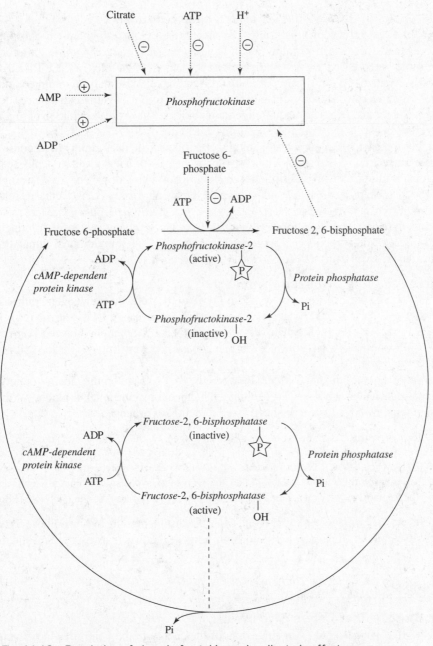

Fig. 11-12   Regulation of phosphofructokinase by allosteric effectors.

EXAMPLE 11.14   Phosphofructokinase is also inhibited by H$^+$.

Phosphofructokinase rarely operates at maximum velocity which only occurs at about pH 8.5. This is a safety valve for the preservation of skeletal muscle because when the muscle is active, it devours a lot of glucose and produces heat and lactate. The formation of lactate (and H$^+$) inhibits phosphofructokinase which causes glycolysis to slow down, thereby protecting the muscle from overheating.

Overall, *glycogen synthase* is stimulated by insulin, and a falling cellular energy charge stimulates *phosphofructokinase*. Appreciation of the fact that glycogen synthesis is an anabolic process and consumes ATP allows us to see that if insulin stimulates glycogen synthesis, then it must also decrease the concentration of ATP, which will stimulate phosphofructokinase. Therefore, insulin stimulates glycogen accumulation directly but also indirectly stimulates glycolysis. This is an excellent example of how flux through an anabolic pathway is linked by regulatory processes to flux via a catabolic pathway.

11.5   Regulation of Glycogen Production

Tissue Differences in the Regulation of Glycogen Synthesis

Glucose uptake into skeletal myocytes is insulin-dependent (Sec. 11.4), and glucose 6-phosphate concentrations do not rise greatly because of its inhibition of hexokinase; this *product inhibition* is a form of *negative feedback control* of glucose flux via hexokinase. Even if there are high rates of GLUT-4 mediated glucose uptake into cells, if glucose 6-phosphate accumulates, then hexokinase will be inhibited and glucose will exchange back out of the cells. However, insulin also activates glycogen synthase that places demand (a *sink*) on glucose 6-phosphate and releases the inhibition of hexokinase. Thus the stimulation of glycogen synthase by insulin diverts glucose to glycogen in skeletal myocytes.

In contrast, in hepatocytes the concentration of glucose 6-phosphate rises rapidly in response to an increase in blood glucose concentration. Elevation of glucose 6-phosphate is sufficient to allosterically activate glycogen synthase, even in the absence of any insulin-induced dephosphorylation of the enzyme. The high intracellular glucose concentration exerts a stimulatory effect on protein phosphatase 1, via an increased release of it from an inactive complex with another glycogen-metabolizing enzyme, *glycogen phosphorylase* (see more in Chap. 13). Thus, a high blood glucose concentration promotes glucose into glycogen synthesis. In principle, increased synthesis of glycogen could occur just in response to hyperglycemia, but the additional stimulation of glycogen synthase by insulin provides a further boost to the rate of glycogen synthesis.

Other Factors Affecting Glycogen Synthesis

Figure 11-13 shows more details (compared with Fig. 11-10) of the pathway of glycogen synthesis. The reaction between glucose 1-phosphate and UTP that generates the activated precursor UDP-glucose is a *priming* reaction that involves the formation of pyrophosphate (PPi). Pyrophosphate is rapidly hydrolyzed via *pyrophosphatase*, to generate two orthophosphate ions (Pi); since this reaction is effectively irreversible, the hydrolysis drives the formation of UDP-glucose.

The formation of a glycosidic bond occurs between the 4-OH group on the glucose moiety at the end of the glycogen molecule and the activated 1-position of the glucose residue in UDP-glucose. As in nucleic acid and protein synthesis, glycogen synthesis has a fixed direction of propagation.

EXAMPLE 11.15   There are basic similarities between glycogen synthesis and the synthesis of some other key macromolecules.

The reactions of glycogen, DNA, RNA, and protein synthesis all use activated precursors, UDP-glucose, dNTPs, NTPs, and amino-acyl tRNAs, respectively. However, unlike the others, glycogen synthesis does not use a template in its propagation. And during the formation of glycogen, branch points are introduced into the emerging polymer (Fig. 11-10).

For a tissue to synthesize glycogen, *glycogen synthase* must be present. White adipose tissue has little of this enzyme, so even though glucose uptake into white adipose tissue is responsive to insulin, little glycogen is made there.

11.6   Glycolysis

Fate of the Glucose That Enters Glycolysis

The reactions of glycolysis lead to extracting some of the energy in the bonds of glucose and storing it in the high-energy terminal *phospho-anhydride bond* of ATP. For each molecule of glucose that passes through

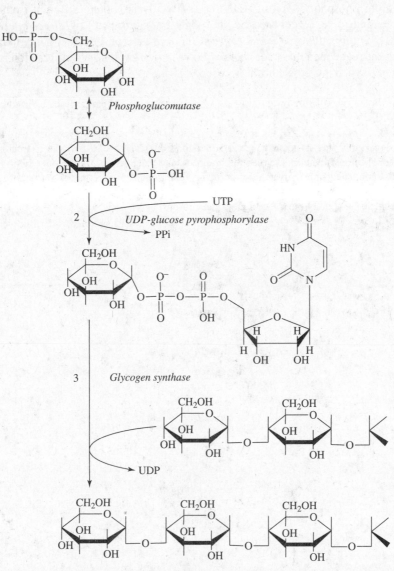

Fig. 11-13 Chemical details of glycogen synthesis. The process of chain branching is shown in Fig. 11-10.

glycolysis, a net 2 molecules of ADP are phosphorylated (with the special exception of the red blood cell; see Prob. 10.35). The glycolytic pathway resides in the cytoplasm, but the full ATP yield from glucose is only obtained when pyruvate passes into the mitochondria and is fully oxidized to CO_2 and water. In addition, glycolysis via its product pyruvate provides the key building block, acetyl-CoA, for fatty acid synthesis. In the liver, and adipose tissue, conversion of acetyl-CoA to fatty acids and then to *triglycerides* occurs at a high rate.

PFK and the Second Stage of Glycolysis

The molecular details of glycolysis are shown in Fig. 10-8. From one molecule of glucose, the reactions leading to the formation of fructose 1,6-bisphosphate use 2 molecules of ATP; fructose-1,6-bisphosphate undergoes *aldol cleavage* to form two 3-carbon sugar phosphates, the *triosephosphates*, that are rapidly interconverted by the relatively high concentration of *triosephosphate isomerase* that exists in the cytoplasm. In the next reaction, one of the triosephosphates, *glyceraldehyde 3-phosphate*, is oxidized by NAD^+ to yield NADH and a doubly phosphorylated carboxylic acid. Then one of these phosphate moieties is transferred to a molecule of ADP to give ATP, leaving a monophosphorylated carboxylic acid. In a second dephosphorylation reaction, another conversion of ADP to ATP takes place, and the resulting nonphosphorylated compound is pyruvate.

The mechanism of phosphorylation of ADP during glycolysis is quite different from that which takes place in the mitochondria. In glycolysis, the phosphate transfer occurs by *direct interaction* between a metabolite and ADP and is called *substrate-level phosphorylation*; on the other hand, in mitochondria ATP synthase mediates the reaction in the process of *oxidative phosphorylation*. This reaction is closely linked to the consumption of oxygen in mitochondria (see Sec. 10.8).

EXAMPLE 11.16 Is the overall flux of carbon atoms through glycolysis markedly influenced by the three-carbon stages of the pathway?

With the exception of *pyruvate kinase*, the reactions involving the three-carbon phosphates are freely reversible, so this part of glycolysis can undergo net flux in the reverse direction from phosphoenol pyruvate to fructose-1,6-bisphosphate (Fig. 10-8). Reversal of the pyruvate kinase reaction does not take place to any significant extent, and yet carbon flux from pyruvate back to phosphoenol pyruvate does occur in some tissues. This requires a group of *specialized enzymes* that are found only in those tissues that can make glucose from pyruvate; this is restricted to those cells and organs capable of gluconeogenesis, notably the liver, kidney, and neurons.

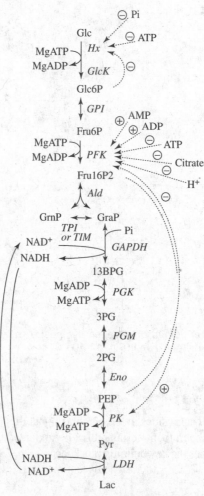

Fig. 11-14 Control of glycolysis. The metabolites and enzymes are denoted by their standard abbreviations (see Fig. 10-8 for the full names). The dashed arrows specify regulation of the enzymes to which they point, and the + and − signs denote activation and inhibition, respectively.

Pyruvate produced in glycolysis undergoes chemical transformations along several different routes. A notable one is transport into the mitochondria where it is oxidized by NAD^+ via the *pyruvate dehydrogenase* complex. Another route involves its reduction via *lactate dehydrogenase*, with cytosolic NADH produced by glyceraldehyde-3-phosphate dehydrogenase in glycolysis, to yield lactate. This reaction is generally a feature of cells undergoing very rapid glycolytic flux, or in those that lack oxygen and therefore have diminished means of oxidizing NADH and hence recycle their limited supply of NAD^+ (as in red blood cells that have no mitochondria; see Prob. 10.35). A third route is via transamination with glutamate to make alanine (see Sec. 14.1).

In the fully oxygenated postprandial state in hepatocytes, pyruvate takes the mitochondrial route. The stimulation by insulin of the *pyruvate dehydrogenase complex* (Sec. 11.7), via dephosphorylation mediated by pyruvate dehydrogenase phosphatase, opens up the pathway to pyruvate metabolism in mitochondria.

11.7　The Pyruvate Dehydrogenase Complex

This enzyme complex constitutes a *point of no return* for carbon atoms derived from glucose in humans and most other higher organisms; there is no pathway that enables the synthesis of carbohydrate from the 2-carbon precursor acetate. This important feature of pyruvate dehydrogenase is crucial to an understanding of fuel selection in exercise and starvation, and is discussed further in Chap. 13.

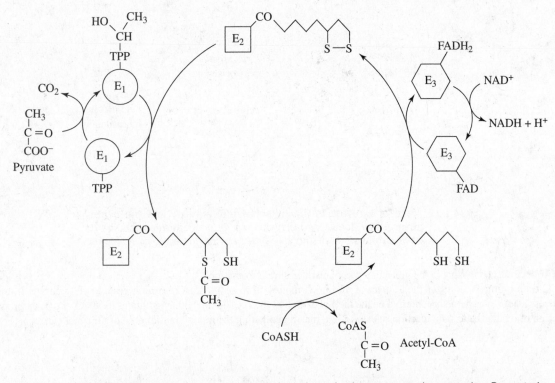

Fig. 11-15　The pyruvate dehydrogenase reaction takes place via *three enzymes* in a complex: Pyruvate is decarboxylated by the E_1 (*pyruvate decarboxylase*) component of the enzyme complex; a key cofactor is *thiamine pyrophosphate* (TPP) that transfers the hydroxyethyl moiety to one of the sulfur atoms on oxidized lipoamide that is covalently bound to E_2 (*dihydrolipoyl transacetylase*). When this transfer takes place, the 2-carbon moiety is oxidized to an acetyl moiety; and then the acetyl moiety is transferred to CoA to yield acetyl-CoA which is then released from the active site of E_2. The reduced lipoamide moiety is recycled back to its oxidized form by donating hydrogen atoms to FAD in E_3 (*lipoamide dehydrogenase*), and the reaction cycle begins over again.

EXAMPLE 11.17　The process of converting pyruvate to acetyl-CoA is highly regulated. Metabolic regulation is almost invariably synonymous with *multimeric proteins*, and this is true of pyruvate dehydrogenase. The three enzymes (Fig. 11-15) exist in a large complex consisting of 24 copies of E_1 (pyruvate decarboxylase), 24 copies of E_2 (dihydrolipoyl transacetylase), and 12 copies of E_3 (lipoamide dehydrogenase). Regulation of flux through the overall reaction is achieved by reversible phosphorylation, as shown in Fig. 11-16.

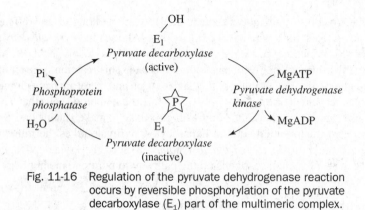

Fig. 11-16   Regulation of the pyruvate dehydrogenase reaction occurs by reversible phosphorylation of the pyruvate decarboxylase (E_1) part of the multimeric complex.

11.8   Krebs Cycle Flux

Acetyl-CoA has many metabolic fates, but there are two that begin with the *condensation* of acetyl-CoA with *oxaloacetate* to give citrate.

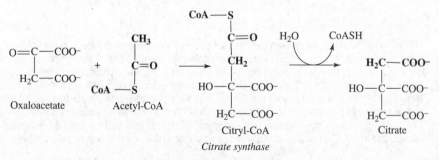

Fig. 11-17   Fate of pyruvate in the mitochondrial matrix. Note the control exerted by acetyl-CoA: elevation of its concentration inhibits its own synthesis and stimulates its own conversion to oxaloacetate.

EXAMPLE 11.18   What is the molecular mechanism of citrate formation?

Citrate synthase catalyzes the transfer of the acetyl moiety from acetyl-CoA to oxaloacetate to yield citrate. In the process a negative charge is conferred on the methyl carbon of the acetyl moiety that facilitates its attack on the carbonyl carbon of oxaloacetate. The reaction releases CoA, thus regenerating the mitochondrial pool of this vital carrier.

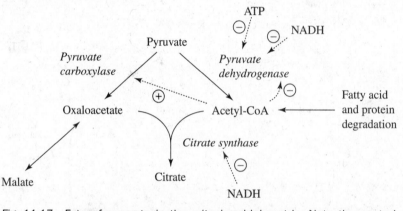

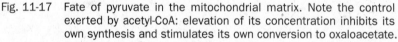

Fig. 11-18   Molecular mechanism of citrate synthase.

The Krebs cycle completes the disassembly of glucose to six molecules of CO_2 by combining the two carbon atoms from acetyl-CoA with oxaloacetate to make citrate; this is then successively transformed to release two molecules of CO_2 and to regenerate oxaloacetate. This reformation of a carrier molecule in a cyclic manner led Hans Krebs to the concept of a *metabolic cycle*; he first observed this with the urea cycle (Sec. 14.8).

The oxidation of the two carbon atoms is accomplished by NAD^+ and FAD, yielding three molecules of NADH and one $FADH_2$. Substrate-level phosphorylation also takes place in which GDP is phosphorylated to GTP. Note that the two carbon atoms that are lost as CO_2 molecules in one turn of the cycle are not both of those present in the original acetate moiety; one is derived from the initial molecule of oxaloacetate. In a subtle turn of events, while chemically this molecule is recycled, structurally it is resynthesized (Prob. 10.17).

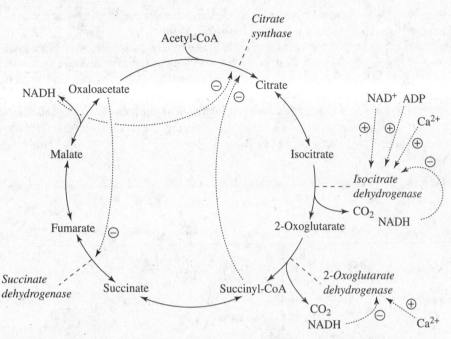

Fig. 11-19   Regulation of flux through the Krebs cycle. Details of the chemical structures and a complete list of enzyme names are given in Fig. 10-9.

The two decarboxylation steps in the Krebs cycle are catalyzed by *2-oxoglutarate dehydrogenase* and *isocitrate dehydrogenase*, and both reactions produce NADH. The rapid diffusion away of CO_2 in water renders the dehydrogenase reactions effectively irreversible. Both enzymes are sensitive to the ratios of NADH to NAD^+ and ATP to ADP. When either ATP or NADH concentrations are low, they are stimulated. Thus these enzymes respond to both the *energy charge* in the mitochondria and the amount of *reductant* available. The cycle is further regulated by feedback inhibition of succinate dehydrogenase by oxaloacetate.

In addition, both 2-oxoglutarate dehydrogenase and isocitrate dehydrogenase are stimulated by a rise in mitochondrial Ca^{2+} concentration; this is important in stimulating the rate of the Krebs cycle during exercise.

EXAMPLE 11.19   Citrate transport into the cytoplasm.

Citrate that is not oxidized by isocitrate dehydrogenase can be transported from the mitochondrial matrix into the cytoplasm. In the cytoplasm of adipocytes and hepatocytes, oxaloacetate and acetyl-CoA are formed from citrate, not by the reversal of the citrate synthase-catalyzed reaction, but by *ATP-dependent citrate lyase*. As the name indicates, the free energy of ATP hydrolysis drives this reaction in the degradative direction.

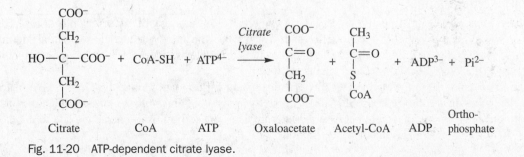

Fig. 11-20   ATP-dependent citrate lyase.

11.9   Metabolic Shuttles

In the cytoplasm, oxaloacetate is reduced by NADH to malate via *cytoplasmic* malate dehydrogenase. Malate can pass into the mitochondrial matrix via special *dicarboxylic acid transporters* that are in the inner mitochondrial membrane. Once in the matrix, oxaloacetate is reoxidized to malate by *mitochondrial* malate dehydrogenase. Thus this series of enzyme and transporter reactions has effectively shuttled reducing equivalents in NADH from the cytoplasm to the matrix. This shuttle constitutes the most efficient way of transferring hydrogen atoms from NADH in the cytoplasm to the mitochondrial matrix, and hence into the electron transport chain (see Sec. 10.12 for the glycerol 3-phosphate shuttle).

An additional shuttle involves cytosolic *malate* which is oxidized by *NADP⁺*, a phosphorylated variant of NAD⁺, via the *malic enzyme*. Malate is decarboxylated, releasing CO_2 that diffuses away, rendering the reaction effectively irreversible. The other products are pyruvate and NADPH. Pyruvate can be transported back into the mitochondrial matrix where pyruvate dehydrogenase produces NADH from it. Thus hydrogen atoms are shuttled from the cytoplasm to the mitochondrial matrix. However, energy is expended to reconvert the pyruvate back into oxaloacetate for further metabolism. This reaction is catalyzed by *pyruvate carboxylase* that is described in greater detail in Chap. 13 (see Fig. 13-9).

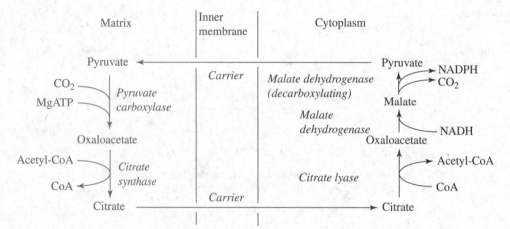

Fig. 11-21   Oxaloacetate transport, as citrate, into the mitochondrial matrix.

EXAMPLE 11.20   How do NADP⁺ and NADPH differ from NAD⁺ and NADH?

These pairs of molecules are identical except for the presence of a phosphate group at the 2′ position on the ribose moiety. This is not a high-energy phosphate but rather a molecular *tag* that enables enzymes to discriminate between the two forms of redox compound. In higher animals there do not appear to be any *NADH transferase* enzymes that catalyze direct transfer of hydrogen atoms from NADH to NADP⁺ or from NADPH to NAD⁺.

NADH and NADPH are equivalent in terms of their *standard redox potentials*, but because redox enzymes are usually selective for one or the other of them, two distinct pools of reductants exist. NADH is used as a source of reducing equivalents for the electron transport chain (ETC) while *NADPH* provides reducing equivalents for many *biosynthetic reactions*. Hence, even within a single spatial compartment such as the cytoplasm, the NADH to NAD⁺ ratio can be very low, favoring oxidation of fuels, while simultaneously the NADPH to NADP⁺ ratio can be very high, facilitating biosynthesis.

11.10   Lipogenesis

In the cytoplasm, the acetyl moiety of acetyl-CoA can enter the reactions of fatty acid synthesis or lipogenesis. As with other biosynthetic processes, this pathway involves the energy-dependent sequential addition of activated precursors to a growing molecule; but in contrast to nucleic acid, protein, and glycogen synthesis, lipogenesis also requires reducing equivalents.

The first step of the pathway involves the ATP-dependent carboxylation of acetyl-CoA to give malonyl-CoA. The reaction is catalyzed by *acetyl-CoA carboxylase* that contains *biotin* as an essential cofactor. The reaction mechanism is remarkable because the intermediates are ferried from one active site to another by means of a long, flexible arm linked to the biotin.

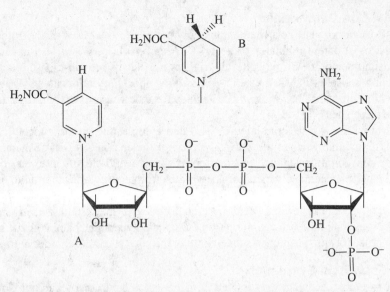

Fig. 11-22   NADP⁺ (A) and the reduced nicotinyl moiety (B) of NADPH.

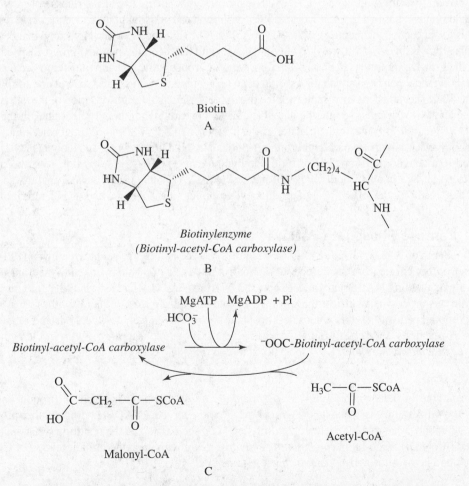

Biotin

A

Biotinylenzyme
(Biotinyl-acetyl-CoA carboxylase)

B

Malonyl-CoA

Acetyl-CoA

C

Fig. 11-23   Mechanism of acetyl-CoA carboxylase. Note the central role of (A) biotin that is attached (B) to the apoenzyme by a Schiff base linkage to the ε-amino group of a lysine side chain. (C) The overall reaction requires energy from the hydrolysis of the Mg²⁺ complex of ATP, and the fixation of CO_2 as HCO_3^-.

Control of Acetyl-CoA Carboxylase

In animals acetyl-CoA carboxylase is a filamentous polymer of M_r 4–8 MDa, made from 230-kDa monomers. Insulin is the most potent regulator of acetyl-CoA carboxylase. When *insulin* binds to an insulin receptor in the plasma membrane of the cell, this triggers a series of protein-kinase reactions that lead to the enzyme becoming phosphorylated. It also has *alternative* phosphorylation sites that are inhibitory; and counterregulatory hormones such as *glucagon* and *epinephrine* decrease its activity by stimulating kinases that phosphorylate these sites.

Acetyl-CoA carboxylase is also stimulated by elevated cytoplasmic citrate concentrations; the citrate effect is an *allosteric* one that leads to the *polymerization* of the enzyme as part of the activation process. Elevation of citrate concentration indicates a situation in which acetyl-CoA is in excess of the capacity of the Krebs cycle to handle it. Hence diversion of acetyl-CoA from energy transduction to energy storage, in the form of fatty acids, is favored.

Malonyl-CoA is converted into new fatty acids by a remarkable enzyme system, the fatty acyl synthase complex. This consists of several individual active sites on the same polypeptide chain, with the intermediates that are involved in the process being positioned sequentially in the correct temporal order in these different sites.

Mechanism of Fatty Acid Synthase

Fatty acid synthase assembles acetyl groups derived from the malonyl portion of malonyl-CoA onto a growing fatty-acyl chain (Fig. 11-24). The growing chain remains attached to the enzyme during the whole process. After each 2-carbon addition, a sequence of *reduction/dehydration/reduction* reactions occurs that reduces the carbonyl carbon to a fully saturated —CH_2—. The processing leads finally to the release of fatty-acyl-CoA

Fatty acid synthase has two free sulfhydryl (—SH) groups on one of its subunits, called the *acyl-carrier protein* (ACP). It is a 4-phosphopantetheine group (as in CoA; Fig. 10-6) attached to a seryl hydroxyl that bears the –SH group. This group is linked to the growing fatty-acyl chain and the incoming malonyl group, respectively, and it positions the growing molecules in exactly the right way for group interaction and transfer to occur optimally.

The reaction sequence begins with the binding of an acetyl moiety from acetyl-CoA, at one sulfhydryl group termed the XXX site, and a malonyl moiety at the other, the YYY site. Decarboxylation of the end of the malonyl residue leaves a very reactive intermediate that attacks the carbonyl carbon in the acetate at the XXX site. This *nucleophilic attack* results in the transfer of the acetyl group onto the end of the former malonyl moiety. Reduction of the acetyl-derived carbonyl group is achieved by NADPH, leaving an alcohol (—OH) group that is removed in a dehydration step. The resulting double bonded —CH=CH— portion is further reduced by NADPH to give a 4-carbon fatty acid that is still attached to the YYY site. Finally, the nascent fatty acid moves to the XXX site, ready for the arrival of another malonyl group into the XXX site and, then a repeat of the cycle.

11.11   Pentose Phosphate Pathway (PPP)

The major source of NADPH used in fatty acid synthesis is the pentose phosphate pathway (PPP).

The transport of citrate from the mitochondrial matrix into the cytoplasm is linked to the transfer of reducing equivalents yielding NADPH via malate decarboxylation (Fig. 11-21). However, the amount of NADPH produced in this process is insufficient to provide all that is required for fatty acid synthesis.

The additional pathway diverts glucose 6-phosphate from the first step of glycolysis and reduces $NADP^+$ in two redox reactions (Fig. 11-25). This reaction sequence is called the *oxidative part* of the pathway or the *oxidative hexose phosphate shunt*. It is especially active in *lipogenic* cells such as hepatocytes and adipocytes.

Oxidative PPP

The first enzyme in the pathway, *glucose-6-phosphate dehydrogenase* is strongly product-inhibited by NADPH. It oxidizes glucose 6-phosphate using $NADP^+$ and generates NADPH with the other product being 6-phosphoglucono-δ-lactone. The latter is hydrolyzed via δ-*lactonase* and the resulting 6-phosphogluconate is oxidized by $NADP^+$ via *6-phosphogluconate dehydrogenase* with the concomitant release of CO_2, and the production of a ketopentose phosphate, ribulose 5-phosphate.

Nonoxidative PPP

The remainder of the pathway consists of a series of *isomerase* and *group transfer* reactions (Fig. 11-26). These produce sugar phosphates ranging in size from the 3-carbon glyceraldehyde 3-phosphate to the 7-carbon sedoheptulose 7-phosphate. Also derived from ribulose 5-phosphate is ribose 5-phosphate, an essential component of *ribonucleosides* and *ribonucleotides*. The group exchange reactions are catalyzed by *transaldolase*

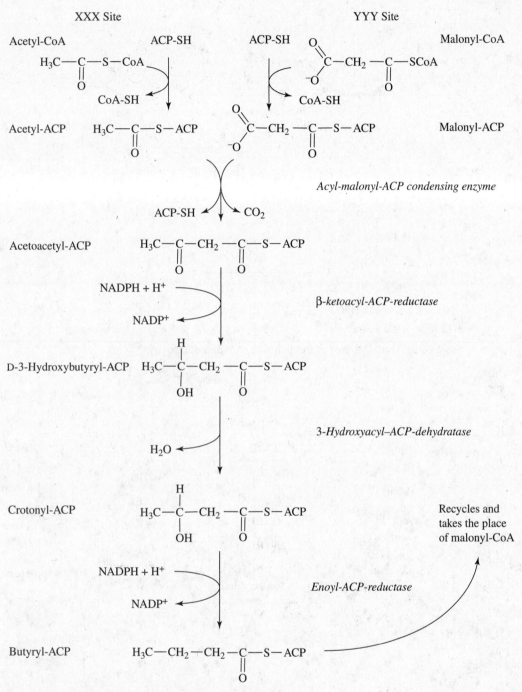

Fig. 11-24 Mechanism of fatty-acyl-CoA synthesis.

and transketolase; the latter interestingly contains the prosthetic group thiamine pyrophosphate (TPP). Transketolase transfers a 2-carbon *glycolaldehyde* moiety from a ketose phosphate donor to an aldose phosphate acceptor. Transaldolase transfers a 3-carbon *glyceraldehyde* moiety from a ketose phosphate donor to an aldose phosphate acceptor. Residual flux of carbon atoms back into glycolysis occurs via glyceraldehyde 3-phosphate and fructose 6-phosphate.

11.12 Metabolism of Two Other Monosaccharides

The two major monosaccharides, other than glucose, that enter the bloodstream from the diet are *fructose* from sucrose and *galactose* from lactose. In both cases these hexoses are metabolically transformed and enter the early stages of the *glycolytic* pathway.

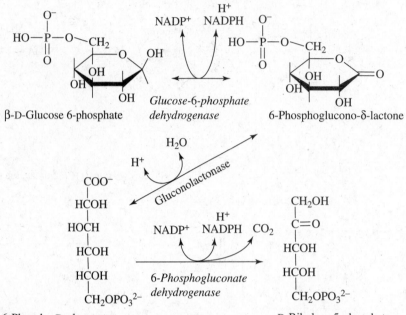

Fig. 11-25   Oxidative part of the pentose phosphate pathway.

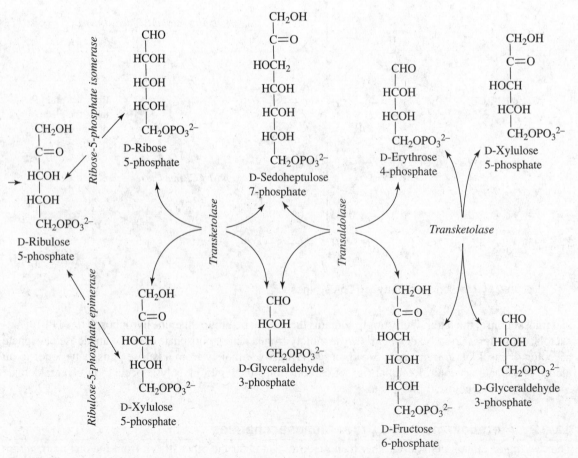

Fig. 11-26   Nonoxidative pentose phosphate pathway. Note the four different enzymes.

Fructose

After absorption from the gut, fructose is taken up into tissues via GLUT-5 transporters in the plasma membranes of most cells. In the muscle (and other peripheral tissues) fructose is converted to fructose 6-phosphate which is simply an early intermediate in glycolysis. The liver, via its portal vein, is the first tissue to encounter fructose as it is absorbed from the intestine; but it does not contain sufficiently high hexokinase activity to handle all the fructose load, although it does phosphorylate some of it. Instead the liver has the fructose-specific enzyme *fructokinase* that yields fructose 1-phosphate in the presence of ATP. From here, aldolase B, an *isozyme* of the main aldolase in glycolysis, cleaves fructose 1-phosphate to *glyceraldehyde* and *dihydroxyacetone phosphate*. The glyceraldehyde enters glycolysis after phosphorylation by ATP via the enzyme *triokinase*.

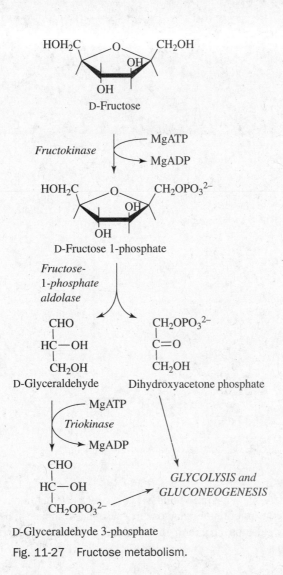

Fig. 11-27   Fructose metabolism.

Galactose

In contrast to fructose, galactose is metabolized primarily in the liver. The liver contains both the enzyme galactokinase (which catalyzes the conversion of galactose into galactose 6-phosphate) and a suite of enzymes that are necessary to convert galactose 6-phosphate into glucose 6-phosphate. The latter enzymes belong to a class called the *epimerases*. Galactose and glucose are epimers of each other, differing in absolute configuration only around the carbon atom in position 4 (Sec. 11-2, Fig. 11-1)). The epimerization takes place while the monosaccharide is conjugated to UDP, thus galactose is substituted for glucose on UDP-glucose.

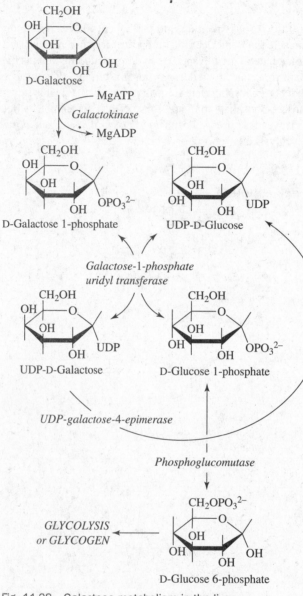

Fig. 11-28   Galactose metabolism in the liver.

In a manner similar to fructose, some individuals have a *genetic defect* in one of the enzymes involved in galactose metabolism; and consumption of galactose by these individuals can be detrimental to their health. The most common defect in galactose metabolism is with *galactokinase*, and not with the epimerase.

11.13   Food Partitioning

After a meal, there are several possible fates of the ingested carbohydrate. The regulatory influences dictate whether carbohydrate will be stored as glycogen or triglyceride, or oxidized to carbon dioxide.

Given the limit on the size of the glycogen molecule, it is reasonable to assume that, after a meal, glycogen stores would be maximized first with the excess carbon atoms from glucose being diverted to lipogenesis. However, leading nutrition scientists contend that lipogenesis is not very active in people eating a Western diet. This is so because the expression of lipogenic enzymes is down-regulated by consumption of triglycerides. Thus most of the triglyceride in white adipose tissue comes from the diet and is not synthesized de novo. Recent research indicates that glycogen concentrations can, temporarily, become very high in the liver after a high-carbohydrate meal.

SOLVED PROBLEMS

SOURCES OF DIETARY CARBOHYDRATE

11.1. In foods that have high starch contents, are mono- and disaccharides and nondigestible fibers also high?

SOLUTION

No. In fact along with the average values of starch content given in Sec. 11.1 are the following: (1) 100 g of boiled peeled potato has 12.8 g of carbohydrate that is made up of 12.4 g starch and 0.4 g sugar, and there is 1.9 g of fiber; (2) 100 g of boiled white rice has 28 g of carbohydrate that is made up of 27.9 g starch and 0.1 g sugar, and there is 0.5 g of fiber; (3) 100 g of cooked pasta has 24.6 g of starch and 0.0 g of sugar, and there is 1.8 g fiber; and (4) 100 g of white bread has 44.7 g of carbohydrate of which 42.4 g is starch and 2.3 g is sugar, while there is 3 g of fiber.

NOMENCLATURE OF CARBOHYDRATES

11.2. Of the compounds shown in Fig. 11-29, which are carbohydrates?

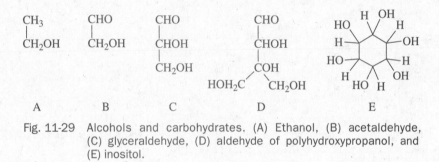

Fig. 11-29 Alcohols and carbohydrates. (A) Ethanol, (B) acetaldehyde, (C) glyceraldehyde, (D) aldehyde of polyhydroxypropanol, and (E) inositol.

SOLUTION

A and B are not carbohydrates because they have only one hydroxyl group each; C, D, and E are carbohydrates because they have the general formula $(CH_2O)_n$ and are polyhydroxylic.

11.3. Derive the structure of β-methylfructofuranoside. (1) Write the structure for D-fructose; (2) convert this to the five-member Haworth ring form (Fig. 3-8); and (3) take the β-anomer and substitute the anomeric hydroxyl with a methyl group.

SOLUTION

See Fig. 11-30.
1. Straight chain representation of D-fructose.
2. Haworth projection of D-fructose.
3. Haworth projection of the methyl derivative of D-fructose.

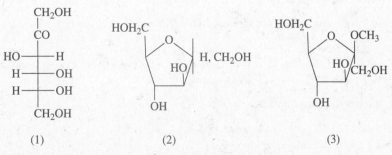

Fig. 11-30 The structure of β-fructofuranoside and its methyl derivative.

11.4. The structures of two different disaccharides, both composed of glucose, are shown in Fig. 11-31. Why are the glycosidic bonds drawn the way they are?

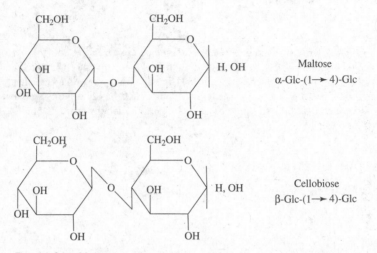

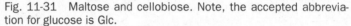

Fig. 11-31   Maltose and cellobiose. Note, the accepted abbreviation for glucose is Glc.

SOLUTION

Consider a disaccharide formed between two monosaccharides, A and B, in which the anomeric hydroxyl of A is used to glycosylate the hydroxyl group at C-4 of B:

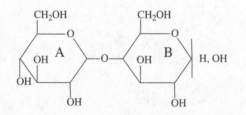

This structure is ambiguous in two respects. It does not show the configuration at C-1 of A, i.e., whether the glycosidic bond is α or β. Nor does it show the configuration at C-4 of B, and therefore the identity of B is not revealed; B could be either glucose (with the glycosidic O below the ring B) or galactose (with the glycosidic O above the ring B). Thus maltose and cellobiose are written as shown to indicate clearly (1) whether the glycosidic bond is α or β with respect to the glycosyl component and (2) what the identity of

the other sugar is. The printing of the glycosidic bonds as $\overset{C}{\underset{O}{\llcorner}}\overset{C}{\lrcorner}$ and $\overset{C}{\diagup}\overset{O}{}\overset{C}{\diagdown}$ is a pictorial device: it clearly gives the correct configuration of the chiral carbon atoms; of course in reality the bond is not bent.

11.5. What are the systematic names for maltose and cellobiose?

SOLUTION

Maltose is α-D-glucosyl-(1→4)-D-glucose or, more specifically, α-D-glucopyranosyl-(1→4)-D-glucopyranoside. Cellobiose is β-D-glucopyranosyl-(1→4)-D-glucopyranoside.

11.6. Is maltose a reducing carbohydrate?

SOLUTION

Yes. Although it is a glycoside, the second glucose unit possesses an anomeric carbon atom, and its ring can open to give an aldehyde. For the same reason, solutions of maltose display mutarotation.

11.7. Why does pure sucrose, a disaccharide, not have reducing properties?

SOLUTION

Sucrose, the main sugar, in cane and beet is a disaccharide in which the anomeric hydroxyl group of α-D-glucose is condensed with the anomeric hydroxyl group of β-D-fructose. It is therefore both an α-glucoside and a β-fructoside. Neither unit possesses an anomeric hydroxyl, and neither ring can open to give an aldehyde group.

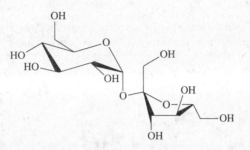

11.8. A solution of D-glucose contains predominantly the α- and β- anomers of D-glucopyranose; in fact the ratio is ~36:64. Both forms are not reducing so why is a solution of glucose a strong reducing agent?

SOLUTION

Because there is some open-chain glucose present with reducing properties. As this reacts, the equilibria between it and the nonreducing forms are disturbed, causing more of the open-chain form to appear. Ultimately, all the glucose will have reacted with an oxidant via the open-chain form.

11.9. The disaccharide shown is lactose, the main carbohydrate of mammalian milk. Give (a) its full name and (b) its abbreviated name.

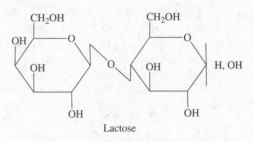

Lactose

SOLUTION

(a) β-Galactopyranosyl-(1→4)-glucopyranoside.
(b) β-Gal-(1→4)-Glc.

DIGESTION AND ABSORPTION OF CARBOHYDRATES

11.10. How are the different solubilities of sucrose, glucose, and fructose employed in making confectionary?

SOLUTION

A solution of equal parts of glucose and fructose is more soluble than an equal mass of sucrose. A paste of sucrose can, when hydrolyzed into glucose and fructose, become a solution. Soft-centered chocolates are created by coating a semisolid sucrase-treated sucrose paste, and over several weeks, the sucrose becomes hydrolyzed to give a liquid center.

11.11. What happens to amylose starch that is not fully hydrolyzed in the small intestine? What might be the clinical consequences?

SOLUTION

Undigested amylose passes into the large intestine (colon) where it is fermented by bacteria that produce short-chain fatty acids, hydrogen and methane. These compounds cause intestinal discomfort and intestinal bloating; and their production explains the well-known association between flatulence and the consumption of baked beans. Baked beans also contain complex oligosaccharides, some of which are not hydrolyzed in the small intestine and hence enter the colon and lead to the same symptoms as with undigested starch.

11.12. Sucrase deficiency comes about either by profound damage to the small intestine or more usually from an inherited defect. The gene for *sucrase* resides on chromosome 3, and homozygous individuals for the defective gene have *sucrose intolerance*. The total world incidence of the inherited intolerance is ~1100, so it is very rare. What do you think would be the signs and symptoms of this enzyme defect?

SOLUTION

Sucrase is associated with the brush border of the intestinal mucosal cells. It catalyzed the hydrolysis of sucrose to D-glucose and D-fructose. Its absence means that sucrose passes through the small intestine where it enters the large intestine. There it interferes with water absorption because it is osmotically active and leads to the retention of water in the bowel lumen. This gives rise to abdominal cramps and watery diarrhea. Treatment involves limiting sucrose in the diet and more recently the ingesting of a proprietary enzyme, Sucraid.

BLOOD GLUCOSE HOMEOSTASIS

11.13. What are the molecular and clinical consequences of glycation of proteins?

SOLUTION

The presence of covalently attached glucose residues generally causes a protein to malfunction. This has serious effects on the eye and the kidney. In the eye some of the proteins have slow turnover, such as crystallins in the lens and structural proteins in the retina. In the kidney, structural proteins in cells and in the extracellular matrix are exposed to high concentrations of glucose from the blood and the urinary filtrate. Damage to these tissues leads to blindness, vascular disease with high blood pressure, and nephropathy, respectively.

11.14. Which foods have a low GI?

SOLUTION

Amylose-containing legumes are the *classical* low-GI foods. In a seemingly paradoxical way, foods that contain sucrose and lactose are often seen to have low or medium GI values. This arises because one-half of the carbohydrate in these disaccharides is not glucose but, respectively, fructose and galactose; and these are not detected by the glucose assay. Nevertheless they are rapidly absorbed and potentially exacerbate hyperglycemia. More scientific work is needed in this area.

Dairy foods also have a low GI because they elicit an early extra insulin (blood-glucose lowering) response via the amino acids that are released by digestion of proteins; the amino acids enter the bloodstream with glucose and, like it, stimulate insulin release from the β-cells of the pancreas.

11.15. What is the merit of knowing the GI of a food?

SOLUTION

Maintenance of euglycemia is not achieved in patients with insulin resistance and Type I diabetes. For these individuals, eating low-GI foods obviates large surges in blood glucose concentration after a meal. Knowing the GI of food helps in planning a diet with an appealing range of different foods, which leads to better control over blood glucose concentration without necessarily the recourse to drug and hormone treatment to control hyperglycemia.

11.16. Predict what might happen to GLUT-4 once the insulin stimulus for its incorporation into the plasma membrane of a cell has been removed.

SOLUTION

GLUT-4 transporters reenter the cytoplasm by invagination of the plasma membrane and the formation of vesicles via endocytosis. Thus the number of GLUT-4 molecules on the cell surface is reduced, leaving only GLUT-1 to mediate a basal rate of glucose transport.

11.17. Glucose uptake into the liver is not dependent on insulin, but glucose concentration inside a hepatocyte rises after a carbohydrate meal. Are GLUT-4 transporters likely to be involved?

SOLUTION

In the liver (and pancreas) a high rate of glucose uptake occurs after a meal. But instead of using the insulin-responsive GLUT-4 system, hepatocytes have a relatively large number of GLUT-2 transporters that are always active in the plasma membrane. Thus glucose transport into the hepatocytes is always rapid, and the concentration in the cytoplasm closely mirrors that in the bloodstream (i.e., plasma and red blood cells).

11.18. In what way do the properties of GLUT-2 and glucokinase complement each other in the metabolism of glucose by the liver?

SOLUTION

GLUT-2 is not regulated by insulin, and it mediates the rapid uptake of glucose into the liver from the bloodstream; thus the glucose concentration in the cytoplasm of hepatocytes is virtually equal to that in the portal vein. The high K_m of glucokinase means that the flux through it, when intracellular glucose concentration rises, responds in direct proportion to the increase. Thus GLUT-2 and glucokinase work together to bring about rapid assimilation of glucose into hepatocytes.

11.19. Since the three kinase enzymes of glycolysis are effectively irreversible (Fig. 11-32), speculate on which the main flux control enzymes in glycolysis are.

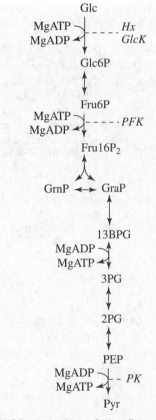

Fig. 11-32 Location of the flux-controlling kinases in glycolysis.

SOLUTION

The glycolytic pathway down to pyruvate involves 10 enzyme-catalyzed steps with three kinases that use ATP (Fig. 11-32). The reaction catalyzed by phosphofructokinase (PFK) plays the major part in controlling the overall flux of the whole pathway. It catalyzes the phosphorylation of fructose 6-phosphate (Fru6P) to fructose 1,6-bisphosphate (Fru16P$_2$). Hexokinase and pyruvate kinase (PK) have relatively higher maximal velocities. PFK is the target for more effector molecules than the other two kinases (see Fig. 11-14).

11.20. What are the general properties of enzymes that have high flux control?

SOLUTION

Reactions that have a lot of control over the overall flux through a metabolic pathway are of course relatively slow, but they also tend to be effectively irreversible, such as the kinases. Another feature is that they are often saturated by their substrates; in other words, their substrate concentrations under normal steady-state conditions are at 10 times their K_m, so they are unresponsive to minor changes in substrate concentration. Flux through the enzyme is then controlled by altering its intrinsic properties via effector molecules.

11.21. Use the metaphor of passenger movement, or flow in a busy railway station, to illustrate flux control in a metabolic pathway.

SOLUTION

Suppose that the city railway station has many tracks but a single set of five automatic, ticket-operated exit gates. The gates constitute a single step in the "pathway" that commuters must take from their homes to work. At morning peak hours many trains arrive, bringing thousands of passengers, all of whom must pass through the exit gates. It is clear that, at this time, these gates are likely to become saturated with commuters. At this point, increasing the number of commuters trying to leave the platforms will not increase the flux of commuters via the exits. In this saturated state, flux through the gates is less dependent on the absolute number of commuters and much more dependent on the intrinsic activity of the gates themselves. It is also clear that the movement of commuters through the gates is effectively irreversible. Unless an alternative set of gates is provided for passengers wishing to enter the station, the prevailing pressure of commuters, that is akin to concentration in a metabolic pathway, will overwhelmingly drive the reaction in the "exit" direction. Of course the metaphor with irreversibility works even better if the gates formally allow movement in only one direction.

There are several ways of regulating flow through the gates. First, the station could have a larger complement of gates and open a larger number of them during peak times. This is analogous to a metabolic step in which an enzyme is switched from being fully inactive to fully active, something that is often achieved metabolically by reversible phosphorylation of the enzyme. The total amount of enzymes (gates) does not change, just the proportion of enzymes (gates) in the active form does.

Second, each individual gate could be made to work faster. For the enzyme, this might be achieved by a change in the conformation of the active site, such as might be induced by the binding of stimulatory effectors to allosteric sites (Chap. 5). Third, each morning, construction staff could erect a completely new set of gates for the peak periods, dismantling them just a few hours later, making the space available for flower sellers and buskers. While this latter approach may seem inefficient, cells often respond to situations by increasing the transcription and translation of genes and thus make more enzymes that are relevant to a new situation. Just such a course of action would generally only be taken in the station in response to alternative needs for space; and regulation of concentrations of flux-controlling enzymes via changes in gene expression constitutes such a longer-term response.

11.22. Use the metaphor in Prob. 11.21 to illustrate whether an enzyme with high flux control always catalyzes the major point of flux control in a metabolic pathway.

SOLUTION

Outside of peak hours, the exit gates will no longer be saturated with people. Therefore the main flux-controlling step of the pathway will have shifted to some other process such as the rate of arrival of trains, or even the rate at which people are leaving their homes. This illustrates the point that different steps in a complex pathway can become more important in controlling flux under different steady-state conditions.

Because no single enzyme in any known pathway has absolute control over the flux through it, the old notion of a single "rate-limiting step" has given way to the more refined and mathematically rigorous notion of *flux control coefficients* in metabolic control theory or analysis (MCA). For example, in the station metaphor at peak hour, the flux of patrons through the exit gates could be *equally limited* by the width of the passageways leading to the gates as to the gates themselves.

11.23. What are the kinetic characteristics of an enzyme that has low flux control in a metabolic pathway?

SOLUTION

Such an enzyme under normal steady-state conditions tends to have the concentrations of its substrates and products at or near to their equilibrium values. Any enzyme enhances equally both the forward and the reverse rates of its catalyzed reaction. Those enzymes that catalyze seemingly irreversible reactions usually involve hydrolysis; and since the water concentration in cells and tissues is thousands of times greater than metabolites, the equilibrium position of these reactions is poised in favor of the forward or hydrolytic process. In reactions not involving water, the net direction of the reactions depends on the relative concentration of the substrates and products. If the activity of the enzyme is sufficiently high, relative to others in a metabolic pathway, altering the activity of the enzyme simply makes both the forward and reverse reactions go faster, thus maintaining a *pseudo-equilibrium*.

REGULATION OF GLYCOGEN PRODUCTION

11.24. What is the likely limit to the size of a glycogen molecule?

SOLUTION

The best way to visualize the situation is via the construction of a 3D model of a growing glycogen molecule; as the molecule becomes larger, the branches begin to interfere with one another. The extent of steric hindrance is sufficient to impair the activities of glycogen synthase and the branching enzyme, which are buried within the growing polymer. Glycogen synthase also must be in close association with glycogenin possibly via *adaptor proteins* to catalyze the addition of new glucose molecules; as the polymer becomes larger, this protein-protein interaction is weakened. Inspection of any treelike structure reveals that toward the extremities packing constraints dictate that the branches become shorter; when the chains become too short, the branching enzyme ceases to function.

11.25. How many molecules of ATP are required to store one glucose molecule as glycogen?

SOLUTION

Figures 11-10 and 11-13 appear to indicate that as the glucose molecule is incorporated into glycogen, one molecule of UTP is converted to UDP and pyrophosphate (PPi). Phosphorylation of a molecule of UDP uses one molecule of ATP; the reaction is simply UDP + ATP ⇔ UTP + ADP. However, one molecule of ATP is used in the synthesis of glucose 6-phosphate. Therefore two molecules of ATP are required for the addition of each glucose molecule that is stored as glycogen. Another way of viewing this is to note that PPi has a high-energy phosphate bond, and it takes a molecule of ATP to reinstate the energy loss that occurs when PPi is hydrolyzed by *pyrophosphatase*.

GLYCOLYSIS

11.26. What is the fate of cytosolic pyruvate when it is reduced by cytosolic NADH?

SOLUTION

Reduction of pyruvate by NADH via *lactate dehydrogenase* yields lactic acid. The carboxylic proton readily and reversibly dissociates in a reaction with a pK_a of ~4; therefore at pH 7 the molecule exists mostly as the lactate anion. Lactate undergoes facilitated diffusion into and out of cells via an integral membrane protein, the *monocarboxylate transporter*. When there is net loss of lactate from a cell, it is mostly taken up by the liver and the heart. In the liver it is turned back into pyruvate and then via the gluconeogenic pathway (Sec. 13.7) to glucose. In the heart the conversion to pyruvate is followed by oxidation via pyruvate dehydrogenase, the Krebs cycle, and oxidative phosphorylation in mitochondria.

Some investigators believe that the major route for liver glycogen synthesis involves this pathway. Thus glucose that enters muscle cells after a meal proceeds through glycolysis to lactate; this is released from the muscle and is taken up by the liver where gluconeogenesis leads to glycogen synthesis. This is referred to as the *indirect route* of postprandial glycogen synthesis.

KREBS CYCLE FLUX

11.27. What factors influence the metabolic fate of citrate in the mitochondria?

SOLUTION

If there is demand for ATP in a cell, citrate enters the Krebs cycle. If there is a stimulus for fatty acid synthesis, citrate is exported from the mitochondria to the cytoplasm where lipogenesis takes place. As occurs with the reciprocal relationship between glycolysis and glycogen synthesis, the two fates of citrate are complementary.

11.28. Why is ATP required for the ATP-citrate lyase (ACL) reaction but not for the citrate synthase reaction?

SOLUTION

This difference illustrates the fact that the thioester bond in compounds that contain CoA (like acetyl-CoA) has a high free energy. Similarly, when fatty-acyl CoA molecules are produced during the priming/trapping phase of fatty acid oxidation, ATP bond energy is also supplied to drive the reaction forward (Sec. 10-5).

METABOLIC SHUTTLES

11.29. In the redirection of citrate carbon atoms in the mitochondrial matrix back to acetyl-CoA for fatty acid synthesis in the cytoplasm, why is acetyl-CoA itself not transported out of the mitochondria?

SOLUTION

The large CoA molecule renders complexes containing it unable to cross normal membranes. In Chap. 10, it was noted that fatty acids conjugated to CoA could not pass into the mitochondria; they require transfer to carnitine before transport from the cytoplasm can take place.

11.30. Are there two separate metabolic pools of CoA in most cells, one in the mitochondria and the other in the cytoplasm?

SOLUTION

Yes. Because CoA cannot freely cross membranes, not only do the cytoplasmic and mitochondrial compartments contain separate pools of CoA, but also the acetyl CoA-to-CoA ratio can be quite different in each compartment. Similarly, mitochondrial and cytosolic NAD^+ and NADH pools are wholly separate; and the NADH to NAD^+ ratio on one side of the mitochondrial membrane can be different from that on the other side.

11.31. How does oxaloacetate that is generated from citrate released from the mitochondrial matrix return there?

SOLUTION

A temporary deficiency of oxaloacetate in the matrix reduces the rate of disposal of acetyl-CoA, but cytosolic oxaloacetate produced via ATP-dependent citrate lyase returns to the matrix, thus overcoming the deficiency. Oxaloacetate itself does not cross the inner mitochondrial membrane; it is converted to compounds for which there are specific transporters.

LIPOGENESIS

11.32. Malonyl-CoA inhibits the transport of fatty acids into the mitochondria. How might this assist insulin in promoting glucose oxidation?

SOLUTION

Although the balance between glucose and fatty acid oxidation is described in Chap. 13, it is relevant to note here that malonyl-CoA inhibits carnitine acyl transferase I (CAT-I), the enzyme that catalyzes the exchange of fatty acids for carnitine as part of the cytosol-to-matrix fatty acid transport system. Inhibition of CAT-I occurs when acetyl-CoA carboxylase is activated by insulin. By inhibiting the uptake of fatty acids into mitochondria, malonyl CoA favors the oxidation of glucose and prevents fatty acids from being oxidized at the same time as they are being synthesized.

11.33. How many malonyl-CoA and NADPH molecules are required to produce a 16-carbon fatty acid molecule?

SOLUTION

Refer to Fig. 11-24: Starting with one acetyl-CoA molecule to fill the XXX site (left side of the diagram) and a malonyl-CoA to fill the YYY site (right side of the diagram), a 4-carbon fatty acyl chain will be formed by also using two molecules of NADPH. Each subsequent addition of two carbon atoms requires a molecule of malonyl-CoA and two more molecules of NADPH. Thus a 16-carbon fatty acid molecule, *palmitic acid*, requires 1 acetyl-CoA, 7 malonyl-CoA, and 16 NADPH molecules for its synthesis.

11.34. What is the mechanism of release of fatty acids from fatty acid synthase?

SOLUTION

When the growing fatty-acyl chain reaches 16 carbon atoms long, it is transferred onto a molecule of CoA. This produces *palmitoyl-CoA*, or what is more generically called *fatty-acyl-CoA*.

11.35. What is the metabolic fate of fatty-acyl-CoA?

SOLUTION

Because carnitine acyl transfertase I (CAT-I) is inhibited by fatty-acyl-CoA, these molecules are not normally oxidized in the mitochondria. Instead, fatty-acyl-CoA donates its fatty acyl moiety to the 3-carbon backbone of a glycerol 3-phosphate molecule, producing mono-, di-, and then triacyl glyceride. The latter resides in the cytoplasm of many cell-types as lipid droplets.

Precursors of membrane phospholipids are diglycerides formed from glycerol 3-phosphate. These molecules are made by reducing dihydroxyacetone phosphate from glycolysis with NADH in the cytoplasm. In the liver, glycerol 3-phosphate is also produced from glycerol itself by ATP-dependent phosphorylation via *glycerol kinase*. This enzyme is notably absent from other tissues.

11.36. How many molecules of ATP are hydrolyzed during the synthesis of one molecule of palmitoyl-CoA?

SOLUTION

Refer to Fig. 11-24: None. However, recall that one molecule of ATP is hydrolyzed in the formation of malonyl-CoA, one of the substrates of the reaction pathway. For this reason malonyl-CoA can be viewed as an activated acetyl-CoA. Hence 7 molecules of ATP are used in the formation of 1 molecule of palmitoyl-CoA.

11.37. Does the carbon atom in carbon dioxide that condenses onto acetyl-CoA in forming malonyl-CoA, via acetyl-CoA carboxylase, reside in the final fatty acid?

SOLUTION

Refer to Figs. 11-23 and 24. No. The same carbon atom that was condensed onto acetyl-CoA is released during the chain elongation phase.

11.38. What is the process involved in forming unsaturated fatty acids?

SOLUTION

These fatty acids are formed by desaturation of saturated fatty acids. The process occurs after the release of the saturated fatty acid from fatty acid synthase, and it requires a special enzyme, *fatty-acid desaturase*, which uses FAD as a cofactor. The enzyme only creates —C=C— double bonds between carbon atoms less than nine away from the carboxyl end. Thus many nutritionally important unsaturated fatty acids that contain double bonds at higher positions along their carbon chain, such as linolenic acid, which is unsaturated at the C9, C12, and C15, must be derived from the diet. Such fatty acids are called *essential*, as is the case for those amino acids for which there is an obligatory requirement in the diet.

Omitting the second reduction phase in a particular cycle of fatty acid synthesis would produce unsaturated fatty acids, but this seems not to occur in nature. Furthermore, in such a process double bonds would be placed at every second carbon atom in a fatty acid molecule, and yet another means would be required for additional desaturation steps between the intervening carbon atoms.

PENTOSE PHOSPHATE PATHWAY

11.39. What regulates carbon flux through the pentose phosphate pathway?

SOLUTION

The main control of flux in the oxidative pentose phosphate pathway under normal conditions is the profound product inhibition by NADPH on the first enzyme, glucose-6-phosphate dehydrogenase (G6PDH). NADPH concentrations can become low due to active lipogenesis. Then G6PDH will increase in activity.

Note that NADPH is also a substrate for glutathione reductase, regenerating the powerful antioxidant glutathione in conditions of oxidative stress.

11.40. How might the PPP, lipogenesis, and the Krebs cycle interact and influence flux through one another's reactions?

SOLUTION

The insulin-stimulated drive to increase lipogenesis and triacylglycerol synthesis creates a demand for ATP, NADPH, and glycerol 3-phosphate. ATP demand is satisfied by an increased activity of the Krebs cycle that occurs in response to a fall in ADP concentration in the mitochondrial matrix. A fall in the concentration of NADPH in the cytoplasm stimulates flux via the oxidative PPP. The use of glycerol 3-phosphate in esterification of fatty acids to make phospholipids stimulates glycolytic flux. Thus, by directly stimulating lipogenesis, insulin indirectly stimulates the PPP, the Krebs cycle, and the first four reactions of glycolysis.

11.41. Beriberi is a neurological and cardiovascular disorder that is caused by a *deficiency of thiamine* (also called vitamin B_1). It has been a serious health problem in Asia and continues to be in those places where *rice* is the main staple food. The problem is exacerbated if the rice is dehusked (*polished*) because only the outer layers of the seeds contain appreciable amounts of thiamine. Beriberi also occurs in some malnourished chronic alcoholics, so to avoid this problem in some countries certain alcohol-containing drinks are fortified with thiamine. Beriberi is characterized by pain in the limbs, weak muscles, abnormal skin sensation, and an enlarged heart with inadequate cardiac output. Which biochemical processes are affected by thiamine deficiency?

SOLUTION

Thiamine pyrophosphate (TPP) is the prosthetic group in three main enzymes in humans: pyruvate dehydrogenase; 2-oxoglutarate dehydrogenase; and transketolase in the pentose phosphate pathway. The common feature of the three enzymes is the transfer of a 2-carbon activated aldehyde unit. In beriberi the plasma concentrations of pyruvate and 2-oxoglutarate are elevated; the pyruvate concentrations are especially high after glucose ingestion. The low activity of transketolase in the red blood cells is diagnostic of beriberi.

METABOLISM OF TWO OTHER MONOSACCHARIDES

11.42. An inborn error of liver fructose-1-phosphate aldolase (aldolase B) leads to a condition known as *fructose intolerance.* The condition is characterized by life-threatening liver damage that can occur after consuming fructose in the diet. Why is it life-threatening?

SOLUTION

Fructokinase catalyzes the formation of fructose 1-phosphate from fructose and ATP. It is a very rapid reaction that has minimal product inhibition by fructose 1-phosphate. Normally, fructose 1-phosphate enters glycolysis after aldolase B has catalyzed its scission to yield glyceraldehyde and dihydroxyacetone phosphate; then dihydroxyacetone phosphate passes via triosephosphate isomerase to glyceraldehyde 3-phosphate and then into the final part of glycolysis, generating pyruvate. This pyruvate leads to regeneration of ATP. If aldolase B is inactive, then phosphate becomes trapped in fructose 1-phosphate which seriously compromises ATP regeneration. As a result, ATP concentrations in the liver fall dramatically, leading to a failure of the many ATP-dependent reactions including those that pump ions across the plasma membrane. This leads to irreversible damage of the hepatocytes. Even in normal individuals, the activity of aldolase B is sometimes a little lower than that of fructokinase so, in general, ingesting large doses of fructose is not advisable.

11.43. What are the metabolic and likely clinical consequences of a deficiency of galactokinase?

SOLUTION

This deficiency causes an inability to trap galactose inside the hepatocytes. Thus galactose is not efficiently cleared from the bloodstream. The accumulation of galactose is especially damaging to sensitive tissues such as the eye lens and the retina, because the open-chain aldehydic form, which is present in dynamic equilibrium with the closed pyranose forms, reacts with exposed amino groups. This causes *glycation* of many different proteins including those in the lens, leading to cataracts and retinal impairment. Thus an end-stage complication of galactosemia is blindness.

SUPPLEMENTARY PROBLEMS

11.44. Restorers of old machinery sometimes place rusty items in a large barrel of molasses, the syrup from cane sugar, for several months. Why do they do this?

11.45. Most evolutionarily higher plants produce nectar that is secreted in their flowers. This attracts bees that collect it and in the process transfer pollen from the male part of the flower to the female part. The bees transfer the nectar back to the hive where it is stored and concentrated by airflow from their buzzing wings. This increases the osmolality of the solution rendering it uninhabitable by most microorganisms. But another biochemical process rapidly doubles the osmolality. What is it?

11.46. A standard test for amylose is to add a solution containing potassium iodide and iodine. If amylose is present, the solution turns a deep blue. What is the explanation for this effect?

11.47. The glycemic index of a loaf of bread is not the same for the crust compared with the soft inner part. It is higher for the crust than the interior. Why?

11.48. In humans the total complement of red blood cells (~2 kg in an adult of 70 kg) consume ~20 g of glucose a day. For what is the energy from this glucose used in these cells?

11.49. Glucose entry into human red blood cells is mediated by the GLUT-1 transporter. How many of these transporters are there per cell, and what is the mean residence time of a glucose molecule in the cell?

11.50. A glycogen particle and a starch grain both consist of glucose polymers. But are they composed only of carbohydrate?

11.51. How many glucose molecules pass through glycolysis in one human red blood cell in a second?

11.52. Are any of the enzyme components of the pyruvate dehydrogenase complex coded for by the mitochondrial genome?

11.53. Is it true that Hans Krebs' paper in 1937, reporting the discovery of the citric acid cycle, was rejected by the journal *Nature*, so it was submitted to the journal *Enzymologia* were it was published?

11.54. Are there possible alternatives to the non-oxidative pentose phosphate pathway (PPP) shown in Fig. 11-26?

ANSWERS TO SUPPLEMENTARY PROBLEMS

11.44. Molasses is highly concentrated syrup of sucrose. Its osmolality is so very high, like honey, that microorganisms do not grow in it. In the presence of iron oxide some of the sucrose is hydrolysed to glucose and fructose. These, in turn, act as reducing agents and reduce the iron oxide of the rust, loosen it, and expose the underlying iron.

11.45. Bee saliva contains the enzyme *invertase*. This catalyses the hydrolysis of sucrose into glucose and fructose thus doubling the number of molecular particles in the solution, thus doubling the osmolality.

11.46. In solution, amylose forms a helical structure, and iodine atoms and ions fit snugly down the central cylinder. This produces electron delocalization that has an absorption-energy bandwidth that encompasses the red to green wavelengths of white light. Photons from white light can be absorbed by the electron system, leaving the blue light that we see.

11.47. The higher temperature attained by the outer part of the loaf during baking disrupts the outer starch grains more than those inside. This means that digestive amylase gains more rapid access to the amylose and amylopectin inside them, releasing glucose more rapidly than for the starch granules in the interior of the loaf.

11.48. It is known that ~40% of the ATP generated in glycolysis in the red blood cell is consumed in driving the Na, K-ATPase that maintains the ionic disequilibrium across the plasma membrane; the K^+ concentration inside is ~100 mM while Na^+ concentration is ~10 mM. The converse is approximately true for outside in the plasma; $[Na^+]$ is ~140 mM and $[K^+]$ is ~10 mM. Other reactions that consume the ATP include those of glutathione synthesis, and Ca^{2+}-ATPase that pumps Ca^{2+} out of the cell. However, these consume only an additional ~10% of the ATP and it is curious that the remaining ~50% of turnover is unaccounted for; although some of it appears to be used in maintaining the biconcave-disc shape of these cells.

11.49. There are ~200,000 copies of GLUT-1 per human red blood cell. The mean residence time of a glucose molecule was shown by Jennifer Potts and colleagues in 1987, using a special nuclear magnetic resonance (NMR) method called magnetization transfer, to be ~1 second. Since the hexokinase reaction is relatively slow, the fast transmenbrane exchange implies that only one in about a thousand entries of a glucose molecule has it become phosphorylated and then metabolised via glycolysis.

11.50. No. In glycogen there is the core *protein* glycogenin, the glycogen synthetic enzymes, and those engaged in glycogenolysis. In starch grains there is some endogenous amylase but the hydrolytic enzymes are not present to the same extent as in glycogen.

11.51. ~30. The demand for ATP in the red blood cell appears to control the flux via glycolysis. ATP consumption by Na, K-ATPase is at a rate of ~3 mmol $[L cells]^{-1} h^{-1}$. Since this ATP turnover constitutes ~40% of the total turnover (Prob. 11.48) and knowing the volume of one red blood cell to be 86 fL, we can compute the number to be ~30.

11.52. No. Only 13 proteins are coded for by the mitochondrial genome in humans and all of these are components of the electron transport chain (ETC).

11.53. Yes. In fact he had the rejection letter from *Nature* framed and hung in his office in Oxford. The Nobel Prize committee and colleagues around the world clearly had a different opinion of the work than the editors of *Nature*.

11.54. Yes. The pathway that appears in most biochemistry textbooks is that in Fig. 11-26. It was described by Bernard Horecker in 1955. It appears to be the pathway that operates in adipocytes, red blood cells, and many other cell types; hence its name the F-type (for fat-type). However, the possibility exists that other forms of group transfer reactions could take place via transketolase and aldolase, in the absence of transaldolase. It is thought that this more complicated reaction scheme operates in the liver, so it was called the L-type (for liver-type) pentose phosphate pathway by its main proponent John Williams.

CHAPTER 12

Fate of Dietary Lipids

12.1 Definitions and Nomenclature

Question: What fundamental chemical features distinguish *lipids* from the other *macronutrients*, proteins, and carbohydrates?

In Sec. 3.5 we noted that lipids are defined as water-insoluble compounds that can be extracted from living organisms by weakly polar or nonpolar solvents. Lipids are a structurally diverse group of compounds, and the fact that they are not water-soluble means that they can serve as a barrier between two aqueous compartments (as self-assembling membranes) or as compact energy reserves (as droplets).

Revise some of the ideas presented in Chap. 3, by considering the following.

EXAMPLE 12.1   Which of the compounds in Fig. 12-1 are lipids?

Compounds 1, 3, and 5–9 are lipids because they are biological in origin and are soluble in organic solvents (such as benzene). The latter property arises because they contain a high proportion of carbon and hydrogen and are therefore insoluble in water. Compound 4 is not a lipid because it does not occur in living organisms. Compound 2 is water-soluble, but because it is a member of the same series of compounds as compound 1, it is usually considered to be a lipid.

Classes of Lipids

A common feature of all lipids is that biologically their hydrocarbon content is derived from the polymerization of acetyl units followed by reduction of the chain that is formed. (However, this process also occurs in the synthesis of some compounds that are not lipids, so this property cannot be used as a definition of lipids.) Polymerization of acetyl units gives rise to the following:

1. Long, linear hydrocarbon chains:

$$n\text{CH}_3\text{COO}^- \longrightarrow \quad \longrightarrow \text{CH}_3\text{COCH}_2\text{CO} \cdots \longrightarrow \quad \longrightarrow \text{CH}_3\text{CH}_2\text{CH}_2\text{CH}_2 \cdots$$

The products are *fatty acids*, $\text{CH}_3(\text{CH}_2)_n\text{COOH}$, which in turn can give rise to amines and alcohols. Lipids that contain fatty acids include *glycerolipids*, the *sphingolipids*, and *waxes*.

2. Branched chain hydrocarbons via a five-carbon intermediate, isopentene (*isoprene*):

$$3\text{CH}_3\text{COO}^- \longrightarrow \quad \longrightarrow \left(\text{H}_3\text{C} - \text{HC} = \overset{\overset{\text{CH}_3}{|}}{\text{C}} - \text{CH}_2 - \right) \longrightarrow \quad \longrightarrow \text{terpenes}$$
(including *steroids* and *carotenoids*)

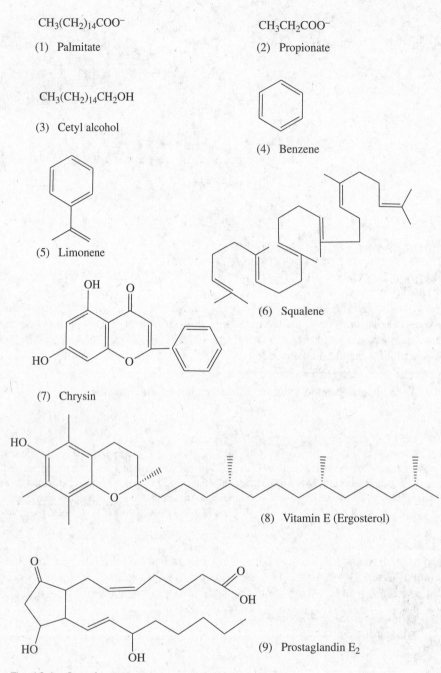

CH$_3$(CH$_2$)$_{14}$COO$^-$

(1) Palmitate

CH$_3$CH$_2$COO$^-$

(2) Propionate

CH$_3$(CH$_2$)$_{14}$CH$_2$OH

(3) Cetyl alcohol

(4) Benzene

(5) Limonene

(6) Squalene

(7) Chrysin

(8) Vitamin E (Ergosterol)

(9) Prostaglandin E$_2$

Fig. 12-1   Set of compounds, some of which are lipids.

3. Linear or cyclic structures that are only partially reduced:

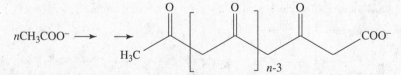

nCH$_3$COO$^-$ →

These are called *acetogenins* (or sometimes *polyketides*) and many are *antibiotics*. Many of these compounds are aromatic; and their pathway of formation is the principal means of synthesis of the benzene ring in nature. Not all are lipids, because partial reduction often leaves oxygen-containing groups that render the product soluble in water.

Fatty Acids

These are the main energy-rich part of the triacylglyceride molecule. More chemical details are given in Chap. 3, and note the use of the numbering system to describe the various fatty acids.

EXAMPLE 12.2 Following are some important fatty acids:
(a) Saturated:

$$CH_3(CH_2)_{14}COO^- \qquad CH_3(CH_2)_{16}COO^-$$

Palmitic acid   Stearic acid
(hexadecanoic acid)   (octadecanoic acid)
16:0   18:0

(b) In unsaturated fatty acids, the double bond nearly always has the *cis* conformation:

$$CH_3(CH_2)_5CH{=}CH(CH_2)_7COOH$$

Palmitoleic acid
(*cis*-9-hexadecanoic acid)
$16:1^{\Delta 9}$

(c) In polyunsaturated fatty acids, the double bonds are rarely conjugated (consecutive):

$$CH_3(CH_2)_4CH{=}CH{-}CH_2{-}CH{=}CH(CH_2)_7COOH$$

Linoleic acid
(cis, cis-9, 12-octadecadienoic acid)
$18:2^{\Delta 9,12}$

A numbering notation that is used widely for indicating the structure of a fatty acid is shown under the names of the fatty acids in Example 12.2. To the left of the colon is shown the number of C atoms in the acid; to the right, the number of double bonds. The position of the double bond is shown by a superscript Δ followed by the number of C atoms between the double bond and the end of the chain, with the carbon of the carboxylic acid group being called 1.

Another numbering system that is frequently used by nutritionists is the *omega* system. With this system the carbon atom farthest from the carboxyl carbon (the methyl carbon) is denoted ω; and counting back along the chain of carbon atoms gives $\omega 1$, $\omega 2$, $\omega 3$, etc. E.g., a fatty acid with a double bond between the third and fourth carbon atoms from the methyl carbon is called an $\omega 3$ fatty acid.

Glycerolipids

Glycerolipids are lipids that contain glycerol in which the three hydroxyl groups are substituted. *Triacylglycerols* are neutral glycerolipids and are also known as *triglycerides*; and the three hydroxyl groups of glycerol are each esterified, usually by a *different* fatty acid (also see Chap. 3).

$$
\begin{array}{c}
CH_2O \cdot OCR \\
| \\
R'CO \cdot O {-} CH \\
| \\
CH_2O \cdot OCR''
\end{array}
$$

EXAMPLE 12.3 The structure of 1-oleoly-2-palmitoyl-*sn*-glycerol is

$$
\begin{array}{c}
CH_2O \cdot OC(CH_2)_7CH{=}CH(CH_2)_7CH_3 \\
| \\
CH_3(CH_2)_{14}CO \cdot O {-} CH \\
| \\
CH_2O \cdot OCR''
\end{array}
$$

This is a *diacylglycerol*. Diacyl- and monoacylglycerols are found in cells, but only in small amounts; they are metabolites of *triglycerides* and *phospholipids*.

Triglycerides are the most abundant lipids in animals. They form *depot fat*, and hydrolysis of the ester bonds releases fatty acids and glycerol from adipose tissue. *Phospholipids* are the main structural lipids in cell membranes, while *glycoglycerolipids* exist in cell membranes they are much less abundant.

12.2   Sources of Dietary Triglycerides

Triglycerides are the main constituents of vegetable oils, butter, and margarine. They are a significant proportion of processed foods such as cookies (25–30%) and pastries (40%) that are made with butter or oil. Since triglycerides are stored in the body in white adipose tissue, animal flesh is a rich source, with meat such as bacon consisting of over 40% by weight.

EXAMPLE 12.4   Most fruits and vegetables do not contain significant amounts of triglyceride. Some common plant foods are exceptions: avocados are approximately 22% by weight triglyceride, and nuts such as macadamias are up to 75% by weight triglyceride.

EXAMPLE 12.5   How much triglyceride is consumed in an average day by a person on a typical Western diet?

Some people consume large amounts of food to go ("take away" in some other countries) that is deep-fried in vegetable oil, and they may obtain well over 70% of their daily energy intake as triglycerides. Other people are careful about what they eat and regulate their injestion to ~10% of their daily energy intake. On average ~100 g of triglyceride is consumed by an adult on an affluent Western diet; this constitutes 30–50% of the daily energy intake.

12.3   Digestion of Dietary Triglyceride

Hydrophobicity

The hydrophobic nature of triglycerides means that special molecular adaptations have evolved for their digestion, absorption, and intertissue transport.

EXAMPLE 12.6   When vegetable oil is shaken vigorously with water, an *emulsion* is formed, but in a short time the triglyceride and aqueous phases separate. In making a salad dressing, the addition of an *emulsifying agent* ensures that the tiny oil droplets remain suspended in the aqueous medium. The oil is not dissolved in the water, but the mixture forms a stable macroscopic system.

EXAMPLE 12.7   What is the chemical nature of an *emulsifying agent*?

Molecules that have both hydrophilic and hydrophobic characteristics often form spherical self-assembled structures called *micelles* (Fig. 12-2). These enclose lipids and interact with the surrounding water at their surface; they are also called *detergents*. Household detergents, such as washing-up liquid and soap, dissolve hydrophobic oils within the hydrophobic core of their micelles. Molecules that have both hydrophobic and hydrophilic characteristics are variously called *amphiphilic*, *amphiphobic*, and *amphipathic* (Greek *amphi*, both sides; as in *amphitheater* in which the audience sits on both sides of the stage).

Micelles, Vesicles, and Bilayers

By both increasing the surface area of the lipid-water interface and providing a point of contact for digestive enzymes, the digestion of triglycerides is facilitated by the formation of micelles in the small intestine. *Bile salts* are the body's detergents involved in the process of dissolving triglycerides and amphipathic nutrients such as phospholipids. The latter form *mixed micelles* in which there is more than one type of amphipathic molecule forming the micelle structure.

More generally, both micelles and bilayers arise spontaneously through the operation of two opposing forces: (1) attractive forces between the hydrocarbon chains (van der Waals forces) drawing the chains together and (2) repulsive forces between the charged head groups that nevertheless interact with and order water molecules in close proximity to them.

Bile Salts

Bile acids are synthesized from cholesterol in hepatocytes (Chap. 3), and the conjugation of the carboxyl group with glycine or taurine converts them to the strongly *amphipathic* bile salts; these are strong detergents that are essential for dissolving fat in digestive fluids, making them susceptible to hydrolytic attack by lipases.

Hepatocytes secrete bile salts into the *bile canaliculi* that lead into the common bile duct that discharges its contents into the duodenum. The gall bladder that is attached to the bile duct serves as a reservoir, and outside meal times, it stores the continual stream of solutions of bile salts from the hepatocytes. Immediately after a meal,

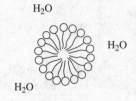

Micelle

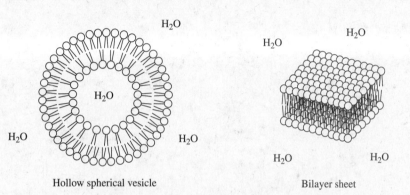

Hollow spherical vesicle

Bilayer sheet

Fig. 12-2 A micelle, a vesicle, and a portion of a lipid bilayer. The *hydrophilic* head groups are represented by spheres while the *hydrophobic* hydrocarbon chains are represented by solid lines.

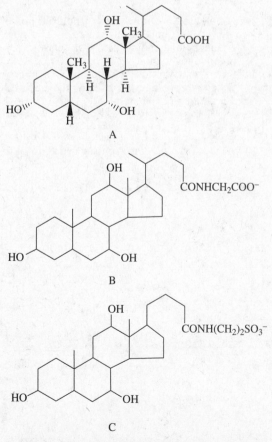

A

B

C

Fig. 12-3 Bile acid and bile salt detergents. (A) Cholic acid drawn showing the stereochemistry of carbon atoms in the system of fused rings, (B) glycocholate, and (C) taurocholate.

the arrival of products of digestion causes, via the action of the gastric hormone *cholecystokinin*, the smooth muscle in the walls of the gall bladder to contract; and a solution of bile salts is squirted into the duodenum.

Cholesterol

Bile salt production and the esterification with a fatty acid are the only *metabolic fates* of cholesterol. It is not oxidized to carbon dioxide, so any excess is excreted in the bile.

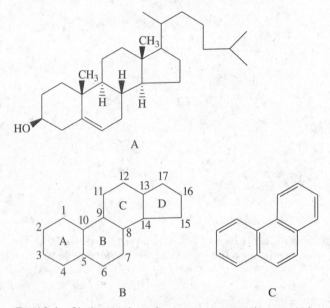

Fig. 12-4 Cholesterol and some structural nomenclature. (A) Cholesterol structure showing key aspects of bonding at chiral centers. (B) The numbering system used in the 4-ring structure. (C) Phenanthrene that formally is chemically, although not biosynthetically, the basis of the structure of cholesterol.

EXAMPLE 12.8 Structurally cholesterol is classified as a *steroid*. Steroids are structural derivatives of the aromatic hydrocarbon *phenanthrene* (Fig. 12-4); they are reduced and contain an additional five-member ring hence the name *cyclopentanoperhydrophenanthrene*.

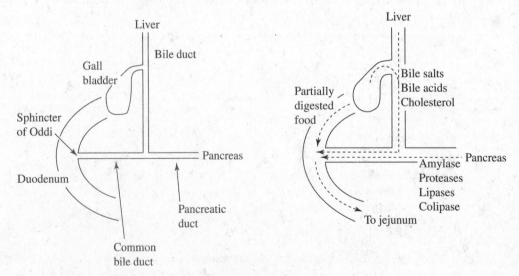

Fig. 12-5 Gall bladder and pancreatic secretions.

The contents of the small intestine, with its bile salts and dietary triglycerides, are mixed by the continual churning brought about by *peristalsis* in the smooth muscle walls of the small intestine; this hastens the formation of micelles. Once emulsified, triglycerides are hydrolyzed by *pancreatic lipase*. This enzyme is synthesized in the exocrine cells of the pancreas and is secreted along with other digestive enzymes into the duodenum. The nature of the interaction between the lipase and the triglycerides in the micelles is intriguing because the active site of the enzyme must bind to a hydrophobic substrate while the enzyme as a whole is immersed in an aqueous environment (see Fig. 12-6).

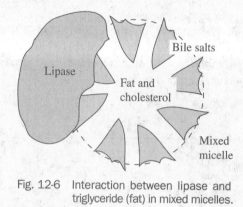

Fig. 12-6   Interaction between lipase and triglyceride (fat) in mixed micelles.

EXAMPLE 12.9   What are the products of lipase-mediated hydrolysis of triglycerides?

Lipase hydrolyzes the ester bond between the fatty acid residues and the glycerol backbone of triglycerides. Complete hydrolysis is neither necessary nor generally achieved prior to absorption from the intestine. Instead, the enzyme mainly produces a mixture of free fatty acids and mono- and diacylglycerides. Since all these components are amphipathic, they remain associated with the micelles.

Fully and partially digested triacylglycerol, along with the *micellizing* bile salts, is absorbed by the epithelial cells of the small intestine. In the cytoplasm of these cells, mono- and diacylglycerides are reesterified with activated fatty acids to form triglycerides. These are packaged into *chylomicrons* for export in lymph into the *thoracic duct* from which they pass to the subclavian vein and enter the bloodstream, and pass to tissues throughout the body. The bile salts are also salvaged in this process and are absorbed from the blood by the liver.

EXAMPLE 12.10   About 20 g of bile salts are secreted by the liver into the duodenum each day. Only a small proportion (less than 2 g) enters the feces because the uptake from the intestine into the bloodstream and transport back to the liver are very efficient. This is called the *enterohepatic circulation* of bile salts.

The biochemical processes involved in triglyceride digestion and absorption have recently been targeted in two weight-loss strategies. They reduce the amount of triglyceride that enters the body from the gut.

1. Inhibition of pancreatic lipase prevents the hydrolysis of triglycerides and reduces the absorption of fatty acids. Side effects that are similar to gall bladder blockage result from the passage of triglycerides into the large intestine. So uncomfortable are the side effects that these drugs act partly as *aversion therapy* in conditioning subjects to avoid fatty meals.

2. The *Olestra* molecule consists of a fatty acid covalently linked to a sucrose molecule. It is not hydrolyzed by pancreatic lipase, yet tastes and behaves as a natural triglyceride. Cookies, pastries, and fries made with Olestra do not contain any absorbable triglycerides.

3. Gall bladder blockage and the inhibition of pancreatic lipases decrease the breakdown of triglycerides in the small intestine, whereas the ingestion of Olestra results in the provision of an oil which cannot be broken down. The result is that the triglycerides and Olestra are evaluated as oily feces accompanied, in some cases, by anal leakage of feces.

EXAMPLE 12.11   Not only does consumption of food made with Olestra have the same side effects as the lipase inhibitors but also an adverse behavioral outcome is that its use does little to promote changes toward a healthy lifestyle. Food that contains Olestra must be labeled with a warning of both the intestinal consequences and the complication that the passage of Olestra into the large intestine can impede the uptake of the fat-soluble vitamins. For this reason foods that contain Olestra are usually supplemented with the lipid soluble vitamins A, D, E, and K.

12.4   Transport of Dietary Triglycerides to Tissues

After reesterification of fatty acids in the enterocytes, the resulting triglycerides self-assemble into the core of a sphere that has a shell of phospholipids that is interwoven with a molecule (or sometimes more) of *apolipoprotein*. There are several types of apolipoproteins and different tissues make particular types.

As described in Secs. 3.11 and 12.3 on membrane structure, phospholipids are amphipathic, consisting of a polar head group and a fatty-acyl tail so the outer face of the phospholipid shell is hydrophilic while the whole particle remains in solution in the bloodstream. The inner core also contains cholesterol that is both in its free form and esterified to a long-chain fatty acid.

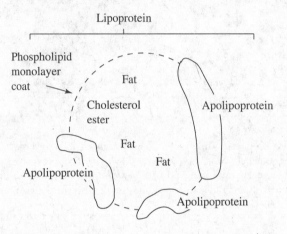

Fig. 12-7   Lipoprotein structure and assembly.

Lipoproteins produced in the intestinal epithelium are called *chylomicrons*. Chylomicrons are the largest lipoproteins and are particularly rich in triglyceride.

Different types of lipoprotein vary in size and contain contrasting ratios of cholesterol to triglyceride.

12.5   Uptake of Triglycerides into Tissues

Once in the bloodstream, chylomicrons can bind to *lipoprotein lipase* that is integral to the plasma membranes of endothelial cells that make up the capillaries in the heart, muscle, adipose, and other tissues. The enzyme projects into the bloodstream and hydrolyzes the triglyceride that is contained in chylomicrons, to yield fatty acids and glycerol. In the process, the chylomicron is reduced in size, and the fatty acids enter nearby cells via specific transport proteins or by simply dissolving in the membrane bilayer. It might have been anticipated that the glycerol would also enter nearby cells, thus providing substrate for the reformation of triglyceride. However, reesterification requires glycerol 3-phosphate that is synthesized via glycerol kinase; but most peripheral tissues do not contain this enzyme. The source of glycerol 3-phosphate in most tissues is dihydroxyacetone phosphate from glycolysis. Therefore glycerol from the chylomicron lipid is released into the bloodstream and is taken up primarily by the liver that does have glycerol kinase.

EXAMPLE 12.12   What is the metabolic fate of the fatty acids that are released from lipid digestion of triglycerides in *chylomicrons*?

After entering the cytoplasm, the fatty acids are trapped in the cell via the action of thiokinase that yields fatty-acyl-CoA. The activated fatty acids are either oxidized after transport into the mitochondria or reesterified with glycerol to give triacylglycerols that are stored in lipid droplets in the cytoplasm. The esterification may be only partial, giving diacylglycerols that are intermediates in phospholipid synthesis.

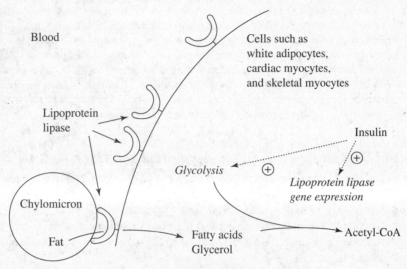

Fig. 12-8   Fates of fatty acids derived from chylomicrons.

As the chylomicrons lose lipids, the ratio of cholesterol to triglyceride within the core increases. This makes the *chylomicron remnant* more compact and physically dense.

The remnants are taken up by hepatocytes. Specific receptors on the hepatocyte membrane bind to one of the particular apoproteins, *apoB-48*, in the remnants. The whole receptor-remnant complex enters the cell by endocytosis. Through fusion with lysosomes, the remnants are digested, liberating fatty acids and cholesterol ester into the cytoplasm. It can be seen that this is the way dietary cholesterol eventually reaches the liver.

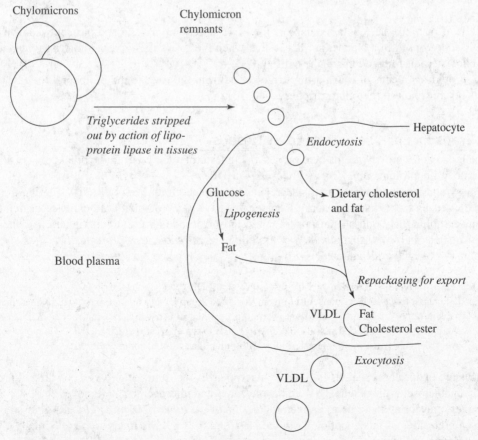

Fig. 12-9   Processing of chylomicron remnants by the liver.

EXAMPLE 12.13   Which tissue takes up most of the fatty acids from triglycerides in chylomicrons?

Transport of triglyceride and cholesterol from the small intestine to the blood and then to the tissues is often referred to as the *exogenous triglyceride transport system*. The tissue that receives most of the triglyceride varies with the individual, but generally it is the white adipose tissue. Insulin, a hormone secreted by the pancreas, stimulates the expression of lipoprotein lipase in the endothelial cells of the capillaries around white adipocytes. A consequence of the fatty acid uptake is that the chemical composition of triglycerides stored in adipocytes closely reflects the chemical composition of those ingested in the diet. Accumulation of triglycerides in tissues such as skeletal muscle and liver can be damaging to those cells, whereas adipose tissue has potentially a huge capacity for storage.

12.6   Export of Triglyceride and Cholesterol from the Liver

One of the metabolic fates of the cholesterol that arrives in the liver is conversion to bile salts (Sec. 12.3).

The liver also synthesizes cholesterol and repackages both the diet-derived and endogenously synthesized forms into lipoproteins for export to the peripheral tissues.

The liver synthesizes large amounts of triglyceride using precursors such as glucose as the source of the building block acetyl-CoA. The triglyceride is transported to the periphery in lipoproteins, and from these it enters adipose and other tissues.

The type of lipoprotein assembled and secreted by the liver is *very low-density lipoprotein* (VLDL). It contains a high ratio of triglyceride to cholesterol. The main apoprotein in VLDL is *apo-B100* which is derived from the same gene as the chylomicron-specific *apo-B48*. The latter apoprotein is slightly shorter because the mRNA in the intestinal cells is posttranscriptionally altered to introduce a premature stop codon.

Secretion of VLDL by hepatocytes into the bloodstream occurs by membrane budding, *exocytosis*.

EXAMPLE 12.14   What is the metabolic fate of VLDL?

As with chylomicrons, VLDLs interact with lipoprotein lipase in the endothelial cells of capillaries in tissues such as muscle, heart, and white adipose tissue. This enzyme strips triglycerides from the lipoproteins, leaving cholesterol-dense particles called *low-density lipoprotein* (LDL).

The cells of many tissues contain receptors for LDL; upon binding, the complex between LDL and the receptor is endocytosed in a manner similar to that when the liver takes up chylomicron remnants. Subsequently, cholesterol is released inside the cell.

VLDL provides a means of transporting triglyceride from the liver to the peripheral tissues while LDL transports hepatic cholesterol to the periphery.

12.7   Transport of Cholesterol from Tissues

Excess cellular cholesterol in plasma membranes, or cholesterol released from the breakdown of cells, enters another type of lipoprotein, *high-density lipoprotein* (HDL).

HDL is synthesized in the liver and is secreted as a phospholipid/apoprotein disk. During transit in the blood, HDL acts as a sink for cholesterol. Hepatocytes have receptors that bind cholesterol-rich HDL particles, thus completing a cycle of transport of cholesterol from the liver to the periphery and back again to the liver. The latter half of this *metabolic loop* is called *reverse cholesterol transport*.

A summary of triglyceride and cholesterol transport around the body is given in Fig. 12-10.

EXAMPLE 12.15   Why is HDL called "good" cholesterol and LDL "bad" cholesterol?

Answer: In contrast to LDL, HDL concentrations in the blood are inversely related to the risk of heart disease. HDL is involved in the return of cholesterol to the liver where it is excreted. It is not high concentrations of cholesterol per se that are necessarily damaging to blood vessels via *atherogenesis*, but a high ratio of LDL:HDL. When physicians assess cholesterol levels, they are often more interested in the ratio than the absolute *concentrations*.

Atherogenic lipoproteins such as LDL enter macrophages within the blood vessel wall and promote the growth of an atherosclerotic plaque. HDL in the plasma is antiatherogenic and removes cholesterol from the macrophages, preventing the growth or even regression of the *atherosclerotic plaque*. Aggressive targeting of lipids on both sides of this equation, both the LDL and the HDL, is likely to be maximally effective in reducing cardiovascular risk.

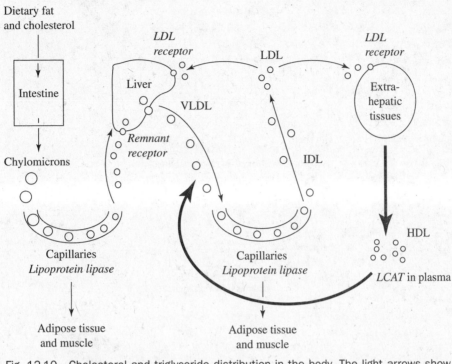

Fig. 12-10 Cholesterol and triglyceride distribution in the body. The light arrows show the route of both triglycerides and cholesterol. The two heavy arrows denote cholesterol export from peripheral plasma membranes into LDL and via IDL (*intermediate-density lipoprotein*) and VLDL back to the liver.

The passage of HDL cholesterol back to the liver is not without interruption. HDL particles interact with both LDLs and VLDLs, and in so doing they exchange cholesterol for triglyceride via the actions of a protein called *cholesterol ester transfer protein* and the enzyme *lecithin-cholesterol acyltransferase* (LCAT).

Cholesterol ester transport protein depletes HDL of cholesterol while concomitantly increasing the amount of cholesterol in the outward-going VLDL and LDL particles. At first glance, it may seem disadvantageous for cholesterol to remain in the atherogenic LDL and VLDL fractions of the lipoproteins. However, the mechanism scavenges cholesterol from the periphery, thus relieving cells of the metabolically expensive process of de novo synthesis.

12.8 Cholesterol Synthesis

Since the *lead* compound in cholesterol synthesis is acetyl-CoA, and mitochondria produce this, almost any cell with mitochondria can synthesize cholesterol. The pathway of synthesis of the 27-carbon, four-ringed molecule from the two-carbon precursor is long and complex. The main flux-controlling step is early in the pathway, and it is subjected to many forms of regulation.

In the mitochondrial matrix, acety-CoA molecules are condensed to produce 3-hydroxy-3-methylglutaryl-CoA (HMG-CoA). The next step, catalyzed by *HMG-CoA reductase*, is the major flux-controlling step. HMG-CoA reductase is modulated by both reversible phosphorylation and allosteric factors, and the activity of the enzyme even shows a *circadian rhythm*. The regulating influences are summarized in Fig. 12-11, but the most germane factor is the level of cholesterol itself, which acts as a negative feedback inhibitor. Therefore, cells respond to a lack of cholesterol both by expressing more LDL receptors and by increasing their own synthesis of cholesterol.

Drugs that inhibit HMG-CoA reductase have been developed for the treatment of *hypercholesterolemia* (high blood cholesterol). These drugs are based on a class of fungus-derived molecules called *statins*. One such chemical structure is shown in Fig. 12-12; note how part of the molecule is similar in shape to HMG-CoA, and it is via this moiety that it binds to HMG-CoA reductase.

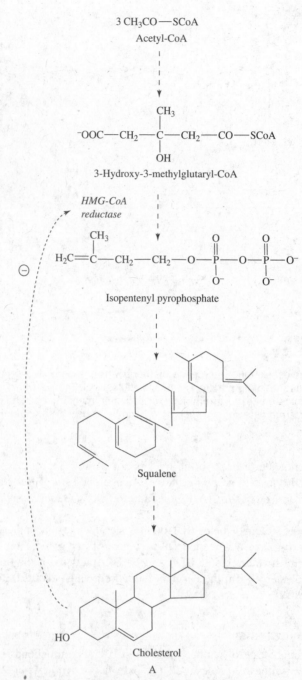

Fig. 12-11 Cholesterol synthesis and the regulation of *HMG-CoA reductase*. (A) Overview of the pathway showing negative feedback control of HMG-CoA reductase by cholesterol. Dashed straight arrows denote more than one enzymic reaction. (B) Synthesis of HMG-CoA, in two steps. (C) Details of the conversion of HMG-CoA into *isopentenyl pyrophosphate*, the building block for cholesterol and terpenes (Sec. 12.1). (D) Conversion of isopentenyl pyrophosphate to the long linear molecule *squalene* that folds up to make cholesterol. (E) Extensive rearrangement of squalene to make cholesterol.

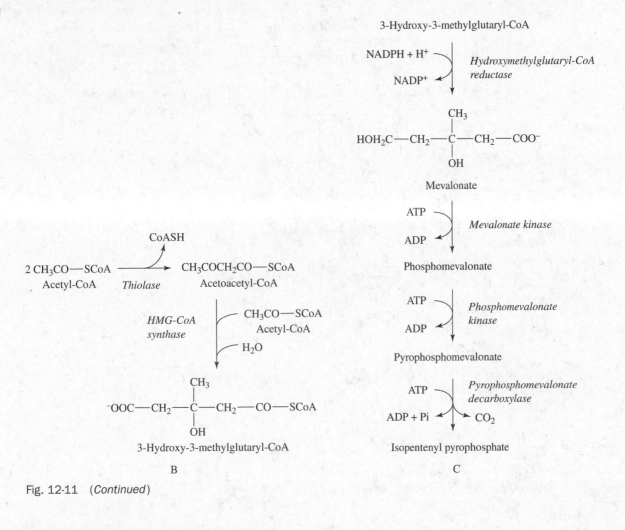

Fig. 12-11   *(Continued)*

12.9   Cholesterol and Heart Disease

Atherosclerotic Plaque Formation

If the concentration of LDL is high and HDL is low in the blood plasma, then there will be an increased risk of heart disease. LDL is implicated in the formation of *atherosclerotic plaques* that are a buildup of fatty deposits in the walls of medium-sized arteries. Plaques can severely impede blood flow or block it entirely; they form by the migration of macrophages that become laden with LDL into the inner layers of the walls of arteries. Because of the large number of lipid droplets in their cytoplasm, that are visible under the light microscope; the macrophages look as if they contain foam, hence the name *foam cells*. Macrophages do not control their uptake of LDL, so they readily become transformed into foam cells when LDL concentrations are high for prolonged periods.

Plaque formation is dangerous not only because blood vessels become occluded, but also because the cellular activity associated with the macrophages stimulates an inflammatory response in the walls of the blood vessel, which in turn promotes the formation of a blood clot, or *thrombus*, inside the vessel. In an artery that is not totally occluded, the thrombus can dislodge to become an *embolus* and travel to a narrower vessel and occlude it.

The rate of uptake of LDL into macrophages and the inflammatory response are greater when the LDL particles have become *oxidized*.

Trans Fatty Acids

These are unsaturated fatty acids in which the hydrocarbon chains on either side of a C=C double bond are oriented in the *trans* configuration. The overwhelming orientation around such bonds in biologically produced fatty acids is *cis*, and the enzymes of the β-oxidation pathway are selective for *cis* fatty acids.

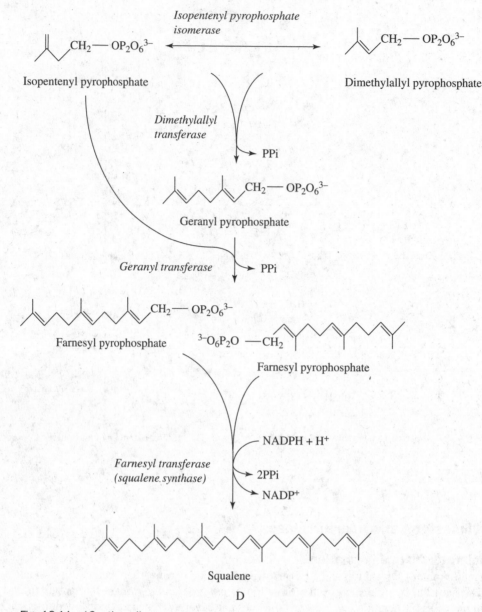

Fig. 12-11 (*Continued*)

Trans fatty acids are formed inadvertently during the manufacture of margarines in a process called *hydrogenation*; this converts polyunsaturated fatty acids with a low melting temperature, such as those present in canola oil, into the saturated fatty acids that have a higher melting temperature and form solid spreads. Hydrogenation uses a nickel catalyst with hydrogen gas under high temperature and pressure. As well as saturating existing double bonds, the process introduces new trans double bonds into the fatty acids.

Trans fatty acids are oxidized only slowly in human cells. Their accumulation has been implicated in *macular degeneration* in the eye and in *atheroma* formation.

12.10 Strategies for Lowering Blood Cholesterol

Cholesterol Balance

Intuitively, we might suppose that lowering the dietary consumption of cholesterol would automatically result in a decreased concentration of cholesterol in blood plasma.

Squalene

Squalene
monooxygenase
(2,3 epoxidizing)

$\frac{1}{2}O_2$

NADPH + H⁺ → NADP⁺

H₂O

Squalene-2,3-oxide
(Squalene epoxide)

2,3-Oxidosqualene
lanosterol cyclase

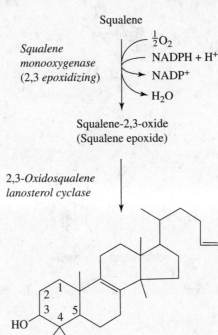

Lanosterol

Several steps involving
oxygen, NADH, and NADPH
with removal of methyl
groups as carbon dioxide,
reduction of carbon atoms
to remove two double bonds
and formation of one other

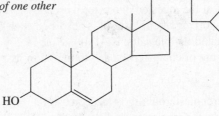

Cholesterol

E

Fig. 12-11   (*Continued*)

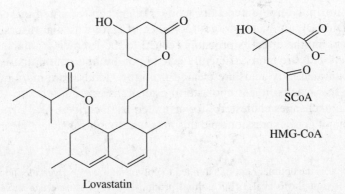

Lovastatin

HMG-CoA

Fig. 12-12   The statin Lovastatin and for comparison with its
structure, HMG-CoA.

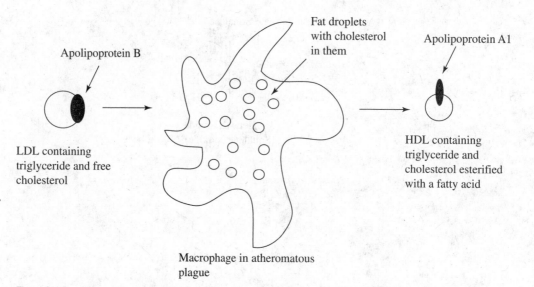

Fig. 12-13   Atherogenesis by lipids and macrophages that turn into *foam* cells.

EXAMPLE 12.16   What are the main dietary sources of cholesterol?

Cholesterol is not present in plants, but plants do contain analogs of cholesterol called *phytosterols* (Greek *phytos*, plant). These phytosterols inhibit the uptake of cholesterol from the gut, and some types of margarine contain them and contribute to this outcome. Meat and dairy products are rich in cholesterol, with cheese and some meats containing up to 100 mg per 100 g.

The recommended upper limit of dietary intake of cholesterol in an adult human is less than 400 mg per day, but it is not uncommon for a Western diet to contain 1 g per day.

Approximately one-half of the ingested cholesterol escapes absorption from the intestine and passes into the feces. Thus only ~200–500 mg of cholesterol is absorbed each day; this is small in comparison with the whole body pool which, including bile salts, is ~140 g. Since <2 g of bile salts is lost to the feces each day, the body synthesizes ~500 mg of cholesterol a day to maintain its balance.

Treatments

One idea for treating hypercholesterolemia is to decrease the reabsorption of bile salts from the intestinal contents by ingesting anion-exchange resin that retains the bile salts in the intestinal lumen (Sec. 12.2). The liver, however, responds by synthesizing more cholesterol so the treatment is not as effective as might have been anticipated.

The most effective treatment strategy is to block cholesterol synthesis by using *statins* that inhibit HMG-CoA reductase. Most cholesterol-lowering treatment regimens use a combination of diet with low cholesterol, anion-exchange resin, and a statin.

The consumption of polyunsaturated fatty acids, rather than saturated ones, is usually associated with a favorable HDL:LDL ratio and a lower incidence of cardiovascular disease. The precise reasons for this are unknown, but the effect is probably related to the following points: (1) Lipids containing polyunsaturated fatty acids are more efficiently acted upon by lipoprotein lipase. Hence chylomicrons containing polyunsaturated fatty acids are cleared from the bloodstream more rapidly than if the fatty acids are saturated; this results in less cholesterol ester transfer from HDL to VLDL. (2) Cholesterol ester transfer protein exchanges cholesterol for saturated triglycerides. (3) Polyunsaturated fatty acids are potent modulators of gene expression, and this may lead to more efficient clearing of LDL lipid from the blood.

EXAMPLE 12.17   What is the optimal ratio of saturated to polyunsaturated triglyceride in the diet?

The optimal ratio is thought to be 1:1, but animal products such as cheese and baked products that contain butter and oils contain over 20-fold more saturated triglycerides than this. Certain types of fish are the notable exception.

12.11   Cellular Roles of Cholesterol

Apart from being a precursor of bile salts, cholesterol is a major component of cell membranes where it modulates membrane fluidity. Integration of cholesterol into a lipid bilayer renders it less leaky to small solutes and ions. Conversely, it makes very rigid membranes more flexible.

Cholesterol is used by some cells such as the adrenal gland and the ovary and testis in the synthesis of corticosterones and sex hormones, respectively.

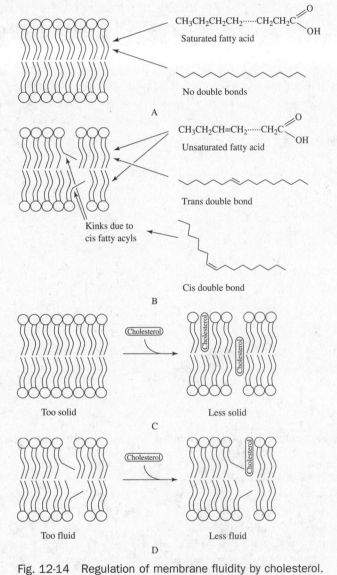

Fig. 12-14   Regulation of membrane fluidity by cholesterol. (A) Representation of a lipid bilayer in which the fatty acyl groups of the phospholipids are all *saturated* and hence in an almost *crystalline* phase. (B) Representation in which some of the fatty acyl chains are unsaturated, being either trans (straight) or cis double bonds, the latter giving rise to a kinked chain of carbon atoms and making the membrane *more fluid*. (C) Cholesterol *fine-tunes membrane fluidity*, making membranes with saturated fatty acyl chains more fluid. (D) Membranes with unsaturated fatty acyl chains become less fluid.

DEFINITIONS AND NOMENCLATURE

12.1. For the compounds in Fig. 12-1, the routes of synthesis, as defined under Classes of Lipids, are well understood. Postulate which route is taken for each of the compounds.

SOLUTION

Compounds 1, 3, and 9 are made via route 1; compounds 5 and 6 are made via route 2; compound 7 is made via route 3, while compound 8 has a mixed origin via routes 2 and 3.

12.2. From Solved Problem 12.1, for the lipids synthesized by route 2, postulate the way in which the isoprene units would have been condensed together to make the final compounds.

SOLUTION

The dotted lines indicate the segments of the respective molecules that are the original isoprene units.

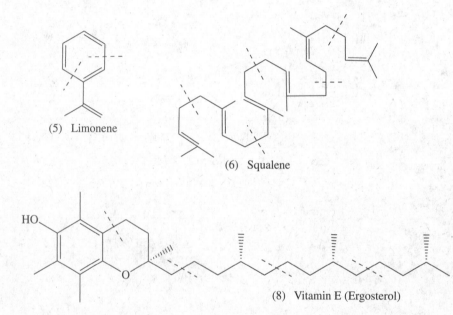

(5) Limonene

(6) Squalene

(8) Vitamin E (Ergosterol)

12.3. Give the systematic name and number notation for the following fatty acids that have commonly used *trivial* names:

    1. $CH_3(CH_2)_7CH{=}CH(CH_2)_7COOH$
               Oleic acid

    2. $CH_3CH_2CH{=}CH{-}CH_2{-}CH{=}CH{-}CH_2{-}CH{=}CH(CH_2)_7COOH$
                       α-Linolenic acid

    3. $CH_3(CH_2)_4CH{=}CH{-}CH_2{-}CH{=}CH{-}CH_2{-}CH{=}CH{-}CH_2{-}CH{=}CH(CH_2)_3COOH$
                       Arachidonic acid

SOLUTION

The systematic names and corresponding number notations are (1) *cis*-9-octadecanoic acid, $18{:}1^{\Delta 9}$; (2) all *cis*-9,12,15-octadecatrienoic acid, $18{:}3^{\Delta 9,12,15}$; and (3) all *cis*-5,8,11,14-eicosatetraenoic acid, $20{:}4^{\Delta 5,8,11,14}$.

12.4. Depot fat has a relatively high content of unsaturated fatty acids. What advantages does this have for the cell?

SOLUTION

The greater the extent of unsaturation, the lower the melting point of the lipid. Solid fat would present only a small surface area for enzymes in the cytoplasmic water that mobilize it. Also, solid fat would make the adipose tissue rigid and unyielding during mechanical stress.

SOURCES OF DIETARY TRIGLYCERIDE

12.5. Below is a table of the fatty acid compositions of selected common edible fats and oils.

Percent by Weight of Total Fatty Acids in Dietary Sources of Fat

Oil or Fat	Unsat./Sat. ratio	Saturated acids					Mono-unsat. acid	Polyunsaturated acids	
		Capric C10:0	Lauric C12:0	Myristic C14:0	Palmitic C16:0	Stearic C18:0	Oleic C18:1	Linoleic C18:2 (ω6)	α-Linoleic C18:3 (ω3)
Almond oil	9.7	—	—	—	7	2	69	17	—
Beef tallow	0.9	—	—	3	24	19	43	3	1
Butterfat (cow)	0.5	3	3	11	27	12	29	2	1
Butterfat (human)	1.0	2	5	8	25	8	35	9	1
Canola oil	15.7	—	—	—	4	2	62	22	10
Cocoa Butter	0.6	—	—	—	25	38	32	3	—
Coconut oil	0.1	6	47	18	9	3	6	2	—
Cod liver oil	2.9	—	—	8	17	—	22	5	—
Corn oil (maize)	6.7	—	—	—	11	2	28	58	1
Lard (pork fat)	1.2	—	—	2	26	14	44	10	—
Olive oil	4.6	—	—	—	13	3	71	10	1
Palm oil	1.0	—	—	1	45	4	40	10	—
Peanut oil	4.0	—	—	—	11	2	48	32	—
Safflower oil	10.1	—	—	—	7	2	13	78	—
Sesame oil	6.6	—	—	—	9	4	41	45	—
Soybean oil	5.7	—	—	—	11	4	24	54	7
Sunflower oil	7.3	—	—	—	7	5	19	68	1
Walnut oil	5.3	—	—	—	11	5	28	51	5

1. Notice from the table that human and cow milk fats have a relatively high content of shorter-chain (C10–C14) fatty acids. If you were to make a milk supplement using a plant source of oil, which might you use?
2. α-Linoleic acid is an essential fatty acid, meaning that humans cannot synthesize it, and yet it is absolutely required for normal health. Which two oils would you recommend to ensure a good dietary supply of this fatty acid?
3. Oleic acid (Latin *olea*, olive) is present in abundance in olive oil. The triglyceride is called *triolein*. But if found in abundance in other oils, which are they?
4. Given a choice between safflower oil and sunflower oil, which might you choose in your diet?

SOLUTION

1. Coconut oil. From the table it is seen to have a similarly high content of short-chain fatty acids to those of cow and human milk.
2. Canola and soybean oil have a relatively high content of the essential fatty acid α-linoleic acid.
3. Oleic acid is the most abundant fatty acid in triglycerides in humans and most mammals. Hence it is found in abundance in beef fat (tallow), pork fat (lard), and butter (see the table); but it is also present in abundance in almond oil, peanut oil, and palm oil (see the table). This high content with a lower proportion of saturated fatty acids makes these fats have a low melting temperature; hence they are liquid (oils) at room temperature. On the other hand, the animal fats tend to be solid as a result of also having a high content of saturated fatty acids.
4. It is good for health to ensure a steady supply of essential fatty acids such as α-linoleic acid. Since safflower oil has very little (or none according to the table) of this fatty acid, but sunflower oil has some, then sunflower oil would be the preferred choice, all other things being equal.

DIGESTION OF DIETARY TRIGLYCERIDE

12.6. Which of the following lipids are amphiphilic: fatty acids, acylate ions, triacylglycerides, cholesterol, or phosphoglycerides?

SOLUTION

Fatty *acids*, triacylglycerides, and cholesterol are not amphiphilic. What polarity they possess is extremely weak. All the others, and notably the *acylate ion* of fatty acids, possess at least one formal charge or an abundance of hydroxyl groups in one part of the molecule.

12.7. Which compounds other than triglycerides might be absorbed into detergent micelles?

SOLUTION

Any hydrophobic or substantially hydrophobic compound such as cholesterol and fat-soluble vitamins will integrate into detergent or bile-salt micelles.

12.8. Are there other forms than micelles that amphiphilic lipids can adopt in water?

SOLUTION

Yes, see Fig. 12-2. A bilayered structure in the form of a closed, water-filled sphere is also possible. This type of structure is called a *vesicle* and occurs naturally in nearly all cells. The primary concept of a vesicle is two sheets of lipid with their hydrocarbon chains opposed, forming a *bilayer*. An isolated bilayer cannot exist as such in water because exposed hydrocarbon chains would exist at the edges of the sheet. However, this situation is obviated by the sheet curving around to form a *self-sealing* sphere.

12.9. How might interruption of the *enterohepatic* circulation of bile salts lead to reduction of the total pool of cholesterol in the body?

SOLUTION

Strategies for lowering blood cholesterol are discussed fully in Sec. 12.9. Since the liver synthesizes bile salts at a steady rate, preventing bile salt reabsorption from the small intestine, by using anion-exchange resin, leads to the liver synthesizing bile salts from endogenous cholesterol. This increases the overall rate of cholesterol loss from the body since dietary cholesterol is not available for the synthesis of bile salts. The ion-exchange resins are also called sequestrants; in several cases they are derived from plants.

12.10. Predict the clinical effect of an obstruction in the bile duct.

SOLUTION

The gall bladder sometimes becomes almost filled with *gall stones* that are composed of crystalline cholesterol, or compounds derived from bilirubin metabolism. These *stones* obstruct the rapid secretion of bile salts into the duodenum after a meal. The lack of a bolus of bile salts at the time of the meal leads to incomplete digestion of triglycerides which then pass into the large intestine where the resident bacteria metabolize them to short chain fatty acids. These fatty acids irritate the intestinal cells. The person then experiences abdominal pain, flatulence, and loose stools that contain a large amount of triglyceride. This is the condition known as steatorrhea (Greek, *steat*, fat). The stools often float in the toilet bowl as a result of their low-average density due to fat and trapped gas (so called *Card's sign*). Patients who have had their gall bladder removed also need to regulate their fat intake to avoid steatorrhea.

TRANSPORT OF DIETARY TRIGLYCERIDES TO TISSUES

12.11. Chylomicrons enter the bloodstream via the *thoracic duct* that is part of the lymphatic system. The thoracic duct drains fluid from the mesentery of the small intestine and passes from the abdominal cavity, along the *mediastinum* in the thorax, into the subclavian vein near the neck. What are the metabolic consequences of this route of delivery into the blood?

SOLUTION

When *carbohydrates* are absorbed from the intestine, they pass directly into the blood that drains via the portal vein to the liver, so it is the first major organ to gain access to these nutrients. The delivery of chylomicrons into the bloodstream in the subclavian vein, rather than into the portal vein, means that the first tissues to encounter chylomicrons are not the liver. Lipids in chylomicrons first encounter the other tissues such as the heart, skeletal muscle, and adipose tissue; and these interact with other chylomicrons and lipoproteins in their *first pass* through the blood circulation. This competition with the liver for "first grab" at the food supply, however, is unlikely to be a major factor in the overall distribution of fuel to cells. As the mean circulation time of blood in the human is only ~1 min the chylomicron pool is rapidly distributed throughout the body.

12.12. Which apoproteins form the molecular scaffolding for chylomicrons?

SOLUTION

As stated in Sec. 12.5, the only protein present in chylomicrons is apoprotein B-48. It is synthesized in the enterocytes (lining cells) of the small intestine.

UPTAKE OF TRIGLYCERIDES INTO TISSUES

12.13. *Lipoprotein lipase*, like many enzymes, has several *isozymic* forms that differ from one tissue to the next. Insulin is known to enhance lipoprotein lipase synthesis in the capillary endothelium next to adipocytes, whereas it has no such effect in the myocardium. Why might this have come about?

SOLUTION

Adipocytes, being storage cells for fat, respond to variations in supply from the bloodstream. On the other hand, the heart beats incessantly and has a constant need for fatty acids as a fuel; so the uptake, which is high, is not regulated in the short-term.

EXPORT OF TRIGLYCERIDE AND CHOLESTEROL FROM THE LIVER

12.14. What would be the metabolic consequences of cells not expressing LDL receptors?

SOLUTION

For a cell to take up cholesterol esters, it must have LDL receptors on its surface. In the absence of these receptors, cells might still synthesize their own supply of cholesterol, or obtain free cholesterol from that which is bound to serum *albumin*; but LDL particles from the blood could not be *endocytosed*. If the problem exists in all cell types of the body, then LDL concentrations in the blood are high. In this way a defect in the LDL-receptor gene causes hypercholesterolemia.

   This inborn error of metabolism, familial *hypercholesterolemia*, is dangerous because high LDL concentrations are linked to *atherosclerosis* and heart disease. The patients normally die before the age of 25 years.

CHOLESTEROL METABOLISM

12.15. Cholecalciferol (vitamin D$_3$) is derived from cholesterol. How and in which tissues does the conversion occur?

SOLUTION

With normal exposure to sunlight, 7-dehydrocholesterol is converted to cholecalciferol in the skin.

12.16. Cholecalciferol is metabolized to produce other steroidal vitamins/hormones. How and in which tissues does this occur?

SOLUTION

Cholecalciferol is hydroxylated at three positions in its carbon skeleton; 1, 24, and 25. In the liver, cholecalciferol is hydroxylated to 25-hydroxycholecalciferol. Further reactions occur in the kidney, resulting in the formation of three new metabolites. These are 1,25-dihydroxycholecalciferol; 24,25-dihydroxychole-calciferol; and 1,24,25-trihydroxycholecalciferol. 1,25-Dihydroxy- and 1,24,25-trihydroxycholecalciferol are active hormones involved in calcium-ion uptake from the intestine.

CHOLESTEROL SYNTHESIS

12.17. How is the biosynthesis of cholesterol regulated by the amount of cholesterol in the diet?

SOLUTION

A *negative feedback* mechanism operates in which intracellular free cholesterol inhibits *HMG-CoA reductase* (Fig. 12-11). When the diet is rich in cholesterol, intracellular cholestrol concentrations increase in the liver and the biosynthesis of cholesterol is suppressed. Conversely, a low-cholesterol diet, but one with adequate triglyceride, stimulates cholestrol synthesis.

12.18. Why do mono-oxygenase reactions require the reductant NADPH as a cosubstrate?

SOLUTION

Mono-oxygenase reactions catalyze the introduction of only one of the two oxygen atoms from molecular oxygen to form a hydroxyl or keto group in the substrate. The other oxygen atom ends up in water. Both the substrate and the NADPH act as proton and electron donors. Mono-oxygenase reactions occur in the endoplasmic reticulum (ER) and involve *iron-sulfur proteins* (as in the mitochondrial electron transport chain), *ferredoxin* (a small redox active protein), and *cytochrome P$_{450}$.*

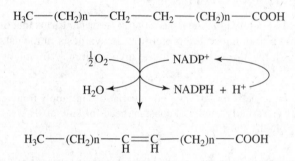

12.19. How does the expenditure of ATP maintain the active form of HMG-CoA reductase in the liver? (*Hint*: The system of regulation is similar to that of glycogen phosphorylase, Sec. 11.5.)

SOLUTION

See Fig. 12-15. ATP is a cosubstrate in phosphorylation reactions that covalently modify *protein kinases* and *protein phosphatases*. Two phosphorylation reactions are involved in the modification of HMG-CoA reductase:
1. HMG-CoA reductase is phosphorylated in a reaction catalyzed by *HMG-CoA reductase kinase*.
2. *cAMP-dependent protein kinase* phosphorylates *HMG-CoA reductase kinase*, converting it to its active form. Subsequent dephosphorylation of HMG-CoA reductase and its *kinase* releases inorganic phosphate (Pi). Each molecule of HMG-CoA reductase is phosphorylated via one molecule of ATP. Similarly, one molecule of ATP is used in the initial phosphorylation of *HMG-CoA reductase kinase*. However, one molecule of active HMG-CoA reductase kinase can catalyze the phosphorylation, and hence activation, of many molecules of HMG-CoA reductase, constituting an *enzymic amplification* process.

CHOLESTEROL AND HEART DISEASE

12.20. Coronary heart disease and stroke are medical conditions with seemingly myriad potential causes. How have the major causative agents been identified?

SOLUTION

This has been done within several major population studies. The most famous is the one initiated over 60 years ago in the United States. The Framingham Heart Study began in 1948, to try to delineate those factors that underlie heart attacks and strokes. The study established that high blood cholesterol concentration is a

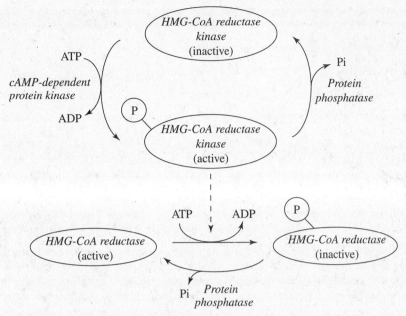

Fig. 12-15 Regulation of HMG-CoA reductase by phosphorylation and dephosphorylation.

risk factor for coronary heart disease (CHD). Results of the Framingham study showed that the higher the cholesterol concentration, the greater the risk of CHD. On the other end of the spectrum, CHD is uncommon at total serum cholesterol concentrations below 3.9 mM. A direct link between high blood cholesterol concentration and CHD was confirmed by the Lipid Research Clinics-Coronary Primary Prevention Trial in 1984. It showed that lowering total and LDL ("bad") cholesterol concentrations significantly reduces CHD. A series of more recent trials of cholesterol lowering using statins demonstrated conclusively that lowering total cholesterol and LDL cholesterol reduces the chance of having a heart attack, needing bypass surgery or angioplasty, and dying of CHD-related pathologies.

MEMBRANE FLUIDITY

12.21. Why is membrane fluidity important for cell function?

SOLUTION

For cell membranes to be effective permeability barriers, they must be flexible and allow relatively free motion of proteins that are embedded in or linked to them. Integral membrane proteins often diffuse laterally, and many receptor-mediated solute-uptake pathways involve endocytosis that entails phospholipid rearrangement in the membrane. Hormone secretion and other protein trafficking processes involve exocytosis; and it is usual for membrane vesicles to fuse with each other in a process that also involves the lateral diffusion of membrane constituents. The activity of some receptors is strongly linked to the extent of fluidity of the membrane around them.

12.22. Will the melting point of *lactobacillic* acid ($C_{19}H_{36}O_2$, a cyclopropane fatty acid) be higher or lower than that of the linear, saturated fatty acid of the same chain length?

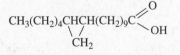

SOLUTION

The melting point will be lower; the cyclopropane group decreases the tendency of an array of molecules to pack regularly. The melting points of lactobacillic acid and the corresponding 19:0 fatty acid are 28 and 69°C, respectively.

SUPPLEMENTARY PROBLEMS

12.23. What determines the lower limit of the micellar size of a detergent?

12.24. What determines the upper limit of micellar size of a detergent?

12.25. (a) Define the term *glycolipid*. (b) Give two examples.

12.26. Write the structures of the following fatty acids: (a) myristic acid (14:0); (b) myristoleic acid (14:1$^{\Delta 9}$); and (c) ricinoleic acid (18: :1$^{\Delta 9}$ C-12 hydroxylated).

12.27. How many different molecules of triacylglycerol can be made from glycerol and four different fatty acids?

12.28. Write the structures of two triglycerides, one of which is (a) solid and one of which is (b) liquid at 37°C.

12.29. A solution of 1-palmitoyl-2-stearoyl-3-myristoylglycerol and phosphatidic acid (glycerol 3-phosphate with two fatty acyl moieties, attached to C-2 and C-3) dissolved in benzene is shaken with an equal volume of water. After the two phases separate, which lipid will be in the higher concentration in the aqueous phase, and why?

12.30. Predict the effects of the following operations on the *phase-transition temperature* (the temperature when the membrane becomes fluid on heating) and the mobility of the phospholipid molecules in vesicles made from the phospholipid *dipalmitoylphosphatidylcholine*: (a) Introducing *dipalmitoleoylphosphatidylcholine* into the vesicles; (b) introducing *cholesterol* into the vesicles; and (c) introducing *integral membrane proteins* into the vesicles.

12.31. What might be the consequences of abnormal deconjugation of bile salts if bacteria invade the *small* intestine? (Bacteria are normally not abundant in the small intestine, but are present in vast numbers in the large intestine.)

12.32. What is the mechanism of stimulation by triglyceride in the diet of the synthesis of cholesterol?

12.33. Why does feeding compounds such as betaine, that act as a methyl donor, to patients with fatty liver alleviate the condition?

12.34. 3-Hydroxy-3-methylglutaryl-CoA (HMG-CoA) is an intermediate in the synthesis of acetoacetate and cholesterol in the liver. How does this intermediate become available to each biosynthetic pathway?

12.35. How are cholesteryl esters synthesized?

12.36. What are the physical chemical reasons that fatty acids are transported in lipoproteins in blood plasma?

ANSWERS TO SUPPLEMENTARY PROBLEMS

12.23. The hydrophobic effect. A minimum number of hydrocarbon chains must associate before the water-hydrocarbon interface is eliminated. This association is a cooperative one so the micelle has a minimum size.

12.24. The length of the hydrocarbon chains. The longer they are the larger the diameter of the micelle. But there is a limit, as chains that are very long relative to the head size do not stack together in a stable way.

12.25. (a) A lipid that contains carbohydrate. (b) Galactosylceramide, a glycosphingolipid; and 6-α-D-galactosylpyranosyl-β-D-galactosyldiglyceride, a glycoglycerolipid.

12.26. (a) $CH_3(CH_2)_{12}COOH$
(b) $CH_3(CH_2)_3CH{=}CH(CH_2)_7COOH$
(c) $CH_3(CH_2)_5CHOHCH_2CH{=}CH(CH_2)_7COOH$

12.27. 64. Or 24 if the triglycerides must contain three different fatty acids.

12.28. (*a*)   (*b*)

$$CH_2O{-}OC(CH_2)_{14}CH_3$$
$$|$$
$$CH_3(CH_2)_{14}CO{-}OCH$$
$$|$$
$$CH_2O{-}OC(CH_2)_{14}CH_3$$
Solid

$$CH_2O{-}OC(CH_2)_7CH{=}CH(CH_2)_7CH_3$$
$$|$$
$$CH_3(CH_2)_{14}CO{-}CH$$
$$|$$
$$CH_2O{-}OC(CH_2)_7CH{=}CH(CH_2)_7CH_3$$
Liquid

12.29. Phosphatidic acid, because its phosphate group can ionize, making the molecule amphiphilic.

12.30. (a) Lowers, (b) raises, (c) raises the transition temperature. (a) Increases, (b) decreases, (c) decreases the phospholipid mobility.

12.31. The pH of the contents of the lumen of the ileum is between 6.0 and 8.0. Bile salts in the lumen are therefore ionized. E.g., taurocholate has a pK_a of ~1.5 owing to the conjugation of taurine with the cholate, while glycocholate has a pK_a of ~3.7 owing to its conjugation with glycine. Deconjugation of either bile salt leaves free cholate with $pK_a = 5.0$. The higher pK_a value reduces its solubility in the aqueous environment of the lumen, compared to the bile salts which are readily soluble. Reabsorption of the bile salts in the ileum will be decreased, and the bile acids will be excreted from the body.

12.32. Cholesterol is the precursor of bile salts, and their secretion into the intestine is stimulated after eating food and during the digestion and absorption of triglycerides.

12.33. Methyl groups are used in the de novo synthesis of choline that enters phosphatidyl choline, a process that decreases the availability of 1,2-diacylglycerol for triacylglycerol synthesis.

12.34. *Cytosolic* HMG-CoA synthase produces HMG-CoA for cholesterol synthesis, while the *mitochondrial* isozyme HMG-CoA synthase produces HMG-CoA that is converted to acetoacetate, a *ketone body*.

12.35. Cholesteryl esters arise from the activity of acyl-CoA-cholesterol: acyltransferase which catalyzes the formation of the esters from acyl-CoA and cholesterol, and also from the activity of lecithin-cholesterol acyltransferase (LCAT) that catalyzes the formation of the ester from a fatty acyl group on phosphatidyl choline. The first enzyme is *cytoplasmic* while the second one is associated with HDL in *blood plasma*.

12.36. Long-chain fatty acids are relatively insoluble in polar media, but they still form salts, some of which act as detergents (they are *soaps*), and thus they associate with hydrophobic lipids in lipoproteins.

CHAPTER 13

Fuel Storage, Distribution, and Usage

13.1 Fuel Stores

Question: Under normal physiological conditions, in what form are fuels stored in the body?

Fuel is stored primarily as droplets of triglyceride in adipocytes, and as glycogen particles in both hepatocytes and skeletal myocytes; other tissues have little fuel storage capacity and primarily rely on a continuous supply of fuel from the liver via the bloodstream.

Triglyceride stores vary widely in size from less than 5% of the body weight in *elite marathon runners* to more than 60% in the very obese. *White adipocytes* are unique in their ability to change size as they store or release triglycerides. An average healthy human male has ~20% of body mass as triglycerides, with the proportion being higher in females (~25%). This means that a 60 kg female of normal proportions possesses ~15 kg of stored triglyceride. In contrast, the amount of glycogen stored is very small; the *liver* normally stores ~100 g of glucose as glycogen while the muscles, in total, store ~250 g of glycogen.

The fuel demands of all tissues are mismatched with respect to the amount of fuel stored in them. The brain, for example, has an obligatory requirement for glucose, so the maintenance of a blood glucose concentration of 5 mM is essential for brain function (Sec. 11.4). Typically, the brain (weighing ~1.3 kg) consumes ~120 g of glucose per day; in contrast, the ~2 kg of red blood cells in the body consume 20 g of glucose per day.

EXAMPLE 13.1   Tissues such as muscle and white blood cells are very dependent on glucose for their energy but also oxidize fatty acids; red blood cells have no mitochondria, and in humans they depend almost exclusively on glucose for their energy. The renal medulla and the skin also require large amounts of glucose, with the skin in particular often being overlooked as an important metabolic consumer.

Although humans store most of their energy as fatty acids within triglycerides, metabolic machinery to convert these into carbohydrates is not present. Fatty acids are catabolized to acetyl-CoA via β-oxidation (Sec. 10.5), and the overall reaction of the pyruvate dehydrogenase complex is irreversible.

Question: Many seeds and nuts from plants have energy stored almost exclusively as triglycerides. How is it possible for these stores to be made into carbohydrate in the germination process?

The conversion of acetyl-CoA into carbohydrate is required during germination when the seed's energy reserves are rapidly mobilized. Seeds and nuts contain two enzymes in special subcellular organelles that catalyze the condensation of two 2-carbon acetyl units into a precursor that ultimately becomes glucose. The metabolic pathway is called the *glyoxylate cycle*.

In mammals the mismatch between small glucose stores and large glucose requirements means that special fuel selection strategies have evolved for maintaining euglycemia (that is, having a glucose concentration at a constant 5 mM): (1) carbohydrate stores are conserved for the brain, red blood cells, and other glucose-requiring tissues; and other organs switch to fatty acids as a fuel when the blood glucose concentration is low; (2) even if glucose enters cells, it can be removed if it is not converted into glucose 6-phosphate; and (3) new carbohydrate can be synthesized from some amino acids and lactate, together with glycerol derived from stored triglycerides.

13.2 Fuel Usage in Starvation

Postabsorptive Period

After a meal, the ingested food continues to be digested and absorbed for 2–4 h. The beginning of *starvation* is normally considered to be ~5 h after the last meal. Before all the nutrients have been absorbed from the intestine, the rate of uptake of glucose by tissues, from the bloodstream, will be greater than the rate of absorption from the intestine. Under these circumstances glucose stores, especially in the liver, are mobilized, releasing glucose into the blood and thus maintaining *euglycemia*.

EXAMPLE 13.2 It is important to distinguish between a nondangerous decrease in blood glucose concentration that stimulates a metabolic response and an *overtly hypoglycemic* episode. During the postabsorptive period, blood glucose concentration falls to ~4 mM, and this is sufficient to stimulate the appropriate hormonal responses that, in turn, stimulate the mobilization of glycogen stores.

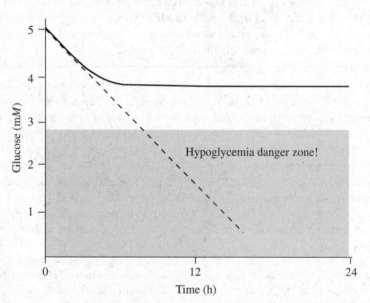

Fig. 13-1 Blood glucose concentration during postabsorptive period.

When the blood glucose concentration falls below ~5 mM, secretion of insulin by β-*cells* in the islets of Langerhans in the pancreas ceases. The α-*cells*, also situated in the islets of Langerhans, commence secretion of *glucagon*; the blood glucagon concentration rises to 7 pM while the insulin concentration falls below 90 nM.

It is within the liver that glucagon initiates glycogen breakdown, via *glycogenolysis*. Although all the skeletal muscle in the body, collectively, has the largest store of glycogen, it does not possess glucagon receptors. Also muscle does not contain glucose 6-phosphatase that hydrolyzes glucose 6-phosphate into glucose; so it cannot be a net exporter of glucose as the phosphorylated glucose remains trapped inside the cells.

13.3 Mechanism of Glycogenolysis in Liver

A major flux-controlling step in glycogen breakdown is catalyzed by *glycogen phosphorylase* which catalyzes the attack of phosphate on 1→4 glycosidic bonds in glycogen, thus releasing glucose 1-phosphate; this is rapidly converted into glucose 6-phosphate by *phosphoglucomutase*.

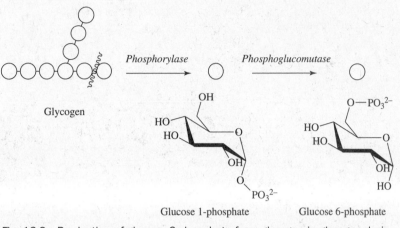

Glycogen

Phosphorylase

Phosphoglucomutase

Glucose 1-phosphate   Glucose 6-phosphate

Fig. 13-2   Production of glucose 6-phosphate from glycogen in glycogenolysis.

Enzyme Activation by Phosphorylation

Question: How does glucagon bring about an increase in glycogen phosphorylase activity?

    Glycogen phosphorylase is regulated by reversible *phosphorylation*. In contrast to glycogen synthase, it is fully active when phosphorylated, and inactivated when dephosphorylated. Glycogen phosphorylase is phosphorylated by *phosphorylase kinase*; this enzyme itself must first be activated by phosphorylation via *protein kinase A*.

    Protein kinase A is also known as *cyclic AMP-dependent protein kinase* because it is stimulated whenever intracellular cAMP concentrations rise. The binding of glucagon to specific receptors on the plasma membrane of hepatocytes stimulates the activity of *adenylate cyclase* that catalyzes the production of cAMP from ATP. Thus, glucagon stimulates glycogen phosphorylase via a chain of enzyme phosphorylations which *amplify* the initial stimulus at each stage of the chain.

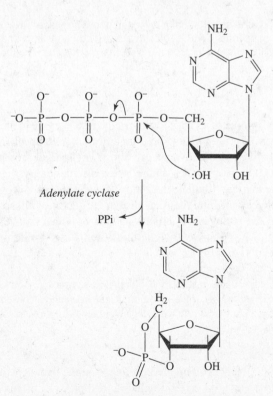

Fig. 13-3   Synthesis of cAMP by adenylate cyclase.

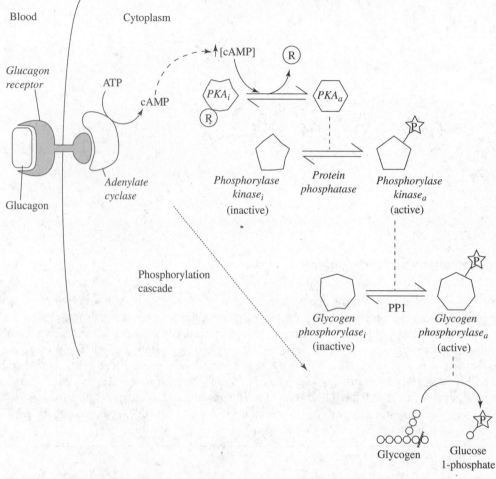

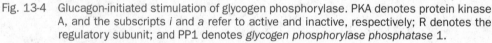

Fig. 13-4   Glucagon-initiated stimulation of glycogen phosphorylase. PKA denotes protein kinase
A, and the subscripts *i* and *a* refer to active and inactive, respectively; R denotes the
regulatory subunit; and PP1 denotes *glycogen phosphorylase phosphatase* 1.

Enzyme Cascade

An enzyme that, once activated, produces activated forms of the next enzyme in the pathway, and so on, produces
a *cascade*. Thus the initial signal of glucagon binding is greatly *amplified*. Specifically, each molecule of *protein
kinase A*, once activated and before it is deactivated, can phosphorylate and activate *hundreds* of *phosphorylase
kinase* molecules that, in turn, can activate many hundreds of molecules of *glycogen phosphorylase*. Thus, just a
few molecules of glucagon can rapidly stimulate the action of *thousands* of glycogen phosphorylase molecules.

An enzyme that is controlled by the binding of an allosteric effector or phosphorylation allows fine-tuning
of a stimulus at each step of the pathway of activation. This provides an avenue for modulation by other
chemical communication pathways. Many cell-signaling systems use similar multienzyme phosphorylation
cascades (e.g., HMG-CoA reductase, Fig. 12-15).

EXAMPLE 13.3   During the first few hours of starvation, blood glucose concentration falls from ~5 m*M*, but only a very
small decrease of ~1 m*M* is sufficient to trigger the secretion of *glucagon* and a consequent *large increase in glycogenolysis*. If the response of glycogen phosphorylase were dependent on a simple mass-action effect of glucose, it would
only increase in activity by a few percent.

Enzyme Compartmentation

Glucose 6-phosphate is ultimately produced by glycogenolysis in the liver (via glucose 1-phosphate), and it is
hydrolyzed via *glucose-6-phosphatase* to give free glucose and phosphate; this enzyme is located inside the
endoplasmic reticulum, and a specific glucose 6-phosphate transporter allows its entry into this compartment.

Compartmentation of glucose-6-phosphatase ensures that its product, glucose, is isolated from direct rephosphorylation by *glucokinase* in the cytoplasm; if this did occur, it would form a *futile cycle*, non-productively consuming ATP. Glucose is transported from the endoplasmic reticulum to the cytoplasm through the selective transporter, GLUT-9, that delivers it away from the location of glucokinase.

Because of the high V_{max} and K_m of GLUT-2 transporters in hepatocytes, their cytoplasmic glucose is in quasi-equilibrium with that in the blood. Therefore as tissues consume glucose from the blood, they effectively withdraw newly formed glucose from the liver.

Enzyme Inhibition by Phosphorylation

The phosphorylation cascade that stimulates glycogenolysis also inhibits *glycogen synthase*. Phosphorylase kinase and protein kinase A phosphorylate and thus *inactivate* glycogen synthase. The simultaneous action of glycogenesis and glycogenolysis is therefore prevented; in reality, neither of these opposing pathways is ever fully "switched off." There is always some *futile cycling* with glucose 6-phosphate being made into glycogen and then back into glucose 6-phosphate again. *Futile cycling* adds sensitivity to control of the pathways and adds metabolic inefficiency that contributes to thermogenesis (see Sec. 10.10).

Debranching of Glycogen

Hydrolysis of the α 1→6 bond of glucose residues in glycogen is catalyzed by a special enzyme evocatively named *debranching enzyme*. It operates only at the ends of degraded glycogen chains, and it is *not* under any regulatory control. Rather than catalyzing *phosphorolysis* as with phosphorylase, debranching enzyme catalyzes a *hydrolytic* reaction that releases pure glucose. Since branch points occur every ~10 residues in glycogen, ~10% of the glucose from a disassembled glycogen molecule appears as unphosphorylated, free glucose.

Postabsorptive Period

The liver releases glucose to the blood, thus maintaining euglycemia in the first few hours of the postabsorptive period after a meal. Measurements of the amount of glycogen stored in the liver (~100 g) show that glucose demand by key peripheral tissues cannot be maintained for more than a few hours by the liver alone. After an overnight fast, the liver glycogen is depleted so metabolic strategies have evolved for the conservation, recycling, and resynthesis of glucose.

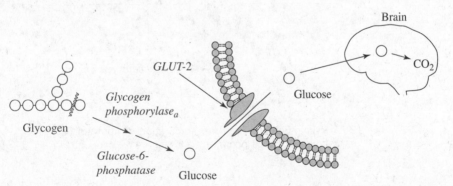

Fig. 13-5   Glucose release from glycogen in the liver into the blood in the *postabsorptive period* after a meal, and its use by the brain.

Early Starvation

Although there are no distinct times after a carbohydrate meal at which a particular metabolic process begins or ends, the near depletion of liver glycogen and the mobilization of fatty acids as an alternative fuel to glucose occur after about 1 day of starvation.

13.4   Mechanism of Lipolysis

As well as stimulating glycogenolysis, a rise in blood glucagon concentration increases triglyceride breakdown in liver and white adipose tissue. This occurs via activation of *hormone-sensitive lipase* that is regulated by phosphorylation via *cAMP-dependent protein kinase*, which makes it fully active.

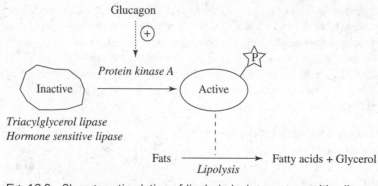

Fig. 13-6   Glucagon stimulation of lipolysis by hormone-sensitive lipase.
Note that the hydrolytic reaction is shown in Fig. 10-25C.

Glucagon is not the most important regulator of lipolysis, since the concomitant decrease in blood insulin concentration provides a larger stimulus to the elevation of cAMP concentrations in white adipocytes.

EXAMPLE 13.4   The concentration of any metabolite in a cell is the result of the balance between its synthesis and its degradation. For cAMP, the activity of *adenylate cyclase* determines its rate of production whereas the activity of *phosphodiesterase* determines its rate of breakdown. If the activity of adenylate cyclase is greater than the activity of phosphodiesterase, then the concentration of cAMP will rise. Insulin is a potent stimulator of phosphodiesterase so that, in the fed state, the cAMP concentration in adipocytes is kept low. During starvation when insulin concentrations decrease, phosphodiesterase will not be activated. Therefore, even if adenylate cyclase is not stimulated, the cAMP concentration still rises in the absence of insulin. This outcome becomes important in diabetes when, even in the presence of high blood glucose concentrations, the lack of insulin leads to uncontrolled lipolysis from white adipose tissue.

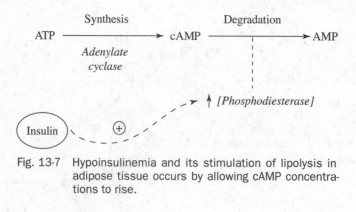

Fig. 13-7   Hypoinsulinemia and its stimulation of lipolysis in adipose tissue occurs by allowing cAMP concentrations to rise.

Hyperglucagonemia (high blood glucagon concentration) and *hypoinsulinemia* (low blood insulin concentration) stimulate the rapid release of fatty acids and glycerol from white adipose tissue.

Fatty acids are *amphipathic* and form micelles like other detergents (Sec. 12.3), and they are transported in the blood bound to albumin. This is the most abundant plasma protein, and each molecule of M_r 68,500 contains four fatty acid binding sites.

13.5   Fatty-Acid-Induced Inhibition of Glucose Oxidation

Even though hypoinsulinemia leads to a depletion of GLUT-4 carrier proteins in the skeletal-myocyte membrane, GLUT-1 is *constitutively* expressed, thus allowing *some* glucose uptake by these cells at all times. Fatty acid uptake by muscle cells leads to metabolic competition with glucose oxidation; but the acetyl CoA formed in β-oxidation directly prevents the maximal rate of oxidation of glucose by inhibiting *phosphofructokinase* (Sec. 10.6) and by inhibiting of pyruvate dehydrogenase.

EXAMPLE 13.5 *Pyruvate dehydrogenase* catalyzes an irreversible step in carbohydrate oxidation. In glycolysis, prior to the conversion of pyruvate to acetyl-CoA, the intermediates can all be converted back into glucose, provided that the *three kinase reactions* of glycolysis are bypassed; this is achieved by the special enzymes of *gluconeogenesis*. In starvation, the conservation of glucose through the inhibition of the oxidation of pyruvate is important for survival.

Pyruvate dehydrogenase is regulated by reversible phosphorylation; its activity is a balance between the activity of *pyruvate dehydrogenase kinase*, which catalyzes *inhibitory phosphorylation*, and *pyruvate dehydrogenase phosphatase*, which *activates* by dephosphorylation. Pyruvate dehydrogenase kinase is strongly activated by a rise in the ratio of acetyl-CoA to CoA, the former resulting from rapid β-oxidation of fatty acids. Therefore, when fatty acids are oxidized in muscle mitochondria, pyruvate dehydrogenase is inhibited and the rate of pyruvate conversion to acetyl CoA is reduced.

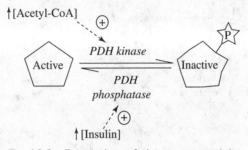
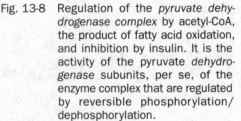

Fig. 13-8 Regulation of the *pyruvate dehydrogenase complex* by acetyl-CoA, the product of fatty acid oxidation, and inhibition by insulin. It is the activity of the pyruvate *dehydrogenase* subunits, per se, of the enzyme complex that are regulated by reversible phosphorylation/dephosphorylation.

Fatty acids, which are amphipathic, can freely diffuse across a phospholipid membrane; but recent evidence suggests that there are specific *fatty acid transporters* in most cell membranes. When not in demand for fatty acid uptake, these transporters are located in the membranes of vesicles in the cytoplasm. In response to hormonal stimuli, they are translocated to the plasma membrane where fusion of the vesicles takes place with it.

Fatty acid diffusion into cells is also facilitated by a mass-action effect whereby their binding to a cytosolic *fatty acid binding protein* reduces the *free* cytosolic concentration, thus promoting movement of fatty acids into the cell. This binding step needs to take place prior to activation of fatty acids to fatty-acyl CoA.

In conclusion, fatty acid oxidation inhibits glucose oxidation and provides acetyl-CoA to the Krebs cycle; it also ensures that any glucose that enters skeletal myocytes is not rapidly oxidized, but is converted into lactate that leaves the cells and is transported in the blood to hepatocytes and cardiac myocytes. Although this conservation of glucose occurs in skeletal myocytes and other tissues, it does not occur in the brain because fatty acids do not cross the *blood-brain barrier*. Thus even after 2 days of starvation, the brain continues to use ~120 g of glucose per day.

13.6 Glucose Recycling

Hepatocytes absorb lactate from the blood via monocarboxylate transporters in the plasma membrane and *lactate dehydrogenase* rapidly catalyzes its oxidation to pyruvate. In starvation, the liver, like muscle and other tissues, largely oxidizes fatty acids, and pyruvate dehydrogenase is inactive; thus, pyruvate formed in hepatocytes from exogenously produced lactate will not be acted upon by pyruvate dehydrogenase. The pyruvate is converted to glucose by net flux in the reverse direction of glycolysis with the assistance of enzymes that bypass the irreversible kinases, in a process called *gluconeogenesis*.

The last step, the release of glucose from glucose 6-phosphate, is catalyzed by *glucose-6-phosphatase*.

EXAMPLE 13.6 Bypassing the glycolytic reaction in which phosphoenolpyruvate is converted to pyruvate entails two separate enzymes that are coupled with *transport* of intermediates into the mitochondrial matrix and back into the cytoplasm.

The first step is the transport of pyruvate, via a *monocarboxylate transporter*, into the mitochondrial matrix. This is followed by the carboxylation of pyruvate via *pyruvate carboxylase*; this enzyme, like *acetyl-CoA carboxylase*, uses the

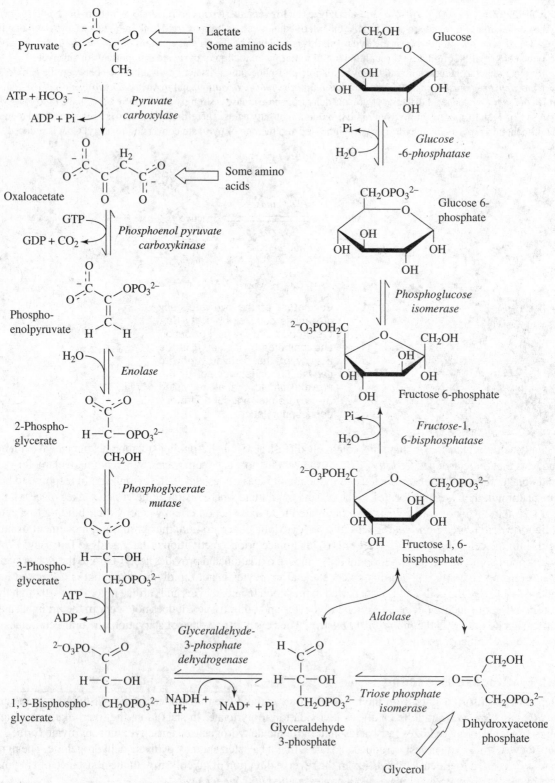

Fig. 13-9 Gluconeogenesis. Note the use of an alternative representation of the carboxylate ions in the metabolites from those given in Chap. 10.

cofactor *biotin* and the input of energy from ATP. One of the products is *oxaloacetate* which does not permeate the inner mitochondrial membrane (Fig. 10-24). One way in which its constituent carbon atoms can leave is after the conversion of oxaloacetate to *malate*; but an alternative route is via conversion into phosphoenolpyruvate by the matrix enzyme *phosphoenolpyruvate carboxykinase*. This reaction is driven by both ATP and the release of the carbon dioxide that had previously been added to the pyruvate by pyruvate carboxylase. Phosphoenolpyruvate leaves the matrix and enters the intermembrane space via specific transport proteins in the inner membrane; from there it passes via *porins,* in the outer membrane of the mitochondrion, to the cytoplasm.

If malate is transported to the cytoplasm, it is converted into oxaloacetate, and then via a *cytosolic isozyme* of *phosphoenolpyruvate carboxykinase* into phosphoenolpyruvate.

EXAMPLE 13.7   Conversion of fructose 1,6-bisphosphate into fructose 6-phosphate is more straightforward than the previous bypass of a kinase reaction. It involves simply the hydrolysis of a phosphate group. Nevertheless, the enzyme *fructose-1,6-bisphosphatase* is subject to very complex regulation.

Gluconeogenesis provides excellent examples of the many regulatory paradigms that exist in metabolism: allosteric modulation, reversible phosphorylation, mass-action via substrate supply across membranes, and *variable expression* of the genes of the enzymes involved.

EXAMPLE 13.8   Fatty acid oxidation strongly *activates* pyruvate carboxylase by the allosteric action of acetyl-CoA. Thus an increased rate of hepatic β-oxidation favors the routing of pyruvate through pyruvate carboxylase, rather than through pyruvate dehydrogenase.

EXAMPLE 13.9   Although not sensitive to allosteric activation, the expression of the gene for *phosphoenolpyruvate carboxykinase* is strongly stimulated in early starvation, thus increasing the total amount of the enzyme present and hence its maximal velocity.

EXAMPLE 13.10   Both the conversion of fructose 6-phosphate to fructose 1,6-bisphosphate and the reverse-bypass of this reaction in gluconeogenesis are sensitive to the regulatory metabolite *fructose 2,6-bisphosphate*. This is not an intermediate in either glycolysis or gluconeogenesis but is formed by a separate ATP-dependent kinase, *phosphofructokinase-2*.

The hydrolysis of fructose 2,6-bisphosphate is catalyzed by *fructose-2,6-bisphosphatase*, but curiously phosphofructokinase-2 and fructose 2,6-bisphosphatase are the *same* enzyme: phosphorylation of phosphofructokinase-2 by *protein kinase A* converts the enzyme into a phosphatase, whereas dephosphorylation makes it operate as a kinase.

When the concentration of fructose 2,6-bisphosphate is high, such as when this dual enzyme is in the phosphofructokinase-2 form, the glycolytic phosphofructokinase-1 is activated. This situation will prevail when protein kinase A is active, such as during starvation. Fructose 2,6-bisphosphate not only stimulates phosphofructokinase but also inhibits fructose-1,6-bisphosphatase.

If fructose 2,6-bisphosphate concentrations are reduced, then gluconeogenesis is favored over glycolysis.

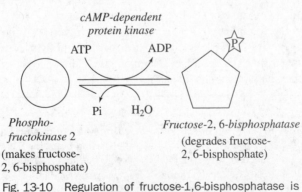

Fig. 13-10   Regulation of fructose-1,6-bisphosphatase is via fructose 2,6-bisphosphate. It is synthesized by the allosterically regulated tandem enzyme that is both a kinase and a phosphatase. Fructose 2,6-bisphosphate is an inhibitor of phosphofructokinase and an activator of fructose-1,6-bisphosphatase. A more complex description of the inhibition of phosphofructokinase by fructose 2,6-bisphosphate is given in Fig. 11-12.

EXAMPLE 13.11   As with *phosphoenolpyruvate carboxykinase*, the activity of glucose-6-phosphatase is mainly modulated by activation of the transcription and translation of its gene.

   Many hours after a meal, and also during starvation, glucose is removed from the blood by muscle and other tissues, and lactate is produced by them. This leads to an increase in the rate of gluconeogenesis from lactate by hepatocytes. The glucose that is produced this way, however, only constitues recycling of the carbon atoms; and gluconeogenic enzymes also convert other 3-carbon compounds into glucose.

   The passage of glucose from the liver to other tissues, and from them back to the liver (as lactate) is called the *Cori cycle*.

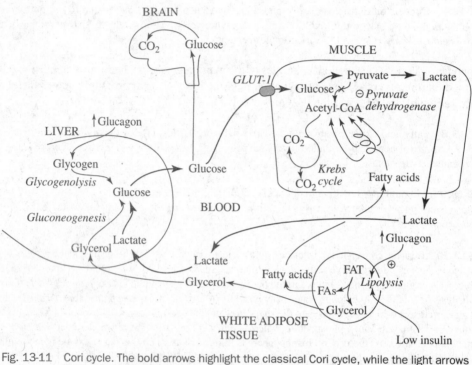

Fig. 13-11   Cori cycle. The bold arrows highlight the classical Cori cycle, while the light arrows indicate the routes of hepatic glucose delivery and metabolism in the periphery and the return of glycerol to the liver as a contributor to gluconeogenesis. FA denotes fatty acid.

Question: Is the liver the only tissue that carries out gluconeogenesis?

   No, the kidney also has the crucial bypass steps that allow the reversal of the carbon flux of glycolysis and thus enable gluconeogenesis. The kidney contributes to whole-body glucose production only during starvation. Other tissues have some, but not all, of the enzymes of gluconeogenesis, and in those tissues the bypass steps have roles other than in gluconeogenesis.

EXAMPLE 13.12   The expression of *phosphoenolpyruvate carboxykinase* provides adipose tissue with an additional route for the formation of glycerol 3-phosphate that is the starting point for fatty acid esterification and then their storage as *triglycerides*. It is unclear why white adipose tissue has acquired another mechanism for producing glycerol 3-phosphate, since it is already able to synthesize it from *dihydroxyacetone phosphate*; despite this, phosphoenolpyruvate carboxykinase is constitutively expressed in white adipose tissue, thus further *stimulating triglyceride* accumulation.

EXAMPLE 13.13   *Pyruvate carboxylase* equips a cell to produce more of the key carrier metabolite *oxaloacetate* for use in the Krebs cycle. Even though oxaloacetate is recycled, a low concentration potentially limits the rate of acetyl-CoA oxidation. In strenuous exercise, flux within the Krebs cycle is increased by the addition of the amount of oxaloacetate via this "filling" or *anaplerotic* reaction (Greek *ana*, again; *pleros*, to fill). Pyruvate carboxylase is stimulated by a rise in acetyl CoA concentration in the cell, and this occurs when the rate of its production exceeds its loss by oxidation.

13.7 De Novo Glucose Synthesis

Although the conversion of lactate to glucose in the *Cori cycle* (Fig. 13-11) regenerates this central energy source, it only constitutes a recycling of the same carbon atoms. However, the liver also converts glycerol (obtained from the blood, released from the mobilization of triglycerides in adipose tissue) into glucose (also as shown in Fig. 13-11). This pathway constitutes de novo or new glucose synthesis from carbon atoms that were previously stored as triglyceride; but note, not from the fatty acid components but only from the glycerol moiety of the triglyceride.

After transmembrane exchange of glycerol into the blood from the liver, it is converted into glycerol 3-phosphate via *glycerol kinase* in an ATP-dependent reaction. Glycerol 3-phosphate is then oxidized to dihydroxyacetone phosphate that is an intermediate of gluconeogenesis.

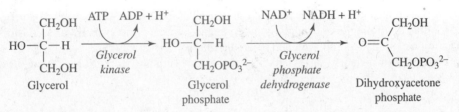

Fig. 13-12   Entry of glycerol into gluconeogenesis via dihydroxyacetone phosphate.

The other precursors that contribute to de novo gluconeogenesis are called *glycogenic* or *glucogenic*. During periods of hypoinsulinemia the rate of proteolysis in all tissues increases. Insulin is a potent stimulator of protein synthesis and an inhibitor of protein breakdown. Therefore lack of insulin leads to protein degradation, and after deamination, the carbon skeletons of the glycogenic amino acids enter gluconeogenesis.

EXAMPLE 13.14   Amino acids taken up from the blood by the liver are deaminated by a class of enzymes called *transaminases* or *aminotransferases*. These enzymes catalyze the conversion of the carbon atom containing the amine (—NH_2) group to a ketone (2-oxoacid), and in the process a 2-oxoacid is converted to an amino acid. The commonly produced 2-oxoacids are pyruvate, oxaloacetate, and 2-oxoglutarate. (Transamination reactions are discussed more fully in Sec. 14.1.)

2-Oxoacids are referred to as *carbon skeletons* of their corresponding amino acids; and some 2-oxoacids enter the Krebs cycle in *anaplerosis* that balances the flux of oxaloacetate into gluconeogenesis.

Some 2-oxoacids are converted into glycolytic, and thus glucogenic, intermediates. But there are some that are only catabolized to acetyl CoA, so there is no net flux of carbon atoms into glucose. The amino acids that lead to these 2-oxoacids are called *ketogenic*.

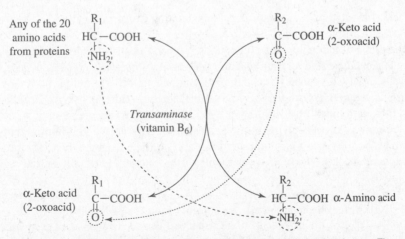

Fig. 13-13   Synthesis and catabolism of 2-oxoacids via transaminase. The dashed arrows indicate the reciprocal exchange of 2-oxo and 2-amino groups. Each of the reactions is freely reversible with an equilibrium constant near 1. The R groups are any of the ~20 side chains of amino acids found in proteins.

EXAMPLE 13.15 How many grams of protein must be catabolized to generate 1 g of glucose in a normal human liver?

Because not all amino acids are *glucogenic*, and because entry of carbon-skeleton metabolites into the Krebs cycle results in the release of carbon atoms as carbon dioxide during conversion to phosphoenolpyruvate, greater than 3 g of protein is required to make 1 g of glucose.

EXAMPLE 13.16 Can muscle glycogen be mobilized during starvation when net protein hydrolysis is taking place?

An increase in glucagon concentration in the blood, such as occurs during starvation, does not provide a strong stimulus for muscle glycogenolysis; but the concomitant hypoinsulinemia inhibits new glycogen synthesis. Therefore, every time muscle glycogen is used in muscle contraction, it is not immediately replaced; so the concentration of glycogen in muscles steadily declines over the first few days of starvation.

Providing fatty acids as an alternative fuel to glucose, increasing the rate of glucose recycling, and de novo glucose production all lead to the maintenance of the normal blood glucose concentration during starvation. The main persistent drain on glucose supply is the brain, and massive loss of body protein is obviated during starvation by metabolism being switched to an alternative fuel supply. Fig. 13-11 gives a summary of the metabolic features of the early stages of starvation, and it emphasizes the role of the Cori cycle in the reutilization of lactate via hepatic gluconeogenesis.

13.8 Ketone Body Synthesis and Oxidation

After several days of starvation, the rate of fatty acid release from adipose tissue reaches its maximum. Tissues such as muscle and liver oxidize fatty acids and produce ATP, but its rate of production may not change or it can become lower as a consequence of increased efficiency in starvation. Therefore the fatty acid concentration in the blood rises as the rate of release of fatty acids from adipose tissue exceeds that of tissue usage. In contrast to other tissues, the liver continues to perform β-oxidation even if the resulting acetyl-CoA is not consumed by the Krebs cycle. It is this feature of its metabolism that gives rise to the production of *ketone bodies* which serve as an alternative fuel for the brain and other tissues.

EXAMPLE 13.17 In skeletal muscle, the rate of acetyl-CoA production via β-oxidation cannot exceed the rate of consumption of acetyl-CoA via the Krebs cycle for extended periods. This is so because a constant rate of CoA supply is necessary for both the conversion of fatty acids to fatty-acyl CoA and the cleavage of acetyl-CoA molecules from fatty-acyl chains in β-oxidation. The CoA concentration in the mitochondrial matrix falls unless CoA is regenerated via citrate synthase in the first step of the Krebs cycle.

Although fatty acid oxidation raises the acetyl-CoA:CoA ratio in the mitochondrial matrix, the production of acetyl-CoA cannot exceed the activity of the Krebs cycle indefinitely. Carbon flux through the Krebs cycle is strongly negatively regulated by the ATP concentration, so β-oxidation in muscle is almost solely driven by ATP demand.

In the liver, there is an alternative mechanism for regenerating CoA from acetyl-CoA: two acetyl-CoA molecules react to form a 4-carbon compound called a *ketone body*. (Naming a class of molecules *bodies* is a quaint hangover from the past, but in reality these compounds "embody" the molecule of acetyl-CoA.) The enzyme in the hepatocyte that catalyzes the relevant reaction is *hydroxymethylglutaryl CoA synthase*. The consequent release of CoA from acetyl-CoA enables β-oxidation to continue rapidly. The ketone body that is formed first is *acetoacetate*; it is reduced to β-*hydroxybutyrate* by NADH; and the oxidation of NADH further stimulates flux via the fatty acid β-oxidation pathway. Recall that β-oxidation requires regeneration of NAD^+ (Sec. 10.5).

In summary, the conversion of acetyl-CoA molecules into acetoacetate and β-hydroxybutyrate transforms acetyl groups into water-soluble ketone bodies which readily diffuse from the liver into the bloodstream and then into the peripheral tissues. The brain, in particular, uses ketone bodies as a source of energy, reducing its reliance on glucose.

EXAMPLE 13.18 After diffusion into the matrix of a mitochondrion in a peripheral tissue, acetoacetate is converted into acetoacetyl-CoA, using CoA from succinyl-CoA. This process constitutes an input of energy into the assimilation of a molecule of ketone body. Even though the GTP-forming step of the Krebs cycle is bypassed in this process, the energy investment is reclaimed after CoA-mediated thiolysis of the product yields two molecules of acetyl-CoA. The acetyl-CoA then enters the Krebs cycle and generates NADH and $FADH_2$ which supply electrons to the electron transport chain. When β-hydroxybutyrate enters a cell, it is first oxidized to acetoacetate, thus yielding an additional molecule of NADH for electron transport.

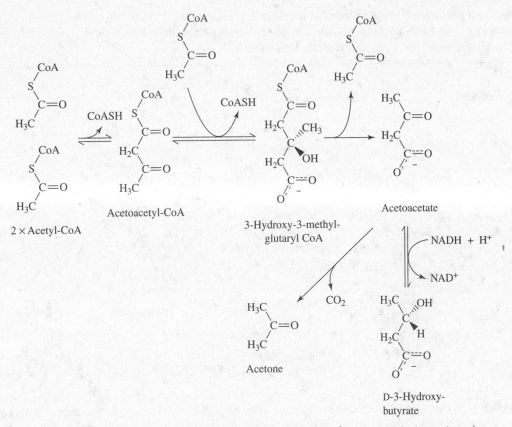

Fig. 13-14   Ketone body synthesis. Note that the conversion of acetoacetate to acetone is a slow *spontaneous* (not enzyme-catalyzed) decarboxylation reaction.

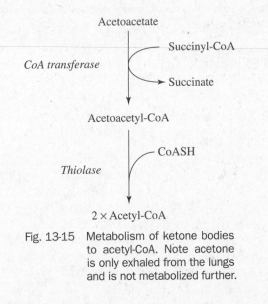

Fig. 13-15   Metabolism of ketone bodies to acetyl-CoA. Note acetone is only exhaled from the lungs and is not metabolized further.

Question: What is the mechanism whereby the oxidation of ketone bodies decreases the oxidation of glucose in the brain?

An increase in the concentration of ketone bodies in the blood raises the cellular concentration of acetyl-CoA, thereby inhibiting the activity of *pyruvate dehydrogenase*. The rate of acetyl-CoA supply exceeds the flux through the Krebs cycle which elevates the citrate concentration that in turn inhibits glycolysis by inhibiting *phosphofructokinase*. In other words, decreased use of fructose 6-phosphate leads to a buildup of glucose 6-phosphate via net reversal of the reaction catalyzed by glucose phosphate isomerase. In turn, this causes *product inhibition* of *hexokinase*. Thus during oxidation of ketone bodies, the brain does not necessarily produce lactate, as occurs in skeletal muscle.

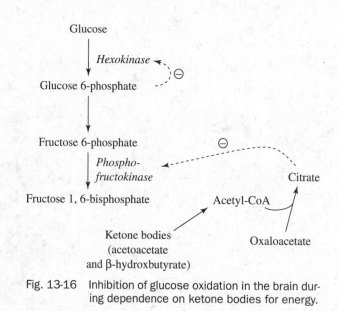

Fig. 13-16   Inhibition of glucose oxidation in the brain during dependence on ketone bodies for energy.

Synthesis of ketone bodies by the liver during starvation reduces the glucose requirement by the brain from ~120 to ~30 g per day. Even when ketone bodies are supplied in excess, the brain still has this basal usage of glucose, and this can be met by de novo gluconeogenesis from glycerol (Sec. 13.7). However, other tissues such as red blood cells have an obligatory requirement for glucose, so even with ketone body oxidation, proteolysis and gluconeogenesis from amino acids must occur. Elevated plasma ketone body concentrations have an inhibitory effect on proteolysis.

13.9   Starvation and Exercise

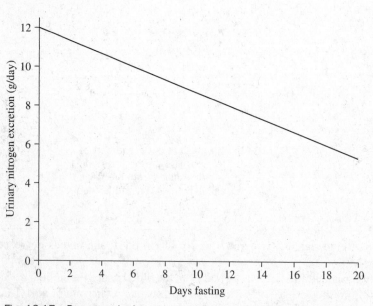

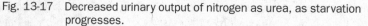

Fig. 13-17   Decreased urinary output of nitrogen as urea, as starvation progresses.

Established Starvation

After ~3 days of starvation, whole-body metabolism reaches a new steady state, as depicted in Fig. 13-18. The long-term problem for survival is the incessant loss of total protein mass.

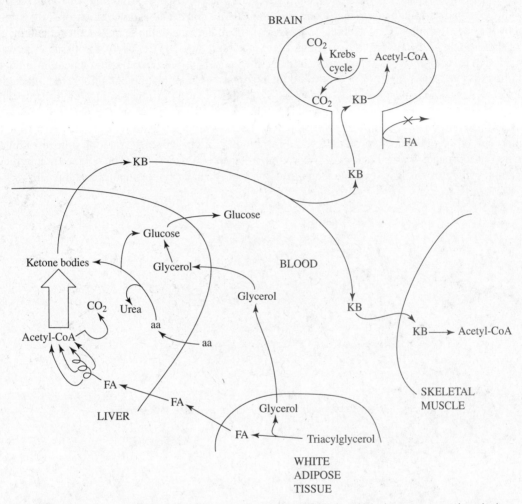

Fig. 13-18 Major metabolic interorgan fuel flow during established steady-state starvation. Amino acids are indicated by aa, fatty acids by FA, and ketone bodies by KB.

Time Course of Metabolic Changes in Starvation

It would be incorrect to assume that the changes described above follow a reproducible chronological pattern. While the production of ketone bodies is associated with starvation, it is possible that ketone body formation occurs much earlier. Similarly, processes such as gluconeogenesis occur even in the fed state, but the net contribution of these pathways becomes more important as starvation progresses.

Refeeding after Starvation

If metabolic fuel becomes available after several days of starvation, the metabolic response is one that reinstates the depleted carbohydrate and protein stores.

EXAMPLE 13.19 Pyruvate dehydrogenase is inhibited during starvation as a consequence of the increased activity of *pyruvate dehydrogenase kinase*. Although phosphorylation of only one of the regulatory serine residues is required for full inactivation of the enzyme, prolonged starvation results in the phosphorylation of all *three* sites. This makes pyruvate dehydrogenase more resistant to reactivation, so the return to carbohydrate oxidation does not occur unless carbohydrate ingestion is sustained.

Skeletal Myocytes and Muscle Contraction

Exercise involves muscle contraction which is brought about by the relative movement of filaments known as *myofibers* within muscle cells. A nerve impulse arriving at the *neuromuscular junction* in the plasma membrane of the myocyte causes a wave of dissipation of the membrane potential (*depolarization*) that is conveyed into the cytoplasm to the network of membrane-enclosed spaces called the *sarcoplasmic reticulum*. This compartment contains a high concentration of Ca^{2+} ions. The accumulation of Ca^{2+} is brought about by very active pumps (Ca^{2+}ATPases) that reside in the membrane of the sarcoplasmic reticulum; operation of these pumps accounts for the very high basal metabolic rate (BMR) of muscle tissue. The wave of electrical depolarization causes the opening of calcium channels in the sarcoplasmic reticulum membrane, and these allow the rapid flow of Ca^{2+} ions into the cytoplasm. Under resting conditions, the interaction of *actin* and *myosin* filaments is normally prevented by the intervention of a group of proteins (*tropomyosin and troponin*) that form the *troponin* complex. The binding of Ca^{2+} to troponin displaces the complex and allows actin and myosin to interact, and ATP to power the relative movement of one protein across the other. An important aspect of contraction is the rapid reabsorption of Ca^{2+} back into the sarcoplasmic reticulum, thus allowing further rounds of contraction and relaxation, as occurs in *locomotion*. The obvious requirement for ATP in many muscle cells is reflected in the large number of capacious mitochondria in these cells.

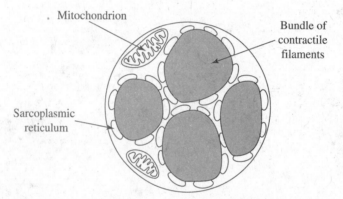

Fig. 13-19   Schematic cross section of a skeletal muscle cell.

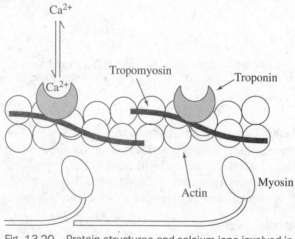

Fig. 13-20   Protein structures and calcium ions involved in *actomyosin fiber* contraction in a muscle cell.

Muscle Fiber Types

Individual muscle cells in different locations of the human body differ in several ways, but it is *functionally relevant* to divide them into two main categories based on: (1) the speed with which they can contract; (2) the density of their blood supply; and (3) the number of mitochondria per cell.

EXAMPLE 13.20 *Type I muscle fibers* are often referred to as *red muscle* fibers because they are colored a distinct reddish brown by their relatively large numbers of mitochondria that contain colored cytochromes in the electron transport chain (Chap. 10; Fig. 10-17). They are also characterized by their association with a *dense blood supply* and a high concentration of the red-colored oxygen-binding protein, *myoglobin*. On arrival of a nerve impulse, these cells contract relatively *slowly*; so they are often referred to as *slow-twitch* muscle fibers. Thus, type I fibers have evolved for slow, endurance contractions such as are used for *maintaining posture*.

EXAMPLE 13.21 Type II muscle fibers are subdivided into type IIa and type IIb. Type IIa can use both aerobic and anaerobic metabolism to produce ATP whereas type IIb fibers use only anaerobic metabolism. In contrast to type I muscle fibers, *type IIb fibers* contract rapidly after stimulation by a nerve impulse. They have evolved for short-lived, *powerful* contractions by the possession of characteristically active myosin ATPases and a *dense packing of contractile filaments*. So much of the cytoplasmic space is taken up with filaments that little exists for mitochondria. Similarly, these fibers are associated with a relatively *poor blood supply*. Type IIb fibers are also known as *white* and *fast-twitch* muscle fibers and are adapted for short-lived but *powerful contractions*. The relative paucity of mitochondria and the poor blood supply impose obvious constraints on the generation of ATP during exercise.

In the human body, most muscles are composed of a *mixture* of type I and type IIb fibers, but among other animals there are examples of muscles that consist almost entirely of one particular type of fiber.

EXAMPLE 13.22 The best example of muscles that are composed largely of type I fibers is the pectoral flight muscles of migratory birds; these persist even in domestic chickens, namely, the white "breast" meat that many folk like to eat. Another familiar example is the lobster tail that sustains a single, or only a few, powerful bursts of contraction during the backward propulsion in the animal's escape response.

Light Exercise

With the onset of light exercise such as walking, type I muscle fibers are mostly used. Their plentiful blood supply ensures that bloodborne fuels such as glucose and fatty acids are readily available for oxidation. Under normal circumstances, glucose is much more available to skeletal muscles from the blood than are fatty acids. The process of contraction provides a strong stimulus for the recruitment of GLUT-4 transporters to the myocyte plasma membrane from within the cytoplasm of the cell. Fluctuations in intracellular Ca^{2+} concentrations, that when averaged over time reflect a mean elevation, are paralleled by a rise in mitochondrial Ca^{2+} concentration that stimulates *pyruvate dehydrogenase phosphatase*, thus activating the enzyme complex. This stimulates the conversion of glucose into acetyl-CoA.

In the initial stages of light exercise, therefore, the demand for ATP is met by the full oxidation of glucose through the Krebs cycle.

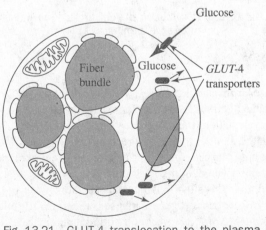

Fig. 13-21 GLUT-4 translocation to the plasma membrane enhances glucose uptake into the myocyte in the first few minutes of light exercise.

A few minutes into light exercise, the appearance of fatty acids in the blood provides the muscle with an alternative fuel to glucose. The preferential oxidation of fatty acids has much the same effect as it does in starvation. Namely, β-oxidation of the fatty acids leads to an increase in the acetyl-CoA:CoA ratio, and this stimulates *pyruvate dehydrogenase kinase*. At a later time, the activity of pyruvate dehydrogenase kinase exceeds that of *pyruvate dehydrogenase phosphatase* so the pyruvate dehydrogenase complex will be phosphorylated and hence inactivated. In this way, fatty acids prevent glucose from being wastefully oxidized even though the stimulus for glucose uptake is still present, as is evident from the presence of GLUT-4 transporters in the plasma membrane.

Fate of the Glucose in Muscle in Light Exercise

As in starvation, inhibition of *pyruvate dehydrogenase* in skeletal muscle is characterized by an increase in the conversion of pyruvate to lactate followed by its export into the bloodstream. Although lactate production is increased, light exercise does not result in a large or even detectable increase in blood lactate concentration. This is so because the liver and heart very efficiently absorb lactate from the blood.

(This metabolic scenario is a good example of why caution must be employed when drawing conclusions from the steady-state concentration of metabolites: the fact that the concentration of a compound does not change in a certain metabolic situation does not imply that its rates of production and disposal have remained constant.)

After a few minutes of light exercise, the fuel uptake profile in skeletal muscle shifts so that the oxidation of fatty acids is dominant and most glucose taken up into the muscles is recycled in the *Cori cycle*. This situation is highly sustainable as very little carbohydrate is lost and there are usually large reserves of triglycerides in the body. Humans have evolved to do a lot of walking (light exercise); it is possible to walk very long distances (many miles) before exhaustion occurs.

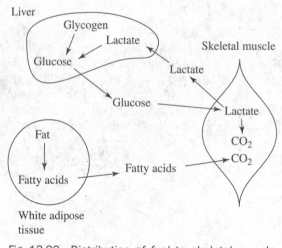

Fig. 13-22 Distribution of fuel to skeletal muscle after several minutes of light exercise.

Moderate Exercise

If the pace of exercise increases from a walk to a *light jog*, the rate of fatty acid oxidation by the muscles also increases. This is a consequence of Krebs cycle flux increasing in response to elevated rates of NADH consumption and oxidative phosphorylation. Increased activity of β-oxidation is dependent on both an adequate supply of fatty acids to the mitochondrial matrix and responsive β-oxidation enzymes.

During more strenuous jogging, the enzymes that catalyze fatty acid oxidation soon reach their maximum velocity, and in most individuals, β-oxidation will not provide acetyl-CoA sufficiently rapidly to drive the Krebs cycle at its maximum rate. In this situation, the concentration of acetyl-CoA in the matrix falls. As the concentration of CoA falls, pyruvate dehydrogenase kinase is no longer stimulated by acetyl-CoA, and *Ca²⁺-activated pyruvate dehydrogenase phosphatase* becomes dominant; this *reactivates* pyruvate dehydrogenase and allows glucose oxidation to increase again.

Even though the inhibition on glucose oxidation is relieved, the rate of fatty acid oxidation remains high. β-Oxidation still proceeds at its maximum rate, but it is insufficient for the supply of all the energy, so the muscle cells burn a *mixture* of glucose and fatty acids to sustain repeated contractions.

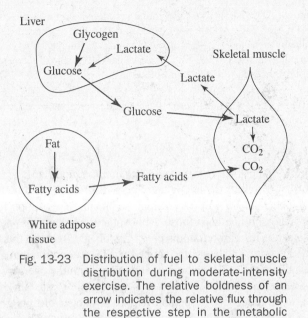

Fig. 13-23 Distribution of fuel to skeletal muscle distribution during moderate-intensity exercise. The relative boldness of an arrow indicates the relative flux through the respective step in the metabolic process.

Strenuous Exercise

As the intensity of exercise increases further, such as occurs in a *competitive marathon* race, both fatty acid oxidation and glucose oxidation determine the rate of ATP supply. Muscle glycogen is mobilized, and its concentration steadily decreases at a rate that is proportional to the intensity of the exercise.

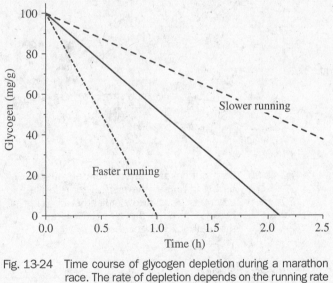

Fig. 13-24 Time course of glycogen depletion during a marathon race. The rate of depletion depends on the running rate as indicated by "faster running" and "slower running."

EXAMPLE 13.23 Which biochemical signals activate *glycogenolysis* in muscle?

Muscle *glycogen phosphorylase*, like its counterpart in the liver, is *activated* by phosphorylation via *phosphorylase kinase*. Even in its dephosphorylated state, glycogen phosphorylase is activated allosterically by adenosine monophosphate (AMP). AMP concentrations rise whenever ATP concentrations fall (Example 13.24), so if the combined effects of both fatty acid and glucose oxidation are unable to sustain normal ATP concentrations in contracting muscle, AMP concentrations rise quickly and stimulate glycogen phosphorylase.

EXAMPLE 13.24 The concentrations of AMP, ADP, and ATP in the cytoplasm of cells are interconnected via *adenylate kinase*. This enzyme catalyzes the transfer of the terminal phosphate of one ADP molecule onto another, thereby converting two molecules of ADP into one of ATP and one of AMP. The reaction is very rapid in both directions, and a very small change in the ratio of ATP:ADP is translated into a very large change in the concentration of AMP; e.g., at rest, the concentrations of ATP, ADP, and AMP are ~4.8, ~0.2, and ~0.001 mM, respectively. During strenuous exercise, in a skeletal muscle these values change to ~4.2, ~0.5, and ~0.3 mM. Even though the ATP concentration does not change very much, the AMP concentration increases ~300-fold. This makes AMP a very effective signal via allosteric activation of enzymes that respond rapidly to changes in ATP concentration.

The energy charge (EC) of a cell is a parameter that is used to express a cell's energetic status. The value is given by

$$EC = ([ATP] + 0.5[ADP])/([ATP] + [ADP] + [AMP])$$

At very low values of EC, when AMP is elevated it is *deaminated* via *AMP deaminase* to inosine monophosphate (IMP). This further displaces the adenylate kinase reaction in the direction of ATP synthesis. The IMP is dephosphorylated by *nucleotide phosphatase*, and the inosine is phosphorylyzed via *purine nucleotide phosphorylase*, releasing hypoxanthine and ribose 1-phosphate. The latter is metabolized via the pentose phosphate pathway, and most of the carbon atoms enter glycolysis. Because this course of events depletes the overall adenine nucleotide pool, and hence the scope for ATP production in the longer term, it represents a metabolic "last ditch stand" by the cell to extract energy even from the energy currency itself!

If muscle glycogen is depleted completely, then it is impossible to sustain contraction and it is likely that liver glycogen will also be reduced. The person will be in danger of hypoglycemia; and exercise will be solely reliant on fatty acid oxidation. The person will be able to only walk, not run. Under conditions of glycogen depletion, the runner is often said to have "hit the wall."

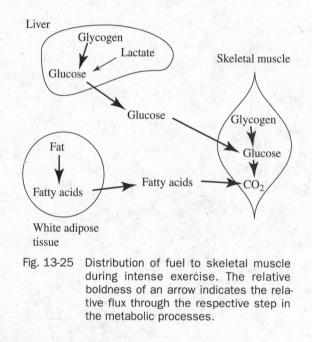

Fig. 13-25 Distribution of fuel to skeletal muscle during intense exercise. The relative boldness of an arrow indicates the relative flux through the respective step in the metabolic processes.

13.10 Control of Muscle Glycogen

It could be a distinct advantage for an athlete to start a race with more muscle glycogen than the competitors. It would also be an advantage if the athlete could conserve some glycogen by making greater use of fatty acids, both during the race and right at the start when, even at walking pace, blood glucose is the preferred fuel.

EXAMPLE 13.25 During the 1960s it was observed that glycogen resynthesis was especially rapid after exercise-induced glycogen depletion, and the extent of new glycogen synthesis exceeded the initial preexercise level. This overshoot in glycogenesis was termed *glycogen supercompensation*. Its discovery stimulated much research in nutrition to find the most potent means of increasing prerace muscle glycogen content. Elite athletes now routinely use such special diets.

EXAMPLE 13.26 Manipulation of glycogen concentration by exercise or dietary intervention is often referred to as *carbohydrate loading*. The strategy favored in the late 1960s was a highly invasive program that involved two exhaustive bouts of exercise between periods of low-carbohydrate intake, to fully deplete muscle glycogen; this was followed by the consumption of a high-carbohydrate diet. Although this strategy is effective in raising muscle glycogen concentrations, it clearly interrupts training and is potentially dangerous since there is a high risk of hypoglycemia on the second bout of exhaustive exercise. Today, athletes favor a less proactive regime, simply relying on the natural propensity for glycogenolysis to be followed by a period of glycogen overshoot, provided that a high-carbohydrate diet is consumed.

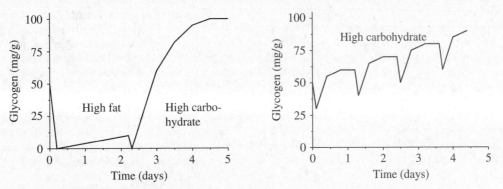

Fig. 13-26   Comparison of glycogen-loading strategies.

EXAMPLE 13.27   If muscle uses fatty acid oxidation to supply ATP, then less glycogen is mobilized; so any exercise/diet strategies that increase the proportion of energy derived from fatty acids should save glycogen. Training increases the activity of the β-oxidation enzymes (Sec. 10.5), and a good supply of carnitine should also assist in fatty acid catabolism.

Carnitine supplements are effective in augmenting fatty acid oxidation, especially in subjects who may be naturally prone to carnitine deficiency, such as vegetarians.

EXAMPLE 13.28   To prevent muscles from wastefully using carbohydrate during the first few minutes of exercise, it may be beneficial to raise plasma fatty acid levels even before the race begins. Fatty acid release from adipose tissue can be stimulated by caffeine although competitively one would have to be wary of this strategy because, above certain levels, caffeine is considered to be an illegal performance enhancer. Caffeine may also have undesirable diuretic effects.

Fitness

As well as providing a higher capacity for β-oxidation, the muscle mitochondria of well-trained athletes appear to be larger and to have more electron transport proteins. At the physiological level, a more efficient cardiovascular system and increased vascularization of muscles allow for a better delivery of fuels and oxygen. Endurance training may even lead to remodeling of muscle fiber composition so that muscles contain a higher proportion of type I fibers (Example 13.20).

Very High Intensity Exercise

The forces generated by very rapid and/or powerful contractions associated with sprinting or weight lifting are mainly generated by type IIb muscle fibers (Example 13.21). These cells generate ATP very quickly, despite having relatively few mitochondria and a lesser blood supply than for type I fibers. The latter reduces their reliance on bloodborne fuels. The relative density of mitochondria in type IIb cells imparts a low capacity for fatty acid oxidation. There is also a delay in the metabolic response because it takes several minutes to recruit GLUT-4 transporters from the cytoplasm.

In a *flight or fight* situation, it would not be desirable for a delay while GLUT-4 molecules were recruited to the plasma membrane.

The cells use endogenously stored glycogen, which circumvents the requirement for many glucose transporters; and they oxidize the glucose produced in glycogenolysis via anaerobic glycolysis.

13.11   Anaerobic Glycogen Usage

The conversion of glucose to lactate is a relatively inefficient process in that the molecules that are produced still contain much free energy in their covalent bonds. Only a net two ATP molecules are produced per glucose molecule, or three if one considers the starting point for the catabolism to be of glycogen.

Glycolysis in skeletal muscle can attain very high fluxes, so even though the yield of ATP per molecule of glucose is low, the rate at which ATP is produced is high. The incomplete catabolism of glucose generates a large amount of the end product, lactate. Lactate is produced from pyruvate and regenerates cytosolic NAD^+ so a high rate of glycolysis is maintained. Although glycogenolysis and glycolysis are very rapid, it still takes several seconds for the flux-controlling enzymes, notably glycogen phosphorylase and phosphofructokinase, to reach their maximum activities.

EXAMPLE 13.29   How might glycogen phosphorylase and phosphofructokinase be stimulated?

At the onset of very rapid muscle contraction, ATP levels fall. This causes an increase in AMP concentration. Both phosphofructokinase and glycogen phosphorylase are sensitively stimulated by AMP. After several seconds, glycogen phosphorylase becomes fully activated because of the arrival of epinephrine in the blood that stimulates the cAMP cascade. Epinephrine is rapidly secreted at the onset of high-intensity exercise and is a mediator of the fight or flight response.

The low-capacity blood supply to the type IIb fibers (Example 13.21) may limit the amount of epinephrine available to bind to the receptors, but the operation of the phosphorylation amplification cascade more than compensates and rapidly leads to full activation of glycogen phosphorylase.

The accumulation of lactate is often cited as a cause of fatigue during intense muscle contraction; but the effect is actually due to a low pH in muscles. Protons dissociate in a reversible manner from lactic acid, glycolytic intermediates, and the purine nucleotides, thus contributing to a net increase of protons in solution. A marked drop in pH is not conducive to efficient operation of the contractile machinery, as well as inhibiting hexokinase and phosphofructokinase in glycolysis.

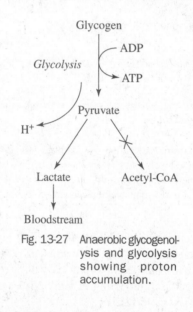

Fig. 13-27   Anaerobic glycogenolysis and glycolysis showing proton accumulation.

13.12   "Buying Time" with Creatine Phosphate

ATP Buffering

Even though AMP-induced activation of glycolysis and glycogenolysis is rapid, cellular reserves of ATP would only allow vigorous contraction of skeletal muscle for ~1 s. An instantly available store of high-energy phosphate is provided by creatine phosphate. Creatine kinase is exceptionally active and maintains the reaction between creatine and ATP, and creatine phosphate and ADP, in rapid dynamic equilibrium. This pool of creatine phosphate serves as a buffer for ATP that occurs without any activation of metabolic pathways.

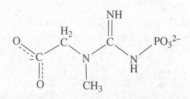

Fig. 13-28   Creatine phosphate.

During periods of physical inactivity, creatine phosphate is formed from creatine and ATP simply by reversal of the creatine kinase reaction.

Creatine is synthesized in an interorgan metabolic pathway that spans the kidney and liver. In the kidney, arginine and glycine are condensed to form *guanidinoacetate*, which is exported from the kidney and taken up by hepatocytes in which it is *methylated*. Creatine phosphate is chemically unstable and spontaneously cyclizes to give *creatinine* and phosphate; it cannot be reverted back to creatine, so it is a metabolic end product that is excreted in the urine. Because the size of the creatine phosphate pool is relatively constant, the amount of creatinine produced in 24 h is also relatively constant. Thus, the amount of creatinine excreted in the urine is used clinically to gauge renal excretory function.

The amount excreted becomes an unreliable measure of renal function in subjects who have a very large muscle mass or in those taking creatine dietary supplements, such as athletes.

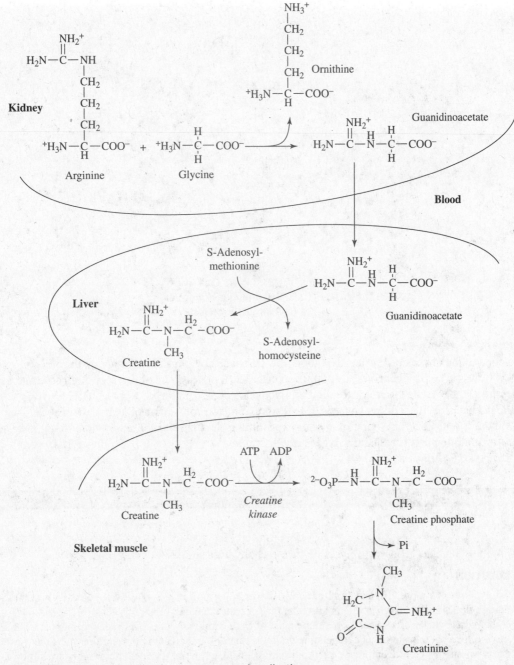

Fig. 13-29   Creatine synthesis, transport, and cyclization.

EXAMPLE 13.30   Creatine phosphate concentration in the cytoplasm of skeletal muscle is ~15 m*M*. Since the rate of ATP consumption during intense exercise is ~3 mmol L^{-1} s^{-1}, there is potentially a 5 s supply of creatine phosphate. Many sprinters and power lifters attempt to increase the amount of creatine phosphate in their muscles by ingesting creatine as a dietary supplement. There is strong evidence to suggest that this strategy is effective, but the long-term effects on general health, particularly kidney function, are yet to be determined.

Very high intensity exercise is characterized by rapid glycogen breakdown, glycolysis, and lactate production, with almost instantaneous ATP buffering by creatine phosphate.

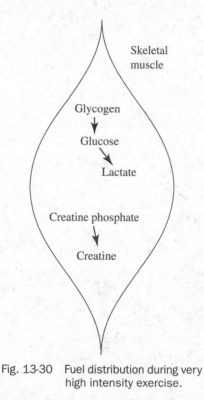

Fig. 13-30   Fuel distribution during very high intensity exercise.

Postexercise Recovery

During contraction of skeletal muscle, the blood flow is reduced by physical pressure on the blood vessels, so the blood flow to type IIb fibers increases after exercise. The increased rate of delivery of glucose and oxygen and the removal of lactate lead to restoration of glycogen stores, creatine phosphate, and reestablishment of cytosolic pH back to ~7.2. This resynthesis of fuel stores, and the conversion of lactate to glucose in the liver, implies there is a postexercise burst of energy expenditure. This is reflected in an increase in postexercise oxygen consumption that is called the *oxygen debt*.

SOLVED PROBLEMS

FUEL STORES

13.1.   Why is a greater mass of triglyceride than carbohydrate stored in the human body?

SOLUTION

Triglyceride is a more efficient store in terms of energy per unit of mass, or even volume; this is true even though the density of triglyceride is less than that of water and carbohydrates. The full oxidation of 1 g of carbohydrate yields 17 kJ whereas the same mass of triglyceride produces over twice this amount (38 kJ g^{-1}). In vivo, glycogen is stored as cytoplasmic granules that are associated with a lot of water; this lowers the effective energy yield from a glycogen particle to ~6 kJ g^{-1}. Triglycerides, being very hydrophobic, are stored in the absence of water.

While there is a limit to how much glycogen can be stored in a cell, there is no limit to the size of triglyceride stores. When adipocytes become full, new adipocytes are formed from preadipocyte precursor cells that exist in adipose tissue.

MECHANISM OF GLYCOGENOLYSIS IN LIVER

13.2. A relatively small number of humans have been discovered with a deficiency in one or the other of the enzymes of glycogen metabolism. The combined incidence of these diseases is ~1:40,000 live births. These conditions are tragic for the patients and their families, and yet they have furthered the understanding of normal carbohydrate metabolism. A defect in the gene coding for an enzyme may lead to the lowered stability of the protein, a small amount of enzyme being produced, or altered substrate binding affinity or turnover number in the active site of the enzyme (Chap. 5). In the case of diseases of glycogen metabolism, this can result in either a high or low content of glycogen of normal or abnormal structure and is generally associated with muscle weakness; and in some cases the accumulation of glycogen in the tissues that have the defective enzyme. Seven of the ten well-described types of glycogen storage disease are given in the table.

Deficient enzyme	Name	Type	Tissue site of defect
Glucose 6-phosphatase	Von Gierke disease	I	Liver and kidney
Lysosomal α-glucosidase	Pompe disease	II	All tissues
Amylo-1,6-glucosidase	Limit dextrinosis	III	All tissues
Branching enzyme	Amylopectinosis	IV	All tissues
Glycogen phosphorylase	McArdle disease	V	Skeletal muscle
Glycogen phosphorylase	Hers disease	VI	Liver
Phosphofructokinase		VII	Skeletal muscle and erythrocytes

1. In McArdle disease (type V glycogen storage disease) the first patient was a young man who was weak and developed severe muscle pain on doing modest exercise. Biopsy of his muscle showed accumulation of glycogen, and enzyme assays revealed low glycogen phosphorylase activity. Predict the effect of exercise on the lactate concentration in such a patient.
2. In von Gierke disease (type I glycogen storage disease), the liver of the young patient was enormously enlarged. The failure to release glucose from the liver means that the brain is deprived of glucose between meals and the patient suffers severe brain damage. Why might this occur and would the structure of the glycogen in the liver be normal?
3. In Pompe disease (type II glycogen storage disease), there is accumulation of normal glycogen in the lysosomes of almost all tissues. Early death usually results from heart failure. The enzyme that is defective is in the lysosomes, and it would normally hydrolyze both the $1\rightarrow4$ and $1\rightarrow6$ linkages of glycogen. Why might it be that almost all tissues are affected?
4. In amylopectinosis (type IV glycogen storage disease), all tissues are affected by the accumulation of glycogen that has a structure similar to amylopectin, the form of starch that has a branched structure with a large number of glucose residues between branches and long branches. Why is this so?
5. In limit dextrinosis (type III glycogen storage disease), the glycogen that accumulates has an abnormal structure. Based on the information given in the table, explain what this structure might be and why it comes about.

SOLUTION

1. The concentration of lactate scarcely rises since glycogen is broken down very slowly, due to low activity of glycogen phosphorylase, to provide glucose for glycolysis and ATP production to drive muscle contraction.
2. Since in von Gierke disease the liver and kidney, the two gluconeogenic tissues, cannot convert glucose 6-phosphate to glucose, the effect of the elevated glucose 6-phosphate provides mass-action backpressure on the glycogen phosphorylase reaction. This leads to *lactic acidosis* (high lactic acid concentration in the blood), the accumulation of glycogen of normal structure, and hypoglycemia that starves the brain of fuel.

3. The discovery of Pompe disease highlighted the fact that there is significant flux of glycogen through the lysosomal system of all cells, and especially in macrophages as they ingest cells that have undergone apoptosis. The glycogen that accumulates is of normal structure.

4. In amylopectinosis, the defective enzyme is the branching enzyme. In normal glycogen a branch occurs every 7–10 glucose residues; in the starch, amylopectin this is usually every ~12–20 residues. A defect in the branching enzyme leads to a decrease in the frequency of branch points and the glycogen having a structure like amylopectin, hence the name of the disease. The enzyme carries out a complicated combination of processes (see Fig. 11-10) that involves first excising a linear segment of ~7 glucose residues from the parent glycogen, carrying this segment further into the polymer, and then catalyzing the condensation of the linear segment with the 6—OH of a glucose residue. Clearly there are many steps in which a mutated enzyme could be defective and still lead to amylopectinosis.

5. In limit dextrinosis, the defective enzyme is amylo-1,6-glucosidase. Dextrin is a general name for polymers of glucose. A *limit dextrin* is one in which the branched glucose polymer, in this case glycogen, has multiple branches but they are all very short. This is the consequence of the inability of the cell to remove the branch points. Since glycogen phosphorylase operates only on the ends of linear chains with the 1→4 linkage, the limit dextrin accumulates in the affected tissues. The failure of rapid glycogen mobilization leads to hypoglycemia, muscle weakness, and brain damage, depending on the extent of the enzyme deficiency.

13.3. Does the production of cAMP that is central to the control of glycogenolysis significantly reduce the ATP concentration in muscle cells?

SOLUTION

The amount of ATP used is tiny in comparison with the size of the ATP pool. The intracellular cAMP concentration fluctuates around the nM range that is several orders of magnitude smaller than the ATP concentration. Thus hormone-stimulated cell-signaling pathways provide a much more sensitive means of regulating enzyme activity than direct control by mass-action effects of the reactants of an enzymic reaction.

MECHANISM OF LIPOLYSIS

13.4. Where in the alimentary tract does lipolysis begin to occur?

SOLUTION

A lipase that hydrolyzes triglycerides, hence a true *triglyceridase*, is secreted by Ebner's glands in the tongue.

FATTY-ACID-INDUCED INHIBITION OF GLUCOSE OXIDATION

13.5. If pyruvate dehydrogenase is inhibited in white adipocytes and skeletal muscle, what happens to the cytoplasmic pyruvate concentration?

SOLUTION

Even if glucose were converted into pyruvate by glycolysis, the pyruvate would be reduced by cytosolic NADH into lactate. Lactate leaves the cytoplasm by carrier-mediated diffusion and enters the bloodstream, from which it is taken up by the liver and heart muscle.

13.6. How does a rise in fatty acid concentration in the blood lead to the stimulation of fatty acid oxidation in skeletal myocytes?

SOLUTION

It may seem logical that a rise in fatty acid availability will cause an increase in the rate of fatty acid oxidation. However, the rate of oxidation of fuel is matched purely to the demand for ATP; and if glucose oxidation provides sufficient ATP, the extra supply of fatty acids is not metabolized. Fatty acid oxidation can be regulated by controlling the rate at which the fatty acids enter the mitochondria, and this, in turn, is dependent on the activity of carnitine acyl transferase I. This transferase is inhibited by malonyl CoA, the production of which (by acetyl-CoA carboxylase) is stimulated by insulin. So, under conditions of hypoinsulinemia, malonyl-CoA concentrations fall and carnitine acyl transferase I is activated. This stimulates the uptake of fatty acids into the mitochondrial matrix and promotes β-oxidation. It is not so much the rise in fatty acids in the blood that stimulates β-oxidation, but the fall in insulin concentration.

GLUCOSE RECYCLING

13.7. Is the conversion of oxaloacetate to phosphoenol pyruvate more likely to occur in the mitochondria or the cytoplasm of skeletal myocytes, and or hepatocytes?

SOLUTION

For cytoplasmic conversion to phosphoenolpyruvate, the oxaloacetate must leave the matrix as malate. Since the conversion to malate goes against the normal direction of Krebs cycle flux, by involving reduction with NADH, it is more probable that the conversion will occur in the mitochondria.

DE NOVO GLUCOSE SYNTHESIS

13.8. What fraction of the glucose that is synthesized from triglyceride-derived glycerol occurs during early starvation?

SOLUTION

At the maximum rate of lipolysis, the amount of glycerol released from white adipose tissue generates ~30 g of glucose per day. This is only one-quarter of the glucose required by the brain and, of itself, is insufficient to achieve euglycemia.

KETONE BODY SYNTHESIS AND OXIDATION

13.9. In acute diabetic ketoacidosis it is usual to be able to smell acetone on the breath of the patient. How does this come about?

SOLUTION

Figure 13-14 shows that the decaboxylation of the ketone body *acetotacetate* yields acetone. If acetoacetate concentrations are high in the body, due to a switch to metabolism that uses ketone bodies, rather than glucose, then the spontaneous first-order kinetic production of acetone is high. Acetone has a low boiling point and emerges in the exhaled breath of the patient.

STARVATION AND EXERCISE

13.10. How long can a steady state of protein degradation be maintained during starvation?

SOLUTION

Given that 3–4 g of protein can be converted to 1 g of glucose, even a 20 g per day mismatch between glucose production and usage will lower protein reserves by 60–80 g per day. Although most tissues contain some redundant protein mass, there is obviously a limit to how much protein a cell can lose before it begins to malfunction. The total protein reserves vary between individuals, but it is generally ~8 kg. Even if one-half of this protein could be lost without ill effect, it would only allow survival for 1–2 months; this is about the length of time that humans have been known to survive without food, given adequate supplies of water. The most likely causes of death after prolonged starvation result from a compromised immune system and general malfunction of salt balance and temperature control.

13.11. What is the consequence of glucose use by muscle on blood glucose concentration in the initial stages of light exercise?

SOLUTION

Blood glucose concentration falls, but euglycemia is maintained by liver *glycogenolysis*. As exercise continues, and the blood glucose concentration falls to ~4 m*M*, glucagon is released by the α-cells of the islets of Langerhans in the pancreas, while insulin concentration in the blood falls. The latter stimulates the mobilization of fatty acids from adipose tissue (Sec. 13.9).

13.12. Which metabolic factors might limit the ability of muscle to use fatty acids as the intensity of exercise is increased?

SOLUTION

The rate of transport of fatty acids into the mitochondria is determined largely by the availability of carnitine that is used as a carrier. The rate of β-oxidation is also limited and this is especially pronounced in unfit individuals. One of the beneficial effects of exercise training is that it brings about an increase in the expression of the genes of the proteins of the β-oxidation pathway.

The availability of oxaloacetate, which acts as the *metabolite carrier* in the Krebs cycle, may also be limited. The production of oxaloacetate is achieved by acetyl-CoA-induced stimulation of pyruvate carboxylase (Sec. 11.8; Fig. 11-17).

13.13. What happens to the rate of liver glucose metabolism during moderate-intensity exercise?

SOLUTION

An increase in the rate of glucose usage by the skeletal muscles increases the rate of depletion of muscle glycogen. The rate of glycogenolysis in the *liver* rises as well, supplying glucose, via the blood, to the muscles for oxidation. Less glucose recycling occurs via the Cori cycle as pyruvate is oxidized in the muscles.

The situation is more complicated in unfit individuals who produce much more lactate when they change from walking to running. This is related to a lower maximal rate of oxidative phosphorylation (Sec. 10.11).

13.14. Is the consumption of glucose likely to be effective in preventing the loss of muscle glycogen during exercise?

SOLUTION

In high-intensity exercises, glycogen in skeletal myocytes is mobilized because the combined effects of glucose supply from the blood, that is then oxidized, and fatty acid oxidation cannot provide sufficient acetyl-CoA to the Krebs cycle. Glucose uptake from the blood is determined not by the concentration of glucose there but by the number of glucose transporters in the plasma membrane of the myocytes. Thus increasing the blood glucose concentration has little effect on the rate of ATP production. The elevation of blood glucose concentration stimulates insulin secretion by the pancreas, which decreases the rate of lipolysis, so decreasing the availability of fatty acids.

Carbohydrate-containing drinks definitely increase athletic endurance. One explanation is that the drinks are effective in restoring liver glycogen. Also the rise in blood insulin concentration is much less than expected during exercise because *stress hormones* (e.g., epinephrine) that are secreted during intense physical activity inhibit insulin secretion. If glucose is absorbed from the intestine at exactly the same rate as it is used by the muscle, the drink will be beneficial. The value of glucose drinks taken before exercise is more controversial. Early evidence suggested that prerace glucose consumption leads to inhibition of lipolysis that precipitates hypoglycemia during exercise; recent studies have contradicted that finding.

CONTROL OF MUSCLE GLYCOGEN

13.15. Are there any functional disadvantages to having large stores of glycogen in muscle cells?

SOLUTION

Glycogen is a relatively inefficient fuel reserve in terms of energy stored per unit of mass; it is stored in large intracellular granules that are associated with a lot of water, so its bulky presence is not necessarily conducive to efficient muscle contraction. Muscle fatigue can occur during a marathon race even though glycogen is not totally depleted, implying that not all glycogen is equally accessible to breakdown.

13.16. What is the likely metabolic response to exercise in skeletal muscle by an *unfit* individual?

SOLUTION

The major factor impacting on ATP generation in muscles of unfit subjects is a suboptimal blood supply. If the delivery of fatty acids and glucose is compromised, then the only readily available fuel will be muscle glycogen. But a suboptimal delivery of oxygen will render oxidative phosphorylation unable to keep pace with the demand for ATP. Under these circumstances greater reliance is placed on glycolysis as a means of generating ATP. Thus glycolytic flux will rise, resulting in the production of a large amount of lactate. This situation, which involves the *anaerobic* generation of ATP, is similar to fuel metabolism of muscle during a sprint.

ANAEROBIC GLYCOGEN USAGE

13.17. Account for the fact that three ATP molecules are produced from one molecule of glucose that is derived from glycogen when it is catabolized via glycolysis.

SOLUTION

Glycolysis commences with glucose being phosphorylated by ATP to glucose 6-phosphate; thus one molecule of ATP is "invested" to initiate glycolysis. In glycogenolysis, orthophosphate is used in a *phosphorolysis* reaction (instead of water in hydrolysis) to cleave glucose residues from glycogen; this yields glucose 6-phosphate. Thus glucose is phosphorylated and is ready for glycolysis without the requirement for the initial use of ATP.

"BUYING TIME" WITH CREATINE PHOSPHATE

13.18. Would a diet that gives rise to glycogen loading in muscle be of benefit to a sprinter?

SOLUTION

Even during longer sprint events, such as 400 m, the race is completed before muscle glycogen stores have become depleted by ~50%. If multiple races are to be run, adequate glycogen resynthesis between each event is important, so the consumption of rapidly digested carbohydrate has been shown to be useful for the best performances.

13.19. Would the use of pH buffers help prevent muscle fatigue during exercise?

SOLUTION

It would be difficult to deliver a pH buffer to muscle cells in vivo under normal conditions; but an indirect way involves ingesting sodium bicarbonate. This has been trialed with some success. By increasing the pH-buffering capacity of the blood, bicarbonate has been shown to reduce the time to run 400 m by 1–2 s. However, this procedure is dangerous because an overdose of bicarbonate can cause respiratory alkalosis that gives rise to a reduced oxygen supply to the brain.

SUPPLEMENTARY PROBLEMS

13.20. For type VII *glycogenosis* (Prob. 13.2) explain the likely symptoms due to this inborn error of metabolism, and give the nature of the accumulated glycogen.

13.21. For Hers disease, a *glycogenosis*, (Prob. 13.2) explain the likely symptoms of this inborn error of metabolism and describe the nature of the accumulated glycogen.

13.22. Why does the brain use ketone bodies as metabolic fuel during starvation when there are abundant fatty acids available from the blood?

13.23. Apart from glucose, how are carbohydrates in the diet digested and processed in metabolism?

13.24. In a 100 m sprint, what do the skeletal muscles of an elite athlete use to provide ATP in abundance?

13.25. Why do sprinters breathe heavily and deeply immediately after a 100 m race?

ANSWERS TO SUPPLEMENTARY PROBLEMS

13.20. The defective enzyme is *phosphofrucokinase in skeletal muscle and erythrocytes*. Therefore there is muscle weakness, and the glycogen has normal structure. The patients normally live into adulthood as hepatic gluconeogensis is not affected and brain fuel supply and metabolism are normal.

13.21. The defective enzyme is *glycogen phosphorylase in the liver*. Therefore the liver is enlarged; it is swollen with glycogen of normal structure. The patient will usually have hypoglycemia between meals, and potentially brain damaged due to long-term intermittent hypoglycemia.

13.22. Fatty acids are transported in the blood bound to serum albumin. Since the blood-brain barrier excludes all proteins from entering the interstitial spaces, fatty acids cannot be delivered there in the large quantities that would be required to supply adequate amounts of energy. On the other hand, ketone bodies are small and very soluble in water. They readily traverse the blood-brain barrier via specific transporters.

13.23. Starch and glycogen are first hydrolyzed by α-amylase which is secreted by the salivary glands. This particular enzyme has the common name *ptyalin*. Up to 10% of a starch meal such as potato is digested by this enzyme before the reaction is stopped by the low pH in the stomach. The products of digestion are the disaccharide *maltose* (Glc-Glc), maltotriose, maltotetrose, and smaller amounts of other oligosaccharides.
The gastric contents pass into the duodenum where they encounter secretions from the pancreatic duct. Another α-amylase from the pancreas continues the hydrolytic attack on the starch and glycogen.
The disaccharides that are most common in the human diet are *sucrose* (e.g., cane and beet sugar; Glc-Fru), *lactose* (milk sugar; Glc-Gal), and from starch and glycogen, *maltose* (Glc-Glc). A specific enzyme for each of these disaccharides is located on the outer surface of the *microvilli* of enterocytes in the *jejunum* and *ileum*; the enzymes are called *sucrase*, *lactase*, and *maltase*, respectively.

The monosaccharides that are released by this enzyme action are absorbed into the enterocytes via sodium-dependent cotransporters (also called *sodium symporters*). From the enterocytes, the monosaccharides enter the *portal vein* and are taken up by the liver where they are processed further in ways described in this chapter.

13.24. The muscles use three major energy sources: (1) creatine phosphate yields high energy phosphate to ADP to generate more ATP; this occurs over ~4 s; (2) muscle glycogen produces glucose 6-phosphate; and (3) the blood delivers glucose from the liver that is used in anaerobic glycolysis. Since the blood supply during the strong contractions of extreme exertion is interrupted, both the oxygen and the glucose supplies from this source are marginal, hence the myocytes rely on creatine phosphate for the initial burst of ATP, and endogenous glucose from glycogen for most of the remainder.

13.25. Anaerobic metabolism yields lactic acid which is subsequently metabolized by the liver. This metabolism incurs a debt of oxygen. One mole of glucose yields 6 mol of CO_2 and a theoretical maximum of 38 mol of ATP. Therefore there is a huge amount of glucose used in the sprint and a lot of lactic acid to be processed after the race. The lowering of the pH of blood by the lactic acid stimulates a *hyperventilation* response from the brain.

CHAPTER 14

Processing of Nitrogen Compounds

Question: Nitrogen atoms are located in many molecules of biological origin. How do they become incorporated into animals?

Animals are dependent for growth on a source of *fixed* nitrogen from other animals or plants, fungi and micro-organisms; plants in turn are dependent on bacteria for fixing nitrogen, that is, converting N_2 from the atmosphere into nitrite, nitrate, and NH_4^+ which can be incorporated into organic molecules. Humans require fixed nitrogen, which must come from the diet, normally as protein, particularly for protein and nucleic acid synthesis but also for synthesizing many specialized metabolites such as porphyrins and phospholipids.

14.1 Synthesis and Dietary Sources of Amino Acids

The *amount* of protein or fixed nitrogen that we ingest determines our state of *nitrogen balance*. Humans, like other animals, will excrete nitrogenous compounds when they are fed a protein-free diet, because not all nitrogenous compounds can be recycled. We are then in *negative nitrogen balance*. The amount of protein an adult needs to stay in nitrogen balance is not easy to define because not all amino acids found in proteins, particularly plant proteins, are equally important for animal metabolism.

EXAMPLE 14.1 Why are plant proteins not as useful as animal proteins for dietary purposes?

Cereal proteins are only ~70% efficient for replacement purposes. The reason is that cereal proteins are deficient in lysine, an *essential amino acid* for humans. Thus a diet based on one source of protein, e.g., corn, can lead to malnutrition. A partial solution to the problem has been the breeding of high-lysine corn. Other plant proteins, particularly those from the pulses (beans and lentils), are deficient in the sulfur-containing amino acids. A successful vegetarian diet will be balanced in cereals and pulses.

The generally accepted amount of protein required to maintain nitrogen balance is 28 g day^{-1} for a 70 kg man; i.e., ~3.8 g of nitrogen. This is estimated by measuring the N excretion over 6–7 days on a protein-free diet. If the protein were coming from cereal, then the daily intake would have to be increased to ~40 g day^{-1} for a 70 kg man. The difference is due to the variable amounts of essential amino acids found in proteins. The amount required by growing children is larger; the accepted figure is ~0.6 g kg^{-1} day^{-1}.

Question: Is too much protein in the diet harmful?

Eskimos, who have a high protein intake, do have a shorter life span than Europeans, but there is no clear correlation of this with dietary protein.

Nitrogen Fixation

The fixation of nitrogen is the most fundamental biochemical process after photosynthesis. It is the process whereby *atmospheric nitrogen* is reduced to *ammonia*. Nitrogen fixation can be carried out by blue-green *algae*, some yeasts, and especially bacteria. The reduction of nitrogen

$$N_2 + 3H_2 \rightarrow 2NH_3 \qquad \Delta G^{O'} = -33.5 \text{ kJ mol}^{-1}$$

is a strongly *endothermic* reaction accomplished in the laboratory at high temperature (600°C) and pressure (1000 atm). The biological process occurs at 1 atm and 25°C. In bacterial systems, the reaction is catalyzed by the enzyme *nitrogenase*.

EXAMPLE 14.2   What are the sources of the energy and the electrons necessary for the reduction of nitrogen in biological systems?

The energy is provided by the hydrolysis of 12 ATP molecules. Eight electrons are required for the reduction of nitrogen, which is always accompanied by the evolution of H_2.

$$N_2 + 8e^- + 8H^+ \xrightarrow[]{16(ATP + H_2O) \quad 16(ADP + Pi)} 2NH_3 + H_2$$

The electrons can be supplied by several donors including NADH, flavoproteins, or NADPH.
Ultimately all higher organisms are dependent on this bacterially produced ammonia for their nitrogen metabolism.

Question: How do higher organisms obtain ammonia?

Many plants, particularly legumes (peas and beans), have a symbiotic relationship with nitrogen-fixing bacteria, which live in special nodules on the roots. There are about 14,000 species of leguminous plants, all of which have symbiotic bacteria of the genus *Rhizobium*. Some *insects* (termites and cockroaches) also have symbiotic nitrogen-fixing bacteria in their intestines.

Assimilation of Ammonia

Ammonia can be *condensed* with 2-oxoglutarate and thus converted to glutamate via the enzyme *glutamate dehydrogenase*; this enzyme is of highest activity in the liver and kidney. Glutamate is produced from 2-oxoglutarate and ammonia as follows:

$$NH_4^+ + \text{2-oxoglutarate} + NADPH \rightleftharpoons \text{glutamate} + NADP^+ + H_2O$$

Glutamate dehydrogenase can also use NADH. This reaction is freely reversible: the direction of *net flux* through the reaction is determined solely by the relative concentrations of the reactants. Thus, the reaction has two equally important functions: the assimilation of ammonia or the removal of ammonia from metabolites.

Glutamate is also produced in some bacteria via reactions catalyzed by the enzymes *glutamine synthetase* and *glutamate synthetase* acting together. *Glutamine synthetase*, as the name implies catalyzes the synthesis of glutamine, in virtually all organisms. In humans, it is particularly active in the liver; glutamine is transported from the liver to other tissues in the blood.

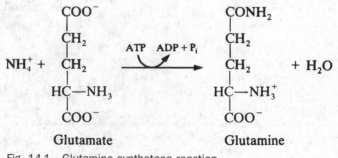

Fig. 14-1   Glutamine synthetase reaction.

Glutamate synthetase, which is not present in humans but is found in bacteria, catalyzes the formation of glutamate as follows.

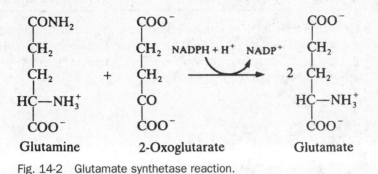

Fig. 14-2   Glutamate synthetase reaction.

This coupled enzyme system is used by blue-green algae and by *Rhizobium*. The amide group of glutamine provides the ammonia for the synthesis of many *N*-containing compounds, e.g., purines and pyrimidines.

Glutamate provides the amino group for the synthesis of many other amino acids through *transamination* reactions. This occurs in all cells. These amino acids are then used for protein synthesis and other aspects of nitrogen metabolism. The majority of animals are dependent on plant or animal proteins for fixed nitrogen for their nitrogen metabolism.

Transamination

This is the process whereby an amino group is reversibly transferred between an amino acid and a 2-oxoacid. The reaction is catalyzed by *aminotransferases*. These enzymes bind *pyridoxal phosphate* as a *coenzyme*. Pyridoxal phosphate and *pyridoxamine phosphate* are the coenzyme forms of *vitamin B_6*.

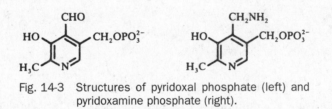

Fig. 14-3   Structures of pyridoxal phosphate (left) and pyridoxamine phosphate (right).

Question: What is the role of the coenzyme in transamination?

The aldehyde group of pyridoxal phosphate accepts the amine group from an amino acid by formation of a Schiff base (Chap. 1). In this process the amino acid is converted to a 2-oxoacid, and pyridoxal phosphate is converted to pyridoxamine phosphate. The amine group on pyridoxamine phosphate can be transferred to another 2-oxoacid, converting it to an amino acid. In this second reaction, the pyridoxamine phosphate is reconverted to pyridoxal phosphate.

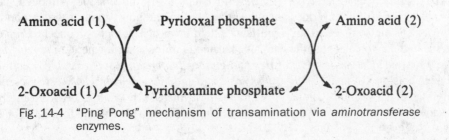

Fig. 14-4   "Ping Pong" mechanism of transamination via *aminotransferase* enzymes.

The overall reaction is

$$\text{Aminoacid (1)} + \text{2-Oxoacid (2)} \rightleftharpoons \text{2-Oxoacid (1)} + \text{Amino acid (2)}$$

2-Oxoglutarate is the normal acceptor of the amine group. In the aminotransferase reaction, 2-oxoglutarate is transaminated to give glutamate. There are at least 14 different *aminotransferases* in humans, but their specificities are not all known. The most important are *aspartate aminotransferase* which has high affinity for the compounds in the following reaction (Fig. 14-5):

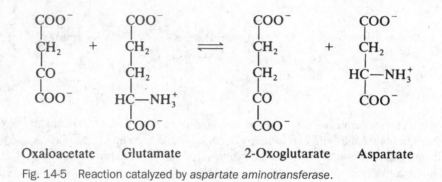

Fig. 14-5   Reaction catalyzed by *aspartate aminotransferase*.

and *alanine aminotransferase* which catalyzes the formation of alanine from pyruvate (Fig. 14-6):

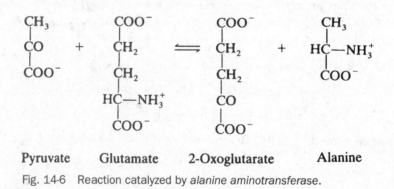

Fig. 14-6   Reaction catalyzed by *alanine aminotransferase*.

EXAMPLE 14.3   Aspartate aminotransferase and alanine aminotransferase are released into the blood when tissues are damaged. For example, they are used as diagnostic tools when heart or liver damage has occurred, such as after a *heart attack* (myocardial infarct) or in *hepatitis*, respectively. Following tissue damage and cell death, these enzymes (and others) are released into the blood. Damage to heart muscle is further characterized by the presence of *creatine kinase* (Sec. 13.12) in the plasma.

The in vivo significance of the *aminotransferases* is not always understood. Although specific *aminotransferases* exist for histidine, serine, phenylalanine, and methionine, none of the carbon backbones of these amino acids is metabolized to any significant extent in vivo. The highest concentration of the *aminotransferases* is in the cytoplasm, but they are also located in mitochondria where *glutamate dehydrogenase* is exclusively located. The *aminotransferases* and *glutamate dehydrogenase* catalyze central reactions in amino acid metabolism. The major *aminotransferases* and *glutamate dehydrogenase* are present in all tissues in relatively high concentrations compared with other enzymes, such as those involved in glycolysis. The reversible nature of both reactions allows a rapid exchange of amino groups and formation of 2-oxoacids as follows (Fig. 14-7):

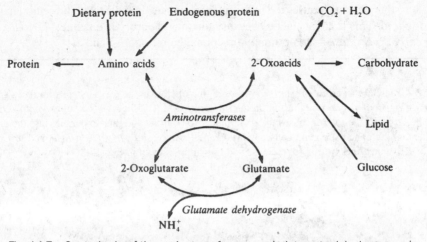

Fig. 14-7   Central role of the *aminotransferases* and *glutamate dehydrogenase* in nitrogen metabolism in humans.

Question: How does the scheme in Fig. 14-7 operate in starvation?

In starvation (or fasting), both protein and carbohydrate may be in short supply. The *net* effect is that endogenous proteins (from muscles) are hydrolyzed, releasing amino acids for protein synthesis and for oxidation to provide energy. The 2-oxoacids produced by the *aminotransferases* either enter gluconeogenesis (Chap. 13) or undergo *respiration* (Chap. 10) and are metabolized to CO_2 and H_2O. The amount of stored lipid and glycogen determines the extent of net degradation of endogenous protein. *Glutamate dehydrogenase*, again, catalyzes the release of ammonia from amino groups as the amino acids are broken down.

14.2   Digestion of Proteins

Dietary protein is the principal source of fixed nitrogen in higher animals. Digestion is the process whereby proteins are hydrolyzed to peptides and amino acids, which are absorbed from the lumen of the small intestine. The hydrolysis is enzyme-catalyzed and is brought about by a series of hydrolytic enzymes in the stomach and the small intestine. These enzymes are known collectively as *proteolytic enzymes* or *proteases* and belong to the class of enzymes called hydrolases (Chap. 5). The *proteases* differ in their substrate specificities, which are broad.

Zymogens

The proteolytic enzymes are secreted in the gastric juice or from the *pancreas* as inactive precursors called *zymogens*. In the case of *trypsin*, one of the pancreatic enzymes, the zymogen *trypsinogen* is synthesized on the *endoplasmic reticulum* and secreted in a zymogen granule. This is produced in the Golgi apparatus and consists of trypsinogen molecules surrounded by a lipid-protein membrane. The zymogen granules are secreted into a duct leading into the duodenum. The pancreas also produces a *trypsin inhibitor* that ensures that the pancreatic cells are not autodigested.

EXAMPLE 14.4   In the disease *pancreatitis* that occasionally follows a bout of mumps, the proteolytic enzymes secreted by the pancreas are prematurely activated and digest the cells of the pancreas itself.

The entry of protein into the stomach stimulates the release of a hormone, *gastrin*, into the bloodstream, which then causes the release of hydrochloric acid from the *parietal cells* and *pepsinogen* from the *chief cells*. *Pepsinogen* is another zymogen (the names all start with *pro-* or end in *-ogen*) that is converted in the gastric juice to the active form *pepsin*.

Question: What is the function of hydrochloric acid in digestion?

Hydrochloric acid lowers the pH of the stomach contents to pH ~2, and this causes the release of another hormone, secretin, from the cells of the small intestine into the bloodstream when the stomach contents pass into the small intestine. Secretin causes the release of bicarbonate in the pancreatic secretion that neutralizes the hydrochloric acid. This is advantageous because the main hydrolytic enzymes—*trypsin*, *chymotrypsin*, *elastase*, and *carboxypeptidase*—are optimally functional between pH 7 and 8.

EXAMPLE 14.5   There are a variety of *peptide hormones* that operate in the gut: *gastrin* stimulates gastric acid (HCl) secretion; *secretin* and *somatostatin* inhibit the production of gastrin. *Cholecystokinin* and *somatostatin* inhibit gastric acid secretion directly, and the former causes the gall bladder to contract and thus expel bile into the duodenum.

In the duodenum, the pancreatic zymogens *trypsinogen, chymotrypsinogen, proelastase*, and *procarboxypeptidase* are converted to active enzymes by enteropeptidase and trypsin, as shown in Fig. 14.8.

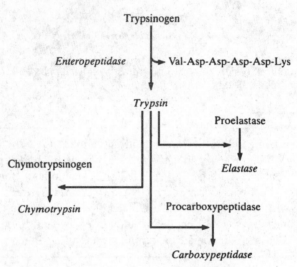

Fig. 14-8   Activation of pancreatic zymogens.

The activation of all the zymogens involves cleavage of peptide bonds and release of peptides, enabling conformational changes and formation of a functional active site.

Question: What is the actual sequence of chemical events involved in zymogen activation?

Trypsinogen, chymotrypsinogen, proelastase, and *procarboxypeptidase* are all synthesized as single polypeptide chains of around 25–30 kDa. The initial step in the activation is the hydrolysis of a hexapeptide from the N terminus of *trypsinogen*. This hydrolysis produces trypsin and is catalyzed by *enteropeptidase* (Fig. 14-8), an enzyme on the membranes of brush border cells of the small intestine.

Question: How are zymogens other than trypsinogen activated?

The activation has been studied in detail; that of chymotrypsinogen is shown in Fig. 14-9.

Chymotrypsinogen, a single polypeptide chain of 245 amino acid residues, is eventually converted to α-chymotrypsin, which has three polypeptide chains linked by two of the five disulfide bonds present in the *primary structure* of *chymotrypsinogen*. Also π- and δ-*chymotrypsin* have proteolytic activity (Fig. 14-9). In contrast, the conversion of *procarboxypeptidase* to *carboxypeptidase* involves the hydrolytic removal of a single amino acid.

Specificity of Proteases

Theoretically there are $20 \times 20 = 400$ possible different combinations of amino acid residues adjacent to one another in a polypeptide. If each possible combination needed a specific protease, then 400 different proteolytic enzymes would be required. However, the proteolytic enzymes have broad specificities, largely confined to groups of amino acids with similar side chain geometries, and therefore only a few different types of enzyme are encountered.

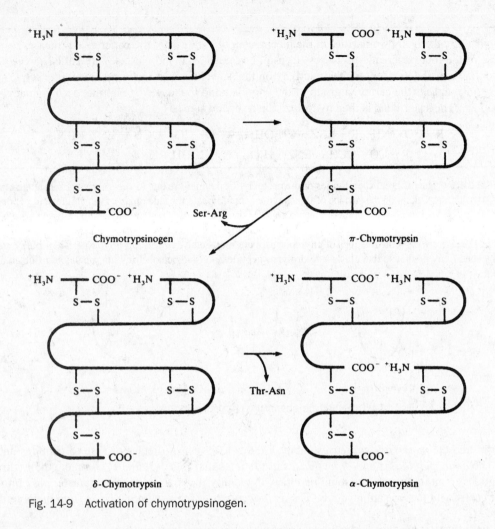

Fig. 14-9   Activation of chymotrypsinogen.

Question: What determines the substrate specificities of the proteolytic enzymes?

   Proteolytic enzymes all catalyze the hydrolysis of peptide bonds as follows:

$$R\text{—}CO\text{—}NH\text{—}R' \rightleftharpoons R\text{—}COO^- + NH_3 + \text{—}R'$$

   The specificities are determined by the side chains of the amino acids on either side of the peptide (or amide) bond that is hydrolyzed in the polypeptide chain. For the *endopeptidases*, it is the side chain of the amino acid contributing the *carbonyl* group of the peptide bond that determines whether the substrate will bind. Thus, chymotrypsin hydrolyzes peptide bonds where the carbonyl group is from one of the *aromatic* amino acids, namely, phenylalanine, tyrosine, or tryptophan. The specificities are listed in Table 14-1.

Table 14-1   Specificity of Proteolytic Enzymes

Enzyme	Specificity
Pepsin	Phe, Tyr, Trp; also, Leu, Glu, Gln
Trypsin	Lys, Arg
Chymotrypsin	Phe, Tyr, Trp
Carboxypeptidase	A bulky, nonpolar, carboxy-terminal residue
Elastase	Ala, Gly, Ser
Aminopeptidase	Any amino-terminal residue except proline

Question: Are there any similarities in the mechanism of catalysis of the pancreatic proteases?

Three of the four pancreatic proteases (trypsin, chymotrypsin, and elastase) are called *serine proteases* because they are all dependent for their activity on the side chain of a *serine* residue in the active site. This serine residue attacks the carbonyl group of the peptide bond to cleave the peptide, giving an acyl-enzyme intermediate. This ester bond is then hydrolyzed in a second step:

$$R—CO—NH—R + ENZ—CH_2OH \rightleftharpoons R—CO—OCH_2—ENZ + RNH_2$$

$$R—CO—OCH_2—ENZ + H_2O \rightarrow R—COOH + ENZ—CH_2OH$$

EXAMPLE 14.6   The different specificities of the proteolytic enzymes are due to *specificity pockets* at the binding site (Fig. 14-10). These pockets on the surface of the enzyme accommodate the side chain of the amino acid residue located on the carbonyl side of the scissile bond of the substrate. In trypsin, a *serine* residue present in chymotrypsin is replaced by an *aspartate* residue. This allows the binding of cationic *arginine* and *lysine* residues instead of bulky aromatic side chains. In elastase, two *glycine* residues of chymotrypsin are replaced by *valine* and *threonine*. Their bulky side chains block the specificity pocket so that elastase hydrolyzes peptide bonds adjacent to smaller, uncharged side chains.

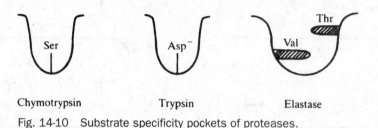

Fig. 14-10   Substrate specificity pockets of proteases.

Pepsin and the *pancreatic proteases* catalyze the conversion of dietary protein to peptides and amino acids. The *aminopeptidases* and *dipeptidases* in the intestinal mucosa almost complete the hydrolysis of the peptides to amino acids, but some peptides, especially those containing glutamate, pass into the gut mucosal cells with the free amino acids. The *aminopeptidases* remove amino acids from the N terminus of a peptide.

The hydrolysis of proteins in the process of digestion is summarized in Fig. 14-11.

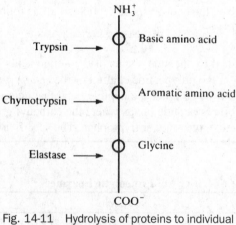

Fig. 14-11   Hydrolysis of proteins to individual
amino acids in digestion.

Amino Acid Transport

Amino acids, dipeptides, and some tripeptides are transported from the lumen of the small intestine through the membrane of the absorptive cells of the brush border, where the peptides are hydrolyzed to amino acids. *Transport of peptides and amino acids is active* and analogous to glucose transport in the intestine; i.e., they are transported by specific protein carriers, together with Na^+ across the cell membrane and they are called *sodium symporters*.

A concentration gradient exists between the gut lumen and the cell that is maintained by Na, K-ATPase. The Na^+ concentration is lower in the cell than in the gut lumen, ensuring that the amino acids and peptides will be transported across the membrane even though their concentration gradient might be in the opposite direction. There are at least seven different protein carriers involved in the transport of the full range of amino acids.

EXAMPLE 14.7   How do seven carriers transport 20 different amino acids? The carriers have overlapping specificities. Thus there is one carrier (called *system L*) for leucine and neutral amino acids with branched or aromatic side chains, another for basic amino acids (the *Ly system*), and a low-activity carrier (the *dicarboxylate system*) for dicarboxylic amino acids.

Some of the amino acids diffuse into the bloodstream where they are transported to the liver and elsewhere. Others, particularly glutamate, glutamine, aspartate, and asparagine, are metabolized by the cells for energy.

Amino Acid Synthesis

RNA base-triplet codes (codons) exist for the 20 amino acids that are normally involved in protein synthesis (Chap. 9). The special cases of selenocysteine and pyrrolysine are worth noting too, but only a few proteins have these strange amino acids in their sequences. The ability of an organism to live and grow is dependent upon protein synthesis and hence on a supply of all the amino acids. Higher plants are able to synthesize all 22 amino acids, but many microorganisms and higher animals can only make considerably fewer. Specifically, humans make 10 of the 22 amino acids; the remainder must be supplied in the diet, usually in the form of plant or animal protein. These amino acids that are essential for us to survive are termed the *essential amino acids*. Those that we synthesize are called the *nonessential amino acids*. The essential and nonessential amino acids are listed in Table 14-2.

Table 14-2   Nonessential and Essential Amino Acids for Humans

Nonessential	Essential
Glutamate	Isoleucine
Glutamine	Leucine
Proline	Lysine
Aspartate	Methionine
Asparagine	Phenylalanine
Alanine	Threonine
Glycine	Tryptophan
Serine	Valine
Tyrosine	Arginine
Cysteine	Histidine

Question: On what are the precursor molecules of the nonessential amino acids dependent?

The synthesis depends on the availability of the appropriate *carbon skeletons* and a source of *ammonia*. Glucose is primarily the source of the carbon skeleton for most of the nonessential amino acids. Two of the essential amino acids are used to form nonessential amino acids. These are *phenylalanine* and *methionine* which are used to synthesize *tyrosine* and *cysteine*, respectively. As ammonia is available in the fed state, amino acids become essential to our diet when we are not able to synthesize their carbon skeletons.

Production of 2-Oxoacids for Amino Acid Synthesis

Certain 2-oxoacids are necessary for the synthesis of the nonessential amino acids; they are listed in Table 14-3.

Four of the amino acids—*alanine, aspartate, glutamate,* and *serine*—are formed by *transamination* of their corresponding oxoacids. The other nonessential amino acids are then derived from these four amino acids.

Table 14-3   2-Oxoacids that are Precursors of the Nonessential Amino Acids

2-Oxoacid	Amino Acid
Pyruvate	Alanine
Oxalacetate	Aspartate, asparagine
2-Oxoglutarate	Glutamate, glutamine
	Proline, arginine
Pyruvate, 3-hydroxy pyruvate	Serine

Arginine

Arginine is synthesized from aspartate and ornithine during the formation of urea. *Argininosuccinate synthetase* and *argininosuccinate lyase* catalyze the condensation and cleavage reactions, respectively, that result in the formation of arginine.

Serine

Serine is formed from the glycolytic intermediate 3-phosphoglycerate (Fig. 14-12). Serine is also synthesized from glycine in a reaction catalyzed by *serine hydroxymethyltransferase*:

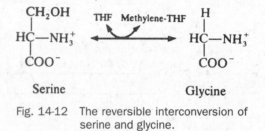

Serine   Glycine

Fig. 14-12   The reversible interconversion of serine and glycine.

N^5,N^{10}-Methylenetetrahydrofolate (methylene-THF) is one of the *folic acid* coenzymes. Note that this reaction is readily reversible; in fact, net flux is usually in the direction of *glycine* synthesis. Thus this amino acid can arise from glucose, and it does so via serine.

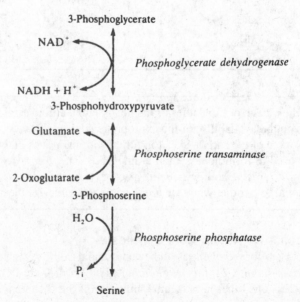

Fig. 14-13   The major pathway of serine synthesis.

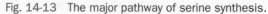

Synthesis of Tyrosine and Cysteine

Two of the *nonessential* amino acids, tyrosine and cysteine, are *derived from essential amino acids* and may be considered to be breakdown products of them, as they are intermediates in the normal degradation pathway of these amino acids. Provided sufficient quantities of the two essential amino acids, *phenylalanine* and *methionine*, are available in the diet, then *net synthesis* of tyrosine and cysteine occur.

Tyrosine

Tyrosine is synthesized from phenylalanine in a reaction that is catalyzed by *phenylalanine hydroxylase*, which catalyzes two reactions as follows. The reducing power for the reaction comes from NADPH, and the oxygen comes from molecular oxygen.

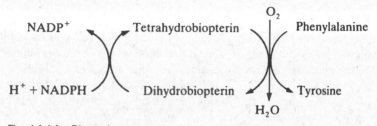

Fig. 14-14   Biopterin as a redox intermediate in the oxidation of phenylalanine to tyrosine.

The overall reaction is

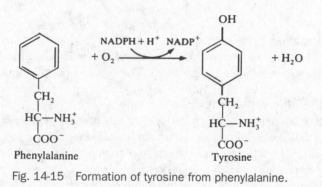

Fig. 14-15   Formation of tyrosine from phenylalanine.

EXAMPLE 14.8   The first enzyme activity (*dihydrobiopterin reductase*) in Fig. 14-14 catalyzes the transfer of hydrogen to *dihydrobiopterin* which is thereby reduced to *tetrahydrobiopterin*. The second enzyme activity is a *hydroxylase* containing two Fe^{3+} atoms, and this catalyzes the reduction of O_2 such that one oxygen atom is incorporated into phenylalanine to form tyrosine, and the second is incorporated into water. At the same time tetrahydrobiopterin is oxidized to dihydrobiopterin. Phenylalanine hydroxylase is an example of a *mixed-function oxidase*. A deficiency of phenylalanine hydroxylase results in an accumulation of phenylalanine which is not converted to tyrosine but is excreted as *phenylpyruvate*. This pathological condition is known as *phenylketonuria* and is associated with severe mental retardation.

Biopterin, like folic acid, contains a pterin ring.

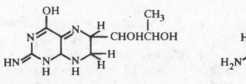
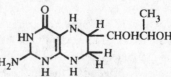

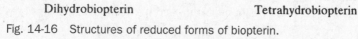

Dihydrobiopterin   Tetrahydrobiopterin

Fig. 14-16   Structures of reduced forms of biopterin.

Cysteine

Cysteine is synthesized from homocysteine (see Sec. 14.5) and serine. Condensation of these two amino acids produces cystathionine that is cleaved to produce cysteine.

14.3 Dynamics of Amino Acid Metabolism

In addition to being synthesized or produced by the hydrolysis of dietary protein, amino acids are released by the hydrolysis of tissue proteins, e.g., intestinal mucosa and muscle. Amino acids enter protein synthesis (Chap. 9); they also enter gluconeogenesis, lipogenesis, or are degraded to provide energy, as well as being used for synthesizing compounds such as *purines*, *pyrimidines*, and *porphyrins*. They are precursors of specialized metabolites such as *epinephrine* and *creatine* (Fig. 13-29).

This metabolic activity is achieved by a turnover of amino acids and proteins that is as rapid as that of lipids and carbohydrates. In an adult human ~400 g of body proteins is turned over each day. Of this ~50 g replaces digestive enzymes and ~15 g replaces hemoglobin. The amino acid concentration in plasma is small (total 3.2 mM, of which ~25% is glutamine); but the turnover of ~400 g day^{-1} of protein is equal to the uptake and release back into the plasma of 4.6 mol of α-amino-N, so that the average lifetime of an amino acid in the plasma is ~5 min. Plasma amino acids are turned over with the same kind of rapidity as plasma glucose or free fatty acids. Like plasma glucose, the plasma amino acid concentration is remarkably constant, but it is not understood how this is regulated.

14.4 Pyrimidine and Purine Metabolism

The synthesis of nucleotides is important not only because of the crucial role nucleic acids play in protein synthesis and in the storage of genetic information, but also because of the role nucleotides such as FAD, NAD(P)H, CoASH, cAMP, and UDP-glucose play in metabolism.

Biosynthesis of Pyrimidine Nucleotides

The atoms of the pyrimidine ring are derived from *carbamoyl phosphate* and *aspartate*; the de novo biosynthesis of pyrimidine nucleotides is shown in Fig. 14-17. The first completely formed pyrimidine ring is that of *dihydroorotate*. Only after oxidation to *orotate* is the ribose attached to produce orotidylate. The compound 5-phosphoribosyl 1-pyrophosphate (P-Rib-PP) provides the ribose phosphate. L-Glutamine is used as a substrate, donating nitrogen atoms at reactions 1 and 9, catalyzed by *carbamoyl phosphate synthetase II* and *CTP synthetase*, respectively; a second amino acid, L-aspartate, is a substrate for reaction 2, catalyzed by *aspartate transcarbamoylase*. P-Rib-PP is an activator of carbamoyl phosphate synthetase II and a substrate for reaction 5, which is catalyzed by *orotate phosphoribosyltransferase*.

The end product of the pathway, UTP, is a potent inhibitor of carbamoyl phosphate synthetase II, and the substrate, ATP, also activates this enzyme. The enzymic activity of carbamoyl phosphate synthetase II is low relative to subsequent enzymes in the pathway (Fig. 14-17), and under normal conditions, flux through the de novo pathway may be regulated by cellular levels of P-Rib-PP, UTP, and ATP; i.e., carbamoyl phosphate synthetase II catalyzes the reaction that has the highest *control coefficient* (Chap. 5) in the pathway.

There are two multifunctional proteins in the pathway for de novo biosynthesis of pyrimidine nucleotides. A *trifunctional* protein, called *dihydroorotate synthetase* (or *CAD*, where the letters are the initials of the three enzymic activities), catalyzes reactions 1, 2, and 3 of the pathway (HCO$_3^-$ → CAP → CA-asp → DHO in Fig. 14-17). The activities of carbamoyl phosphate synthetase, aspartate transcarbamoylase, and dihydroorotase are contained in discrete globular domains of a single polypeptide chain of 243 kDa, where they are covalently connected by segments of polypeptide which are susceptible to digestion by proteases such as trypsin.

A *bifunctional enzyme, UMP synthase*, catalyzes reactions 5 and 6 of the pyrimidine pathway (orotate → OMP → UMP; Fig. 14-7). Two enzymic activities, those of *orotate phosphoribosyltransferase* and *OMP decarboxylase*, are contained in a single protein of 51.5 kDa that associates as a dimer.

Dihydroorotase dehydrogenase, the enzyme that catalyzes the dehydrogenation of dihydroorotate to orotate (reaction 4 of the pathway; Fig. 14-17), is located on the outer side of the inner mitochondrial membrane. This enzyme has FAD as a prosthetic group, and in mammals electrons are passed from it to ubiquinone (Fig. 10-17).

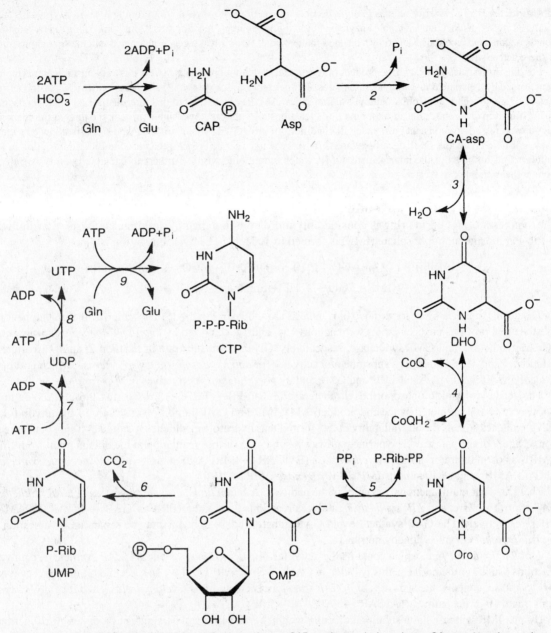

Fig. 14-17   De novo pyrimidine biosynthetic pathway. CAP, carbamoyl phosphate; CA-asp, *N*-carbamoyl-L-aspartate; DHO, L-dihydroorotate; Oro, orotate; OMP, orotidine-5′-monophosphate. Enzymes: (1) carbamoyl phosphate synthetase II; (2) aspartate transcarbamoylase; (3) dihydroorotase; (4) dihydroorotate dehydrogenase; (5) orotate phosphoribosyltransferase; (6) OMP decarboxylase; (7) nucleoside monophosphate kinase; (8) nucleoside diphosphate kinase; (9) CTP synthetase.

The de novo pyrimidine pathway is thus *compartmentalized*; dihydroorotate synthesized by trifunctional DHO synthetase in the cytosol passes across the *outer* mitochondrial membrane to be oxidized to orotate, which in turn passes back to the cytosol where it is a substrate of the bifunctional UMP synthase.

Mammalian cells contain two carbamoyl phosphate synthetases: the *glutamine-dependent enzyme* (*CPSase II*) which is part of CAD and an ammonia-dependent enzyme (*CPSase I*) which is localized in the mitochondrial matrix and which is used in urea and arginine biosynthesis. Under certain conditions (e.g., hyperammonemia), carbamoyl phosphate synthesized in the matrix by CPSase I may enter pyrimidine biosynthesis in the cytoplasm.

EXAMPLE 14.9   In bacteria, such as *E. coli*, the first six reactions of the de novo pyrimidine pathway (Fig. 14-7) are catalyzed by six distinct and separable enzymes; but in higher animals, reactions 1, 2, and 3 are catalyzed by a trifunctional enzyme, and reactions 5 and 6 by a bifunctional enzyme. What advantages might there be in the spatial proximity of these active sites?

For dihydroorotate synthetase, the product of reaction 1, carbamoyl phosphate (CAP), is very unstable but is rapidly transformed by aspartate transcarbamoylase that is 50 times more active (per active site) than carbamoyl phosphate synthetase. High concentrations of carbamoyl aspartate (CA-asp) may be toxic, but this intermediate is rapidly consumed by the high dihydroorotase. Because the first three reactions are catalyzed by a single protein, the three different active sites are expressed in a constant ratio under all conditions of growth; this maintains CAP and CA-asp at low concentrations. For UMP synthase, OMP decarboxylase is far more active (per active site) than orotate PRTase, resulting in low cellular concentrations of the intermediate, OMP, which would otherwise be subject to enzymic hydrolysis (in cells from higher animals).

Biosynthesis of Purine Nucleotides

The synthesis of the purine ring is considerably more complex than pyrimidine synthesis. Starting with P-Rib-PP, inosine monophosphate (IMP) is formed in 10 steps. The overall reaction is

$$P\text{-Rib-PP} + 2Gln + Gly + 2,10\text{-formyl THF} + HCO_3^- + Asp + 4ATP$$
$$\rightarrow IMP + 2Glu + 2THF + fumarate + 4ADP + PP_I$$

The details of the pathway for de novo biosynthesis are shown in Fig. 14-18. The amino acid L-glutamine is the substrate that provides nitrogen atoms for reactions 1, 4, and 14, catalyzed by *amido phosphoribosyltransferase*, FGAM synthetase, and GMP synthetase, respectively. Glycine is a substrate in reaction 2, and L-aspartate in reactions 7 and 11. P-Rib-PP is a substrate and activator for *amido phosphoribosyltransferase*, which is subject to *feedback inhibition* by AMP, IMP, and GMP and by *polyglutamate* derivatives of *dihydrofolate*.

The activity of amido phosphoribosyltransferase (P-Rib-PP → PRA) is low so flux through the de novo pathway in vivo is regulated by the end products AMP, IMP, and GMP. Inhibition of reaction 1 by dihydrofolate polyglutamates signals the unavailability of N^{10}-formyl tetrahydrofolate, which is required as a substrate in reactions 3 and 9 of the pathway. The purine pathway is subject to further regulation at the branch point from IMP; XMP is a potent inhibitor of *IMP cyclohydrolase* (FAICAR → IMP), AMP inhibits *adenylosuccinate synthetase* (IMP → AMP), and GMP inhibits *IMP dehydrogenase* (IMP → XMP).

There are four multifunctional enzymes in the pathway: A *trifunctional enzyme* consisting of *GAR synthetase, GAR transformylase*, and *AIR synthetase* catalyzes reactions 2, 3, and 5 (PRA → GAR → FGAR, FGAM → AIR), respectively. The GAR synthetase and GAR transformylase domains may be separated by digestion of the *trifunctional* enzyme with chymotrypsin.

A *bifunctional* enzyme, which contains the activities of *AIR carboxylase* and *SAICAR synthetase*, catalyzes reactions 6 and 7 of the purine pathway (AIR → CAIR → SAICAR; Fig. 14-18). A second bifunctional enzyme, *IMP synthase*, contains the activities of *AICAR transformylase* and *IMP cyclohydrolase*, and it catalyzes reactions 9 and 10 of the pathway (AICAR → FAICAR → IMP).

Human IMP synthase has a subunit molecular weight of 62.1 kDa and associates as a dimer. A trifunctional enzyme, *C_1-THF synthase*, containing N^5,N^{10}-methenyl tetrahydrofolate (5,10-CH-THF) cyclohydrolase and N^{10}-formyl tetrahydrofolate (10-CHO-THF) synthetase, catalyzes the reactions 5,10-CH$_2$-THF → 5,10-CH-THF and THF → 10-CHO-THF. The N^{10}-CH-THF produced is a substrate for GAR and AICAR transformylases catalyzing reactions 3 and 9 of the pathway. In higher eukaryotes, the dehydrogenase and cyclohydrolase activities are located in one domain of the protein, which is fused to a larger synthetase domain, forming a *trifunctional* enzyme.

There is a fifth bifunctional enzyme that catalyzes reactions 8 and 12 of the purine pathway, but *adenylosuccinate lyase* has *one* active site with dual specificity, catalyzing both reactions (SAICAR → AICAR, sAMP → AMP). All 14 enzymic activities of Fig. 14-18 are *cytosolic*, and there is a variety of evidence for association of subsets of these activities in vivo.

The existence of a "pathway particle" or "metabolon" for de novo purine biosynthesis in intact cells has been proposed.

EXAMPLE 14.10   There is evidence for the existence of a metabolon for de novo purine biosynthesis that contains the 14 enzymes of the pathway (Fig. 14-18) and four additional enzymes that are involved in the synthesis of N^{10}–formyl tetrahydrofolate.

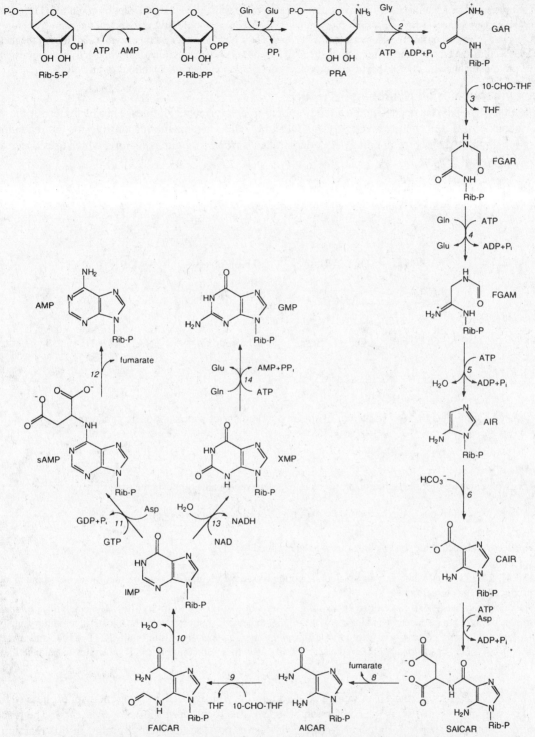

Fig. 14-18 De novo purine biosynthetic pathway. Rib-5-P, ribose 5-phosphate; P-Rib-PP, 5-phosphoribosyl 1-pyrophosphate; PRA, 5-phosphoribosylamine; 10-CHO-FH$_4$, N^{10}-formyl tetrahydrofolate; GAR, glycineamide ribotide; FGAR, *N*-formylglycineamide ribotide; FGAM. *N*-formylglycineamidine ribotide; AIR, 5-aminoimidazole ribotide; CAIR, 4-carboxy-5-aminoimidazole ribotide; SAICAR, *N*-succino-5-aminoimidazole-4-carboxamide ribotide; AICAR, 5-aminoimidazole-4-carboxamide ribotide; FAICAR, 5-formamidoimidazole-4-carboxamide ribotide; sAMP, *N*-succino-AMP. Enzymes: (1) amido phosphoribosyltransferase; (2) GAR synthetase; (3) GAR transformylase; (4) EGAM synthetase; (5) AIR synthetase; (6) AIR carboxylase; (7) SAICAR synthetase; (8) adenylosuccinase; (9) AICAR transformylase; (10) IMP cyclohydrolase; (11) sAMP cyclohydrolase; (12) adenylosuccinase; (13) IMP dehydrogenase; (14) GMP synthetase.

Possible selective advantages of this association of catalytic sites in the course of evolution could be: (1) *channeling* of unstable intermediates, such as phosphoribosylamine (PRA), between successive enzymes of the pathway before they diffuse away from the confines of the metabolon; (2) *coordinated regulation* of several enzymic activities of the metabolon by effectors that bind at a single regulatory site; and (3) *coordinated expression* of enzymic activities expressed in a single protein, maintaining their catalytic activities in a constant ratio under all conditions of growth.

Deoxyribonucleotide Synthesis

The synthesis of DNA is dependent on a ready supply of deoxyribonucleotides. The substrates for these are the ribonucleoside diphosphates ADP, GDP, CDP, and UDP. The enzyme responsible for the reduction of these substrates to their corresponding *deoxy* derivatives is *ribonucleotide reductase*, which uses *thioredoxin* as a *cosubstrate*.

EXAMPLE 14.11 Thioredoxin is a protein of 12 kDa that donates two electrons by the oxidation of two *cysteine sulfhydryl* groups to cystine. Oxidized thioredoxin is reduced by NADPH.

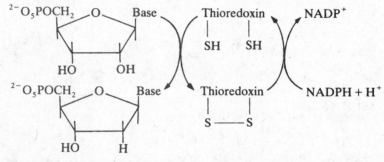

Fig. 14-19   Reduction of the ribosyl moiety of a nucleotide to make a deoxynucleotide.

The overall reaction for the synthesis of, for example, deoxyadenosine diphosphate (dATP) is

$$ATP + NADPH + H^+ \rightarrow dATP + NADP^+ + H_2O$$

The deoxyribonucleoside diphosphates are phosphorylated by ATP.

EXAMPLE 14.12 How is the activity of ribonucleotide reductase regulated to ensure that the deoxyribonucleotides are produced in the correct ratio?

The enzyme contains two catalytic sites, two regulatory sites, and two specificity sites. The catalytic site binds the substrates, thioredoxin (reduced by NADPH + H$^+$), and the nucleoside diphosphates. The allosteric regulatory site binds ATP as an *activator* in competition with dATP as an *inhibitor*. The specificity site binds dGTP, dTTP, and dATP but not dCTP and modulates ribonucleotide reductase activity selectively for the four NDP substrates to balance the four dNTP pools.

Cells that are synthesizing DNA must also be able to synthesize deoxythymidine triphosphate (dTTP). The key step in the synthesis is the conversion of dUMP to dTMP *via thymidylate synthetase*. The reaction requires a source of N^5, N^{10}-*methylene tetrahydrofolate* to provide the methyl group. In this reaction the tetrahydrofolate is oxidized to dihydrofolate. Dihydrofolate is reduced to tetrahydrofolate via *dihydrofolate reductase* so more methylene N^5, N^{10}-tetrahydrofolate is made from serine in a reaction that is catalyzed by *serine hydroxymethyltransferase*. These three reactions, which are essential for the formation of dTMP, are shown in Fig. 14-20.

Salvage Synthesis of Nucleotides

The de novo synthesis of pyrimidines and purines, particularly purines, is energetically expensive so most (~80%) of the purines and pyrimidines obtained from the degradation of nucleic acids, particularly RNA, are salvaged for reuse. Human cells contain three *phosphoribosyltransferases* (PRTases) that convert *preformed*

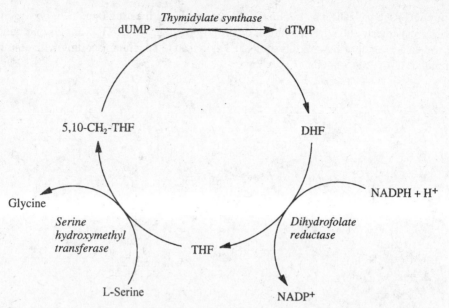

Fig. 14-20   Formation of dTMP from dUMP in a reaction that involves DHF and THF in methyl donation.

nucleobases to the equivalent nucleoside 5′-monophosphate (NMP). They are adenine-, hypoxanthine-guanine-, and orotate-(uracil) PRTase, respectively:

$$\text{Nucleobase} + \text{P-Rib-PP} \rightarrow \text{NMP} + \text{PPi}$$

P-Rib-PP is an activated form of ribose 5-phosphate (Rib-5-P). The equilibria of these reactions favor nucleobase + Rib-5-P, but the pyrophosphate (PPi) formed is hydrolyzed to phosphate by pyrophosphatase. Therefore, NMP is formed from the corresponding nucleobase.

While the PRTases salvage nucleobases within cells, nucleosides such as *adenosine* and *uridine* are present in the blood at much higher concentrations (~1 μM) than their corresponding nucleobases, adenine and uracil. Indeed, the brain synthesizes pyrimidine nucleotides (UTP and CTP) via salvage synthesis from uridine that is produced by the liver and released into the circulation. Human cells may contain at least three types of nonspecific nucleoside transporters; and nucleosides are taken up into the cells from the blood more rapidly than nucleobases.

Once inside the cell, nucleosides are converted to the corresponding NMP: adenosine by *adenosine kinase* and uridine by *uridine kinase*. The reaction is as follows:

$$\text{Nucleoside} + \text{ATP} \rightarrow \text{NMP} + \text{ADP}$$

EXAMPLE 14.13   In some diseases, excessive amounts of purines are produced in the body, leading to accumulation of urate. Patients with *Lesch-Nyhan syndrome* lack the enzyme hypoxanthine-guanine phosphoribosyl-transferase (HG-PRTase). Children born with this disorder are mentally retarded and prone to self-mutilation. They produce excessive amounts of purines due to accumulation of P-Rib-PP which stimulates the first enzyme of the purine synthesis pathway, amido PRTase (Fig. 14-18). Patients with Lesch-Nyhan syndrome may also suffer from gout, which is due to an accumulation of urate in the body with deposition of crystals of sodium urate in the joints and kidneys, or due to accumulation of P-Rib-PP for reasons other than a deficiency of HG-PRTase.

Nucleotide Antagonists as Anticancer Drugs

To grow and divide, cancer cells duplicate their chromosomes that are composed of deoxynucleoside 5′-monophosphates (dNMPs) polymerized into unique sequences. Cancer cells differ from normal body cells by growing more rapidly or by "cycling" and dividing continuously. Inhibitors of nucleotide biosynthesis have *selective toxicity* for such cancer cells due to a depletion or imbalance in the cellular stores of dNTPs that are required for DNA synthesis, which would be more pronounced than in normal cells. A selective depletion of one of the four dNTPs (e.g., dTTP) by treatment of cancer cells with a drug (e.g., *5-fluorouracil*) may cause the arrest of DNA synthesis and consequent cell death. Alternatively, if dTTP is not absent, but decreased in amount, the imbalance in the cellular pools of dNTPs may lead to genetic miscoding with consequent mutations that are fatal for the cancer cells.

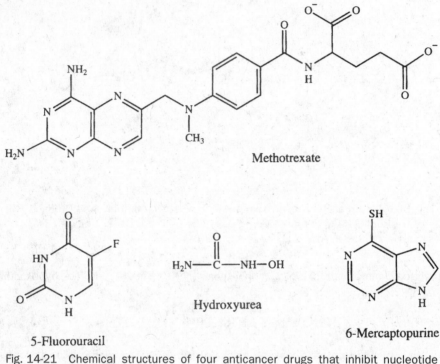

Fig. 14-21   Chemical structures of four anticancer drugs that inhibit nucleotide biosynthesis.

The chemical structures of four commonly used anticancer drugs are shown in Fig. 14-21. Methotrexate was the first highly specific anticancer drug. It was first synthesized in 1949 and has been in clinical use for the treatment of a variety of cancers since the early 1950s. It is a potent inhibitor of *dihydrofolate reductase* with an inhibition constant (K_i) for interaction with the enzyme of 10^{-9} M. Inhibition of this enzyme in a cell leads to dramatic accumulation of dihydrofolate (DHF) to concentrations around 2.5 μM, and minor decreases in tetrahydrofolate (THF). More marked decrease in THF may not be seen due to the release of bound THF in methotrexate-treated cells. The high concentrations of DHF are toxic to the cell, inhibiting the reaction catalyzed by thymidylate synthase,

$$dUMP + 5,10–CH_2–THF \rightarrow dTMP + DHF$$

and the first reaction of *de novo* purine biosynthesis catalyzed by amido PRTase,

$$P\text{-Rib-PP} + \text{L-glutamine} \rightarrow PRA + \text{L-glutamate} + PP_i$$

In leukemia cells treated with methotrexate, levels of dTTP decrease, and there may be less marked decreases in dATP and dGTP resulting from inhibition of amido PRTase. The consequent imbalance in nucleotide pools results in genetic miscoding and cell death.

EXAMPLE 14.14   Methotrexate remains an anticancer drug of major importance for *combination chemotherapy*. A number of mechanisms by which cancer cells gain resistance to methotrexate have been identified.
   (a) Amplification of the gene which encodes the target enzyme, dihydrofolate reductase.
   (b) Mutation of the folate transporter which translocates methotrexate into cells.

(c) Mutation of dihydrofolate reductase so that the binding of the substrate, dihydrofolate, is retained but the binding of methotrexate is weaker.

(d) Loss of activity of the enzyme *folylpolyglutamyl synthetase*; this enzyme adds a polyglutamyl tail to methotrexate, thus retaining it in the cancer cell.

Such methotrexate-resistant cells are found in cancer patients who had been given methotrexate as a single agent, where remission is followed by relapse with drug-resistant cancer.

5-Fluorouracil (FU) is also a very useful anticancer drug that is taken up by cells and metabolized in the following way:

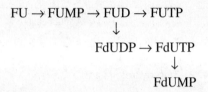

The primary mechanism of action of FU may be inhibition of thymidylate synthase (dUMP → dTMP) by 5-fluorodeoxy UMP (FdUMP). FdUMP binds to thymidylate synthase with the other substrate 5,10-CH$_2$-THF forming a tight *ternary complex*. A cysteine residue at the active site of the enzyme attacks the natural substrate, dUMP, forming a transient covalent bond. In FdUMP this bond cannot be broken due to the presence of the 5-fluoro group on the pyrimidine ring. Thymidylate synthase is thus permanently inactivated by this *suicide inhibitor*, with a consequent depletion of dTMP and thus dTTP in the cells. In addition, 5-fluorouracil may kill cancer cells by two other mechanisms: (1) FUTP that accumulates in cells may be incorporated into RNA, thus causing *genetic miscoding*; or (2) FdUMP may be incorporated into DNA, again leading to *fatal mutations*.

Hydroxyurea is a simple molecule (Fig. 14-21) which inhibits *ribonucleotide reductase*. This enzyme binds to the four NDPs—UDP, CDP, ADP, and GDP—as substrates and catalyzes their reduction to the corresponding dNDP. The mechanism of catalysis involves the formation of an unusual *tyrosyl radical cation* that induces the formation of a *radical* of the NDP substrate. Hydroxyurea *quenches* this tyrosyl radical cation intermediate, leading to depletion of all four dTNPs, which are required as substrates for the synthesis of DNA.

6-Mercaptopurine (MP; Fig. 14-21) is one of many drugs discovered by the Nobel Laureates Gertrude Elion and George Hitchings. MP was first synthesized in the early 1950s and remains a very useful anticancer drug. Like 5-fluorouracil, MP has several mechanisms of toxicity that vary from one cell type to another. MP enters cells and is metabolized in the following way:

MP → MP—MP → MP—DP → MP—TP
↓
MX—MP
↓
MGMP → MGDP
↓
MdGDP → MdGTP

The 6-mercaptopurine 5′-monophosphate (MP-MP) formed is a potent inhibitor of *amido PRTase*, and thus de novo purine biosynthesis (Fig. 14-18) is blocked. The 6-mercaptodeoxy GTP (MdGDP) is incorporated into DNA and causes genetic miscoding.

14.5   One-Carbon Compounds

Folic Acid Derivatives

Several processes described above use one-carbon derivatives of *tetrahydrofolic acid* (Fig. 14-22). E.g., the synthesis of the purine ring (Fig. 14-18) requires N^{10}-*formyl tetrahydrofolate*. Thymidylate synthetase, a key enzyme in pyrimidine synthesis, uses N^5,N^{10}-*methylene tetrahydrofolate* both as a donor of a methyl group and as a reducing agent. This compound is perhaps the most important in one-carbon metabolism; it is also involved in the synthesis of serine and glycine. All these compounds are derivatives of 5,6,7,8,-tetrahydrofolic acid, which is the reduced form of the vitamin folate (or folic acid).

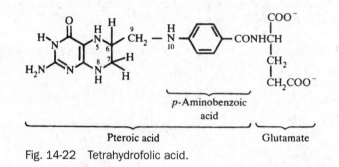

Fig. 14-22   Tetrahydrofolic acid.

The *pteroic acid* moiety of tetrahydrofolate consists of a reduced *pteridine ring* and p-aminobenzoic acid. Folic acid from the diet is absorbed by the intestinal mucosa, and in two enzymic steps is reduced to tetrahydrofolate which is the active form of the coenzyme. Mammals cannot synthesize folate; this normally does not present a problem because microorganisms of the intestinal tract do so in sufficient quantities. The two steps in the reduction of folic acid to tetrahydrofolate are catalyzed by *dihydrofolate reductase*. Both of these reactions require NADPH as a source of electrons.

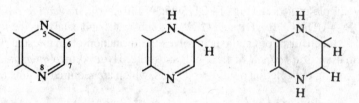

Fig. 14-23   Folate, dihydrofolate, and tetrahydrofolate.

To understand the bewildering array of reactions involving tetrahydrofolate, it is essential to realize that in biological systems, one-carbon compounds exist in *five* different oxidation states. The most *reduced* form is methane, CH_4, and the most *oxidized* form is CO_2. In between these two extremes are *methanol* (CH_3OH), *formaldehyde* (CH_2O), and *formate* ($HCOO^-$).

Question: Are all the above folate compounds involved in one-carbon metabolism?
    Methane and carbon dioxide are the exceptions. Methane is an end product of anerobic metabolism in many microorganisms, and carbon dioxide (for carboxylation) is handled by *biotin*-containing enzymes.

Table 14-4 lists the various one-carbon groups that are carried by tetrahydrofolate derivatives.

Table 14-4   Tetrahydrofolate (THF) Derivatives

Group carried	THF derivative
—CH_3	N^5-methyl THF
—CH_2OH	N^5,N^{10}-methylene THF
—CHO	N^5-formyl THF
—CH=	N^5,N^{10}-methenyl THF

These *C1 groups* may be attached to *N* atoms in positions 5 or 10 (Fig. 14-23) or may form a bridge between the two. N^5-Methyl THF is formed in mammals by a virtually irreversible reaction that is catalyzed by the enzyme *methylene THF reductase*; the other THF derivatives are interconverted through a series of oxidation-reduction and hydration-dehydration reactions.

$$N^5\text{-methyl THF} \rightarrow N^5,N^{10}\text{-methylene THF} \rightarrow N^5,N^{10}\text{-methenyl THF} \rightarrow N^{10}\text{-formyl THF}$$

Question: What is the major reaction that replenishes one-carbon units in THF?

With the exception of N^5-methyl THF, the THF derivatives are directly synthesized from a C1 unit in the appropriate oxidation state and THF. The major *anaplerotic* reaction is that catalyzed by *serine hydroxymethyltransferase*.

Biological Methylation

Many biochemical reactions involve the transfer of methyl groups. The introduction of a methyl group into a molecule is an important way of modifying biological activity, as in the case of *epinephrine* versus *norepinephrine*. The methyl groups originate from N^5-methyl tetrahydrofolate, although this compound is involved directly in only one methylation reaction. The simplest form of this reaction occurs in plants where it is catalyzed by the enzyme *homocysteine transmethylase*.

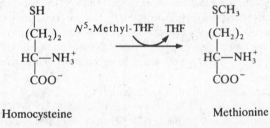

Homocysteine

Methionine

Fig. 14-24 Generation of methionine from homocysteine in plants.

The synthesis of methionine in mammals is more complex than in plants and requires *cobalamin*, a coenzyme form of vitamin B_{12}. Because methionine is an essential amino acid, it must be supplied in the diet; methionine that is used for methylation is converted to homocysteine, and this is *remethylated* to regenerate methionine. These reactions merely *recycle* methionine and do *not* constitute a means of *net* synthesis.

EXAMPLE 14.15 Vitamin B_{12} does not exist in plants, and strict vegetarians risk succumbing to vitamin B_{12} deficiency. Thus, humans are dependent on animal and bacterial sources for vitamin B_{12}.

Cobalamin is a complex molecule that contains an atom of cobalt (Co). In the mammalian synthesis of methionine, *cobalamin* acts as a coenzyme by accepting the methyl group from N^5-methyl THF and transferring it to homocysteine. The reaction is catalyzed by *cobalamin-N^5-methyl THF:homocysteine methyltransferase*. The overall reaction is (Fig. 14-25):

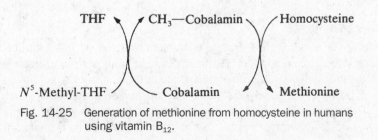

Fig. 14-25 Generation of methionine from homocysteine in humans using vitamin B_{12}.

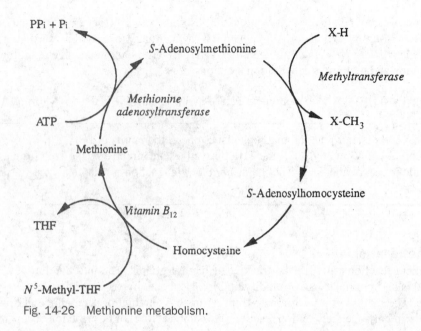

Fig. 14-26   Methionine metabolism.

EXAMPLE 14.16   Vitamin B_{12} deficiency results in the accumulation of N^5-methyl THF. N^5-Methyl THF is synthesized in mammals via an irreversible reaction (as shown in Fig. 14-26); if it cannot be utilized because of a deficiency of vitamin B_{12}, then it accumulates. This causes a depletion of the other forms of THF, resulting in a deficiency of THF.

     Megaloblastic anemia (pernicious anaemia) results from a deficiency of cobalamin and THF.

     The methyl group on methionine is activated when methionine is converted to *S-adenosylmethionine*. It is the methyl group of *S-adenosylmethionine* that is the immediate donor in biological methylations. Important reactions in which *S*-adenosylmethionine acts as the methyl donor are the syntheses of creatine, *epinephrine*, and phosphatidyl choline.

EXAMPLE 14.17   Creatine is synthesized in the liver and transported in the blood to skeletal muscle where it enters the cells and is converted, by creatine kinase and ATP, to creatine phosphate (Fig. 13-29). The reaction is reversible so that creatine phosphate, during muscle activity, produces ATP. Creatine is synthesized from guanidinioacetate (which is synthesized from glycine and arginine).

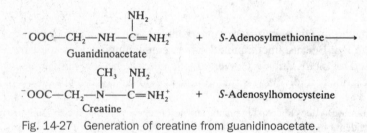

Fig. 14-27   Generation of creatine from guanidinoacetate.

     The carbon skeleton of homocysteine is salvaged and used to synthesize methionine. Alternatively, homocysteine is used to synthesize cysteine.

14.6   Porphyrin Synthesis

The synthesis and turnover of porphyrins that are precursors of heme are important because of the central role of heme proteins, hemoglobin, and the cytochromes in reactions with oxygen and in electron transfer. Quantitatively, hemoglobin synthesis is a major part of the nitrogen economy in humans.

     The first step of porphyrin synthesis is the *condensation* of succinyl-CoA and glycine to form δ-*aminolevulinate*. The reaction takes place in mitochondria, where succinyl-CoA is available. The reaction is irreversible and requires pyridoxal phosphate and Mg^{2+}. It is catalyzed by δ-*aminolevulinate synthase*.

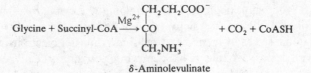

δ-Aminolevulinate

Fig. 14-28   The δ-aminolevulinate synthase reaction.

Subsequent reactions occur in the cytoplasm, and they are *irreversible*. Two molecules of δ-aminolevulinate are condensed via *porphobilinogen synthase* to form the tri-substituted pyrrole *porphobilinogen*. Two enzymes, *uroporphyrinogen synthase* and *uroporphyrinogen cosynthase*, condense four molecules of porphobilinogen into the porphyrin *uroporphyrinogen III*.

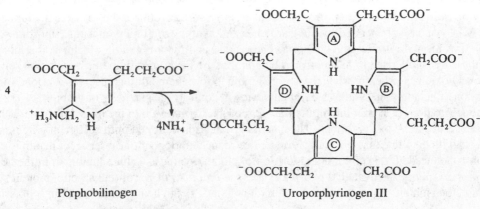

Porphobilinogen   Uroporphyrinogen III

Fig. 14-29   Porphyrin biosynthesis.

Note that uroporphyrinogen III is *not* a symmetric molecule. During its synthesis one of the pyrrole rings (ring D) is reversed in its orientation, with the result that the acetate and propionate side chains are not symmetrically arranged around the porphyrin ring.

The key porphyrin intermediate in cytochromes and hemoglobin synthesis is *protoporphyrin IX* (Fig. 14-30).

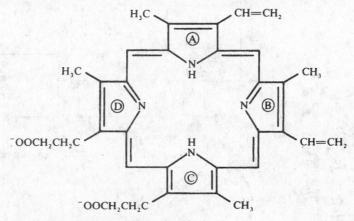

Fig. 14-30   Structure of protoporphyrin IX.

The synthesis of protoporphyrin IX involves two alterations to the side chains of uroporphyrinogen III: (1) *decarboxylation* of the *acetate* groups to methyl groups; and (2) *decarboxylation* of the propionate residues in rings A and B to *vinyl* groups ($-CH=CH_2$). The first decarboxylations take place in the *cytoplasm* while the formation of the vinyl groups and the conversion of the methylene bridges ($-CH_2-$) to the unsaturated methene ($=CH-$) bridges are *mitochondrial*. The final product from these reactions is the fully aromatic, planar *protoporphyrin IX*. The final reaction in the mitochondria is the *chelation of Fe^{2+}* to form heme, a reaction that occurs *spontaneously* although the enzyme *ferrochetalase* accelerates the rate.

Heme is the functional group in *hemoglobin* and *myoglobin*, the *cytochromes*, and the enzymes catalase and peroxidase. These molecules all have distinctly different functions but mostly involve oxygen: Hemoglobin carries oxygen, myoglobin stores oxygen, the cytochromes transfer electrons, and catalase catalyzes the decomposition of hydrogen peroxide to release oxygen, while peroxidase catalyzes the oxidation of specific molecules by peroxides.

EXAMPLE 14.18   What determines the function of the heme group in different proteins?

Although there are differences in the way heme is attached to various proteins, it is the amino acid sequences of the proteins that determine the function of the heme in these molecules.

Regulation of Heme Synthesis in Reticulocytes

Heme synthesis is controlled primarily by δ-*aminolevulinate synthase* (ALA synthase). There are two mechanisms of control, and each involves a process that affects the *concentration* of the enzyme. First, the half-life of ALA synthase, as shown by experiments in rat liver, is very short (60–70 min). Like many mitochondrial proteins, ALA synthase is encoded by nuclear genes and synthesized on cytoplasmic ribosomes, and the enzyme is translocated into the mitochondria. The second and main regulating factor is the inhibition of ALA synthase by *hemin*. Hemin differs from heme in that the Fe atom is in the Fe^{3+} oxidation state. Heme spontaneously oxidizes to hemin when there is no globin to form hemoglobin; it serves a second function in the regulation of hemoglobin synthesis in reticulocytes: It controls the synthesis of globin.

High concentrations of hemin inhibit the transport of *ALA synthase* into the mitochondria, where one of the substrates, succinyl-CoA, is formed. Thus, heme synthesis is inhibited until sufficient globin is synthesized to react with the heme that is already formed. Low concentration, or the absence, of hemin is the signal that globin is not needed; this protein (and, therefore, globin) synthesis is then inhibited. In the absence of hemin, a *protein kinase* is activated; it phosphorylates the *initiation factor* of (eukaryotic) protein synthesis, *eIF-2,* which then inhibits polypeptide chain initiation (Chap. 9) and hence inhibits globin synthesis.

14.7   Amino Acid Catabolism

The catabolism of amino acids is complex; there are too many differences between the amino acids for any useful generalization to be made about the processes except for the turnover of the amino group.

Some of the carbon skeletons of the amino acids, with the exception of *leucine*, are used in gluconeogenesis. The fates of the carbon atoms are summarized in Fig. 14-31.

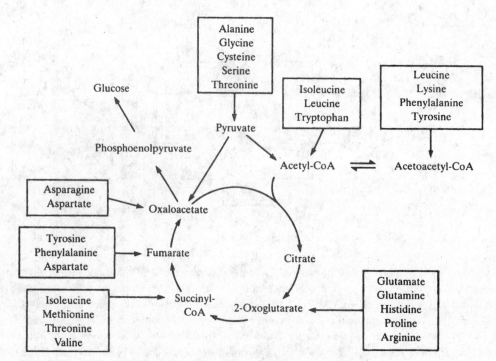

Fig. 14-31   Fates of carbon skeletons of amino acids.

Amino acids that can eventually give rise to pyruvate, which can then be used in *gluconeogenesis*, are often referred to as *glucogenic amino acids*. Pyruvate can be converted to glucose, but it can also produce acetyl-CoA. A ketogenic amino acid is one that can be degraded into an intermediate of the Krebs cycle. The one amino acid, leucine, that does not give rise to any intermediates of gluconeogenesis (i.e., it is only ketogenic) is degraded to acetoacetate and acetyl-CoA. Several amino acids—phenylalanine, tyrosine, tryptophan, and isoleucine—are both *glucogenic* and *ketogenic*. Thus all of the amino acids except leucine are at least *glucogenic*.

The pathways involved in the catabolism of the individual amino acids range from one-step reactions, such as with aspartate, glutamate, and alanine, which use the appropriate amino transferases, to multistep pathways of the aromatic amino acids and lysine (e.g., tyrosine is degraded in four steps to *acetoacetate* and *fumarate*).

EXAMPLE 14.19 Tyrosine, itself a degradation product of phenylalanine, is initially converted to *3,4-dihydroxyphenylalanine* (DOPA) and the corresponding *DOPA quinone* by the copper-containing enzyme *tyrosinase*. Tyrosinase is located in *melanocytes* and is a *mixed-function oxidase*.

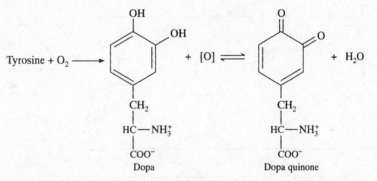

Fig. 14-32   Tyrosine is oxidized to DOPA and then to DOPA quinone.

DOPA-quinone is a precursor of *norepinephrine* and *epinephrine* in the adrenal medulla.

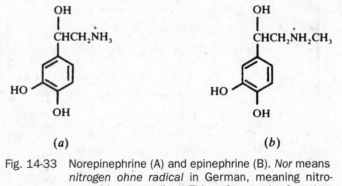

Fig. 14-33   Norepinephrine (A) and epinephrine (B). *Nor* means *nitrogen ohne radical* in German, meaning nitrogen without a radical. This refers to the fact that epinephrine has a methyl group on the side chain nitrogen and norepinephrine does not.

Amino acid catabolism is particularly important during starvation. Because of the mass of muscle, amino acid catabolism is particularly important in this tissue which, in starvation, supplies the liver with most of its gluconeogenic precursors (see also Fig. 13-11). Amino acids resulting from proteolysis during starvation are interconverted in the muscle so that ~60% of the amino acid mass that leaves the muscle is either *glutamine* or *alanine*. The branched-chain amino acids *valine*, *leucine*, and *isoleucine*, which are all essential amino acids, are *deaminated* in muscle by a specific aminotransferase, and the corresponding 2-oxoacids are transported to the liver for further metabolism via *branched-chain 2-oxoacid dehydrogenase* (BCOADH). The aminotransferase is inactive in the liver, and this ensures that the peripheral tissues are supplied with valine, leucine, and isoleucine.

In times of plenty, the activity of BCOADH, which oxidatively decarboxylates all three amino acids into CoA derivatives, in a reaction analogous to that catalyzed by the pyruvate dehydrogenase complex (it also uses thiamine pyrophosphate, TPP), is regulated by *phosphorylation*; this leads to the inactive form. The enzyme is regulated in accordance with the cellular demand for branched-chain amino acids. The control is overriden during starvation when the demand for glucose, for survival, becomes paramount.

In starvation, the kidney uses glutamine as an energy source, and glutamate derived from it is used as a source of ammonia to buffer ketone bodies which are excreted in the urine. Some ammonia passes to the liver and is used in urea synthesis.

The carbon skeleton, 2-oxoglutarate, is used in gluconeogenesis. The *intestine* preferentially uses *glutamine, glutamate, aspartate*, and *asparagine* for energy metabolism in both normal times and in times of starvation. The intestine has a high demand for cell division due to the continuous sloughing off of intestinal cells, and glutamine is used as a source of nitrogen for purine synthesis. Some glutamine is used to make *citrulline*, which travels to the kidney where it is converted to arginine for later use by the liver in urea synthesis, and the remainder is converted to alanine which enters the portal vein. Figure 14-34 summarizes amino acid metabolism in the tissues discussed, and the origin of nitrogen for urea synthesis in the liver.

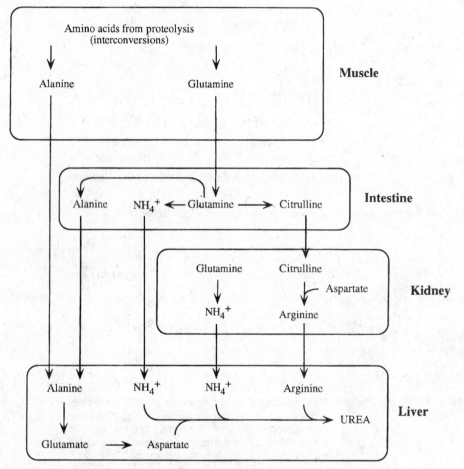

Fig. 14-34   Transfer of nitrogen components of amino acids from various tissues to the liver.

14.8   Disposal of Excess Nitrogen

Question: Why is nitrogen excreted?

Apart from that which is incorporated into functional compounds, there are no stores of nitrogen in the body that are *comparable* in form to lipids and glycogen; i.e., any nitrogen in excess of growth requirements is *excreted*. If we ingest less nitrogen than we require for normal growth and tissue repair, then we use the nitrogen that is stored in muscle proteins.

Amino acids that exist in excess of metabolic requirements are degraded to their carbon skeletons, which, as discussed in the preceding section, enter energy metabolism or are converted to other compounds and *ammonia*; the latter is excreted as such or is converted to *urea* and then excreted. This is the situation with humans, but there are major species differences as to the means by which excess ammonia is discharged from the body.

In aquatic animals, ammonia diffuses out through the skin, but land animals excrete excess ammonia as either *urea* or *uric acid*. Ammonia is excreted by humans who are on high-meat diets as a strategy to conserve Na^+ and K^+. Excess PO_4^{3-} and SO_4^{2-} that are produced from phosphoproteins and sulfur-containing amino acids are excreted as ammonium salts; Na^+ and K^+ are exchanged for NH_4^+ in the kidney. The excretion of urea requires a plentiful supply of water as it is normally excreted in solution, whereas uric acid is very insoluble and is excreted as a solid. Thus in animals in which weight, or the conservation of water, is important (e.g., birds and desert animals), excess ammonia is excreted as uric acid. This is the white material in bird droppings.

Urea, NH_2CONH_2, is highly water-soluble (~10 mol L^{-1}), nontoxic, and high in nitrogen content (47%). Normal humans excrete about ~30 g d^{-1} on a Western diet, but on a high-protein diet, this can increase to 100 g per day. Humans, and other primates, excrete only a small amount of uric acid as the end product of purine metabolism. Thus, humans *excrete* excess nitrogen as *ammonia, urea,* and *uric acid*.

Several other nitrogen-containing metabolites, notably the bile pigments, are also excreted. These are degradation products of hemoglobin and various porphyrin-containing molecules.

Formation of Ammonia

The major enzyme involved in the formation of ammonia in the liver, brain, muscle, and kidney is *glutamate dehydrogenase*. It catalyzes the reaction in which ammonia is condensed with 2-oxoglutarate to form glutamate (Sec. 14.1).

Small amounts of ammonia are produced from amine-metabolites such as epinephrine, norepinephrine, and histamine via *amine oxidase* reactions. Ammonia is also produced in the degradation of purines and pyrimidines and in the small intestine from the hydrolysis of glutamine.

The concentration of ammonia is regulated within narrow limits; the upper limit of normal in the blood of humans is ~70 μM. At quite low concentrations it is toxic to most cells; hence there are specific biochemical mechanisms for its removal. The reasons for ammonia toxicity are still not understood.

The activity of the urea cycle in the liver maintains the concentration of ammonia in peripheral blood at ~20 μM.

In tissues and other aqueous solutions, ammonia and the ammonium ion are in rapid equilibrium:

$$NH_3 + H^+ \leftrightarrow NH_4^+$$

At physiological pH, ~7.2, ~99% of ammonia is in the ionic form. The un-ionized form diffuses across cell membranes. It was previously thought to simply pass via the phospholipid bilayer but it is now known to use specific transporters; in human erythrocytes it is one of the rhesus-antigen proteins (*rhesus associated glycoprotein*) that mediates the exchange. The NH_4^+ ion is transported much more slowly via another carrier-mediated process.

A large fraction of the ammonia that is converted to urea in the liver comes from metabolism in the extrahepatic tissues, although only a small fraction leaves these tissues as ammonia. The absorptive cells of the small intestine are exceptional in this respect, in that they release ammonia into the portal vein; there the ammonia concentration may reach 0.26 mM, accounting for 30% of the urea synthesized in the liver.

Urea Synthesis

Urea is synthesized in the liver by a series of reactions known collectively as the *urea cycle* (Fig. 14.37). One nitrogen is derived from ammonium, the second from aspartate; the carbon is derived from CO_2. The synthesis of urea requires the formation of *carbamoyl phosphate* and the four enzymic reactions of the urea cycle. These take place partly in the mitochondrion and partly in the cytoplasm. The enzymes involved in the synthesis of urea are discussed next.

Carbamoyl phosphate synthetase I

The formation of carbamoyl phosphate ($NH_2COOPO_3^{2-}$) takes place in the matrix of mitochondria:

$$NH_3 + HCO_3^- + 2ATP \rightarrow NH_2COOPO_3^{2-} + 2ADP + Pi + H^+$$

The ammonia can come indirectly from glutamate via *glutamate dehydrogenase*, and the HCO_3^- comes from respiration.

Ornithine carbamoyltransferase

The first reaction of the urea *cycle*, as such, takes place in the matrix of mitochondria and is catalyzed by *ornithine carbamoyltransferase*:

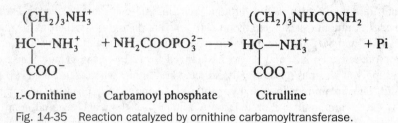

$$\text{L-Ornithine} \qquad \text{Carbamoyl phosphate} \qquad \text{Citrulline}$$

Fig. 14-35   Reaction catalyzed by ornithine carbamoyltransferase.

Both ornithine, which is a homolog of *lysine*, and citrulline are L-amino acids, but neither has a genetic codon, and both are found only as *posttranslational modifications* of arginine residues in some proteins such as *keratin*. Citrulline leaves the mitochondria by the same transport system that facilitates the entry of ornithine from the cytoplasm inter-membrane space.

EXAMPLE 14.20   Citrulline takes its name from the watermelon genus (*Citrillus*) in which it was first found in 1930. It was also discovered the same year as a bacterial degradation product of arginine. Hans Krebs (Nobel Prize, 1953), who elucidated the reactions of the urea cycle, demonstrated that citrulline was an intermediate between ornithine and arginine. The urea cycle was the first metabolic cycle to be discovered. In Krebs' words, "it revealed a new pattern of the organization of metabolic processes."

Argininosuccinate synthetase

Argininosuccinate synthetase (the second enzyme of the cycle) and the remaining two enzymes of the cycle are located in the cytoplasm. *Argininosuccinate synthetase* catalyzes the condensation of *citrulline* with *aspartate* to form *argininosuccinate*. The reaction requires one molecule of ATP, which is hydrolyzed to AMP and PPi. Pyrophosphate is a strong inhibitor of the reaction ($K_i = 6.2 \times 10^{-5}\ M$), but inhibition is normally not evident because of pyrophosphatase activity.

$$\text{Citrulline} + \text{aspartate} + \text{ATP} \rightarrow \text{argininosuccinate} + \text{AMP} + \text{PPi}$$

Argininosuccinate lyase

Argininosuccinate lyase (the third enzyme of the cycle) reversibly catalyzes the cleavage of argininosuccinate to arginine and fumarate:

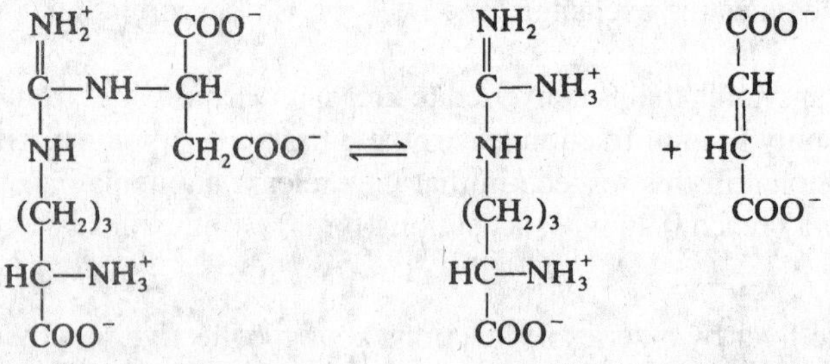

Argininosuccinate   Arginine   Fumarate

Fig. 14-36   Reaction catalyzed by argininosuccinate lyase.

This reaction also provides arginine for protein synthesis. Any arginine removed from the cycle in this way must be replaced in order for the cycle to operate. This is done by synthesizing ornithine from glutamate.

The fate of fumarate depends on its demand from gluconeogenesis. If glucose is required, fumarate is converted via cytosolic fumarase and malate dehydrogenase to oxaloacetate, and then to phosphoenolpyruvate and glucose. If the fumarate is not required for gluconeogenesis, it can be converted to oxaloacetate and then transaminated by *aspartate aminotransferase* to provide aspartate for a further round of the urea cycle.

Arginase

Arginase, a manganese-containing enzyme, is the last (fourth) one in the urea cycle. It catalyzes the hydrolytic cleavage of arginine to yield urea and ornithine:

$$\text{Arginine} + H_2O \rightarrow \text{urea} + \text{ornithine}$$

Urea passes out of the hepatocytes via a transport protein, into the blood, and is conveyed to the kidneys where it enters the glomerular filtrate, from which it is excreted in the urine.

The reactions of the urea cycle are summarized in Fig. 14-37.

The overall reaction of the urea cycle is

$$3ATP + NH_4^+ + CO_2 + 2H_2O + \text{Aspartate} \rightarrow 2ADP + 4P_i + AMP + \text{Fumarate} + \text{Urea}$$

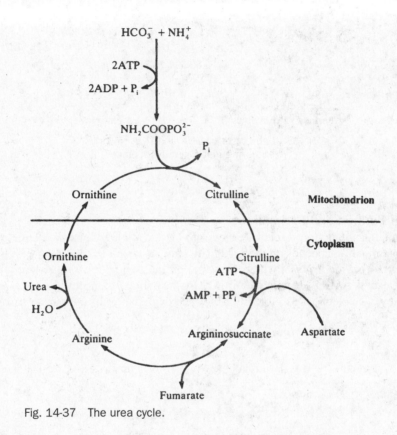

Fig. 14-37   The urea cycle.

EXAMPLE 14.21   Why is the urea cycle compartmentalized?

The main reason is probably that the system evolved to keep the fumarate concentration low, because fumarate (and arginine) inhibits *argininosuccinate lyase*. Since this enzyme is cytoplasmic, it should not be inhibited by the high concentration of fumarate that exists in conjunction with the TCA cycle. The latter pool of fumarate is in the mitochondrial matrix.

Nucleic Acid Degradation

The general scheme for the degradation of nucleic acids has much in common with that of proteins. Nucleotides are produced by hydrolysis of both *dietary* and *endogenous* nucleic acids. The endogenous (cellular) polynucleotides are broken down in *lysosomes*.

DNA is not normally broken down, except after cell death and during DNA repair. RNA is turned over in much the same way as protein. The enzymes involved in breaking down both types of polynucleotides are the *nucleases*, or more specifically *deoxy-ribonucleases* and *ribonucleases*; they hydrolyze DNA and RNA, respectively, to oligo-nucleotides which can be further hydrolyzed (Fig. 14-38) so eventually purines and pyrimidines are formed.

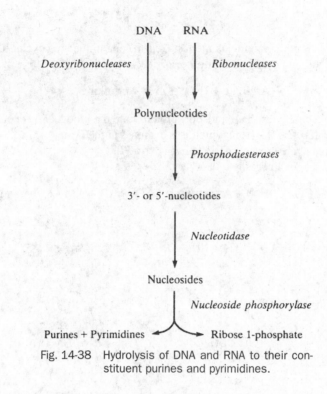

Fig. 14-38   Hydrolysis of DNA and RNA to their constituent purines and pyrimidines.

Degradation of Purines and Pyrimidines

Purines and pyrimidines that are present in excess of cellular requirements are degraded; the extent of the chemical transformation depends on the organism. Humans cannot degrade purines beyond uric acid because we lack the enzyme *uricase*, which splits the purine ring to form *allantoin*; but this occurs in dogs. In humans, excess AMP is deaminated to IMP by the action of a specific *AMP deaminase*. IMP is then hydrolyzed by 5′-nucleotidase to form *inosine*. The degradation of the purine bases to uric acid is shown in Fig. 14-39.

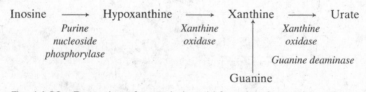

Fig. 14-39   Formation of urate/uric acid from inosine and guanine.

Thus, because we lack uricase, we excrete uric acid continuously, albeit in small amounts. The liver synthesizes ~0.8 g of uric acid per day, but 20–50% enters the gut in gastric secretions and in the bile, and is degraded by microorganisms in the gut lumen. For some animals, i.e., the *uricoteles* such as birds, uric acid is the form in which excess nitrogen is excreted (Sec. 14.8). Unless there are enzymes missing, as is the case in humans, nonuricotelic organisms can degrade purines to urea, ammonia, and carbon dioxide. Pyrimidines are also salvaged to some extent, but they are ultimately degraded, with the nitrogen released as NH_4^+.

EXAMPLE 14.22   Overproduction of uric acid can cause *gout*. Crystals of uric acid accumulate in the joints and the kidney. How can this condition be treated?

Patients suffering gout are prescribed the drug *allopurinol*. This compound is an inhibitor of *xanthine oxidase*, the enzyme that oxidizes xanthine to uric acid, so that the production of uric acid is decreased.

Excretion of Creatinine

During skeletal muscular activity, a lot of ATP is required and stores of creatine phosphate are converted to creatine while ADP is converted to ATP. It is estimated that the amount of ATP produced in this manner can maintain muscular activity in a 100-m sprinter for ~4 s. The large amount of free creatine is rephosphorlyated by ATP via creatine kinase during a rest phase.

Creatine phosphate undergoes slow but spontaneous phosphorolysis during which it irreversibly cyclizes to give *creatinine*, which is very water-soluble and is excreted in the urine.

EXAMPLE 14.23   What are the major nitrogenous components of normal human urine?

The major nitrogen-containing metabolites are urea (~84% of total nitrogen), uric acid (~2%), creatinine (~5%), ammonia (~5%), amino acids (~4%), protein (trace), and degradation products of porphyrins (trace, a few tens of mg). The amounts of these substances can vary. E.g., the amount of urea will increase during starvation and when a person is eating a high-protein diet; and creatinine excretion will increase after physical activity.

Degradation of Hemoglobin

The life span of the human erythrocyte is ~120 days (Chap. 1), in other words with ~0.85% of that total are broken down each day in the reticuloendothelial (RE) cells of the spleen, liver, and bone marrow. The erythrocytes are lysed inside the digestive vesicles of the *reticuloendothelial* (macrophage) cells and the hemoglobin is hydrolyzed. The globin is hydrolyzed to amino acids, and the heme is metabolized as follows.

The porphyrin ring is oxidatively cleaved between rings A and B to form a linear tetrapyrrole, *biliverdin,* which is a green colour (Italian, *verde* green). The complete reaction requires molecular oxygen and NADPH; the final product is *bilirubin* (which is an orange-red color; Latin, *ruber* red). The Fe^{2+} is salvaged via *transferrin* and stored within the protein *apoferritin,* and the methene bridge between rings A and B is removed as carbon monoxide, CO.

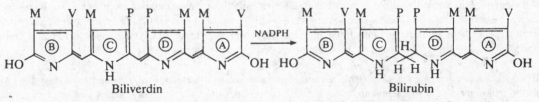

Fig. 14-40   Formation of bilirubin from biliverdin. M = methyl group, V = vinyl group, and P = propionate.

Biliverdin and bilirubin are bile pigments and are familiar as the green and orange coloring of bruises. Bilirubin, a water-insoluble molecule, is released into the plasma where it binds to *serum albumin* and is transported to the liver. In the liver it is solubilized by being converted to bilirubin diglucuronide (90%) and bilirubin sulfate (10%). Bilirubin diglucuronide is excreted from the liver in the bile and thence into the duodenum. Within the bowel it is hydrolyzed, and the bilirubin is reduced to *urobilinogen* and *stercobilinogen.* These compounds are excreted in the urine as *urobilin* and in the feces as *stercobilin*; the pigments give urine and feces their characteristic yellow and brown colors, respectively.

14.9   Metabolism of Foreign Compounds

Foreign compounds, also known as *xenobiotics*, are defined as those substances that are ingested or absorbed, which are not used as an energy source or for cell maintenance. Most xenobiotics are not deliberately ingested; they include food additives, preservatives, *colorants*, industrial and household chemicals, insecticides, and *pesticides*. However, pharmaceuticals, or drugs, are ingested intentionally. Nearly all foreign compounds undergo modification *in vivo*, which makes them less toxic (by masking or modifying functional groups) and/or more water soluble so that their metabolite(s) are excreted in the urine. This process is called *detoxification.*

While not all foreign compounds contain nitrogen, the majority of pharmaceuticals do; but as they are ingested in small doses, their contribution to nitrogen excretion is minor. There are essentially four processes of detoxification; *conjugation, oxidation, reduction,* and *hydrolysis,* and more than one process may occur with any particular foreign compound.

Conjugation

Conjugation involves the addition of a normal cellular component, or a modified form of a normal component, to the foreign compound. Glucuronic acid that is derived from glucose forms *glucuronides*; an acetyl group from acetyl-CoA produces an acetate derivative; and a sulfate group from a reactive AMP-sulfate gives rise to sulfate esters. Amino acids may also be added as conjugates; e.g., glycine and cysteine.

EXAMPLE 14.24   What is an example of conjugation with glycine?

Sodium benzoate and benzoic acid are food preservatives. Benzoate is metabolized by conjugation with glycine. The metabolite is *N*-benzoyl glycine, or *hippuric acid*, which is more water soluble than benzoate itself.

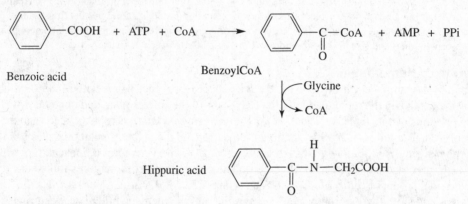

Fig. 14-41   Formation of hippuric acid by conjugation of benzoic acid with glycine.

EXAMPLE 14.25   How is cysteine involved in conjugation?

Alkylating agents are very reactive chemicals and can covalently link to many cellular components. The liver contains a variety of enzymes known as *glutathione S-transferases*, which protect against alkylating agents by covalently linking them to a molecule of *glutathione*. Glutathione is a tripeptide, γ-glutamylcysteinylglycine, and it is the thiol group of the cysteine residue that is involved in the conjugation reaction, thereby sacrificing itself to the alkylating ability of the foreign compound.

The glutathione conjugate passes into the bile and is secreted into the duodenum where proteases involved in protein digestion hydrolyze off the γ-glutamyl and glycyl residues to produce the *S*-alkylated cysteine conjugate. This conjugate is absorbed from the intestine and is excreted in the urine. Also, in the hepatocyte it may be acetylated, using acetyl-CoA, to produce the *S*-alkylated cysteine *N*-acetate, that is called a *mercapturic acid*, which is also excreted in the urine.

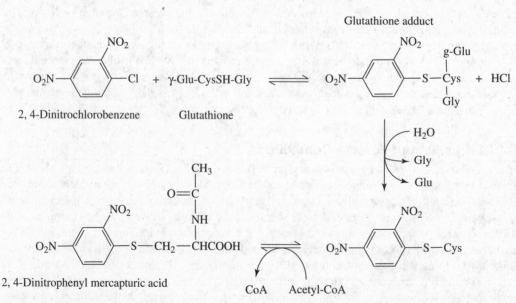

Fig. 14-42   Conjugation of xenobiotics with glutathione to form mercapturic acid.

Oxidation

Molecular oxygen is used in a variety of oxidative detoxification reactions; aromatic hydroxylation; aryl oxidation; *O*- and *N*-dealkylation; deamination; and sulfoxidation. These reactions either modify functional groups or add oxygen to the foreign compound, forming metabolites that lack pharmacological activity and which are more rapidly eliminated in the urine because of increased water solubility.

Reduction

Double bonds can be reduced; nitro groups can be reduced to amino groups; and azo dyes can be reduced to amino compounds.

EXAMPLE 14.26 Soft drinks contain colorants to make them more visually appealing. How are the colorants metabolized?

Some colorants contain an azo group that links two aromatic rings. This conjugated system of double bonds is a *chromophore*; i.e., it is colored. Liver enzymes that use NADPH as the reductant convert the azo group to a *hydrazo* group and then to two amino groups that may be acetylated.

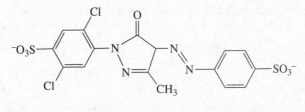

Yellow E107

A

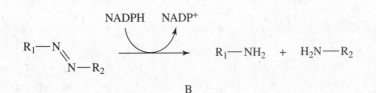

B

Fig. 14-43 A representative azo food dye (A) yellow E107 and,
(B) its reduction by NADPH to two amino compounds.

Hydrolysis

Water-soluble carboxylic esters are not constituents of normal metabolism and are hydrolyzed. There exist specific esterases for carboxylic esters, but ingested amides are hydrolyzed by proteases in the duodenum.

EXAMPLE 14.27 Local anesthetics such as *procaine* are carboxylic acid esters. How can these have local anesthetic activity if they are metabolized by esterases in the blood?

Local anesthetics would have minimal activity as they are rapidly hydrolyzed by esterases in the blood. So they are injected as a mixture with epinephrine, which is a vasoconstrictor, and this action reduces the rate at which the anesthetic diffuses from the site of injection.

EXAMPLE 14.28 Phenacetin, in combination with aspirin, was used for many decades as an *analgesic* (relieves pain) and *antipyretic* (reduces temperature), but with continual ingestion over a few years it exhibited toxicity. A study of its metabolism revealed that it was metabolized by two pathways: (1) The major pathway is an oxidation reaction (*O*-dealkylation) followed by conjugation with *glucuronic* acid in the liver. (2) The minor pathway is a hydrolysis (deacetylation) that yields a metabolite that is toxic. It causes methemoglobinemia (hemoglobin which does bind oxygen). Studies with the primary metabolite of the major pathway, *N*-acetyl-*p*-aminophenol, showed it to be nontoxic and to have both analgesic and antipyretic activity. This compound is paracetamol, which is in widespread use today as a "pain killer".

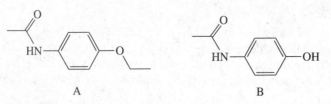

Fig. 14-44   (A) Phenacetin and (B) paracetamol.

SOLVED PROBLEMS

SYNTHESIS AND DIETARY SOURCES OF AMINO ACIDS

14.1. The majority of ingested proteins are composed of L-amino acids, but some plant and microbial proteins contain D-amino acids. How does the human body deal with these amino acids?

SOLUTION

In the liver, *D-amino acid oxidases* convert D-amino acids into the corresponding 2-oxoacid and ammonia. The 2-oxoacids, which no longer have a chiral carbon atom at position 2, can then be transaminated to the L-form via the main (L-specific) *aminotransferases*, or used in metabolic pathways that operate on 2-oxoacids.

14.2. What effect will high concentrations of NADPH and 2-oxoglutarate have on the assimilation of ammonia?

SOLUTION

Either or both of these compounds in high concentration will favor glutamate synthesis in the reaction catalyzed by glutamate dehydrogenase. This shift of the chemical reaction to the right will result in assimilation of ammonia.

$$NH_3^+ + 2\text{-Oxoglutarate} + NADPH \rightleftharpoons Glutamate + NADP^+ + H_2O$$

14.3. How does the TCA cycle operate if oxaloacetate and 2-oxoglutarate are removed for amino acid synthesis?

SOLUTION

Any oxaloacetate or 2-oxoglutarate removed from the TCA cycle must be replaced. Pyruvate is converted by *pyruvate carboxylase* to oxaloacetate, which can then enter the TCA cycle to yield 2-oxoglutarate. Also 2-oxoglutarate can be produced from glutamate and glutamine by *transaminases*.

14.4. In the fed state, what is the direction of the net carbon flux in transamination?

SOLUTION

In the fed state, in which there is abundant protein and carbohydrate, dietary protein is hydrolyzed to free amino acids that are absorbed into the circulation. Those amino acids that are not required for protein synthesis are converted to 2-oxoacids via their specific *aminotransferase*. The 2-oxoacids are then converted to lipids and carbohydrate for storage.

14.5. What determines the fate of pyruvate that is produced in muscle from metabolism of amino acids?

SOLUTION

In the normal fed state, pyruvate is oxidized by the pyruvate dehydrogenase complex (PDH), but in starvation, PDH is inactivated. Thus, pyruvate is converted to alanine which enters the blood and is conveyed to the liver where *gluconeogenesis* takes place.

DIGESTION OF PROTEINS

14.6. What is the fate of the proteases after their role in protein digestion?

SOLUTION

The proteases and other pancreatic enzymes such as pancreatic lipase are eventually also degraded by proteases. Digestion is responsible for the turnover of ~50 g of endogenous protein per day. This comes from the breakdown of the proteases and the pancreatic enzymes, as well as the epithelial cells of the gut, which are replaced every 24 h.

14.7. Why are there six types of digestive proteases when they all catalyze essentially the same reaction?

SOLUTION

While all proteases convert proteins to amino acids, each enzyme acts on a particular section of the protein. *Endopeptidases* hydrolyze peptide bonds that are adjacent to specific amino acid side chains, thus converting long protein chains into many shorter peptides. The *exopeptidases* hydrolyze peptide bonds at either the carboxyl- or amino-terminal ends of these peptides. The *endopeptidases*, therefore, produce more substrates for the exopeptidases so that the rate of protein digestion accelerates almost like a chain reaction and then declines as the hydrolytic processes approach completion.

PYRIMIDINE AND PURINE METABOLISM

14.8. Uric acid crystals can be deposited in the joints, causing the painful condition known as gout. What, causes the deposition of the crystals?

SOLUTION

Gout is caused either by an overproduction of purines, which leads to the overproduction of uric acid, or by a failure of the kidneys to excrete uric acid. Because of its very low solubility in water ($< \sim 2$ mM at 37°C), uric acid precipitates in the joints, and the sharp, needlelike crystals cause inflammation.

14.9. *Lesch-Nyhan syndrome* is a distressing inherited disorder that includes neurological abnormalities, self-mutilation, and overproduction of uric acid. Why might the uric acid be overproduced?

SOLUTION

Lesch-Nyhan syndrome is caused by a deficiency of the enzyme *phosphoribosyltransferase* that is involved in the salvage pathway of hypoxanthine and guanine (HGPRTase). The accumulation of P-Rib-PP stimulates purine biosynthesis.

14.10. What is the biochemical basis of *hereditary orotic aciduria*?

SOLUTION

The disease results from an inherited deficiency of orotate phosphoribosyltransferase that causes the accumulation of orotate/orotic acid and the excretion of the excess in the urine.

14.11. Why does a deficiency of *adenosine deaminase* result in *severe combined immunodeficiency* (SCID)?

SOLUTION

Patients who lack adenosine deaminase are unable to efficiently degrade adenosine to inosine, or deoxyadenosine (dAdo) to deoxyinosine. Elevated concentrations of dAdo are converted to nucleotides as follows:

$$dAdo \rightarrow dAMP \rightarrow dADP \rightarrow dATP$$

Millimolar concentrations of dATP kill T- and B-lymphocytes, resulting in immunodeficiency.

ONE-CARBON COMPOUNDS

14.12. The sulfonamides are antibacterial compounds that are sulfur-containing analogs of *p*-aminobenzoate. The simplest of these is sulfanilamide. What is the biochemical mechanism of sulfonamide action?

SOLUTION

Sulfonamides are *competitive inhibitors* of the incorporation of *p*-aminobenzoate into *folic acid* by bacteria. Without folic acid, the bacteria cannot grow. Humans are unable to synthesize the aromatic ring of benzoic acid so we must obtain folic acid in the diet. Therefore, sulfonamides have no effect on human metabolism.

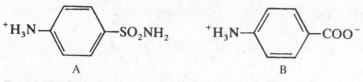

Fig. 14-45   Sulfanilamide (A) and *p*-aminobenzoate (B).

AMINO ACID CATABOLISM

14.13. Pyridoxal phosphate is a coenzyme in amino acid decarboxylations. What is a likely mechanism of the decarboxylation, and what are the products?

SOLUTION

As with transamination reactions, the first step is the formation of a *Schiff base* between the amino acid and the vitamin B_6 derivative, *pyridoxal phosphate*:

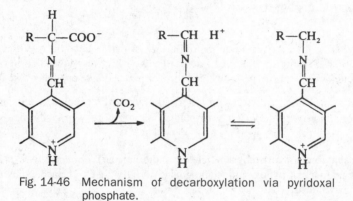

Fig. 14-46   Mechanism of decarboxylation via pyridoxal phosphate.

The quaternary nitrogen acts as an electron sink, which facilitates the decarboxylation. Further electron and proton shifts produce a Schiff base between the amine and pyridoxal phosphate, which is then hydrolyzed. Amino acid decarboxylations are involved in the synthesis of several metabolically important amines, e.g., *5-hydroxytryptamine* (serotonin) from tryptophan, *histamine* from histidine, and γ-aminobutyric acid (GABA) from glutamate.

14.14. The inherited disease *phenylketonuria*, which causes severe mental retardation, is characterized by the urinary excretion of phenyl-pyruvate, -lactate, and -acetate. How are these metabolites formed?

SOLUTION

Phenylketonuria is due to an inborn error of phenylalanine metabolism. Typically, it is due to a deficiency of phenylalanine hydroxylase (which converts phenylalanine to tyrosine). Less commonly it is caused by a deficiency of *dihydrobiopterin reductase* and a resulting inability to synthesize *biopterin*. All these conditions cause an accumulation of phenylalanine; this can be transaminated to phenylpyruvate which is converted to phenyl lactate and phenyl acetate.

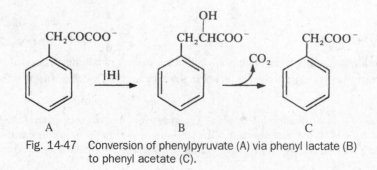

Fig. 14-47   Conversion of phenylpyruvate (A) via phenyl lactate (B) to phenyl acetate (C).

Phenylpyruvate can be reduced to phenyl lactate and oxidatively decarboxylated to phenyl acetate, both of which are also excreted in the urine.

14.15. Amino acid oxidases exist for both D- and L-amino acids. They catalyze the following reaction:

$$R\text{-}CH\text{-}COOH + 1/2\ O_2 \rightarrow R\text{-}CO\text{-}COOH + NH_4^+$$
$$\underset{NH_3}{|}$$

What metabolic roles do they serve?

SOLUTION

They exist with relatively low activity in *peroxisomes* in the liver and kidney. The most important D-amino acid oxidase is glycine oxidase, an FAD-containing enzyme that catalyzes the formation of glyoxylate and also acts on D-amino acids to form their corresponding 2-oxoacid. Glyoxylate is further oxidized to CO_2 and formate, $HCOO^-$, which is used in one-carbon (C1) metabolism.

14.16. Phenylalanine is ultimately catabolized to *acetoacetate* and *fumarate*, so it is both *ketogenic* and *glucogenic*. Initially, phenylalanine is *hydroxylated* to tyrosine, then transaminated to *p*-hydroxyphenylpyruvate. This is further oxidized to *homogentisic acid* and then to fumarate and acetoacetate. What happens to a patient if the enzyme that is required for the cleavage of the aromatic ring is absent?

SOLUTION

Alkaptonuria is a rare inborn error of metabolism caused by a lack of the enzyme *homogentisic acid oxidase*. The deficiency causes a failure to oxidize *homogentisate*, which is excreted in the urine in abundance. Polymerization of the metabolite, especially under alkaline conditions in the presence of oxygen, leads to the production of a black polymer. This makes the urine black if it is exposed to air for a few hours; and in vivo, cartilage and other connective tissues become pigmented and take on an orange color (hence the name *ochronosis* for this state of the tissues; the ocher color is readily seen postmortem). In later years the patients develop severe arthritis.

14.17. Normally, homocysteine is either remethylated to methionine with N^5-methyltetrahydrofolate (N^5-Me-THF) or converted to cysteine via cystathionine, but abnormally it can be excreted as homocystine. What does urinary excretion of homocystine indicate?

SOLUTION

Homocystinuria is a biochemical abnormality caused either by a deficiency of *cystathionine β-synthase* or impaired activity of N^5-*methyltetrahydrofolate-homocysteine methyltransferase*. The classical homocystinuria occurs when the conversion of homocysteine to cystathionine is limited by a deficiency of cystathionine β-synthase, with accumulation of methionine and homocysteine and a decrease in cysteine.

DISPOSAL OF EXCESS NITROGEN

14.18. Under what conditions does citrulline, argininosuccinate, or arginine accumulate in the urea cycle?

SOLUTION

The accumulation of any of these amino acids is due to a lack of the enzyme that operates on it, resulting in decreased metabolite flux through the reactions of the urea cycle. Inborn errors of metabolism are known for deficiencies in all the enzymes of the urea cycle. Decreased flux through the urea cycle results in elevated concentrations of ammonia in the blood, a condition known as *hyperammonemia*. It causes nausea, vomiting, and, at high concentrations, fits, spasticity, and loss of consciousness.

14.19. Can hyperammonemia be clinically controlled?

SOLUTION

Feeding low-nitrogen diets where the essential amino acids are ingested as their 2-oxoacids will reduce ammonia concentrations as the ammonia will then be used for amino acid synthesis.

14.20. Predict the form in which excess ammonia would be excreted in the following organisms: tadpoles, frogs, birds, and mammals.

SOLUTION

As aquatic animals, tadpoles lose excess ammonia by simple diffusion, but the amphibian frog and the reptiles with skins that have evolved to retain water and prevent dehydration excrete urea. Birds do not have any spare water (it represents extra weight) and so they excrete uric acid. In most mammals excess ammonia is excreted as urea.

14.21. Inborn errors of metabolism are normally associated with a deficiency or absence of an enzyme. Can excessive production of an enzyme result in an inborn error of metabolism?

SOLUTION

Excessive production of liver δ-amino levulinate synthetase causes two forms of congenital *porphyria*. These diseases are characterized by overproduction of porphyrins and excretion of large amounts of δ-amino levulinate and porphobilinogen. Some populations, such as Turks, are susceptible to this disease, and in these people acute attacks are brought on by barbiturates and other compounds which induce synthesis of the enzyme.

METABOLISM OF FOREIGN COMPOUNDS

14.22. Cyclamates, saccharin, and aspartame are artificial sweeteners. What is the metabolic fate of these compounds when they are ingested in food?

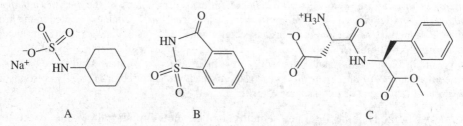

Fig. 14-48   Structures of three commonly used food additives: (A) cyclamate (cyclohexane sulfamate); (B) saccharin; and (C) aspartame.

SOLUTION

Cyclamate and saccharin are rapidly excreted in the urine, mainly unchanged. Aspartame, a monomethyl ester of aspartylphenylalanine, is degraded by digestive enzymes into its constituent amino acids. Phenylketonurics should limit their intake of aspartame due to its conversion to phenylalanine in the intestine.

14.23. Some patients have an inborn error of metabolism that involves a defective enzyme, or enzymes of the urea cycle. This results in reduced efficiency to excrete their waste nitrogen. The patients are prescribed sodium *phenylbutyrate* (buphenyl) (~30 g per day). What is the action of sodium phenylbutyrate?

SOLUTION

Phenylbutyrate mimicks a medium-chain fatty acid, and is transported into liver mitochondria, and undergoes one round of β-oxidation to produce phenylacetic acid. Humans conjugate this acid with glutamine, and the conjugate is excreted in the urine. This lowers the amount of glutamine whose amines cannot be processed by the urea cycle.

SUPPLEMENTARY PROBLEMS

14.24. Why would a diet that is rich in energy but low in nitrogen result in malnutrition?

14.25. Would you expect a diet in which cheese had replaced meat to be nutritionally adequate in nitrogen?

14.26. Which proteases would be required to hydrolyze the following peptides to completion?
    (a) Tyr-Phe-Gly-Ala
    (b) Ala-Arg-Tyr-Glu
    (c) Leu-Trp-Lys-Ser

14.27. Glutamine derived from the diet and from muscle during fasting can be converted to alanine in the intestine. Which enzymes are involved in the conversion?

14.28. Why is arginine classified as an essential amino acid in humans when it is synthesized in the urea cycle?

ANSWERS TO SUPPLEMENTARY PROBLEMS

14.24. A person eating this diet would be in *negative nitrogen balance* and could not sustain normal metabolism.

14.25. Yes, because cheese contains animal proteins.

14.26. (a) Chymotrypsin and elastase; (b) elastase, trypsin, and chymotrypsin; and (c) pepsin, chymotrypsin, and trypsin.

14.27. Glutaminase, aspartate aminotransferase, TCA cycle enzymes, citrate lyase, malate dehydrogenase, and $NADP^+$-linked malate enzyme.

14.28. The concentration of free arginine in the liver, and hence its release into the bloodstream, is insufficient to sustain growth in children, so a dietary source of arginine is essential.

Index